MW01098105

CARRY ON

THE LATTER-DAY SAINT YOUNG WOMEN ORGANIZATION 1870–2024

LISA OLSEN TAIT
AMBER C. TAYLOR
KATE HOLBROOK
JAMES GOLDBERG

THE CHURCH
HISTORIAN'S
PRESS

Copyright © 2025 by Intellectual Reserve, Inc. All rights reserved.
The Church Historian's Press is an imprint of the Church History Department of The Church of Jesus
Christ of Latter-day Saints, Salt Lake City, Utah, and a trademark of Intellectual Reserve, Inc.

www.churchhistorianspress.org

Art direction: Garth Bruner.
Cover, jacket, and interior design: Heather G. Ward.
Typography: Ashley Woodworth Skinner.

Jacket image: Girls at Brighton Camp, Utah, ca. 1929. Church History Library, Salt Lake City.

Library of Congress Cataloging-in-Publication Data

Names: Tait, Lisa Olsen, author. | Taylor, Amber, author. | Holbrook, Kate, author. | Goldberg, James, author.
Title: Carry On: The Latter-day Saint Young Women Organization, 1870–2024 / Lisa Olsen Tait,
Amber C. Taylor, Kate Holbrook, James Goldberg.
Description: Salt Lake City, Utah: The Church Historian's Press, [2025] | Includes bibliographical references and index. | Summary: "A history of the Young Women organization of The Church of Jesus Christ
from its founding in 1870 through the present day"—Provided by publisher.
Identifiers: LCCN 2024030276 | ISBN 9781639933747 (hardback)
Subjects: LCSH: Young Women (The Church of Jesus Christ of Latter-day Saints)—History. | Latter-day
Saint youth—Religious life—History. | Teenage girls—Religious life—History.

Classification: LCC BX8643.Y6 T35 2025 | DDC 248.8/3—dc23/eng/20240828

LC record available at https://lccn.loc.gov/2024030276

Printed in the United States of America on acid-free paper.
10 9 8 7 6 5 4 3 2 1

CHURCH HISTORY DEPARTMENT EXECUTIVES
Kyle S. McKay

Hugo E. Martinez

Matthew J. Grow

DIRECTOR OF PUBLICATIONS
Matthew S. McBride

CONTRIBUTORS TO THIS VOLUME

EDITORIAL STAFF
Riley M. Lorimer

Nicole Christensen Fernley

Keaton Reed

Hannah Lenning

Laura S. Rawlins

RESEARCH SPECIALISTS
Brittany Chapman Nash

Nicholas Shrum

CONTENTS

Introduction xi

PART 1: THE YOUTH OF ZION
(1870–1930)

1. Retrenchment and Improvement, 1870–1890 3
2. The New Young Woman, 1891–1910 27
3. Making the MIA, 1911–1930 59

PART 2: TRUE TO THE FAITH
(1930–1984)

4. Modern Mutuals, 1930–1948 105
5. Showcasing Youth, 1948–1961 143
6. A Program of Defense, 1961–1972 177
7. YWMIA to Young Women, 1972–1984 203

PART 3: DAUGHTERS OF HEAVENLY PARENTS
(1984–2024)

8. Standing as Witnesses of God, 1984–1992 231
9. Engaging the World, 1992–2012 267
10. Disciples of Christ, 2013–2024 299

APPENDIXES

Appendix A: Chronology 327

Appendix B: Young Women General Presidencies 333

Appendix C: Class Chart and List 339

REFERENCE MATERIAL

Acknowledgments 345

Notes 347

Works Cited 401

Index 417

ILLUSTRATIONS

Brigham Young Family Homes, Salt Lake City 8

Ten of Brigham Young's Daughters 11

Our Little Gem Newspaper, Front Page 17

Elmina Shepard Taylor and YLMIA General Board 32

Maud May Babcock Demonstrating Physical Culture 41

Cover Illustration, Young Woman's Journal 44

Alpine Stake MIA Orchestra at June Conference 66

Hawthorne Ward MIA Drama Winners 85

Banners at the MIA Jubilee 88

Brighton Summer Home 91

Bee-Hive Girls of the Zwickau Branch 111

Kidderminster MIA Conference 126

Members of the Linden Lionettes at the Lion House 137

Rose Tying Ceremony, Aurora, Utah 147

Singers at the Danish Mission MIA Convention 153

Blackfoot Fourth Ward YWMIA Softball Team 154

June Conference Dance Festival, University
    of Utah Ute Stadium 157

Gold and Green Ball, New Zealand 162

MIA Chorus at the Hollywood Bowl 170

Cover Illustration, *For the Strength of Youth* Booklet 186

Centennial Commemorative Linen Dish Towel 195

Rexburg Fifth Ward Honor Night 198

APMIA Organization Charts 200

APMIA Presidencies and Advisers 207

Youth Service Project, Bountiful, Utah 219

Young Women Fireside and Worldwide

     Satellite Broadcast 249

The Rising Generation Worldwide Young Women

     Celebration, Buenos Aires, Argentina 252

Ardeth Greene Kapp with Young Women Logo and

     Personal Progress Booklet 257

Young Women of Italy Hiking as Part of

     Fiaccola Novanta 263

Zandile Qinisile after Sunday Church Meetings,

     South Africa 270

Cultural Celebration for Mexico City Mexico

     Temple Rededication 286

Young Women Camp in Mongolia 289

Young Women Raising Virtue Banner, California 297

Young Women Participating in Worldwide Indexing

     Event, Salt Lake City 304

Youth at Temple Devotional, California 306

Youth Temple Trip, Guayaquil, Ecuador 309

Youth Community Service Project, Philippines 311

Service Activity, Guatemala City, Guatemala 316

INTRODUCTION

I n July 1885, members of the Young Ladies' Mutual Improvement Association in the East Bountiful Ward in northern Utah Territory issued their own hand-written newspaper. An association member named M. A. Willie wrote that she felt self-conscious at first about writing for the project, but living in a culture that prized collective industry, she also felt a strong need to contribute to the shared work. "The Kingdom of God is a progresive Kingdom and it will wait for none of us," she reflected. "I want to be one with my sisters." Setting her insecurities aside, she cast her generation's experience in heroic terms that echoed those used for their parents, the pioneers who had worked to build up their religious Zion in the Great Basin of the American West. "I think we as daughters of Zion have a great labor at home with ourselves," she wrote. "There has never been a better time for woman to improve her talents than at the present time. We have oportunities that our mothers were deprived of for the improvement of our minds. Then let us as wives, as mothers and as daughters of parents that we have reasons to be proud of, improve every oportunity that is afforded us, that we may be honored instruments in the kingdom of God."[1]

Fifty years later, Jantje Copier, who lived in the Netherlands, expressed her excitement over the church's Bee-Hive Girls program for young women. "Begun in Utah, it has now penetrated to the little village in Holland where I live and gather my honey of knowledge. How thankful I am for the great privilege of being a Bee-Hive Girl," she wrote. "It has brought me that for which my soul seeks. It has brought me faith in life, in love, in joy, and in helpful work. . . . May our Father bless the Bee-Hive work that it may bring happiness to this and future generations."[2]

In 2006, teenagers in Panama City participated in the Personal Progress program in their Young Women organization. "Personal Progress hasn't taught me only about the Church," said sixteen-year-old Andrea Navas. "It has helped me realize who I am, that we're daughters of God." It was equally meaningful to Mayka Moreno: "Personal

Progress helped me to understand the doctrines of the gospel. It strengthened my testimony a lot about Christ's Atonement and other things I didn't understand. . . . I'm not the same person I was. I'm better. . . . The Lord wants us to be better, shine brighter. He wants us to develop our talents, to be a light on the hill. . . . That's why we have this program."[3]

Although separated by generations and nationalities, these young women are united through their participation in the Young Women organization of The Church of Jesus Christ of Latter-day Saints. For more than 150 years and through varied name and programming iterations, the organization has played a pivotal role in cultivating a sense of divine identity, purpose, and belonging for the rising generation of Latter-day Saint women in their respective eras. Preparing young women for a lifetime of discipleship in the gospel of Jesus Christ, encouraging them to make and keep covenants with God, and cultivating their engagement within the Latter-day Saint faith have been central to the purpose of the organization's programs. The Young Women organization also nurtured young women who would become its future leaders. Understanding what individuals like M. A., Jantje, Andrea, and Mayka experienced in Young Women helps reveal what Latter-day Saints valued at different times in their efforts to keep faith alive and build up the kingdom of God on the earth.

Early histories of the Latter-day Saints seldom mentioned the Young Women organization, focusing instead on the prophets and apostles who serve as the faith's central and most visible leaders. Over the past half century, however, scholars have been increasingly interested in the ways women have influenced religious practice and the transmission of faith traditions, a focus that has coincided with Latter-day Saint women's interest in and subsequent efforts to recover the history of their foremothers. These efforts were first characterized by a strong emphasis on biography and life writings and on the Relief Society, the church's first women's organization.[4] More recently, scholars have published important studies of the religious lives of Latter-day Saint women, and the Church History Department of The Church of Jesus Christ of Latter-day Saints has established women's history as one of its primary areas of focus.[5] A growing body of scholarship and commentary has shed light on the roles of women in the church and on their relationship to men and to the priesthood as the church has grown and changed since it was established nearly two hundred years ago.

Still, little of this scholarship has examined perhaps the most potent intersection of all these historical inquiries: the history of the church's Young Women organization. It is in this organization that adult Latter-day Saints have most consistently worked to define and model what it means to be a woman who follows Jesus Christ and lives the ideals of Latter-day Saint faith. Throughout its history, the organization's female leaders have worked in concert with and under the direction of the church's presiding male priesthood leaders to determine how to respond to cultural change and international growth. While the Young Women organization published its own official histories in 1911–1955, no full, scholarly history of this important organization has yet been written.[6] *Carry On: The Latter-day Saint Young Women Organization, 1870–2024* enters this virtually unplowed field to examine the aspirations and anxieties that have shaped the organization and its members.

The history of the Young Women organization, while unique, can serve as a case study of the ways religious groups wrestle with generation gaps, gender roles, and the tension between fidelity to tradition and adaptation to modernity. In addressing these issues, *Carry On* draws on scholarship about the history of childhood and youth and on scholarship probing Latter-day Saint communal boundaries and relations with the outside world. With this foundation, this history shows how successive generations of Latter-day Saints defined youth, femininity, and spirituality and how a succession of female leaders both studied social trends and sought divine guidance as they set a course for their organization and solidified its place in the larger church.

This volume is essentially an institutional history.[7] While the Young Women organization has sought to adapt to the local circumstances of its members around the world, the organization is headquartered in Salt Lake City, and thus the cultural changes and contexts that have molded it most throughout its history overwhelmingly reflect those of the United States. Additionally, because adults have led the organization and shaped its records, this volume most often reflects the concerns of adults *about* girls. This narrative covers the full span of the organization's history from 1870 to 2024, but it is not a comprehensive history of every change and program in the organization, which has been dynamic and fluid since its beginning. *Carry On* focuses on programs, initiatives, changes, and details that are particularly significant or illustrative of larger themes and trends in the history. The appendixes to the book, in print and online, supplement the narrative by providing a timeline and charts outlining the organization's general presidencies, classes, and awards.

This book draws on a rich base of source material preserved in The Church of Jesus Christ of Latter-day Saints' central archive, the Church History Library (CHL). These sources include board meeting minutes and other executive files, personal files of presidencies and board members, statistical reports, scrapbooks, handbooks and manuals, pamphlets and circulars, and church periodicals such as the *Woman's Exponent*, the *Young Woman's Journal*, the *Improvement Era*, the *MIA Leader*, the *Church News*, the *Latter-day Saints' Millennial Star*, and *MIA in the Missions*. The CHL also holds an extensive collection of local records, including minute books and local publications. Because leadership changes regularly and participation in the organization is intentionally limited to certain ages, materials that might document individuals' experiences are often considered ephemeral, and the CHL contains comparatively few records created by everyday young women and their leaders. To supplement the core institutional history with personal perspectives, researchers scrutinized correspondence collections, community and family histories, and oral histories, including those at other repositories such as the University of Utah and Brigham Young University. Church History Department staff also conducted oral history interviews and solicited personal materials for use in this book. These sources help ensure that, while this volume focuses primarily on the history of the central Young Women organization, the stories of individual young women and local organizations provide important illustration.

This volume traces the development of the Young Women organization in three parts:

PART 1: THE YOUTH OF ZION (1870–1930)

The first Young Ladies' Department of the Ladies' Cooperative Retrenchment Association was founded in 1870. The word *retrench* meant to economize or simplify, though it was also used in military contexts to refer to fortifications. Both senses fit the times. Many of the earliest members of these young women's groups had parents who experienced religious persecution in the eastern United States or marginalization in Europe and crossed the Great Plains to build up distinctively Latter-day Saint communities in Utah. By 1869, however, the arrival of the transcontinental railroad meant the end of an era of relative isolation for the Saints. They responded to the change with concerns over encroaching outside influences and perceived spiritual erosion, yet they were also interested in what could be gained from closer connection to the outside world. These opposing impulses—defense against assimilation and engagement with the larger culture—would recur throughout the organization's history.

Initially, "junior retrenchment," as the young ladies' groups were sometimes known, spread as a grassroots movement, and in its beginnings, local organizations included married and single young women in their teens and twenties and existed only in congregations in Utah and the surrounding areas. Though unified in purpose, young women created and led their own organizations without any central governing body. By embracing retrenchment, Latter-day Saint women and girls intended to resist worldly influences, foster spirituality, and band together in economic and temporal solidarity. By the mid-1870s, however, these local associations had expanded their focus to intergenerational mentoring, practical work and service, and development of skills in reading, writing, and public speaking. After the mid-1870s, local retrenchment associations also began to develop closer ties with the recently organized

Young Men's Mutual Improvement Association (YMMIA) and formally adopted a parallel name: Young Ladies' Mutual Improvement Association (YLMIA). In 1880, church president John Taylor established a YLMIA general presidency in Salt Lake City to offer centralized leadership to local associations. The shift in identity from retrenchment to mutual improvement echoed the recurring impulses toward defense and engagement. In the organization's early years, its leaders also wrestled with ongoing questions as to whether the YLMIA's focus should be on its role as a women's organization alongside the church's other female-led groups or a youth organization working in close collaboration with the church's organization for young men.

At the close of the nineteenth century, YLMIA leaders worked to meet the needs of the church's young women through greater centralization and unification, including the advent of standardized lessons and programs overseen by an expanding and ambitious general board. As centralization progressed, the YLMIA and YMMIA began cooperating extensively in their programs and activities, which led to a growing self-perception of the two as a single youth organization. The close association of the two groups at the turn of the century required female leaders to navigate overlapping responsibility and authority with men, a diplomatic dance with long-term implications.

By the 1910s, rapid urbanization was transforming life in Utah and the surrounding Latter-day Saint–majority areas. As the United States reached the height of the Progressive Era, the surge in popularity of clubs and social programs led the YLMIA to see itself as an alternative to secular community organizations, extending the Saints' nineteenth-century goal of self-sufficiency into the cultural and social realms. Local YLMIAs were subdivided into Bee-Hive Girls and Gleaner Girls programs to offer a more structured approach to both achievement and adolescent development. Leaders of the YLMIA and YMMIA (known collectively as "the MIA") developed a theory of "teaching the gospel through activities," drawing on Latter-day Saints' expansive theology of the interrelationship of the physical, spiritual, and social to argue that the MIA's cultural and athletic programs fostered spiritual development. The MIA was assigned to oversee recreation for the church in 1922, though questions about the proper balance between activities and more overtly religious pursuits persisted.

PART 2: TRUE TO THE FAITH (1930–1984)

By the 1930 centennial of the church's organization, the pioneer culture of the nineteenth century had waned. Immigration to Latter-day Saint population centers had declined, and Latter-day Saints were better accepted in American society. In the records of the renamed Young Women's Mutual Improvement Association (YWMIA), honoring spiritual heritage and cultivating belief in the miraculous events of the faith's founding emerged as key purposes of the organization alongside its robust slate of recreational and cultural activities. Given the declining focus on migration to Utah, this period also witnessed significant development of the MIA in Europe, Latin America, and the Pacific. In the United States, mobilization for World War II in the early 1940s heightened MIA leaders' awareness of the world's interconnectedness and raised new questions about how to address sexuality and track a young population in motion.

During the 1950s, the YWMIA was central to the church's public image. Even as the organization enjoyed relative autonomy within the larger church, the YWMIA collaborated closely with the YMMIA to disseminate the church's message and showcase the benefits of gospel living through the wholesome activities and achievements of its youth. Massive festivals, coordinated to occur during the MIA's yearly June Conference, brought tens of thousands of youth, leaders, and spectators to watch the young people dance, sing, perform plays, and participate in other cultural events, some of which were televised to a still larger audience.

Within the Young Women organization, leaders created more subdivisions—adding the Mia Maids and Junior Gleaners—and adjusted age requirements within existing groups, in keeping with current thinking on stages of adolescent development and teenage life patterns. Reflecting the high marriage rates and relatively young marriage ages of the era as well as Latter-day Saint theology on family, preparation for marriage continued to be a major emphasis of instruction and activities for young women in their teens. Additionally, because the MIAs included members in their twenties and also sponsored groups for adults, the organizations served as the social hub for Latter-day Saints of all ages. To support both instruction and activities among these varied groups, the MIA organizations and their subdivisions printed thousands of pages of instructional materials each year to distribute to members and leaders.

In the 1960s, YWMIA leaders responded to rapid social change and church growth with an increasing emphasis on spiritual and leadership development. Even as time-honored traditions such as June Conference remained in place, concerns that church programs were too large and elaborate, combined with the international growth of the church and worries about the trajectory of the broader culture, caused leaders to drastically rethink the YWMIA. Though the church's correlation committees had worked through the 1960s toward centralizing and streamlining all church organizations, including the YWMIA, the impact of those efforts began to be felt largely in the 1970s. Departing from the outward-facing, elaborate programs of the 1950s and 1960s, changes under the correlation movement generated a period of simplification and an even stronger emphasis on spirituality. The

YWMIA was redefined and renamed to become the Young Women organization. Its recreation focus was curtailed, and its demographic scope narrowed to include only girls up to age eighteen. In the wake of correlation-related changes, leaders developed the church's programs for young women and young men in different directions. The dramatic changes that came with closer integration into the shared structure of the church highlighted tensions regarding the place of women's organizations within the priesthood hierarchy and the church's expanding bureaucracy.

PART 3: DAUGHTERS OF HEAVENLY PARENTS (1984–2024)

Following the profound change and reorganization at all levels of the church in the previous decades, leaders in the 1980s worked to stabilize the Young Women organization within the new, correlated church structure. Seeking to foster a specifically Latter-day Saint identity, leaders redesigned the personal achievement program and introduced a theme and a set of values that would define the organization for more than three decades. In the 1990s and 2000s, leaders largely maintained the framework established by their predecessors and worked to help young women resist what leaders saw as increasing threats to traditional gender norms and family roles. And with rapid expansion of church membership throughout the world, they looked for new ways to make the Young Women programs accessible and relevant in settings with major economic, social, cultural, and demographic differences.

While marriage remained theologically important, the early 2000s saw marriage rates decline and average marriage ages increase substantially relative to the mid-twentieth century. By the 2010s, the Young Women organization increasingly worked to prepare young women for potential missionary service and emphasized service within the church and larger community. At the end of that decade and into the next, a series of dramatic changes within the organization and the larger church reoriented Young Women programs around integrating youth more fully into the work of the church, taking previous generations' vision of youth leadership to a new level. Some of these changes consciously broke with the organization's history, while others preserved and modified existing traditions. In general, the changes reduced the differentiation between the church's organizations for young women and young men, bringing the two closer together than they had been since the mid-twentieth century. As they worked to make these adjustments, leaders turned consciously to the organization's history, seeking not to replicate past practices but to find inspiration in them.

The organization's recent reimagining demonstrates both the continuity and the dynamism that characterize the history of the Young Women organization. *Carry On: The Latter-day Saint Young Women Organization, 1870–2024* narrates that history, offers insights into the challenges of imparting religious faith and promoting human flourishing, and analyzes the processes that produce religious inspiration and motivate organizational change. Taken as a whole, this history is one of young believers who worked to shape their lives around their religious ideals and of leaders who carried on a long tradition of seeking out inspiration and introducing intentional change to further the organization's consistent purpose—to raise up righteous women who would follow the teachings of Jesus Christ, blessing the church and the world.

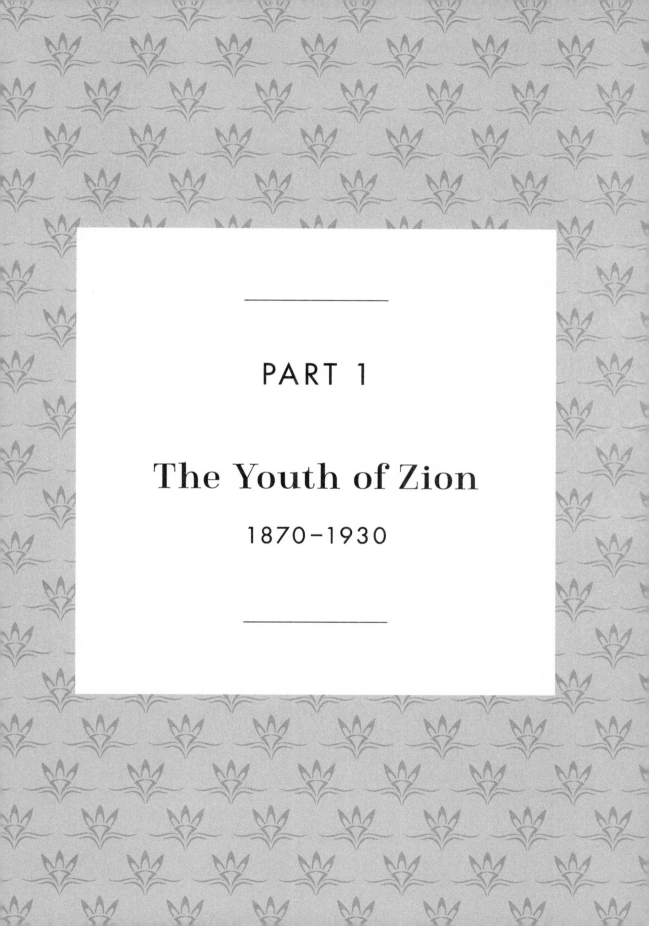

PART 1

The Youth of Zion

1870–1930

RETRENCHMENT AND IMPROVEMENT

1870–1890

On Sunday, 28 November 1875, seventeen-year-old Henrietta Lunt took charge of the telegraph office in Cedar City, Utah Territory. Like many other members of The Church of Jesus Christ of Latter-day Saints at the time, her father, Henry, practiced plural marriage. Henrietta was the eldest child of Mary Ann Wilson Lunt, Henry's second wife. His first wife, Ellen Whittaker Lunt ("Aunt Ellen" to Henrietta), usually ran the office, which occupied one room in the large Lunt home. But on this day, Ellen and Mary Ann were at an important church meeting for the women of the area.[1] Elvira Stevens Barney, a medical doctor from Salt Lake City and a "leading sister" in women's work in the church, was stopping in Cedar City as part of a nine-hundred-mile tour of the settlements in southern Utah.[2] Barney's address in Cedar City focused on promoting a cooperative economic system called the United Order. Latter-day Saint leaders hoped this system would help the Saints build up Zion, a religious ideal espousing righteous communities where people took care of one another, and be strengthened against growing influences from the outside world.[3] Probably most of the women of this small, isolated town attended the meeting to hear Barney speak.

Barney brought a feast of spirit and principle to the women of Cedar City. She spoke encouragingly of women's work within the cooperative system, making no distinction between the temporal and spiritual—in typical Latter-day Saint fashion. But she was particularly interested in the young women. A report of her visit recorded that "her heart was full to overflowing . . . when she looked at the faces of the daughters of Zion, whose bright eyes beamed with intelligence."[4] Helping those young women establish their own organization in their local congregation, or ward, was one of the primary reasons for Barney's visit.

The telegraph office could not be left unattended during the meeting, so Henrietta did not hear any of Barney's remarks. After the meeting, she saw Barney and several other women coming toward her house. Perhaps thinking that she should leave the adult women to their discussions, Henrietta stepped outside as they arrived. But when she entered the hall to return to the office, Barney was there, looking for her. Placing her hand on the girl's shoulder, Barney turned to the other women and said, "This is our President." Henrietta Lunt had just been chosen to lead the Young Ladies' Retrenchment Association in Cedar City.[5]

Although Henrietta must have heard about this organization that had been taking form within the church for the past five years, she was taken aback by the assignment. "I never will forget the feeling that came over me," she later wrote, "the thoughts of such a responsibility, and to be expected to teach the Gospel, which I didn't understand myself."[6] The church provided no outlines or lesson plans, and the Cedar City Ward, her local congregation, was over 250 miles from church leaders in Salt Lake City. Still, with her father serving as bishop, the lay leader of the ward, and her mother and Aunt Ellen serving as leaders in the ward's Relief Society organization for adult women, Henrietta was surrounded by people who could support and guide her as she fulfilled her new assignment.

Latter-day Saints had sought since their beginnings to involve young people in the life and work of the church. In the 1830s and 1840s, Latter-day Saints in Kirtland, Ohio, and Nauvoo, Illinois, like members of other Christian denominations, held Sunday schools where young people were taught from the scriptures.[7] In winter 1843, apostle Heber C. Kimball led a short-lived Young Gentlemen and Ladies Relief Society of Nauvoo, apparently inspired by the adult women's society.[8] A few years later, the Latter-day Saints began migrating to the valley of the Great Salt Lake; shortly thereafter, a movement to establish Sunday schools for children began, eventually resulting in the implementation of a churchwide Sunday school organization for young people in 1867.[9] Newspapers occasionally reported meetings of "juvenile relief societies," perhaps patterned after the adult organizations.[10]

By 1870, there were over eighty-eight thousand church members, and the need to educate youth took on new urgency. Latter-day Saints had been in the Intermountain West, where a great majority of them immigrated to be removed from the rest of society, since 1847.[11] Completion of the first transcontinental railroad in 1869 promised to transform their interactions with the outside world as well as their national and local economies. Church leaders both welcomed and feared this revolution. Cheaper, faster transportation would hasten the gathering of converts from the eastern United

States and abroad, and it would make many necessities and comforts more affordable and available to the Saints in Utah Territory. But the Saints feared that the railroad would also bring imported goods, materialistic values, and additional residents who did not share their faith. During the five years before Henrietta was selected for leadership, these concerns led to a new movement designed to encourage communitarian cooperation, promote spiritual pursuits, and foster a distinctive Latter-day Saint identity. The movement would be called *retrenchment*.

ORIGINS OF RETRENCHMENT

On an 1869 tour of the settlements in central and southern Utah, church president Brigham Young became concerned that women were spending too much time and too many resources on elaborate meals and, to a lesser extent, on their clothing. While he was in Gunnison, Utah Territory, he spoke about his concerns with Mary Isabella Hales Horne, Relief Society president in the influential Salt Lake City Fourteenth Ward and a leading figure in women's work in the church. He asked her to lead a movement to reform dining, dress, and housekeeping. Young then took up the topic in public meetings upon his return to Salt Lake City. Lamenting that church members were taking lightly their spiritual opportunities and duties, he said that humans were weak and shortsighted, prone to give themselves up "to the grovelling things of the world." He then invited female audience members to work "a revolution" by preparing simpler meals and establishing a plainer style of dress. Young taught that this "practical religion" would help them save time for spiritual and intellectual development and improve the health of their families.[12]

Women were the natural focus for this effort in part because they were the primary decision makers in their homes and communities in matters of food and dress. Horne herself was the mother of fifteen children, including three sets of twins; she was well acquainted with the intricacies of domestic labor and therefore well placed to oversee domestic reform.[13] For Saints in Utah at the time, it was not enough simply to issue calls for reform. In an era of institution building, their impulse was to *organize*, to create a voluntary society or association. Nineteenth-century Americans joined such societies and associations in great numbers with the hope of addressing perceived social needs, and Latter-day Saints similarly embraced that inclination in their commitment to communal solidarity and the idea of cooperation.[14]

On 10 February 1870, Horne invited a dozen Relief Society presidents from Salt Lake City wards to form a retrenchment organization, which they called the Ladies' Cooperative Retrenchment Society.[15] Following group discussion, Eliza Roxcy Snow, who oversaw all women's work in the church, worked with two other women to draft six resolutions for the society. One read, "*Resolved:—*That by carrying out the principles of retrenchment, the time, strength and means, redeemed from useless labor and waste, shall be devoted to noble purposes—such as instructing each other and the rising generation in the principles of physical and intellectual improvement, dietetics, &c."[16] Horne later described the movement's purpose as being "to lighten the labors of the women and give them more time to devote to mental and spiritual culture."[17]

Some of the language in the resolutions appears to have applied mainly to people who were financially stable—those who had comfortable resources from which to retrench. Addressing the Saints in the less developed town of St. George, Utah Territory, apostle Erastus Snow admitted as much. "We have not needed so much in this part of the land the sermons on retrenchment," he said with some understatement.[18] One woman in southern Utah recalled being taught retrenchment by a wealthy visitor from Salt Lake City. "They told us how it was the wish of the President that we should do away with all our extravagances in dress and habits," she remembered. She looked around at the women in the audience and contrasted their coarse, faded homespun clothing with the speaker's silk dress adorned with wide bands of velvet ribbon and lace edging. She sat and listened as long as she could stand it and then asked wryly, "Which do you want us to retrench from, Sister Young, the bread or the molasses?"[19]

The founders of the retrenchment movement demonstrated at least some awareness that many Relief Society members lived in poverty. The fourth resolution shows a determination that retrenchment would promote unity by reducing class distinctions and diminishing the opportunity gap for those with lower household incomes: "*Resolved:*—That inasmuch as many of our good and worthy citizens are deterred from inviting company by the consideration that they cannot compete with their more affluent neighbors, and are thereby deprived of many rich and profitable interviews, we say that henceforth any table neatly spread, with no matter how plain, but wholesome, food, *shall be considered fashionable.*"[20]

Although the Retrenchment Society was an entity distinct from the Relief Society, the two organizations were still closely allied. Horne continued to serve as president of the Fourteenth Ward Relief Society while she was president of the Retrenchment Society. The Retrenchment Society was formally established only in Salt Lake City, but leaders visiting Latter-day Saint settlements throughout the West broadcast the message of retrenchment. In the city, retrenchment meetings provided a forum for ward Relief Society presidents to come together and discuss matters of common concern. In this way, retrenchment meetings functioned as an unofficial governing board for Relief Society until the establishment of higher-level leadership in the late 1870s and early 1880s.

JUNIOR RETRENCHMENT

A few months following the launch of the Ladies' Cooperative Retrenchment Society, Eliza R. Snow composed resolutions for another new society—this one for young women.[21] As a plural wife of Brigham Young, Snow lived in the Lion House with many of Young's wives and children. Every evening around seven thirty, Young or one of the children rang the bell that called the fifty or so family members living at the Lion House into the parlor for their nightly prayers. Each mother and her children took their assigned place, and the family knelt as Young led them in prayer. Then the little ones went to bed while the others stayed behind to sing or discuss the day's affairs. Snow often took a leading role in these discussions and used the time to consult with Young about women's interests.[22]

At one such gathering, his daughters remembered, Young stressed the need for his family members to lead by example in needed reforms. Church members watched his family, including his popular older daughters, and were influenced by what they did. He criticized church members for competing with one another for status and his daughters for following worldly fashions. He encouraged them to instead make their own fashions and establish those as models for Latter-day Saint young women to follow.[23]

Sources attribute contradictory dates to this discussion. Much later in their lives, daughters Susa Young Gates, Zina Young Williams Card, and Maria Young Dougall remembered it as happening in November 1869, shortly after Young returned from the southern tour during which he discussed retrenchment with Horne. It is possible that Young did discuss retrenchment with his family at this time when the subject was clearly on his mind. But other sources show that the formal organization took place six months later. When published in the *Deseret Evening News*, Snow's resolutions for a new Young Ladies' Department of the Ladies' Cooperative Retrenchment Association were dated 27 May 1870.[24]

"Realizing ourselves to be wives and daughters of Apostles, Prophets and Elders of Israel," the resolutions began, "we feel to unite and co-operate with, and do mutually pledge ourselves that we will uphold and sustain each other in doing good." While the adult women's society focused primarily on table reform, the resolutions proposed for the Young Ladies' Department emphasized dress reform as their organization's main purpose. "Inasmuch as the Saints have been commanded to gather out from Babylon and 'n[o]t partake of her sins,'" the resolutions declared, "we feel that we should not condescend to imitate the pride, folly and fashions of the world." The young women committed to set an example for others by following scriptural counsel regarding dress and adornment; they would enhance real beauty through plain dress and reject

Brigham Young family homes, Salt Lake City. 1865. The Lion House, with its distinctive gabled windows, is shown from the side. The original Young Ladies' Department of the Ladies' Cooperative Retrenchment Association was organized in the parlor of this house on 27 May 1870. (Church History Library, Salt Lake City.)

waste, extravagance, and extremes in fashion.[25] Pledging to support each other in this movement was the cooperative part of the endeavor. They resolved not only to wear homemade items but to exercise a united influence in rendering them fashionable.[26] Seven of Brigham Young's daughters signed the original resolutions of the Young Ladies' Department: Ella Young Empey, Emily Young Clawson, Zina Williams, Maria Dougall, Caroline Young Croxall, Dora Young, and Phebe Young.[27] Ella, the eldest, was selected as president of the new association, and she chose the other six as her counselors.[28]

Implicit in their commitment to exercise influence was the understanding that this new movement would spread beyond the Young family. Within a few days of the inaugural meeting, Dora—one of the counselors in the new association—spoke glowingly of the new initiative to her close friend Lona Pratt, a young schoolteacher. Lona gathered many of her friends and pupils and organized an association in her ward; their resolutions were published in the newspaper alongside those of the original meeting.[29] Within weeks, several Salt Lake City wards organized young ladies' retrenchment associations. Within months, many outlying communities did the same, and over the next decade, most wards in Utah established young women's organizations, sometimes known as Junior Retrenchment or simply Young Ladies' Associations.[30] Adult leaders helped found young ladies' retrenchment associations throughout the church, as Elvira Barney did in Cedar City, and the idea of retrenchment in the church at large became identified with the young women.[31]

THE FIRST LATTER-DAY SAINT ADOLESCENTS

One aspect of this founding period has remained central to young women's programs to the present day: a desire among the older generations to instruct and safeguard youth from the dangers of the world. As an insular community seeking to transmit its founding principles to the young, the Latter-day Saints were particularly sensitive to generational issues in the years surrounding the coming of the railroad. While worrying about external influences, they also recognized demographic challenges. By 1870, the fruits of conversion, gathering, and natural increase (including, of course, plural marriage) had multiplied the Latter-day Saint population substantially, resulting in large numbers of children and youth. In one representative community in northern Utah, for example, 67 percent of the population was under age twenty-five, and youths from ages ten to twenty-four accounted for 27 percent.[32] As social and material conditions in the community changed, parents saw their children facing issues very different from their own pioneer experience.

Generational conflicts are, by definition, recurring, and while there is nothing new about adults worrying and complaining about children, factors specific to any given social moment shape the form and expression of those concerns.[33] In the church community of the late 1860s, leaders worried that pioneer-era parents had not sufficiently attended to their children's spiritual development. Eliza R. Snow attributed the failure to difficult living conditions. Carving a living out of a challenging landscape demanded much of the time and energy of the generation that crossed the Great Plains, and their relative isolation in the West made it easier to avoid unworthy distractions. But as their children began to come of age, parents and leaders worried that the spirit of the world had crept in among their young people.[34]

Residents of the Lion House were experiencing firsthand the community's generational tensions, inflected by concerns about gender. Between 1847 and 1860, nineteen daughters and eleven sons had been born into the Young family. Most of those girls were adolescents by 1870 and lived either in or near the Lion House, where the household also included, at any given time, as many as twenty women who had married Young (some of whom adopted children or brought children from previous marriages). In the 1860s, then, the majority of the household was female, and at prayer time, Young was surrounded by up to forty women and girls.[35] The Young parents had worked hard to provide a comfortable, secure home for the family, but the resultant ease and privilege had a downside. "The girls in the Lion House, took life too easy," one of the daughters recalled. While the boys helped work the farm, the girls had few chores to occupy their time, since their mothers took care of most of the housework.[36] The time not devoted to school lessons was often given to various kinds of recreation, such as parties and plays, with all the attendant focus on what to wear, including dresses, ribbons, and bows. Given these dynamics at home, it is not surprising that Young encouraged his own daughters to inaugurate another cooperative endeavor within the community.[37]

While Snow, Young, and others expressed concerns about the young people, the parameters of that group were not yet well defined. At the time Young's daughters inaugurated the organization, Ella was twenty-two, three others were over twenty, two were in their late teens, and one was fifteen. Five of these women were already married—all before turning twenty. In the early decades of the organization, society often considered girls quite juvenile well into their teens,[38] but the definition of young womanhood continued to shift over time and only gradually settled into the clear categorizations based on age and marital status reflected in the twenty-first century Latter-day Saint recognition of young women as unmarried girls ages twelve through seventeen.

The term *adolescence* would not come into common use until the end of the nineteenth century. Several trends converged to make that new life stage visible. The rapid growth of urban and middle-class life shifted social, educational, economic, psychological, and familial patterns and gradually created a discrete space between

Ten of Brigham Young's daughters. 1865. As social leaders in the Latter-day Saint community, these young women were positioned to lead the new junior retrenchment movement. Ella Young Empey, center front, served as the first president of the Young Ladies' Department of the Ladies' Cooperative Retrenchment Association. Maria Young Dougall, top right, was one of Ella's counselors and later served as a counselor in the YLMIA general presidency from 1887 to 1904. (Church History Library, Salt Lake City.)

childhood and adulthood. Freed from some of the domestic labor that defined earlier generations' lives, middle-class girls found new opportunities to go to school, spend time shopping and visiting with friends, and engage in cultural and literary activities—developing new life patterns that would bridge the growing-up years. The Lion House, situated at the heart of Salt Lake City, in many ways epitomized those developing circumstances in Utah.[39] The Young family members were eager patrons of the growing cultural opportunities, including theater productions and music and dance training, and they enjoyed an increasingly prosperous household, with access to businesses—some of which the family owned—to serve their needs. Nineteenth-century American girls have been called the first adolescents; the daughters of the Young family—and those of the other prosperous families of the community—may well have been the first *Latter-day Saint* adolescents.[40]

No one in the Lion House in May 1870 was thinking explicitly of identifying a new age group for young women. Still, their views of young women aligned with patterns of nineteenth-century thinking about girls and women. Relationships among female members of households and communities were often characterized by generational interdependence, in which girls were seen as apprentices to be mentored by adult women and a mother's work and identity were tied up in her relationship with her daughters. These relationships provided girls instruction on what it meant to be female and feminine. Girls learned not only domestic skills but also the social and emotional patterns of womanhood from the adult women in their lives. Mothers and daughters identified strongly with one another, each seeing in the other an image of herself.[41]

Intergenerational mentoring was the bedrock upon which the organization for young women was originally founded. When Cedar City's Young Ladies' Retrenchment Association became official on 9 December 1875, Henrietta Lunt had six young women to serve with her as counselors, as well as a treasurer and two secretaries. Even with all those positions filled, she also had three adult women to act as superintendents and then added a "mother" over the society.[42] Ann Blunt Alldridge filled the mother position, and Henrietta later remembered that they "certainly did appreciate her good advice and counsel."[43] Alldridge spoke frequently in the meetings, as did Mary Ann Lunt, Henrietta's actual mother and a counselor in the Relief Society presidency.[44] In the spirit of intergenerational bonds, the new young women's organizations were considered something of a daughter to the Relief Society. The Young Ladies' Retrenchment Association of Virgin City in southern Utah Territory, for example, reported that it was established "under the guardianship of the Relief Society."[45]

DRESS REFORM

In keeping with the founding impulse toward dress reform, young women in ward after ward began adopting resolutions to dress neatly and attractively, to avoid indulging in ornate styles, and to create their own fashions.[46] In practical terms, retrenchment in dress saved time and money, both of which they thought could be put to better use. But the focus on women's clothing was also something more. In discussing women's fashion, Latter-day Saints participated in a much broader cultural conversation taking place in the nineteenth century—one that was on the minds of other reform movements as well. Other American reformers of the period denounced women's clothing as unhealthful, impractical, socially and politically restrictive, and just plain ugly.[47] The Saints' emphasis on the economics of dress seems to have been unique among such movements. One of the most famous clothing reform efforts of the nineteenth century was the adoption of the Bloomer costume by women in the Perfectionist community of Oneida, New York.[48] Latter-day Saint women were never quite so far reaching in their clothing reform as groups like the Perfectionists. Despite a momentary effort in the mid-1850s to incorporate trousers into a Deseret Costume for women—named after Utah's nickname of Deseret—Latter-day Saint women's retrenchment in dress followed a much more conservative approach.[49]

In the end, the rhetoric around retrenchment in clothing faded rapidly, likely because reform impulses could not outweigh the broader societal norms surrounding appropriate dress for women. Clothing was an important avenue by which individuals expressed their sense of self and their relationship with the social order in which they lived.[50] Within American society, presenting oneself as proper and refined through one's clothing and appearance was not only personally but also morally significant.[51] National media in 1870 regarded Latter-day Saint women as sexually degraded, downtrodden slaves of their polygamous masters.[52] Maintaining allegiance to accepted standards of clothing, therefore, was an important assertion of legitimacy and respectability.

Latter-day Saint women also soon found that retrenchment in dress could lead to increased contention rather than unity. Many early members of the young ladies' retrenchment organizations felt a sense of isolation and restriction in adopting retrenchment styles, and they hesitated to invite their friends to join. They even experienced ridicule from some of their peers—both for embracing the strange new clothing and for not embracing it enough.[53] Maria Dougall recalled that a neighbor told her sister Zina, dressed in the new style, she looked like "a yard of pump water."[54] On another occasion, Maria attended an early retrenchment meeting with another sister, Ella, the new president of the Young Ladies' Department of the Ladies' Cooperative

Retrenchment Association. Ella had dressed plainly, with only one small pink bow on her white collar; still, one woman criticized her for wearing that much finery.[55]

For some young women, the association's message of dress reform failed to catch on simply because the rhetoric addressed a problem they could hardly fathom. Speakers generally offered frequent but vague comments about moderation, eliminating trimmings, and avoiding competition.[56] Yet, outside of the more established and prosperous cities, women and girls in towns and settlements were living at a far more modest level where there were few luxuries from which to retrench. So while dress reform was an impermanent goal of the new retrenchment associations, the rhetoric established fashion and female self-presentation as enduring points of tension and as boundaries between young Latter-day Saint women and the outside world.

FROM RETRENCHMENT TO IMPROVEMENT

As the new young ladies' organization grew beyond the focus on dress reform, leaders and speakers attributed broader meanings to retrenchment. Louisa Barnes Pratt did so for the young ladies of Beaver, Utah Territory, for example.[57] Pratt, a leader in the Beaver Relief Society, explained that the term signified a cooperation of effort in restraining from extravagance. Yet it also meant working toward communal harmony and establishing a "wise, prudent, and refining intercourse with each other."[58] In another ward, a young woman testified that retrenchment encompassed everything that would make them wise, useful, and happy by teaching women to live their religion and align their lives with God's will.[59]

Seen in this light, retrenchment encouraged intellectual and spiritual development. This, like the impulse to organize a voluntary association to address social needs, reflected broader American sensibilities. In post-Revolutionary America, associations and even academies for educating young women had proliferated, seeking not only to instill refined comportment but also to properly educate mothers of the new republic and increase women's access to political discussions in the growing nation.[60] Leaders of Latter-day Saint young women similarly wanted their meetings to cultivate the girls' minds and abilities.[61] Eliza R. Snow stressed the need for spiritual development and warned young women to depend on neither their parents nor their future husbands for salvation.[62]

Mary Ann Burnham Freeze, who went on to become the president of the Salt Lake Stake young women's organization, later remembered the spiritual purpose in positive terms.[63] "Many can look back to their first associations in these societies," she testified, "as to the dawning of a new and happier life, because of having become acquainted with their heavenly Father, and the principles of the holy gospel which bringeth joy and peace that the world can neither give nor take away." Those who were faithful to their duties in young women's retrenchment societies could expect a continual growth in the things of God, she promised. If they applied the things they learned, they would become great and mighty women in the kingdom of God and attain final exaltation in His presence.[64]

The term *improvement* was soon used to express this more positive emphasis for the young women's organization. Early in 1874, the Young Ladies' Retrenchment Association of the Sixteenth Ward in Salt Lake City adopted it as their motto; the girls of Richfield, Utah Territory, followed suit a few months later.[65] *Improvement* reframed the retrenchment movement's essentially negative mindset—rejection of the world—to a more positive, outward-reaching effort to increase spirituality and refinement among young people. As one young woman expressed it, *improvement* applied to all aspects of life: "We need to improve our minds, our persons, our habits, and our language. We should improve in true politeness, socially and morally," she said. "As members of the church and professors of the Gospel, we should improve in the spiritual graces . . . and thus bear testimony to all, that we love virtue and truth."[66]

Latter-day Saints were not alone in aspiring to improvement. The term was used widely in the nineteenth century to denote a desire to progress, not only in moral matters but also in physical, secular, and religious ones.[67] And if improvement was a widely held value, *mutual improvement* was a social expression of that ideal—the idea that by engaging together in worthy pursuits, people could build each other while improving themselves. This sense of mutual improvement stretched back to the seventeenth century; it was applied to numerous groups, formal and informal, encompassing a wide range of purposes and social classes.[68] A directory of women's clubs in the United States shows how ubiquitous the term had become by the end of the nineteenth century. A page listing clubs in Iowa and Kansas, for example, shows that of the sixty-two clubs listed, sixteen indicate "mutual improvement" as their purpose, with another seventeen employing one term or the other ("mutual" or "improvement").[69]

Not surprisingly, then, the Latter-day Saint young women's associations soon began replacing *retrenchment* with *improvement* in their names. On 9 November 1876, the Young Ladies' Retrenchment Society of Virgin City in southern Utah Territory, which had only just been organized in March of that year, changed its name to Young Ladies' Mutual Improvement Association (YLMIA).[70] The trend quickly spread, with some also changing the word *Association* to *Society*.[71] A report from young women in Goshen, Utah Territory, provides a snapshot of the expanding nature of the improvement program. Their resolutions called for each member to participate by reading, writing essays, or praying. They were to dress attractively, engage in worthy types of dancing, observe the Word of Wisdom (the church's dietary code), attend church meetings, display good manners, and develop charity.[72]

Self-expression, both spoken and written, quickly became one of the primary emphases for young women. They were now invited, even expected, to speak publicly. Although the prospect was daunting for many, Latter-day Saint women wanted to hear their sisters speak. "I think we should try to overcome this timidity which keeps us on our seats," exhorted Hilda Stark in the Brigham City, Utah Territory, Third Ward meeting.[73] Older women hoped the associations would provide young women with both experience and confidence. For her part, Mary Ann Freeze was pleasantly surprised at the talent she saw emerging at the young ladies' meetings. She remarked that young women who had thought it impossible to contribute through their writing or their speech were doing both well.[74]

A staple of young ladies' meetings was the reading of essays written by members. Some of these essays found their way to publication in the *Woman's Exponent*, a semimonthly newspaper for Latter-day Saint women established in 1872, which provided a forum for articles and poetry written by women on both religious and secular topics. Publishing in the *Exponent* made young women's writings available to be used as readings by other groups.[75] In many locations, the outlet for girls' literary ambitions took the form of manuscript newspapers sponsored by the young ladies' associations. These were amateur periodicals, handwritten and circulated person to person, with editorship often rotating among the group. Dozens of such publications existed at one time or another in the last quarter of the century, sometimes providing the first outlet for promising writers.[76] The young women of Goshen established their own manuscript paper, the *Young Ladies' Gem*, featuring writing by the young people themselves.[77] Julia Ivins Macdonald, who was later widely published in Latter-day Saint periodicals under her own name and under the pen name Cactus, first wrote as "Juie Ivins" in the *Little Girls' Magazine* of St. George in the late 1870s.[78] These papers were inherently ephemeral, and most have been lost, but they were taken seriously by their readers and writers and provided a significant venue for young women to develop their literary talents and sense of agency.

IMPROVEMENT MEETINGS

Back in Cedar City, where families were generally poor compared with those in Salt Lake City, improvement was an effective rallying cry for the girls of Henrietta Lunt's ward.[79] The focus on intellectual and spiritual improvement readily shaped their aspirations, and after organizing their association, the girls immediately set to work. Meetings for the young women in the Cedar City Ward, held at first every other Monday in the Social Hall, which served as Cedar City's meetinghouse,

***Our Little Gem* newspaper, front page.** December 1881. This manuscript newspaper was created by young women from the Ovid Ward, Bear Lake Stake, in Idaho Territory. Such handwritten newspapers—containing essays, poems, and stories written by local members—were popular among Young Ladies' Mutual Improvement Associations. (Church History Library, Salt Lake City.)

consisted largely of singing, reading aloud, exhorting, and sharing testimonies. Young women and older women attended together. Henrietta recalled that they bore testimony to the truth as they understood it and depended on the Spirit of the Lord to direct them.[80]

Their meeting on 20 March 1876 was typical of their meetings and representative of other young women's meetings being held throughout the church. After Henrietta called the meeting to order, they sang a hymn, had a prayer, and sang another hymn.[81] As president, Henrietta then told the girls that she wished "to see all the girls make good use of their time and try and improve in their habbits as actions speak louder than words." Following her remarks, several pieces from the *Woman's Exponent* were read, after which Rachel Corry, one of Henrietta's counselors, instructed the girls, and Mary A. Smith expressed her desire to help the association all she could and try to attend its meetings. Henrietta then assigned five young women, including her younger sister Ellen, to procure readings for the next meeting. Another girl offered a benediction, and the meeting was dismissed.[82]

The scope of the organization expanded over time to encompass practical work, service, and social activities.[83] Henrietta recalled that they made straw hats—hat making was a common home industry among Latter-day Saint women—and on one occasion some of the young women drove a team of horses and wagon to another settlement to procure better quality straw. They made a quilt and other items, which were sold to raise funds to donate toward temple construction.[84] In September 1878, four young women were appointed "teachers" in the association. Their assignment likely paralleled that of teachers in the Relief Society and in Aaronic Priesthood quorums of the church, whose assignments included visiting church members in their homes and, in the case of the Relief Society, collecting charitable donations. The YLMIA teachers made visits throughout the ward to obtain the names of all young women who wished to join the organization.[85] Subsequent minutes show the teachers reporting on their visits and bringing donated items.[86] By 1879, the young women had begun meeting jointly with the young men on occasion and producing their own manuscript newspaper.[87]

The girls of Cedar City also stepped into politics. Late in 1878, several young women, including Henrietta, joined the older women in a meeting to protest the anti-polygamy movement gaining traction in the United States. They drafted their own resolutions, which endorsed those adopted by a mass meeting of women in Salt Lake City, and submitted a report to the *Exponent*.[88] "The Young Ladies' Association has a beneficial effect among our young people," Mary Ann Lunt wrote in a joint report of the Cedar City women's organizations to the *Exponent*. "Their meetings are also well attended and a good spirit prevails."[89]

A PARALLEL ORGANIZATION FOR YOUNG MEN

As Henrietta and her peers in Cedar City organized themselves to foster improvement, other wards in the church became interested in forming similar organizations for young men, likely because members observed the momentum gathering around young women's groups. Debating societies, literary clubs, and the like were popular among young men in the United States at this time, and by 1875 a number of such groups had been established in Salt Lake City, including the Institute in the Twentieth Ward, the Instructive Association in the Sixth Ward, and the Literary Association in the Tenth Ward.[90] Some of these groups included both men and women, like the Wasatch Literary Society, which was made up of some of the sons and daughters of leading Salt Lake City families and featured poetic and dramatic readings, lectures, debates, musical exercises, and even spelling matches.[91] But the idea of a religious organization for young men was relatively new.[92]

In June 1875, Brigham Young determined to organize the young men, and he assigned twenty-one-year-old Junius Wells to undertake this task. Junius was a son of Daniel H. Wells, counselor to Brigham Young in the church's First Presidency, and was thus well known among church leaders. But he had also gained leaders' respect on his own merits. He had graduated from the University of Deseret at age seventeen and then served a two-year proselytizing mission in Great Britain.[93] Upon returning home, Wells visited various wards in Salt Lake City to teach young men how to prepare for missionary service, hoping to spare others the embarrassment of inexperience he felt early in his mission. Even before Young approached him, Wells noticed the work being done with young women and spoke with Eliza R. Snow about the need to organize the young men.[94]

Young envisioned the new organization preparing young men for church service, particularly as missionaries. He wanted them to have opportunities to speak publicly, especially to bear testimony.[95] A letter from the First Presidency—the highest governing body in the church—to representatives of the new organization emphasized this purpose, adding that young men should broaden their comprehension of the gospel. Training in public speaking and gospel principles became the basis for every association.[96] Young reportedly came up with the name for the new young men's organization on the spot. Wells remembered him saying, "We want to organize the young men into an association—an improvement association—a mutual improvement association—Young Men's Mutual Improvement Association. There's your name."[97]

Wells and other newly appointed leaders mounted an ambitious campaign, traveling throughout Utah Territory to preach mutual improvement and organize local young men's groups. Working as "missionaries," they traveled for days at a time, filling prearranged appointments in various congregations.[98] The Young Men's Mutual Improvement Association, or YMMIA, continued to appoint such missionaries periodically for several years, giving practical experience to many young men and bringing them to the attention of church leaders as candidates for proselytizing missions.[99] While the men's efforts were similar to those of women leaders who established retrenchment associations half a decade earlier, the men were apparently more systematic and comprehensive in their approach, setting out on trips specifically designed to establish associations in each congregation rather than organizing them in whatever settlements they happened to be visiting on other business.

The YMMIA developed a strong churchwide organization almost from the start. A central committee was established in 1876, and in 1880 three members of the Quorum of the Twelve Apostles were appointed as general superintendents to oversee the organization.[100] This meant that the young men's organization enjoyed a close relationship with church officials at the highest levels, and this strong centralized leadership facilitated the rapid spread of the YMMIA. By April 1876, not even a year after Young's original assignment to Wells, there were 57 YMMIAs spread throughout the territory.[101] Three years later, there were 20 stake organizations, comprising 230 associations and a membership of over 9,000; by comparison, in 1881 there were 193 young women's associations with 7,102 members.[102]

THE YOUNG LADIES' MUTUAL IMPROVEMENT ASSOCIATION

The establishment of a young men's organization proved influential for young women. While the full extent of that influence took decades to build, some effects were immediate. The first and most visible influence was a change in names. *Improvement* had already made its way into the young women's parlance for their groups, and in fall 1877, a name change became official, perhaps due to the influence of YMMIA. A *Woman's Exponent* report of the Salt Lake City First Ward young ladies' association indicated that Eliza R. Snow initiated a change in the name of the organization, explaining that Brigham Young had wished it.[103] Shortly before his death in August 1877, Young had written in a letter to his sons, "We have lately changed the old style of the Retrenchment Societies of the Young ladies to conform in name, as we also wish them to conform in spirit, to the Mutual Improvement Societies."[104] After reading the First Ward's declaration, other associations voted to change their names as well.[105] Since there was no strong central administration for the young women's associations, the name change proceeded along the same lines as the original organization—that is, according to local initiative and timing—but reports published in the *Exponent* soon employed the new terminology.[106]

By the late 1870s, the YLMIA had become firmly established throughout the church alongside the Relief Society and the Primary Association, collectively constituting a vibrant Latter-day Saint women's sphere of work and relationships. Under the leadership of Eliza R. Snow, these organizations functioned cooperatively with each other and were largely autonomous. Ties to governing priesthood leaders and structures were informal in the women's organizations; no apostles or ranking male leaders exercised formal oversight, as they did in the YMMIA. Leaders of the women's organizations were from Salt Lake's leading families and often had access to male leaders through family relationships or church assignments.[107]

At this same time, the church was undergoing a movement, initiated by Brigham Young and carried forward by his successor, John Taylor, to organize priesthood quorums—groups of male church members who hold the same office in the priesthood—in a more structured and uniform way. This movement brought about significant developments for the women-led organizations by establishing layers of standardized leadership for them at the stake and general levels.[108] In 1877, Jane Snyder Richards became president of the Weber Stake Relief Society organization, the first stake Relief Society in the church. Young appointed Richards to take charge of all the stake women's work, including the YLMIA, shortly before his death later that year.[109] In December 1877, a Relief Society presidency was appointed for the Salt Lake Stake, and thereafter presidencies were established in other stakes.[110]

While these early stake Relief Society presidents initially had stewardship over the young ladies' associations in their stakes, separate stake presidencies of the YLMIA were soon established. No definite, central directive concerning this step survives; the earliest reported stake YLMIA presidency was formed in the Davis Stake in July 1878 under Snow's direction at a quarterly Relief Society conference.[111] In September of that year, Mary Ann Freeze became president of the large and influential Salt Lake Stake YLMIA, and the organization of YLMIA presidencies in other stakes continued over the next two years.[112]

The next major step in establishing general leadership for the associations was the appointment of central committees (soon to be known as general presidencies) to oversee the Relief Society, YLMIA, and Primary Association. These presidencies, which had responsibility for their organizations on a churchwide level, were appointed by church president John Taylor at a Salt Lake Stake Relief Society conference on 19 June 1880. In the morning session, Snow and the women she had chosen as her counselors were sustained and set apart by Taylor to preside over the Relief Society.

For Snow, the formal setting apart made official the position in which she was already acting, but this was not the case for other leaders appointed that day. When conversing with a group of women over the midday meal, Snow informed a surprised

Elmina Shepard Taylor that Taylor was to become general president of the YLMIA, a position that had not previously existed. "Have you chosen your counselors?" Snow asked. Taylor must have thought quickly because she was sustained that afternoon alongside counselors Margaret Young Taylor and Martha "Mattie" Horne, with Louisa "Louie" Wells as secretary and Fanny Young Thatcher as treasurer.[113] A native of New York, Elmina Taylor joined the church in 1856 as a young schoolteacher, and her newfound faith became the guiding force in her life. "When I was confirmed by the laying on of hands I received the testimony of its truth which I have never lost from that day to this," she recorded.[114] When she became general president of the YLMIA, Taylor, age forty-nine, lived in Salt Lake City, where her husband, George Taylor, was a businessman and rising church leader who practiced plural marriage. At the time of her appointment, Elmina Taylor was simultaneously serving as secretary of her ward Relief Society, president of her ward YLMIA, and counselor in her stake Relief Society presidency; she continued to serve in the Relief Society positions well into the 1890s, even as she led the YLMIA.[115]

On a structural level, the establishment of stake and general leadership for the church's women's organizations solidified their position in the church and further aligned them at all levels with men's organizations. Establishing general and stake leadership for the women's organizations also placed them on a trajectory to become separate entities with their own lines of authority. While the YLMIA and Primary had been considered daughters of the Relief Society, all three eventually became parallel sister organizations. These implications, however, were not yet clear in the summer of 1880, when Taylor took her place as one of the church's leading women, in close cooperation with the presidencies of the Relief Society and Primary.

Throughout the 1880s, the presidency members' main occupation was to visit the stakes, usually at quarterly conferences, and offer support, teaching, and spiritual uplift.[116] This required frequent travel, and Taylor joined Snow and other women leaders in an exhausting schedule of journeys, making over three hundred visits in her first decade in office. A history of the YLMIA memorably described the interconnected labors of these women: "They traveled thousands and thousands of miles, mostly in carriages or wagons, holding two and sometimes four meetings a day, organizing branches of the Retrenchment or Mutual Improvement Associations, meeting with the Relief Societies, 'preaching up' silk, or the loyal support of home industry; securing subscribers to the *Woman's Exponent*; urging the women and the girls to study well their responsibilities, as mothers, wives and daughters."[117]

The women-led organizations of a stake customarily met on the Friday before quarterly stake conferences, often with visiting leaders in attendance. Typically, Primary meetings occupied the morning, Relief Society the afternoon, and YLMIA the evening. A history noted that the audiences, speakers, and topics at all these meetings were very similar, engendering "unanimity and harmony" among the "three sister organizations."[118]

Beyond making visits, organizing new associations, and speaking at meetings, the duties of the central committee were not well defined or extensive. Until her death in December 1887, Snow acted as the leader of women's work in the church, and other general-level leaders acted under her direction, nominally in charge of their designated organizations but acting cooperatively to lead women's work. This may be the reason that Taylor and her counselors were not formally set apart in their positions by the First Presidency until 1888, nearly eight years after their appointment and shortly following Snow's death.[119]

PARTNERSHIP WITH THE YMMIA

While the establishment of central leadership made the YLMIA a peer with the other women-led organizations, it also nudged the YLMIA toward partnership with the YMMIA. Even before the formal founding of the YMMIA, young women and young men had sometimes met together. One report, for example, mentioned an evening meeting in Ogden in which twenty-eight young women and nineteen young men gave remarks, thanking their instructors and the Lord and bearing testimony.[120] Combined activities, known as "conjoint" meetings, now began to proliferate. Socializing was a major draw for young people, and in many smaller towns, where the total numbers of young men and young women were often low, meeting together meant a better turnout. By 1880, however, YMMIA leaders were lamenting that people of both sexes and all ages attended many of their meetings, making them more like weeknight ward gatherings than YMMIA meetings.[121]

Both female and male leaders resisted the tendency toward mixed membership, insisting on the importance of retaining the distinctive character of each gender-based organization. The young women's leaders feared it would become even more difficult to get their members to participate, presumably because the presence of the opposite sex made some girls self-conscious.[122] Moreover, existing gender norms meant that young men could expect to take a more dominant public role, likely pushing young women to the margins. Mixed groups also presented an obstacle to the more serious purposes of the associations. Junius Wells recalled that at the very beginning of the movement to organize the young men, Brigham Young discouraged the idea of combining the associations for young women and young men: "If the Associations are mixed, they will become mere courting meetings, the boys will go to take the girls home and the girls will go to be took, and I shall have nothing whatever to do with them."[123] Young wanted the organizations to create serious, strong church members, and Wells himself noted that when young men and young women met together, the gatherings tended toward amusement instead of serious study and presentation.[124]

After becoming general president of the YLMIA, Elmina Taylor worked to preserve gender-specific meetings for the young women, but questions about conjoint meetings continued to arise. In 1888 at a conference in Sanpete County, Utah Territory, one local leader said she thought the weekly meetings had become more interesting and beneficial since they began meeting with the young men. This admission prompted Taylor to stand and offer clarification: "The rule is that we should meet separately. . . . In the first place, we all need a testimony for ourselves, or we cannot withstand temptation and persecution; and for this reason a part of our exercises should consist of bearing testimony, but it is very embarrassing for our bashful girls to speak their feelings in the presence of the opposite sex. Also certain subjects pertaining to our mortal lives should be taught by our presidents and older sisters, which could not be done in a mixed assembly."[125]

In her final line, Taylor referred to life experiences unique to women, such as menstruation and childbirth, and the practices surrounding those events, which would have been part of the wisdom and training mature women passed to the younger generation. But her objection was not just about the need to discuss woman-specific subjects. She also argued for a female space in which young women could express themselves and focus on developing individual faith in Jesus Christ and knowledge of the gospel.

The answer to this dilemma was to establish one conjoint meeting a month. In 1879, while speaking to a conference of the YMMIA, Joseph F. Smith, an apostle and a counselor in the YMMIA general superintendency, expressed his view that separate meetings of the young men's and young ladies' associations would bring advantages; he suggested that holding joint meetings only monthly would foster a spirit of emulation between the societies.[126]

Four years after Henrietta Lunt completed her service as YLMIA president in Cedar City, Utah Territory, local young women and men met in the Social Hall on a Saturday in late November 1884 for mutual improvement. This was only their second official conjoint meeting. Ada Wood read poetry, Hyrum Jones spoke about repentance, Florence Lunt sang a song, Mary Ann Hunter read prose, John Tait sang a song, Rosy May Sherratt and William Houchen both gave recitations, May Macfarlane performed a song, and Priscilla Barnhurst gave a selected reading.[127] Readings, musical performances, and testimony bearing became typical of joint meetings, as did exhortations from adults for young people to do their duty. Young people themselves frequently professed a desire to do so—to "improve" or "press forward." In Cedar City, young people had conjoint meetings only a few times a year, but throughout the 1880s, monthly conjoint sessions became well established throughout the church, with the expectation that they would feature greater variety and be entertaining.[128] As they had in Cedar City, these lively meetings showcased an impressive array of talents and generally included a balance of male and female participants. Despite the fairly equal numbers of male and female presenters at such conjoint sessions, gender norms did seem to play a role in what each did. Women were more likely to sing and present lighter literary selections, while men were more likely to deliver speeches and lectures on weighty subjects.[129] Still, those lectures were relatively few compared with the more artistic fare.

In October 1879, the first issue of the *Contributor* magazine was published, with Junius Wells as editor. Billed as the organ of both the YMMIA and YLMIA, the *Contributor* was intended to encourage the literary talent of young Latter-day Saints. "This is the mission of the Contributor, the name of which has been chosen," Wells said, "that it might say to every young man and every young lady among our people, having literary tastes and ability, *Write*." Wells believed "that the thoughts and expressions of the young people of the Territory will be interesting to their companions, and that in writing for the press their thoughts will gain volume and solidity."[130]

In reality, the *Contributor* featured little writing by young people and focused on YMMIA organizational concerns, which were covered in its monthly "Association Intelligence" columns. Though it published a few resolutions of young ladies' associations, the magazine never contained any reports or organizational communications from the YLMIA; female authors were very seldom featured in the *Contributor*, and no women worked on its editorial staff. Perhaps this was due in part to women submitting their writing to and reporting their activities in the *Woman's Exponent*. The *Contributor* seems to have modeled itself after the monthlies of national stature, featuring high-toned articles on religious, historical, scientific, and geographic topics.[131] Though the magazine struggled financially, it was highly regarded as modern, interesting, and progressive.[132] By the end of its first decade, the *Contributor* began to open its pages to the developing genre of home literature, or Latter-day Saint fiction written for didactic purposes.[133] This paved the way for more content written by women in the 1890s, though by then the YLMIA had its own magazine.

The two organizations also began to collaborate on regular churchwide meetings. The YMMIA established its own general conferences (initially called the general semiannual meeting) in the late 1870s and eventually began to draw women's participation. At first, leaders of the YMMIA planned and took charge of these meetings.[134] By the 1880s, women leaders were invited to speak at some of the meetings, and YLMIA leaders were sustained as part of the regular business of the conference.[135] While the women's organizations continued to hold conferences in conjunction with stake conferences, the YMMIA conferences were held on the general level in conjunction with the church's general conferences in April and October, which created greater visibility and connection with the general priesthood leaders.[136] Participating in conferences with the young men's organization began reorienting the YLMIA toward a parallel relationship with the YMMIA and away from the umbrella of intergenerational women's organizations.

By 1890, the YLMIA had established a lasting position in the Latter-day Saint community. General, stake, and local leaders guided 300 associations with a total membership of 8,300.[137] The economic separatism that had helped motivate the retrenchment movement was unsustainable in the long term—increasingly, the Saints' sense of separateness and self-containment would be expressed in moral and cultural terms. The shift from *retrenchment* to *improvement* helped foster that distinctive identity and focus young women on personal achievement, setting up a fundamental duality of purpose that would ebb and flow throughout the organization's history.

THE NEW YOUNG WOMAN

1891–1910

In the decades surrounding the turn of the century, Fanny Rowland came of age in the third generation of Latter-day Saints—a generation noted for its large size.[1] "There were young boys and girls in every home of the neighborhood," Rowland wrote in an autobiographical sketch, "and so many games to play that my mother felt that her children were of little help to her." Like many of her peers, Fanny was the daughter of two immigrant converts; both her parents had joined the church in England. Fanny's father crossed the plains with an ox team pioneer company in 1862. Her mother, who made the journey just seven years later, was among the first to cross the plains entirely by train. The family settled in Springville, Utah Territory, where her father and his brother owned a peach orchard and an alfalfa field.[2]

In 1892, about the time sixteen-year-old Fanny became a member of the YLMIA, the Springville Ward was divided into four wards to accommodate growth. In her new ward, she was invited to serve as a YLMIA counselor in 1894 and helped determine the direction the local organization would take as it served the needs of the many young women in its ranks.[3] In her young adult life, Fanny's experience would be shaped by the changing central administration in the YLMIA and the church and by evolving models of femininity and women's roles.

Organizational changes in the church and the YLMIA at the turn of the century were a response to transitions unfolding in the Latter-day Saint community and the larger society. The 1890 Manifesto announcing the end of plural marriage and Utah's achievement of statehood in 1896 profoundly altered Latter-day Saint life. "We are certainly undergoing radical changes," one writer observed in 1891.[4] The Saints' self-perception and their relationship to society at large were transformed—after decades of isolation, they were redrawing the boundaries of their relationship with the outside world.[5] Moreover, the Latter-day Saints were reaching a critical demographic turning point. The church had grown to over 195,000 members, with 32 stakes and 409 wards and branches in the Intermountain West, and 12 missions and 332 additional branches outside of the region.[6] By the 1890s, more members were born into the faith than were converted by missionaries, a pattern that would prevail until the mid-twentieth century.[7]

At the end of the nineteenth century, the Latter-day Saint community in Utah comprised three dominant generational cohorts, defined in terms of each generation's relationship to the experiences of conversion and emigration.[8] Many general leaders in the church were from the pioneer generation and were shaped by their experiences of breaking away from society to cross the plains, embrace plural marriage, and settle in the West. This generation was elderly and receding by the 1890s, but their example loomed large. The children of the pioneers, who provided the bulk of local leadership, were the frontier generation, having grown up in the West in Latter-day Saint communities. For many members of this generation, building the kingdom of God did not represent a radical break with a corrupt society; it was simply a fact of their everyday life. Many were children of plural marriage, and a substantial number had entered plural marriages themselves. Finally, the railroad generation were the young people of the community who were just coming of age. While their parents had witnessed the rapid changes and upheaval brought about by the coming of the railroad, this generation had grown up amid those changes and knew no different—they were mostly native-born Latter-day Saints who had never known the isolation, insularity, and privation their parents experienced. This generation would need to find new ways to relate to their faith and their changing economic and political environment, even as the previous generations measured them against the example of the pioneers.

Many in the pioneer and frontier generations feared that the young people of the railroad generation were not living up to their heritage and were instead becoming materialistic, self-indulgent, and spiritually indifferent, or even rebellious. "The implicit confidence in God, which enabled the parents to perform deeds of valor and mighty works; which planted their feet in the desert and converted it into a garden of comfort and cheer," one writer lamented, "is seldom thought of by the children, and the grand-children are forgetting it altogether, with their attention turned toward the goal of wealth and luxury without labor."[9] These concerns were not unique to Latter-day Saints. Boundaries between the Saints and broader society were, in fact, fading, and the Saints' increasing integration into society meant new circumstances for their young people.[10]

Preparing young women to meet those circumstances fell in large part to the YLMIA, which had to evolve to meet new needs. In 1890, the Young Ladies' Mutual Improvement Associations (usually referred to in the plural) were a loose federation of largely autonomous local groups, each more or less a law unto itself, in one characterization;[11] by 1910, the Young Ladies' Mutual Improvement Association (by then often rendered in the singular) had developed a strong central core anchored in the leadership of the general board, with standardized schedules, lessons, programs, and leadership structures, all animated by elements of the New Woman ethos, a progressive view of women then gaining traction in the United States. The YLMIA was also inextricably linked with the YMMIA and charged with helping young people develop their own religious convictions.

THE *YOUNG WOMAN'S JOURNAL*

In 1888, Susa Young Gates wrote to several friends from Laie, Hawaii, where she had been living with her missionary husband and three small children for over two years. She asked for ideas about how she might build a literary career. One friend suggested she start a monthly magazine for the YLMIA, in which Gates could "show up to the world the immense & brilliant work that is piling up like a magnificent coral reef of intelligence" and "pouring forth from these associations continually."[12] A daughter of Brigham Young and Lucy Bigelow, Gates was fourteen when her family members formed the first Young Ladies' Department of the Ladies' Cooperative Retrenchment Association in 1870. Since she had been studying shorthand at the time, she was appointed as general reporter at an early meeting and took the minutes.[13] In the ensuing eighteen years, she had seen the retrenchment associations, and then the Mutual Improvement Associations, grow to the stature mentioned in her friend's letter.

Enthusiastic about the magazine, Gates initiated a flurry of letters between Laie and Utah, seeking approval for the plan. Drawing on her personal connections to church leadership, she wrote to Joseph F. Smith and Wilford Woodruff of the church's First Presidency, both of whom responded favorably. Woodruff made it clear that, like other Latter-day Saint publications, the new magazine would have to stand upon its own resources and be independent of any church aid other than moral support.[14] Since the magazine would represent the organization they led, Gates also wrote asking approval of the general presidency of the YLMIA—Elmina Taylor, Maria Young Dougall (Susa's half sister), and Martha Horne Tingey.[15] Their response is not extant, but apparently it was affirmative. By the time the Gates family returned from Hawaii in the spring of 1889, plans for the magazine were well underway.[16]

The first issue of the *Young Woman's Journal* appeared in October 1889 and contained thirty-two pages of stories, poetry, recipes, and articles on health and dress. The general presidency of the YLMIA also included a letter in the issue, expressing care for the young women and hope that the magazine would enable them to communicate with local associations.[17] In an editorial, Gates solicited submissions and subscriptions from readers and expressed an ambitious vision for the magazine: "Let its field of usefulness be extended from Canada to Mexico, from London to the Sandwich Islands; and then as the years go by, let us send it forth on its mission of love and peace to every nation under the sun, bearing with it a message of freedom to every daughter of woman."[18] While the international scope of the young ladies' organization was still in its infancy, Gates's global vision for the magazine, undoubtedly shaped by her own missionary experience in Hawaii, expressed broader Latter-day Saint hopes for the spread of the gospel message.

Like other American women's magazines, which saw exponential growth in the nineteenth century, the *Young Woman's Journal* created a public female space for its readers.[19] The *Woman's Exponent*, a newspaper closely associated with the Relief Society, had functioned similarly since 1872 to create a forum for adult Latter-day Saint women's voices and concerns. The magazine format of the *Journal* was more modern, and its affiliation with the YLMIA positioned it to reflect the dynamic, forward-looking ideas of the times.

The *Journal* gave voice to the organization and facilitated a new level of mutual awareness among leaders and members throughout the church. Articles, reports of conferences, and letters from the general presidency created a sense of community—local leaders who could not attend the semiannual officers' meeting in Salt Lake City during the church's general conference could now read detailed reports of the proceedings, and general leaders could ensure that their instructions were widely disseminated. In this way, the magazine both created and reflected a broader trend at the turn of the century, in the YLMIA and beyond—a shift from localized initiative to centralized organization.

ESTABLISHMENT OF THE GENERAL BOARD

As American society expanded and became more complex, people sought order, organization, and new ways to relate to each other in the face of rapid and bewildering change. By the 1920s, a rise in bureaucratic order regulated by professionalized rules and administrative procedures had woven together communities that had previously been self-contained.[20] Within The Church of Jesus Christ of Latter-day Saints, a similar process played out as the informal administration of church leaders and a few clerks underwent administrative modernization that brought standardization, classification, and interconnection to church operations and entities.[21]

Leaders of the YLMIA embraced this structural transformation. Throughout the 1880s, the general leadership of the organization consisted of the president, her two counselors, a secretary, and a treasurer. These leaders were called the central board until 1892, when they voted to use the term *general board* instead.[22] Their primary duties were visiting stake conferences, usually in company with the general leaders of the Relief Society and the Primary Association, and hosting meetings for local leaders twice a year in Salt Lake City in conjunction with the church's general conferences. The new decade brought heavier demands on YLMIA general president Taylor and her counselors. Requests for visits to stakes multiplied at a time when neither counselor could undertake much travel due to health troubles and family demands. Rapid growth in the associations also meant many calls for help, and reviewing content and conducting correspondence for the *Journal* occupied an increasing portion of Taylor's time.[23]

To meet these needs, in 1890 Taylor appointed four women as aides to the board: Adella Woolley Eardley, Lelia "Lillie" Tuckett Freeze, Agnes Campbell, and Sarah Eddington.[24] All these women were part of the frontier generation and in their thirties, younger than the presidency members; Campbell and Eddington were single. All four had significant leadership experience in women's organizations. The aides were considered part of the board from the time of their assignments,[25] but they seem to have been thought of initially as traveling missionaries, perhaps similar to those who had served the YMMIA for years. Their primary function was to visit stake conferences and impart the kind of encouragement and advice dispensed by the presidency. The aides' importance within the organization grew with their service and paved the way for further growth.[26]

The expansion of the general board provided a base from which new organizational initiatives could be launched—and those initiatives, in turn, required more oversight and leadership. Simple numbers tell the story. In 1892, the board numbered eleven (including the presidency and secretaries); seven years later, in 1899, it had grown to twenty-two. By the end of the following decade, the board consisted of over thirty women, including a music director and two organists, and it was divided into several subcommittees overseeing every aspect of an increasingly elaborate organization.[27] Fanny Rowland's local leadership experience coincided with these developments. She served as president of the Springville Fourth Ward YLMIA before becoming a stake board member and then president of the Kolob Stake YLMIA, in Springville. In those capacities, she likely consulted personally with visiting general board members, strengthening ties between the local and central organizations.[28]

The members of the general board also developed strong bonds with one another. They met every few weeks, and the minutes show the leaders took affectionate interest

Elmina Shepard Taylor and YLMIA general board. 1898. Taylor (front center) was the first general president of the YLMIA, serving from 1880 until her death in 1904. She is pictured here with her counselors, Martha Horne Tingey (left of Taylor) and Maria Young Dougall (right of Taylor), and members of the general board. (Church History Library, Salt Lake City.)

in each other's lives, often praying and fasting for each other and sometimes speaking in tongues and laying on hands to bless each other.[29] At one officers' meeting, Elmina Taylor said she had asked God to help her know the best women to serve on the board and testified, "I have yet to see the first one called into my Board that He has not called there."[30]

INTRODUCTION OF STANDARD LESSONS

By the early 1890s, some stake YLMIA leaders wished to coordinate the work in their wards and began creating outlines and publishing bulletins that gave instructions to ward leaders.[31] Meanwhile, in 1891, the YMMIA published a manual that outlined a year's worth of lessons in four areas of study: theology, history, science, and literature.[32] Evidently some local YLMIAs began using the manual created by the young men's organization to structure their weekly work, and some local leaders even urged the YLMIA at the general level to adopt it wholesale.[33] Noting these developments, Susa Gates offered to prepare a guide containing lessons specifically for the young women. After many discussions with the board and much fasting and prayer on her own, Gates completed a manual titled *Guide to the First Year's Course of Study*, issued early in 1893, around the same time Fanny Rowland's sprawling ward was divided into four smaller units.[34]

The *Guide* joined spiritual learning with secular and scientific knowledge. With outlines for twelve lessons in each of three subjects, the *Guide* also revealed what kinds of knowledge leaders felt was foundational for young women's lives: theology (topical treatment of gospel subjects), history (of Joseph Smith and the founding of the church), and human physiology or "hygiene" (study of the body's systems).[35] A list of recommended reference works included the Bible and Latter-day Saint scriptures, George Q. Cannon's *Life of Joseph Smith*, Orson F. Whitney's *History of Utah*, and textbooks on physiology and health.[36] In contrast to Henrietta Lunt, who had worked without support materials in the 1870s, Fanny and her peers had access to detailed and wide-ranging materials to study.

Perhaps uncertain the *Guide* would be universally welcomed, Gates wrote in the preface, "It is designed only as an aid in your work, and should not be relied upon to take the place of personal research and study."[37] She offered suggestions for flexible implementation of the new lessons and encouraged leaders to intersperse their lessons with music and literature and allot time for testimony bearing, business, and other activities—all established features of YLMIA meetings.[38] The push for uniform lesson material seems to have come from both general and local leaders, but general leaders wanted to tread carefully and not entirely supplant the tradition of local autonomy. Use of the *Guide* was uneven at first; the board lamented a year later that the lessons were not being used as much as they had hoped, so they established classes to train local leaders in using the manual. Brigham Young Academy, a church-sponsored school in Provo, Utah Territory, later offered similar classes for stake leaders.[39] A second *Guide* was published in 1896; those two manuals were used until 1900, when lessons began to be published in the *Young Woman's Journal*.[40] The lessons in the *Guide* and the *Journal* largely maintained the lecture format that had long structured YLMIA meetings, but some changes were intended to elicit more active participation from the young women. "The great object of 'the Guide,'" Gates said in one board meeting, "is to set the young ladies to thinking."[41]

Lessons in the *Guide* and the *Journal* consisted of a brief summary or statement of the subject, followed by review questions.[42] Theology lessons included scriptural references; history lessons referred to chapters in Cannon's *Life of Joseph Smith*. Physiology lessons did not make specific reading assignments but drew on information that could be looked up in any of the suggested textbooks. Many of the questions required memorization of information, as might have been typical in a school setting ("Where and when did the first baptism occur in this dispensation?"[43]), but others encouraged personal reflection and application. Prompts such as "How may a testimony of the truth be gained?" and "Give personal illustrations of testimonies received from the Lord" offered young women a chance to speak about their own experiences.[44]

Lessons about theology and church history were meant to help young women develop strong testimonies, or personal convictions of the gospel, and commitment to the church. As YLMIA leaders worked to strengthen the organization, their driving purpose was to help young women build individual faith in Jesus Christ and His gospel. Early Latter-day Saints had eagerly sought what they called the gifts of the gospel, charismatic demonstrations of spiritual power such as miraculous healing and speaking in tongues, that evinced the truth and efficacy of the restored gospel, and a strong tradition of seeking and sharing such manifestations developed. In one *Young Woman's Journal* article, Zina D. H. Young, then serving as general president of the Relief Society, shared her experience in the 1830s of receiving an instantaneous witness of the Book of Mormon's truth through a vision, which led to her baptism and experiencing the gift of tongues.[45] Stories about such gifts remained a part of the church's youth culture at the turn of the century. One young woman from Pleasant Grove, Utah, for example, testified that she was living proof of God's power. She had suffered from poor health most of her life, at one point becoming totally blind. "Through the faith and prayers of myself and friends," she affirmed, "my Heavenly Father has restored my eyesight." She declared that this miracle would be a testimony to her forever.[46] Personal testimonies and accounts of manifestations of the Spirit were frequently published and shared in young women's meetings.[47]

Latter-day Saints in this period also began to emphasize a less spectacular, more private witness of the Holy Ghost as the foundation of testimony. "It is necessary that you shall *know*, not think nor suppose nor believe, but *know* that God lives and that He is your Father," Gates declared to readers of the *Young Woman's Journal*.[48] So important were these spiritual witnesses that church leaders indicated they should be the primary focus of each ward YLMIA president.[49] "The thing of the utmost and deepest importance," wrote Gates, "is the obtaining of a testimony." Not only would it strengthen each girl's own desire to remain faithful, but it would also make meetings more enjoyable. "The testimonies bourne by the members present will seem like music to her ears, although couched in homely and, perchance, ungrammatical language," wrote Gates.[50] In fact, she believed polished speeches would be less effective than the simple, heartfelt sharing of personal experiences. "Do not preach prosy sermons upon the subject," she advised, "but give occasionally stories of those who have received their testimonies of the truth." She asserted that the young women would enjoy this more and would more effectively learn true principles.[51]

Once young women built up their testimonies, they were encouraged to share them. The general board advised leaders to make such sharing opportunities a regular part of the schedule, and the first meeting of each month became the time usually set aside for testimony meetings.[52] Such was the practice of the Pleasant View Ward in Provo, Utah. On Monday, 7 February 1898, several leaders and young women met—despite stormy weather—and took turns sharing their feelings. Their testimonies included retellings of experiences that affirmed their beliefs and their faith in Jesus Christ. The association's president, Louisa Foote, spoke of her abundance of daily blessings, and Mary Peterson shared her gratitude for the goodness of the Lord. Counselor Ann Cluff spoke on achieving a prudent marriage, encouraging the young women to pray to the Lord to lead them in choosing a companion. Others related their experiences of being healed, while still others expressed their love for all the officers and members and the desire to do their duty.[53] Stories in the *Journal* and local YLMIA testimony meetings taught young women how they might develop the kind of faith that would endure any circumstance.

THE NEW WOMAN

The circumstances young women might expect to encounter in their lives were changing rapidly in the late nineteenth century. In the United States, one of the signal developments of that period was the emergence of the New Woman. The term first came into use in the 1890s, reflecting a phenomenon that was already underway and that would play out over the early decades of the new century. In the popular imagination, the New Woman was young, well-educated (often at college), independent, spirited, athletic, assertive, and seeking to move into the economic, political, and social realms formerly reserved for men. However, laws, customs, and attitudes still circumscribed the spheres within which women operated, often limiting their opportunities. Women still worked in traditionally feminine occupations for little pay, endured unequal conditions at home and in public, and paid a disproportionate price for transgressing social boundaries. Moreover, the opportunities of the New Woman were more available to girls in urban, middle-class settings than to those who lived in rural areas or had no choice but to labor in menial work to support themselves. Nevertheless, American culture showed real change in this era, and the sense of possibility reached Latter-day Saints in Utah.[54]

Many Latter-day Saint women, especially leaders such as Susa Gates whose voices shaped the public discussion, enthusiastically embraced the opportunities represented by the New Woman and used YLMIA channels to encourage young women to do the same. Gates wrote in the *Journal*, "All these broadening, upward movements made by women, either here or elsewhere in the world, react directly upon you and me. They serve to open new doors of thought, of progress, and of development for women everywhere."[55] This feeling of progress vitalized and uplifted both the lives of individual women and the trajectory of the YLMIA in ways that began to reshape the organization itself.[56]

Foremost among the new opportunities for young women was education. Girls were going to school in ever-increasing numbers, with secondary schools seeing an especially dramatic increase. Nationally, the number of public high schools increased 750 percent and attendance increased by 700 percent in the decades around the turn of the century.[57] By 1900, girls made up 60 percent of the student population in high schools.[58] In Utah, the last decade of the century was particularly significant for the expansion of public education.[59] Latter-day Saints established a system of church-sponsored schools for young people, affording another avenue for young women to seize educational opportunities.[60] When the Brigham Young Academy building opened in Provo in 1892, Gates exhorted her readers to set their sights on obtaining as much education as possible and to pray to God for the power to do it.[61]

Whether at a church-run academy or a public high school, attendance and advancement at school had profound effects on the development of young women. Since virtually all schools were coeducational, girls attended and competed alongside boys, showcasing their intellectual, physical, and social abilities. School reoriented young women's day-to-day lives away from the domestic realm and attuned them to a peer culture in which they could develop and express their individuality.[62] When a new high school opened in the 1890s and a territorial law made education free for all students, Fanny Rowland was in the first cohort of students to graduate from public high school in Springville. In fact, she represented Springville graduates by giving an address during a larger recognition ceremony held in nearby Provo. Her subject, reflective of the widening horizons of the era, was "An Aim in Life."[63]

Opportunities for higher education also expanded. By 1910, 73 percent of colleges and universities in the United States were either coeducational or women's colleges, and 140,000 women were enrolled in them. This represented 40 percent of the student body overall. In absolute numbers, only 3.8 percent of American women ages eighteen through twenty-one enrolled in higher education, but the numbers had increased significantly over the past four decades and would more than triple in the next twenty years.[64] A small but visible cohort of young Latter-day Saint women and men traveled to the eastern United States to study in the decades around the turn of the century; in the process, these students modeled a way for others to enter mainstream American life without relinquishing their essential identity and faith commitments.[65] They even encouraged their peers' aspirations by writing about their experiences for church periodicals. The *Young Woman's Journal* featured one such model in a series written by a medical student at the University of Michigan. Calling herself Cactus, Julia Macdonald wrote vividly of her experiences with enrollment and registration, living arrangements, coursework, and social and religious life on campus, providing encouragement and practical advice for any who wanted to follow.[66] Even for young women who were not able to attend full-time college at home or in the East, options for women to receive some education were expanding. In Springville, Fanny took correspondence and extension courses in finance, public speaking, and literature, and she qualified for a teaching certificate.[67]

With this increase in educational opportunities came aspiration to professional vocations. Women—especially immigrant women, women of color, and women from the laboring classes—had always worked. Many Latter-day Saint young women in the 1890s had immigrant mothers who helped provide economically for their children in the context of plural families or were involved in farm work or other labor. But the types of work women could pursue were changing. In the late 1890s and early 1900s, white-collar jobs were expanding rapidly, and an increasing number of white, middle-class, native-born young women began spending a period of years in such jobs between school and marriage. Others aspired to professional careers in formerly all-male fields. Their numbers were not large, but they were visible and growing.[68] A series in the *Journal* entitled "Professional and Business Opportunities for Women" described various careers—medicine, law, stenography and typewriting, photograph retouching, dentistry, and merchandising—that young women could consider. The articles were long on exhortation and short on practical guidance, but they signaled new aspirations for women.[69] By 1904, an article in the *Journal* mentioned that in larger cities, "most of our girls are engaged in office work."[70] Fanny was among them: after missing an opportunity to teach because of a yearlong struggle with typhoid fever, she became a clerk for a local department store and soon earned promotions to cashier and bookkeeper, then assistant buyer.[71] Likewise, in 1897, Estelle Neff, recently the top graduate in her class at Brigham Young Academy, was hired to work as the business manager for the *Young Woman's Journal*.[72] From that point forward, the *Journal* and the YLMIA depended on hired female office staff.

Throughout the country as well as in Utah, these new trends in education and employment led to changing marital patterns for women, many of whom chose to marry later compared to earlier generations, or not at all. The generation of American women born between 1860 and 1882—those in the leading edge of the New Woman cohort—married at a higher average age than women of any other generation until the late twentieth century, and 9 percent remained single.[73] To be sure, most women did marry; moreover, prevailing norms and even laws meant that women often had to stop working when they married.

Latter-day Saint women coming of age in the 1890s still married about two years earlier than their national counterparts.[74] Latter-day Saints considered marriage a fundamental part of their theology and practice. Beginning with Joseph Smith, Latter-day Saint leaders taught that a woman and man must be sealed together in a holy temple, through a sacred ceremony administered by someone with the proper priesthood authority, to attain eternal exaltation. Latter-day Saints also believed that this sealing bound the couple together eternally, beyond death. These beliefs led Latter-day Saints to reverence marriage, particularly marriage in the temple, and this likely influenced their lower participation in larger trends around marriage.[75]

For her part, Fanny Rowland never married.[76] While many members of Susa Gates's generation had worried about the reduction in marriage prospects for young women in Fanny's generation after the end of plural marriage, Fanny's autobiography expressed no regret about not having married. "I am happy to have lived, to have worked, to have played, and to have done some things for others," she wrote.[77]

As the rhythms of young women's lives changed, a number of Latter-day Saint women received assignments to serve as full-time missionaries. Since the earliest days of the church, full-time proselytizing had been exclusively within the male sphere, though women had served in some limited ways. But after a Latter-day Saint woman visiting Great Britain gave a powerful sermon to a gathered crowd, mission leaders in Europe wrote to Salt Lake City requesting female missionaries.[78] Initial assignments of young, single "lady missionaries" focused on articulate young women who had taken advantage of new educational opportunities: In March 1898, Inez Knight and Lucy Jane "Jennie" Brimhall of Provo—both graduates of Brigham Young

Academy—were appointed as full-time missionaries and set off together to prose-lytize in Great Britain. Before long, several notable YLMIA leaders at the local and general levels came from the ranks of those who had proved their faith and efficacy in the mission field.[79]

Women who married later or not at all found themselves with a broad window for potential missionary service. In April 1908, after years of experience in local YLMIA leadership, Fanny was asked if she could serve a mission. "It would be perfectly agreeable to my feelings," she replied, but she noted that she was "a work-ing girl" and asked for a few months more to help support family members before leaving her source of income. From a spiritual perspective, she felt ready. "I have a testimony of the Gospel," she stated.[80] Fanny served in Colorado and Nebraska from 1908 to 1910.[81]

NEW WOMEN SHAPE THE YLMIA

A strong cohort of young, educated women began to influence YLMIA lead-ership at all levels. Of the twenty women serving on the general board in 1901, six began serving while in their twenties.[82] One of these, Ann Mousley Cannon, was at the leading edge of the first generation of New Women in the church. At age twenty-two in 1891, she became YLMIA general secretary. While in her early teens, Cannon had learned business methods from her brother, working in his real estate office for several years during her time off from school. After graduating from the University of Deseret at age seventeen, she began working in the Salt Lake County Recorder's office, eventually becoming deputy recorder and later working in banking for over twenty years.[83] Cannon brought professional perspective to her service on the YLMIA board, which spanned four decades, and she created the first standardized report forms for use at all levels of the organization.[84] Cannon, who never married,[85] took care of her parents in their old age and helped raise her sister's four children, try-ing out new programs for the young women on the girls.[86] Cannon was not unique—three other women on the board never married but made careers of office work with church, county, and business entities.[87] Within a few years, other women with similar backgrounds joined the board; collectively, their education, professional training, and modern outlook contributed significantly to the development of the organization.

Women in the New Woman generation also embraced a range of reforms in their physical lives, insisting that robust physical activity—and clothing that enabled it—was an essential mark of progress. The *Journal* ran many articles about hygiene (or health) and dress reform, especially the abandonment of the corset. A quarter of a century after the original retrenchment movement, dress reform reemerged as a topic of discussion, but this time in terms of health, freedom, and aesthetics, with less concern for economics and distinctiveness.[88] Susa Gates had studied physical culture, or gymnastics and calisthenics, at a Harvard summer school. There she recruited a young teacher named Maud May Babcock to come to Utah and establish new initiatives in the field. Reporting on this effort, Gates published a series of articles promoting physical culture—some illustrated with photographs of Babcock in her gymnasium costume, demonstrating various exercises.[89]

One of the most significant effects of the New Woman ethos was women's participation in the public and political realms, and Latter-day Saint women eagerly embraced these opportunities. In 1888, to commemorate the fortieth anniversary of the landmark Seneca Falls Convention for women's rights, leaders of the National Woman Suffrage Association had called an eight-day meeting of representatives of women's organizations from around the world to form an umbrella organization called the International Council of Women. In 1891, the United States' National Council of Women (NCW) had been formed.[90] The Relief Society and the YLMIA were charter members of both councils; as such, their presidents and other representatives served as officers of the councils and regularly attended the triennial conventions and other meetings, reporting on Latter-day Saint women's activities and contributing to discussions of women's views of issues in education, labor, politics, medicine, social customs, and many other topics. To represent itself as a national organization like the other groups in the NCW, the YLMIA during this period often referred to itself as the Young Ladies' National Mutual Improvement Association.[91]

Susa Gates and other YLMIA leaders relished the visibility and connections their participation in the councils brought. Gates became heavily involved in the NCW and wrote lengthy accounts of the triennials and other meetings for the *Journal*, drawing young women into awareness of both women's issues and their leaders' involvement in addressing them.[92] When a delegation of leading Latter-day Saint women took part in the women's congress held in conjunction with the Chicago World's Fair in 1893, Gates exhorted young women to support their leaders with earnest, mighty prayer on their behalf and suggested that they mark the day with fasting and prayer.[93] The Salt Lake Tenth Ward held a special fast for the cause.[94]

Despite their enthusiastic participation in outside organizations, Latter-day Saint women retained a sense of their distinctness.[95] "My dear girls," wrote Gates about one meeting, "I heard no one there who could fill you and thrill you with the real eloquence of the Spirit, or who could pour out such a flood of heartfelt words as can our own beloved Sister Taylor. I just longed for an opportunity for her to arise and speak to them under the inspiration of the Holy Ghost."[96] As they did in so many other realms during this period, Latter-day Saint women made bold advances into the

Maud May Babcock demonstrating physical culture. 1894. Illustrating the progressive and athletic New Woman ethos, in 1894 the *Young Woman's Journal* published a series of "educational gymnastics" demonstrated by Babcock, an instructor of physical culture at the University of Utah. The exercise depicted here was intended to improve posture. (Courtesy Special Collections, J. Willard Marriott Library, University of Utah, Salt Lake City. Maud May Babcock Photo Collection, P0083, 61.)

outside world and sought to build new bridges, but their commitment to their faith and their community remained primary.

FUNDING THE YLMIA

The growth of the YLMIA in its third and fourth decades meant a substantial increase in expenses, the bulk of which were used for board members' travel to visit the stakes. Records do not survive to show details of the organization's funding before the 1890s.[97] Stakes and wards evidently raised whatever money they needed on an individual, ad hoc basis through events such as balls, raffles, auctions, bazaars, and confectionary and ice cream sales. Those stakes that could afford it paid travel expenses for the general leaders to visit their conferences.[98] This meant that there was substantial disparity between wealthier stakes, which tended to be in easier-to-reach locations, and those that had fewer means and were more remote. Yet the poorer, rural stakes needed the encouragement and training of general leaders all the more. At some point, likely around 1890, the general board began requesting that each stake contribute annual dues to help defray the board's expenses; in 1892, this amount was set at two dollars.[99] A year later at the officers' meeting in October 1893, the board requested that each stake give an entertainment—that is, some kind of fair or community celebration—as a fundraiser on behalf of the board. This initiative raised $763, which they invested, using the interest to pay travel costs. But expenses continued to outpace revenues.[100]

The following year, Elmina Taylor and Sarah Eddington traveled to a conference in Wyoming with George Goddard and George Reynolds of the Sunday School general board. The men were surprised to learn that the YLMIA operated entirely without help from the church. "Women are always independent if they have half a chance," Taylor replied. From this conversation came the idea that the young women themselves should be asked to make an individual contribution to YLMIA funds. Since 1891, children who attended the church's Sunday Schools had been asked to pay five cents on an annual "Nickel Day," but that seemed too little to ask of the older girls. "By doing without chewing gum for a month," Reynolds suggested, the young women ought to be able to pay ten cents each once a year.[101] Upon their return, Taylor and Eddington discussed this idea with the board, and they formulated a plan to establish an Annual Day—also known as Dime Day—on or near the twelfth of September to honor Taylor's birthday.[102] This would be a day of celebration, when new officers might be appointed and a special effort made to invite all young women to participate. It would also be the day for each girl to bring her dime and contribute to funding the organization. Ward YLMIAs had sometimes held annual celebrations on the anniversary of their founding; the designation of a single day for all associations to gather and support the general organization was another step in the move toward centralization and standardization.[103] This annual contribution from young women would remain a backbone of the organization's funding for many decades.

The other major financial problem confronting the YLMIA in the 1890s was the *Young Woman's Journal*, of which the organization had become part owner in the early 1890s. Gates had founded the magazine with the hope that it would provide an income for her and also help support the organization. Neither of these hopes was realized for many years.[104] Two thousand copies of each issue were published each year, even though subscriptions fell considerably below this number. By 1897, despite YLMIA membership surpassing sixteen thousand, subscriptions to the journal still numbered less than three thousand. At an annual price of two dollars—equivalent in 2020 to just over sixty dollars—subscriptions to the magazine were likely out of reach for many girls and their families. In some cases, associations might pool their resources to pay for a single subscription and then pass the magazine around for members to take turns reading. Unsold volumes piled up on the publisher's shelves, and the low subscription numbers meant that the magazine was heavily in debt.[105] Meanwhile, the country was experiencing the most severe economic depression in its history, exacerbating financial difficulties all around.

In summer 1896, tragedy struck with the unexpected death of Abraham Cannon, the *Journal*'s publisher. Cannon had managed the publishing business and other enterprises in his family's financial portfolio and had also served as an apostle in the church's leadership. He had patiently supported the magazine and encouraged Gates and Taylor even when its prospects seemed bleak, subordinating financial concerns in the service of a community enterprise. Upon his death, his successors began pressing for payment, no doubt prompted by the dire financial situation of the times. "What shall we do? *Must we abandon the Journal?*" Taylor wrote despairingly to Gates in October.[106]

YLMIA leaders mounted an ambitious plan to travel to the stakes throughout the church, selling off the back issues and recruiting new subscribers and advertisers. Gates, by this time a member of the general board, took the first trip herself, traveling for several weeks to northern Utah communities. Soon other board members followed suit. This effort yielded thousands of dollars, and together with an amicable settlement offer from the publisher, it enabled the *Journal* to essentially start over on a new, more prosperous basis.[107] In 1898, the magazine was redesigned with more attractive formatting. When a new Guide department was added in 1900, replacing the separate lesson manuals that had been published earlier, the journal became an indispensable part of the organization. The subscription price was reduced by one-half. By 1901, circulation had increased to ten thousand and continued to climb,

Cover illustration, *Young Woman's Journal.* June 1890. Susa Young Gates founded the magazine in 1889 to serve as the official organ of the YLMIA and provide an outlet for her own and others' literary talents. (Church History Library, Salt Lake City.)

providing a steady source of revenue and a continued voice for the organization for another thirty years.[108]

Meanwhile, Cannon's death brought about the demise of the YMMIA's *Contributor*. He had become the editor of that magazine in 1892, and it ceased production almost immediately after his passing. One year later, leaders of the young men's organization launched a new publication, the *Improvement Era*, which debuted in November 1897.[109] Although the magazine retained its identity as the YMMIA magazine, the *Era* quickly expanded in scope to become the leading venue for discussion of doctrinal, social, political, and general church matters.[110]

INVITATIONS TO COLLABORATE

Early in April 1896, YLMIA president Elmina Taylor called her board members together to discuss a special invitation. Thomas Hull and George Pyper, secretaries of the YMMIA, had approached YLMIA secretary Ann Cannon about the possibility of the young women and their leaders joining the YMMIA's annual conference in June. Board members generally supported the idea, thinking that cooperation would be productive and promote harmonious relations. Taylor also supported the initiative, though she had some concerns about logistics. Still, in light of the potential benefits, a motion to accept the invitation passed easily. Soon planning was underway, with a committee of two women and two men from each organization making arrangements.[111]

The invitation to work together on the Conjoint Conference, as it was called, was significant. Questions about the relationship of the young men's and young women's associations had lingered almost from their founding. Conjoint meetings were already taking place in many wards and stakes. On the general level, leaders and members of the YLMIA were sometimes invited to participate in the YMMIA's general conferences, but those events were planned and conducted solely by YMMIA leaders. The YLMIA had held its own annual conferences in 1890 and 1891, and officers' meetings for stake leaders occurred every six months in conjunction with the church's general conferences.[112] These were all-female gatherings. The conference of 1896, which became a yearly tradition, was the first truly joint effort on the general level, setting a precedent for cooperation and parity.

The YMMIA's request came out of a sense that the organization was in crisis. In contrast to the growth of the YLMIA, young men's attendance at MIA meetings was dwindling, with one report estimating the attendance of young women at ten to one compared with the young men.[113] Even energetic efforts to systematize the curriculum and send out missionaries to boost enthusiasm in the stakes failed to drive up participation. So concerned were the leaders of the Salt Lake Stake YMMIA that they began meeting monthly to discuss ways they might resuscitate the organization.[114] In some areas, the YMMIA leaders regularly asked the young women to meet with them, claiming "they could not get along without them."[115]

The first annual Conjoint Conference of the YLMIA and YMMIA took place on Saturday and Sunday, 30 and 31 May 1896. Officers and general leaders of the YLMIA and the YMMIA gathered in the Tabernacle at Temple Square in Salt Lake City. Shaped from the beginning as a joint effort between the two organizations, the conference represented a new direction in gender dynamics, and its program and structure would set the precedent for future conferences. The conference opened with a joint session in which both Joseph F. Smith, a counselor in the First Presidency and the assistant superintendent of the YMMIA, and Elmina Taylor, president of the YLMIA, gave addresses. In all the joint sessions, both men and women spoke in roughly equal numbers. In the Saturday afternoon joint session, the officers of both organizations were presented to the congregation for a sustaining vote. Susa Gates appeared on the Sunday evening program alongside prominent church authority B. H. Roberts, and various women also spoke to the combined groups. These included Luisina "Lucy" Hoving of the Cache Stake in northern Utah, renowned as a magnificent speaker, and Elizabeth "Libbie" Noall, who spoke on "Woman in the Missionary Field," based on her well-known missionary work in the South Pacific with her husband.[116] In separate officers' meetings, each association gave instruction to its own officers, whereas during the joint sessions men and women came together to instruct and be edified by each other.

While most women's speaking opportunities had previously come in local, informal, single-gender settings, the Conjoint Conference represented a prominent church setting for female speaking in an era when public speaking by women was rising as a norm.[117] George Q. Cannon of the First Presidency congratulated female participants on their strength in speaking and giving prayers.[118] Their performance represented a noteworthy step forward in women's opportunities to address mixed-gender audiences.

The Conjoint Conference was considered a great success. As they reflected on the conference, YLMIA leaders were pleased, believing the combined efforts would produce much good in the mutual improvement cause.[119] The conference did, indeed, mark the beginning of an important development; thereafter, the annual Conjoint Conference became a significant focal point and vibrant tradition for both organizations. It also brought them into a closer relationship with one another.

Local conferences, such as the one held by the Utah Stake in Provo in November 1896, included a similar kind of parity.[120] After separate officers' meetings on Saturday, the three sessions on Sunday were combined, with the YLMIA and the YMMIA taking turns conducting each meeting. General leaders from both the YLMIA and YMMIA sat on the stand alongside general and stake priesthood leaders. In his address, church apostle John Henry Smith said he "did not think the labors of the sisters are appreciated by the brethren as they should be," and Lillie Freeze remarked that the organizations had "lived too far apart in our Mutual Improvement work."[121] Conjoint conferences (or conjoint sessions at conferences) were not entirely new, but these remarks suggest that participants perceived something new was happening. The conjoint movement was bringing a new sense of appreciation and cooperation.[122]

By 1897, the boards of both organizations had taken several steps toward even closer working relationships. In January of that year, the YLMIA's general leaders sponsored a sociable, or informal social gathering, for the YMMIA board with the hope that better acquaintance would lead to better cooperation.[123] Later, in March, the two general boards began meeting together regularly, forming committees with equal membership from each board to plan for the second annual general Conjoint Conference.[124]

Amid this new level of collaboration, at least one YMMIA leader proposed the union of the YMMIA and YLMIA. In a letter published in the *Young Woman's Journal*, Thomas Hull, then the acting general secretary of the YMMIA, presented the idea as the only way to revive the young men's organization.[125] His primary rationale was that the young men needed the good influence of the young women to improve both attendance and behavior. Implicit in Hull's proposal was the perception that the young women's associations were more vigorous and effective than the young men's. Knowing that YLMIA leaders might be reluctant to fully join with the young men, he framed the proposal as an opportunity for young women to become more confident at speaking in front of men.[126] Even as he acknowledged that a union of the associations was liable to create the flirtatious "sparking meetings" denounced by Brigham Young, he insisted, "For my own part, I would much rather see a young man sitting in a mutual improvement meeting, indulging in a little harmless 'sparking,' than to see him standing on the street corner with a cigar or cigarette in his mouth, or to find him in a still worse place." If problems arose, he argued, they could be appropriately addressed.[127]

Taylor and the YLMIA leaders refused Hull's proposal, which Gates had published in the *Journal* without Taylor's approval.[128] At an officers' meeting, Taylor discouraged talk about merging the associations, arguing that no one with authority had instructed them to do so. "Our prophet has said we should hold conjoint meetings once a month," she explained, adding that separate organizations were essential in order to study subjects particular to each group.[129] While invoking prophetic authority,

Taylor's reasoning may have also reflected a desire to preserve the autonomy the YLMIA had so far enjoyed.

Even without merging the organizations, collaboration raised urgent questions concerning gender, hierarchy, and precedence. The YLMIA, like the church's other organizations, patterned its leadership structure after that of the priesthood quorums, with a presidency (a president and two counselors) at the general, stake, and local levels.[130] The YLMIA was subject to priesthood governance by bishops, stake presidents, and general authorities, and female leaders readily acknowledged this order. In practice, however, YLMIA organizations, like the other organizations run by women, operated autonomously. They launched initiatives, planned their own programs, and presided at their own meetings with minimal input from male leaders.

The relationship of the YMMIA to the priesthood in this period, however, was more complex. Most adult males were ordained to the church's lay priesthood, which was organized in two orders—the Melchizedek Priesthood and the Aaronic Priesthood—and further subdivided into quorums. In the late nineteenth century, it became more common to ordain teenage boys to the Aaronic Priesthood.[131] The YMMIA thus became tightly interwoven with Aaronic Priesthood quorums and their activities, though the two would never become synonymous. The YMMIA was not a priesthood quorum, and membership was not based upon priesthood ordination, though Melchizedek Priesthood office was seen as a prerequisite for some leadership positions. At the stake and general levels, these leaders were called superintendents; at the ward level, they were known as presidents. At the general level, it was customary for the president of the church to serve as superintendent of the YMMIA.[132]

At the first joint meeting of the general boards in 1897, Joseph F. Smith addressed questions of gender and hierarchy using principles that he would continue to emphasize after becoming president of the church four years later. "There can't be two heads," he declared. "Where Priesthood is, they have the authority to preside." Even though both the YMMIA and YLMIA had presidents and officers, they were not equal in authority. Smith taught that since the male YMMIA leaders also held priesthood office, they should be considered the presiding authority when the two organizations met together, though he did not explicitly define what it meant to preside.[133] In practice, presiding at a joint meeting primarily meant having the prerogative to conduct the proceedings oneself or delegate that responsibility to someone else. On multiple occasions, Smith insisted that while a YMMIA officer always presided when the organizations met together, the YLMIA leaders should be given equal chances to conduct.[134] These principles were codified in the pamphlet *Instructions to the Y. L. M. I. A. Officers* and remained in YLMIA handbooks through the 1926 edition.[135]

YLMIA leaders accepted this instruction, but they focused on the sense of companionship and cooperation offered by their relationship with the YMMIA. Comparing the organizations' partnership to a marriage, Elmina Taylor explained, "The interests of husband and wife ar[e] best served when they are made one, and so it will be in this society."[136] Susa Gates, in an editorial, also referenced spousal dynamics, emphasizing harmony and unity in the relationship: "It was the unity which always exists in a perfect home. The man quietly at the head, because he is worthy and ordained, the woman close at his side, perfectly independent in her sphere, and acting harmoniously with her companion."[137] In this view, unity was based on priesthood order.

For YLMIA leaders, then, the conjoint movement raised both hopes and fears. Joining with the men meant new opportunities for leadership and recognition, which they celebrated. Gates asserted that the joint work of the YLMIA and YMMIA was "the only place or portion, in the Church organization, outside of Temple work, where women possess an actual equality of work and interest with the brethren."[138] But leaders also worried that the close collaboration could lead to the subordination of women and loss of their gender-specific priorities. "Let them [the YLMIA] retain the individuality and autonomy of their own organization, and its work," Gates wrote, "for absorption means loss of power and finally of existence, except as an echo."[139]

PLANNING LOCAL CONJOINT ACTIVITIES AND CONVENTIONS

Despite its complexities, the conjoint movement broadened at all levels and helped shape a period of rapid development in the first decade of the twentieth century, bringing the YLMIA and the YMMIA closer together and invigorating them both. Stake conventions—a practice first introduced by the Sunday Schools—became a key event on the YLMIA and YMMIA calendars.[140] The YMMIA held its first stake conventions in 1900; by 1902 the YLMIA joined in a plan to make conventions a joint affair to be held each fall at the beginning of the "Mutual season," which ran parallel to the American school year from fall to spring.[141] During these annual meetings of all stake leaders, visiting general board members conducted leadership training and introduced the centrally prescribed program for the upcoming year. Conventions provided practical training in procedures, record keeping, splitting the associations into age-specific groups, and similar matters; they also sometimes included model classes to demonstrate effective teaching methods. General sessions featured spiritual messages and encouragement. Just as general board leaders visited the stakes and offered training and assistance, stake leaders did the same for the wards in their stewardship. Conventions helped prepare them for these duties.[142]

Conventions facilitated standardization of stake and ward programs, raised the quality of leadership, and created important relationships between general and stake leaders within each organization and across gender lines. They also represented significant expansion of general board duties, since board members were now expected to visit the stakes for conventions, held in August and September, and for stake conferences, held in the winter and spring. In 1903, for example, YLMIA board members visited at least forty-five stake conventions and fifty-one stake conferences in Utah, Idaho, Wyoming, Arizona, Canada, and Mexico.[143] Even with the availability of train travel, this was an ambitious and taxing undertaking for the board. As it became increasingly difficult to meet these demands, they gave preference to the conventions.[144]

The Utah Stake in Provo provides one robust example of what stake conventions looked like. Their fourth annual convention on Sunday, 23 September 1906, was an all-day affair with three separate sessions. Elen Wallace and George Brimhall represented the YLMIA and YMMIA general boards; church apostles Francis M. Lyman and Anthon H. Lund attended the evening conjoint meeting. In the morning and afternoon, stake and local officers of the YLMIA and the YMMIA met separately in sessions geared toward practical discussion of methods and suggestions in their respective organizations; YLMIA leaders considered ways to present the season's work. Three bishops made congratulatory remarks, as did the stake Relief Society president. The afternoon session unfolded in a similar format, with discussions titled "Example of Officers" and "What shall we do with our leisure moments[?]" According to the minutes, Wallace punctuated the local leaders' discussions "with timely and fitting suggestions." Many musical numbers were interspersed between the talks. The evening session was a devotional meeting. Wallace, Lyman, Lund, and stake YMMIA leader Bryant Hinckley addressed the large congregation, which included many stake and local officers. Music was provided by the Provo tabernacle choir and a well-known local soloist.[145]

As programs became more standardized, monthly conjoint officers' meetings became increasingly important.[146] For example, officers of the Utah Stake YLMIA and YMMIA met conjointly on the third Sunday of each month. They listened to reports of leaders' visits to wards in the stake, planned visits for the upcoming month, and discussed other matters of concern. After the conjoint session, the YLMIA leaders met separately to discuss their particular business, primarily more visits to ward associations; they also met with the ward leaders on the third Sunday of each month.[147] On occasion, the conjoint officers' meetings took up special topics. In December 1906, for example, a special session was held to discuss the subjects of reverence, order, and punctuality, resulting in a renewed and determined effort to help the associations improve along these lines.[148]

As mixed-gender interactions increasingly shaped leaders' service at the turn of the century, the dynamics of conjoint activities also became a more regular part of individual members' experience. Ward associations conducted a monthly conjoint meeting on a Sunday evening, and stake-level YLMIA and YMMIA associations sponsored a conjoint meeting on the Sunday evening of each quarterly stake conference.[149] The young women's and young men's organizations also started meeting together for preliminary programs at the beginning of their weekly meetings. These programs were an innovation introduced in the 1901–1902 YMMIA manual to include recreation along with musical and literary instruction, similar to popular literary societies and clubs of the time, and similar to the content of the monthly conjoint meetings that MIAs had held since the 1870s.[150] Each weekly program featured prayer and singing, followed by three short items: a five-minute talk about current events, ten minutes of extemporaneous talks or literary recitations, and a five-minute musical number.[151] These programs gave young people opportunities to develop musical, literary, and public-speaking abilities and became a popular and long-lasting element of weekly MIA meetings.

Meanwhile, the size of the church was expanding, and the organization was changing. Around the turn of the century, wards and stakes were divided and organized to create smaller units that would serve as members' spiritual and social bastions against the encroachments of the world, and many wards and stakes developed strong, cohesive identities with an attendant sense of loyalty and belonging among the members. Institutional activity likewise became more important and more extensive, such that, in the words of one study, "hardly a night went by when the lights of the meetinghouse were not ablaze," and ward-centered activities filled the free time of many members. The intensive focus on church commitments set apart the Saints in the Intermountain West from their neighbors at a time when they were coming to resemble their fellow Americans in many other ways. The YLMIA and YMMIA played prominent roles in the calendars of Latter-day Saints, providing regular opportunities for them to come together.[152]

DEFINING YOUTH

The conjoint movement not only filled young people's time with wholesome activities, but it also helped define them as a discrete group. While gender differences remained important, the *young* in "young people" was a unifying characteristic of girls and boys that served to bring them together in a single category—one that was receiving increasing scrutiny and definition in American culture at the time.

Most famously, in 1904 G. Stanley Hall published his watershed study, *Adolescence: Its Psychology and Its Relations to Physiology, Anthropology, Sociology, Sex, Crime,*

Religion, and Education. Based on more than a decade of his own study as well as earlier work from other researchers, Hall characterized adolescence—the years from puberty to adulthood—as a time of inner stress and conflict, with rapid physical and emotional change brought on by biological forces.[153] People had long known that the years from puberty to adulthood were prone to turbulence, but Hall offered extensive scientific analysis to identify this period as a distinct biological and psychological life stage. Since adolescents could be volatile and vulnerable, Hall argued, they needed unhurried time to grow up in controlled environments, such as school, where adults could monitor and direct their growth.[154]

Such notions appeared in the work of YLMIA and YMMIA leaders of the time as well. In the annual conference of 1904, Josiah Hickman, superintendent of the Utah Stake YMMIA in Provo, Utah, spoke to officers of both organizations about their weighty responsibility to guide the youth. As a longtime teacher, Hickman knew well the coalescing discourse about this newly recognized life stage. Youth was, he explained, a dangerous time when people could easily be lured from safe paths, but it was also a precious period when they shaped their character and established their lives' directions. Hickman asserted, "It is the period when the young receive with greatest readiness, if rightly presented, their deepest religious convictions."[155]

The idea that adolescents often experience intense religious awakening extended back centuries, but many social scientists, including Hall, were exploring the idea around the turn of the century. Hickman specifically cited the work of George A. Coe, a professor at Northwestern University near Chicago, who was then publishing influential research about adolescents and the psychology of religion.[156] Coe had found, Hickman noted, that 80 percent of young people experienced religious conversion between ages twelve and twenty, and a full 50 percent between ages sixteen and eighteen. "This would indicate," he summarized, "that youth, early man-hood and woman-hood, are the periods of life when we get our religious impressions."[157] For Hickman, and Latter-day Saint leaders of youth generally, the implications were clear: the unique needs of young people should shape the structure and content of the church's youth organizations.

In part as a result of conversations about these ideas, leaders grew increasingly aware of the distinctions between young women of different ages in the YLMIA. The age range for "young ladies" eligible to participate in YLMIA was not rigidly defined in the nineteenth century. Hall's definition, however, specified that adolescence comprised the years from fourteen to twenty-four years old.[158] While he offered little explanation for or analysis of these boundaries, they show that in the prevailing view, "youth" extended into the early twenties. From early on, girls were considered old enough to enter the YLMIA around age fourteen, a boundary solidified and reiterated in the 1890s by Elmina Taylor in her responses to repeated inquiries from local leaders.[159] An upper age limit remained undefined but clearly extended into the years when young women might be attending college, working, and marrying. Young women of a considerable age span, therefore, might assemble for a YLMIA meeting. In 1903, YLMIA leaders began recommending that local associations grade, or subdivide, their ranks into junior and senior classes—juniors being ages fourteen to sixteen and seniors ages seventeen and older.[160] Junior lessons began to be published in a special *Guide for the Junior Department*, but senior lessons continued to appear in the *Young Woman's Journal*. Since, as the first *Guide* noted, younger girls were often timid in meetings with the older ones, leaders hoped that everyone would benefit from smaller, peer-group classes in which they could actively participate.[161]

LEADERSHIP TRANSITION AND LOCAL CONTINUITY

As with the appointments of members of the First Presidency, Quorum of the Twelve Apostles, and Relief Society general presidents at the time, Elmina Taylor's appointment as YLMIA general president lasted until her death on 6 December 1904.[162] During the twenty-four years of her presidency, she expanded the organization's structure and helped a collection of largely autonomous local units develop a stronger shared identity. Amid the organization's growth, she worked to maintain a spiritual core for young women's lived experience in the YLMIA. "We should have a reverence for everything that is sacred," she taught, urging young women to address such subjects in their meetings. For Taylor, spiritual purposes connected with the aim of individual and mutual improvement. "Everyone of us should be an angel of charity, every kind act we do will come home to us in blessings, not only in after life but in this life; it will have a sanctified influence upon our character," she said.[163]

Taylor's death marked the end of an era in more than one sense. She was typical of the church's pioneer generation: she was born in 1830, joined the church after profound spiritual experience despite disapproval in her community, and migrated west before the completion of the railroad.[164] Forty-seven-year-old Martha Horne Tingey became the organization's next general president.[165] A daughter of Mary Isabella Horne, retrenchment and Relief Society leader, Tingey was a precocious learner. At age sixteen, she took up the trade of typesetting, in which she worked expertly until her marriage, four years after her appointment as counselor to Taylor in 1880. A spiritually minded young woman, she joined her local young ladies' association, taught in Sunday School and Primary, and sang in the Tabernacle Choir. She was also known for her talent in giving public readings. Having grown up among the Saints in Salt Lake City, Tingey represented the frontier generation, taking up the torch from her convert-pioneer forebears.[166]

Tingey chose for her counselors Ruth May Fox and Mae Taylor Nystrom, both of whom had served on the YLMIA general board, were proponents of women's suffrage, and were active in other women's organizations. Nystrom, in fact, was a daughter of Elmina Taylor and something of a New Woman herself, having graduated from the LDS College and worked as director of a school for physical culture.[167] When the new presidency began their service, the YLMIA had a well-defined organizational structure, a standardized calendar of lessons and meetings, and the expectation of conjoint work with the young men. For local organizations such as the Springville Fourth Ward, where Fanny Rowland served as president, the transition to a new general presidency brought little change in their week-to-week experience. The minutes of the Fourth Ward for the 1906–1907 season provide rich illustration of what those local meetings looked like.

In this small community fifty miles south of Salt Lake City, young ladies' associations had been organized for at least thirty years by 1906 and were woven into the fabric of the community. That year, the Fourth Ward had over forty young women attending YLMIA meetings.[168] Born between 1874 and 1892, most of the girls grew up in the dawning age of the New Woman, and their lives reflected it. Nearly half attended high school, and most of those graduated; eight went to college.[169] Others worked, before or after marriage, and a few enjoyed distinguished professional careers. Four of the women never married, and the rest married on average at age twenty-three, a full four years older than the average age of their mothers when they married.[170]

During the Mutual season, the Fourth Ward YLMIA gathered each Tuesday evening, with an average attendance of thirty-three. At thirty years old, Fanny Rowland presided over nineteen junior and twenty senior girls. One of Fanny's counselors, Melvina Tew, was two years her senior, but the other, Lola White, was only twenty-two—well within the age range of the senior class over whom she had charge. Other members of the association's leadership were likewise young women themselves, the youngest being Vida Houtz at fifteen.[171]

In late August 1906, as another Mutual season was approaching, the young women of Springville had a special visit from Tingey, Fox, and Nystrom, along with general board member May Booth Talmage.[172] The ward had invited the general leaders, and Tingey, who had been encouraging such visits, obliged.[173] In keeping with the concerns of the time, Tingey cautioned the girls against what she called "the evils of familiarity with boys" and counseled them on how they dressed. Fox explained the young women's responsibilities as daughters of Zion, while Nystrom and Talmage got straight to business, discussing the plan of work for the upcoming Mutual season.[174]

That plan went into effect the third Tuesday of September, when the Springville YLMIA launched the first of their regular meetings for the season. Each week was dedicated to a specific focus: they held testimony meetings on the first week of the month, the senior class studied literary subjects and the junior class ethical subjects on the second week, and both classes held theological lessons on the third and fourth weeks. The theological lessons were essentially a New Testament course on the teachings of the Savior. The senior class occasionally also enjoyed a lecture, even though this was not part of the official outlines.[175]

Each week the young women first met together with the young men for a preliminary program before separating for their classes. When they met at the ward meetinghouse at seven o'clock in the evening on 22 January 1907, Alva Zabriskie, president of the YMMIA, presided, and Fanny Rowland conducted. After an opening song and prayer, they sang another hymn, "For the Strength of the Hills." Next, a seventeen-year-old young man gave a reading, followed by a young woman, age eighteen, singing a solo. After this brief preliminary program, the young men left for their classes, but they would return after their lessons for a joint closing hymn and prayer. Meanwhile, the young women remained and held their own opening exercises—something that seems to have been customary—which consisted of roll call and approval of the last meeting's minutes. This was followed by another literary selection that was read aloud by Melvina Tew.[176] The junior and senior young women studied the same lesson: "How Jesus taught by parables No. 2," covering several parables about treasures. The lesson period included time for class members to discuss questions such as "How do these parables inspire hope in the final outcome of God's work?"[177]

The association followed this meeting pattern for the rest of the regular YLMIA season, which lasted through May for the young women (the young men adjourned on 1 April). When the season ended, leaders faced a perennial question: What to do during the summer? Summer was seen as a time of extra temptations for young people, with school out and long, pleasant evenings to fill. But it was also a time for relaxation, sociability, and a change of pace from the rest of the year. Sometimes the YLMIA general board published outlines for summer work, but recently they had relinquished the decision about summer activities to stake and local officers, recommending only that they meet at least monthly and do what they could to maintain an influence on the girls.[178]

In summer 1907, the Springville young women continued to meet weekly. They held monthly testimony meetings and often presented recitations and musical numbers; some weeks they had literary lessons or discussed business matters. A major segment of each meeting was taken up by reading aloud from the *Journal*. The girls seem to have taken turns doing the reading; the others possibly tied a quilt as they listened, as they had the previous summer.[179] The first reading selection that summer, which occupied most weeks from May to July, was a serialized novel, *The Western Boom*.[180] It told of a young Latter-day Saint woman who married a man who was not a member of the church and moved with him to California, where she experienced suffering and tragedy because of her unwise choice. *The Western Boom* was published in the first volume of the magazine, 1889–1890, making it almost two decades old by this time.[181] The Springville Fourth Ward's use of it suggests that the back issues of the magazine continued to be valued.

The Springville young women also enjoyed a few special events throughout the summer. On the fourth Tuesdays of June and July, all the young women of the four wards in town met together, and on 20 August they took an excursion to Sumsion's Grove, a local picnic spot.[182] In mid-July, the Fourth Ward girls hosted an event for the women of their ward Relief Society, which included many of their mothers, presenting for them a model lesson and the subjects for the next season's study, before sharing the musical numbers and refreshments they had prepared.[183]

By early September 1907, it was time to kick off another season. On 10 September, the four Springville wards again met together for their Annual Day. The following week, on 17 September, the Fourth Ward YLMIA leadership was reorganized. Fanny Rowland had been assigned to the stake YLMIA board. She was replaced as president by her sister Louisa. The new president, counselors, and secretary were set apart by their bishop in the meeting. One week later, on 24 September, the Fourth Ward YLMIA resumed its regular meetings and lessons, although the first conjoint session did not take place until 15 October, when the young men's season began.[184]

MAKING HISTORY

Believing that the YLMIA had reached a point of development that warranted recognition, Susa Gates spent much of the first decade of the twentieth century writing the *History of the Young Ladies' Mutual Improvement Association*—a 488-page volume, generously illustrated, that was published in 1911.[185] The *History* gave a unified identity to the organization, celebrating its origins, landmarks, and formative leaders. Most consequentially, the *History* gave the YLMIA an origin story, a past rooted in prophetic leadership that could be used to shape the future.

Up to this point, there had been little discussion of the founding of the young women's organization. In 1892, Gates had published a "Historical Sketch of the Y. L. M. I. A." in the *Young Woman's Journal*, in which she described an iconic scene recounting her father's instruction to his wives and daughters. "All Israel were looking to his family and watching the example set by his wives and children," she reported Brigham Young explaining. He proclaimed that "our daughters are following the vain and foolish fashions of the world" and then exhorted his wives and daughters to make their garments plain and to set the styles for the rest of the world to follow and further to simplify their food and avoid light-mindedness in speech and thought. He called for his family to organize a retrenchment association, which, in this telling, was effected immediately.[186]

When Gates published the official *History* almost two decades later, she inserted much of the 1892 account into the book, but she also made two consequential additions. First, she dated the founding meeting in the Lion House to 28 November 1869. While this date cannot be corroborated from contemporary sources, it nonetheless became the generally recognized anniversary because it appeared in the official history.[187] Second, in the middle of Young's speech to his family, Gates added this statement, "There is need for the young daughters of Israel to get a living testimony of the truth. Young men obtain this while on missions, but this way is not opened to the girls. More testimonies are obtained on the feet than on the knees. I wish our girls to obtain a knowledge of the Gospel for themselves."[188]

It appears that Gates adapted this statement at least in part from an account of the founding of the YMMIA given by Junius Wells, which Gates included later in the *History*. Wells reported that Young told him, "We want to get our boys into the habit of trying to say something in the name of the Lord. More people have received testimonies on their feet than down on their knees praying for them."[189] Gates may have wished to give the young women's organization a charge parallel to the one given to the young men.

These words entered the YLMIA with great force, giving the organization a founding purpose that transcended the retrenchment movement. The young women's organization was to impart a living testimony and knowledge of the gospel of Jesus Christ to young Latter-day Saint women. Its purpose was fundamentally spiritual, reflecting the YLMIA's emphasis on building a personal witness of truth. Attributing the importance of testimony to a prophet and making it part of the organization's founding story gave it added weight and staying power.

No matter where the statement attributed to Young originated, it certainly expressed an idea that resonated deeply. Leaders began to use the *History* almost immediately to invoke the founding account in teaching about the organization's purpose.[190] The account figured prominently as the organization observed its fiftieth anniversary in 1919 (based on the 28 November 1869 date in the *History*). In her commemorative article, May Talmage recounted the founding meeting and quoted Young's exhortation about testimony; Ruth May Fox incorporated it into a short fictional story.[191] The excerpt from the *History* quoting Young was republished in handbooks and manuals for decades and became part of the organization's fundamental self-definition.[192] The YLMIA would consistently strive to keep young women on their feet *and* on their knees, seeking spiritual knowledge through service and study.

The *History* was an important marker of the development of the YLMIA over the preceding two decades. Against the backdrop of turbulent transitions in the Latter-day Saint community—notably the end of plural marriage, which raised urgent concerns about young women's marital prospects—the organization had established a bedrock emphasis on helping girls find their own spiritual witness that would motivate them to remain firmly in the community and make good choices for their lives. Both the leadership and the young members of the organization increasingly reflected the ethos of the New Woman in their lives and service. From a loose confederation of localized groups organized under the same banner, the YLMIA had become a centrally directed organization, with its own magazine and standardized lessons, calendars, and leadership structures.

At the 1909 annual Conjoint Conference of the MIAs—increasingly known simply as the June Conference—longtime YMMIA leader George Q. Morris expressed a fundamental conceptual shift that was taking place in Latter-day Saints' thinking about the MIAs. "In all my work in this cause," Morris declared, "I have assumed that it is one organization—the Mutual Improvement Association—and that the Young Men's association is but one department of that work; that the Young Ladies' is another." While recognizing that they were, in fact, individual organizations, he insisted, "If we work upon this basis, and keep this principle in mind, we can not help but co-operate, because we are one, and we act and work and plan together."[193]

YLMIA leaders embraced this vision and gladly joined in close cooperation with the YMMIA. At the same time, they recognized the need to maintain their distinctness and keep sight of the particular needs of young women. For the time being, leaders struck a successful balance between cooperation and autonomy, and Morris's comments captured a dynamic that would shape the young women's and young men's organizations for another sixty years. They were becoming known simply as the MIA.

MAKING THE MIA

1911–1930

On the morning of Sunday, 4 June 1911, a congregation of church youth leaders assembled in the Tabernacle on Temple Square in Salt Lake City for the annual June Conference of the Mutual Improvement Associations. The topic for the meeting was social affairs. At the time, patterns of social interaction were in flux as more and more people moved from rural areas to cities. Edith Rossiter Lovesy, a thirty-five-year-old YLMIA board member, was born in Salt Lake City when it had about twenty thousand residents. The city's population had surpassed fifty thousand by the time she moved away at age twenty-five in 1901. Over the next decade, Salt Lake City's population nearly doubled: when Lovesy returned to speak at the 1911 conference, the population was approaching one hundred thousand.[1] Evidence of change was everywhere. The Utah Light and Railway Company had built a massive new facility, known as Trolley Square, to house 144 streetcars that helped people move across the city to work, study, shop, and socialize.[2] A growing number of businesses, including dance halls, catered specifically to young people. Amid the growth came a continued influx of establishments thought to be disreputable, such as billiard halls, saloons, theaters for vaudeville and silent movies, and even brothels.[3]

Salt Lake City was hardly the only city to experience such growth and the accompanying social challenges in this period. The rapid urbanization of recent decades had brought throngs of young people, particularly single young women, to cities across the United States to work, and most of them lodged in boardinghouses if they had no relatives in the city.[4] Weekly working hours for many in turn-of-the-century

America were decreasing, allowing more time for the pursuit of leisure activities, and businesses advertised new and alluring ways for young people to spend their wages and free time.[5] Single young working women, with enough money or a generous date, could enjoy commercialized recreation where genders regularly mixed, often without supervision, in places like dance halls, amusement parks, and movie theaters. A new national culture of consumption and leisure was developing alongside looser norms of female-male relations, and young people readily participated.[6]

As technologies reduced the time and energy needed for transportation and domestic labor, new doors opened for young people. They attended at least some school as a matter of course; increasing numbers graduated from high school and even went on to college. Athletics, entertainment, and cultural events proliferated, as did the financial means and freedom of movement to enjoy them.[7] Everyday life and national systems alike were being remade by developments such as electricity, telephones, indoor plumbing, household appliances, prepackaged food, ready-made clothing, and modern medical care.[8]

Membership in The Church of Jesus Christ of Latter-day Saints grew steadily and gradually expanded beyond its Utah center. In 1910, about 80 percent of the church's 400,000 members lived in the Intermountain West. By 1930, there would be 670,000 members, with just over 70 percent living in the Intermountain West.[9] As the church expanded in other parts of the United States and the world, new leaders instituted organizations for their young women. The Mapusaga branch in Samoa organized a YLMIA by 1909; Gaffney, South Carolina, had one in 1914; and the Puketapu branch in New Zealand formed a YLMIA in 1921.[10]

Societal changes rippled into individuals' lives and family dynamics. Camilla Eyring, who turned sixteen in 1910, lived in a Latter-day Saint settlement in rural northern Mexico. She attended school and learned about evolution in a biology class—this during a time of heightened concern in the church community about the issue. "I swallowed the new daring theory hook, line and sinker and delighted to argue with father and mother," she wrote. She also argued with her father over young women's growing tendency to go to social events in groups that included young men. "I always went with them at his protest," she said. Her time of return was another issue. "Sometimes when I came home later than I should I would take my shoes off and sneak up the stairs to bed," she said. The technique, though, was imperfect. "The stairs were sure to squeak before I could get up to the top step and father wake to scold me a bit." Camilla experienced similar differences outside her home: she remembered MIA-sponsored dances as a negotiation between the adult generation, concerned about which dance forms to permit and prohibit, and young participants looking for ways to dance with closer physical contact than their elders appreciated.[11]

In the United States, this complex period of industrialization, urbanization, and immigration, spanning the late nineteenth and early twentieth centuries, became known as the Progressive Era. This era was characterized by the work of reformers known for both their zeal for curing social ills and their optimism about their ability to do so. They organized for social improvement, creating new government institutions and voluntary associations and seeking to apply scientific expertise to solve problems.[12] Some worked to improve employment and living conditions for workers by organizing labor unions and mutual aid societies. Organizations like the Young Women's Christian Association (YWCA) and Girls' Friendly Society, both nondenominational religious groups, offered safe and highly supervised boarding options for women, as well as free libraries, classes in subjects like cooking and sewing, and even concerts and other entertainments designed to contend with the wanton appeals of dance halls and movie theaters.[13]

For their part, many American Latter-day Saints found that their theology of eternal progression aligned well with other Americans' progressive mood and optimistic outlook. As the twentieth century entered its second decade, Latter-day Saints, having weathered the initial shocks of cultural change within their community, were poised to join the rapidly developing modern American order. Like others, Latter-day Saints at this time emphasized progress through the application of scientific methods, technological discoveries, and systematic social organization in virtually every realm of life. It was a time of great optimism—about science and technology, about education and culture, and most of all about human potential.[14] In this context, Latter-day Saint belief in unlimited human potential and in the power of collective effort to achieve idealistic goals offered a way for the Saints to reconcile their faith with the national culture they aspired to join.

Early indications of this progressive approach to social concerns were evident in MIA leaders' speeches at the 1911 June Conference. In her address, Edith Lovesy declared, "It is natural that youth should be joyous, and needful that they should be given relaxation, and diversion." But she added a warning: "Let us be morally thoughtful about the forms of amusements we encourage or patronize."[15]

Following Lovesy, YMMIA leader Edward Anderson reflected on the place of the MIA in an era of change. "We are large enough," he said, "to exercise great influence for good, healthful, clean amusements, self-respect, politeness and conduct among our communities." In expressing his confidence that the MIA had the tools to act as a pillar of local life, Anderson noted that many stakes and wards had taken up wholesome activities, including debates, dancing, home socials, calisthenics, athletics, music, oratory, storytelling, drama, and nature outings.[16] Zina Bennion Cannon, president of the Granite Stake YLMIA in Salt Lake City, spoke of specific efforts in her stake, including hiring a teacher from the University of Utah to give dance instruction to representatives from each ward, who then shared what they had learned with their members.[17] Rachel Grant Taylor, who would soon join the YLMIA general board after years of service on the local level, closed the session by urging leaders to become better acquainted with young women so they themselves would stay young in spirit and thereby wield greater influence.[18]

The speakers in this session did not announce a new program or different direction for the MIA, but their preoccupation with recreation reflected an increasing focus of the MIA. Susa Gates's history of the YLMIA up to 1910 noted the organization's roots in the retrenchment movement, which involved resisting outside influences through restraint, simple living, and study. By 1911, the tides had shifted toward engaging with the current interests of youth and channeling their energy for spiritual and communal ends. For the next six decades, an emphasis on recreation shaped the identity of the MIA as its leaders' fundamental goal became teaching the gospel through activities. The organizations sought to blend the spiritual and the temporal, bringing young people more securely into the church by offering them a fun and uplifting place to belong. "I know that where we have control of the amusements of the young people we have more influence with them," Zina Cannon observed. "If we mingle with them in their amusements, we become better acquainted with them, and a fellowship grows up between us that would not otherwise exist."[19]

TEACHING THE GOSPEL THROUGH ACTIVITIES

Recreation was an important theme of Camilla Eyring's experience as a young woman in her teens and early twenties. She recalled feeling isolated when she arrived in Provo, Utah, as a refugee, having left her home in Mexico during the Mexican Revolution. She felt so self-conscious about her clothes, which didn't match Provo fashions, that she initially wouldn't go to Sunday School or activities. However, after she secured some income and learned to sew dresses in local styles, recreation became a central mode of her relationship-building. Her autobiography recounts hikes, church dances, movies, parties at private dance halls, and membership in a sorority. Organized recreational outlets, whether religious, academic, or commercial, were particularly valuable to people like Camilla, whose young adult lives were marked by constant movement. Between her first church dance in 1909 and her marriage in 1917, Camilla lived in Colonia Juárez, Chihuahua, Mexico; El Paso, Texas; Provo, Utah; Hinckley, Utah; San Francisco; Pima, Arizona; Logan, Utah; and Salt Lake City.[20] While MIA organizations were more fully developed in majority Latter-day Saint communities, MIAs also had a long-standing presence, often led by missionaries, in branches like the one in San Francisco.[21] For young women like Camilla, MIA activities could be an accessible, low-stakes way to meet new people.

MIA leaders had higher aims than merely facilitating young people's social lives. Like Edith Lovesy, they believed recreation could bring religion into young people's hearts, and their rhetoric shows how comprehensively they defined recreation.[22] "Social affairs," one writer explained in the *Young Woman's Journal*, "embrace the highest economic and ethical principles that can be applied to the problems of collective living."[23] Recreation was physical, moral, spiritual, and social in nature. It developed talents and abilities. Therefore, it encompassed almost any organized activity—but the *organized* aspect was essential.

Progressive recreation reformers also saw a close connection between physical, social, and moral development. By developing people's individual character, constructive recreation improved society. Reformers worried that children and youth who spent their time in school and adults who worked all day in offices and factories were becoming physically unfit, their nerves overstrained and their bodies underdeveloped. They also worried that children in the city had too little to do and needed supervised public spaces with open air to channel their energies away from vice.[24] Public parks, playgrounds, and organized sports leagues were outgrowths of this movement. The *Young Woman's Journal* ran several articles noting local developments on this front.[25] And in 1910 the church opened the Deseret Gymnasium in downtown Salt Lake City, giving local Latter-day Saints a state-of-the-art facility for pursuing wholesome recreation.[26]

Religious thinkers in the wider society had seized on such ideas to explore ways of combining physical activity with religious programming. For decades, American religionists had sought ways to energize their churches by employing athletics to instill good habits and ideals among those who might not otherwise engage in religious practice, with the ultimate goal of guiding them more firmly into the Christian fold. The YWCA and Young Men's Christian Association (YMCA) were among the national organizations seeking to synthesize the religious and the recreational and thereby attract participation in religion.[27] For Latter-day Saints, church-sponsored recreation presented a possible path to retaining young people who might be less spiritually inclined, while at the same time helping Latter-day Saint youth achieve greater respectability in American society in the years following the end of plural marriage.[28]

Latter-day Saints also developed a unique theological basis for their sponsorship of recreation, in keeping with their longstanding belief in the spiritual significance of the physical and material aspects of life.[29] Addressing MIA leaders at the 1912 June Conference, B. H. Roberts invoked scriptures defining the soul as the spirit and the body combined in one and teaching that God views all things as spiritual.

He insisted that the body is holy and that pursuing physical development is just as sacred a part of the work of mutual improvement as efforts at spiritual and moral improvement.[30]

In 1915, YLMIA board member Mary Connelly laid out an even more explicit rationale in a June Conference address titled "Teaching the Gospel through M. I. A. Activities." Quoting the account of Brigham Young's founding charge to the MIAs, Connelly reminded leaders, "More testimonies are obtained on the feet than on the knees." While some worried that recreational activities took the MIA's focus away from gospel learning, Connelly insisted that idea was mistaken. She used the example of competitive activities. "Isn't there an opportunity there for teaching brotherliness, justice, honesty, truth, integrity, glorying in the success of others?" Debating, music, and storytelling, she argued, all likewise brought spiritual growth. "All through the work everywhere is the Gospel standard," she insisted. It was MIA leaders' duty to "teach [youth] the Gospel of Jesus Christ, which embraces all truth," she exhorted, "the Gospel of being and of doing." Young people would learn spiritual truths and values by applying those truths and values as they participated in activities in the MIA. Connelly's language—"teaching the gospel through activities"—gave expression to the foundational understanding of the MIA's goals, an expression that would persist for the next six decades.

ESTABLISHING YOUTH CONTESTS

One of the clearest indicators of the 1910s' rapid expansion of recreation in the MIAs was the rise of "contest work" on the ward, stake, and general levels. Contests grew out of stakes' annual MIA Days, large community events held in the spring to mark the end of the Mutual season.[31] General leaders of the MIA observed such events and advocated for more areas to adopt similar practices. In his 1911 talk, for example, Edward Anderson noted that an increasing number of stakes were holding these celebrations, which featured contests in athletics, dance, music, oratory, and storytelling, as well as presentations of lectures and exercises from the manuals.[32]

The general boards of the YLMIA and YMMIA had also begun sponsoring athletic contests at the annual June Conference. The first MIA Field Day held during June Conference was in 1906, featuring a baseball game between the young men's teams from the Box Elder and Weber stakes in northern Utah and a basketball game between two young women's teams from Salt Lake City, as well as some footraces.[33] In 1911, a fourteen-stake MIA track meet featured young men competing in individual and relay races, jumping, pole vaulting, and shot put.[34] On the preceding day, young men's basketball games and wrestling matches had been held at the Deseret Gymnasium, along with classes of women and girls demonstrating calisthenics and folk dancing.[35]

The associations also held music contests, which gave young women more opportunity for participation. The Granite Stake in Salt Lake City had pioneered large-scale music contests in the MIA in 1909 when it held a song festival intended to stimulate interest in music.[36] Wards entered contestants in twelve categories, including chorus, trio and quartet, vocal solo, and violin, piano, and organ performance.[37] Again, the YLMIA general board worked to spread local innovation. In a 1912 article, board organist Mattie Read Evans described contests in the Granite, Jordan, and Salt Lake stakes and said that "every stake in the church should inaugurate the same system and take up the work in the same spirit."[38] By 1913, contests had become a large focus at the annual June Conference. Finals in storytelling, oratory, and quartet singing (male and female) took place on Saturday evening, 7 June, in front of a large audience in the Assembly Hall on Temple Square in Salt Lake City. Several female quartets competed, and the young women from the Wasatch Stake in Heber City, Utah, took first place.[39]

Unsurprisingly, performances in competition became a source of local pride. A Utah County paper praised two local 1913 finalists in oratory, who narrowly lost out to boys. "Two pretty Y. L. M. I. A. girls, Miss Lisle Lindsay of Heber City and Miss Lethe Coleman of Midway, won the popular, if not the judicial decision," the report read. Lisle's story was entitled "Theodosius's Pearls," and Lethe's oration on Utah was described as patriotic and full of love for her state.[40] Contest success could also bolster personal aspirations, and both young women mentioned in the newspaper continued to cultivate their talents. Lisle went on to teach dramatic arts and physical education classes at Brigham Young College in Logan.[41] Lethe went on to appear in numerous church-related film productions, including *How Near to the Angels*, the first dramatic film produced by the young women's organization.[42] Lethe's most famous performance came when she was eighty-three years old, starring in a church video called *The Mailbox*.[43]

A culture of performance and contests opened the door for independent performance groups to enter church settings. For example, in the western Utah town of Iosepa—populated mainly by Hawaiian church members—MIA minutes mention a variety of musical numbers by MIA members alongside performances by local groups like the Kawailani Glee Club and the Hawaiian Troubadours of Iosepa.[44]

As contests grew more prominent in the MIAs—bringing with them the potential for controversy and hurt feelings—leaders felt it necessary to explain how they helped the organizations achieve their goals. Speaking at the joint officers' meeting of the 1913 June Conference, Oscar A. Kirkham, a YMMIA board member, took up the subject. Contests provided both individual and group benefits, he said. They inspired young people to give their best and ended the MIA season on a climactic

Alpine Stake MIA orchestra at June Conference. 1927. This orchestra composed of MIA members from Utah County won second place in its division at the music contest finals. Churchwide contests in music, speech, drama, and dance were highly anticipated features of the annual MIA conference. (Church History Library, Salt Lake City.)

note. They also taught young people how to compete graciously. "Life is a series of contests," he declared, and it was good for young people to learn the life lessons of winning and losing among friends and fellow Saints. Finally, Kirkham envisioned the ultimate purpose of contests: "If the officers and members get the proper spirit of this movement," he exhorted, "they will realize that it is not to win or lose, but to grow, that matters." He saw meaningful victory in the hours of preparation and improvement that contests required.[45] May Green, speaking on behalf of YLMIA leaders, agreed. "The idea of contest is not the main thing," she said. "It is only a means to an end." The main goal was helping young people improve their talents and desire advancement.[46] Local leaders and members shared this enthusiasm for contest work, and a large majority of stakes expressed clear appreciation for it.[47]

The stakes that implemented contest work saw the added benefit of increased youth engagement and participation in MIA activities, in some cases quadrupling regular attendance.[48] Throughout the decade, contest work flourished in the MIAs, both reflecting and contributing to the momentum of a recreational focus. In 1915, the finals at the June Conference featured public speaking, storytelling, quartet recitals, choral performances, and a short drama.[49] In 1916, leaders introduced an award system: each ward earned points when its members participated in or won a contest, and each stake awarded a pennant "to the ward scoring the greatest number of points in proportion to its enrollment."[50] As the United States entered World War I in 1917, the YLMIA sponsored contests reflecting the ethic of the times. Young women could earn a share of $300 in prize money for preserving the most dried corn, peas, or fruit.[51] The scope, content, and configuration of contests varied from year to year, but they became a standard element of the organizations' programs.

ORGANIZING THE FIRST GIRLS' CAMP

Since the MIA season officially ran from fall to late spring, the question of what recreational activities to sponsor during the summer—if any—was a perennial one. Meanwhile, the idea of summer homes and camps as a restorative response to the demands of modern city living was taking hold all over the United States, often with a distinctively religious bent. The Salvation Army, for example, had been developing "fresh air" camps since 1897, and in 1898 the Young Women's Bible Training Movement established a camp, later known as Camp Pinnacle, overlooking the Hudson Valley in New York. By the turn of the century, the YWCA had also opened camps that offered experiences in outdoor skills and sports, with a focus on transforming character and "ministering to the whole person."[52]

Latter-day Saints in Utah also became interested in using the summer months to give girls some time away from city life. In 1912, the newly appointed president of the Liberty Stake YLMIA, Emily Hillam Higgs, resolved to organize a girls' summer camp. As a young woman, Higgs had worked in various positions and attended LDS College for a year and a half. After her husband died in 1905, she became a secretary at an insurance company to support her family. It was likely during this time as a single mother that Higgs gained an appreciation for the benefits of outdoor life. Her oldest son, Brentnall, developed tuberculosis, and the doctor prescribed outdoor living. So the family built a small "sleeping house" behind the regular house. This sleeping house allowed for constant fresh air, and the family often slept in it year-round. Later, Higgs and two of her siblings purchased land in Emigration Canyon, east of Salt Lake City, where they built a cabin similar to the sleeping house behind the family's home in the city.[53]

Higgs and her stake board recognized that many of the young women in their stake were employed in various jobs in the city or studying in school, and they believed these young women would benefit from some time in what they called "nature's luxuries." Yet they also recognized that commercial summer resorts were unaffordable for many.[54] Therefore, in addition to planning for the camp itself, the board began raising funds to pay for their own campsite. Fundraising events included a stake outing to Saltair, a church-owned resort on the shores of the Great Salt Lake, as well as activities at the Deseret Gymnasium. The stake presidency also contributed, and eventually the stake raised $365.27 toward the camp (the equivalent of $9,746 in 2020).[55]

Early in 1912, Higgs and her counselors rode all over the Salt Lake Valley with the stake president, Hugh Cannon, in his automobile to scout for an appropriate location. The place they chose was in a glen about a mile east of Murray, on the farm of James and Fannie Jones Godfrey, who had lived there for several decades.[56] Though the site was only a twenty-minute walk from the streetcar line, it felt sufficiently remote from civilization.[57] The Godfreys agreed to host the camp on their property and widened and deepened a portion of a stream on their property to make a swimming hole for the young women. One evening each week at camp, one of the Godfreys' sons acted as a teamster and took the campers for a hayride on country lanes. In addition to the money raised by the stake, each camper paid twenty-five cents to the teamster and twenty-five cents toward upkeep of the camp.[58]

With the money they raised, the stake YLMIA leaders built modest sleeping quarters for the girls. The building's walls were made of boards halfway up and then connected to the roof with netting, and the cabin could sleep about twenty girls on cots and straw mattresses. A member of the stake donated his labor to install electric lights, and a music company in Salt Lake donated a piano. Swings and hammocks were strung out among the trees.[59] Next to the swimming hole, leaders furnished a tent so that the girls could change in privacy, and atop a fifty-foot cottonwood pole hung an American flag.[60]

Three rules governed the new campsite, called Liberty Glen: (1) The girls must be present and ready for meals at appointed times. (2) The girls must not leave camp without permission from their leader. (3) Camp must be kept sanitary and left clean. Otherwise, in keeping with the goal of giving young women a vacation, camp life was largely unstructured. The campers took turns cooking the meals according to a menu that the leaders had planned and the young women had practiced at home. Likewise, camp responsibilities rotated among participants: While one group of three girls cooked, another group served the food and washed dishes, and still another group made the beds and did necessary cleaning.[61] Everyone else enjoyed free time. Parents and ward leaders were invited to visit the camp one day during the week and join in activities like bonfires, candy pulls, concerts and performances, and open-air dances.[62] The young women also received some outdoor training. One afternoon during the week, Joshua Hughes Paul, who was the president of LDS University, came to teach the young women about flowers, insects, and birds.[63]

Liberty Glen Camp proved immediately popular, and the YLMIA general board took notice. They interviewed Higgs to learn how she had organized the camp, and in 1916 Higgs herself became a member of the general board.[64] That first year, eighty-two young women and fifteen officers attended the camp, taking turns attending in groups of twenty for a week each. The next year, the number rose to ninety-eight, and the stake added a dining lodge next to the dormitory.[65] Higgs later recalled what summer camp would come to mean as it grew into an integral program for the young women: "The girls wake each morning in their new world. Their busy life has been left behind. There is time and opportunity to think and feel," she said. Higgs saw shared time in that setting as nurturing social development. "They become a united family of friends. Their social instincts begin to develop." She also felt camp revealed and nurtured a foundational spirituality. "Morning is the time for daily devotional prayer," she wrote. "Their hearts easily attune to their Heavenly Father."[66]

SCOUTING AND THE MIA

The desire to teach young people values through experiences in nature extended beyond Higgs's efforts. Around the same time the Liberty Stake YLMIA was establishing its camp, the YMMIA was investigating the possibility of affiliating with the Boy Scouts of America (BSA), which attempted to reconnect boys with pre-urban skills and train them to be leaders.[67] By 1911, YMMIA leaders had formed a committee headed by church general authority B. H. Roberts to study the matter and report back to the board. The committee saw much good in the Boy Scouts program but initially advised against joining. They were concerned about diverting engagement from church-sponsored activities and convinced that the Latter-day Saint youth program had the resources necessary to achieve their goals.[68]

The Scouting idea was too popular and attractive to drop altogether, and YMMIA leaders continued to explore options. The director of physical training at Brigham Young University (BYU) proposed creating a Scouting-inspired organization specific to Latter-day Saint boys. Writing in the *Improvement Era*, he suggested the "Boy Pioneers of Utah" as an adjunct to the YMMIA. It would teach all the same outdoor skills as the Boy Scouts, but it would also incorporate an emphasis on the Saints' pioneer legacy.[69] This idea never came to fruition, but it represented a growing desire to give better shape and a name to boys' activities. In late 1911, YMMIA leaders voted to give the name MIA Scouts to the scouting-inspired activities the organization was beginning to sponsor.[70] Local leaders were to continue with regular lessons from the class manuals, but they were also to organize local MIA Scouts units, adapting guidelines from the Boy Scouts handbook though they were not affiliated with the organization.[71]

The new MIA Scouts program continued through 1912, but by 1913, the BSA began working to bring all the various Scouting movements—which were then only somewhat loosely connected as a system—together into a central organization. S. A. Moffat, the field secretary of the BSA, visited Salt Lake City over 7 and 8 January 1913 to pursue the goal of affiliating the YMMIA with the Boy Scouts.[72] It was apparently a fruitful visit. When the general board leaders met for another round of discussions in February 1913, B. H. Roberts favored affiliation, and the board voted with him.[73] But Church leaders wanted to maintain some autonomy. At the insistence of the YMMIA, the BSA agreed to commission John H. Taylor, who had overseen MIA Scouts, to oversee all Boy Scout work in the church through the YMMIA, preserving its distinct identity within the national organization.[74]

The YLMIA and YMMIA had some shared practices with Scouting, such as using brief statements like a motto, a slogan, and a law to communicate core values.[75] The YMMIA and YLMIA already each had a motto: The scriptural phrase "The Glory of God Is Intelligence" had appeared on the nameplate of the YMMIA publication *Improvement Era* since its initial 1897 issue, and a 1904 article noted that the YMMIA in Norway had taken the phrase as its official motto.[76] That same year, the *Young Woman's Journal* began publishing its own phrase on each issue's title page: "Improvement our motto, Perfection our aim." This motto went back as far as 1880.[77] Beginning in 1914, the YMMIA and YLMIA jointly adopted a slogan for each mutual improvement year.[78] Some slogans reflected progressive engagement on social issues. For example, the 1916 slogan—"We stand for state and nationwide prohibition"—expressed Latter-day Saint support for a progressive reform intended to improve health and home life by eliminating the alcohol industry. Slogans also encouraged spiritual and religious growth, such as "divine guidance through individual and family prayer," "attendance at sacrament meetings" (Sunday worship services where members partake of the Lord's Supper), and "a testimony of the divine mission of Joseph Smith."[79]

Each year the general boards of the YLMIA and YMMIA prayerfully considered current needs and conditions and formulated the slogan, which they introduced at June Conference with a talk explaining its meaning and application. The congregation then stood and repeated the slogan, literally "standing for" its message. At every session of the conference, leaders repeated and discussed the slogan, and they often also printed it on buttons for all to wear. Thus fired with enthusiasm for the new slogan, stake and ward officers returned home to implement it in their organizations through talks, music, readings and scripture recitations, dramatizations, testimony meetings, and class work.[80] The slogans became a prominent focus each year, emphasized in the handbook as "the rallying cry that concentrates M. I. A. effort to live by gospel standards."[81]

BEE-HIVE GIRLS

Both nationally and locally, the development of boys' outdoor programs led many to call for similar opportunities for girls. The Girl Guides originated in Britain when girls demanded to be included in Boy Scout activities; it was adapted as Girl Scouts in the United States in 1912. In the same year, another organization called the Camp Fire Girls was established.[82] YLMIA leaders quickly recognized the potential of these movements to provide a framework for their organization's summer work. Ann Cannon of the general board led out in investigating the feasibility of affiliating with one of the girls' organizations.[83] During the summer of 1913, the Ensign Stake YLMIA in Salt Lake City experimented with some aspects of Camp Fire Girls, and the Box Elder Stake in northern Utah tested the Girl Guides program.[84]

At the time, Camp Fire Girls was the largest girls' organization and the focus of YLMIA leaders' investigations. Founded by the recreational reformers Charlotte and Luther Gulick and a group of likeminded associates, Camp Fire Girls sought to address what Luther Gulick called "a new relation of women to the world."[85] The Gulicks believed that modern culture had contributed to a disassociation between girls and their domestic nature. Their program sought to arouse girls' womanhood by featuring activities centered on the campfire, which represented the hearth fire and women's imagined primeval role as conservators of the home.[86] Spending time in nature and tending the fire, the Gulicks believed, would help girls internalize an archetypal femininity. The Camp Fire Girls incorporated stereotyped Native American imagery, and rather than adopt a slogan, Charlotte Gulick used a kind of acronym she thought sounded like an Indigenous word, coining the term *Wohelo* from the first letters of the three words that the organization stood for: *work, health,* and *love*.[87] The program was based on practical activities, many of them taking place outdoors, that would develop these ideals, with participants proceeding through three ranks and being rewarded with beads for completing requirements in seven areas.[88]

Camp Fire Girls proved influential with YLMIA members and leaders. In 1914 the general board published a detailed outline of possible activities based on the Camp Fire Girls program. The work was optional, but it did provide practical mutual improvement work for the summer.[89] Madelyn Stewart, Ann Cannon's niece, was thirteen at the time. Over the next year, she completed requirements in the seven outlined areas, including practicing correct horse-riding form, planning a balanced vegetarian diet for a week, memorizing five folk songs, identifying twenty wildflowers, making a pair of pajamas, and earning money to pay for a Camp Fire Girls uniform and beads.[90] Meanwhile, Cannon and her committee corresponded with Luther Gulick about the possibility of official affiliation with the Camp Fire Girls organization, along the same lines as the YMMIA's adoption of the Boy Scout program.[91]

Leaders soon decided not to affiliate, however. Like their male counterparts, YLMIA leaders wanted autonomy, and they were unconvinced that affiliation would allow it. Cannon explained that they felt it was necessary for the YLMIA to keep control of their program and not cede oversight to a national organization. YLMIA leaders also worried that the charter fees and annual dues would burden the members and be difficult for leaders to collect, and they saw the potential for Camp Fire Girls activities to overtake the YLMIA's other priorities. Representatives from the Camp Fire Girls did not make the same sort of follow-up recruiting visit BSA representatives had made. Instead, with Luther Gulick's blessing, the YLMIA leaders decided to create their own version of the program.[92]

The result was the Bee-Hive Girls program, which was announced in March 1915.[93] Honeybees had long been a symbol of biblical significance in the United States, including through references to the country as a New Canaan, flowing with milk and honey.[94] The image of the beehive was embraced by early frontier communities for its powerful imagery of communal harmony and by Freemasons as a symbol of industry and thrift. For Latter-day Saints, the beehive, or *deseret* as it was called in the Book of Mormon, was an integral representation of industry and collective effort.[95] Ruth May Fox, a counselor in the YLMIA general presidency, was the first to suggest the honeybee as a symbol of YLMIA.[96] When board member Elen Wallace discovered a book by Maurice Maeterlinck, *Life of the Bee,* the board realized the symbol could work well with the program. Maeterlinck's detailed exposition of the workings of bees and beehives provided a framework for the ideals and skills the program would teach. "It seems almost as if it had been written to meet our especial need," they later wrote.[97] Wallace testified that the experience of finding the beehive symbolism and mapping it onto the new program was inspired by God.[98]

The Bee-Hive Girls program became the summer work for all young women in the YLMIA. "Swarms" of eight to twelve young women met weekly under the direction of an adult "Bee-Keeper." The bees' work, as Wallace explained it, was animated by an unseen force directing the bees' united efforts, known as the spirit of the hive. Likewise, young women began their membership in the swarm by learning and reciting a theme titled "Spirit of the Hive," which laid out the ideals Bee-Hive Girls should strive for in their subsequent development:

Have Faith
Seek Knowledge
Safeguard Health
Honor Womanhood
Understand Beauty
Know Work
Love Truth
Taste the Sweetness of Service
Feel Joy[99]

After completing a certain number of requirements, Bee-Hive Girls advanced in ranks. The three ranks were modeled after roles and dynamics related to the beehive: some worker bees establish the hive by building cells from wax, others go out into the fields to gather pollen, and the human beekeeper oversees the work of the whole hive. Likewise, Bee-Hive Girls moved from Builder in the Hive to Gatherer of Honey to Keeper of the Bees, progressing from acquiring individual knowledge and skills to becoming a leader who could help direct the work of others.[100] Each requirement was called a cell, as a beehive is made up of cells, and young women filled cells in seven fields, as a bee gathers pollen in fields of flowers. The fields were religion, home, health, domestic arts, out-of-doors, business, and public service. Leaders were encouraged to complete requirements alongside the young women to promote mutual understanding.[101] Requirements encouraged good health ("For at least one month, refrain between meals from candy, chewing gum, sundaes, sodas, and commercially manufactured beverages"), domestic skills ("Keep a written account of all money received and spent during one month, classifying it under the heads of food, clothing, amusements, tithing, reserve fund, etc."), and artistic sensibilities ("Commit to memory a poem of not less than twenty-five lines").[102]

As the founders of the Camp Fire Girls had done, YLMIA leaders expressed the culture and aims of the new organization through a watchword: *Womanho*, made up of the first letters of the words *work*, *mankind*, and *home*. Two original Bee-Hive Girls songs appeared in the first handbook, and light blue, gold, and brown were designated the official colors.[103] Uniforms were not required at first, although it was suggested that young women wear a shorter skirt (or bloomers when hiking), a sailor-style blouse, and a necktie, in some combination of the official colors.[104] At the end of the season, each group celebrated the Day of the Swarm by meeting as a stake group to demonstrate and celebrate their accomplishments. On 14 September 1915, the first Day of the Swarm ceremony was held in the Assembly Hall on Temple Square in Salt Lake City.[105] Madelyn Stewart, who had faithfully fulfilled the Bee-Hive Girls program requirements, was among the first to receive the Builder in the Hive rank.[106]

The Bee-Hive Girls program was the first personal achievement program for Latter-day Saint young women, cementing the YLMIA's commitment to self-improvement. In its early years, the program's combination of group activities and personal advancement made it a close corollary to the Boy Scouts, only more rooted in Latter-day Saint imagery and goals. "The purpose," the Bee-Hive Girls handbook declared, "is to perfect our womanhood,—to hold the faith of our fathers and develop it in our individual womanhood, drawing from all good sources to do so."[107] That purpose statement balanced the perennial impulses toward retrenchment and improvement: the program was meant both to anchor youth in an inheritance of Latter-day Saint faith and to open new horizons for them in a larger world. By adapting an outside program for their own use, YLMIA leaders gathered the best the world had to offer and brought it home to use in building Zion.

AUXILIARIES TO THE PRIESTHOOD

The same striving for balance that guided the YLMIA—preserving the faith of the forebears while drawing innovations from all good sources—was also playing out elsewhere in the church organization. The MIA, Relief Society, and Sunday School had each built up their own fundraising systems, publications, leadership lines, and sometimes even buildings. They were all learning from and partnering with outside organizations, and they operated mostly autonomously.[108] As the church grew in numbers and complexity, church presidents could no longer rely on networks of personal relationships to ensure coordination. Church president Joseph F. Smith recognized the challenges of leading nearly half a million Latter-day Saints, concentrated in the area around Utah but expanding in the Pacific, Europe, and Mexico, with smaller branches in the Ottoman Empire, South Africa, and Japan.[109]

In response to these challenges, Smith instituted a priesthood reform movement. Priesthood quorums had been structured inconsistently—sometimes reporting to stake leaders, sometimes to ward leaders—and participation in them was low. In 1913, reported priesthood meeting attendance was just 16 percent.[110] Smith oversaw the restructuring of priesthood quorums so that reporting lines were the same throughout the church, and he consistently emphasized that priesthood quorums were the core of the church—all else was peripheral.[111]

During Smith's administration, leaders increasingly used the term *auxiliary* to describe the relationship between the canonical priesthood bodies and the vibrant organizations that had developed in response to social and religious needs. Within the church, auxiliaries were regarded as helps to priesthood quorums, with an understanding that these entities were *not* part of the priesthood and were subordinate to it. The term was applied to the YMMIA by the 1880s and to other church organizations by the 1890s.[112]

"Our auxiliary organizations, what are they?" Smith asked in an April 1913 address. "Helps to the standard organizations of the Church." Without taking issue with their innovations or outside partnerships, Smith emphasized that their primary accountability was to priesthood leadership. "I want to say to the Young Men's and Young Ladies' Mutual Improvement Associations, and to the Relief Society, and to the Primaries, and to the Sunday Schools, and Religion Classes, and all the rest of the organizations in the Church, that not one of them is independent of the Priesthood of the Son of God, not one of them can exist a moment in the acceptance of the Lord when they withdraw from the voice and from the counsel of those who hold the Priesthood and preside over them," he said.[113] Moreover, he envisioned that the day would come when the priesthood quorums would better understand their duties and assume much of the work of the auxiliaries.[114]

In keeping with this model, church leaders experimented with different ways to coordinate and direct the work of the auxiliaries. In 1916, for example, Smith noted ongoing concerns about new fashions that conflicted with commonly held views of modest dress, and what he referred to as "unbecoming positions in the dance"; he announced a reform movement to be headed by the general boards of the women-led organizations, under the umbrella of the Relief Society.[115] Three women from each board convened as the newly formed Social Advisory Committee and began discussing how to respond to such issues. They adopted resolutions affirming their commitment to teach modesty by example and principle and wrote two documents: a

"Communication on Dress" and "Instructions on Social Work" (primarily dancing), which were published in the church magazines and issued separately as pamphlets.[116]

While a specific directive from priesthood leaders had created the Social Advisory Committee, its influence quickly broadened beyond the original concerns. Within a short time, the committee expanded to include representatives from the YMMIA, the Sunday School, and the program of after-school religion classes for children, giving it largely balanced gender membership and the potential to coordinate action between the church's auxiliaries. An apostle, Stephen L Richards, was assigned to chair the committee, which continued to function for six years.[117] During that time, it would become a leading influence in bringing progressive methods and ideals to bear on modern social problems within the Latter-day Saint community. Auxiliary leaders' proactive collaboration with each other and with priesthood leaders—and their engagement in seeking the good in the world around them—would help Latter-day Saints navigate the social turbulence of the coming years.

RESPONDING TO CRISIS AND CHANGE

America's reluctant involvement in World War I in 1917 disrupted regular YLMIA activities, but classwork continued as the young women directed their work toward the war effort. Members of the YLMIA board were appointed to National Defense Committees, and they recognized ways the young women could contribute. Girls were encouraged to knit, sew, and work on other needed items during local meetings.[118] Leaders introduced a new war service pin for Bee-Hive Girls, which they could earn for twenty-four hours of volunteer service in the war effort. In addition to knitting, sewing, and making surgical dressings, they harvested and preserved food through bottling and drying, and raised funds for Liberty Bonds and war service stamps.[119]

Young women rose to the cause in remarkable numbers. In 1918, the young women of the Utah Stake in Provo dried nearly 3,000 pounds and canned over 24,000 quarts of fruits and vegetables.[120] That same year, the general board also held a conservation contest to encourage greater effort. Five thousand young women from forty-three stakes and one mission participated.[121] The young women's combined volunteer hours totaled over 370,000, through which they grew 36,000 pounds of food, dried nearly 100,000 pounds of fruits and vegetables, canned 600,000 quarts of fruits and vegetables, and stored an additional 450,000 pounds of fruits and 175,000 bushels of vegetables for the winter. This was in addition to donations of money, jam, Christmas boxes, and 225,000 dressings and garments—all of which they had made themselves—to the American Red Cross.[122]

The influenza pandemic in 1918–1919, which had a disproportionate mortality rate for young adults, also impacted MIA activities. "The conditions through which we are now passing should give rise to serious reflection on the part of all of us. Perhaps never before has it happened that quarantine well nigh Church-wide has existed, preventing the holding of religious gatherings," the *Young Woman's Journal* reported in December 1918.[123] The first wave of infections caused the MIA season to be suspended for different lengths of time in different areas, and the January 1919 issue of the *Young Woman's Journal* gave directions on adjusting lesson schedules, filing delayed reports, and lowering the thresholds for certain awards. At the same time, the *Journal* noted that meetings might be canceled again in some areas, leaving young women to study lessons alone at home. "It behooves each officer and member to exercise faith and to be cheerful and courageous," the journal said. Though its past editorial policy had been not to publish death notices, the *Journal* promised to publish short sketches honoring stake-level MIA leaders who had died over the previous six months.[124]

In the March 1919 issue, as a deadly winter drew to a close, a three-part editorial reflected on the war and pandemic. The first section, titled "The Art of Adjustment," addressed the feeling of ongoing disruption. "Changes now come so quickly and suddenly into the lives of all," it said. The editorial complimented women's wartime economic mobilization, including in traditionally male labor roles. "They met the difficulties of war nobly, they adjusted themselves splendidly," it noted, while adding, "We wonder how they will adjust themselves to the changed peace conditions." The next section, "The Art of Nursing," encouraged young women to enroll in the nursing courses offered by the Relief Society. Many people "could not get help however much they were willing to pay, for every nurse was kept employed constantly and could not begin to take all the cases she was called upon to nurse," the editorial noted. "Wise are the girls that take this work." The final section, "Trust," addressed the existential questions raised by the death toll. "We do not know why so many of the best people have been stricken, why so many in the prime of life have been summoned hence, but we must not let doubts darken our lives." Rather than invoking heavenly rest, the editorial asked readers to consider the meaning of a short life. "If one's earthly work is finished, what matters it whether the sojourn on earth has been long or short. 'One crowded hour of glorious life is worth more than sluggish years,'" it said.[125]

The upheaval of war and pandemic intensified and accelerated the profound social change happening at this time, resulting in generational strain in American culture that extended into the 1920s. Young people—those in secondary school and college—were seen as different than their parents had been at the same age. "What ails our youth?" one influential 1924 book asked.[126] Tension points were not difficult to see: young people were rejecting the formal manners of the past and taking up jazz music, fast dancing, dating (in place of traditional courting), speaking in slang, and racing in automobiles. Young women were going out joyriding with young men, bobbing their hair, and wearing short skirts, low necklines, and cosmetics. Smoking and drinking seemed especially popular, and new ideas about sex and birth control seemed to be breaking down traditional morals.[127]

Many adults reacted by denouncing young people's behavior and calling for authoritative efforts to control it. Others took a positive, progressive view, recognizing that cultural change had brought new realities and celebrating the potential of young people to bring improvement to society and human nature. They acknowledged that there were serious challenges, but they insisted that improved understanding of psychology, sociology, and physiology would offer modern solutions to modern problems.[128] While some Latter-day Saints were shocked and alarmed by the ways of the youth, church leaders quickly mobilized the MIAs to create a positive, optimistic outlook on the youth and their future, without ignoring the challenges of social change.

During the early 1920s, the Social Advisory Committee made recommendations and issued guidelines for what it called "social work." The committee's understanding of this term was very broad. "The common idea of the word 'social' must be enlarged," explained one editorial in the *Young Woman's Journal*. "Heretofore it has held for many of us only the thought of recreation but the term really implies all of the relations of man which make for normal life." By this definition, charitable work and efforts to address problems of health, labor, or delinquency belonged under the heading of social work along with recreational activities.[129] Social work thus encompassed virtually all activities and reforms intended to improve community standards and prevent societal problems. The committee subdivided its areas of emphasis into three broad subjects: teacher training, social and educational leadership, and charity and relief work.[130] The MIA representatives particularly emphasized the second. As a result, YLMIA leaders were exhorted to see themselves as social workers, or leaders in improving community standards and activities through working directly with the young people. The committee established several avenues for developing this kind of leadership in the church.

One of these efforts took place in spring 1920. The Forty-Seventh Annual Conference of Social Work commenced in New Orleans on 14 April that year, and among its nearly two thousand attendees was Clarissa A. Beesley, the general secretary of the YLMIA. She had departed for the event four days earlier, along with Stephen L Richards and other members of the Social Advisory Committee, and found herself rubbing shoulders with notable activists in social work, including Jane Addams and Felix Adler.[131] Beesley was a well-known figure in the Latter-day Saint community. At forty-one, she had been involved in ward and stake leadership for over twenty years, working mostly with the young women, and after serving a successful mission in the central United States, she had been invited to join the YLMIA general board in 1912. Beesley was unmarried and had taught school for several years after earning her teaching degree from the University of Utah. She was a popular speaker and frequent contributor to MIA lessons and articles in the *Young Woman's Journal*.[132] Attuned to the social issues among youth, Beesley relished participating in this grand congregation of like-minded individuals working for social improvement.

At the conference, social workers' methods and their forthright acknowledgment of the shortcomings inherent to their approaches impressed Beesley. "They are among the most earnest and energetic people of the Nation," she wrote. They so inspired her that she wrote a *Journal* article to share details of their insights with young women and their leaders. Yet she also returned even more impressed with the Church of Jesus Christ, believing it to be beautiful and complete, the perfect plan for social healing and progress.[133]

After attending the conference, Beesley and other members of the Social Advisory Committee worked to disseminate similar training widely within the church. In summer 1920, they sponsored three concurrent five-week courses at BYU focused on teacher training, social and recreational leadership, and charities and re-lief work. Each stake sent three representatives (presumably one for each course), and those who completed the course satisfactorily received college credit. Arthur Beeley, a professor of sociology at the University of Utah and the secretary of the Social Advisory Committee, directed the courses on social and recreational leader-ship, which included lectures from experts in psychology, sociology, drama, music, pageantry, games, dancing, and physical education.[134] Beeley felt the courses' success showed that a scientific and religious approach to social problems was both possible and desirable.[135] Attendees were expected to take what they had learned back to their stakes and use it to train local leaders. Minutes of the Social Advisory Committee indicate that committee members attended many of those conventions and reported favorably on their results.[136]

The committee conducted several studies using modern statistical and scientific methods, including a study that compared urban and rural adolescent activity in the church. The study found that large numbers of adolescents of both sexes were not being reached by the church, and adolescent disengagement from the church was highest in large cities.[137] Beeley also studied social dance and concluded that boys liked sports even better than girls liked dancing, although dancing was the second-place choice of a large majority of the boys. Both girls and boys ranked "as-sociation" and "meeting new people" as their top reasons for enjoying dancing.[138] In response to Beeley's studies on the nature of female adolescents, the Social Advisory Committee recommended that the MIA hold a wide variety of activities, such as music, dance, drama, oration, party hosting, sewing, athletics, and the study of so-cial problems. Finally, the committee advocated for religious influences that would appeal to young people's hearts and intellects, recommending weekly supervised recreation either in conjunction with MIA meetings or on another weeknight.[139]

Out of the Social Advisory Committee emerged a vision of making the ward the social center for members of the church. The ward building would serve as a kind of community center, perhaps something like the settlement houses established by progressive activists to bring recreational, cultural, and educational facilities to urban neighborhoods.[140] Stephen L Richards said in one meeting that the ward amusement hall should become the social center for church members, appealing to young people's interests and thereby drawing them back from commercial gathering places.[141] One writer explained that the committee sought to make the wards "interesting community units providing dressmaking, millinery classes, physical recreation and all other activities which go to make up an interesting group unit."[142]

While the idea of using the ward building as a fully equipped social center did not come to pass as envisioned, changes to meetinghouses did facilitate the centering of social activities in the ward. Over the first decades of the twentieth century, a new building pattern took hold in which the formerly separate buildings for Relief Societies, "cultural halls" for social activities, and chapels or assembly halls for general meetings were consolidated into a single structure. These new buildings incorporated classrooms, Relief Society rooms, and recreation halls, which often included a stage for performances.[143] Just as all church auxiliaries were being brought under the jurisdiction of central priesthood authority, church buildings consolidated all church entities and functions into a single architectural space.

In November 1920, the Social Advisory Committee was consolidated with the Correlation Committee, which had been working (under various titles and in various forms) for most of the decade to study and coordinate the work of the organizations within the church, attempting to reduce overlap and increase efficiency.[144] The new Correlation–Social Advisory Committee considered social matters, structural relationships between church entities, and the potential for duplication of efforts.[145] Two years later, in 1922, the First Presidency issued a circular letter that reflected the outcome of these efforts, laying out the purpose and function of each auxiliary in the church. The auxiliaries were to provide a place to study the gospel and participate in literary and social activities. The MIAs were to teach the gospel, help young people obtain testimonies, and establish clearer guidelines and oversight for social activities.[146] Significantly, the MIAs were also designated to function as the church's chief recreational agencies.[147] In 1923, the MIAs began publishing the *Recreation Bulletin*, reflecting their assumption of this responsibility; the bulletin was a forerunner of increasingly elaborate handbooks that continued to articulate expansion of the recreation focus.[148]

The efforts of the Correlation–Social Advisory Committee emphasized and codified standards and guidelines for dances, activities, and personal conduct—including modest dress—while also communicating to MIA leaders the breadth of their commission. Stephen L Richards exhorted the committee to ensure that church activities aimed to do more than entertain. Their greater purpose was to help the young people develop faith. "The dancing manager is not employed merely to see that the young people have the correct position in the dance," he said. "To be successful he must see behind his work for the future of the boy and the girl and help them to accomplish their great work in life."[149]

ACTIVE LIVES AND CHANGING STYLES

YLMIA leaders' interest in strengthening the faith of young women through recreation guided them as they navigated social tensions over changing women's styles and patterns of self-presentation. During leaders' lifetimes, dresses rapidly lost the weight, length, and shapes of late nineteenth-century fashions. Corsets and long, heavy skirts were gone. Sleeves grew shorter and high necklines receded. Latter-day Saints disapproved of the standards the 1920s flapper represented—smoking, drinking, and sexuality—but they ultimately accepted many of the era's fashion changes.[150]

Modern activities required modern clothing and hairstyles. The first Bee-Hive Girls manual's 1915 reference to bloomers as appropriate attire for hikes was followed in the 1920s by references to knickerbockers and trousers.[151] In a 1924 article in the *Young Woman's Journal*, Fern Chipman Eyring celebrated the growing involvement of women in outdoor recreational activities once considered masculine. "They now share the out-of-doors to the fullest extent with their brothers, thus strengthening both mind and body."[152] Eschewing long hair done up in elaborate twists, knots, or buns, many Latter-day Saint young women—and their mothers—embraced the trend of bobbing their hair, cutting it to shoulder length or higher. "Nowadays, one often cannot tell by the hairdress whether Mary is sixteen or sixty, for the grandmothers are bobbing too!" one article noted approvingly.[153] In 1926, another writer insisted, "Today, no one thinks about thinking of bobbed hair at all." The writer explained, "The coming of short hair certainly has been a great relief to the athletic girl."[154]

This modern feminine ideal was founded on new ideas about the physical self. The modern girl was to be active and robust. She was to understand the principles of health, nutrition, and sanitation. YLMIA leaders enthusiastically incorporated these principles into lessons, articles, and activities. In 1925, for example, Bee-Hive Girls were encouraged to keep a monthly health diary that included the following tasks:

> Slept out of doors or with windows open and made an average of nine hours a night each week.

Cleaned finger nails and pushed back cuticle this morning.

Washed my hair (to be checked every 2 or 3 weeks).

Tried to sit and stand straight.

Chewed my food thoroughly, and ate slowly today.

Walked 100 miles this month.

In addition, they could participate in swimming or basketball.[155]

In the 1910s, Latter-day Saint leaders had wrestled over what to do about changing fashions, which raised questions unique to the community. Since the introduction of temple ordinances under Joseph Smith's direction in the 1840s, adult Latter-day Saints have been encouraged to prepare for and participate in an endowment ceremony in the temple, which is seen as both a bestowal of spiritual power and a step necessary for exaltation. The ceremony includes making special covenants, receiving eternal blessings for their continued faithfulness to those covenants, and being clothed in a sacred undergarment that endowed members are to wear throughout their lives as a symbol of their sacred commitments.[156] In the early twentieth century, the garment was a one-piece item with sleeves extending to the elbow, legs extending to the ankle, and a very high neckline up to the throat. The new fashions were clearly incompatible with the garment, creating a dilemma for many Latter-day Saint women.

"We frequently receive letters asking to what extent our Mutual girls should adopt the prevailing fashions of the day," wrote the YLMIA presidency in early 1916. "Our answer is, only so far as is consistent with our professions as Saints of God."[157] In 1918, the First Presidency sent a letter to bishops, reiterating that the garment should be worn as intended and not altered.[158] Some YLMIA members in their twenties had received their endowments and covenanted to wear the garment, and younger members who had not received their endowments were encouraged to follow comparable limits in their styles.[159] Even as they supported the direction of the First Presidency regarding wearing the temple garment, YLMIA leaders were sympathetic to modern styles. "We want to be progressive," general president Martha Horne Tingey affirmed in 1917. "We love to look like other people, we love to take up the new things that come along; and it is all right in a sense, but we must never go to extremes."[160]

Ultimately, church leaders found ways to accommodate most of the changes in fashion. After a period of prayer, study, and discussion, senior church leaders concluded that the symbolic meaning of the garment, the principles it represented, and the covenants it reminded wearers to keep were more important than its specific form. It could be redesigned to be less cumbersome and more in keeping with changing dress styles. In 1923, they authorized a new design for both women and men with shorter sleeves and legs and a lower neckline.[161] Because of the concern about dress, the term *modesty* became enduringly associated primarily with clothing rather than character, but expressions of censure about young women's clothing decreased considerably after the temple garment change.[162] Some photographs of young women at activities in the late 1920s even show them wearing pants.[163]

While YLMIA leaders were largely supportive of changes in hair and clothing, they were less welcoming of the dramatic cosmetic styles young women were adopting. In the 1920s, mass production and advertisement of beauty products created new ideals of beauty.[164] YLMIA leaders were unenthusiastic about the heavy use of rouge and powder on the faces of their young women. "Why, Oh Why?" lamented one editorial. "It is sickening to see young girls cover the glowing cheeks of health and the satin smooth skin of youth with drug store concoctions."[165]

Some MIA activities overtly addressed changing ideas about female presentation as a way to connect generations. For example, at a 1925 stake day in St. George, Utah, a "dressing race" was held in which a grandmother raced to don a flapper dress and a young woman hurriedly put on the grandmother's clothes. That race ended in a tie.[166] Other wards held activities such as a bridal fashion show, with daughters modeling their mothers' wedding dresses, as well as a fashion show in which two young women dressed up in costumes representing "the girl of yesterday" and "the modern 1927 miss," followed by piece-by-piece removal of the clothing (presumably with other clothing underneath) to demonstrate the stark differences in the number of pieces and their respective weights. The modern girl undressed in just a few seconds, and her clothing weighed less than one pound, while the old-fashioned girl took twenty minutes to shed her ten-pound costume.[167] These mother-and-daughter activities, which became part of the regular YLMIA summer program in 1923, were felt to bring the generations together in camaraderie and mutual understanding.[168]

GOLD AND GREEN BALLS

The MIA emphasis on recreation saw the inauguration of several iconic Latter-day Saint traditions that would be cherished for generations. Many activities became more than youth events, involving the whole ward or branch and becoming a prominent part of Latter-day Saint life rhythms. Foremost among these were Gold and Green Balls. In 1922, a joint committee of the general boards decided to adopt official colors for the MIA: green to symbolize "life's springtime" of youth and gold to symbolize light and knowledge.[169] Gold and Green Balls began as local events in the mid-1920s, but by 1927 they were listed as one of the expected events on the MIA season calendar published by the general board.[170] By 1928, the MIA handbook stated that the Gold and Green Ball stood out "for its beauty and cultural tone."[171] These dances were usually held early in the year and, in keeping with standard practice of the time, generally required attendees to purchase tickets. Reports and photographs of the dances, which often became gala productions, appeared in the *Young Woman's Journal* and the *Improvement Era*. Common elements included elaborate decorations, selection of a queen of the ball, a formal procession, creative invitations and refreshments, and performance of a standard gold and green waltz or cotillion. While the MIA sponsored and organized the dances, they were usually community events to which all were invited.

Even small, rural towns staged elaborate Gold and Green Balls. For example, in the Garfield Stake in southern Utah, the queen, dressed in gold and green, opened the stake's 1927 ball with a grand march. MIA officers and teachers participated in the procession, eventually marching into the shape of the letter *M*. The queen spoke briefly about the MIA colors, and senior classes of both young men and young women, also dressed in gold and green, performed a folk dance. Then everyone joined in social dancing for the rest of the evening. In addition to decorating the room in which the ball was held in gold and green, the MIA served refreshments of gold- and green-colored lemonade and cookies frosted in green with the gold letters *M*, *I*, and *A* on top.[172]

Dances in Salt Lake City were no less impressive. On 25 January 1929, the Pioneer Stake held a Gold and Green Ball at a venue called Rainbow Gardens. Each ward's queen took her place on the platform in a beautiful gown. Following a speech by the stake president, a little girl dressed in a white satin fairy costume brought in a jeweled crown on a gold and green pillow and gave it to the queen of the ball. Gladys Huber, the queen from the Mexican Branch (a unit within the stake for Spanish-speaking Saints), was the winner. Two flower girls then entered, distributing corsages and boutonnieres to Gladys, her attendants, and their partners, who then led a procession around the room to form three sets for dancing the cotillion.[173]

ROAD SHOWS, DRAMAS, AND PAGEANTS

Performance became a major emphasis of the MIAs in the 1920s, with local groups putting on plays, pageants, tableaux, and all forms of drama. Latter-day Saints had long embraced drama as a wholesome cultural outlet; the grand Salt Lake Theater, built under Brigham Young's direction sixty years earlier, still stood as a monument to the power of theater in the Saints' community-building efforts.[174] Now, in the Progressive Era, the MIA took up the cultural work of drama. Building on the work of Maud May Babcock, who had become a pioneering theater professor at the University of Utah, YLMIA leaders explained that drama promoted mental, moral, and physical improvement and uplifted performers who portrayed worthwhile characters.[175] Young women could also develop positive attributes through drama.

Hawthorne Ward MIA drama winners. 1924. Members of the Hawthorne Ward in Salt Lake City, pictured here in costume, won the Granite Stake Merry-Go-Round drama event. Over 250 participants traveled by automobile to perform their acts at the various ward buildings in the stake, setting the pattern for MIA road shows that would thrive for more than fifty years. ("Hawthorne Blossoms," in "Preaching the Gospel of Better Recreation," *Young Woman's Journal*, May 1924, 258, copy at Church History Library, Salt Lake City.)

"Practicing and playing the part of a refined, lady-like person in one of our M. I. A. plays might have a lasting uplifting influence on a naturally rowdy, careless girl," one article in the *Young Woman's Journal* argued.[176] Leaders believed that young people would learn about the gospel and high moral standards more by doing than by being lectured to. Besides all that, putting on plays was fun.

Road shows, in which productions toured to multiple local audiences, became the hallmark feature of MIA drama. The Granite Stake in Salt Lake City originated the idea in 1924 with its "merry-go-round," in which eighteen troupes of performers traveled around the stake, presenting their short plays to audiences totaling over 2,500. Road shows were enabled by improved roads and the widespread availability of automobiles. In the Granite Stake, it took thirty-five cars to transport everyone from ward to ward, but they did so on schedule and without any accidents.[177] Conditions in rural areas sometimes made for challenges, but many stakes rose to the occasion. In the Panguitch Stake in southern Utah, bad weather in January 1927 made the roads unusable, so performers held their road shows on two separate nights, a week apart. Still, the weather did not discourage performers or audiences—stake leaders reported the event had elicited greater participation than anything they had done before.[178] The MIA had tapped into a social need and was shaping the culture. While the MIA sponsored the road shows, the variety of onstage roles and need for offstage help with the production often drew in participants of all ages and made the plays a true community enterprise.

The YLMIA incorporated drama in many of its programs for young women as well. Original plays gave them the opportunity to embody principles they could aspire to. For example, *A Bee-Hive Girl's Fantasy* was a short play written in verse by Marguerite Gordon and Velma Wing, who were Bee-Keepers in Honolulu. In the production, a Bee-Hive Girl slipped away from her group to avoid helping with the work. After falling asleep, she was visited by the ideals of the Bee-Hive, such as Faith, Knowledge, Health, and Beauty, who each bestowed their emblems upon her. When Work, Service, and Joy entered, however, they were unable to give her their badges. Awakening, the Bee-Hive Girl recognized the lesson of her dream. "And now I know what I must do," she said. "Work and Service my motto shall be / For surely Joy will then come to me."[179]

The June Conference provided another venue for dramatic performances by YLMIA members. At the 1925 June Conference, young women performed a play called *The Latter-day Saint Girl*. In this elaborate production, the Spirit of Mutual Improvement (a young woman dressed in the MIA colors) joined three young women representing the Bee-Hive Girl, Junior, and Senior (or Gleaner) classes and gave each in turn a charge to enact the ideals of her class. The representative figures then took seats at the back of the stage, and scenes depicting the activities of each age group followed. Finally, a "True Latter-day Saint Girl" stepped forward and was proclaimed "the culmination of the Bee-Hive Girl, Junior, and Senior years."

"O, Spirit of Mutual Improvement," she exclaimed. "Through you I have found expression in literature, in music, in the manual arts, and above all in our glorious religion. It is to you largely that I owe my testimony of the divinity of that religion." The girl then bore her testimony, focusing on the divinity of Jesus Christ, and led the audience in repeating the year's slogan: "We Stand for an Individual Testimony of the Divinity of Jesus Christ."[180]

Similar presentations carried out at the local level struck a meaningful chord. Elizabeth Eames King, president of the Raymond Second Ward YLMIA in Alberta, Canada, reported to the *Journal* that her young women had prepared productions as part of a conjoint evening with the young men. "These were *very* much appreciated by the audience," she reported, "and gave an opportunity to use about forty-four girls."[181] Through drama, the YLMIA built relationships between young women, offering them shared memories and opportunities to work together.

MIA JUBILEE

By 1925, the annual June Conference was well established as a highlight in the MIA calendar, and the vibrant scope of the MIA organizations was on full display at the June Conference of 1925, which was the focal point of yearlong celebrations. This year marked the fiftieth anniversary of the founding of the Young Men's organization—the Young Ladies' organization had celebrated its fiftieth anniversary in 1919—and since the two organizations' joint relationship had continued to intensify, the boards of both organizations felt it was appropriate to join in a single, massive commemoration.[182]

Events commemorating the Jubilee extended throughout the year with two particular initiatives. First, the organizations mounted a drive to increase the rolls of the MIAs to one hundred thousand members—fifty thousand each for the Young Men and the Young Ladies.[183] Second, they promoted 1925 as "a year of testimony" in the MIA. Invoking Brigham Young's founding charge that "more testimonies are obtained on the feet than on the knees," the goal was to have all members and leaders of the MIAs "stand on their feet and tell of what they believe and know" about the gospel of Jesus Christ. Even if such expressions were "halting" and "timid," leaders believed that individuals who stood to express themselves would receive a more powerful spiritual witness.[184]

In addition to these ongoing efforts, each local association was to hold a special joint program on Sunday evening, 7 June. At least by aspiration, this meant the entire

Banners at the MIA Jubilee. 1925. This celebration marked the fiftieth anniversary of the MIA organizations, specifically the organization of the young men's association in 1875. Participants from local units made banners to represent the MIA in their stakes and marched in a grand parade during June Conference in Salt Lake City. (Church History Library, Salt Lake City.)

membership of the MIAs would be meeting simultaneously to commemorate the Jubilee. The suggested program featured historical sketches of the general and local organizations, a review of the MIAs' purposes, and testimonies of its accomplishments and influences by members, both men and women. All who had served in the MIAs over the years were to be invited and recognized during the meeting.[185]

As the highlight of the Jubilee year, the celebration at June Conference triumphantly exceeded all expectations. Following the regular leadership sessions held over the weekend on 6–7 June, several big events took place on 8–10 June. During the YLMIA session on Monday, young women presented the play *The Latter-day Saint Girl*. That evening, a pageant entitled *The Torch of Inspiration* presented the origin, growth, and potential of the MIAs in the past, present, and future.[186]

On Tuesday, stake bands, choruses, and speakers performed in tryouts during the afternoon; winners were announced and all participants joined in a "grand concert" that evening. A capacity crowd eagerly filled the Tabernacle to witness the gala program, which included ensemble performances by fourteen bands, thirty-six ladies' choruses, and twenty-two male choruses, as well as impressive addresses from young women and men participants in the public speaking contest. The audience was thrilled: "It was Mutual Improvement work at its height!"[187]

The next day's events soared even higher, as over twelve thousand participants in fourteen divisions joined in a grand parade on the streets of Salt Lake City. For a full ninety minutes, the procession, stretching over two miles in length, paraded past spectators and an official reviewing stand on the steps of the Church Administration Building on South Temple Street, where Church authorities, government officials, and MIA leaders were seated. One reporter described the "floats, banners, standards, flags; groups in costume, in uniform or bearing significant trophies" who made a "demonstration unprecedented" that impressed the tens of thousands of spectators who crowded the parade route.[188]

As each unit passed the reviewing stand, its flag bearer dropped out and joined the others in formation on the side of the street opposite the stand. Eventually over two hundred flag bearers stood six deep, their banners bearing slogans, mottoes, and insignia of the various groups and programs in the MIA—an "impressive moment" in the event.[189] "The Mutual Improvement Association has borne testimony to the world, that the Gospel as taught by the Latter-day Saints is a marvelous work and a wonder," exulted a *Young Woman's Journal* editorial about the Jubilee events.[190]

EXPANDING CAMP

Continued emphasis on recreation led to the expansion of camp programs. Throughout the 1920s, camping in the YLMIA remained centered on summer homes built by various stakes, usually in a mountain setting. Newspaper articles touted the summer home for Latter-day Saint girls in Brighton, Utah, as a beautiful, affordable recreation site.[191] Nestled in the Silver Lake Basin atop Big Cottonwood Canyon some twenty miles southeast of Salt Lake City, the camp at Brighton connected to several trails and mountain destinations, including Lakes Mary, Martha, and Catherine. In 1927, camp attendance had reached five thousand, and by 1928, eleven homes had been built by seventeen stakes to accommodate young women from the Utah-Idaho border in the north and into Arizona in the south.[192]

Leaders planned camp experiences carefully to foster a sense of camaraderie and wonder in participants, and they worked to develop camp traditions. One of these traditions at Brighton was the sunrise hike, such as the one held on Thursday, 12 July 1929. At two o'clock in the morning, a leader gently woke the sleeping young women. They quickly dressed, then filed down the stairs to gather in front of the cold fireplace. Leaders distributed "bugs," or large tin cans fitted with candles and a wire handle, and soon the girls were on their way. The destination was Mount Majestic, now known as Clayton Peak, a little over three miles up a steep, rocky trail.

The young women hiked along in single file, crossing creek beds and brushing past trees in the darkness as their bug lanterns lit the path a few feet ahead. They stopped periodically to catch their breath and admire the low-hanging moon. As dawn began to cast its light on the western mountains, the young women hung their bugs on tree limbs and began the final scramble, using both hands and feet to reach the summit. Once atop the peak, they rested and watched as rose-colored clouds gradually faded, creating a pale glow on the mountains below, until finally, shortly after five o'clock in the morning, the sun peeked over the eastern ridges and fully lit their view.[193]

In addition to hiking, typical camp activities included swimming, boating, games, races, stunts, performances, storytelling, and an evening bonfire with group singing. Camp was intended to be busy in a good way—it was not a place for loafing but for change and recreation.[194] Camp also contributed to the growing trend of ritualizing Latter-day Saint history: for one evening, camp leaders were instructed to organize a Camp Fire Ceremonial, a program that included a poem, recited lines, dances, and lighting of the fire, with themes commemorating the Saints' pioneer heritage.[195] To help leaders blend recreation and spirituality, several summer homes hosted recreational institutes for leaders, led by Elva Moss, a college-educated returned missionary who served on the YLMIA general board as field secretary to the camp program.[196]

Writing after two years as chair of the camp committee for the Cache and Logan stakes in northern Utah, Claire N. Hulme laid out a religious rationale for camp as a valuable element of the YLMIA's programs. Summer camps had brought joy, spirituality, and ethical values into the lives of hundreds of girls, she wrote, and they were one

Brighton summer home. 1924. This large, new summer home in Big Cottonwood Canyon, east of Salt Lake City, welcomed its first campers in 1921. It was built through the combined efforts of the Ensign, Liberty, Pioneer, and Salt Lake stakes and was among the first permanent facilities for Latter-day Saint young women's camps. (Church History Library, Salt Lake City.)

of the best activities the association could provide its members. Camp activities harmonized physical, social, and religious life and created a happy, healthy atmosphere. The fresh air, comfortable setting, and engaging activities promoted good health and high moral standards. Girls developed leadership, self-control, teamwork, cooperation, consideration for the rights of others, respect for law and order, and sportsmanship. Most of all, camp developed a spiritual awareness by fostering a deeper acquaintance with the works of the Creator. "Through sleeping among the tree-tops, as we do in our camp, with the stars shining upon our beds, there are moments when the most thoughtless girl realizes, if but dimly, the wonder and glory of it all."[197]

QUANTIFYING RELIGIOUS COMMITMENT

While the MIA in the 1910s and 1920s focused on strengthening spiritual development indirectly through recreation, progressive thinkers in the organization also wanted to use modern methods to track and address more overtly religious behaviors. The data they obtained worried them. One major concern was a decrease in the number of Saints marrying in a temple. One study reported that the 1920 percentage of temple marriages was among the lowest in the twentieth century, despite the highest total number of marriages ever recorded. About a quarter of church members who married chose non–Latter-day Saint spouses, and of those marrying outside the faith, three-fourths were women. If these trends continued, temple marriages would account for only 40 percent of Latter-day Saint weddings by midcentury.[198]

The 1920 study cited "lack of faith" as the primary reason for the declining temple marriage rates.[199] The reality was more complicated than a single statistic might suggest. Lethe Coleman was married civilly at age forty-one and did not have children, but she was active in the church and passed on her religious identity to the next generation through service in the Primary and Young Women organizations.[200] There were also many women who married outside the faith and raised committed Latter-day Saint children. For example, in 1906 Nellie Marie Rasmussen married John William Hunter, who was not a member of the church. Their son, Howard W. Hunter, later became the church's fourteenth president.[201] Studies of temple marriage rates might miss some couples who were initially married civilly, for whatever reason, and sealed in the temple later. Camilla Eyring, for example, married Spencer Kimball civilly while his military draft group was awaiting possible deployment to Europe. Because his unit's deployment was postponed, they were able to make the rail journey to Salt Lake City to be sealed in the temple shortly before she gave birth to their first child.[202] However, because church leaders believed marriages outside the temple might represent a risk in religious transmission, leaders and programs would increasingly emphasize temple marriage.

Worry over their young people's marriage choices was not new for Latter-day Saints. Earlier generations had warned against marrying outsiders while trying to maintain community boundaries. In the 1910s, lessons on marriage tended to focus on principles and lofty ideals; by the 1920s the ideals were still important, but the lessons drew on sociological and scientific research about marriage and family life.[203] The sociological language of the time often reflected the larger society's assumptions about gender and race, which also appear in the lessons. In the 1921 introduction to the courtship course of study for the Senior class, for example, YLMIA leaders explained, "Most scientific authorities agree that for our race and climate the best age for marriage is on the average from 22 to 26 years for the young man and from 18 to 24 years for the girl."[204] The writers of the manual assumed that all Latter-day Saints were of the same race (white) and that men and women of approximately the same age should be referred to differently (as *young men* and *girls*).

While marriage was some years off for many participants in the MIA, leaders sought ways to connect Latter-day Saint young women to the temple as they grew up. Interest and participation in genealogy and temple work had been growing significantly in the church since the early decades of the century,[205] and at the April 1928 general conference, church president Heber J. Grant encouraged Saints to spend more time at the temple.[206] By the end of the 1920s, many young women had experienced a new tradition of youth temple trips to perform baptisms for the dead, a distinctive aspect of Latter-day Saint theology in which church members conduct genealogical research and then enter the temple to be baptized for their relatives and others who died without receiving the gospel and its ordinances. Young people who had themselves been baptized were qualified to perform vicarious baptisms for the dead, and leaders hoped temple visits to perform proxy ordinances would offer powerful spiritual experiences and a reminder of the covenants and blessings associated with church membership.[207]

In 1928, the same year Grant made his remarks on temple attendance, Bee-Hive Girls in the Deseret Stake in central Utah participated in a temple trip. Each young woman contributed one dollar, and the group raised additional funds by selling paper flowers. Fifteen young women attended, traveling to the temple in Manti, Utah. The evening before they entered the temple, the Bee-Hive Girls met with their leaders on the tree- and grass-covered temple hill, which overlooked the city. They listened to a talk on the construction of the temple, and some of the Bee-Hive Girls gave a program. The next morning the girls were baptized for 160 deceased individuals. One of the leaders, Zola Woodbury Bunker, reported, "Our trip to the Temple was surely worth all the effort that we had put forth."[208] Several months later, an article in the *Young Woman's Journal* tied baptisms for the dead to increased spiritual maturity among the youth: "The principle of universal salvation becomes full of spiritual significance to the MIA girls or boys who go in large numbers to the temple and are baptized for the dead."[209]

CLASS TOPICS AND STRUCTURE

Lessons on courtship and temple marriage were only one part of a larger constellation of YLMIA curriculum. Young women received consistent messages that marriage and motherhood were women's most important missions, but YLMIA instruction also included preparation to engage in the world beyond the walls of a home.[210] The wide array of lesson topics also shows that leaders paid increasing attention to stages of young women's development, aided by their engagement with scientific studies in this area.[211] The leaders' progressive attitudes and understanding, along with consistent feedback from young women and their leaders on the local level, spurred the general board to create more age-group divisions for young women than ever before.[212]

Between 1919 and 1936, the board implemented over a dozen changes or adjustments in the age groupings, their corresponding names, and the lessons and work or activities recommended for them. In 1919, Bee-Hive Girls work was adopted as the program for the Junior class, ages fourteen through seventeen, though the specified ages initially fluctuated.[213] By 1923, entrance into the Bee-Hive Girls was equated with entrance into the YLMIA; the first edition of the *Y. L. M. I. A. Hand Book*, which was published in 1923, codified the age range for the youngest class (called Bee-Hive Girls) as fourteen to fifteen, while the Junior class covered ages sixteen and seventeen.[214] Even though boys were entering Scouts at twelve, YLMIA general leaders maintained the age of entry into the young women's program at fourteen.[215] An exception could be made in the case of a physically and mentally advanced girl of younger age who had the permission of her parents, YLMIA leaders, Primary leaders, and bishop. But in this period, girls of twelve and thirteen were still seen as juvenile, and leaders insisted that the YLMIA was not a children's organization.[216] Also by 1923, a shift had occurred in how leaders viewed the Bee-Hive Girls program in relation to YLMIA classes. The *Young Woman's Journal* announced that the Bee-Hive Girls would no longer serve as the program for the Junior class's "work" (though a woman of any age could still enroll in the program), and leaders and young women soon began using the Bee-Hive Girls name to refer solely to the youngest age group in the organization. A 1931 supplement to the Bee-Hive Girls handbook advised that MIA officers could allow girls of twelve and thirteen to join, with parental approval, but that officers were not to actively invite girls of that age. Those who did enter at age twelve were called Nymphs, with special officers to guide them in transitioning to the Bee-Hive Girls program.[217]

Now distinct from the Bee-Hive Girls program, the Junior class began to take on an identity of its own. Each Junior class could choose from two outlines of "courses" (readings on a particular topic), both of which also contained a required course specific to gospel study. The courses were available in small booklets, but each course was also printed in one of the monthly editions of the *Young Woman's Journal*, as were the courses for the Senior and Advanced Senior departments.[218] Through these courses, Juniors might learn about such topics as "Social Conduct," "Studies in Nature," "Parables and Miracles of the Savior," "Some of the Songs We Sing," and "Music Appreciation."[219] Juniors also participated in several social activities throughout the year, such as the yearly Mothers' and Daughters' Day and the MIA Day, but by 1926, the general board offered lists of specific monthly activities for these young women, such as a fashion show, where they could bring and display items of clothing they had made themselves; a music appreciation evening (the main list also included opera and composer nights), which was facilitated by the Victrola or a local member with musical ability; or a Junior Outing, during which they might hike, swim, or travel to see various sites.[220] A common summer activity for young women in Junior classes was growing flowers, which they were then encouraged to share, perhaps by providing decoration in sacrament meeting or taking them to the sick and sorrowing.[221]

As with the Bee-Hive and Junior classes, the year 1923 was also momentous for young women in the Senior class, those ages eighteen to twenty-three.[222] In 1922, leaders had established Senior class organizations as a way to "make the M. I. A. more vital" in the lives of older young women. The work of these organizations supplemented the regular studies of the Senior classes and provided opportunities for leadership, self-expression, and group association. Members of these organizations, which were led by the young women themselves, participated in activities during the last half-hour of weekly MIA meetings.[223] In 1923, YLMIA leaders announced the name *Gleaners* for this program, beginning a tradition associated with that name that would carry on for decades.[224] Referring to the Old Testament story of Ruth, program instructions noted that, as Ruth gleaned grain from the fields, Senior girls gleaned knowledge from many sources.[225] In the Gleaner program, young women *gleaned* sheaves by gaining knowledge and *bound* those sheaves by putting the knowledge into action. By gathering knowledge, Gleaners were to raise their standards, gain self-mastery, and build character. Suggested sheaves, or goals, included controlling one's temper, leaving one's room in order, avoiding criticizing others, cultivating a hobby for half an hour each day, and reading from the Bible each night. The young women were to write out their chosen goal, hand it to their leader, then work on it for one month, after which they were to report back on their success. This made the program almost entirely self-determined and individually motivated.

In addition, ward Gleaner groups could choose a collective sheaf, and a general sheaf was recommended for all Gleaners to bind during each MIA season.[226] In the 1927–1928 season, the general Gleaner sheaf was "I Will Endeavor to Cultivate My Graces," for which young women sought to understand their gifts and cultivate further cultural, physical, and intellectual talents.[227] Several years after the introduction of the Gleaner program, ward Gleaner groups began participating in sheaf-binding ceremonies, which celebrated a Gleaner class having achieved 100 percent enrollment of all eligible girls (ages seventeen to twenty-three).[228] These ceremonies were often elaborate affairs, with carefully scripted and highly choreographed programs that included young women, attired in formal gowns and corsages, walking in a procession to the front of the gathering. There, they explained the Gleaner program and the Gleaner sheaf, which after 1937 had become an official code for living. Written by board member Rose Wallace Bennett and based on Psalm 24, it encouraged young women to possess a clean body, a pure heart, a humble and obedient spirit, and an honest mind.[229] The sheaf-binding ceremony frequently incorporated music provided by combined girls' groups or local soloists, but the focal point was always the moment when the girls brought their individual sheaves of wheat and tied them together, symbolizing both their declared commitment to the ideals set forth in Bennett's creed and the camaraderie they shared in maintaining those ideals.[230] As with the Bee-Hive Girls program, *Gleaners* soon replaced *Senior* as the name of the department for young women of this age.

The most ambitious curriculum was reserved for the Advanced Senior department, introduced in 1917 for MIA members over age twenty-five.[231] Advanced Senior classes, later termed Adult classes and then, interestingly, Seniors (after that class had become Gleaners), were for combined groups of women and men, with a curriculum that included lessons on travel, literature, ethics, music, art, civics, and science.[232] The program proved popular as people responded to leaders' aspiration to enrich young adults' social and intellectual lives.[233] Lessons were progressive and high minded, presented through a gospel lens and geared toward helping people make sense of their rapidly modernizing world. In the 1923–1924 MIA season, for example, the course of study was "Life's Visions and Purposes," which included the topics of education, marriage, service, aesthetics, physical fitness, and spirituality.[234] Topics for discussion also included more secular subjects that could be taught by local experts, such as "All about Radium," "The Advance of Surgery," and "The Struggles for Sanitation."[235] In addition to lessons, classes were to hold socials and include time for bearing testimonies.[236]

The Advanced Senior class was the culmination of leaders' aims to develop youth into model Saints and citizens, and the efforts of those aims were woven into the curriculum and activities of each class. This oldest class participated in a sophisticated curriculum and an elaborate slate of activities that seemed more developmentally appropriate for an older age range.

BALANCING THE SPIRITUAL AND RECREATIONAL

The MIA's inclusion of secular topics in the curriculum and focus on elaborate activities made some members wonder whether recreation was overtaking the organization's spiritual mandate. General leaders reported on questions they received: "Are we not to teach religion any more?" and "Are we not to do more than devote our energies to secular studies and play?"[237] A new handbook released in September 1928 responded to those questions by defending the organization's heavy recreation emphasis.[238] While previous handbooks had built up to the 1928 handbook, this handbook laid out a comprehensive, progressive view of the mutually reinforcing roles religion and recreation could play in the development of a new kind of womanhood and manhood.[239]

The handbook was the work of the Community Activities Committee, a joint subcommittee of the YLMIA and YMMIA general boards that consisted of twelve board members.[240] Foremost among the progressive thinkers on the committee were Charlotte Stewart and Ephraim Ericksen. Stewart began her twenty-five years of service on the YLMIA board in 1914, when she was assigned specifically to use her knowledge of recreational leadership. She was head of the women's physical education department for the Utah Agricultural College (now Utah State University) and director of physical education for Salt Lake City public schools; she would go on to do graduate work at New York University, Columbia, and Stanford and to represent Utah and the YLMIA at numerous national recreation conventions.[241] Stewart was attuned to the needs of young women and brought their case to the board insistently: "We must take care of our girls and must find a way to meet their needs," she said.[242] She believed that recreation was vital to growth, as did Ericksen.[243] Ericksen received a PhD in philosophy from the University of Chicago with a dissertation later published as *The Psychological and Ethical Aspects of Mormon Group Life*. A professor at the University of Utah since 1915, he joined the YMMIA general board in 1922 and was quickly appointed to head the recreation committee. Thoroughly imbued with the outlook of progressive recreation, Ericksen believed it to be what he called a "spiritual agency," and he felt a sense of mission in his work on the board.[244] Supported by the other members of the committee, Stewart and Ericksen drew on their expertise to set forth a religiously based program of progressive recreation for the MIA.

Like earlier publications, the handbook quoted Brigham Young on the founding purposes of the YLMIA and YMMIA, drawing on the accounts in Susa Gates's history of the YLMIA and other sources. In addition to the traditional statements on gaining testimonies, however, the handbook included additional passages from the origin stories of the organizations. To the young men, Brigham Young had mentioned the need to develop "the gifts within them" and to cultivate "a knowledge and an application of the eternal principles of the great science of life." He had told the young women to "retrench in everything that is bad and worthless, and improve in everything that is good and beautiful" in order to be happy in this life and the next.[245] The handbook connected these statements to recreation, endowing it with prophetic approval.

The handbook listed the following purposes for the MIA, in addition to cultivating young people's testimonies:

> To aid them in obtaining all true knowledge; to teach the young people to preside over public assemblies; to express themselves before the public; to enable them to study and practice civil, vocational, social, scientific and educational affairs; and also to train them in all that pertains to religious, moral, social, physical and intellectual advancement.[246]

Nevertheless, the handbook repeatedly insisted that the MIA's top priority was spiritual. "Directly or indirectly, all the activities under the direction of our Church organizations should contribute to the making of true Latter-day Saints," it said. It also indicated that the recreational activities should "emphasize the fundamental ideals and standards of the church."[247] But this goal would be realized through action. The MIA's recreation program would be applied religion—what they called "the gospel of doing rather than of theorizing."[248] It would reach out to young people who might not currently be interested in religion and, through its activities, draw them in to spiritual awakening. Recreation was a means, not an end.[249]

The MIAs were charged, the handbook said, "to assist every man and woman to complete living on the foundation of faith in God and His great Latter-day work."[250] The idea of "complete living" powerfully blended Latter-day Saint and progressive ideals. It expressed a belief in the church as an agency of social, physical, intellectual, and spiritual development, rooted in the Saints' aspiration to create a unified, all-encompassing community—or in Latter-day Saint parlance, to build Zion. At the same time, it captured a progressive vision of promoting human flourishing through organized means and application of modern insights.

Substantial leadership training programs connected with that vision were necessary, the handbook argued, for Latter-day Saints to engage young people who had so many other options for how to spend their free time. "Recreation has been so generally commercialized that it is going to be no easy matter to develop the leadership which can compete with commercialized recreation," another section of the handbook observed. Church leaders did not desire to eradicate commercialized recreation, but they did wish to have some influence in raising standards. Above all, they sought to protect their own young people from the damaging influences they perceived in commercial environments.[251] For those concerned about social boundaries, the handbook suggested that an effective, church-sponsored recreation program would eliminate the need for young women and young men to look elsewhere to satisfy their legitimate desires for recreation.

While boundaries governing social interactions were critical, MIA leaders did look outward to design their recreation plans. In setting forth the extensive programs for each age group within the organizations, the handbook drew explicitly on sociological theory that attributed to human beings seven fundamental needs, which it called urges: social, rhythmic, dramatic, linguistic, physical, environmental, and constructive. Effective recreational activities would satisfy each of these urges—music for the rhythmic urge, sports and games for the physical urge, community beautification for the environmental urge, and so forth. Because the theory asserted that these needs manifested in different ways at various stages of life, the manual outlined specific needs and corresponding activities for each age group.[252]

While some needs and activities were different for the young women and young men, the 1928 handbook presented the YLMIA and YMMIA as distinct but thoroughly integrated. The organizations were structured around complementary divisions between the female classes and their male counterparts: Gleaners and M Men, Juniors and Vanguards, Bee-Hive Girls and Scouts. Contests included a few sex-segregated categories, primarily in vocal music, but playwriting, dance orchestra, drama, and dancing were all open to participants of both sexes.[253] Commenting favorably on the new manual, apostle Richard R. Lyman observed that, given the joint nature of their programs, perhaps it was time to start referring to the two organizations as the "M.I.A. of the Church," echoing George Q. Morris's statement from two decades earlier.[254] The handbook also reflected the increasingly common practice of referring to the meetings and activities of both organizations as *Mutual*.[255]

YLMIA leaders generally enjoyed their joint leadership in the MIA. For them, it reinforced the sense that women had taken their rightful place in the modern world. Ruth May Fox celebrated women's leadership in the MIA and in the church at large. "Women have become teachers of the Gospel and have been brought into closer co-operation with the priesthood of the Church," she noted. "Both men and women have broadened their attitude toward each other and have a larger understanding of the great problems of life." She thought the work of women in the church had elevated them to stand shoulder to shoulder with the men of the church.[256] Men still presided at meetings and took the lead in other ways, but the relative parity between the YLMIA and YMMIA struck her as significant.

MERGING THE JOURNALS

The clear integration of the YLMIA and YMMIA presented in the 1928 handbook made further changes possible. The Saturday morning session of the 1929 June Conference was just winding down when the gathered officers of the various local and stake MIAs received a surprising announcement. Looking at their programs, they saw that the next event was "A Delightful June Ceremony," but they were wholly unprepared for what this meant. It was, in fact, a "story book wedding"—at least, that is how the news was presented to them. Melvin J. Ballard, now serving in his tenth year as a church apostle and also in the role of assistant superintendent of the YMMIA, explained to the congregation that the *Young Woman's Journal* and the *Improvement Era* were to be joined into a new *Improvement Era*.[257]

Despite the momentum toward an integrated program, the journals' merger seemed sudden. Clarissa Beesley, who had served as the *Journal*'s managing editor for most of the 1920s, had guarded the magazine's independence and impressed upon her successor, Elsie Talmage Brandley, the need to prioritize YLMIA lines of authority and not get swept up by every conjoint proposal. "One of the important lessons I have had to learn in this work is to stifle energy and initiative and wait until I am told what to do—and then do it—and be sure it is the right authority by whom I am asked," Brandley wrote. "If the Young Men's organization representative asks me to do things—refuse until it comes through the recognized channel of power."[258] Given that YLMIA leaders had turned down merger proposals in previous years, the rapid move toward union of the journals was a surprise.[259]

The journey toward merging began early in 1929, when the YMMIA general board appointed a committee to study the status of the *Improvement Era*, which had been its official magazine since 1897. The result was a ten-thousand-word report confirming that the magazine was losing money and subscribers.[260] The committee had studied trends in national magazine publishing and made several recommendations: enlarge the *Era* to standard magazine size, add more colorful covers and increase illustrations throughout, and incorporate advertising alongside reading matter in the back half of the magazine. They also recommended launching a more intensive subscription drive led by a representative in each ward. If these recommendations were adopted, the committee wrote, they felt sure that the *Improvement Era* would become the most prominent regional magazine, with the finest, most influential content.[261]

Up to this point, nothing had been said about joining with the *Young Woman's Journal*. The committee met with the YMMIA general board on 8 May, and the general board accepted the committee's recommendations. But then Ballard suggested merging the *Era* with the *Young Woman's Journal*, and the board decided to pursue the idea with the YLMIA. That same day, Ballard met with YLMIA leaders and showed them the plans for the new, improved *Improvement Era*. The minutes of the YLMIA general board meeting record that Ballard "asked if the Young Ladies would like to make this a joint magazine, doing away with the Young Woman's Journal." The board agreed to consider the proposal and vote on it at their next meeting.[262]

That meeting was held on 14 May, but records leave no insight as to YLMIA leaders' assessments of the proposal. The minutes record only this: "The amalgamation of the Improvement Era and Young Woman's Journal was considered. Rose W. Bennett moved that the consolidation take place, which was seconded and passed."[263] The next evening at a joint board meeting of the two organizations, Ballard announced that the YLMIA board had voted to combine the *Improvement Era* and the *Young Woman's Journal*.[264]

It is unclear why the YLMIA board accepted the merger and whether they had reservations about doing so. At the time, the *Journal* was flourishing. General board minutes show that the *Journal* made money for the YLMIA, which they were able to use for other purposes in the organization. Each issue featured between sixty-four and seventy-four pages of content, with twelve pages of advertising.[265] Board members often expressed satisfaction that the magazine was edited and managed by women, and they exhorted young women to regard the *Journal* as theirs and take pride in it. In the atmosphere of the late 1920s, however, perhaps YLMIA leaders saw having a single magazine for both genders as a mark of progress, signifying women's equal position with men. Perhaps they felt it simply reflected the reality that an ever-increasing portion of MIA work was undertaken jointly.[266]

At least initially, representatives from the two organizations collaborated closely in editorial leadership of the merged periodical. Brandley shifted from working as the managing editor of the *Young Woman's Journal* to working as the associate editor of the *Improvement Era*, while Hugh Cannon of the YMMIA continued as its managing editor. "We worked together in harmony and friendliness," Brandley recorded in her journal. She appreciated Cannon's faith and perspectives and felt his death two years later as a personal loss. "From the time of his death on, I think my own faith was stronger," she reflected, "for having known the man, and realized that such as he could not cease living—he was too much a soul to be perishable, as a body might be perishable."[267]

FACING FORWARD WITH OPTIMISM

On 28 March 1929, Heber J. Grant attended a special meeting of the YLMIA general board to announce the release of Martha Horne Tingey as president of the organization after almost fifty years of service in its presidency.[268] Ruth May Fox, then serving as Tingey's first counselor, was appointed as the new president. It was not exactly a generational changing of the guard; at age seventy-five, Fox was four years older than Tingey. But she was vigorous in mind and body and had proven herself an imaginative, capable leader. After announcing her appointment, Grant handed Fox a poem that read, in part: "But if from life you take the best / And if in life you keep the zest / If love you hold; No matter how the years go by, / No matter how the birthdays fly, / You are not old."[269] Fox served as president for eight years, and she lived for three more decades.

The new presidency anchored the YLMIA with tradition and experience. First counselor Lucy Grant Cannon had served almost continuously for thirty years as a YLMIA leader since becoming president of her ward association at age eighteen.[270] Since 1916, she had served on the general board and had worked extensively on the *Guide* committee (which compiled the lessons) before becoming second counselor to Tingey in 1923. Clarissa Beesley, Fox's second counselor, had a long record of service in the organization and had been a key participant in the MIA's embrace of progressive methods as a member of the Social Advisory Committee. Both had served missions.[271] These collaborators presided over a vibrant organization of over fifty-four thousand members in nearly twelve hundred local associations.[272]

The YLMIA faced modern conditions with a sense of optimism. "We believe sagacity, foresight, vision, stability and faith are not foreign to youth—*our* youth," wrote an editorialist of the *Young Woman's Journal* in 1929. "They are making a contribution to the world."[273] Picturing the faces of the young people of the church, Richard R. Lyman had proclaimed that no other institution was giving as much experience and training to its youth. This generation would be stronger and better because of the modern methods of the MIA. Fifty years ago, he said, his generation had been born into a world of "dirt, ugliness, disease." Now the world embraced cleanliness, beauty, and health. The MIAs, he said, "provide that recreation, training, and education which are necessary to produce well rounded and successful lives."[274]

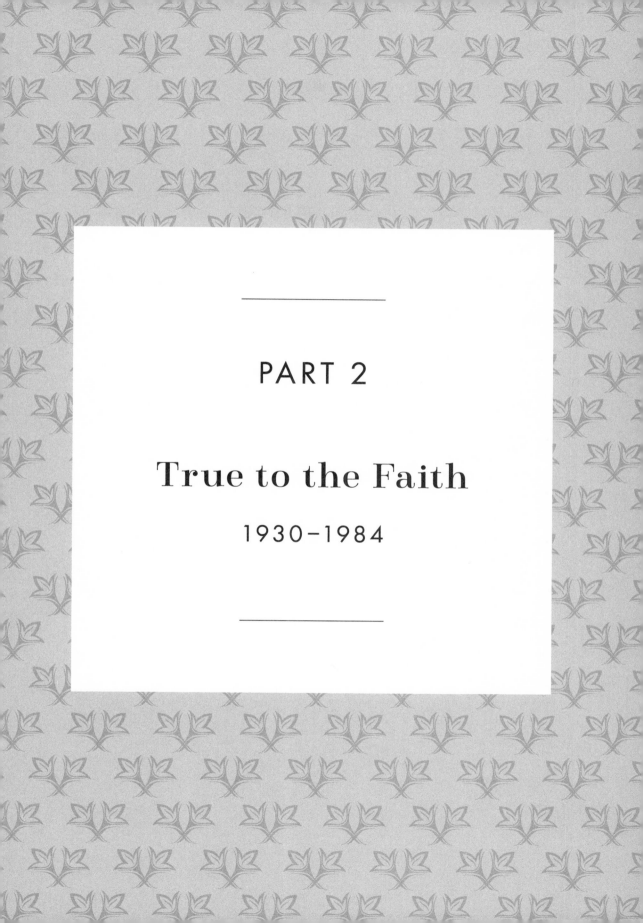

PART 2

True to the Faith

1930–1984

MODERN MUTUALS

1930–1948

In 1930, Latter-day Saints felt a sense of optimism that shaped their celebration of the church's centennial anniversary. The church had grown to include nearly seven hundred thousand members, and both the institution and its people were gaining public acceptance in the United States.[1] Technological and social development had dramatically increased most members' standard of living. For YLMIA president Ruth May Fox, the establishment and growth of the church and concurrent advances in secular fields such as science were not coincidental. For the April 1930 issue of the *Improvement Era*, she wrote a poem entitled "The Heavenly Gift." In her poem, the personified figure of Faith opened heavenly gates at the time of the church's founding and awakened Progress and enlivened Science.[2]

Some members felt concerned, however, that the church might drift from the spiritual power of its roots. If opposition had helped turn early Saints and pioneers toward God, would the comforts of modern society lead to complacency? To balance a sense of forward momentum with a connection to the past, MIA leaders chose "Onward with Mormon Ideals" as the theme for the 1930 June Conference. In preparation for the conference, they sent out an open call for submissions of original songs to reinforce the spirit of the event. None of the submissions, however, met their hopes, and board members worried about how to close the program. "I guess I'll have to see what I can do," Fox commented after one meeting. That afternoon, she returned with the words for a new hymn entitled "Carry On."[3]

On the final evening of the June Conference, M Men and Gleaners—young men and women ages seventeen to twenty-three—presented a program featuring music, talks, and performances. Divided into two parts, the program addressed the "Contribution of Youth in the Past" and "The Young People of Today."[4] The themes of heritage and youth today also echoed through Fox's new hymn, invoking the mountains and deserts of the Utah landscape, pioneer ancestors, and new efforts to build:

> Firm as the mountains around us,
> Stalwart and brave we stand,
> On the rock our fathers planted
> For us in this goodly land. . . .
> And we hear the desert singing,
> Carry on, carry on, carry on.
> Hills and vales and mountains ringing,
> Carry on, carry on, carry on.

As young women and men sang the chorus, they enacted the final verse's call to hold aloft their colors by lifting papers in MIA gold and green. "O youth of the noble birthright," they sang, "carry on, carry on, carry on."[5]

In the *Improvement Era*, MIA leaders expressed their hope that every stake in the church would hold a similar program, representing the theme "Onward with Mormon Ideals."[6] The idea of being guided by uniquely Latter-day Saint values would have an extended influence on the MIA. For Fox, *onward* also meant outward: she used her 1930 June Conference address to report on the establishment of MIA organizations outside the Latter-day Saint heartland.[7] The 1930s were a decade of both internal definition and international expansion for the MIA—until, at the close of the decade and in the early 1940s, the world faced another global war.

PRESERVING MEMORY TO PROMOTE FAITH

As YLMIA leaders prepared for the centennial, they sought ways to promote the sort of reflection that would link modern young women with the church's pioneer roots. One of these was Treasures of Truth, a class project that became an enduring and cherished part of the Gleaner experience. The church published an official multi-volume account of its history in 1930, and leaders intended the Treasures of Truth project to give young women an opportunity to write the religious history of their families.[8] The young women were to collect and write their own or their ancestors' conversion experiences and reflect on the influence of those stories of faith. Where applicable, they were encouraged to include details about the pioneer trek west, missionary service, and the establishment of settlements in what would become Utah. They were to include pictures of the relevant people and places wherever possible to illustrate their books.[9] To link young women with their future families, leaders encouraged them to compile the book with durability in mind.[10] If the pioneer era had produced spiritually valuable experiences, the centennial era had produced the right circumstances to widely document them. By the 1930s, young women had the literacy, leisure time, and access to inexpensive consumer goods—notebooks, paper, and even photographs—that made such a project possible.[11]

Leaders worried that the emphasis on inspiring stories could lead young women to seek out stories valued more for their thrill than for the depth of personal conversion they represented. In the Gleaner manual, therefore, leaders instructed that all the stories should be well documented. Young women were to list the sources of their information and, when possible, obtain signed statements from those who provided the stories. "Great care should be taken that stories changed or exaggerated through a number of repetitions find no place in the book," the manual warned. "The record will be valuable only as it is entirely true."[12]

While not all young women in the Gleaner class took on the project, extant Treasures of Truth books demonstrate that many took the work seriously. Eleanor Larsen, an eighteen-year-old Gleaner from Spring City, Utah, started work on her book in 1932 and dedicated it "to my mother and her future generations." Eleanor used her book primarily for genealogical information: beginning with her maternal great-great-grandparents, she documented ancestors and extended family, noting births, deaths, and migrations from Denmark to Utah. Multiple types of ink and later dates indicate she continued to update the book long after her initial efforts. Eleanor noted births, marriages, and deaths through the 1940s. The last date in the book is for her own 1950 wedding. Her focus on key dates is rarely interrupted by comments, but some are poignant. Under the entry for her mother's June 1944 death, Eleanor noted, "All the flowers she loved were in full bloom. She died of a heart attack. I was alone with her at the time. I am thankful I was there."[13]

Some Treasures of Truth books were kept not by individuals but by Gleaner groups collectively. These books, which mix personal stories with histories of the local MIA organizations and wards and narrative writing with poetry and hand-drawn art, give insight into the mix of stories that shaped a local religious identity. A 1935 Treasures of Truth book created by the Gleaners in the South Davis Stake (which included Bountiful, Farmington, and Centerville, Utah) offers organizational histories in place of a family genealogy. The book's compilers dedicated a section to each of the stake's wards, giving space to photos of ward YLMIA members and poems or narratives written by them. The West Bountiful Ward's section demonstrates how a distinctive local MIA memory was being preserved and passed on. A short dedicatory verse mentions both past Gleaners and those who died before becoming Gleaners. Later in the section, the compilers included a poem written by ward member Jessie Stirling Pack about her daughter Belle, who had been active in the local YLMIA when she passed away in 1905, thirty years earlier. The poem's inclusion suggests that the mother or daughter had made a deep impression on local YLMIA identity. A local newspaper reported that members of the YLMIA had served as pallbearers at Belle's funeral, which might explain why this particular poem continued to resonate as the West Bountiful Ward constructed their history.[14]

The local spiritual history documented by the young women also sheds light on changing expressions of spirituality. Treasures of Truth books show young women forging a link with the miraculous, even after charismatic practices such as speaking in tongues and women's healing blessings had fallen out of favor. A 1931–1932 Treasures of Truth book compiled by the Jefferson Ward in Salt Lake City, for example, features stories about sickness or accidents from multiple generations. LaVern McClellan Lloyd shared an extended account of her mother's experiences with a son's health crisis in 1914. This story includes a revelatory dream and a healing in the temple. "At that time they were giving blessings in the Temple for the sick," the account notes, indicating LaVern's awareness of how Latter-day Saint healing practices had changed in a generation. The later stories are more subtle and focus on experiences such as the incidental effects of mothers' prayers. Bertha Blechert wrote about being hit by a truck on 16 September 1929 and regaining consciousness lying underneath it, but with only a few scratches. Bertha credited her mother's prayer for her protection with preserving her from serious injury.[15]

The year following the introduction of Treasures of Truth, a similar project was introduced for the Junior classes: My Story—Lest I Forget. Like its sister project for the older young women, My Story gave fifteen- to sixteen-year-olds the opportunity to make a record and tell their own and their loved ones' stories.[16] Bee-Hive Girls—young women ages fourteen and fifteen, plus twelve- and thirteen-year-olds whose parents had given them permission to participate—were likewise encouraged to keep a scrapbook showing the activities they had engaged in to complete their requirements. Such scrapbooks might include drawings, recipes, games, songs, pressed flowers, small crafted items, programs, clippings, and pictures.[17] Participants could even enter their scrapbooks in a stake contest.[18] My Story and the scrapbook for Bee-Hive Girls were natural extensions of the idea behind the Treasures of Truth books and ensured that YLMIA members of all ages had a common experience.

By 1940, the general board had collected numerous responses to the My Story effort that they included in a series of lessons in the *Junior Manual* to encourage young women to embrace the exercise. "It's the most precious thing I own," one young woman said. Another said that her book was an inspiration to her: "I've written some of the things I've thought and believed about life and now it's interesting to see how some of my views have changed." Another mentioned the value of learning more about her family history: "I wrote some stories in my book that my grandmother told me about her early life. She died several years ago and I'm the only one in the family who has much written about her." One young woman said that her book had become a "real friend" to her on her mission as she found inspirational things she had recorded in her book that gave her courage.[19]

In practice, young women experienced significant overlap between their My Story and Treasures of Truth work. In 1947, a new manual said the entire project for Juniors and Gleaners would be called Treasures of Truth, and "My Story" would appear on the title page.[20] For decades to come, Treasures of Truth remained part of each program, shaping the identity, spirituality, and aspirations of young Latter-day Saint women.[21]

ADOPTION AND ADAPTATION OUTSIDE THE UNITED STATES

The Treasures of Truth and Bee-Hive programs had been designed largely around the needs of young women in Utah, where large Latter-day Saint youth cohorts were the norm and pioneer ancestors were commonplace. By the 1930s, however, these programs were expanding well beyond the Intermountain West. Increased migration out of Utah in the early decades of the twentieth century had led to growing Latter-day Saint communities in California and in eastern urban centers like New York City and Washington, DC. Church leaders were no longer encouraging converts to immigrate to Utah, which led to further development of branches outside the Intermountain West and the United States.[22] Despite the pressures of a deepening economic depression, the 1930s marked an increasingly visible investment by the church in its national and international presence, as witnessed by the replacement of rented meeting rooms with the first custom-built Latter-day Saint meetinghouses in many locations around the world.[23]

The YLMIA provided a crucial place of belonging for young Latter-day Saint women throughout the world. Louise Puenzieux recalled belonging to the first Gleaner cohort in French-speaking Switzerland in the mid-1930s.[24] As their peers in Utah did, Gleaners in Lausanne, Switzerland, documented their spiritual history in Treasures of Truth books. An excerpt from Louise's book was deemed important enough to the collective memory of Latter-day Saints in her area that it was preserved in the mission president's files.[25]

In her book, Louise recorded an account from when she was five months old and her parents were recent converts to the church. She was suffering from tuberculosis, and the family's doctor told her parents she might not survive the night. Despite the concern, her father fulfilled his responsibility as a local deacon to go heat the meeting hall for the annual district conference. Their landlord, a Mrs. Perrenoud, came by while he was gone and brought up their new faith. "Look, you have your Mormons," she said. "Let them come and heal this child, then maybe we will believe what they have to say." Louise's mother asked for priesthood bearers to bless the child, hoping they would come immediately. She was disappointed when they promised to come after the conference. When Perrenoud said that the men would purposely wait to come until after Louise had died, however, Louise's mother asserted her continuing faith. "They will raise her from the dead," she responded. But the elders soon arrived, and Louise's condition improved shortly after they blessed her, astonishing the doctor.[26]

As was common in Utah examples, Louise's story focused on a miraculous healing. In her piece, however, the references to her father's commitment to church service and her mother's responses to their landlord's challenge emphasize fidelity in the face of skepticism, social marginalization, and disappointment. The story served not only as evidence of divine presence but also as justification for the family's religious identity. While Louise signed the statement, the document also notes attestations of its accuracy by her parents and one of the elders who helped with the blessing. For Louise, the dynamics of conversion provided a comparable substitute for the pioneer experiences that the Treasures of Truth program was initially designed to capture.[27]

Bee-Hive work was also expanding internationally and becoming part of the YLMIA experience around the world. In Germany, thousands of Latter-day Saint women were involved in auxiliary work over the course of the 1920s and 1930s. At the time, YLMIA membership was becoming established as a marker of religious identity for the growing cohort of young women raised in the church in Germany.

On 24 October 1934, fourteen-year-old Helga Meiszus in Tilsit (then in the German state of Prussia; now Sovetsk, Russia) placed a seal in the health section of her Bee-Hive handbook. It was her first seal—a mark of achievement in the program, earned by going three consecutive months without missing a day of school or work due to illness. In the months that followed, she passed off additional requirements and pasted seals into the sections in her manual for religion, home, health, handicrafts, out-of-doors, business, and public service.[28] Around the same time, the Nazi party began strongly encouraging young women her age to join the League of German

Bee-Hive Girls of the Zwickau Branch. 1924. In Germany, the *Zwickauer Bienenkorbmädchen*, or Bee-Hive Girls of the Zwickau Branch, developed a robust program during the 1920s and 1930s, including these matching uniforms with beehive insignia. Several young women kept their Bee-Hive Girls scrapbooks among the few treasured possessions they brought when immigrating to new lands. (Courtesy Glenn Fassmann.)

Girls. Helga asked her mother if she might enlist. Her mother told her no. "You are a Beehive girl," she explained. "You don't need to belong to that group."[29] Over the next four and a half years, Helga passed off dozens of Bee-Hive requirements. Like all participants in the Bee-Hive program, she chose a special name. Hers was "Edelmut," a combination of *Edelweiss*, the personal symbolic flower she chose as part of her Bee-Hive program, and *Mut*, the German word for courage. She drank warm water each morning as recommended in the health section, attended sacrament meetings, bore her testimony at fast and testimony meetings, made clothing, performed household chores, prepared meals, visited local sites of interest, and completed dozens of other requirements. Almost a century later, her carefully preserved German Bee-Hive manual, decorated with hand-colored illustrations, attests to her dedication in performing these tasks and her reverence for her Bee-Hive membership.[30]

Although there were already groups of Saints in Germany before the founding of the YLMIA in the 1870s, the book Helga used was among the first efforts to translate a YLMIA manual into a language other than English. In 1926 a woman in the church in Hamburg translated a few parts of the English handbook and organized a few girls into a swarm. That same year, Sarah Richards Cannon, who led the Swiss-German Mission alongside her husband, Hugh, proposed integrating the Bee-Hive program into the existing MIA work of the mission. She gathered a committee to work out a translation of the handbook, which included alterations to meet the particular needs of the young women in that area, and it was published early in 1927.[31] The committee, including three native German speakers, published an improved and enlarged second edition in 1928.[32] This second German edition of the Bee-Hive Girls handbook was the one Helga used to guide her work.

The 1928 handbook represented an adapted editorial vision rather than a simple translation. The German version of the handbook omitted altogether some sections found in English, such as descriptions of awards. Some sections were shortened—for example, only five of the thirteen songs in the handbook used by young women in the United States were translated into German. Other sections were extended. The German handbook contained coursework for three full years rather than just one, as was the American custom. The German version also included supplemental material to help young women understand the principles behind the program's requirements. There was, for example, only one line in the English version instructing young women to "know what a girl of her age ought to know of the physiology of her own body." In the German version, there was an entire chapter on the subject, which credited a Swiss medical doctor for his review of the material.[33]

Some parts of the manual indicate clearly that the committee sought to adapt the handbook to German culture. At the end of one article, for example, the committee added a verse by the well-known German writer Friedrich Rückert to poetically express and summarize the ideas:

> *Vor jedem steht ein Bild des, was*
> *er warden soll:*
> *So lang er das nicht ist, ist nicht*
> *sein Frieden voll.*

> Before each person stands an image
> of what he ought to be:
> And for as long as he's not that,
> he'll never know peace fully.[34]

The YLMIA general board was delighted with the advancement of MIA work in German-speaking countries. Within a few months of the January 1927 publication of the Bee-Hive handbook in German, the *Young Woman's Journal* reported that the young women of the Basel Branch in Switzerland had "made remarkable progress and shown much enthusiasm for the new activity." Two swarms had been created, with swarm names and symbols, under the guidance of well-trained local Bee-Keepers.[35] By 1929, the organizations not only in the German-speaking missions but also in the Netherlands Mission had run consistently for two full years, and several swarms in Great Britain were likewise approaching two-year anniversaries.[36] By the early 1930s, translations of the Bee-Hive handbook were in full swing across the European missions. Girls in France were also forming swarms, and young women in Denmark and other Scandinavian countries quickly followed. When they began their work, they did so from books in their own languages.[37]

The growing emphasis on establishing MIA programs outside of Latter-day Saint–majority areas increased the responsibilities placed on mission leaders, who oversaw all church work outside of stakes in the western United States and Canada and reported to leaders at church headquarters. At the time, mission presidents' wives acted as Relief Society mission presidents and were responsible for overseeing the work of Relief Society, YLMIA, and Primary in the missions and improving the experience of women and children in mission branches.[38] These responsibilities could be daunting. At a conference of Relief Society mission presidents in Europe, some of the women felt they were attempting to accomplish extraordinary tasks and expressed the need for help in effectively running the growing organizations. These mission leaders then wrote to the First Presidency in Salt Lake City, requesting that they send trained women from Utah, perhaps even female missionaries, to help.[39]

The First Presidency responded by encouraging them to find local women to train as leaders. "It is not at all necessary," wrote the First Presidency, "for the mission president's wife to supervise all women's work in the mission." They believed that many local members, though new to the organization of the church, could successfully serve in the auxiliaries.[40] Relief Society mission presidents heeded that counsel and resolved to appoint local presidents for each auxiliary, along with two counselors and a secretary. They also chose district supervisors and worked toward finding more leaders.[41] Once assigned, local leaders in Europe collaborated with mission leaders to adapt, implement, and expand the YLMIA.

In other regions, too, the YLMIA was often run by local members, while many priesthood leadership positions were filled by missionaries from Utah and other areas heavily populated by Latter-day Saints. When the mission in Japan closed in 1924 because of political tension, mission leaders directed the handful of Latter-day Saints in the country not to hold any meetings other than those for the MIA. Japanese Latter-day Saints organized a joint MIA the month after missionaries left. The first issue of their newsletter expressed hope that the MIA would be a path to light in the present darkness. That hope proved crucial—MIA meetings and newsletters were the primary church contact for Latter-day Saints in Japan until after World War II.[42]

In Mexico, where criticism of foreign clergy had become an important part of the national discourse, disagreements about the urgency of appointing local leaders led to a period, from 1936 to 1946, in which about one-third of local Latter-day Saints refused to recognize mission leadership and instead established a break-off church group known as the Third Convention.[43] Although the MIA organizations were relatively new to Mexico at the time of the schism—efforts to establish MIAs across central Mexico began in 1934—Third Convention members nevertheless installed MIAs in their congregations.[44] That a break-off group concerned with asserting Mexican leadership and culture continued with MIA activities suggests that, despite being shaped by norms of congregations in the United States, the organizations were valued locally rather than being perceived primarily as a colonial incursion. Years later, when most members of the Third Convention rejoined the body of the church, MIA programs of drama, speech, dance, and music were featured prominently at the reunification conference. Rather than being passive spectators to the end of a decade-long division in the church, young women in Mexico played an active part in bringing their religious community back together.[45]

A CRISIS OF MODERN SPIRITUALITY

The MIAs' successful movement outward unfolded at the same time as anxieties increased over what it would mean for Latter-day Saint youth to move "onward with Mormon ideals." As the 1929 stock market crash in the United States gave way to a lingering economic depression rather than the rapid recovery many had hoped for, it grew harder to sustain the effusive confidence of the Progressive Era. While the terms *progress* and *progressive* had animated developments in the MIA in recent decades, now the term *modern* came to the fore, reflecting the sense that the Saints were living in a new world and a new social order—one with a difficult-to-define mix of progress and peril. In the Intermountain West, where a large percentage of Latter-day Saints lived, unemployment was rampant, reaching 35.9 percent in Utah in 1932, and per capita income had fallen by almost 50 percent since 1929.[46] Nationally, young people suffered the highest unemployment rate of any group— only an estimated 6 to 10 percent of recent high school graduates could find work.[47] College enrollments grew in the absence of job opportunities, but students subsisted from semester to semester, living on meager rations and unsure whether they could afford to continue classes.[48] While the emotional toll of shrinking household incomes affected each family differently, a collective strain was clear. By 1932, some two hundred thousand young Americans had left their homes altogether to wander the country.[49] In one joint MIA board meeting, YMMIA board member Oscar Kirkham estimated despairingly that over five thousand young Latter-day Saint men were drifting without schooling or employment.[50]

MIA leaders brought different life experiences and perspectives to bear on the challenges of the era. Through the early twentieth century, the impulse to engage with the world had dominated the MIA's focus. Faced with the crises of the 1930s, leaders were divided over what to do. Several YMMIA board members were university professors, and their campus experience and academic training influenced the discussion. This meant that much of the concern focused on youth ages eighteen to twenty-four and especially on college students, who were confronting challenges to their faith in their studies, especially in philosophy and science. While this segment of the Latter-day Saint population was certainly a numeric minority, it did fall within MIA age, and leaders believed these young people represented general trends in the church and society.[51]

YLMIA board member Elsie Talmage Brandley shared many perspectives with the professors on the boards. Brandley's background predisposed her to feel open to intellectual change rather than embattled by it. Her father, James E. Talmage, was a geologist and university president who became an apostle when she was fifteen. In contrast to her contemporary and college friend, Camilla Eyring, she'd had little cause to argue with her parents over perceived conflicts between science and religion, because in Brandley's home, the two fields had existed in harmony.[52]

In October 1933, Brandley and her husband attended a dinner social for members of the general boards of the YLMIA and YMMIA and their spouses. J. Reuben Clark Jr., a former MIA board member and newly appointed counselor in the church's First Presidency, attended. Since joining the First Presidency that spring, he had reviewed church policies, conducted church business, and represented the church in secular affairs.[53] He now turned his attention to the MIA. "President Clark had been invited to speak, and made the most of it by speaking with alarming frankness about MIA work," Brandley noted. "It had the admirable effect of waking up the Boards, both of which have needed some waking for a long time," she added.[54]

Though no one appears to have taken detailed notes on what Clark said to "wake up" the boards, subsequent discussions at board meetings make clear that he reproached them for not being sufficiently grounded in the spiritual and religious truths of the restored gospel. Just two weeks later, apostle John A. Widtsoe, recently returned from presiding over the European Mission, issued a similar rebuke. While overseeing the translation of MIA manuals, he thought they contained too much material that resembled university extension courses. "Unless we flavor all we do, all we have, with the message of the Prophet Joseph Smith," he insisted, "we are far afield."[55]

Such critiques were not new. Concerns about the potential to underemphasize spirituality had arisen alongside the organizations' recreation emphasis, and leaders had worked all along to fortify the testimony-building purposes of their programs. Given their official assignment of overseeing recreation for the church, the MIAs had taken pains to articulate the importance of teaching the gospel through activities while simultaneously offering a great deal of explicitly religious content. In the 1920s, slogans—and their accompanying talks, discussions, and activities—had proclaimed belief in divine guidance, the divinity of Christ, the truth of Joseph Smith's work, and the divine origin of the Book of Mormon.[56] Critique from a counselor in the First Presidency and an apostle, however, could not be ignored. Clark's address to the MIA boards represented a forceful new iteration of the impulse toward spiritual retrenchment.

Shaken but mobilized by Clark's and Widtsoe's charges, the boards appointed a joint Survey Committee, headed by Widtsoe. The committee was to conduct a thorough evaluation of the YLMIA, the YMMIA, and their programs to root out redundancy and gauge whether they were sufficiently focused on spiritual matters. The committee set to work right away, meeting at least twice a week between November 1933 and March 1934. Meanwhile, other committees immediately began reorienting the curriculum then in development toward distinctly Latter-day Saint teachings.[57] Having received what they considered authoritative guidance from ranking priesthood leaders, they quickly aligned themselves.

As the boards waited for the results of the Survey Committee's work, they began to address Clark's and Widtsoe's concerns in the early months of 1934, engaging in a series of far-reaching discussions about youth, the changing world, and the church. Their discussions revealed diverging assumptions and approaches—between the church and the world, certainly, but also within the church itself.[58] At the first general board testimony meeting of the year, Elsie Brandley observed that some of the differences between leaders' responses might reflect their own generational perspectives. "There is always much said that is helpful," she wrote. "Always much to make the young ones realize that they are too impulsive; always much to make us realize that some of the old ones have lost the touch of youth and the understanding and tolerance necessary if they are to touch the lives of youth at all."[59] Brandley also reflected on generational considerations during local visits to youth. At one local discussion of chastity with a group of Junior class members, she noted differences from her own still-recent youth. "They asked questions which, 15 years ago, we should not have known enough to ask, and, if we had, would have been too embarrassed to mention," Brandley noted.[60] Meeting with another Junior class on the same subject, she found herself reflecting on the MIAs' messaging power. "As I looked at them I wondered how many of them were believing a word of what I was saying," she wrote. "With the floods of moving pictures, books and magazine stories which paint the matter of sex contacts so alluringly, it is small wonder that old ideas of morality go down. I should like to know how the older generation who think they would be so strong under any conditions would have reacted to the powerful influences of today—in their own youth."[61]

Brandley heard others at board meetings raise related observations about the challenges young people faced. Helen Spencer Williams observed that young people wanted new ways of doing things and they felt that changing situations made information obsolete unless it was adjusted to meet the changes.[62] Arthur Beeley noted that economic uncertainty was a major factor in young people's mindset: "The young people today are facing many problems and are truly wondering whether there is any future for them."[63] In keeping with the paradigm of improvement through engagement, George Q. Morris pointed out that the Saints did not live in isolation and needed to engage with the world around them.[64] BYU president Franklin Harris agreed: "We want to make our teaching in MIA, and our preaching, and all of our work fit the modern world just as much as we can."[65]

Many other board members, though, worried like Clark and Widtsoe that too much fealty to worldly ideas eroded young people's foundational witness of the distinctive aspects of Latter-day Saint belief. In particular, board members worried that young people did not believe in Joseph Smith's first vision of Deity and the other miracles that led to the establishment of the church, the revelation of divine truths, and the restoration of priesthood authority.[66] This concern registered a sense that modern ways of thinking posed a threat to belief in God's direct intervention in the world. Leaders did not blame perceived spiritual shortcomings solely, or even primarily, on youth. "I consider that our teaching is poor," said Rose Bennett.[67] While they criticized poor leadership, some board members were also concerned about teachers who contradicted spiritual truth claims. Nicholas G. Smith said that one of his sons had told him about an Aaronic Priesthood leader with openly divergent beliefs, explaining, "He doesn't believe in Joseph Smith's visions; he doesn't think there is anything divine about what has come to pass in the organization of our Church."[68] Herbert Maw noted particular concern on behalf of college students, who also faced unbelieving professors and fellow students who actively tried to undermine their faith.[69] Joseph Fielding Smith, son of former church president Joseph F. Smith, related his experience with one young man at the University of Utah who Smith said was "literally going through Gethsemane with his faith," wanting to believe but finding it rationally impossible.[70] Since the MIA was the only contact many young people had with the church, he said, it was critical that youth leaders guide their attitudes correctly.[71]

Smith also noted a desire among many young people to gain experience of their own through meaningful church service. "I need a project," one young man had lamented, wishing for something on par with the heroic undertaking of the pioneers.[72] Bennett and others noted that returned missionaries especially wanted a chance to lead and participate meaningfully in the church.[73] Board members had also observed that young people wanted the church to take a more active approach to dealing with the economic devastation occurring all around. The discussions among board members revealed that there were, indeed, deep-seated disagreements about what the church should do—even what it should *become*—in the face of modernity.[74]

This debate among Latter-day Saints reflected larger currents in the American religious landscape of the 1930s. Mainline Protestant denominations experienced a "religious depression" as they lost their once-dominant place in society amid a wave of spiritual decline and skepticism rooted in the disillusionment that followed World War I. Mainline Protestantism had in recent decades sought to reconcile faith and science, emphasized ethics over doctrine, and prioritized unity over a distinction between the church and the world. Meanwhile, seemingly marginal fundamentalist and evangelical movements were vibrant and growing, offering resistance to both secular modernism and mainstream Protestantism.[75] Catholicism was also rising in numbers and influence as millions of Catholics immigrated to the United States. It was a critical period for the development of American religious pluralism, and most religious groups were working to respond to challenges posed by science (especially evolution), sociology, and philosophy—challenges exacerbated by the seeming inadequacy of religion to address the acute devastation of the Depression.[76] "A change has come over the spirit of our times, and the old faiths and hopes no longer carry conviction, when stated in the old terms," lamented one Protestant theologian, echoing the sense of religious crisis that Latter-day Saints perceived in their community.[77] After several young women were invited to share their feelings in a board meeting, Brandley observed that "some of the girls are almost tragic in their feeling that the Church is not feeding them the bread of life."[78]

During the February 1934 board meetings, divisions among YMMIA board members deepened. Arthur Beeley and Ephraim Ericksen, who had served faithfully on the board for many years, both believed the church needed to adapt to the modern world, which to them meant emphasizing the ethical, social, and broadly spiritual aspects of the gospel. Addressing both MIA boards, Beeley suggested that the youth of the church felt "some of the very literal things, such as faith, repentance, baptism, etc." were less important than the vision laid out in the thirteenth article of faith, which indicated that the goal of a religious life was to find goodness and beauty.[79] Similarly, Ericksen believed the church's teachings had the potential to produce the best young people in the world and build a community committed to beauty, truth, and justice. These fruits, he felt, would demonstrate that Joseph Smith was a prophet.[80]

Ericksen and Beeley did not believe that modernity had to be resisted. They interpreted their religion through modernist lenses, less concerned with visions, angels, and miracles than with the application of spiritual truths and religious energies to create a community focused on human flourishing. Like Protestant modernists, they believed that modern times required a modern reinterpretation of the gospel to make it relevant—even comprehensible—to the rising generation. Clark and Widtsoe, on the other hand, believed that the new social order brought about by modernity required the church to stand apart from the culture and assert its independence as a corrective to the secularizing tendencies threatening to overtake religion's unique claims. In their view, a proclamation of visions, angels, and miracles was exactly what the modern world needed. Above all, these were the basis for Latter-day Saints' identity and for their mandate to offer something uniquely true to the world. Latter-day Saints were at a crossroads in the early 1930s, and the MIAs were at the forefront as the church navigated the new territory of modernity.

CONFIRMING AND CODIFYING WITH THE SURVEY REPORT

At the joint board meeting on 14 March 1934, Elsie Brandley read the Survey Committee's full thirty-page report aloud.[81] "Changes of great extent and deep import have come over the world since the founding of the Mutual Improvement Associations," the introduction read. "A different religious outlook has seized upon humanity." The church was trying to keep pace without yielding fudamental principles.[82] The report affirmed the purposes of the MIAs, including the goal of making true Latter-day Saints and teaching the gospel through applied religion.[83]

A substantial section of the report presented a more focused philosophy for MIA activities. In the past, and in keeping with the Saints' goal of being a self-sufficient community, leaders had attempted to keep young Latter-day Saints entirely within the auspices of the church by creating programs that offered alternatives to popular clubs and commercial facilities. But times had changed. The report asserted that the MIAs should no longer attempt to duplicate or compete with the many social offerings sponsored by private and public entities, including recreation and extension programs offered by schools and colleges. Though the MIAs were advised to continue holding activities, the report instructed them to focus on their own purposes and treat secular subjects only under special circumstances and with a spiritual focus. This change was a recognition that Latter-day Saints in Utah coexisted with secular institutions to a far greater degree than they had in prior generations.[84]

The report affirmed Clark and Widtsoe's view that faith in distinctive elements of Latter-day Saint belief was of paramount importance. Along with repeatedly emphasizing the importance of the spiritual orientation in all MIA activities and offering recommendations for enhancing it, the survey report insisted on spiritual qualifications for MIA leaders: "All MIA officers and other MIA leaders [shall] be chosen with reference to their fitness for MIA service," the report stated, including "their acceptance of the principles of the Gospel of Jesus Christ as restored by the Prophet Joseph Smith—that is, they must be real Latter-day Saints."[85]

As the board discussed the report, questions arose as to what the committee meant by "spiritualizing our program."[86] In response, Widtsoe clarified at the next meeting. Spiritual things dealt with the influence of the Spirit or the sacred things of the church, he said. Cultural matters could impart moral training but did not account for the sacred nature of the church and its doctrine. Spiritualizing MIA programs meant that every part must increase faith in God, Jesus Christ, the plan of salvation, and the restoration of the gospel of Jesus Christ, as well as the fundamental claims and principles of the Latter-day Saints. Furthermore, activities should be conducted in harmony with Latter-day Saint practices, and leaders were to teach the place of every activity in the gospel plan. "Any subject which cannot be so treated should not form part of the MIA program," Widtsoe argued.[87] This definition explicitly laid out ideas and imperatives that had been expressed before but never fully codified. Now there was a clear standard for moving forward.

YOUTH AND THE NEW DAY

On Saturday, 9 June 1934, Elsie Brandley delivered an address titled "The Religious Crisis of Today" to over three thousand stake and ward MIA leaders gathered in the Assembly Hall on Temple Square in Salt Lake City for the annual June Conference. "In the religious situation confronting us today the world finds old conditions inadequate," she declared. "The Church of Jesus Christ of Latter-day Saints is having no more and perhaps much less difficulty in making religious adjustment than are others, but it is no longer possible for the Church to remain apart from the world." As she described how young people were asking questions, discovering new ideas, and pushing back against the ideas of past generations, as youth had ever done, she related the story of a geologist who—when loose shale suddenly shifted under his feet—avoided a deadly fall by clinging to the roots of a tree. "To the fundamental roots of Church belief we cling; to them we anchor our faith; in them we believe." At the same time, she said, young people needed room to find their own ways to reconcile fundamental beliefs with an openness to new ideas and innovations. "Instead of making religious truths a bone of contention and source of differences, should we not, as leaders and individuals, try to make them a means of bringing order and harmony out of apparent confusion?" Leaders and parents must allow a legitimate place for inquiry in building a testimony, she affirmed, pleading with adults to listen empathetically to the concerns and questions of young people. "Never bid them be silent but inspire them to cry out to you the innermost questions of their souls."[88]

Brandley's talk was one of four delivered in the morning session by MIA leaders, all of which reflected the theme of the conference: "Youth and the New Day." The talks and the theme grew out of the discussions about spirituality and modernity that had occupied the general boards for much of the year.[89] Melvin J. Ballard spoke about "Morality and the New Day," affirming the need for chastity despite deteriorating standards in society.[90] Oscar A. Kirkham reflected on new challenges facing Latter-day Saint youth in his talk, "Latter-day Saint Youth and the New Day," and Joseph Fielding Smith addressed "The Glorious Possibilities for Us of the Religious Crisis." The essence of revelation, Smith proclaimed, was "to interpret truth in terms of present world conditions for the immediate benefit of mankind." He agreed with the other speakers that the church, with its access to continuing revelation through divinely inspired prophets, was uniquely positioned to respond to the modern world.[91] All four speakers also emphasized that MIA workers must respond to the needs of youth and be willing to adapt to present conditions.

The new slogan for the 1934–35 year, which was announced at the conference, was "By My Actions I Will Prove My Allegiance to the Church." Acknowledging that the slogan had grown out of board discussions about youth problems, leaders said they chose it because of its "especial appropriateness to the present time" in hopes that it would "serve to awaken a new standard of loyalty to Mormon ideals on the part of both the young and old."[92] The slogan and the talks were optimistic and affirming, but by implicitly acknowledging deep concerns, they revealed the tension that underlay them. It is impossible to know how individual local leaders interpreted the messages; certainly interpretations varied. But it seems likely that the ambivalence the talks reflected was widely felt in the community.

Delegates to the MIA conference learned the results of the board's discussions and the recommendations in the Survey Committee report about changes to programs. In an engaging talk likening the boards to architects and local leaders to builders and decorators, Clarissa Beesley affirmed that they were all working together to build a great MIA program. This year the architects had reviewed the blueprints more carefully than ever and had determined upon some significant remodeling to the MIA "house." No longer would cultural activities revolve around contests. These events had been popular features of the MIA for two decades, but like a home's formal parlor, contests were exclusionary—eventually there was only one winner among hundreds of hopeful contestants. Board members wanted instead a "joyous 'living room'" where all were welcomed and valued without competition. "Life *is* a contest," Beesley acknowledged, "but it was never meant to be a struggle of individual against individual."[93] In that "sweet Gospel spirit," the contests at June Conference would eventually be replaced by grand festivals in which thousands could participate.

Beesley announced that individuals would receive recognition in their wards for MIA participation and attendance and that the Tuesday-night MIA schedule would now alternate between lessons and cultural activities instead of trying to fit both into each weekly meeting. To complement this change, manuals would be written more simply and guided more distinctly by Latter-day Saint principles.[94]

In addition to the changes Beesley announced, other important changes to MIA programs and structures resulted from the same discussions about the changing religious landscape that had led to the formation of the Survey Committee and their report. Among the most significant of these for the YLMIA was a change in its name, a move that had been considered for at least two years.[95] On 28 March 1934, the board voted to rename the organization the Young Women's Mutual Improvement Association (YWMIA).[96] Two months later, Ruth May Fox and her counselors sent a letter to the First Presidency requesting approval. In the letter, the leaders explained that they thought the term *women* was more up to date than *ladies*—it was stronger and more dignified.[97] These comments suggest that the name change reflected the recent discussions of modernity. In considering the conjoint relationship of the MIAs, *young women* apparently seemed parallel to *young men* in a way that *young ladies* no longer did. Five days later, the First Presidency replied, approving the change.[98] It was announced in the *Deseret News* with little fanfare shortly thereafter.[99]

One direct result of the Survey Committee report was a recommendation that the *Improvement Era* become the official magazine to represent the voice of the church's leadership to the members. Each monthly issue would contain a message from the First Presidency.[100] The recommendation was taken, and over the ensuing years, the magazine continued to run monthly columns containing "Mutual Messages," but the magazine itself became less youth oriented, and the perspectives and voices of women became even less prominent than they had become since the *Era*'s merger with the *Young Woman's Journal*. To fill the need for a regular means of communication with stake and ward leaders, the MIAs took another suggestion from the Survey Committee report and started their own monthly newsletter, the *MIA Leader*, in August 1934. The *Leader* published program and organizational announcements and the kind of practical details that were no longer appearing in the *Era*.[101]

CONVENING YOUNG PEOPLE IN THE CHURCH'S MISSIONS

Even after the Survey Committee's injunction to spiritualize the MIAs, local organizations continued to facilitate socialization among the youth in their areas. Outside of Utah, especially, MIA participation created opportunities for young Latter-day Saints who often lived as part of a tiny minority to associate with other members of their faith. Geographically separated branch MIA groups traveled to meet for games and dances. In many areas, attending MIA activities was also an accessible way for people outside the church to become acquainted with the church and its members. Many missions began holding large MIA conferences like those in Utah, where church members gathered for contests (which proved persistent at the local level even after being discontinued at June Conference) and training in MIA programs.

In September 1934, Elsie Brandley embarked on a three-week trip to visit MIA organizations in Arizona, northern Mexico, Texas, and California.[102] The trip powerfully demonstrated the role MIAs played in the church's missions as both a meeting place for youth and a bridge to the larger community. While staying in the Safford, Arizona, home of her college friend, Camilla Eyring Kimball, Brandley met a local MIA board member who was not a church member. His interest in drama had led him into the MIA.[103] At a stop in northern Mexico, a government education official attended every session of the MIA conference. Since Mexico's laws at the time limited the activities of foreign clergy, Brandley suspected the official's role was to watch for actions that might be violations. "Naturally we all were slightly worried as to what impression he might be getting," she wrote. The official's address at the conclusion of the conference, however, put such fears to rest: "He stated that the program of this organization was one which Mexico might borrow to put into their own system for culture and education combined was the ideal toward which they were striving."[104]

Nineteenth-century Latter-day Saint relations with neighbors of other faiths had often been characterized by conflict. Now MIA events were helping Latter-day Saints position themselves as a welcome minority. In the southern United States, where there were relatively few members and a history of prejudice, MIA activities became a vital community outreach program. A Halloween party for a Tallahassee, Florida, MIA group with only seven enrolled members drew a total attendance of seventy people from the community.[105] The stake in Oahu, Hawaii, timed one MIA conference to coincide with larger community musical events. Different wards were assigned songs to prepare as part of a shared MIA program featuring Chinese, Japanese, Korean, Spanish, Samoan, Hawaiian, and American music.[106] In such events, Saints were showing they could contribute something in addition to the gospel message to their communities. In Ottawa, Canada, an MIA for people who were blind drew large crowds to its bowling nights and other events. Almost none were members of the church.[107] "Some of our Mutual organizations are entirely among the non-members of the Church," Adelaide Thompson Poananga of New Zealand reported. People who were not members of the church also made up the majority of attendees at a Gold and Green Ball in New Zealand, which was so popular by the late 1930s that some guests traveled three hundred miles to attend.[108]

While nineteenth-century church leaders had warned against the MIA becoming a place for romance and courting, the potential of the MIA to foster romantic relationships and marriages between Latter-day Saints became increasingly important in the twentieth century. In central Mexico, MIA gatherings attracted hundreds of participants.[109] Members from church branches in different towns and cities came together to play sports, perform in dramas, and dance. At one 1935 conference in San Marcos, Hidalgo, a young woman named Porfiria Monroy helped receive visiting youth when they arrived. Guillermo Balderas, who had just moved from El Paso, Texas, to Mexico City, fondly remembered that conference, which was his first in the country. After dinner and an evening program, he and other youth from Mexico City were invited to stay and sleep on the chapel benches. In the morning, they rose early for a breakfast of bean tacos and orange tea. Guillermo and Porfiria met and developed a romantic relationship at that conference, and Guillermo looked forward to future MIA conferences as chances to see Porfiria again. Soon, they began writing each other between conferences. Guillermo treasured the memory of giving Porfiria a first gift at one of the conferences—a pair of earrings. The two were married the next year.[110]

Participating in MIA events also helped Latter-day Saints from smaller branches form a religious identity and feel like part of a broader religious community. In many areas, simply gathering young Saints was a major goal of MIA. For years, Latter-day Saints in New Zealand had gathered for an annual six-day conference and cultural event known as the *Hui Tau*. By the late 1930s, roughly twenty-five hundred people attended each year.[111] In addition to participating in sport and song, MIA members performed *haka* and *poi* dances. These performances allowed for a fusion of Latter-day Saint beliefs and Māori modes of expression. As Adelaide Poananga wrote in a published report, "Our *hakas* are given with a Gospel theme being the foundation. Our *poi* dances and action songs are all based upon some beautiful theme in the scriptures." Youth speakers also addressed the massive Hui Tau crowds. Poananga praised the young people's speeches for their oratorical craft. "Many of them are extremely clever," she wrote.[112]

In the Puget Sound district, located in Washington state and British Columbia, young Latter-day Saints gathered together across the border between the United States and Canada for basketball tournaments, banquets, dances, and special events like a snow carnival.[113] At a conference in Sweden, members celebrated the publication of a Swedish MIA handbook and joined voices in MIA songs translated into Swedish.[114] In 1936, seven hundred German-speaking youth from across central Europe gathered in Berlin, where Gleaners danced with M Men at a Gold and Green Ball and eighty people sang in a choir.[115] Hundreds of Dutch church members traveled by bicycle, bus, train, boat, and even hitchhiking to the seaport city of Rotterdam for an annual Primary and MIA conference. In addition to engaging in various competitions among the MIA members, participants gathered to watch several rugby matches, cheering on their various local teams until a hailstorm eventually forced them indoors. For young Latter-day Saints from small branches, the experience of being with so many peers who shared their faith was striking.[116]

In Britain, the MIA brought young Latter-day Saints together to forge a shared identity. On Saturday, 8 June 1935, for example, MIA members and leaders from Scotland, Ireland, Wales, and "the four corners of England" assembled in Kidderminster in Worcestershire, England, for a huge three-day conference.[117] The event had been heralded in the *Millennial Star* for months in an ambitious attempt to give British Latter-day Saints an experience similar to that of the annual June Conference in the United States.[118]

Kidderminster MIA conference. 1935. Youth from throughout the British Isles gathered in Kidderminster Town Hall for the first festivities of an MIA conference held in Kidderminster, England. One attendee reminisced, "The sweetest days that I ever knew, I spent then in Kidderminster" (A. Leslie Derbyshire, "On the Road to Kidderminster," *Latter-day Saints' Millennial Star*, 11 June 1936, 384). (Church History Library, Salt Lake City.)

Events were designed for individual young women and young men to share their stories and mingle. Saturday included young women's choral performances, M Men public-speaking competitions, and strolls through exhibitions of Bee-Hive scrapbooks and Gleaner Treasures of Truth books. Though British Latter-day Saints did not drink tea, MIA events maintained the custom of a teatime break and small meal immediately after the contests.[119] MIA members gathered for a "gala MIA flannel dance," to which they wore casual cotton clothing rather than formal evening wear and danced to the music of a live band.[120] Sunday involved testimony meeting and general sessions with discourses from MIA board members and mission leaders. Even in such sessions, the theme of British Latter-day Saint identity remained. Reports on numbers of participants varied from three hundred to over four hundred, enough for reports to emphasize the "psychology in numbers" that members from small branches experienced by attending.[121] In reports on the 1935 and 1936 Kidderminster conferences, the themes of group identity, local acculturation, socialization and the hope of marriage, and improved public relations were all on display.[122]

In June 1937, YWMIA president Ruth May Fox and her counselors, Lucy Cannon and Clarissa Beesley, traveled to Europe with church president Heber J. Grant and a number of other church leaders. They disembarked from their ship, *Empress of Australia*, in Cherbourg harbor on the northwest coast of France, beginning a two-month tour of the European missions that would culminate in Preston, England, with a celebration of the hundred-year anniversary of the church's presence in Britain. It was the first time a sitting YWMIA president had visited church members in Europe.[123]

For Fox, the tour had personal meaning. She was born in England and had left the country as a young girl, crossing the plains with a pioneer company at the age of thirteen in 1867. Shortly before her departure from Salt Lake City, she spoke of the tour at June Conference, mentioning her lifelong desire to return and visit the country of her birth.[124] Once in Britain, she visited her hometown and, as part of the British centennial celebration a few days later on the banks of the River Ribble, told members that many of the same landmarks remained from her childhood memory, including a lake near her home that still had swans swimming in it. As part of a ceremony for the celebration, an Irish church member presented her with the Union Jack.[125]

Various MIA events took place as part of the celebration. On Saturday, 31 July, Grant held a discussion with hundreds of young people and then heard speeches by several M Men and Gleaners. In addition to viewing sports events for the M Men, Gleaners, and Bee-Hive Girls, attendees at the celebration watched a baseball game in which the church president threw the first pitch. The local members had prepared a pageant, entitled *The Everlasting Doors*, that played to a capacity crowd and was repeated the next night because hundreds had been turned away the first evening.[126] Fox would remember the celebration for a long time to come.[127]

The tour also made a powerful impression on Lucy Cannon, who kept a log of the travel and events along the way.[128] Her log proved to be a chronicle of Fox's last major event as president of the YWMIA. In October 1937, shortly before her eighty-fourth birthday, Fox was released as president, and Cannon accepted the assignment to lead the organization with Helen Williams and Verna Wright Goddard as counselors.[129] Williams had experience in both MIA drama work and writing for local newspapers and church manuals, and Goddard led the YWMIA in the Liberty Stake.[130] For her part, Cannon was a daughter of Heber J. and Lucy Stringham Grant and was well-known for her kindness, her efforts to help those in need, and her ability to entertain guests, from everyday visitors to dignitaries.[131] Cannon had served for decades in the YWMIA, beginning with her service as the president of her ward association at age eighteen and later on the YWMIA general board and as counselor to both Martha Horne Tingey and Fox.[132] Cannon's chance to visit Latter-day Saints in Europe in 1937 was fortuitous. For much of her eleven-year tenure as YWMIA president, such a visit would not be possible.

ON THE SIDELINES OF A WORLD WAR

In September 1939, the expansionist policies of Germany's Nazi government caused the outbreak of a war that seemed likely to engulf Europe. Church leaders in Europe and Utah had to make quick decisions regarding the hundreds of missionaries under their charge. Hugh B. Brown, president of the British Mission (whose headquarters were the church's administrative center in Europe), coordinated with United States and British officials to return over 130 missionaries to the United States.[133] By 26 September, the First Presidency issued an official statement calling all missionaries in Europe home.[134] Brown himself went home in January 1940.[135]

American missionaries' long absence during the war helped put to rest assumptions that American missionary leadership was necessary to develop church organizations in different parts of the world. Members proved more than capable of carrying forward MIA work without American missionaries, even under difficult wartime conditions. In Oslo, Norway, the MIA continued work with its thousand or so youth through years of Nazi occupation, and various other districts and branches throughout the continent did their best to continue as well.[136] In Britain, eight months after the war's outbreak, the Birmingham district held its annual MIA convention. Although it had to be cut short, forgoing the activities of the last day, the young people participated in public speaking, choral contests, and an evening dance. Local MIA leaders received instruction and hailed the vitality and spirituality of the youth.[137] Administrative work also marched on, with presidencies and board members released and assigned. For example, Edith Rees was released from her position on the YWMIA board in the Birmingham district, where she served as the mission Bee Keeper, to accept an appointment as the district's YWMIA president in 1943.[138] Despite the toll of the war, the MIA in the newly formed London branch sponsored a dance in 1945 to raise funds for a seaside excursion for the branch's children, and the Bristol branch MIA held a social where attendees enjoyed games and refreshments.[139] These and other local efforts to maintain organization and activity ensured that after the war there would be a foundation on which to rebuild.

While September 1939 marked a turning point for the MIA in Europe, there were no immediate effects on MIA work in the United States, which did not enter the war until December 1941. Even before the United States' entry into the war, young people's lives were changing rapidly. By 1940, 70 percent of teenage Americans were enrolled in high school, and the school year had expanded to 152 days, intensifying young people's involvement in peer culture and strengthening their sense of distinct identity.[140] Terminology referring to young people was also changing: the term *teen* had come into use, initially mainly for girls, and *teenager* came into use to describe both girls and boys in the 1940s.[141] *Youth* referred to young people in the eighteen- to twenty-four-year-old range. One could be a "youth" independent of marital or school enrollment status.[142]

The 1939–1940 MIA executive handbook offers a sense of the rhythms of MIA activities for American young people during the period. The MIAs conducted an evening service for the whole ward on the first Sunday of each month. During this meeting, MIA members emphasized the annual theme, which for the 1939–1940 MIA year was a quotation from Matthew 22:37–40 exhorting love of God and love of fellowmen.[143] Each Tuesday evening from mid-September to mid-May, members of the MIA met for lessons and activities. Officers met first at 7:00; at 7:30, all gathered for opening exercises, which lasted around ten minutes. After opening exercises, the younger groups dispersed, and the older groups held an MIA assembly. At 8:10, the age groups separated to study lessons from the manual with their respective classes. Everyone gathered again at 9:00 for official dismissal, and then youth could participate in optional music, dance, speech, drama, or other recreational activities. During months with five Tuesdays, the MIA held special programs for the entire evening on the fifth Tuesday: one-act plays in October, an opera in January, and the ward Theme Festival and Honor Night in April.[144]

Previously called MIA Day, the Theme Festival and Honor Night included performances to celebrate that year's MIA theme and work.[145] Individual Honor Night programs varied, but they drew on the same traditions of performance and socializing. A ward in Logan, Utah, began its 1940 Honor Night with a picnic on the church lawn at 6:30 in the evening, followed by an indoor program at 7:30 that included a violin performance, a review of MIA accomplishments, a vocal solo, a story, a demonstration by the Scouts, a song, a dramatization, a speech, and another violin solo. Following the program, attendees socialized with one another and danced.[146] These elaborate annual events proved to be short lived. In February 1942, as the United States' involvement in the Second World War intensified, a letter from the YWMIA general board to stake leaders requested they eliminate the Theme Festival and Honor Night on the stake level but continue to hold it as wards.[147]

In the early 1940s, another tradition for recognizing achievement emerged. Requirements that built toward individual awards had a long history in the Bee-Hive program, and in 1940, the YWMIA also introduced the Golden Gleaner award for older members.[148] Young women had to participate in a minimum of three years of Gleaner work and fulfill requirements in four achievement areas: spiritual, executive, cultural arts, and creative.[149] When receiving their awards, young women in Nephi, Utah, described how they had met the requirements. Their descriptions of obeying the Word of Wisdom, paying a full tithe, serving in local YWMIA leadership, performing in a church play or opera cast, making a Treasures of Truth book, and arranging and living by a personal budget give a sense of how broad the work for Golden Gleaner could be.[150] Ward groups could also earn a related award for enrolling all eligible young women into their Gleaner class.[151]

MOBILIZING FOR WAR IN THE UNITED STATES

The normal patterns of life for young Latter-day Saints in the United States changed substantially after their country entered the war. Military service had a disproportionate impact on the young. Statistics from Utah give a sense of the scale: About 130,000 men in Utah between ages eighteen and thirty-seven registered for the draft. In June 1941, six months before the attack at Pearl Harbor, Hawaii, 7,000 Utahns were enlisted in the United States military, representing about 5 percent of the draftable population. By July 1945, over 60,000 Utah men—nearly half of those who had registered for the draft—had enlisted or been drafted. Just over 1,300 Utah women also served in the military.[152] Virtually all women felt wartime changes as they or their friends and relatives went off for work or military service.

Emma Lou Warner, a Gleaner-age young woman from the Highland Park Ward in Salt Lake City, made frequent trips to the University of Utah library during the war.[153] An undergraduate student, she visited the library for schoolwork, but she also went to read the daily listings of missing, wounded, and dead in the *Salt Lake*

Tribune.[154] One of her brothers was serving in the Naval Air Corps.[155] Though her brother ultimately came home safely, Emma Lou often read the names of people she knew in those listings. "The war was very close," she later remembered.[156] Many of her classmates and their loved ones were off at war. Even those without family in active military service lived with the likelihood that someone they knew would be called up. And, of course, all regularly faced the loss of classmates, acquaintances, and loved ones from causes related to the war. While Emma Lou's studies kept her close to home, many young women's social networks changed as they moved for work. The mobilization of wartime industries finally broke the grip of the Great Depression and put people to work, but most of the work was concentrated around military bases or strategic factories and mines. Teen participation in the workforce tripled between 1940 and 1943, pulling young people into mass migration.[157]

Utah was dramatically affected. The state's available open land and location far from potential attacks from the Pacific theater made it an attractive center for training and military support.[158] By 1943, over 50,000 people were employed in defense industries in Utah, a staggering figure for a state with a total prewar population of roughly 550,000.[159] Many of those employees were young women, who often relocated from farming and ranching areas to take jobs in the defense industry or in supporting swelling populations near military bases or factories.[160] Between 1940 and 1943, Utah's civilian population grew in only seven of the state's twenty-nine counties, with the population in four counties near military installations or strategic mining growing by 20 to 65 percent. During the same three years, the civilian populations of the other twenty-two rural counties fell, with nine of them reduced by 20 to 45 percent.[161]

Mary Lue Knell was one of the YWMIA members who began working in Utah's defense industry. Originally from Cedar City, she decided in 1942 to work for the Ogden Arsenal, some forty miles north of Salt Lake City. Mary Lue and her friends took turns driving from Salt Lake City to the arsenal each day, calling themselves the "Spinsters Club" and packing Spam sandwiches for lunch. They spent their days preparing ammunition for .50-caliber aircraft machine guns by linking the bullets into a belt-like strip and then packing them into metal boxes. On the days they didn't have ammunition to pack, they worked on the railroad to pick up debris with pointed sticks. The job provided good wages, and Mary Lue and her friends continued working there on Saturdays when school started in the fall.[162]

The young women were often joined in their work by Italian prisoners of war being held at the army depot in Ogden. Though the lack of a shared language made communication difficult, Mary Lue trusted the soldiers and enjoyed the Italian food the soldiers cooked for the young women. When Christmas arrived, the two groups overcame the language barrier as they joined in singing carols together, and before long, Mary Lue had learned at least one common expression in Italian: *Ti voglio bene*, expressing affection and friendship. She continued writing some of the Italian soldiers for a few years after the war had ended and they had returned to their homes in Naples.[163]

With so many young people affected by the war, Latter-day Saint youth leaders wasted no time in responding. Immediately following the attack on Pearl Harbor, the *MIA Leader* published an urgent message to stake and ward leaders, outlining priorities and recommendations for maintaining courage and faith. Leaders encouraged MIA members to participate in home defense measures and civilian defense service. MIA programs were to move forward as normally as possible, and leaders were to redouble their efforts to make personal contact with the youth under their stewardship. They were also encouraged to provide opportunities for youth to hear talks from effective speakers that could provide stability and promote faith. "Our duty at the present time is to hold fast to fundamentals," they stressed.[164]

The First Presidency also released specific guidelines that affected MIA programs for the duration of the war. Because travel was restricted, stake leadership meetings, institutes, and conventions were suspended, placing greater responsibility on wards and branches to carry out the work.[165] June Conferences were canceled, and attendance at general conferences was sharply curtailed.[166] Under these difficult conditions, the YWMIA engaged in a memorable period of work and service shaped by a few overriding concerns: keeping track of and caring for young women, discouraging lapses in morality, and giving young women opportunities for meaningful service.

KEEPING TRACK OF YOUNG WOMEN

Reflecting on the sudden scramble to meet the wartime housing demand, the United States National Housing Agency called the war years "the greatest voluntary migration of free men and free women in history." At a 1942 meeting in Ogden, Utah, near Hill Air Force Base, Major George Cressey pled with community and business leaders to prepare housing at an affordable rent (no more than $27.50 per month) for thousands of incoming civilian workers.[167] In such an environment, church leaders were concerned that young women would be unable to find housing that was adequately supervised and respectable. Since 1920, the YWMIA had operated the Beehive House in Salt Lake City as a boarding house for young, single women who came to the city for work or school.[168] The Beehive House was at full capacity throughout the war years, and the YWMIA made other efforts to secure housing for its members, though those efforts met with limited success. In 1943, board member Katie C. Jensen reported the YWMIA had connected just twelve hundred young women with appropriate housing, out of an estimated fourteen thousand young women who had come to the city for work. The low rate may have been related to the appeal of independence in the wartime economy—Jensen thought young women who had left home generally did not want supervision.[169]

YWMIA leaders expressed deep concern about simply keeping track of the church's young women. "They all belong to us!" proclaimed the *MIA Leader*, noting the influx of single young people and families with MIA-age children into many city wards. Local MIA leaders formed committees to coordinate with other auxiliaries to contact the new people—especially members of the church but also people who were not members—and invite them to participate in the church, using MIA social and recreational activities as an attraction.[170] YWMIA leaders were directed to expend every effort to find the young Latter-day Saint women who had moved to cities, including Salt Lake City, Los Angeles, and Seattle. "Go into the thickly populated sections, into apartment houses, and homes and find these girls," the *Leader* exhorted. "No other defense work is so important as this!"[171]

Despite efforts to connect migrants with local MIA organizations, YWMIA enrollment statistics showed an enormous drop by 1944.[172] The general board discussed several possible measures that might address the problem, and the presidency composed a letter for local leaders to give to young women they contacted. "During the past year many of you have changed your way of living; you have left your homes and gone into the homes of strangers, into boarding homes or apartments. You have been to a great extent 'on your own,'" they wrote. The letter stated that young Latter-day Saint women should have a clear understanding of their purpose and mission. Practicing their faith offered protection—attending worship services, paying tithing, keeping the Word of Wisdom, helping the poor, and avoiding the sins of the world would be safeguards to young women. The leaders admonished them to be frugal with their money and choose their friends carefully.[173]

In the 1930s the church had increased efforts to find and keep track of every member. The terms *active* and *inactive* came into use around that time to describe Latter-day Saints' level of participation, and auxiliaries were instructed to keep rolls of members in both categories.[174] During the war, the YWMIA revitalized a transfer card system—initially introduced in the 1920s—to help track the whereabouts of Latter-day Saint young women.[175] Under this system, ward leaders reported to stake leaders the names of young women who moved. Stake leaders compiled and submitted those names on specially printed transfer cards to the general office with their monthly reports. The YWMIA office staff sent those names to the stakes to which the young women had relocated, and the stake leaders then notified ward leaders of new young women to seek out, preferably by involving the other young people in the ward. In February 1944 alone, over two hundred young women were tracked through this system, which became one precursor to the general membership record eventually adopted churchwide.[176]

PROMOTING THE CLEAN LIFE

Implicit in the desire to keep track of young women was a recognition that wartime conditions had created many new temptations. Latter-day Saints had long focused on Word of Wisdom observance as the foundation of clean living. Under Heber J. Grant's continuing presidency, the Word of Wisdom received much emphasis throughout the church, including in the MIA through slogans, lessons, articles, pamphlets, and reports published throughout the 1930s and 1940s.[177] A two-year "Clean Life" campaign culminated in a booklet distributed to young women at a special meeting in May 1941 and a public show of solidarity at June Conference. Ten thousand young women and men stood in the Tabernacle on Temple Square in Salt Lake City to verbally pledge their willingness to live by the high ideals of the clean life, inaugurating a campaign against alcohol and tobacco use that lasted through the war years.[178]

In addition to observing the Word of Wisdom prohibitions on alcohol, tobacco, coffee, and tea, living the clean life meant adhering to high standards of sexual morality, a particularly pressing issue during the war. Wartime mobility fostered loneliness, anonymity, new acquaintances, and an absence of adult chaperones, all of which relaxed traditional sexual norms. In the United States, rates of divorce, births outside of wedlock, and venereal disease substantially increased during World War II, and women were often blamed for these trends.[179] Concerns about changing moral standards were not new. A decade earlier in the discussions surrounding the Survey Committee's report, MIA leaders had lamented a decline in standards since World War I and had exhorted the youth to hold up their standards as a light to the world.[180]

As soon as the United States entered World War II, MIA leaders identified sexual immorality as one of the major problems likely to arise. The boards' letter to local leaders reminded them to emphasize the necessity of clean living, which included holding to strict standards of sexual conduct. Chaste thinking and behavior, board members emphasized, would lead to strength of body and mind and make Latter-day Saint youth an asset to the country.[181] But they recognized that wartime psychology could undermine young people's willingness to adhere to the high standards they had been taught. A pair of editorials in the *Improvement Era* warned against adopting fatalistic thinking during uncertain times, which they explained was "a tendency to shrug the shoulders and indulge, as they are wont to call it, in one 'last fling.'" Such indulgences, the editorials argued, were delusions. They were not satisfying and would only pile up regret and disillusionment.[182] Whatever sacrifices were necessary, those who remained steadfast would reap the rewards of living a good life, making intelligent sacrifices, and enriching their spirits.[183]

While premarital sex was recognized as a sin for both men and women, the two genders received different messages about preventing sexual misconduct. There was a widespread assumption that male sexual desire was harder to control and more opportunistic than female desire. This view intensified the scrutiny of women and shifted responsibility to them for controlling sexuality—their own and men's.[184] A 1942 address by Hugh B. Brown, who was a former Canadian military officer serving as coordinator for Latter-day Saint servicemen during the war, illustrated these assumptions. Titling his talk "To the Girls behind the Men behind the Guns," Brown argued that anyone who allowed a soldier to give in to temptation weakened him and contributed to bringing down one of the nation's "fighting men." Even when men pled with women to give in, they really wanted their girlfriends to say no, he insisted. "To them you symbolize an ideal. Their thoughts of home, family, and the verities of life include you."[185] YWMIA leaders considered the talk so timely and effective that they decided to have it published as a pamphlet for young women throughout the MIA.[186]

Wartime conditions created further incentives to differentiate messages by gender. Because support for the military and patriotism were so intertwined, people were reluctant to criticize soldiers for sexual misconduct.[187] In a call to the broader Salt Lake community for awareness about the shifting sexual conditions young women faced, Marion Kerr, a lifelong member of the church who was then serving as president of the Salt Lake district of the Utah Federation of Women's Clubs, told a local newspaper that girls between the ages of fourteen and sixteen were particularly vulnerable to soldiers who were, she said, "lonesome, eager for a change in their programs, and anxious for companionship."[188] Her language stopped short of condemning male soldiers preying on teenagers, even though sex with a young woman under the age of eighteen was a crime under Utah law.[189] The evidence of rising rates of misconduct was alarming: arrests in Utah for sexual offenses had increased sharply between 1942 and 1943 as the nation continued to mobilize and move troops.[190] Church and community leaders alike wanted to protect young women from the psychological, social, and spiritual risks they faced as local young men left for war or when young women found work in urban centers near military bases.

Not content to simply counsel young women about what not to do, YWMIA leaders worked to create positive alternatives that promoted feelings of connection and contribution in times of uncertainty. *Improvement Era* editor Marba Cannon Josephson asserted that young women's best response to the war was to forget the troubling circumstances by finding something that absorbed their minds, exhausted their bodies, and awakened their spirits.[191] The general board decided to plan social events for the thousands of young women pouring into Salt Lake City for employment. Responding to complaints that there were not enough respectable places in the city, they worked to create more.[192] If fraternization was inevitable, they wanted to make the context as wholesome as possible and find meeting spaces where they could help protect their young women. General leaders of the MIA submitted a plan to the First Presidency and the Salt Lake–area MIA boards, which they thought could be replicated elsewhere. They suggested five social centers be designated in the area, with a monthly dance in each location, totaling five dances a month in the city. Stake and ward boards would make sure "dances were conducted under M.I.A. standards and regulations." They also recommended that these social centers be open every day, including Sunday, and sponsor activities such as games, lectures, plays, book reviews, and music appreciation.[193] These plans apparently went unrealized, but they demonstrate the concerns that preoccupied YWMIA leaders during the war years.

WARTIME SERVICE OPPORTUNITIES

Many on the home front during World War II responded to uncertainty and loss by wanting to do something, and there was plenty to do. The great, pioneer-scale project that youth in the 1930s had longed for had arrived. Like many others during the war, Emma Lou Warner rolled bandages for the Red Cross, just one of many activities young women could participate in to support the war effort.[194] The Lion House in downtown Salt Lake City regularly hosted such service and social activities for young women, either as church-sponsored events or in connection with outside organizations like the Red Cross.

Built between 1854 and 1855 as a residence for Brigham Young's family, the Lion House had a long association with the church's organization for young women.[195] In the Lion House parlor Brigham Young encouraged his daughters to retrench, setting them on the path to create the young women's organization. In the early 1900s, when Young's widows no longer lived in the house, it was converted into classrooms, a teaching kitchen, and a dining facility for students of the LDS University and later for church leaders, employees, and missionaries.[196] In 1932, at the request of YWMIA leaders, the building became a social center for young people.[197] There were rooms for sewing (including a sewing machine young women could use), reading, and gathering.[198] Members of the YWMIA who paid the Lion House's one-dollar annual membership dues could host their friends in rooms there for a fee.[199]

Members of the Linden Lionettes at the Lion House. 1939. The Linden Lionettes club was founded in 1937 by Ruth May Fox, general president of the YWMIA. Club members were typically single working women who moved to Salt Lake City and could not regularly attend MIA meetings due to employment conflicts. They met weekly at the Lion House, which served then as a social center for members of the YWMIA. (Courtesy Michael Morris, copy at Church History Library, Salt Lake City.)

During the war, the Lion House's position on Temple Square—a few hundred feet from the temple and adjacent to the Beehive House—made it an effective contact point for young women arriving in the city as part of the war effort. By January 1942, 150 women and girls were taking first aid classes at the Lion House, and many others had joined war-work clubs that met there. Lion House classes included standard first aid, knitting and hand sewing, and nutrition. Because of a yarn shortage, members of the Out-of-Towners Club unraveled donated garments and then the Defense Club knit them into new items. The Red Cross Service Club requested yarn donations, made afghans for veterans hospitals, and knit sweaters for the Red Cross.[200]

In wards and branches around the church, young women of the YWMIA engaged in countless service projects and war-support efforts. Writing letters to soldiers was one popular activity. The Gleaners of the Mill Creek Ward, south of Salt Lake City, attempted to write to all the young men serving from their ward, but with the number at fifty-six and counting, it was impossible to keep up. Consequently, they compiled a two-page newsletter that included news items, a birthday page, humorous items, and messages from the bishopric, stake presidency, and young men's parents. With funding from the high priests quorum, they mimeographed the letter and sent it to the local young men in the service.[201] Young women in another ward held a clothing remodeling evening, deeming it patriotic to "conserve on clothes."[202] In May 1943, the MIA invited participants to sponsor an aircraft rescue boat by purchasing stamps and war bonds.[203] The Wasatch Ward in Salt Lake City reported that in June and July 1943, forty-eight girls spent 124 hours sewing for the Red Cross, twenty girls attended Red Cross nutrition classes, and eighteen girls wrote letters to soldiers in war zones.[204] Around the same time, the YWMIA distributed a new plan for summer work entitled "The Wartime Summer Way for M.I.A." The first part of the book covered first aid, home nursing, welfare gardens, home kindergarten for neighborhood children, and war bonds and stamps. The second portion covered recreational activities.[205]

FINDING REFUGE AT CAMP

Even in wartime, recreation was an important part of the YWMIA calendar, and camp was no exception. By the beginning of the war, camping was becoming a prominent part of the summer YWMIA program, particularly for Juniors and Bee-Hive Girls.[206] During the 1930s, the MIA general boards had helped spread ideas about summer camps from a few stakes to the broader organization, launching a summer agenda that included sunset services and campfire programs, as well as plenty of outdoor activities such as hiking and folk dancing.[207] In 1940, the efforts of central YWMIA leadership to extend camp experiences throughout the organization marked a turning point. The Bee-Hive committee of the YWMIA general board made their slogan "Every Girl in Summer Camp" and planned a separate camp experience for Bee-Hive Girls.[208] The *MIA Leader* noted, "It is hoped that the [summer] Homes already established will be maintained with new interest and enthusiasm, and that all stakes will plan some activity in the out-of-doors for their girls." More than nine thousand Bee-Hive participants attended camp in the summer of 1940.[209] The crowded 1942 schedule for Mutual Dell, the summer home owned by the Lehi, Alpine, and Timpanogos stakes in Utah, demonstrates the increased popularity of camp during the war years. Mutual Dell was in constant use by these three stakes throughout the summer.[210]

To help leaders produce a good camping experience, the general board introduced a camping manual, *Camp-O-Rama*, which served as the basic manual for summer camp in the YWMIA throughout the next two decades.[211] Subsequent editions contained updates, including supplemental booklets such as *Cooking Out-of-Doors, Camp Standards*, and *Camptivities*.[212] The introduction to *Camp-O-Rama* established what the general leaders hoped young women would experience through summer camping. "The beautiful out-of-doors," it explained, "belongs to all as a gift of the great Creator." In this setting, young women could build deep and lasting friendships.[213] The rest of the manual offered dozens of activity ideas and some detailed instructions on health, sanitation, and first aid, many of which assumed prior camping experience and knowledge. In describing basic sanitation at camp, for example, the book offered advice on disposal of waste, including the use of latrines, but without explaining what a latrine was or how to build one.[214] Recommended foods included peach shortcake, "pioneer roasting corn," "camp chowder," and a version of baked beans.[215] The influence of the Camp Fire Girls and Boy Scouts remained evident: the activities recommended in *Camp-O-Rama* included building a campfire next to a wigwam, or dome-shaped hut, and telling "Indian legends." Other activities included handcrafting items to represent Native and pioneer cultures as wilderness archetypes.[216]

During the war, leaders viewed camp as a vital retreat from troubled conditions and a way to develop leadership skills.[217] Camp, they declared, could help relieve emotional stress and help young people work through their problems. It could also serve as a place to instill qualities in young people that, it seemed, were lacking in their wartime behavior, such as tolerance of other creeds, races, or even those permanently injured in the war.[218] Young people could likewise build leadership through planning and participating in camp activities. The *Camptivities* booklet was intended to help in these efforts.[219] Encouraging leaders to provide a "camp democracy," the booklet recommended including young women in the planning process and providing them several activity options from which to choose as they helped plan their camp.[220]

A NEW WORLD DAWNING

In summer 1945, the Second World War ended with physical and economic devastation in Europe, the aftermath of fierce battles and fallout from two atomic bombs lingering in Japan, and a changed sense of global purpose in the United States. Apostle Ezra Taft Benson traveled to Europe to oversee church relief efforts, and by the end of February 1946, Latter-day Saint women had sent more than eight thousand quilts and blankets to European countries other than Germany, with another one thousand to be sent as soon as shipping to Germany was possible. Women in the Norwegian Mission sent food to church members in Germany and Belgium, while Belgian members shared their welfare supplies with starving German Saints.[221] In Soviet-occupied East Germany, local church leaders used a church meetinghouse in Cottbus and purchased a villa in Wolfsgrün to house members and families who had been driven out of the eastern regions of Prussia, Pomerania, and Silesia.[222] After working and fighting alongside the rest of their nation, American Latter-day Saints at war's end were more fully integrated into the fabric of the country's culture than ever before, and they embraced this integration even as they remained ambivalent about some of its implications.[223]

At the church's first general conference following the end of the war, Stephen L Richards captured the sense of sober hopefulness with which Latter-day Saints faced the new era. "We stand on the threshold of a new day," he said. "We look out into the morning and see the rays of the rising sun tint the sky with the hopes of humanity." The night had been long and the work had been slowed, but sentinels had stood watch and safeguarded the church. "Now in the daylight of peace," he affirmed, "we go back to our work."[224]

As the war reached its close, the YWMIA was ready to enter an era of renewed organization and expansion. Membership stood at nearly seventy-two thousand in 1,056 ward associations—an increase of four thousand over the previous year but still considerably lower than before the war.[225] Average attendance of 65 percent in 1944 and 1945 likely reflected wartime displacement of members. At least in the United States, the Bee-Hive, Junior, Gleaner, and Special Interest (adult) departments were well organized and conducting activities, meetings, and courses.[226] In summer 1945, the boards once again reviewed their programs to determine how they could best meet the needs of the church's young people. They were making plans for the first June Conference since 1941, and development of new manuals and publications proceeded accordingly.[227]

"The hand of the Lord has been in the affairs of the world," Lucy Cannon testified to her board in January 1946. "We should be grateful we have the gospel during such times, for we have had peace in our hearts."[228] But some wartime concerns persisted. "There is a new spirit that has come into the world with this war," J. Reuben Clark Jr. warned YWMIA leaders in 1946. Sexual expectations that had shifted during the war, he felt, were unlikely to change with the decline in military mobilization. Young women would need church support to preserve religious standards.[229] Other leaders focused on countries' increased familiarity with one another. Latter-day Saints had been given a long geography lesson as they followed the course of the war, and many felt that the eyes of the world were on the United States. "The world has come to us," Marba Josephson observed. "We must receive it and teach it."[230]

Twenty thousand youth, MIA leaders, and spectators participated in the 1946 June Conference.[231] General MIA leaders wished to honor returning servicewomen and servicemen. Accordingly, church apostle Harold B. Lee, who chaired the church's servicemen's committee during the war, opened the conference with an official welcome to returning servicepeople, and several speakers at the conference addressed these young people specifically. While introducing the new MIA theme, YMMIA general superintendent George Q. Morris spoke of the devastation of the war, offering it as proof that human wisdom was not enough to promote peace and healing. Only turning to the Lord, he insisted, could do that.[232]

As the world attempted to heal the wounds of war, the church reached another centennial, this time of the arrival of the first Latter-day Saint pioneers in the Salt Lake Valley in 1847.[233] The YWMIA general board expected over twenty thousand Bee-Hive Girls to participate in pioneer-themed summer camps and called on local groups to design their own centennial symbols, the best of which would be honored at June Conference.[234] In the church's missions, local leaders planned events adapted to their identities and environments. In Britain, the commemoration was not planned for 24 July but for the public holiday weekend of Whitsun (Pentecost) in late May, with reenactments focusing on early British converts preparing to emigrate rather than on pioneer arrivals in North America. Young women and men in Hawaii planned to hike to the summit of Haleakalā to sing the hymn "High on the Mountain Top."[235] As the world emerged from years of war, Latter-day Saint youth claimed both the history and the future of the church as their own.

SHOWCASING YOUTH

1948–1961

In December 1955, eighteen-year-old Myrna Petersen typed up the life story she had been working on for many months and inserted it into her Treasures of Truth book. She pasted photographs throughout the book and drew a few illustrations, including a full-page colored map of her family's dairy and beet farm in rural eastern Utah. She titled it "Life Is a Package of Happiness: A Gift from God." This theme ran through her entire scrapbook—she personalized the preprinted divider pages for each section by adding hand-drawn illustrations of gift packages. Myrna's sense that her life was a gift and a blessing had grown during her time in the YWMIA. She wrote that she was about fifteen when "the Church became very important in [her] life." Myrna started praying every day, taking walks alone, and singing hymns to herself until she reached the farm field, where she would sit under a tree by the river and meditate on her blessings. "I know sometimes I felt the Spirit of the Lord was with me because of the contented pleasant feelings I had," she wrote.

Living in Utah, where church was a pillar of social life, Myrna had frequent opportunities to contribute publicly to church life. A skilled pianist, she found herself much in demand as an accompanist and performer at church services and MIA activities. Like many young women in Utah, she competed in speech and drama contests and festivals, gave talks in sacrament meetings, attended firesides and standards nights, danced in the Gold and Green Ball floor show, and enjoyed socials like the "food and fun party" for Junior Gleaners and Junior M Men, which featured Dutch oven cooking and outdoor games.[1] She also attended the central MIA June Conference in Salt Lake City, where she could socialize and worship alongside thousands of fellow Saints and hear from YWMIA general leaders.[2] With her peers, Myrna would have learned that "the standards of the Church are the standards of the Gospel of Jesus Christ" and that church standards included honesty, chastity, and personal purity; faith in a living God; observance of the Word of Wisdom by refusing alcohol, tobacco, and stimulants such as coffee; and "loyalty to the Church, its institutions and its Leaders."[3]

Myrna's experiences in the YWMIA—and her happy, optimistic feelings about her life in the church—are typical of many in the generation of young Latter-day Saints coming of age in the postwar United States. While many parts of the world in the 1950s were focused on rebuilding after the devastation of war, the confidence, well-being, and prosperity of Americans—especially but not only the white middle class—rose sharply amid rapidly expanding economic, educational, and social opportunities. It was a time of sustained economic growth and real financial gains for millions. Americans expressed great confidence in the potential of science, technology, and professional expertise to fuel further progress.[4] In response to the privations of the Depression and war in the previous decades, Americans also developed a focus on the nuclear family that addressed deep emotional needs and encouraged them to seek satisfaction in private life. The promise of prosperity and stability led people to feel that they could marry, buy a home, and have children—that is, they could aspire to middle-class family life, often in the rapidly developing suburbs. The result was a period of intensive marriage, child-rearing, and family stability not seen before or since.[5]

Those high expectations, however, fueled concern about whether youth would attain the good, stable life that seemed so readily available. The American media and economy in the 1950s developed an ever-increasing focus on youth. With most teens attending high school and delaying their entry into the workforce, the rise of a strong and separate youth culture baffled and frightened older Americans. *Teenage* came to signify not just a state of biological and psychological transition but also a distinct set of styles, language patterns, music choices, and social norms.[6] Studies indicated that parents still wielded the greatest influence in the development of teens' behavior and ambitions, but it was clear that the opinions of peers played an increasingly important role in teenagers' daily habits and activities.[7] Despite much outward optimism, these developments created a great deal of anxiety, especially over youth sexuality and delinquency.[8]

Because all the general leaders and a majority of the members of the YWMIA lived in the United States during the 1950s, YWMIA structures, practices, and messaging worldwide reflected both the optimism and the anxiety of American postwar culture. As long as they could keep youth engaged in their programming, leaders believed, MIA recreation, socialization, and instruction would help young women and young men live church standards and prepare for marriage and stable family life, making them examples for the larger culture.[9] "Our Latter-day Saint boys and girls are the finest in the world," apostle Spencer W. Kimball said in a 1951 address. "There is no group anywhere from ocean to ocean that can even compare with them."[10] The church was eager to let its young people's light shine. In an era when adult concerns about the large rising generation occupied public attention, the MIAs became flagship organizations for the church, showcasing the church's two hundred thousand clean, wholesome youth in massive, well-run programs.[11] Focusing on the organizations—not only their numerical and geographical expansion but also their centrality to the church's missionary and recreation efforts—could affirm to church members and others the goodness of the fruit and, thus, the rightness of the faith they embraced. Throughout the 1950s, YWMIA leaders and members extended the reach of the organization through activities, sporting events, camp, and June Conference. The YWMIA used media both new and old to promote messages about temple marriage, chastity, modesty, and femininity.

UPDATING YWMIA CLASS STRUCTURE

Myrna Petersen's early years in the YWMIA—she turned twelve in January 1949—coincided with a period of organizational restructuring, beginning with new general leadership. In spring 1948, the First Presidency appointed Bertha Stone Reeder as the fifth general president of the young women's organization. In contrast to the previous three presidents, who had each served as counselors in the presidency for over a decade before assuming general leadership, Reeder had no experience with the YWMIA at the general level. She had served some years earlier as president of her ward YWMIA, as a counselor in a stake Primary presidency, and for a short period on the Primary general board. Most recently, she had returned from presiding with her husband over the New England Mission.[12] Perhaps reflecting a consciousness of church growth, Reeder's appointment was the first in what became a pattern in the following decades: general leaders for the church's women's organizations increasingly came from the ranks of women who had led missions alongside their husbands. Reeder served with counselors Emily Higgs Bennett, who had served on the YWMIA general board, and LaRue Carr Longden, whose dynamic leadership of the Highland Stake YWMIA in Utah had garnered the attention of general leadership. Reeder knew neither of them personally before their assignments, but the three women worked well together.[13]

These new leaders inherited the task of updating the YWMIA structure for a changed world. In a 1946 report, YWMIA leaders had noted that fourteen-year-old young women were losing interest in Bee-Hive work.[14] Leaders had long been concerned that the needs of young women in their midteens were not being adequately met, so Reeder and her board set about restructuring the YWMIA age groups.[15] In 1950, YWMIA leaders redefined the Bee-Hive class to include only twelve- and thirteen-year-olds.[16] They also introduced two new classes—Mia Maid for ages fourteen and fifteen and Junior Gleaner for ages sixteen to eighteen.[17]

Almost as soon as it was announced, the unusual new name *Mia Maid* demanded explanation. Some local leaders reported that the young women in their wards hissed and booed when the new name was announced.[18] The foreword to the new Mia Maid manual explained that the first part of the name came from the organization's initials (MIA), but some individuals proposed alternative explanations. One local leader sent the board a five-page document she had written, proposing that the name could stand for "My Inner Awakening."[19] The chair of the Mia Maid committee of the general board initially tied the name to the "AIM" ("MIA" spelled backward) of building better wives and mothers.[20] These explanations indicate that the resonance of the phrase "mutual improvement" may have been receding as cultural values changed, reflecting a growing emphasis on personal development and domesticity, rather than collective betterment, as values for women.[21]

Myrna Petersen turned fourteen in 1951, making her one of the first cohort to start out as Mia Maids. The Mia Maids adopted the traditional Junior class symbol of the rose, and Myrna included a leaflet called *The Symbolism of the Rose* in her Treasures of Truth book. The general presidency worked with the rose imagery as they sought to deepen a sense of identity for Mia Maids. YWMIA leaders collaborated with a horticulturist to breed a new variety of rose specifically for the Mia Maids.[22] An image of the resulting pink rose was then printed on various Mia Maid materials, and a new achievement program called Mia Joy allowed young women to work for a rose pin during their first year as Mia Maids. In their second year, they could earn a guard, which was a small gold-plated pin containing the words *Mia Joy* that attached to the rose pin with a chain.[23]

A new formal event called the Rose Tying Ceremony acknowledged group achievement. When Myrna's younger sister LaRene was a Mia Maid in 1954, her ward met the qualifications for the event, which meant that 50 percent of class members had received their individual Mia Joy award and the class as a whole had achieved 50 percent attendance at Sunday School and 35 percent attendance at sacrament meeting that year.[24] Cultural refinement and feminine qualities remained driving YWMIA values: at the 4 June ceremony in which LaRene participated, the young women, dressed in formal gowns, gathered around a "beautifully appointed" tea table to serve candies, punch, and wafers to their

Rose Tying Ceremony, Aurora, Utah. 1948. This Junior Girls class from rural central Utah participated in the annual Rose Tying Ceremony, a formal celebratory evening where young women presented a rose—preferably one they had personally cultivated—whose color or type symbolized their
personal ideals. The roses were then tied together and presented to the president of the ward YWMIA.
This tradition was similar to the Gleaners' sheaf-binding ceremonies, and both were major events on
the YWMIA calendar. (Church History Library, Salt Lake City.)

mothers and friends as they arrived at the ward chapel for the evening's ceremony. Following a program of musical numbers, readings, and talks, attention turned to the rose table, covered with a lace cloth and tiny roses and set with tall green and white tapers in crystal holders; a white satin ribbon lay ready. With Myrna providing piano accompaniment in the background, each young woman in turn presented a rose to the class leader, Catherine Eastin, and expressed a wish for herself and all present—wishes for kindness, understanding, joy, and perseverance, among other things. Catherine accepted the roses, tied them into a bouquet with the white satin ribbon, and presented it to Leah Wells, ward YWMIA president.[25] A churchwide Rose Tying Ceremony at one 1950s June Conference celebrated the fact that 60 percent of Mia Maids throughout the church had received their individual awards, indicating active involvement in the program and adherence to church standards.[26]

The other YWMIA class introduced in 1950 was the Junior Gleaner class, which paralleled the Junior M Men group introduced in the YMMIA. The Junior Gleaner class served young women ages sixteen to eighteen—what would typically be through the end of American high school years, which reflected the emerging cultural significance of high school graduation as a milestone in maturation. These new junior departments carried on much of the same work that the Gleaner and M Men groups continued to do for young people ages nineteen to twenty-five, which for the young women included sheaf-binding ceremonies and a new Silver Gleaner award. In part because dating held a place of prominence in the teen culture of the day and because church leaders wished to foster relationships that could lead to temple marriages, the program for Junior Gleaners and Junior M Men emphasized mixed-gender activities such as dances, parties, firesides, and athletics on ward and stake levels. The two groups also joined in a single course of study called "We Believe." The Silver Gleaner achievement program aimed to help young women become well balanced and happy and develop what it called "sterling qualities." They could also earn a Silver Gleaner pin.[27]

Manuals for the two new classes overtly described how YWMIA leaders saw typical developmental needs in each age range. Young women of Mia Maid age were seen to be at a crucial stage. For many, as for Myrna, it was between the ages of fourteen and sixteen that church either took on added significance or gave way to other priorities. Life for Mia Maids, the manual noted, was "curious, difficult, wonderful, and important," and they found "so many problems to be answered, so many situations to meet, so many thrills to anticipate." The growing-up process was to be the leaders' emphasis in their work with the Mia Maids—with a positive, optimistic tone set by the course of study, "Life to Enjoy."[28]

Junior Gleaners were likewise considered happy, active, and inquisitive. At their age, they began to make decisions that could affect their lives in the long term, so leaders felt they needed direction and guidance. Because Junior Gleaners were likely to be busy with schoolwork and secular activities, leaders were aware their spiritual lives might be neglected. MIA lessons and the accompanying Silver Gleaner program were meant to provide crucial balance in their development.[29]

IMPROVING ATTENDANCE

YWMIA activities could guide young women only if they attended; hence, encouraging attendance grew in emphasis. Since the inception of the young women's organization, membership had been voluntary—the YWMIA attracted many but not all young women in the church. In 1950, however, the church announced a policy of enrolling all young women ages twelve through twenty-five in the YWMIA, including those twelve and older who had not been participating in the organization previously. The policy also underscored the importance of leaders' reaching out to all the young women under their stewardship.[30]

The new policy had its roots in earlier efforts. The wartime transfer card system had tracked young women through moves to help keep them involved in YWMIA. After the war, the church experimented with a "Program for Latter-day Saint Girls" (also referred to as the "Girls' Program") to include young women who did not belong to the YWMIA. The local bishopric and a female leader oversaw the program and selected advisers, who each acted as a "big sister" to groups of no more than fifteen young women. These advisers not only monitored attendance but also established relationships of trust and confidence.[31] In 1950, Reeder, Bennett, and Longden wrote to the First Presidency proposing that the YWMIA assume stewardship over the Girls' Program and laying out a detailed plan for how the merger would work.[32] The YWMIA began appointing new attendance secretaries in each ward; the attendance secretary and the regular YWMIA secretary worked together to keep attendance records and ensure every young woman was accounted for on the rolls.[33]

The YWMIA merged the awards of the Girls' Program with the existing Honor Bee, Mia Joy, Silver Gleaner, and Golden Gleaner achievement programs. Individual award requirements that originated with the Girls' Program and became part of YWMIA achievement programs give a sense of which markers of religious activity postwar leaders prioritized. Requirements included observing the Word of Wisdom (primarily by avoiding tobacco and alcohol), paying tithing, giving a spiritual talk in any church meeting, and participating in a large MIA activity from one of several categories.[34] To receive an award, young women were also required to meet certain attendance thresholds. The attendance goals were set at 75 percent for Mutual and

Sunday School but only 50 percent for sacrament meeting—in 1950, sacrament meeting attendance for young women averaged just 48 percent churchwide, while average YWMIA attendance was already 65 percent, and Sunday School was close behind.[35] As the difference in attendance percentages illustrates, young women participated in the church more through the MIA than through other meetings. One explanation for this difference is that at this time, the sacrament of the Lord's Supper was administered both in Sunday School and in sacrament meetings, so many members of all ages attended only one meeting or the other to participate in that ordinance. Furthermore, there was no Sunday instruction specifically for young women at this time, making weekday YWMIA meetings a primary source of gospel learning for young women. In order to encourage young women to support each other's attendance, the program also gave an award to each class for 50 percent class attendance at MIA meetings and Sunday School and 35 percent at sacrament meeting.[36]

Youth attendance at church meetings did increase over the course of the decade. In 1959, young women's average attendance at YWMIA meetings churchwide rose to 70 percent, and sacrament meeting attendance was up to 60 percent. Overall, attendance was typically higher in historically Latter-day Saint communities in the region stretching from Alberta, Canada, through Idaho, Utah, and Arizona to Chihuahua, Mexico. Attendance percentage gains during the 1950s were most dramatic, however, in areas within the United States where Latter-day Saints were a minority but with an expanding presence due to convert baptisms and migration. In 1950, for example, YWMIA attendance in Oakland, California, averaged 38 percent, but by 1960, it had risen to 63 percent. In Seattle, attendance rose from 49 percent to 64 percent during the same period, and in Chicago, the gain was from 47 percent to 64 percent.[37] Church president George Albert Smith had charged the MIA boards with making young people proud of their religion and proud to be part of the church so that they were happy to participate in its meetings and activities. Increased attendance was one measure of the success of that effort.[38]

The activity structure at the time was designed for consistent rather than intermittent attendance. For young Latter-day Saints and their leaders in the postwar years, the MIAs maintained an ambitious calendar of weekly lessons and activities, all of which necessitated highly structured organizations and detailed instructions. The general boards coordinated the event calendar and instructions for joint efforts but also prepared lessons and manuals specific to each age group in their respective organizations. While the *MIA Leader* offered local leaders ideas for upcoming events, and June Conference provided in-person training and inspiration, the manuals were the source of specific information on coordinating the complex MIA program at the local level. Newly published each year, the sizeable manuals were packed with explanations and details, including the organizational structure and purpose of MIA, weekly activities and lessons, and suggested program outlines for special events. The 1950–1951 *Executive Manual for Officers*, for example, contained a forty-five-page calendar of events and lessons that covered each age group.[39] The manuals kept growing—by 1959, the executive manual was 229 pages. Local leaders studying these manuals for guidance often saw it as their duty to follow the calendars and outlines with careful precision, and general MIA leaders seldom spoke of any room for local adaptation. As one leader reported, "If it was written in the manual it was gospel truth."[40]

The two-hour weekly MIA meeting was to begin at seven thirty in the evening with an assembly program where all the youth gathered for an opening hymn, an opening prayer, the presentation of the year's MIA theme, and sometimes the sharing of a scriptural passage or short thought. From there, the classes went their separate ways to do classwork for fifty minutes.[41] For Gleaners (ages nineteen to twenty-five), this time might be filled with a gospel lesson like the one titled "Take Time to Be Holy"[42] or a combined activity with the M Men, such as a Gleanenight (a word derived from combining *Gleaners*, *M Men*, and *night*). For these activities, the young women and men might participate in a progressive dinner party, traveling together to several different destinations to eat courses of a meal.[43] The calendar for Junior Gleaners similarly included many activities with the Junior M Men, but Mia Maids held fewer mixed-gender social activities. Instead, they held project nights, when young women could work together on their Treasures of Truth books or on goals for their Mia Joy awards.[44] In most months, young women also participated in an activity that included all members of the MIA in the ward. This might be a holiday party, dance, or festival in which young people could showcase their development in music, drama, dance, speech, or athletics.[45] Preparation for these festivals occupied the remainder of most Mutual nights. After the fifty minutes of lesson or project work, the young people of the ward came back together to rehearse for another fifty minutes.[46]

Outside of historically Latter-day Saint communities, young women's experience in the MIA varied based on how established the organization was in their area and how many members lived there. A pamphlet entitled *M. I. A. in the Missions* advised MIA leaders to pattern their Mutual schedules after those of wards in more established areas, but the pamphlet also offered three options for how members living in the church's missions might organize the MIA. For areas in which church members lived at a significant distance from one another, members were advised to conduct "Home Mutuals," where they could participate "in such features of the program as are adaptable to their needs." If a few families lived close together, they could hold "Neighborhood Mutuals," joining at regular intervals to participate in cultural activities like dancing and musical performance. Otherwise, members should organize "Branch Mutuals," patterned more closely after those in a larger ward but combining age groups when numbers necessitated.[47]

Outside the United States, the cultural component of the MIA proved to be a mainstay. Missionwide youth conferences offered a venue for young people to join in sports competitions and to showcase their carefully rehearsed performances in dance, music, drama, and speech. Youth in the West German Mission began saving money months in advance for the July 1956 MIA conference in Wiesbaden. American missionaries participated alongside German youth in choir rehearsals and speech contests. The conference also held a Gold and Green Ball, to which German young women, whose communities were still recovering from the devastation of war a decade earlier, wore gowns donated by Gleaners from wards in Utah, Idaho, and Wyoming. As many as one thousand people reportedly participated in the conference.[48] That same year, the New Zealand Mission reported an attendance of thirty-five hundred at its annual MIA conference, which included plays, speeches, dances, and sporting events.[49]

The Pittsburgh Branch in Pennsylvania, located in the Eastern States Mission, offered a picture of members' creative and consistent efforts to implement MIA programs in their small branch of fewer than eighty-five members. The MIA organized activities for the entire branch, including the Gold and Green Ball in April, an MIA carnival in September, and a drama night in December. Many of these events required a small entrance fee, proceeds of which the youth donated to a fund for building a local chapel. Other activities, such as the annual Rose Prom, were intended only for MIA-age members.[50] Even in such a small branch, MIA work required a large investment of adult leadership. The Pittsburgh Branch assigned fourteen women and twelve men to serve in the branch's MIA organizations in 1955. The branch minutes indicate that an average of seventy people attended sacrament meeting each week; if twenty-six of those served in MIAs, running this complex and dynamic organization involved nearly 40 percent of adults attending the branch.[51]

SPECIAL YWMIA EVENTS

YWMIA leaders were responsible not only for festivals and weekly YWMIA activities but also for special events like sports competitions and camp. When leaders in the early 1950s discovered that some Latter-day Saint young women were joining outside groups to play sports, Bertha Reeder worked to expand MIA sports programs, previously focused primarily on young men, to include more young women. Soon, young women were participating in church-sponsored team sports such as basketball, softball, and volleyball, as well as individual sports like tennis, swimming, and

Singers at the Danish Mission MIA convention. 1956. Young women from Copenhagen, Denmark, participated in a music contest in Aalborg, Denmark. A banner displaying the year's MIA theme is in the background: "I am not ashamed of the gospel of Christ: for it is the power of God unto salvation to every one that believeth" (Romans 1:16). Similar regional conventions were held all over the world. (Church History Library, Salt Lake City.)

Blackfoot Fourth Ward YWMIA softball team. 1953. This team from Blackfoot, Idaho, took home the prize from a stake softball competition. Women's and men's sports were a significant component of the MIA program and were an effective missionary tool to introduce other young people to the church. (Courtesy *Post Register* [Idaho Falls, ID], copy at Church History Library, Salt Lake City.)

archery, all led by newly appointed YWMIA sports directors.[52] In 1956, Reeder reported that the YWMIA had organized fifteen thousand sports events in the last year, with an average of 250 young women in each stake participating.[53]

One of Reeder's major goals was to provide each young woman a camping experience, and she took a special interest in the efforts of the camp committee of the general board.[54] During her time heading the New England Mission with her husband, she had attended meetings of the Camp Fire Girls, consulting with the organization's leadership as YWMIA leaders had done decades earlier, and had worked to institute in the local districts of the church camping programs for young women that incorporated many of the fundamentals of Camp Fire Girls.[55] Reeder was pleased to see so many stakes purchasing sites for summer camps, and she encouraged the leaders of stakes with no such summer camp to procure one.[56] She counseled leaders to provide young women with what she referred to as a "primitive" camping experience, which meant an overnight experience outdoors.[57]

Leaders continued to use *Camp-O-Rama* for guidance, along with other manuals (such as *Camptivities* and *Cooking Out-of-Doors*). These manuals sought to use camping to "create a deeper sense of God as our Maker and a loyalty to His great plan."[58] Building and sharing testimony had become a fundamental part of the young women's camping experience, and fireside testimony sharing had become a beloved tradition. Other camp activities—like the Bee Hive class's inspirational sunrise meetings—also encouraged spiritual development. "Who can spend time in the woods and mountains," the leaders reasoned, "without feeling the majesty and grandeur of the universe!"[59]

Encouraging young women to feel the grandeur of the universe during camp required a great deal of behind-the-scenes planning. The YWMIA provided substantial training and support for local leaders preparing for camp. Articles in the *MIA Leader* and the *Improvement Era* regularly offered ideas and instruction on how to create a satisfying outdoor camp, listing directions for making a tin-can stove and packaging food for easy carrying.[60] Each June Conference provided additional guidance and training for camp leaders and included camp institutes that instructed leaders over two or three days in the fundamentals of camp activities such as nature hikes, camp songs, and games. Since the camp and sports programs were essentially intertwined in this period, leaders who participated in the institute might receive instruction in the young women's sports program in the morning and then later make tin-can camp stoves and sing campfire songs. They might also learn how to engage in specific camp handicrafts such as weaving, ceramics, quilting, rug making, and beading.[61] Helping young women feel a sense of belonging, accomplishment, and pride within the sphere of MIA activities was a major priority.

SHOWCASING YOUTH AT JUNE CONFERENCE

Lia Davis, who attended the Twentieth Ward of the Salt Lake Ensign Stake in the 1950s, felt that church recreation and activities kept her and her cohort out of trouble and fostered strong bonds of friendship among them. "I hope Heavenly Father counts rehearsal time for doing good, because I spent my life in rehearsals when I was younger," she later said.[62] Those rehearsals helped prepare Lia and her peers for regional and central gatherings promoted by Reeder's administration to provide young people with wholesome, church-sponsored entertainment. For over three decades, the annual June Conference in Salt Lake City had featured music, dance, drama, and athletic events. In 1952 and 1953, the YWMIA appointed division and district supervisors for different activities to improve the quality of regional events. Ruth Hardy Funk, who was then serving as the chair of the music committee, remembered youth arriving for June Conference by the carload and busload from about 80 percent of the church's stakes. These young women and men had qualified for the central June Conference by distinguishing themselves at both the local and regional level. "The thrilling thing about June Conference was that it was a culmination of so many local events," Funk said.[63] And all the hours of preparation and competition were hours spent in a protective church environment.

June Conferences were seen as offering both secular and religious benefits to participants. In keeping with the tradition of "teaching the gospel through activities"—or "spiritualized recreation," as it was now often called—leaders hoped the preparation for these events, and the culminating spectacular performances, would plant in the hearts of these adolescents a sense of Latter-day Saint identity and solidarity that couldn't be instilled by any amount of talking.[64] Leaders also believed that as the young women worked together with adult mentors to prepare their performances, they learned important leadership and social skills and developed valuable character traits.

This view of youth leadership development differed from those of both earlier and later periods. Early in the organization's history, the grassroots nature of local associations meant that young women commonly served in leadership positions. Then, as general MIA leaders sought to incorporate their understanding of adolescent development, and especially with the increasing complexity of the programs, the role of young women and men became solely that of participants. Though the needs of small branches in areas where church membership was less established allowed for some exceptions, the massive program required a host of capable and dedicated adult officers and presidencies at the local, stake, and general levels to run it.

June Conference dance festival, University of Utah Ute Stadium. 1963. Spectators of the June Conference dance festival filled the Ute Stadium (now the Rice-Eccles Stadium) to its thirty-thousand-person capacity to watch thousands of youth dance in varying styles and formations. The yearly event became so popular that by the mid-1950s it was televised throughout Salt Lake City. (Church History Library, Salt Lake City.)

This was particularly true as wards and stakes prepared for June Conference, where events also presented an opportunity for leaders to devote their talents to church service, giving religious meaning to their artistic and athletic work. Over two dozen women and men were credited with producing a dance festival associated with the 1956 June Conference; they oversaw everything, including costume design, ticket sales, and sound recording.[65] Each of those general-level producers represented large cohorts of local and regional leaders who devoted their time and talents to helping youth prepare—not to mention all the teaching, coaching, leading, and counseling that went into their work in the other aspects of the program. At all levels, leadership in the MIA engendered strong devotion to and camaraderie within the church.

Between 1953 and 1959, the number of individuals registered for June Conference nearly doubled from around eighty-five hundred to almost seventeen thousand. By 1959, the live audience for the dance festival reached forty thousand. Starting in 1952, the dance festival also began to be broadcast on television, giving the event additional visibility at a time when television was rapidly rising in popularity in the United States.[66] "These were the golden years of festivals," Funk recalled. "There is no question about it. And it was under her [Reeder's] marvelous vision and supervision that this was allowed to grow."[67] The massive performances offered observable, dramatic evidence of the fruits of MIA labor in the form of the many smiling, happy, vibrant young people who sang, danced, spoke, performed, and testified.

As showcases for the church's youth, June Conference spectacles helped the church project confidence at a time when it sought to burnish its public image. While the persecution and social stigmatization that characterized the nineteenth century remained a vivid presence in the faith's collective memory, the 1950s were largely marked by public relations successes. David O. McKay, tall and white-haired, charismatic and forward thinking, became president of the church in 1951 and soon established a national profile as a respected religious leader, forming friendships with United States presidents and high-profile celebrities such as Cecil B. DeMille and Charlton Heston. Ezra Taft Benson, a member of the Quorum of the Twelve Apostles, kept a high profile in United States President Dwight D. Eisenhower's cabinet as the secretary of agriculture. National Boy Scout leaders attended June Conference and praised the church's successes in building young men through its ongoing affiliation with Scouting.[68] In addition to presenting its weekly television and radio broadcast across the nation, the Tabernacle Choir undertook an international tour and released best-selling albums. A number of national publications turned their attention to the Saints, with headlines such as "Those Amazing Mormons" and "A Mighty People in the Rockies." The latter article, published in the *New York Times*, highlighted the church's growth and prosperity and labeled the MIA as "undoubtedly one of the most efficiently organized youth movements in the world."[69]

YWMIA leaders received similar praise firsthand. Reeder's counselor LaRue Longden was well received by attendees and the press at the 1956 World Congress of Recreation and Leisure, where she presented on the church's recreation programs.[70] During the Cold War, physical recreation became a high-profile issue in the United States. Studies suggested that American youth compared poorly with their European counterparts in physical fitness, even as the American military continued to conscript an average of a quarter of a million young men per year. Dwight D. Eisenhower ultimately established the President's Council on Youth Fitness to address the issue.[71] A Latter-day Saint, Ott Romney, was selected as the program's deputy director, while Marion D. Hanks, of the First Council of the Seventy, served on the council. The council's executive director, Shane MacCarthy, not only took time to meet with the MIA boards to discuss how to promote fitness but also praised their pioneer legacy.[72] Elaine Anderson Cannon, a well-known writer and speaker to Latter-day Saint youth audiences, had previously participated in the White House Conference on Youth.[73]

Some of the praise and recognition board members received was directly related to June Conference. Ruth Funk was flattered by the enthusiastic reception she was given by the president of the *Chicago Tribune* when she visited to study the organization of the Chicagoland Music Festival, which the *Tribune* sponsored. Funk showed him a scrapbook of news articles and statistical information on the recent MIA event. "Look what they've done!" she remembered him exclaiming. "Why, they do things we can't even do. She came to learn from me and look what I've learned from them." A similar experience took place in 1956, when distinguished professor of music Grace Spofford came to Utah for a week prior to June Conference. Spofford, who also worked with the National Council of Women and Hull House, was interested in the process of putting on June Conference. "I want to know how it happens and what happens in the lives of people to make it happen," Spofford told Reeder. During her visit, Spofford spent all day with Funk, even helping feed and bathe Funk's children. "It was an extraordinary thing for her to see how a woman could carry on her duties and responsibilities and care for a family and still do all of these things," Funk said. "I told her this was repeated a thousand times all over the Church."[74]

The developing image of Latter-day Saint women drawing on the power of faith to excel in both domestic and cultural activities was not confined to general YWMIA leaders. In 1951, when Colleen Kay Hutchins, a twenty-five-year-old YWMIA member, was crowned Miss America, her faith and values were a recurring theme of media reception.[75] Elated, Latter-day Saint leaders reflected the positive attention back through church media channels. The June 1952 *Improvement Era* featured Hutchins's photo on the cover, and an article in the issue detailed the positive publicity her reign as Miss America was bringing to the church. The magazine praised her as an ambassador for the value of being raised in a good Latter-day Saint home combined with continuous activity in the church. It noted that the pageant's director had called Hutchins "the busiest and most popular of all Miss Americas" and suggested she had garnered the most favorable publicity of any church member of the era.[76]

As a missionary faith, Latter-day Saints considered religious conversion the most highly prized form of attention. By the next decade, "Come to play and stay to pray" had become a common refrain in church articles highlighting the MIA's potential to provide for the world's social and spiritual needs.[77] Church members hoped that the power of their faith demonstrated in the lives of youth could draw others to participate in the MIA organizations and eventually join the church. Examples were easy to find. One stake president reported that thirty-three people in his area joined the church in one year after being introduced to it through the MIA.[78] While that anecdote is noteworthy for its scale, many Latter-day Saints during the period—especially those who lived outside Utah—would have known at least one person who had converted after participating in the MIA. Reflecting on the role of festivals, competitions, and conferences throughout the church, longtime YWMIA board member Marba Josephson expressed hope that the success of these events would assist in the church's missionary work by leading to greater numbers of participants and spectators who would feel the spirit of the occasion.[79]

MAKING VALUES VISUAL

The pride 1950s leaders felt over happy, clean, and committed Latter-day Saint youth was accompanied by anxieties about whether young people would maintain faith in the gospel of Jesus Christ and fidelity to the church's standards. Mindful of the increasingly visual culture youth encountered in television and magazines, leaders began using visual media to express both the ideal and the anxieties. Beginning in the mid-1950s, the foyers in church meetinghouses displayed large posters featuring vivid, colorful scenes of young people, accompanied by aphorisms extolling the virtues of righteous living. A 1956 poster, for example, depicted a happy bride and groom, with smaller images in the background of later joyful family life. The headline on the poster proclaimed, "Virtue Is Its Own Reward." A short text on the benefits of moral living and the dangers of sin appeared on the back of each poster. These posters were also published as pocket-size cards.[80] For some young people, at least, these visual messages resonated. Myrna Petersen's Treasures of Truth book preserves several of these cards, highlighting themes such as respect for parents, careful driving, prayer, and observance of the Word of Wisdom.

The constraints of the poster or card form, however, meant that each could focus only on a single principle. In the mid-1950s, YWMIA leaders turned to film, which offered the potential to create something more holistic. The 1956 film *How Near to the Angels* was a major milestone in the church's efforts to communicate with its youth. Commissioned by YWMIA leadership to showcase the connection between YWMIA programs and temple marriage, the forty-two-minute film was the longest produced at Brigham Young University's Motion Picture Studio to that point.[81] YWMIA leaders advised local units to screen the film as part of their activities calendar, giving it a huge potential audience among members and their families.[82] The YWMIA built on prior theatrical experience as it launched into film. Playwright Ruth Hale, the MIA regional drama director for Southern California, had years of experience mixing church messaging with story in MIA stage productions.[83] In the script for *How Near to the Angels*, she represented both the temptations leaders worried about and the value of YWMIA programming. The finished film is a window into leaders' cultural fears and their organizational responses.

How Near to the Angels opens with a young woman putting on her wedding dress and reflecting on the choices that led her to that moment. The film traces its protagonist, Janet, from her time as a Bee Hive girl to the day of her temple wedding. "I shall always be thankful to my Heavenly Father for those wonderful people who pointed the way for me," Janet says, speaking to a photo of her fiancé. "For without them, darling, I'd never have had you."[84] The interlocking stories of her YWMIA and social experiences then unfold in flashback, giving the film's audience of young women and their leaders an affirming overview of the program.

As a Bee Hive girl, Janet is driven by a longing for peer approval but finds a wise and caring "big sister" in her YWMIA leader and needed perspective through her experience at camp. As a Mia Maid, she dates a high school football star named Ted, who is not a member of the church, only to realize at the Gold and Green Ball how much meaning she finds in her contributions to her religious community. At a later stake athletic event, she meets a Latter-day Saint young man named Kent. The two have an extended romance, but the film depicts their relationship as cut off from the larger community. Kent and Janet spend time alone together rather than with their Latter-day Saint peers. A YWMIA lesson and a personal visit from her leader help Janet rethink this relationship. At a stake fireside, she meets a religiously active and family-oriented Latter-day Saint named Tim. Instead of skipping MIA for time alone together, Tim and Janet court through church activities: a ward outing in the canyon, MIA meetings, an MIA dance, an MIA softball game, and a testimony meeting. Janet sees how Tim interacts with multiple generations of his family members and meets his grandmother, which underscores the importance of family ties. Her choice

Gold and Green Ball, New Zealand. Circa 1949. Young women and young men in New Zealand sashayed around the dance hall as they performed the floor show, observed by dozens of spectators and the ball royalty. These elaborate, formal balls became a cherished annual tradition of Mutual Improvement Associations beyond North America and often involved local church members and non–Latter-day Saints alike, including individuals outside the traditional MIA age. (Courtesy Gordon Woodruff Young, copy at Church History Library, Salt Lake City.)

of a husband who is active in the church community and shows respect for his extended family is presented as her greatest expression of faith.

The depiction of YWMIA teachings on marriage in *How Near to the Angels* leaves no room for doubt as to its centrality as a topic for the era's Latter-day Saints. The film shows a leader asking during a lesson, "What are the three most important dates in your life?" She stands at a chalkboard to record the answers, and the young women quickly supply the desired responses: birth, marriage, and death. Out of these three days, the leader points out, marriage is the only one individuals have much control over. "Never settle for anything less than temple marriage," she admonishes.[85] For young Latter-day Saint women, temple marriage was constantly held up as the foremost goal of their lives, and ages sixteen to eighteen were considered prime courtship years—in the film, Janet is a Junior Gleaner when she makes the choices that will lead her to marriage.

Young adults in the 1950s married younger than their early-twentieth-century predecessors. The median age of first marriage for American women was twenty-two in 1900 but dipped to twenty during the 1950s before rising again to twenty-five by the year 2000.[86] High marriage rates at earlier ages meant that many American YWMIA members in high school were considering marriage or had friends who were. Myrna Petersen's best friend, Wilma Mead, began talking about getting married in their junior year. When Wilma did send out a wedding invitation just after graduation, Myrna placed it in her Treasures of Truth book, a physical indication of how intertwined marriage and YWMIA experience were for 1950s young women.

Some MIA teaching on marriage was not restricted to just young women or young men. A popular series, "If I Were a Teen," ran in most issues of the *Improvement Era* from July 1953 to June 1955, featuring short articles written by youth leaders. Most of the pieces did not identify their audience as male or female and seemed to give counsel meant equally for both. In these pieces, marriage was presented as an ideal for both young women and young men. Carol Hinckley Cannon of the YWMIA board encouraged young people, without reference to gender, to envision their future companion and the day when they would kneel with that companion at the altar of the temple to be sealed together.[87]

ENCOURAGING CHASTITY AND MODESTY

The focus on temple marriage included an emphasis on chastity as a crucial aspect of preparation, and an emphasis on modesty began as an outgrowth of chastity. While the 1950s are often seen as a period of cultural conservatism in the United States, a strong movement for sexual liberalism also took hold, and discussions about sex and morality unfolded alongside it.[88] J. Reuben Clark Jr., a member of the church's First Presidency, had warned that a "new spirit" had entered the world with the war. The bestselling Kinsey reports on human sexuality in the late 1940s and early 1950s detailed high rates of sexual experimentation among thousands of interviewees, thereby weakening taboos against directly discussing sexual subjects. Those taboos, in fact, were blatantly flouted by the advent of sexually provocative magazines and the increasingly open treatment of sexual themes in movies.[89]

Prominent church leaders, such as apostles Mark E. Petersen and Spencer W. Kimball, led out in addressing sexual subjects from a church perspective. Speaking from his own experience interviewing thousands of church members, Kimball decried unchastity and sexual impurity as "the great demon of the 1950s."[90] Petersen gave an address to students at BYU that attempted to help young people understand the admonitions about chastity in a broader context. Sex, he said, was sacred. It was what he called the "spark of the Deity" within each person, through which mortals cooperate with God in His creative work. Misuse of this power before marriage was therefore a serious sin, ranking below only murder and adultery in gravity. Knowing that procreation was one of the most important and sacred parts of God's plan for this life, Petersen taught, Satan sought to exploit it. Satan was inspiring the world to place a demoralizing emphasis on sex, either turning it into a degraded plaything or making sexual sin alluring, both of which destroyed God's great objectives for sex and procreation. Petersen's talk was subsequently distributed as a pamphlet called *The Sacredness of Sex*, extending its influence on Latter-day Saint discourse.[91]

The frankness of discussions of such subjects, especially those using the word *sex* itself, reached new levels in the 1950s, reflecting the urgency with which leaders viewed the problem and, likely, the greater frankness with which sexual subjects were being discussed in the broader society. In the 1940s, the YWMIA had considered but did not publish a booklet on sex and morality, because church leaders believed that discussion of such subjects should be conducted only by parents in the home.[92] But by the next decade, leaders such as Kimball and Petersen spoke openly of "necking and heavy petting" (or passionate kissing and sexual touching), challenging what they believed was a common view that such behaviors were not serious.[93]

In principle, church teachings insisted on the same standard of sexual purity for young women and young men. And indeed, in mixed-gender settings, there was a clear message that young men and young women bore equal responsibility for maintaining sexual morality. "There are no privileged classes, nor is there any privileged sex under the Lord's moral code," stated one lesson designed for both young women and young men.[94] But in discussions directed specifically at young women, the emphasis was often different. One lesson, for example, stated that the sex urge is stronger in boys, "so it is the privilege of you girls to keep the standards high in your association with them."[95] The result was a mixed message that established a single standard of chastity for both genders but also suggested that women bore a disproportionate responsibility to maintain sexual purity in relationships, a view that aligned with the double standard prevalent in the broader culture.

Local YWMIA groups held dedicated events for discussions of sexual standards in the 1950s. Junior Gleaners held Sacred to Me evenings, and Mia Maids attended Dear to My Heart nights, both of which were intended for mothers and daughters to attend together and sometimes referred to informally as "chastity nights."[96] The program might include music, recitation of the class's theme, refreshments, and distribution of a booklet or other handout for the young women to take home. The featured element was a guest speaker who would address the young women on chastity or clean living. How explicit these talks were is hard to gauge and probably depended on the sensibilities of the speakers. If the booklets themselves are any indication, the ideas of clean living and choosing good friends and marriage companions were emphasized, without mention of specific sexual activities.[97] Myrna Peterson taped into her Treasures of Truth book a booklet entitled *Whene'er My Heart Is Pure*, which was intended for distribution to young women and young men at their respective chastity-themed events.

Virtually every talk on chastity by church authorities included comments about modesty as well, since anxieties over sexual behavior gave rise to concern about modest dress and rapid changes in fashion. In the immediate aftermath of the Second World War, French designer Jacques Heim had introduced a new two-piece swimming suit called the *atome*. Playing on the public fascination with atomic energy in the wake of the bombings of Hiroshima and Nagasaki, the piece was advertised as the world's smallest swimming suit, which had been split just like the atom. A competitor, Louis Réard, soon introduced a competing and even more controversial design, called the "bikini" after the United States' nuclear tests on Bikini Atoll.[98] While the new suits were widely viewed as scandalous at the time of their release, they were among the many signals that public norms of appropriate dress were widening.

These shifting norms created both confusion and tension among church members. Lueen Jensen King and her counselors in the Moapa, Nevada, stake YWMIA wrote to Bertha Reeder in December 1950, declaring that they were "a little bewildered." They explained that they had held their Gold and Green Ball near Thanksgiving. "Some of our lovely girls came in formal dresses unbecoming to Latter-day Saints and in total opposition to church standards." What was worse, the inappropriately dressed young women were students at the church-sponsored BYU; young women from the University of Nevada in Reno had all been modestly clothed. "We know this is a very sensitive subject," they wrote, "especially inasmuch as parents do not seem to understand." But they wondered whether church schools were placing adequate emphasis on modesty and whether the YWMIA leaders could do something to help.[99] Reeder and her counselors forwarded the letter from the Moapa leaders to David O. McKay, as well as to Ezra Taft Benson and Mark E. Petersen, the two apostles assigned to oversee the YWMIA. Along with the letter, the presidency sent their own message explaining that the letter was typical of correspondence they'd received from other leaders about the same issue, and they wondered what they could do to remedy it.[100]

Increasingly, church leaders decried immodesty as a gateway to sexual sin. In a 1951 address titled "A Style of Our Own," Spencer W. Kimball pled with female BYU students to keep high standards, denouncing in detail low necklines, form-fitting sweaters, all shorts, immodest evening gowns, and beauty pageants with their bathing suit competitions. Immodesty encouraged what he called "mental adultery" and contributed to the rising tide of sexual immorality.[101] Mark E. Petersen linked the need for modesty to the sanctity of the body, emphasizing that sacred things were not for public display. He reported that young men had told him their downfall began with temptation on the dance floor when they saw parts of young women's bodies that were not covered up.[102] These talks made an impression. For example, Bertha Clark, a sophomore at BYU in 1951, recalled that she and many of her friends altered their dresses to make them more modest in keeping with Kimball's teachings.[103]

Young Women leaders were equally concerned about modesty and sexual morality. In 1955, counselor LaRue Longden published a piece in the *Improvement Era* called "It's Smart to be a Latter-day Saint," in which she took a proactive, positive approach to the subject while upholding its importance. She lamented that many young women felt they were receiving mixed messages on modesty. Some reported that their mothers had told them, "You are only young once; your lovely body is beautiful. It is now or never if you want to wear one of 'those' dresses." In response, Longden quoted Brigham Young exhorting women to cover their bodies neatly and in good taste. Still, definitions of what constituted modest covering were in flux, and some styles that had been considered acceptable were later discouraged. Leaders tried to clarify boundaries without being overly prescriptive. In her article, Longden wrote disapprovingly of young women who would have one kind of dress for church functions but choose more worldly styles for other occasions.

Longden acknowledged the emerging difficulty of finding sufficiently modest dresses in stores and offered several suggestions. Mothers and daughters could make their own clothes, for instance. Longden mentioned one woman who spent every Monday evening helping women design and sew what Longden called "smart and beautiful" dresses that met the right standards. She also told of a young woman in one stake who had started a business tailoring ready-made clothing to make it more modest. Finally, Longden reported that she herself had made a project of collecting pictures of modest clothing for all occasions from top fashion magazines. "Believe it or not," she said, "there were as many modest dresses as there were 'uncovered look' ones." She encouraged each young woman to use her own ingenuity and fix her clothes to fit her personality.[104]

TEACHING A FEMININE IDENTITY

"Women carry the responsibility of blessing the world with their gentleness, their kindness, their mercy," observed the Bee Hive manual in 1956. "It is good to be a girl who will some day grow to be a lovely woman."[105] This statement could stand in for many similar expressions of female aspiration found in YWMIA sources in the 1950s. But while its tone is positive, its substance is ambiguous—what did it mean to be a "lovely woman"? Themes of faith, testimony, high standards, and a positive outlook on life were woven throughout messages disseminated to young women in the YWMIA; the messages took for granted that marriage and motherhood were the source of women's highest honor and aspirations.[106] The most direct messages about gender ideals appeared in the Bee Hive and Mia Maid courses, since the Junior Gleaner and Gleaner programs focused on activities and were almost entirely conjoint with their young men counterparts. Lessons instilled in younger girls the messages about femininity that leaders felt were essential to prepare them for their high school years and life beyond.

The societal focus on family and domestic life in the United States profoundly influenced ideals of femininity. The ideal home and family were built around women creating happy, well-run homes and devoting their lives to service toward husband and children as educator, counselor, cook, nurse, housekeeper, manager, and chauffeur. Homemaking was extolled as a career for women—*the* career for women—and increasingly professionalized through reliance on experts in child-rearing and domestic efficiency.[107] Throughout the country, young women like Myrna Petersen spent considerable hours of their free time learning cooking, sewing, and other domestic skills in clubs and organizations such as 4-H.[108]

YWMIA lessons and programs underscored the importance of homemaking through their perennial emphasis on marriage and through requirements for achievement awards that centered on domestic skills. In the 1954–1955 Bee Hive manual, for example, eight of the ten suggested activities under the category of "Value Work" focused on cooking and cleaning; under "Honor Womanhood," four focused on childcare and household management. "Safeguard Health" likewise included activities in home nursing and planning nutritious meals.[109] Encouraging a serious study of homemaking, board member Marba Josephson wrote that "there is no activity that can mean more to the world as a whole than that of building safe, sound, happy homes."[110]

The emphasis on marriage and homemaking in American culture appears to have also affected educational attainment among women: in the 1950s, two-thirds of women who went to college dropped out before graduating, and fewer women sought advanced degrees or pursued professional careers than in the preceding two decades.[111] Nevertheless, YWMIA lessons did give some attention to choosing a vocation. "You will want to have a feeling of making a contribution to the world," advised one lesson. Women who married would make their greatest contribution through their home and children, it said, but once the family was raised, the mother would want to have a vocation and take up her own interests again. The lesson went on to conduct a substantial discussion about obtaining an education, choosing a career, and starting a business, sprinkled with examples from real women's lives.[112]

In addition to preparing young women for their future lives, YWMIA voices counseled them to develop moral courage and sufficient independence to resist cultural pressures at odds with church norms. At the same time, those voices also reflected other cultural pressures as they encouraged young women to pursue charm and attractiveness. Iris Parker, an associate editor of the *Improvement Era*, asserted that "every girl is beautiful in this happy time of life" and admonished readers to stand tall, let their intelligence shine through, and pray for beauty within. She addressed hypothetical young women in a spirit of helping them overcome their insecurities and highlight their good features. But much of her advice still sounded like it could have come from a teen magazine or a charm class. The slender blonde should "discreetly turn down malts and candy bars" so she could maintain a willowy and trim figure. Young women should be fresh and neat and keep their voices gentle, smiles frequent, and laughter soft. They should wear little makeup, wash their faces nightly, and use a soothing cream.[113]

YWMIA lessons gave heavy emphasis to personality development, including a good amount of popular psychology, and virtually every year young women studied lessons on social skills and etiquette.[114] Such lessons stressed appropriate feminine behavior in various situations. Young women were not to call young men unless absolutely necessary, for example, and they were not to act possessively or expect young men to spend too much money on them. They should let men "see the feminine" in them by waiting for them to open doors, pick up things they drop, and seat them at the table. "Enjoy being looked after," the lesson advised.[115] Such lessons sometimes included lists of dos and don'ts based on surveys of what boys found attractive in girls. "Boys insist that they like a girl who is feminine," according to one such discussion.

"By this they mean that they like a girl who can play a bang-up game of tennis or skate all around them or ski down a mountainside, but who at the same time never forgets for one instant that she is a lady."[116]

MEMBERSHIP GROWTH AND CHALLENGES TO GUIDING ASSUMPTIONS

As church membership expanded rapidly in the 1950s, YWMIA messaging developed in Utah did not always resonate elsewhere. Church growth during the years when Bertha Reeder led the YWMIA was dramatic, with the most rapid growth taking place outside Latter-day Saint majority areas in the Intermountain West. In the 1890s, the church had reached a tipping point in which more members were added by birth than by conversion; in the postwar era, that trend reversed again as missionary work increased substantially around the globe.[117] In 1947, the year before Reeder's tenure as general president began, church membership had reached one million, with just one in three members living outside the Intermountain West. By 1963, two years after Reeder's release, church membership doubled to two million, with half of those members living outside the Intermountain West (though most still lived in the United States).[118] Because of the faith's strong missionary impulse, leaders and members enthusiastically embraced the growth, even as it raised questions about how to adapt to be more representative of members' realities.

June Conference, for example, was scheduled to accommodate youth in Utah—it took place following the school year, during an extended summer vacation. California schools, however, were still in session through June, meaning that prospective participants could not attend the conference unless they took time off from school.[119] This dilemma took on added meaning by the mid-1950s, as California's unusually rapid membership growth meant it accounted for 10 percent of total church membership at that time.[120]

Bernadine Wallace, the stake YWMIA president in the East Los Angeles Stake, and Mark Ross, the YMMIA superintendent from the Glendale Stake, proposed a solution—a separate event, modeled on June Conference, to be held in Southern California in August. The general board supported the plan, pledging to provide the same trainings and speakers as at the central June Conference, while relying on Wallace and Ross to oversee the local organization and fundraising.[121] Around seven thousand young women and men participated in the conference, and around sixteen thousand spectators attended sessions in the Hollywood Bowl in August 1954. On Monday, 9 August, the second page of the *Los Angeles Times* opened with a large photo of the crowd at the Hollywood Bowl and an accompanying article about the event.[122]

MIA chorus at the Hollywood Bowl. 1954. Seeking to make the June Conference experience available to church members outside Utah, leaders in Southern California organized a large conference that drew thousands of participants and spectators. This chorus of 1,500 youth sang at the music festival for an estimated audience of 16,000. (Church History Library, Salt Lake City. Photograph by Vic Stein and Associates.)

A second Southern California conference in 1955 followed the same model, and a third in 1956, with California leadership providing more of the programming. Many leaders viewed the events as successes. YWMIA general leadership even chose the 1956 Southern California conference as the venue to share the first public preview of *How Near to the Angels*.[123] But the conference's success also brought concerns. In 1954, some Arizona Latter-day Saints wondered about coming to the Southern California conference rather than June Conference in Salt Lake City, but church leaders discouraged them because of concerns over housing logistics.[124] Church leaders also grappled with how to balance support for local initiative and adaptation with a desire for more consistency and uniformity. After the 1956 conference, David O. McKay discouraged large-scale events in California out of a concern for fairness to other areas.[125] Without their own high-profile conference, however, California members once again faced the prospect of holding activities designed to build toward a June Conference that most of their youth would not attend.

For youth like those of the El Paso Third Ward in Texas, there were other, more serious obstacles to advancing through regional celebrations to June Conference. The El Paso Third Ward was the church's first Spanish-speaking ward, one unit in an English-speaking stake. Third Ward members took pride in their pioneering position. Many Anglo Latter-day Saints, including leaders like Spencer W. Kimball, were also pleased and saw the advancement of groups with Indigenous American ancestry as fulfilling prophecies in the Book of Mormon. But while Latter-day Saints often formed positive relationships across racial lines through missionary work and shared worship, concerns about interracial marriage and family relationships remained strong and created some anxiety about stake and regional MIA activities where romantic relationships might develop across ethnic lines.[126]

Sensitivities about ethnic distinctions sometimes played out in other ways. According to the process laid out by the general MIA organizations, wards that performed well in drama, dance, athletics, and other activities were supposed to advance to regional competitions, with the winning groups there moving on to final all-church events held in Utah. During the 1950s, however, members of the Third Ward realized that some Anglo leaders involved in the adjudication process were nervous about having them advance. "Instead of helping you out, they would deter you," said Sandra Gonzalez, a YWMIA member from the Third Ward. While MIA activities created positive memories within the ward, she felt that some of the racism that shaped her experience growing up in Texas also affected her experience in stake MIA. This was particularly difficult since church was an empowering aspect of her life, a place where she was encouraged to pursue education to prepare for service in the community and church.[127] "So it left a little acid in your throat when these things happened," she said. Attitudes changed over time, and in the 1960s, a group from the ward was able to participate in a regional competition.[128]

By the end of the 1950s, roughly 10 percent of church members lived outside of the United States, which presented additional challenges to existing assumptions that went well beyond attendance at June Conference.[129] Travel, even within a given country, was often a barrier to full participation in the church, including MIA programs and activities. Growing up in Melbourne, Australia, Margot Butler remembered families in her branch who had to rely on buses and trains—and sometimes a combination of the two—to attend church meetings. "Some who could come on Sundays," she noted, "couldn't come on Thursday [for MIA] because they couldn't get home after. It was too late to come out at night, especially by themselves."[130] Such experiences were common; Utah leaders' assumptions about the accessibility of MIA meetings rarely held up in places where the church's presence was smallest. In most international areas that filed reports, Sunday School rather than MIA had the highest attendance for young women. While in Utah YWMIA attendance exceeded 70 percent in many stakes, international missions reported attendance averaging 50 percent.[131]

Margot herself was able to attend MIA and remembered local leaders providing positive mentoring. She enjoyed activities but noticed gaps between her experience and the assumptions built into YWMIA materials. These gaps were particularly evident to her in lessons taught from YWMIA manuals on topics related to cultural refinement. She remembered local members dutifully carrying out elocution lessons, for example, which involved repeating certain words to practice their pronunciation. Without the unwritten contextual information about differences between Utah accents and the culturally dominant accent many Americans aspired to, Australian members found themselves totally mystified by the word choices and wondered why they were being asked to practice words that everyone they knew pronounced the same way.[132]

Some YWMIA lessons were designed to teach American Latter-day Saints about the wider world. Members outside the United States, then, got a view of the world through an American curriculum writer's frame of reference. "That's why I was disappointed when the manual came out, and it showed the four stars of the Southern Cross—obviously written by a Northerner in Salt Lake who didn't know there were five stars," Margot recalled. While the error was minor, it made her reflect on the overall reliability of what she was learning through MIA. "Maybe we can't trust these manuals," she remembered thinking, "when the only thing I know for sure is wrong."[133]

Experiences like Margot's highlighted the mismatch between centrally produced materials and local circumstances. During the 1950s, YWMIA leaders were more focused on communicating to the historical core of their membership than on adapting to the church's growing diversity. Nonetheless, questions arose during this period that became increasingly urgent through subsequent decades of growth, and leaders gradually became more concerned about how to manage messaging for members' varied circumstances.

Following the release of *How Near to the Angels*, for example, David O. McKay objected to the script's depiction of temple marriage followed by familial bliss. In many countries, Latter-day Saints made up such a tiny numerical minority that the film's narrative seemed unrealistic. "It was my judgment that it would be better not to use it for showing in the Missions of the Church," he wrote of the film, "as it will only intensify the problem that our young girls are now facing with relation to meeting young men who are worthy to take them to the Temple." McKay worried that too heavy an emphasis on temple marriage as the only acceptable path might interfere with members' marrying at all in some areas. In a Utah setting, it was easy to dismiss Janet's passing thought that a boyfriend might convert as wishful thinking, but that same situation would feel different for a global audience. "There is a question in our minds whether it is best for them to go through life unmarried rather than marry outside of the Church as we feel there are many good men in the world that they could marry with the possibility that they may bring them into the Church later," McKay noted.[134] His objection revealed that the combination of church growth with changing use of communications technologies was creating more complex conditions for messaging. In the long term, old systems for coordinating messaging would need to adapt to those emerging dynamics.

REACHING OUT TO YOUTH AROUND THE WORLD

Church leaders began looking for additional ways to help leaders connect with youth around the world. Perhaps the most ambitious media effort of the era was launched in 1960, when general authorities mounted a massive three-month program of weekly firesides to reach as many MIA-age Latter-day Saints as possible in all 290 stakes of the church. A *fireside chat* or *fireside* was a special evening program that aimed to bring speakers and listeners together in a more conversational, intimate tone, similar to United States president Franklin D. Roosevelt's radio-broadcast fireside chats during the Depression and World War II.[135] Established at the local level as early as 1906 and popularized by the 1930s, firesides took on a new role in this 1960 initiative, giving young people opportunities to connect more personally with apostles and members of the First Presidency.[136] The opening event was a general meeting on Sunday, 3 January 1960, held at the Tabernacle on Temple Square in Salt Lake City. It was broadcast by closed-circuit wire to many stake buildings. Audiences farther away received a tape-recorded version. In each location, an hour-long program featuring talks and music by local young women and men, prepared under the direction of MIA leaders, preceded an address by David O. McKay on ideals of courtship and marriage. Conservative estimates placed the total audience for the fireside at two hundred thousand in 170 locations, as far away as New Zealand and Mexico.[137] Twenty radio stations in the western United States, Hawaii, and Canada also broadcast audio of McKay's remarks and the subsequent fireside series.[138] Over the next twelve weeks, youth met each Sunday evening in ward groups to listen by radio to another talk and then engage in a discussion, led by the bishop, about how the counsel applied to their own lives.[139] Speakers included Mark E. Petersen, Spencer W. Kimball, Howard W. Hunter, and Harold B. Lee, of the Quorum of the Twelve Apostles, and Marion D. Hanks, a popular speaker and member of the Quorum of the Seventy.[140] Their messages focused on dating, marriage, and chastity.

Top leaders like those who spoke in the fireside series began to develop a higher public profile. McKay was charismatic and popular, eminently photogenic and quotable. The Quorum of the Twelve Apostles, likewise, featured several vigorous leaders—like Petersen, Kimball, Lee, and Benson—whose strong personalities and prolific output of sermons and writings would shape church culture for the rest of the century. Church media outlets, especially the *Church News*, published as a section of the *Deseret News*, covered their activities assiduously, and church-owned Deseret Book published many of their writings.[141]

These leaders began speaking more directly and extensively to the youth. In past generations, apostles had overseen the YMMIA and had spoken at June Conference, but when it came to direct counsel, young people heard primarily from the leaders of their organizations rather than apostles. As a young girl in Melbourne in 1945, Margot Butler remembered feeling shaken when she heard about Heber J. Grant's death, because his was the only voice representing the whole church that she was accustomed to hearing, and with his death she thought the church was left without such leadership.[142] Now, through such channels as the churchwide fireside program and BYU devotionals, youth heard regularly from apostles and other priesthood leaders, and MIA leaders served a supporting role. Even at June Conference, general authorities took precedence as the featured speakers at many sessions.

As general authorities' voices gained greater prominence in MIA events, their words also became more prominent in publications by or about the MIA. In 1957, for example, the *Church News* coverage of June Conference included excerpts or full-text addresses by seven members of the First Presidency and Quorum of the Twelve

Apostles, and the *Improvement Era* published three of the addresses in full. YWMIA president Bertha Reeder, on the other hand, appeared only in three photographs in the *News*; her words were not reported.[143] By the end of the 1950s, YWMIA leaders were rarely published or featured in church publications, even in relation to their own organization. This broader change in church conventions that allowed youth to hear and read the words of the church's general authorities more often had unintentionally limited the opportunities church members had to hear from female leaders.[144]

In 1960, the *Church News* published a glowing retrospective on the previous ten years. The first decade of David O. McKay's tenure as church president had witnessed the most growth and development of any decade in the church's history, writers exulted. "The Church also stands today on the threshold of a glorious new decade—likely to reach startling proportions in growth and expansion."[145] Rapid membership growth, coupled with praise from outside organizations and individuals, seemed to confirm the sense that something special was happening in the church in general and the MIA in particular. In 1950, the *Deseret News* celebrated when YWMIA enrollment surpassed one hundred thousand for the first time.[146] By the decade's end, the YWMIA had doubled in size to over two hundred thousand participants.[147] And yet, growth also meant that questions arising from geographic and cultural diversity—which had been on leaders' minds for thirty years without being fully addressed—would continue to rise in prominence. As the 1960s began, leaders grappled with the question of whether the same model that had brought the YWMIA increased acceptance and prominence within the United States could continue to carry the organization into the future.

A PROGRAM OF DEFENSE

1961–1972

On the morning of Friday, 29 September 1961, Florence Smith Jacobsen's phone rang. She was busy preparing Thanksgiving dinner, though the holiday was two months away—her sons Stephen and Alan had been called up from the Utah National Guard for active military service in response to the developing Berlin Wall crisis. Stephen had been married for only two weeks, and Alan was days shy of his nineteenth birthday. Though it was the weekend of general conference and she served on the Young Women's Mutual Improvement Association general board, Jacobsen had asked YWMIA president Bertha Reeder for permission to miss Friday's meetings because she wanted her family together for an early holiday dinner the night before Stephen and Alan left.[1]

Jacobsen had already stuffed the turkey when she answered the phone. The secretary to the First Presidency was on the line and asked her to come in that same day. She agreed to an appointment at church headquarters at four thirty in the afternoon, thinking her mother could put the potatoes on to boil at five, and she would be home to finish them at five thirty. She hadn't thought to ask with whom she would be meeting and was surprised when she arrived and was ushered to the office of church president David O. McKay. McKay invited her to sit behind his desk while he sat off to the side and asked her to be the next general president of the YWMIA. When she accepted the assignment, he gave her his card and asked her to call him by seven o'clock the next morning with the names of two counselors.[2]

Jacobsen felt preoccupied when she returned home to finish the potatoes. She knew something of the huge responsibility she was taking on—she had served on the YWMIA general board since 1959, when she returned from leading the Eastern States Mission with her husband. When she was asked to join the general board, she told apostle Harold B. Lee that her initial response had been to say "anything but the MIA."[3] Running the YWMIA could be overwhelming—the organization managed its own budget, curriculum, and publishing program, and it was also both a cultural hub in Latter-day Saint majority areas and a critical tool for building a good reputation for the church in areas with fewer members.

Nurturing the spirituality of young people continued to be of urgent concern in the 1960s, as American culture was undergoing change that seemed little short of revolutionary. The children of the baby boom were entering their teen and high school years surrounded by the largest cohort of peers the United States had ever produced. They would attend college in increasing numbers, cementing university campuses as a center for youth culture, and begin to question the values their parents held.[4] "The order is rapidly fadin'," Bob Dylan sang in 1963, warning parents, "Your sons and your daughters / are beyond your command."

When Jacobsen took up the call to nurture the faith's next generation, change was also coming within the structure of the church. Postwar growth raised questions about how to manage the complex array of programs that had grown organically during the first half of the twentieth century. In the same general conference where those assembled raised their hands to sustain Jacobsen, Margaret Romney Jackson, and Dorothy Porter Holt as the new YWMIA general presidency, apostle Harold B. Lee made a major announcement.[5] The First Presidency felt it was time, he said, that "there should be established an all-Church co-ordinating council and three co-ordinating committees: one for the children, one for the youth, and one for the adults. This council and the three committees will correlate and co-ordinate the total instructional and activity programs of all auxiliaries and priesthood quorums." The new All-Church Coordinating Council, which he chaired, would formulate policy to guide development, coordination, and implementation of curriculum throughout the church. He stated that the three committees' work would be to "plan, provide, write, and co-ordinate curricula and activities."[6] Lee cited the church's growth as a driver of this change but also expressed concern about the church's capacity to respond to alarming changes in the larger culture. "We are in a program of defense," he warned. "The forces of our opposition to the forces of evil must be consolidated in order to give them the most effective possible defense."[7] As the 1960s began, the imperatives to protect youth and prepare them for spiritual conflict quickly rose to prominence.

SERVING ON THE GENERAL BOARD

Shortly after being sustained, Jacobsen and her counselors met with the First Presidency to discuss priorities. As they had in the past, the First Presidency counseled the YWMIA leaders to "guide the destinies of the girls of the church, using gospel principles." In keeping with the long tradition of spiritualized recreation—teaching the gospel through activities—Jacobsen understood that a primary mission of the YWMIA was to help young women build faith and testimony through participation in meaningful activities. During this meeting, Jacobsen and her counselors also asked about changing the size of the YWMIA general board. The First Presidency said they saw no reason for change but deferred to Jacobsen's judgment. Thinking of the many conferences, conventions, and committees run by the YWMIA, Jacobsen determined more board members were required.[8] While Lee's address on a new correlation effort suggested organizational change was on the horizon, Jacobsen's tenure began with the old system virtually intact.

Still, Jacobsen and her counselors were mindful of the growth of the church and changing needs of youth. In considering members for a board, they sought to avoid insularity. "We did not want it to be a little local group," Jacobsen said. Women from California and Idaho joined the board, despite the challenges of semiregular travel to Salt Lake City.[9] Jacobsen also sought out women with a range of life experiences—the board included married, single, and widowed women; professionals and homemakers; and women who were financially affluent as well as those of modest means. All had extensive church service experience, though not necessarily in the YWMIA.[10]

Among those asked to join the general board was Chieko N. Okazaki. The daughter of Japanese American parents, Okazaki had grown up as a Buddhist before joining the church in Hawaii at age fifteen. She and her husband lived in Salt Lake City, where she worked as an elementary school teacher. Many church and community leaders lived in Okazaki's neighborhood, and she had won parents' trust despite widespread postwar prejudice in the United States against Japanese Americans.[11] When apostle Ezra Taft Benson interviewed her for the assignment, he noted that she was the first "non-white" person to serve in that position or any similar position in church hierarchy.[12] Okazaki also appears to have been the first person from a non-Christian background to serve in general church leadership. Before 1960, only white Americans and Europeans had served at the highest levels of church leadership—as apostles, in the Presidency of the Seventy, in general presidencies of the auxiliaries, or on general boards. Okazaki's appointment preceded even the appointment of the first nonwhite mission and stake presidents.[13]

At the outset of Jacobsen's presidency, board members served on a wide range of committees, focused on different age groups or activity programs.[14] For instance, Okazaki was assigned to the committee that focused on the class for young women ages sixteen to eighteen.[15] The decisions of this committee substantially influenced the church experience for young women in this age group. In 1958, for example, the committee had considered how to redefine the identity of the Junior Gleaner group. They wanted the class to feel more like the capstone to a life stage. Committee member Sara Yates presented a plan to make the thirteenth article of faith, with its emphasis on virtuous conduct and the pursuit of goodness, the focus for the group.[16] The class symbol would be the pearl, symbolizing purity, and the course of study would be titled "We Believe," in reference to the Articles of Faith. The first new name proposed for the group was *Zionas*.[17] Ultimately, however, a laurel leaf was added alongside the pearl as a class symbol, and the name *Laurel* was introduced instead. A statement in the new manual with the heading "What It Means to Be a Laurel" emphasized developing integrity and building a foundation of knowledge, good judgment, and connection to the divine.[18] Just as there was a committee to oversee the Laurel program, there were also committees of general board members assigned to the Beehive, Mia Maid, and Gleaner programs.

Florence Jacobsen retained past camp committee members on the new board and gave them permission to introduce a certification program—which Bertha Reeder had been reluctant to adopt—to reinforce a sense of achievement for young women.[19] Bette Lou Sims, who cochaired the committee, recalled taking groups of people to a park up Emigration Canyon, in the foothills of the Wasatch Mountains east of Salt Lake City, to observe them as they practiced different skills the committee was considering teaching to young women.[20] The new certification program, called Campcrafter, focused on outdoor skills, such as first aid, fire making, and knot tying, while also aiming to help young women develop transferrable leadership skills. Jacobsen saw camp as an ideal setting for experiential learning—she felt that if there were flaws in the planning, natural consequences would quickly make them plain.[21] The first certification booklet, published for summer 1963, proclaimed another objective on its cover: "Be Aware of—Not Beware of Nature!"[22] The manual promised that young women could banish fear through expertise, live confidently in the outdoors, appreciate nature, and grow as leaders. Instructions recommended that young women with more camp experience help younger girls complete their assignments.[23]

Other committees managed areas of recreation such as dance, music, and drama. These committees produced publications and trainings, and they prepared activities for the annual June Conference. The work was demanding. Members of the committees served as organizers and producers of elaborate events, and they were serving in a huge, vibrant organization. Enrollment of young women reached 272,370 in 1963, the year in which total church membership surpassed two million.[24] Growth was steady and impressive: young women's enrollment increased by almost one hundred thousand before the decade was out.[25]

For many of the young women who spent weeks in rehearsal, performances became treasured memories. Vicki Noyce, a young woman in the Valley View Stake in Holladay, Utah, remembered rehearsing on the University of Utah football field in sweltering heat for her stake's June Conference dance number, sweating in a costume made by a stake member. "I just remember standing on the field thinking 'Please be done,'" she said. The actual performance, however, culminated for her in a transcendent moment. "At the very end, we sang 'Shall the Youth of Zion Falter?' I'm telling you, we were all in tears," she said. "To be with so many that were in the same mindset and situation as you were. It made you feel like there's a bigger entity out there than even our ward."[26]

BUILDING A VISION FOR CORRELATION

Just before June Conference in 1962, Ruth Funk of the music committee found herself "up to my eyebrows" in coproducing a major musical production, *Papa and the Playhouse*, which was to be rolled out at the conference as a model for churchwide production in local units during the following year. Even by the high standards set in the massive festivals she had worked on since 1947, *Papa and the Playhouse* was ambitious. For the month preceding the conference, Funk practically lived at the huge warehouse where the production was being prepared. When she received a call asking her to attend an unrelated church meeting on a weeknight during this hectic period, it was only with difficulty that she made room in her schedule.

The meeting was an exploratory session, one of three similar gatherings held to gauge the thinking of potential participants in the nascent correlation effort announced by Harold B. Lee in 1961. Funk was distracted and anxious to get back to her work, but near the end of the meeting, the man conducting called on her, saying, "Sister Funk, you haven't expressed yourself." Summarizing her thoughts on the discussion, she said, "I feel that every stop should be pulled to emphasize the strength of the family, to bring our youth back into the cradle of the family as far as possible, to make the father the patriarchal head of the family in every way and put the priesthood where it belongs." She then went back to work on the play. The Monday after June Conference, once her work on the production had ended, Funk received a phone call from apostle Marion G. Romney, who asked her to serve on the Adult Correlation Committee.[27] "Little did I know," she later recalled, "how dramatically this telephone call would change my life."[28]

The original mandate of the All-Church Coordinating Council, issued by the First Presidency in 1960, was to facilitate "a correlation of studies among the Auxiliaries of the Church"—that is, a correlation of the curriculum of each organization, which was how previous correlation efforts had been framed.[29] But Lee brought a much broader vision to his leadership of the council. As the auxiliaries had expanded their vibrant programs in the first half of the twentieth century, they had become largely autonomous entities with independent budgets, curricula, publications, and reporting lines. Overlap, redundancy, and cost had become serious problems, as had the propensity of some auxiliary leaders to advance the missions of their individual organizations rather than pursue a unified direction for the whole church. Lee wanted to use both the council and the new correlation committees for adults, youth, and children—each of which was headed by a member of the Quorum of the Twelve Apostles—to bring a centralizing force into church administration.[30]

In the 1960s and 1970s, the church came to use the term *correlation* for three linked concepts. First, correlation was an ideal—one in which interdependent parts of the church worked together. Critical to this vision was the idea that all church efforts would be overseen at the highest level by ordained priesthood leaders. In service of that ideal, correlation was also a process by which separate organizations working on different problems coordinated to make sure they were contributing effectively to a larger shared vision. Finally, the process of correlation involved oversight committees, which sought to ensure that activities and curricula were aligned across organizations. Thus, the word *correlation* could describe the ideal, the process, or the committees.[31]

A few days after the exploratory meeting, Funk attended an orientation meeting conducted by Harold B. Lee for members of the new correlation committees. Seated amid apostles, stake presidents, former mission presidents, directors of church departments, professors from BYU, and auxiliary general board members, she quickly realized it was no ordinary meeting. In a manner that Funk felt was visionary, Lee described the decadent conditions of the world, the church's destiny to spread Christ's teachings, the growth missionary work would bring, and the need for a strong foundation based on family and home. He spoke of the priesthood in a way Funk "had never heard nor understood before," calling it an all-encompassing force that would guide the affairs of humankind and power the expansion of the church. Lee outlined the necessity for correlation of the church's curriculum and explained the roles of the committees. He then pronounced a blessing upon those present, praying that they would have the capacity to serve God in the work of correlation. "As he spoke, a luminous radiance seemed to emanate from his countenance," Funk recalled. "I had never had such an experience before, and I've never had one since. I knew this was no ordinary man who had been called by the Lord to correlate and orchestrate all the elements of the gospel." From this moment, Funk felt that the term *correlation* took on a sense of "tremendous sacredness and worth."[32]

Like Funk, many women who served on the early correlation committees quickly developed a deep appreciation for the effort and a broad vision of its goals. As correlation efforts advanced, each committee member was released from all other church assignments. The committees operated independently of any other church entity. They acted as a "think tank" organization to thoroughly evaluate every aspect of the church and make recommendations for greater consistency and cooperation among the various quorums and auxiliaries.[33] "It was exciting," recalled Hortense Hogan Child, who, like Funk, had been released from the YWMIA board to serve on the Adult Correlation Committee, "because we were discussing the heartbeat of this Church and the things that would affect its future organization and administration."[34] No topic was off limits, and participants were free to evaluate and critique. Elaine Cannon, who served briefly on the Youth Correlation Committee, considered it a "catalyst situation" that laid the groundwork for future developments, and Ardeth Greene Kapp, who served on the same committee later in the 1960s, felt that the experience helped the participants see the church as a whole organization, rather than focusing on a single part.[35]

Women may have been particularly impressed by their service in correlation because they felt that they were full partners on the committees. In Funk's experience, the Adult Correlation Committee was an open forum where all participants strove to listen with objectivity and without judgment or argumentation.[36] Wendell Ashton, who served with Hortense Child on the adult committee, characterized it as a "great partnership," where women had "equal voice and equal authority."[37] Child concurred, describing "a total committee of men and women who sat around the table and discussed things of a universal nature." Women did not hold leadership positions on the correlation committees, but they apparently felt like full and equal participants. Both Child and Funk were sure Lee had a vision for empowering the women of the church.[38]

While Lee's announcement of the All-Church Coordinating Council and the correlation committees was not the first attempt to streamline church administration, participants felt they had a new vision, and Lee's organizational experience and sense of divine direction energized the effort. Church president David O. McKay, who had been involved in virtually every previous correlation effort, generally supported Lee's vision.[39] Latter-day Saint leaders felt a growing divergence between their values and those of their contemporaries in wider society, and that sense of difference gave urgency to Lee's efforts. His call for a program of defense against the forces of iniquity positioned correlation as a spiritual and theological imperative.[40] Even as it simplified and streamlined programs under priesthood leadership, the correlation movement signified a more defensive posture by Latter-day Saint leaders and a departure from the optimism of decades when they felt more at home in the larger American society.[41]

FOR THE STRENGTH OF YOUTH

In the early 1960s, many Latter-day Saint leaders already shared Lee's sense of the need for a program of defense against emerging dangers. Concerns about sexual standards and modesty in dress continued to proliferate, and leaders worried not just about premarital sex among young people but also about the flouting of societal norms and the general atmosphere of sexual permissiveness. Even before the late-1960s hippie aesthetic emerged, the more formal clothing styles of the 1950s were giving way to the increasingly casual "mod" style of simple miniskirts and shift dresses. Pantsuits and culottes (divided skirts) came into style for women, and slacks were increasingly accepted for everyday women's wear.[42] The Twist dance craze in 1960 paved the way for other partnerless dance styles like the Watusi, which were often considered sexually suggestive.[43] At the same time, a series of court cases involving issues of free speech and obscenity expanded the range of sexual media available in the United States.[44] During the mid-1960s, discussion of sexual behavior became more open, with such dramatic effect that the term *sexual revolution* rose to prominence in American popular media.[45] For Latter-day Saints, who preached abstinence before marriage and fidelity within marriage, combating changing sexual mores was viewed as a fight against evil.[46]

MIA publications advocated a positive, rather than reactive, focus. "Let us teach and promote positive thinking and living, positive seeking, positive choosing," YMMIA leader Marvin J. Ashton urged in 1962.[47] As Latter-day Saints applied this counsel in family discussions and at church events, however, questions about concrete boundaries invariably surfaced. In 1962, church leaders added to the broad counsel to avoid early dating the specific guideline not to date before age sixteen.[48] In 1963, general authorities asked MIA leaders to establish standards for dress, music, dancing, and dating. In response, the MIA general boards consulted about developing trends with, among others, religious educators who worked with young people in high school and college. Initially, the boards resisted taking specific stances, opting instead for a continued emphasis on Latter-day Saint principles and a strong MIA program.[49] "We cannot set hard and fast rules in every little detail such as—how long? How close? How dark? How loud? How wide?" they wrote in the May 1964 *MIA Leader.* "We ask you as MIA leaders to maintain standards of modesty, culture, and refinement in dancing, music, dress, entertainment, and actions."

If the youth were taught correct principles, leaders believed, they would make good choices on their own.[50]

Nevertheless, calls to delineate clear church standards in appearance and behavior only grew. A month after the *MIA Leader* declined to lay out detailed guidelines, apostle Delbert L. Stapley remarked at June Conference that "it seems in the church-prepared lessons the subject of chastity has been somewhat neglected." He warned that the old ways of teaching chastity seemed insufficient: "There has developed among many young people a feeling that it is not too serious to break the law of chastity. . . . Perhaps we need a new personal vision, a new approach, a field of teaching with a positive application for the values and the joys of a clean, moral, and upright life."[51] Spencer W. Kimball, also serving in the Quorum of the Twelve Apostles, believed that general leaders needed to step in. "The time has come when MIA officers and teachers and others should unitedly rise as a single voice to assist parents and youth in changing the pattern of social life among the youth in our communities," he urged in 1965.[52]

That same year, the MIA issued a new booklet: *For the Strength of Youth.* The booklet was created by members from the MIA general boards, a selection of young people, and representatives of the church's educational system (including BYU) and then reviewed by the Youth Correlation Committee.[53] Intended for both young women and young men, the booklet was billed as "an authoritative code of conduct so that all may know what is of Church standard in the way of conduct, speech, dress, etc."[54]

For the Strength of Youth was the first MIA publication on chastity to address youth directly, rather than speaking to their leaders.[55] Leaders still hesitated to discuss sexual matters openly in *For the Strength of Youth*, for fear they would introduce ideas some youth had not yet considered. At the same time, the Youth Correlation Committee expressed concern that if they did not include specific prohibitions, young people might take omission as permission.[56] In the end, the booklet focused more on gateway behaviors that could lead to premarital sex. It included the standard of not dating before age sixteen and encouraged young people to go on group dates before pairing off. Beyond warnings against necking and petting, little was said about sexual behaviors directly.[57]

The booklet placed special emphasis on restraint in dance and dress. *For the Strength of Youth* discouraged the types of movements that had driven recent dance crazes. "The dance should not be a grotesque contortion of the body such as shoulder or hip shaking or excessive body jerking," the booklet said.[58] Florence Jacobsen, who served on the committee that prepared the booklet, reported that they wanted to raise standards of conduct by raising dress standards.[59] Despite an opening disclaimer

For the
STRENGTH
of YOUTH...

Cover illustration, *For the Strength of Youth* **booklet.** 1965. This first edition of *For the Strength of Youth* was divided into sections addressing manners, dating, dancing, dress, and clean living and encouraged all members of the church to be familiar with the standards it advocated. The introduction to the booklet emphasized the importance of remaining different from the world by living according to the high moral standards by which Latter-day Saints were known. (Church History Library, Salt Lake City.)

that modesty could not be defined by inches or fit, the instructions were detailed. Young men were not to wear tight pants and, even when working in the yard, were expected to wear trousers and shirts. Guidance for young women was far more extensive: Shorts were to be worn exclusively for participation in athletic activities. Young women might don slacks or shorts with hems that were not too far above the knee for hiking, sports, and yard work but not for shopping, attending school, going to the library, or dining out. Tight-fitting or "figure-hugging" clothing was never appropriate for a Latter-day Saint young woman, nor were dresses that were backless, strapless, or held up by spaghetti straps. Housedresses were to be worn only at home.[60] *For the Strength of Youth* instructed women to look feminine: "They should not dress like boys or try to give a masculine appearance," it said.[61]

The booklet did not settle all questions, and after its release MIA leaders continued to wrestle over how to offer practicable guidance without seeming too prescriptive or creating unnecessary conflict with youth over clothing choices. In November 1965, after receiving continued queries regarding sleeveless dresses, leotards, and tights, the booklet's writers explained that they had purposefully omitted a pronouncement on sleeveless dresses, adding that blouses and dresses were not immodest so long as shoulders and underarms were covered. "In other words, while we *permit*, we do not *promote* the wearing of sleeveless clothing," they said. Leaders' thinking on sleeveless clothing had evolved quickly—just nine years earlier, the main character in the YWMIA-produced film *How Near to the Angels* wore a sleeveless dress in a climactic scene—but after November 1965, leaders asked that youth wear shirts with sleeves in performances before the public, such as road shows and dance festivals.[62]

Leaders had come to take pride in Latter-day Saint youth—they were the public face of the church as it attained broader acceptance and even acclaim in American society. Leaders wanted youth to belong as Americans in a way that marginalized early Latter-day Saints never had, but the standards they advocated would set Latter-day Saint youth apart from their counterparts outside the church. Leaders believed the standards in *For the Strength of Youth* could help counteract alarming cultural trends—including counterculture, drug culture, and radical student movements—and anticipated that the wholesomeness of their youth would advance the Latter-day Saints' public image. As the booklet explained, "Personal cleanliness of body and cleanliness of one's clothing builds morale and a good name."[63] The final paragraph was even more direct: "The world judges the whole Church by the actions of its youth. . . . They must live up to their responsibilities as members of The Church of Jesus Christ of Latter-day Saints by being kind, clean, thoughtful, refined, dignified, and obedient."[64]

AN EXPANDING GLOBAL PRESENCE

The church experienced rapid growth outside the United States in the 1960s, allowing more people than ever before to judge the church by the actions of its youth. Membership numbers rose in long-established missions in Protestant-majority countries in the Pacific and Western Europe. The church's missionary efforts also expanded in Catholic-majority countries in Latin America and around the world, as well as in some East Asian countries, where Christians were a minority.[65] In all these places, the positive relationships fostered by the MIA attracted new members and gave them a sense of belonging in the church.

When the first full-time missionaries arrived in the Philippines in 1961, the MIA operated under the system outlined in the newly published *Mission MIA Manual*—which gave a comprehensive overview of the elaborate program and guidance for adapting it to different circumstances—and helped make crucial inroads with local communities. "I wasn't a member yet when I first attended the Mutual Improvement Association," recalled Nenita Reyes, who became one of the first people baptized by those early missionaries.[66] In keeping with the MIA counsel to promote local leadership, Nenita was quickly assigned to lead the music at MIA activities. At first, she felt so shy she would hide behind the hymnbook, but she gradually became more comfortable. A young man named Ruben Gapiz attended an MIA caroling activity because he played guitar and thought he might get paid. He soon learned that MIA activities were purely volunteer but decided that being around a singing leader like Nenita was compensation enough. Ruben accepted an assignment as MIA dance director even before his baptism in 1962. He and Nenita became the first Latter-day Saint couple married in the Philippines. Both fondly remembered the sense of community in the MIA. "Everybody in our branch joined us in the MIA," Nenita said, noting that even parents came. "It was beautiful."[67]

Elaine Lewis Jorgensen, an American Latter-day Saint living in Italy, oversaw the YWMIA in the Italian Mission, and just three years after the mission was organized, Jorgensen wrote to Florence Jacobsen to report that every branch in the mission had already organized an MIA group. Jorgensen noted some difficulties in implementation: Many activities outlined in the MIA handbook used in Italy at that time, she wrote, held no cultural relevance for Italian youth.[68] Travel between branches was also an obstacle for her, but she had created a checklist for local leaders and missionaries to fill out and send to her, which helped her monitor progress across the mission. The YWMIA leadership in the mission facilitated travel for members, which connected young Italians from different regions and helped foster a shared sense of Latter-day Saint identity. Despite the challenges of introducing an organization to a new place, there were signs of success. The MIA age group boasted the largest number of church members in Italy, and MIA programs were bringing in friends, parents, and relatives of those who participated.[69]

MIA groups in the church's missions also helped train future leaders in the faith. In 1964, church members Cornelia van Mondfrans and Willy Beekhuizen undertook a last-minute voyage from the Netherlands to the United Kingdom when the mission president invited them to attend a youth leadership conference taking place in Wales. Van Mondfrans was serving as YWMIA president of the Dutch Mission, and Beekhuizen was serving as a young missionary. With less than a day's notice, they made arrangements and set off. At the weeklong conference, the two women participated in trainings on various aspects of the MIA program, including road shows, elocution, and music contests. Afterward, Van Mondfrans and Beekhuizen traveled through the Dutch Mission to train other local leaders. They also planned and conducted a summer camp in 1965 outside the Dutch city of Assen, expressly to mentor future church leaders, both young women and young men.[70] Beekhuizen worked with her future husband there, and after marrying, they continued together to lead camps and train youth and leaders on how to carry out church camping and youth conference events.[71]

Throughout the world, the MIA offered young people an identity and a culture that were distinct from those of their peers. Linda McCahon, a Black Latter-day Saint, remembered that while late 1960s youth culture in her hometown of Birmingham, England, was focused on individuality, it also fueled subcultures based on recognizable shared styles. Taste in clothing and music could identify a person as a mod, a rocker, or a hippie. Youth identity often involved following one's own tastes into the loose fellowship of an established cultural category.[72] Linda herself felt drawn to the community of the YWMIA after meeting Latter-day Saint missionaries in 1966. The first time she attended church, she was aware of how her large Afro, short-sleeved shirt, denim skirt, and flip-flops contrasted with the prevailing Sunday styles in the meetinghouse. She thought she probably struck others as a hippie. "I looked so different," she said. Instead of judgment, however, the members showed curiosity and interest. As Linda attended activities, she quickly found herself fully accepted into the group. "We gelled very, very well," she said. Peers in her MIA group came from different economic backgrounds and different family situations. Some were from Latter-day Saint families, some were the only Latter-day Saints in their families, and some were not members of the church at all. Spending time together, though, gave them a powerful feeling of unity. Linda remembered the young women her age wandering off to sing hymns together, enjoying the feeling of harmonizing.[73]

Among all the other youth subcultures represented in her school, Linda and her friends felt they came across as oddballs for being so enthusiastic about their church activities. At the same time, they noticed that their peers at school were often surprised by how much they did with the MIA. Their travel across Britain for MIA conferences and activities was a particular point of difference. "Our school colleagues were so envious," she said. "Half of them had not been out of Birmingham."

The local leaders and ward members who arranged the trips and invested in the youth played an important role in Linda's life. Her friend Yvonne Bogle's parents often welcomed the whole group into their home. Linda also looked up to her YWMIA leader Maureen Cuthbert. Linda recalled that if she was worried about something, "My first port of call would be Maureen." Cuthbert had a gift for listening without judgment and then sharing scriptures in a way that helped young women find their own answers. Linda treasured that kind of mentoring. "It doesn't just affect your Church life, it carries over into your professional life," she said. Years later, feeling the weight of her responsibility as a senior nurse managing other workers, she continued to imagine how her YWMIA leaders would react to the challenges she experienced. Linda also appreciated the supportive presence of male priesthood leaders. "We knew they cared for us," she said. One week, when Linda and most of her group decided to stop at a newly opened pub for lemonade instead of continuing to MIA, a YMMIA leader arrived to invite them to attend. Rather than feeling intruded upon, Linda felt noticed. For most of her life, her home situation had been difficult. "I needed the gospel in my life at that time. MIA kept me going," she said. "The church became my family."[74]

SHIFTING VIEWS ON AUTHORITY AND COMMUNITY

The sense of belonging Linda felt in her YWMIA experience was not unique. Many young women felt a strong sense of support from their religious community in the organization. Such experiences left them with largely positive attitudes about authority in the church, even as growing numbers of young people became more vocal and even militant in challenging traditional authority in society. "It was like I had two lives," one young woman growing up in California in the late 1960s said. Her church life was highly structured and involved meeting expectations set by adults: "I did the whole Campcrafter thing, got all the awards, and graduated from seminary." In the other part of her life, among her peer group, such traditional structures were viewed with suspicion. "I also was around all these self-styled radicals and Marxists in high school," she said.[75]

As students at the University of Utah in 1968, Carol Clark, Maurine Jensen, and Mary Frances Watson were mostly surrounded by fellow Latter-day Saints and felt somewhat insulated from the international upheaval on college campuses. They were curious, however, about the counterculture. "I wanted to know what other people were so passionate about," Maurine recalled.[76] While serving in student leadership at the University of Utah, they helped approve a series of speakers that included civil rights activist Julian Bond, counterculture poet Allen Ginsberg, and pop artist Andy Warhol, as well as a debate between LSD advocate Timothy Leary and drug researcher Sidney Cohen.[77] Though Utah did not see the same turbulence as campuses in Western Europe and across much of the United States, the same issues captured people's attention. "I also felt like the world was unraveling," Maurine said, but she saw that maybe some aspects of that world did need to change.[78]

The questions about race, war, authority, drugs, sex, and consciousness that were fueling the broader youth counterculture in the 1960s, however, were not generally discussed in church settings. "It was like two communities that in some ways didn't interface all that much," Maurine recalled. Carol felt resistance in one church class when she tried to open a discussion: "I remember asking some questions that were kind of things that were buzzing around campus . . . the teacher just blew me off. It's like, why would you even ask questions like that?"[79]

At times, though, these young women's experiences crossed between those parallel worlds in jarring ways. Maurine's best friend, who had gone through YWMIA with her, became interested in the Vietnam War and began attending antiwar rallies. She became more involved in activism and then surprised Maurine by dropping out of church and other activities they had shared. "She didn't want any more of that structure in any way, shape, or form," Maurine recalled. The women tried to maintain a relationship, but it proved difficult. At the friend's apartment-warming party, the guests sat in a circle and passed around marijuana. Maurine wouldn't take any, and her friend berated her for clinging to the values they'd been taught. "I felt that campus culture at that time in a very real and personal way, because my friend, my sister, my alter ego defected to another way of thinking."[80]

Even for devout church members, attitudes about structure were in flux. Carol was not at all interested in pursuing the Golden Gleaner award or participating in the Gleaner program, designed for young women over eighteen. "None of that was relevant to me. . . . I was very keen, at that point, on exploring more who I was," she said. "I certainly wanted to learn more about the gospel, but that was a very personal thing for me. It wasn't throwing me in another program."[81] Her experience was increasingly typical. The Gleaner program also failed to engage Maurine and Mary Frances. Another young woman, Jan Christiansen, felt that her mother was more invested in young women activities than she was. During high school, Jan had come to feel that she was more a consumer of YWMIA activities rather than an active participant. By the time she was a Laurel, she gravitated toward school clubs where she could take a more proactive role.[82]

In college, each of the four felt more attracted to church organizations where they could have some influence and autonomy. Both Mary Frances and Jan were called into ward YWMIA leadership as teachers for younger classes. Mary Frances, Maurine, and Carol also had positive experiences with the Latter-day Saint Student Association (LDSSA) at the University of Utah, which was launched in 1960 to involve student leaders in fostering Latter-day Saint life on campus through firesides and social events. LDSSA—which was not connected to the MIA—was provided with a budget to cover activities. Student leaders also had open lines of communication with general church leadership.[83] The year Mary Frances chaired the LDSSA Women's Council, the group invited Harold B. Lee to speak. Not only did he accept the speaking invitation, she recalled, but he invited the committee to meet with him in his home to discuss what they wanted him to speak about.[84]

The young women's eagerness to contribute to their church experience corresponded with shifts in the way they saw themselves and their communities. "Being on the campus at the University of Utah in 1968 enlarged my thinking," Mary Frances said. "I was happy with societal traditions and wasn't looking to make changes in the world. However, the changes I saw and the discussions I heard made me realize that I needed to change."[85] She wanted particularly to understand better the experiences of African Americans. The same broadcast media that had brought the dance festivals from June Conference into families' living rooms had also brought searing images of protest and police brutality from the American civil rights movement into homes across the country. "Our world was a white world," Jan Christiansen recalled, but the assassination of Martin Luther King Jr. shook her.[86] Carol Clark didn't know anyone who was Black until after she finished college, and her initial feeling was that the civil rights movement was something happening in the seemingly distant American South. Racial issues became more real for Maurine, however, when she attended a national convention for her sorority and discovered that membership was restricted to white women. Coming from such a heavily white community and school, it had not occurred to her how much racism might be shaping the world around her. On her return, she and her friends began discussing ways their local chapter could lodge complaints about the sorority's national policy.[87]

Postwar patterns of migration also played a role in bringing racial issues into more white Latter-day Saints' lives in the United States. A survey of articles in the *Improvement Era* near the end of the decade offers a few glimpses into the growing individual social connections between white Latter-day Saint women and Black communities: A brief sketch of Gloria Wheeler, a YWMIA officer in Michigan, mentioned that she led a predominantly Black Girl Scout troop.[88] A letter to the editor from another woman, Lucy Caley, noted how she used articles in the *Improvement Era* to answer questions from her students at an all-Black school in Antigua.[89] An article by G. Homer Durham, a Latter-day Saint university president in Arizona, invoked the growing diaspora of educated young Latter-day Saints in multiracial cities to argue that readers had a spiritual stake in addressing the racial inequalities, both social and economic, that young families would encounter. "They cannot stand apart from the issue," he wrote.[90] Though nineteenth-century Latter-day Saints had gathered to Utah precisely to stand apart from the larger society, the combined forces of church growth, migration, and shifting youth culture were making it harder to avoid engaging with broader social issues and trends.

The issue of race affected young women outside the United States as well. As a biracial Latter-day Saint in England—her father, an immigrant from Sierra Leone, was Black—Linda McCahon was personally affected by racial policies and attitudes in the church. Between 1852 and 1978, the church did not ordain Black men to the priesthood or offer the temple ordinances of endowment and marriage sealing to Black women and men of African descent.[91] So although Linda embraced the Latter-day Saint ideal, prominently championed by the YWMIA, of longing for a temple marriage and an eternal family, she was told she would not be allowed to marry in the temple. As a young woman, Linda regularly participated in temple trips to perform proxy baptisms for the dead, but that was the limit of her temple access.

The Latter-day Saint missionaries who taught Linda had told her about the restrictions before her baptism. They were not the only voice on the issue: a classmate sharply questioned Linda's decision to affiliate with a church that the classmate labeled as racist. But as Linda navigated the issue, she was anchored by a feeling of peace she attributed to divine reassurance that all would be well.[92] In her Treasures of Truth book, Linda recorded the feeling she had on the day of her baptism at age fifteen: "I sat on the front row all clothed in white and shaking with fright now the actual baptising was to take place." Nevertheless, she wrote, "As I stepped into the water all my body was at ease."[93] She felt a similar sense of peace and comfort when she received her patriarchal blessing at age eighteen. A patriarchal blessing, given to church members only once in a lifetime and usually when they are teens, gives counsel and promises future blessings. Linda's included a promise that her children would serve missions, which led Linda to conclude that the racial restriction would be lifted within a generation.[94]

BECOMING GOSPEL ACTIVISTS

On Friday, 27 June 1969, at six o'clock in the morning, a chorus of five hundred young women from sixty-two stakes in the Salt Lake Valley—the Centennial Girls' Chorus—lifted their voices to sing at the YWMIA Centennial Sunrise Service in the Tabernacle on Temple Square, performing pieces written specifically for the event. The sunrise performance was one of many special events held in conjunction with June Conference that year to commemorate the one hundredth anniversary of the founding of the young women's organization.[95] The previous evening, over six thousand attendees—including stake, general, and civic leaders—had danced beneath 124 miles of crepe paper that had been strung to create a decorative ceiling in the Salt Palace arena. Attendees could choose from six refreshment parlors and any of three dance floors, each with a live band.[96] On Friday and Saturday, over six thousand young dancers performed in the huge dance festival in front of thirty thousand spectators, and an all-girls dance depicted the theme "An Ideal Girl Is Feminine As Well As Modern."[97]

Connection to the past was a natural theme. Florence Jacobsen and her counselors were dressed in 1869 period costumes as they were presented for a sustaining vote in the afternoon joint executive session.[98] Young women in similar period costumes conducted tours of the Lion House for conference goers, showing off both the historic rooms where the organization had its beginnings and a five-layer cake Jacobsen had baked to share at the conference.[99] Together, the founding home and the cake suggested the spirit of familial closeness the organization still tried to foster. YWMIA board members had commissioned artwork and created publications to celebrate the centennial. Among the items on display were a centennial quilt block designed around the YWMIA symbols; oil paintings of all six YWMIA general presidents; a china plate, linen towel, and medallion, all decorated with an image of a young woman of 1869 side by side with a young woman of 1969; and *A Century of Sisterhood*, a one-hundred-page, lavishly illustrated softcover book recounting the history of the organization year by year.[100] In an article reflecting on the centennial, Jacobsen shared stories of the MIA's influence—stories of young people connecting with each other, adopting a greater vision for their own futures and those of their community, and working to bring their lives into harmony with their values.[101]

Two months later and over two thousand miles away, the iconic rock music festival known as Woodstock also drew young people searching for a sense of belonging in a larger movement, reaching for a greater vision for their future, and wanting to live in harmony with their values.[102] While the YWMIA centennial celebration and Woodstock addressed overlapping human longings, their organizing logics stood in

Centennial commemorative linen dish towel. 1969. The YWMIA commissioned several items to celebrate its centennial, including this dish towel. It features significant iconography: the Lion House, where the first young women's association was organized; the Salt Lake Temple; pioneer symbols of the sego lily and seagulls; and symbols representing the Beehive, Mia Maid, and Gleaner classes. The two young women in the center—one in pioneer clothing, one in modern dress—represent generational unity in the goals of the organization, which was also expressed in the motto for the celebration: "A Century of Sisterhood." (Courtesy Lisa Olsen Tait.)

sharp contrast to one another. Where the MIA celebration promised an orderly, choreographed experience, Woodstock focused on spontaneity to the point of logistical chaos. Both focused attention on dress, sexuality, and drug use, but from opposite points of view. In each area, the MIA championed restraint or abstention, while the counterculture celebrated freedom and experimentation. Though they championed opposing approaches, these two festivals in 1969 provided a vivid demonstration of the rising cultural trends among youth.

Latter-day Saint leaders, while largely critical of the excesses they saw in youth counterculture, did their best to understand youth and anticipate what the rising generation might best relate to. Young people's "great emphasis on genuineness," wrote Latter-day Saint religious educator Kenneth Godfrey, reflected "a genuine concern for that which is really real." Their resistance to authority and institutional mandates grew out of a respect for agency and a desire to be involved in decision-making processes.[103] Recognizing these trends, church leaders sought to engage young people on their own terms, inviting them to become "gospel activists" and channel their energies into strengthening the Latter-day Saint community and finding their identity within it.[104] "Great youth and outstanding leaders can work together within the framework of the restored gospel," Godfrey affirmed.[105]

This impulse was manifest in the establishment of class presidencies in the YWMIA and the creation of the bishop's youth council. Young women already served in leadership roles in their YWMIA classes, but officers and representatives were typically chosen by their peers.[106] The new class presidencies introduced in 1969 were appointed by the bishop instead of elected, in a direct parallel to young men's leadership in priesthood quorums and in keeping with the principles of correlation, which dictated that everything should be done by priesthood authority. The bishop was instructed to counsel with the adult YWMIA president of the ward about whom to appoint as president for each class. New class presidents were then to decide who should serve as their counselors and recommend them to the bishop so that he could issue a formal invitation to serve. Class presidencies were to serve for six or twelve months, at the bishop's discretion.[107]

Class presidents and their counselors were also asked to serve on the bishop's youth council, a new planning body in each ward. An article discussing the new council stated that "a recently conducted survey by the Presiding Bishopric showed that more than 75 percent of the youths questioned, wanted to be more involved in the planning of their own activities." Giving youth greater ownership and responsibility represented a significant departure from decades of MIA practice in which adult leaders, starting with the general boards, outlined, scripted, scheduled, and prescribed Mutual activities, often down to the last detail. The bishop's youth council was intended to enable young women and men to work directly with the bishop to plan activities according to their needs and interests. Leaders also hoped the council would improve communication and provide greater leadership training to youth. Altogether, the bishop's youth council included eighteen young people—three presidency members from each YWMIA class and Aaronic Priesthood quorum. Adult leaders of the youth were invited only when necessary and were "never to dominate the council members."[108]

To foster a culture of youth leadership, the YWMIA also held a leadership conference for Laurels in 1970. A committee of young women, headed by a young woman from a stake in Salt Lake City, was assigned to do the actual conference planning, while a general board committee played a supporting role. The general board committee trained the young women in communicating with others, writing agendas, and conducting meetings. The young women themselves then conducted meetings, organized subcommittees, collected information, and wrote memos. The committee requested that the president of each participating stake select five young women to send to the event. The young women, in turn, were to plan a local leadership conference in their own stakes for all young women ages twelve through seventeen.[109]

More than three thousand young women from the United States and Canada attended the August 1970 conference on the BYU campus.[110] In September, a message in the *MIA Leader* reminded stakes to look to the five young women from their stake who had attended the August Laurel conference for leadership. "Delegates to that conference have information on how to schedule and conduct the stake meetings," the notice said, reminding local adult leaders that their role was to assist and advise.[111] Together with the bishop's youth council, the leadership conference represented a significant attempt to reorient the YWMIA experience toward individual initiative and away from the centrally directed rhythms that had dominated the previous decades.

CORRELATION AND THE WAY FORWARD

Other organizational rhythms were also in flux. Church leaders working on correlation implemented a major overhaul of the church magazines in 1971. The *Relief Society Magazine, Children's Friend, Instructor,* and *Improvement Era* magazines—each published by auxiliary organizations—were all discontinued, to be replaced by three magazines that represented the correlation vision of teaching religious truths to church members in three life stages. The *Ensign* magazine would serve adults, the *New Era* would be for youth, and the *Friend* would be oriented toward children. Elaine Cannon, who had previously helped oversee the Era of Youth section of the *Improvement Era,* became the associate editor of the *New Era,* which offered inspirational and doctrinal content geared toward youth, as well as items of general interest.[112]

Rexburg Fifth Ward Honor Night. 1968. Even as the correlation movement initiated significant changes in the YWMIA, young women maintained time-honored traditions, such as this Beehive Honor Night in Rexburg, Idaho. The young women wore bandoliers—colloquially known as bandlos—personalized with their signature flower and achievement badges. Honor Nights began in the 1930s to celebrate individual achievement. (Church History Library, Salt Lake City.)

The first issue, published in January 1971, presented articles on pop music and an ambitious service project, as well as poetry by young people, crossword puzzles, questions and answers about religious topics, and even recipes. It also highlighted academic work being done by young Latter-day Saints, including studies on young Latter-day Saint women's attitudes toward fashion, factors in successful marriages, and the effect of athletic shoes on performance in basketball. Young men and women from various places were highlighted for their accomplishments.[113] This basic pattern defined the magazine for many years to come. However, the magazine did not always provide equal attention to young women and young men. By April, Cannon had already contacted Young Women general leaders over a concern that the magazine focused on young men more than young women. Leaders were to meet with Cannon and offer suggestions on topics and articles that would be interesting for young women.[114]

One of the most visible effects of Harold B. Lee's vision for correlation was the centralization of auxiliary budgets. Until 1970, each auxiliary, including the YWMIA, had independently raised and disbursed funds within its organizations. Despite the autonomy this fundraising enabled, it was both time consuming and onerous at all levels of the organization. In the latter half of the 1960s, correlation leaders considered ways to bring all church organizations under a central budget as part of their effort to decrease the overlap and burden of these fundraising efforts. Jacobsen felt strongly about keeping the YWMIA budget under YWMIA control. Despite her insistence that elaborate programming elements were necessary and that YWMIA leaders knew the needs of their organization best, all auxiliary money was turned over to a central budget in September 1970.[115] As part of this centralizing effort, the MIA also had to abandon plans to construct a headquarters building in Salt Lake City, and in 1971, the churchwide dance, theater, and sports programs were discontinued, though they continued on the regional level.[116]

Several months after Harold B. Lee became church president in July 1972, Jacobsen and her counselors were asked to come to his office. They had served in the YWMIA presidency for eleven eventful years, and Jacobsen had been telling her counselors she was worn out and ready for a change. During their tenure, they had overseen the highly detailed programs and massive events that had come to characterize the MIA and had helped the organization continue to adapt to international growth. They had helped advocate for newly articulated church standards on dating and modesty while searching for new ways to engage youth during a time of seismic cultural change. The years of work had taken a toll.

When they arrived at the First Presidency's office, they found that the YMMIA superintendent and his counselors were also there. "We've prayed a great deal about

AARONIC PRIESTHOOD—YOUTH STAKE

STAKE PRESIDENCY
HIGH COUNCILORS
AARONIC PRIESTHOOD—MIA

(MUTUAL IMPROVEMENT ASSOCIATION)

- YMMIA-YWMIA Presidencies
- Small Stake Boards For All Youth 12 to 18+

Deacon (Scout) Beehive	Teacher (Venturer) MiaMaid	Priest (Explorer) Laurel

WARD

BISHOPRIC
AARONIC PRIESTHOOD—MIA

(MUTUAL IMPROVEMENT ASSOCIATION)

- YMMIA-YWMIA Presidencies
- Leaders And Teachers Of All Youth 12 to 18+

Deacon (Scout) Beehive	Teacher (Venturer) MiaMaid	Priest (Explorer) Laurel

APMIA organization charts. 1972. These charts published in the 11 November 1972 issue of the *Church News* show the new APMIA organization at the stake and ward levels. They illustrate how the MIA was incorporated into and layered under priesthood lines of authority. (Church History Library, Salt Lake City.)

this," Jacobsen remembered members of the First Presidency saying, "and we feel that we should release all of you from the MIA."[117] While not unprecedented, the choice to replace both leadership groups at once was unusual.

The change in leadership corresponded with changes to how the MIA would fit into the larger church. When Victor L. Brown was appointed presiding bishop of the church in April 1972, he was specifically charged with oversight of both boys and girls of Aaronic Priesthood age—twelve through eighteen years old. By November 1972, when the new general presidencies were announced, the Presiding Bishopric and First Presidency had already agreed that in wards, the bishopric would now oversee the youth, assisted by ward presidencies for the young women and young men. This structure formalized the growing correlation emphasis on the role of bishops by giving them, rather than MIA presidents, ultimate oversight. They had also directed that the large MIA boards of the past be reduced at all levels.[118]

Details remained to be worked out, but the same issue of the *Church News* that announced Jacobsen's release and the appointment of a new presidency also announced changes to the organizations for young people. The 1972 restructuring created a new organization—the Melchizedek Priesthood Mutual Interest Association (MPMIA)—for young people over age eighteen, who had historically been served by the YMMIA and YWMIA. The MPMIA would operate at the stake and regional levels and not have a general presidency. Under this new structure, church members aged twelve to eighteen would still be served by the YWMIA and the YMMIA, but those organizations would be collectively called the Aaronic Priesthood Mutual Improvement Association (APMIA). The division of MPMIA and APMIA at age eighteen reflected that age's growing significance as a marker of adulthood. It was the age at which young men usually advanced from the Aaronic to the Melchizedek Priesthood.[119] It was also the age at which most young people in the United States graduated from high school. The APMIA was to be overseen by the Presiding Bishopric, in keeping with scriptural principles that designated the bishopric as the presidency of the Aaronic Priesthood.[120]

The leaders appointed to replace Jacobsen and her counselors were Ruth Funk, Hortense Child, and Ardeth Kapp. Funk, Child, and Kapp were veteran young women's leaders who had also served on correlation committees.[121] That experience would influence the organization's immediate future. Over the course of the 1960s, the YWMIA had made changes to meet the changing needs of the faith's youth, but during the 1970s, the focus would shift from changes within the MIA to a full realignment of the organization within the structure of the church.

YWMIA TO YOUNG WOMEN

1972–1984

On 29 March 1973, Ruth Funk, Hortense Child, and Ardeth Kapp, general presidency of the YWMIA, met in the Salt Lake Temple with the Young Men general presidency, the Presiding Bishopric, the Quorum of the Twelve Apostles, and the First Presidency. It was the first time, church president Harold B. Lee said, that women had been invited to meet with the senior male leaders during one of their regular council meetings in the upper room of the Salt Lake Temple. Funk and her counselors had fasted and prayed to prepare themselves for the occasion. "The sacredness of the entire setting was almost overwhelming," Kapp recorded.[1] Lee made introductions and gave the youth leaders a moment to speak. Presiding bishop Victor L. Brown, who oversaw the APMIA, then presented the youth leaders' shared recommendations for a complete revision of the church's youth organizations.

Since their appointment in November 1972, Funk and her counselors had been working intensively with their counterparts in the Young Men presidency and their new leaders in the Presiding Bishopric on a proposal to reorient the organization to function within the newly organized APMIA. Their plan would refocus the organization on youth leadership and service, provide flexibility for local adaptation, and be overseen at all levels by priesthood leaders. When Brown finished presenting, Lee asked the general authorities for a vote of approval, and they raised their hands to sustain the plan unanimously. "This program is the most important change you will see in your lifetime in the church," Lee told all the gathered leaders.[2]

The six youth leaders—Funk and her counselors and Robert L. Backman and his counselors—left the meeting after the vote, feeling jubilant. On the way out, they stopped to offer a prayer of thanks in a small alcove in the hallway of the temple. "It was a little hard to think of going out into the real world again after this spiritual experience," Kapp recalled. The Young Women leaders left the temple arm in arm, having received a powerful affirmation of their efforts.[3]

The real world did present many challenges to the Young Women organization and its leadership in the 1970s. The social upheaval of the previous decade in the United States had created a new baseline in behavior for American youth of the 1970s in everything from dress and dancing to sexual morality, and those changes profoundly shaped the way Young Women general leaders perceived the needs of young women around the world. By the middle of the decade, the intensifying women's movement in the United States had especially elicited a sense of crisis as Young Women leaders feared that girls were internalizing messages about womanhood that would lead them away from the fundamental truths of the gospel.

Meanwhile, institutional changes rooted in the correlation movement of the previous decade came to fruition in the church and its auxiliary organizations. Young Women leaders strongly supported these changes and worked tirelessly to implement them, but a transformation of this magnitude could not be effected without tremendous difficulties. Over the decade, Young Women leaders found themselves navigating a dramatically transformed landscape of church structures, processes, and lines of communication, many aspects of which they did not control. Despite their best efforts, it took the rest of the decade for the organization to begin to find a new equilibrium. When it did, the organization was no longer identified with mutual improvement alongside young men—it carried both a new focus and a new name.

SHAPING THE APMIA

Months of intensive effort preceded the meeting in the temple in March 1973. Funk, Child, and Kapp were committed to correlation ideals and came to their new assignments with a willingness to question the status quo and make changes. The APMIA presidencies took office with the mandate to develop a full structure for the new APMIA organization in time to be approved and announced at general conference in early April 1973, with details and materials to be distributed to local leaders at June Conference that same year.[4] It was an almost superhuman task, Child felt, to work everything out so quickly.[5] The executives—Funk and her counselors, Backman and his counselors, and the Presiding Bishopric—met many times between January and March 1973, sometimes working late into the evening to shape a new vision for the church's youth programs.[6]

When Lee appointed the new Young Women leaders, he expressed a need to involve youth more directly in leadership and to orient them toward service more than "fun and games." This directive departed sharply from the 1920s designation of the MIA as the recreation arm of the church and from the longstanding emphasis on teaching the gospel through spiritualized recreation. Church leaders in the early 1970s felt that the youth of the church needed to take more stewardship over their own programs and the activity of their peers.[7] Harking back to Lee's "program of defense," they asserted that Latter-day Saints were living in the "perilous times" foreseen by the apostle Paul and that young people needed a stronger spiritual foundation. "For too many this has been a social gospel," one executive committee member observed, echoing a long history of similar concerns about the youth programs. "We need a program that will help the youth understand that they can draw upon the power of God through personal revelation."[8]

The plan presented to church leaders in the temple envisioned the APMIA being structured around a few basic principles. It would have direction and oversight by priesthood leaders and allow for flexible local administration and leader accountability. It would serve the individual, involve youth in planning, and develop youth leadership through activities focused on service. The bishop's youth committee (a carryover of the bishop's youth council established a few years earlier) would work closely with a small activities committee made up of adults to plan service projects and activities. Local congregations would draw from a "recipe book" of ideas to tailor the program to their needs and resources. "Everything that is done should be done with the purpose of building youth," APMIA leaders emphasized. "Through service leading to spiritual experiences is where youth start to become true Latter-day Saints." The programs would be administered by the ward, with youth presidents of the age groups—still called Beehive, Mia Maid, and Laurel in the Young Women organization—taking the lead, supported by adult leaders.[9] There would be no more detailed, prescriptive calendars and program outlines issued from church headquarters.

After the concept for the realigned organizations was approved and announced at general conference, the APMIA leaders went back to work, sprinting to prepare further guidance for local leaders to be distributed at June Conference, just over two months away. So hurried was the preparation that some of the materials were delivered directly to the Tabernacle from the printshop just before the conference's first session.[10] During the conference, leaders laid out both the goals and the logistics of the APMIA, clarifying the roles of various youth and adult leaders and offering guidance on what materials ought to be used. They explained that traditional recreational events should continue to be part of the program depending on local need, capacity, and desire, while indicating that a major shift in approach was underway.

The report of a panel discussion at the conference shows that stake leaders came with many questions about how the new APMIA organization was going to work.[11]

APMIA TO YOUNG WOMEN

The organization was still in flux when church president Harold B. Lee died suddenly in December 1973. Lee was succeeded by Spencer W. Kimball, a beloved apostle known for his personal ministry to individuals and particularly to Native Americans. Kimball had not been closely involved with Lee on correlation or on the youth organizations. After Kimball became church president, Victor L. Brown approached him with the concern that continued use of the name *MIA* seemed to be keeping ward and stake leaders from recognizing the extent of the changes envisioned.[12] At the 1974 June Conference, Kimball announced that the name *MIA* would no longer be used. The youth organizations had been separated, he said, and would be known simply as Young Women and Aaronic Priesthood. The term *MIA* persisted in colloquial use to refer to youth activities, but its elimination signaled the end of an era in church administration.

Along with the name change, Kimball also announced another structural revision to the youth organizations. Having both the Presiding Bishopric and an APMIA presidency oversee the organization for young men had created a double-layered leadership structure, so the Young Men general presidency was released and discontinued.[13] The Presiding Bishopric was assigned to directly oversee the Aaronic Priesthood organization, and a director of Aaronic Priesthood would serve under the Presiding Bishopric to handle the administrative details of the young men's program. The Young Women general presidency remained in place and would report to the Presiding Bishopric.[14] For three years, the Young Women presidency worked under the direction of and in close collaboration with the Presiding Bishopric. During that time, giving adequate leadership and attention to the youth organizations was the Presiding Bishopric's highest priority.[15] The bishopric developed what Child called a "marvelous working relationship" with the Young Women presidency and board.[16] The bishopric came to Wednesday night board meetings and met regularly with the board committees. That collaboration gave Young Women leaders a strong sense of support and guidance that Child believed could have been a model for helping Young Women leaders at all levels learn to work within the priesthood line.[17]

Ultimately, however, this structure for the youth organizations proved unsustainable. The Presiding Bishopric had extensive responsibilities beyond the youth organizations, and those duties were in the process of being redefined.[18] The Presiding Bishopric expressed concerns about the mismatch between their responsibility for the youth and their overall focus on the church's temporal and logistical needs.

APMIA presidencies and advisers. 1972. From 1972 to 1974, the combined presidencies of Ruth Hardy Funk and Robert L. Backman worked closely with the Presiding Bishopric to reshape and realign the church's youth organizations, then known as Aaronic Priesthood MIA. Seated, left to right: APMIA–Young Women president Funk, Hortense Hogan Child, and Ardeth Greene Kapp. Standing, left to right: presiding bishop Victor L. Brown, H. Burke Peterson, Vaughn J. Featherstone, APMIA–Young Men president Backman, LeGrand R. Curtis Sr., and Jack H. Goaslind. (Courtesy *Church News*, copy at Church History Library, Salt Lake City.)

Furthermore, it did not make sense, as Brown explained, for the Twelve Apostles to "be responsible for the entire ecclesiastical program of the church—except for six years in the lives of boys and girls."[19] In 1977, the Aaronic Priesthood organization was renamed Young Men, and a general presidency was reestablished. Responsibility for the youth organizations shifted from the Presiding Bishopric to a member of the Quorum of the Seventy, Marion D. Hanks, who was made Managing Director of Youth and reported to members of the Quorum of the Twelve.[20] General Young Women and Young Men leaders reported to Hanks.

In contrast to historical practice, the Young Women presidency and their new counterparts, Neil Schaerrer and counselors Roy Doxey and Quinn McKay, never established a strong working relationship. The members of the 1977 Young Men presidency had served as mission presidents, bishops, and stake presidents, but they had little experience working with the church's youth programs. They were unaccustomed to working closely with a women's organization and did not share the women's vision of collaboration.[21] As reflected in the organization's previous official name, Aaronic Priesthood, Young Men programs focused primarily on priesthood duties and missionary preparation, though the organization retained Boy Scouts as a mainstay for activities. Although he did allow that some joint activities were desirable, Schaerrer saw few overlapping interests. "We're not a corresponding organization with the Young Women," he said, "and we ought to have much less activity with the women than there has been over the years."[22]

The years from 1973 through the end of the decade were characterized by rapid administrative change that made collaboration difficult and long-term planning almost impossible. While she supported the overall goals of the organizational changes, Child described these years of change as challenging and dynamic. "First we changed prophets," she recalled, "and secondly we changed from the Bishopric, and then we changed to having a Young Men's presidency whose working relationship with us was very, very scant and brief. And not only that, but the Correlation procedures were changing constantly. . . . We changed names three times. We changed facilities four times."[23]

Kapp acknowledged that from the outside, the Young Women organization must have appeared chaotic and uncertain at times. But Lee had told Funk, Child, and Kapp when they were first appointed that it would take five years for the new youth programs to be understood, and Kapp preferred to look at the bigger picture. "Five years isn't very long in the course of Church history," she said.[24] Both Child and Kapp believed that the period of change ultimately led to youth programs more centered in the church's branches, wards, and stakes and more responsive to local needs.[25]

COMPLICATIONS WITH COMMUNICATIONS

For the first one hundred years of its existence, the Young Women organization had operated through lines of transmission that ran in both directions from the Young Women general presidency to stake and then ward Young Women leaders. Before the 1970s, the annual June Conference had brought Young Women general leaders together with other church leaders who had responsibility for youth to make announcements, explain policy changes, and discuss the year's programs in detail; general leaders' visits to local conventions and conferences had provided further opportunities for training, mentorship, and the building of relationships. They had periodically issued circular letters and published important information in the magazines and the *MIA Leader* and *MIA in the Missions* newsletters. In addition, the general Young Women office received many letters and phone calls from local leaders and responded directly to many of them.

In the first three years of Funk's presidency, almost all these channels of communication were abruptly severed and rerouted to mirror the change in reporting lines.[26] Crucial avenues of communication were lost—right when major changes in the organization and its programs made communication vital.[27] Between June 1974 and October 1975—the period when the structural changes to the Young Women organization were taking hold—general leaders were permitted to send almost no written communication to local leaders, and visits to local units were sharply curtailed. These changes were undoubtedly intended to establish the new order in which local youth leaders were to counsel with their bishops and stake presidents rather than relying on central directives. But the perhaps unintended consequence was almost no communication at all. "There was a vacuum and a dearth of any directing material from headquarters," Child lamented.[28] Bishop Victor L. Brown, feeling the same struggles, observed that the travel and meeting restrictions constrained youth leaders "to the point of eliminating an effective introduction of the program."[29]

The discontinuation of June Conference was felt particularly keenly. Spencer W. Kimball announced the change to a surprised audience of youth leaders during the 1975 June Conference; the Young Women general presidency knew the announcement was coming but had not been informed when it would take place.[30] "With distances growing greater and membership greatly increasing, it seems high time to take another long stride in our decentralization," Kimball declared. Henceforward, the church would focus on reaching people where they were rather than on events in Salt Lake City. "Truly we have become a global church," he said. Even as June Conference had grown in size and scope, it served an ever-decreasing percentage of the globally expanding, increasingly non-English-speaking church membership. It seemed unfair, he said, that so few could attend and get the benefits that so many others wanted and needed. The church had already held area conferences in Europe, Mexico, Brazil, and Argentina and had planned several more. Kimball suggested that such local and regional conferences would replace the need for centralized auxiliary conferences.[31]

Even more than the name change and new reporting lines, the discontinuation of June Conference marked the decisive end of the mutual improvement movement. June Conference had been more than a yearly event—it had been a structuring mainstay for the MIA organizations and their programs. It had long served as a fountainhead of guidance for creating strong programs, and its absence further limited connections between general and local leaders and left local leaders pleading for direction and training.[32] Young Women leaders adhered to the communication protocols of the new priesthood-oriented structure, but it would be a few more years before they could send new guidebooks and training materials to stake and ward leaders.[33]

At headquarters, Young Women leaders found themselves with heavy responsibilities but little decision-making authority and few opportunities to communicate directly with key leaders. Funk recalled that in her early days on the YWMIA board, she found it deeply meaningful to see Lucy Cannon and Bertha Reeder meet regularly with the First Presidency and the organization's apostolic advisers. Her close work with Harold B. Lee in the early part of her administration also brought her great joy because she felt it brought women into what she called "the fold of the Priesthood." With the shift from APMIA to Young Women, however, she found much less opportunity for such interactions. For example, she had only sporadic, informal opportunities to interact with church president Spencer W. Kimball.[34] Especially after the Presiding Bishopric was released from direct oversight of the youth organizations, the presidency found themselves having to implement directives made without their input.[35]

The Young Women general presidency was by this time several layers down the leadership hierarchy, giving them limited access to key decision makers.[36] Even when they managed to arrange a meeting, the interactions were sometimes unsatisfying. Funk and her counselors once requested a meeting with senior leaders; they rehearsed carefully to be concise and effective in their presentation, hoping to receive helpful direction. Instead, Funk began her explanation but was immediately interrupted. "Then the whole meeting became a discussion between those to whom we were to be presenting it, while we just observed," Kapp recalled.[37] Brown likewise recalled meetings in which the Young Women leaders were not allowed to make their presentations without interruption.[38]

Another change the presidency experienced was the need to submit training materials or other documents through proper correlation approval channels before those documents could be published or distributed—a process they unequivocally supported. "Correlation in my mind was like a group of experts who by assignment check your parachute that you yourself have folded before you jump," Ardeth Kapp observed. "Really they protected us from a lot of falls that we could have had without that body of people who were so thorough."[39] At the same time, those approval channels—various reading and review committees and staff gatekeepers—were themselves in process of development. Rapid change created inconsistency, inefficiency, and some unpredictability. After preparing one document and finally seeing it through all the approvals, the presidency would use the same guidelines for their next project, only to find there was a new set of criteria.[40] "It wasn't that we were resisting the direction," Kapp said. "It was that we weren't clear about the direction." The presidency recognized that the problem was not personal. "When I say 'Correlation,' I don't think of it as people who were doing it," Kapp clarified. Their interactions with other staff members were positive and conducted in a spirit of mutual support. The difficulties, Kapp believed, came from "an organizational structure that needed to be refined."[41] Nonetheless, Funk, Child, and Kapp worked persistently to complete projects and secure approvals.

REFRAMING PERSONAL ACHIEVEMENT

Chief among the projects for which Funk and her counselors sought approval was a new goals program. A Personal Achievement Program for youth of both genders had been implemented in 1970.[42] For young women, the core of the 1970 program was a set of seven paperback booklets called journals, one for each year from age twelve to eighteen, that contained guidance and tracking for goal setting. Their titles evoked stages of development: *Beginning, Growing, Discovering, Believing, Aspiring, Achieving,* and *Fulfilling.* These journals, along with envelopes for awards and mementos, were to be placed in a three-ring binder labeled with the traditional title Treasures of Truth. The entire binder was intended to record a young woman's personal history through her goals and their fulfillment.[43] The 1970 program also introduced a central role for the bishop, in keeping with the correlation vision of priesthood oversight. It instructed bishops to interview young women and young men each year, on or near their birthdays, to discuss moral standards and to help youth review and set goals.[44] As interviews with the bishop became a standard feature of young women's experiences, Young Women leaders hoped the regular conversations would better equip bishops to understand and advocate for young women.[45]

By 1974, however, it was clear the achievement program wasn't working. Overburdened bishops struggled to adequately oversee young people's goals, and many local leaders felt parents should take more stewardship over goal setting.[46] The program was too rigid and complex, and most significantly, young people didn't seem to like it.[47] In late 1973, executives of what was then APMIA had discussed a sobering internal estimate that fewer than 10 percent of young Saints were engaging with the program. "Youth want to be involved in goal setting and achievement, and in keeping a record of important events in their life," leaders reported, "but they don't want to do so by answering questions prepared for them by adults."[48] In some international areas, the journals piled up on distribution center shelves because people could not afford to buy them.[49] Leaders recognized the program fell short of its goals and determined that "when something is not working it either needs to be changed or done away with."[50] Early in 1974, they decided to phase out the unpopular Personal Achievement Program.[51]

Eager to move away from the failed program but unwilling to leave local groups without a new one to follow, the Young Women presidency hastily assembled what they said was not a replacement program but rather a "new focus for young women."[52] They called it Behold Thy Handmaiden, a reference to the biblical account of Mary's response upon being told she would become the mother of Jesus Christ. The presidency felt that Mary's submission to God's will was a beautiful ideal for young women.[53] Behold Thy Handmaiden introduced a new framework for the Young Women organization, but it was not yet a fully developed achievement program. It included six areas of focus that would encompass the life of a well-rounded young woman: spiritual awareness, homemaking arts, service and compassion, recreation and the world of nature, cultural arts and education, and personal and social refinement.[54] In the process of creating Behold Thy Handmaiden, Young Women leaders met with teachers in various fields and leaders of organizations such as 4-H and Future Homemakers of America to get a sense of what would best help young women develop spiritual strength, a positive self-concept, and practical skills and talents.[55]

The presidency introduced Behold Thy Handmaiden in a multimedia presentation at the 1974 June Conference, where they distributed a short booklet for young women describing the program and a separate companion guide for leaders.[56] The guidebook for leaders presented ideals in each area of focus and offered suggestions for incorporating those ideals into all aspects of Young Women experiences and activities. It recommended that a "New Beginnings seminar" be held each year to welcome first-year Beehive members, create an atmosphere of love and friendship, introduce class presidencies and adult leaders, and present the areas of focus in creative ways. While Behold Thy Handmaiden introduced some new ideas, it included holdovers from previous programs as well—the guidelines encouraged young women to continue to create Treasures of Truth books and mentioned the availability of binders and the personal achievement journals, but these were offered only as suggestions.[57]

In the *Behold Thy Handmaiden* booklet for young women, each area of focus was introduced in a two-page spread, illustrated with a full-page painting of a young woman. The paintings depicted young women of various races and ethnicities, reflecting awareness of the increasingly multiracial membership of the church. The opening spread also included a relevant scriptural passage, a short aspirational phrase, and a description of the qualities embodied in the area. The spiritual awareness section, for example, cited a Book of Mormon verse exhorting believers to "seek ye first the kingdom of God" and described a spiritual young woman as one who used the scriptures as guidelines for her life, knew she was a daughter of God and looked to Him for comfort and guidance, and recognized the power and authority of the priesthood. The accompanying painting showed an apparently Latina or Indigenous young woman looking up, her face joyously alight, her hands clasped in prayer. "To live thy word, to teach thy word. To praise thy name on high" appeared in calligraphy at the bottom.[58]

Behold Thy Handmaiden responded not only to the shortcomings of the 1970 program but also to changing cultural beliefs in the United States regarding women's place in society.[59] In the early 1960s, Betty Friedan's book *The Feminine Mystique* had sent shockwaves through American culture by arguing that the ideals of domesticity and femininity that structured many women's lives also caused them to suffer from loss of identity and lack of meaning. Around the same time, President John F. Kennedy created the President's Commission on the Status of Women, which investigated the many ways women were disadvantaged in the law, education, employment, and other arenas. Throughout the decade, many efforts began to address these problems through legislation and regulation. The National Organization for Women, founded in 1966 by Betty Friedan and like-minded associates, took on a high profile in pushing for reforms that would dramatically restructure gender relations in American society. Efforts to address issues of equality in employment, education, and legal standing birthed a "rights revolution" for women in the United States.[60] While there was general support in American society for women's equality under the law, some feminists also advocated for the right to abortion and for homosexual rights—causes that were much less popular and sparked heated opposition. By the mid-1970s, many of these energies had become focused on the proposed Equal Rights Amendment to the United States Constitution.

Many women, however, began to see the problem of gender inequality as something that laws and regulations alone could not address. It was a matter of confronting deep structures of society and psychology and of recognizing the norms that led both women and men to internalize the idea that women were inferior and dependent. Women who had participated in the civil rights movement and antiwar protests adopted "liberation" as the watchword for their cause, and the women's liberation movement caught fire. At its core was the idea of consciousness-raising—making women aware of the many manifestations of sexism in their lives and giving them the language to describe it.

Some women's liberation activists took an aggressive approach to confronting sexism in society. They loudly disrupted the Miss America pageant, for example, calling it a cattle auction and crowning a sheep the winner. Such extreme tactics, which played directly against the traditional expectation that women would be polite and agreeable, garnered attention and created a popular image of feminists as radical and threatening. But even feminists with less theatrical methods spoke out strongly about previously taboo subjects such as rape, sexual harassment, and domestic violence, and many advocated for women's sexual freedom and for liberation from what they saw as the oppression of traditional gender roles. Some eschewed marriage altogether.

Latter-day Saints were generally cautious about the women's movement. One group of Latter-day Saint women formed their own discussion group and acknowledged that they read feminist literature with interest. It caused them to search their souls, but ultimately they reaffirmed their commitments to faith and family. As mothers of large families, they were busy working in the church themselves and supporting their husbands' service. They considered themselves "not particularly down-trodden," and they claimed no affiliation with any radical feminist group. "Some of us are so straight as to be shocked by their antics," wrote one participant.[61] Even the most progressive in the group saw themselves as falling somewhere in between the extremes of the day's rhetoric.[62]

Other Latter-day Saint women were even less moved by feminist arguments. Profoundly committed to a view of gender they believed reflected eternal identities, they saw feminist agitation as an attack on women's divinely appointed roles as wives and mothers—roles they believed extended into the hereafter because of the Latter-day Saint belief that the family forms the basic unit of eternal life in God's kingdom. They saw the feminist movement as a tactic inspired by Satan to confuse women and divert their attention away from God's plan of happiness. Apostle Thomas S. Monson criticized the prioritization of personal freedom or professional aspiration over religious duty and gendered roles in family life. "Equality of rights does not imply identity of functions," he argued.[63] Funk assertively aligned herself with this view. "Women of the world can gain the liberation they seek only by recognizing within themselves the gifts of womanhood, the gifts of motherhood, and satisfying them in the natural and divine role as found within the priesthood," she declared. "This is the only key to our identity—the role we play in the priesthood of God." Quoting one of her board members, she added, "I am not interested in liberation. I am interested in exaltation."[64] This positioning would fundamentally structure the Young Women leaders' approach to their service and their messaging to young women.

When they introduced Behold Thy Handmaiden, Young Women leaders warned that "many forces in the world today are trying to destroy or change the feelings of young women about the sacred roles of womanhood." Each young woman was born "uninfluenced by the ways of the world," they said, and had spiritual characteristics that could be diminished by such influences. "The new focus is designed to help the young women regain their celestial status."[65] The next year, in what would be the final June Conference, a handout for Behold Thy Handmaiden took on a more dire tone. "We are exposed on every side to propaganda," it warned, "which is aimed at making women feel that they should seek 'liberation' from their traditional role." This propaganda, it asserted, demeaned marriage and homemaking and offered divorce as "the easy answer to marital problems."[66] Such rhetoric illustrated much of the thinking behind the new program for young women, which sought to dignify caregiving and honor motherhood, in opposition to what leaders saw as misguided and dangerous notions of women's liberation.

After introducing Behold Thy Handmaiden in 1974, the presidency and board continued to work toward a fuller achievement program. They wanted to create something that would provide structure, guidelines, and accountability but also allow girls to have agency and self-direction.[67] They insisted that they did not want to consider it a *program* but rather a *process*, one fully integrated with the total curriculum of the Young Women organization; they especially did not want to structure it around awards but rather around individual progression.[68] "We wanted it to include the mold of the individual award and the detail of the personal achievement programs," Child explained, "but to establish a freedom within it so that every girl, no matter where she was in her development in the gospel, could relate to the program and pick up where she was and move on from there."[69]

As the new program neared completion late in 1976, however, concerns developed about the name. The presidency had intended to retain the title Behold Thy Handmaiden, but in the context of the mid-1970s turmoil over women's rights, the term *handmaiden*, which seemed to imply subservience, felt out of place. Priesthood leaders advised the presidency to reconsider the program's title.[70]

In 1977, the organization introduced the new program, which they called My Personal Progress.[71] It retained the six areas of focus and descriptions of ideals but expanded and structured the program with suggestions for goals in each area and a recording sheet to track progress. The new booklet's first page featured a painting of the Annunciation, in which a young Mary gazes intently at the angel Gabriel—an implicit but clear reference to Behold Thy Handmaiden.[72] The opening sections of the sixty-four-page booklet offered instruction in how to set goals, outlined church standards, and provided guidelines for achieving the yearly certificates of recognition, with space to record attendance at church and weekday seminary classes, keep a journal, and track goals completed. These elements echoed requirements of past programs, but now they were significantly simplified. Yearly certificates were intended as records of progress. Participants became eligible for the culminating Young Womanhood Recognition at the end of their first year as a Laurel. The application for the recognition was found on the last pages of the booklet, where young women could read and reflect on it as a goal throughout their years in Young Women. The recognition application did specify requirements—75 percent attendance at church meetings and two completed goals in each area of focus each year—but bishops were allowed to adjust the requirements. Eligible young women submitted an application to the bishop and discussed it with him in a personal interview. When it was approved, they received the certificate from the bishop in sacrament meeting and could purchase the Young Womanhood medallion, a gold disk engraved with an image of a young woman in a flowing dress—the same image that was embossed on the cover of the new booklet.[73]

With the completion and approval of the My Personal Progress program, the presidency was able to send out several new, much-needed publications to stake and ward leaders: courses of study for the classes (two each for Beehives, Mia Maids, and Laurels), a Young Women handbook for adult leaders, a Young Women guidebook for youth leaders, the *My Personal Progress* booklet, a new resource for youth activities called *The Activity Book*, a new camp manual, and a new manual for physical fitness, sports, and recreation in Young Women and Relief Society. They also released several training tapes and a filmstrip.[74]

Even after the My Personal Progress program was introduced, the concept behind Behold Thy Handmaiden remained largely intact. The emphasis on building young women's identity around their personal relationship with God, their respect for priesthood leaders, and their roles as mothers and homemakers undergirded changes in other aspects of the Young Women organization, including activities and curriculum. The 1977 changes and the materials disseminated to facilitate them helped stabilize the organization and paved the way for it to begin moving forward more effectively after several challenging years of transition.

LEADERSHIP AND SERVICE

Although this decade of extensive change required difficult adjustments for general and local Young Women leaders, and for young women themselves, it was largely one of continuity and personal development. Events like road shows, regional music and dance festivals, sports programs, and camp remained staples of the Young Women experience. Three sisters, Sharon, Karen, and Rama Taylor, participated in all these activities in their ward in Barstow, California, throughout the 1970s. With eleven children in their family, money was tight, so the sisters participated with other ward members in fundraising events, such as selling homemade bread or fried chicken. With the proceeds, they were able to join regional music and dance festivals in venues like a large concert hall in San Bernardino or the Rose Bowl Stadium in Pasadena. The funds also helped send them to youth conferences in distant destinations like Catalina Island off the coast of California and Zion National Park in Utah.[75]

For Dottie Boone in Northern California, strong traditions established in the MIA years likewise remained a central part of her Young Women experience, even though she entered Young Women in 1973, just as APMIA was rolling out. Like the Taylor sisters, she participated in road shows and regional dance festivals. Yet she found the achievement programs in their various iterations between 1973 and 1977 uninspiring and did little with the booklets.[76] In Southern California, Merydith Garfield felt similarly. She entered Young Women the same year as Dottie and felt confused by the frequent changes. She accomplished some goals like learning to crochet and keeping her nails groomed, which she marked in her booklets, but her efforts were sporadic and infrequent, and eventually she gave up.[77] Many young women undoubtedly had more positive experiences with the programs, but anecdotes such as these demonstrate that there was a need for a reevaluation.

While young women were still experiencing traditional MIA activities in their local organizations, general leaders were admonishing local leaders to place less emphasis on recreational and cultural programs and greater emphasis on youth leadership and service within the ward or larger community.[78] The youth organizations sought to put young women and men in positions of leadership, with adults acting as mentors. Leaders wanted youth to have responsibility and accountability not only for themselves but also for other young people.[79] Hortense Child felt that this reorientation toward youth leadership was an inspired step, taken at a time when young people generally were demanding a stronger share of responsibility for themselves and the world. "If we don't give youth the opportunity to carry responsibility, to be accountable for their actions," she said, "we will reap the whirlwind."[80]

The general leaders attempted to introduce the concept of "shadow leadership," in which adults, like a shadow, should be always present but in the background.[81] Largely because of the difficulties in communication at this time, the idea was not well understood. Adopting a paradigm of youth leadership required a significant shift for adult leaders, who were used to doing everything themselves, and some adult leaders seemed to use the leadership focus as an excuse to place responsibility on the young people's shoulders with little support.[82] Shadow leadership was deemed a failure by many.[83]

The inclusion of "service and compassion" as one of the six areas of focus in Behold Thy Handmaiden and then My Personal Progress helped cement service as a major emphasis of the Young Women organization. Service activities and projects began featuring in ward and stake youth programs, for young women separately and combined with young men. Stories of service shared in church publications reinforced the activities' importance. As reported in the *New Era*, the youth of the Torrance California Stake worked to clear a large area of tumbleweeds and trash in preparation for its becoming a park.[84] Young women in Dingle, Idaho, helped three families with cleanup and fundraising after the families' homes had burned down.[85] In Maryland, young women and young men in the Bowie Ward conducted a night of service for the senior citizens' group in their community. They brought the guests to the meetinghouse, where they served a special dinner and presented their road show for the evening's entertainment.[86]

Charlene Holmstrom, who served as the Young Women president in the Ithaca New York Stake throughout the 1970s, felt that the greater emphasis on leadership and service was exactly what young women needed. She saw young women develop strong relationships with their leaders and learn to lead in planning and executing activities. She also believed the changes facilitated a much more spiritual experience for young women and allowed young women and their leaders to spend less time away from home than the earlier elaborate programs had required.[87]

One way many youth served was by working on church-owned farms, which were run by Latter-day Saint volunteers and helped provide food for those in need.[88] In Sharon Taylor's early morning seminary class, announcements asking young women and young men to work at the local church farm were sometimes met with moans. But Sharon dutifully met with other youth at the church early on the appointed Saturday mornings to drive an hour to the farm and pick oranges or grapefruit or pull weeds from among the vegetables. Her sister Karen also went without complaint, despite her dislike of the prickly vines on some of the vegetables and the early morning cold. She did, however, enjoy the smell of the orange groves and was fascinated when she worked in the cannery to see peaches and other fruit go through the preserving process.[89]

Staffing of the youth organizations was pared back to reflect the shift away from culture and recreation and toward leadership and service. Instead of the extensive staff of directors and specialists that had traditionally overseen MIA activities, the youth programs in the 1970s allowed for a small service and activities committee in

Youth service project, Bountiful, Utah. 1974. To commemorate the 145th anniversary of the restoration of the Aaronic Priesthood, youth churchwide were encouraged to help plan local service projects, sporting events, or other group activities. Young men and women in the Bountiful Twenty-Eighth Ward painted the home of a widow in their community. (Courtesy *Church News*, copy at Church History Library, Salt Lake City.)

wards and stakes, which was to serve as a resource to youth and adult leaders in carrying out activities.[90] Speech, music, drama, and dance directors had traditionally taken the initiative in designing and conducting the cultural activities of the MIA; now, in a reversal of previous practice, the service and activities committee was to act only when called upon.

Church members struggled to strike the right balance with cultural activities, which had long been the bedrock of the MIA. With so many rapid changes in the programs, it was probably inevitable some long-held traditions would be lost. Ardeth Kapp acknowledged that recreation and cultural activities essentially fell by the wayside as other matters absorbed leaders' time. Stakes and wards that had strong traditions of MIA programs, with trained, capable leaders, carried on road shows, Gold and Green Balls, and other traditional activities. But in many other places, such things dwindled—a source of much regret by general and local leaders who had overseen or participated in such efforts in the past.[91]

The once-central conjoint relationship of Young Women and Young Men organizations also atrophied during the transition years in the early and mid-1970s. As both organizations scrambled to redefine themselves and deal with the relentless pace of changes—and in the absence of stronger guidance for maintaining conjoint activities and relationships—the two entities continued to find themselves with little relationship to each other.[92] As the organizations began to stabilize in 1977, the newly released *Activity Book* recommended hundreds of potential activities for young women and young men and helped local leaders think about how to align weeknight activities with the current priorities of the youth organizations. Notably, it also provided ideas for combined activities and encouraged casual mixed-gender socialization because it could "help young men and young women develop wholesome and proper relationships in a Church setting."[93]

Painful though the transition had been, it seemed the organization was finding its footing by the time *The Activity Book* and other new materials made it to members. Kapp found that local leaders did eventually take ownership of their programs, adapting them to local needs. One stake president in Arizona told her the new directives had revolutionized his stake's entire youth program—though it had taken two years to get the picture. But the success had come with strain for everyone. In the same note in which he celebrated his stake's success, the president added a simple, weary plea: "Don't let them change it."[94]

NEW LEADERSHIP, NEW INITIATIVES

As the new *Activity Book* made its way into wards and branches, Funk and her presidency turned their attention to one of the most significant issues facing young women in that moment—the deep divisions arising from opposition to the women's movement and the Equal Rights Amendment. In her role as president of the Young Women organization, Funk felt she was almost a magnet to women in the church who felt hurt and confused by the church's ardent opposition to the movement and the Equal Rights Amendment. Many were single and some were not young women at all, but those who communicated with her struggled to see where they fit in the church if their lives had not followed traditional paths into marriage and motherhood.[95] Though she lacked direct access to the church's highest leadership through regular meetings, she took every opportunity she found to discuss these women's challenges with church president Spencer W. Kimball. She felt great love and compassion from him, even as he remained firm in his commitment to the church's stance, and she believed women of the church should hear directly from their prophet as they worked through these issues. By February 1978, Funk had organized a committee to compile Kimball's writings on women from over the years and prepare them for publication, and plans were in the works for him to speak to women and girls ages twelve and up in a churchwide fireside in September.[96]

Funk's expectations were suddenly disrupted, however, when she and her counselors were released and a new presidency was appointed in July 1978, just two months before the special fireside was to take place. Funk felt both surprised and confused. The fireside was only a short time away, and she had served for just six years, while most previous presidents of the Young Women organization had served for a decade or more.[97] Still, plans for the meeting went forward, even as Funk handed leadership over to the new president, Elaine Cannon, and her counselors, Arlene Barlow Darger and Norma Broadbent Smith.

The invitation to serve as president of the Young Women organization was less unexpected for Cannon than Funk's release was for her. In the weeks before receiving the official invitation, Cannon had awakened frequently in the night with a sense that she would serve in that capacity. When she told Spencer W. Kimball of this, he responded, "The time will come when you will be glad to know that it's the Lord Jesus Christ who wants you in this position, and not just me or the Brethren, though we're happy to have you working with us."[98]

The new presidency brought together a range of experience and skills. In addition to Cannon's long experience with church publications and educational work geared toward youth, she had served on several general church committees, including the Youth Correlation Committee and the Young Women general board. Her two counselors likewise had ample experience with youth and church service, though neither had served on the general board. Darger, a longtime friend of Cannon, worked as a psychologist counseling troubled youth. Smith had previously served on the Primary general board and helped write curriculum for the worldwide church.[99]

One of the first things Cannon did after her appointment was change the lettering on the office doors of the Young Women organization. Already four years out of date, the lettering came from a time when Young Women and Young Men leaders shared office space, and it read, "Aaronic Priesthood Young Men and *Young Women of Same Age*."[100] Cannon was a staunch supporter of correlation and had served on one of the correlation committees. At the same time, with all the emphasis on male-held priesthood, she worried that youth programs were not providing young women sufficient opportunity to fully develop their identities within the church. Attendance statistics reinforced her sense that there was cause for concern. A downward trend in attendance among youth had emerged in the mid-1970s as the old MIA model was discontinued at the same time questions over gender roles became more prominent in American society.[101] Cannon felt that her "sole purpose . . . was to give a place and an identity to the young women."[102]

Cannon had been thinking deeply about how the church might best organize to support women since at least 1973, when Harold B. Lee had asked her to propose a new churchwide program for women over eighteen. Cannon had wrestled with how to effectively integrate single women with married women and minister to their needs. She called her proposal an "Overall Womanhood Program."[103] While her proposal was not adopted, the exercise continued to shape Cannon's thinking. "I was already thinking of this concept of looking at the whole woman, from birth till the grave," she said. Cannon and succeeding Young Women presidents would focus on spiritual engagement and confidence for the church's young women *as women*.[104]

At the press conference announcing her appointment, Cannon acknowledged that questions about women were loud and urgent. "There are many unhappy women today and much confusion concerning women's roles," she said. "We want to help our young women discover who they are and what they can do, and understand their relationship with their Father in Heaven."[105] Indeed, Cannon and Funk had both undergone a watershed experience involving women's issues when they participated as delegates to the National Women's Conference in Houston, Texas, in November 1977. Witnessing the strident and uncompromising rhetoric from both conservative and progressive women had been for Funk "a searing and difficult, difficult experience."[106] Funk and Cannon had each experienced the inherent tensions pulling women to opposing sides, and both sought ways to bring women of the church together on common ground during the late 1970s.

The special fireside for women in September 1978 offered Cannon an opportunity to reinforce her message of unity over division. Messages at the fireside focused on the roles of women as wives and mothers and on Latter-day Saint women's responsibility to promote those roles even as they sought peace and unity. Church president Spencer W. Kimball and Relief Society general president Barbara Bradshaw Smith spoke most directly about the political divisions in the United States over women's roles. After encouraging women to follow basic principles such as keeping the commandments and holding family prayer, Kimball told women they should be grateful to be women, particularly at that moment in time. "To be a righteous woman during the winding up scenes on this earth, before the second coming of our Savior, is an especially noble calling," he declared. "The righteous woman's strength and influence today can be tenfold what it might be in more tranquil times."[107] In her message, Smith entreated women to be part of the solutions to society's problems, which she delineated as the issues of abortion, the Equal Rights Amendment, homosexuality, and pornography. She taught that women must work alongside men and use their own talents in every way to do God's work.[108]

Funk and Cannon focused their remarks on fostering peace and unity. Funk, who spoke even though she had recently been released, shared her own harrowing experience of deciding whether to undergo an abortion when serious complications in her third pregnancy became life threatening. She related that she received a spiritual affirmation to continue the pregnancy to delivery, and she eventually gave birth to a healthy boy. "Others in similar situations may well receive a different witness," she noted, in keeping with the church's opposition to abortion except in cases when "the life or good health of the mother is seriously endangered or where the pregnancy was caused by rape and produces serious emotional trauma in the mother."[109] Then, encouraging women to turn to Christ's love as the path toward peace, she said, "May we, as women of all ages, as daughters of God, as wives, as mothers, as contributing members of society whose identities are being challenged, seek to know him well enough to love him, well enough to serve him."[110] Personal revelation and a close personal relationship with Jesus Christ were, in her view, the way to find peace when facing difficult questions.

Cannon's message illustrated her concern over contention and division among the women of the church. She understood that Latter-day Saint women had different life experiences and different perspectives. "We may even clash at times on opinions regarding temporal trends," she said. But she encouraged women to promote harmony over discord. "I urge us all to provide powerful unity as women for those things we can agree upon—family, chastity, accountability to the Lord, responsibility in the community, sharing the gospel." To do that, she felt women must focus first on their own testimony and relationship with Christ, and then they should serve and share.[111]

FINDING A PLACE FOR INSTRUCTION

Moving forward from building unity at the fireside, Cannon turned her attention to the Young Women curriculum. By the late 1970s, young women received religious instruction at least twenty times per year during weeknight meetings, but there was no provision for their Sunday instruction.[112] Young men, in contrast, met with adult priesthood holders on Sundays for instruction in their priesthood quorums. In the 1960s, Cannon and other YWMIA and correlation leaders had proposed adding a Sunday class for young women, but for nearly twenty years the idea remained on the drawing board.[113]

Some leaders felt young women received plenty of instruction—they studied scripture and Latter-day Saint teachings in Sunday School and at weeknight meetings, and those who attended weekday seminary classes studied yet more. Debra Hovik, who participated in Young Women in Atherton, California, valued the instruction she received during weeknight meetings. "The intimate conversations I had during our classes not only taught me about the gospel and helped build my testimony," she said, "but my leaders were so good to me that it helped me believe in my personal value and learn how to love."[114] Cannon valued such settings, where young women could be undistracted and unintimidated by the presence of young men. To her, mixed-gender settings like seminary failed to give young women instruction calibrated specifically to their needs. As for weeknight lessons, she found the environment inconducive to meaningful discussion. Cannon was frustrated knowing that young women and their leaders were trying to discuss spiritual matters with the sounds of pounding basketball games and other young men's activities in the background.[115]

A few years into Cannon's presidency, church leaders introduced a new consolidated meeting schedule churchwide. To save on travel time for members who lived far from a meetinghouse, in 1980 the church consolidated sacrament, Sunday School, Melchizedek and Aaronic Priesthood, Relief Society, Young Women, and Primary meetings into a three-hour block. Under this new Sunday schedule, Young Women and Relief Society members met in their groups at the same time as their male counterparts.[116] This change made Sunday instruction for young women possible.

Cannon was happy to have the more focused Sunday meeting environment for instruction. Her next major focus was flexibility and individual adaptation in the curriculum. Lessons had long been laid out according to a centrally prescribed calendar, but Cannon felt leaders could do more than follow a manual. "You do not teach chastity on the Sunday after one of the girls' mother just died," she said. In her ideal, "a Young Women leader didn't teach the lesson assigned by headquarters for that week. The leader chose a lesson from the unit of study that was relevant to the girls' lives that week."[117]

For many young women, these Sunday lessons became the central aspect of their experience in Young Women. Patty Brown, who grew up in Sandy, Utah, recalled how her leader, Shirley Bradfield, made her feel loved as she entered the Beehive class in 1980. Through Bradfield's well-prepared lessons, Patty began to develop a desire to be married in the temple one day. A few years later, though she participated in a few big activities such as road shows and youth conference, she stopped regularly attending weeknight activities. She had a busy schedule, with drill team, student government, and an after-school job; additionally, she felt disliked by the other young women in her class. She also didn't feel particularly compelled to dedicate serious time and effort to the My Personal Progress program, put off by the notion of doing good things simply to pass off tasks on a list and get an award. Despite this, leaders like Laurel adviser Jacklyn Wheat worked to connect with Patty on a personal level, and Patty frequently felt that Wheat was speaking just to her in her lessons. Those connections were special to Patty, and she carefully arranged her schedule so she rarely missed Sunday classes. In turn, those Sunday lessons and her personal connections with her leaders became foundations of her budding commitment to the church and her witness of the truth of Latter-day Saint teachings.[118]

ESTABLISHING AN IDENTITY AS DAUGHTERS OF GOD

While Cannon and her counselors sought to emphasize family care roles amid significant social change, Cannon's own background did not conform with the church's messaging about the importance of women staying out of the workforce and home with their children. In addition to her career as a writer for the *Deseret News* and her work with the *Improvement Era*, she had launched and operated several small businesses, all as she raised her family and served in the church.[119] Seeking to help young women navigate the tension between economic realities and prophetic counsel, she emphasized not only the sanctity of the home and motherhood but also the theme of preparedness, telling young women, "This is who you are, but this is what you have to be ready for." Women had, of course, always worked, Cannon noted. By the late twentieth century, however, women had fewer opportunities to have their children around them while they worked, putting different pressures on the family. What people needed, she felt, was help learning how to manage those pressures.[120] In this, Cannon was already signaling directions she and future female leaders would take in coming years as they worked to strike a balance between the ideals preached by church leaders and the reality of women's lives.

Rhonda Shelby felt the pressure of those ideals. She joined the church as a seventeen-year-old in 1981 in the rural community of Moses Lake, Washington. Her father's death about a year before her baptism had led to serious financial uncertainty for her family.[121] She had always aspired to a career, and before her conversion, she was determined to maximize her income. After she was baptized and joined Young Women, her priorities shifted. She decided she could be happy with enough income to live comfortably, and her goals expanded to include a temple marriage and a good family life. Rhonda looked at women in her new religious community who were able to balance a career and family life and wondered if she could maintain a similar balance: "It just makes you sit back and think about yourself, 'Can I be a super woman? Can I do this?'"[122]

As a Black Latter-day Saint, Rhonda also found herself navigating evolving racial attitudes in the church. As the only Black member in her ward, Rhonda quickly learned that the emphasis on marrying within the faith clashed with opposition to interracial marriage from some of her fellow Saints. Almost immediately after her conversion, she ran into resistance from Latter-day Saint young men's parents whenever she'd go on a date. "Even if they said they liked me, they had eight or nine fits because they were willing to take me into their house as a member but not as a daughter-in-law," she recalled.[123] She had to find her own way to navigate such conflicting expectations. Because Rhonda accepted the repeated emphasis in Young Women and other church curriculum on dating and marrying within the faith, she learned to look for men who could resist the widespread social pressure and occasional counsel to avoid interracial relationships.[124]

In 1978, just three years before Rhonda's baptism, church president Spencer W. Kimball announced that he had received a revelation extending the opportunity for priesthood ordination to all worthy men regardless of race or color and opening all temple ordinances to Black members. The revelation made it easier for Black young women to join the church in multiracial countries like the United States and Brazil and opened the door for Young Women classes to be organized for the first time in countries like Ghana and Nigeria, as people who had long believed in the church's teachings were finally organized into official branches. The Young Women organization had always sought to prepare girls for the future, and after the 1978 revelation, the contours of a life of church service and participation changed dramatically for Black young women. For the first time, their plans could align with the aspirations encouraged by Young Women lessons. They could receive their endowment and be sealed in the temple, as Rhonda hoped to do and as Linda McCahon had trusted would happen one day. Because missionaries were generally required to receive their endowment before embarking, the revelation also opened the way for young Black women to serve as full-time missionaries. Within months of the revelation's announcement, the first Black female missionary, Sareta Dobbs, was called to serve in Rio de Janeiro, Brazil.[125]

A FOUNDATIONAL IDENTITY IN CHANGING TIMES

Mindful of the toll exacted by changes in the 1970s, Cannon and her board were selective in their modifications to My Personal Progress for a 1983 edition. Rather than asking members to learn a new system, they made some targeted changes to help young women develop a strong identity. First, they replaced the image of Mary with a picture of a contemporary young woman with an open Book of Mormon on her lap, imagining Book of Mormon scenes such as Jesus Christ's appearance in the Americas. Following that opening image came a page where a young woman could insert her own photo with her name underneath. The 1983 edition also included a change in tone. The narrative perspective in the book changed from that of a leader addressing a young woman—"You are a child of God. You have a vital role to fill in God's eternal plan"—to that of a young woman herself—"I am a daughter of God. I have a vital role to fill in God's eternal plan."[126] With these changes, Cannon and her presidency had begun a process—one that would continue to be a focus for subsequent presidencies—of establishing a fundamental identity for young women throughout the world as daughters of God.

The year after the 1983 changes to My Personal Progress were published, Cannon was released as the Young Women general president. Though she had anticipated having a shorter term than some past leaders, the release was bittersweet. Cannon had been involved in efforts at church headquarters since college, when she'd worked on a public relations committee.[127] At the time of her tenure, church leaders wanted the Young Women presidency to be publicly visible to show that women had a place in the church. Cannon traveled extensively with the First Presidency for public conferences held around the world.[128] She and her counselors took part in church press conferences and held their own press conferences.[129] They helped receive visiting dignitaries who came to tour church welfare facilities in Salt Lake City.[130]

By the time of her release, some of the changes she had recommended had not been realized. She wanted to take the September 1978 special women's fireside further by bringing the church's women together regularly in a way that established a more defined place for them in the church framework. While Funk had envisioned a one-time event for the prophet to speak to women, Cannon proposed that a meeting of all the church's women become a regular part of general conference each year.[131] Though this did not happen during her tenure, a yearly meeting for the women of the church, near the time of the October general conference, did become standard for the next several years. She had also proposed that young women and Relief Society women share opening exercises the same way men of different ages met together before dividing into different groups for Sunday instruction and was saddened when an initial decision to introduce the practice was reversed.[132] She took comfort, looking back, from Spencer W. Kimball's counsel that she would need to know it was not he but the Lord who had called her. As she reflected on her role in the church's structure, she thought of a biblical story in which a captive Israelite young woman persuaded the Syrian general Naaman to seek healing from the prophet Elisha. Cannon unequivocally supported the president of the church as a prophet and priesthood leader but saw in that narrative an instigating role for a young woman or the Young Women general president. "The goading and provoking to good deeds and so on is part of our role," she said, "and I'm content with that."[133]

Cannon's concern that certain issues remained unresolved was well founded. Though much progress had been achieved, questions of women's relationship to the priesthood and their place in church structures remained somewhat ambiguous. Still, the Young Women organization had at last achieved a level of stability after significant upheaval and reorganization. The new My Personal Progress program had been established, and with the inauguration of Sunday classes for young women, leaders could take advantage of greater flexibility in teaching and opportunities for spiritual development. Funk's and Cannon's presidencies established a new central priority for the Young Women organization that would guide it for the next several decades: helping young women develop a foundational identity as daughters of God.

PART 3

Daughters of Heavenly Parents

1984–2024

STANDING AS WITNESSES OF GOD

1984–1992

When Ardeth Kapp was released from Ruth Funk's presidency in 1978, she experienced an impression that her work at church headquarters was not finished. By 1984 the feeling had returned with new urgency. She learned why just hours before the Saturday morning session of April general conference, when Gordon B. Hinckley of the First Presidency asked her to serve as Young Women general president. After the sustaining vote later that morning, as Kapp joined the general authorities and other officers of the church on the Tabernacle stand, it felt to her like a historic moment. Until recently, women leaders had been seated in the audience during conference, but now one of the large, red, plush-upholstered chairs on the stand was designated for her, and she walked to it under the gaze of thousands. "It was a long walk," she said. Still, when she took her seat on the Tabernacle stand, Kapp felt she was better prepared for her new assignment and more confident in her abilities than she would have been a few years earlier.[1]

Since her release as a counselor in the general presidency six years earlier, Kapp had undergone a period of personal and professional development that prepared her to take on this new role. She had entered the Latter-day Saint speaking circuit, teaching at Brigham Young University's annual Education Week and traveling around the United States to give presentations at church-sponsored Know Your Religion seminars for adults. A schoolteacher with a master's degree in curriculum design who had previously worked in the College of Education at BYU, Kapp was recruited in 1979 to become coordinator of Student Leadership Development at the university. Kapp also served as chair of the advisory committee on women's concerns at BYU, which brought together women and men from across the faculty to study and address women's issues at the university.[2]

Kapp's work at BYU had involved identifying and applying values as a basis for student leadership. This focus on values carried over into a new professional opportunity in 1983, when she accepted a contract as a consultant for Charles Hobbs, a former church employee who had established himself in the growing field of executive training with an emphasis on values-based time management.[3] Kapp mastered Hobbs's concepts and presentation methods quickly and learned to adapt her teaching style to audiences with various professional backgrounds. It was excellent preparation, she later reflected, for standing with confidence in front of general authorities, knowing what she wanted to say and how to say it effectively.[4]

Kapp also found direction for her assignment in the blessing Hinckley gave her when setting her apart in her new assignment. She recalled him declaring that in the coming years, "we will see the Young Women of the Church awaken like a sleeping giant and rise up and begin to move across the face of the earth in a mighty force for righteousness."[5] Kapp internalized this statement as a prophetic vision for the young women of the church that would guide her presidency as they and the church as a whole navigated the crosscurrents of society in the 1980s. During this time, questions regarding the status of women in the church became increasingly urgent. The women's movement had continued to gain momentum in American society, generating real changes in women's life patterns related to work, education, marriage, and legal status—as well as much loud and heated discussion. Church leaders had voiced strong opposition to the Equal Rights Amendment, and some members had led organized resistance to it. The amendment failed to be ratified, and in the years that followed, the church and its leaders faced intense scrutiny over women's issues.[6] Some Latter-day Saint feminists decried gendered disparities in power and representation at all levels in the church, and correlation changes intensified some of their objections. Even many Latter-day Saint women who generally supported the church's emphasis on motherhood and homemaking longed for women to be more involved in local and general church structures.[7]

Seating women leaders on the Tabernacle stand during general conference, which had begun during Elaine Cannon's tenure, seemed to be one response to such currents. Then, at the April 1984 general conference, four women leaders—including both Kapp and Cannon—spoke in general sessions. It was the first time women had spoken in a general session of conference in fifty-four years.[8] "We were in a period of time when women were seeking more visibility," Kapp recalled.[9] Like Cannon, Kapp was college educated and had worked professionally for most of her adult life, a path women were choosing more frequently, often in combination with marriage and family. Accordingly, Kapp felt it was crucial for young women to develop a solid spiritual identity that would prepare them for any future path.

Kapp also knew that young women in the United States of the 1980s experienced a bewildering level of competition for their attention from television, magazines, and other media. Some of that media seemed intent on undermining young women's sense of self by bombarding them with unhealthy and unrealistic images of women's bodies, which contributed to a sharp rise in eating disorders such as anorexia and bulimia. Church leaders watched these trends with great concern and also worried about rising drug use and increasing sexual activity among adolescents.[10]

At the same time, the number of converts worldwide continued to grow exponentially, which brought both celebrations and challenges.[11] Rapid church growth meant that fledgling branches and districts struggled to fill leadership positions in their local Young Women organizations, even as general leaders in Salt Lake City strove to understand and meet the needs of an increasingly diverse membership. And in many parts of the world, young church members faced their own challenges. Teens everywhere, but particularly in already-impoverished areas, faced stark repercussions of the economic recession of the late 1970s and early 1980s, which led to even higher rates of poverty and the need for many young people, especially young women, to work to help their families get by.[12] As the church expanded, young women's attendance percentages continued to gradually decrease and had dipped below fifty percent.[13] Additionally, the Young Women organization was still seeking stability in the wake of the wrenching changes in the previous decade and also trying to provide clear messaging to young women and their leaders.

Of particular concern to Kapp was her sense that young women struggled to find a grounded sense of identity both in the world and in the church amid the storm of voices and opinions directed at them.[14] Funk and Cannon had successfully brought young women's identity as daughters of God to the forefront of Young Women messaging; Kapp sought a more structured approach to fostering this identity. Sunday instruction during the block meeting schedule had by this time become a key element of young women's church experience. Regular Sunday meetings gave young women and local leaders a sense of continuity even as Kapp set out to rework the activity and achievement programs to make them more globally relevant. To help young women develop a Christ-centered identity, Kapp launched a plan to define core values, overhaul the My Personal Progress program, improve the relationship between the Young Women and Young Men organizations and their members, and harness the power of media to broadcast her vision for young women. The result would be a period of awakening and redefinition for the organization, setting patterns that would define the experience of hundreds of thousands of Latter-day Saint young women for decades to come.

ASSESSING NEEDS

Kapp felt she experienced an outpouring of divine inspiration about her new stewardship almost as soon as she was invited to serve. "I'm seeking to know the Lord's will concerning the mission for young women of the Church at this time in church history, a mission upon which we must base all of our decisions for training, planning, activities, programs, and preparation for their future," she wrote in her journal the week after being sustained in general conference.[15] "It seems to me the heavens are opening and thoughts, directions, spiritual promptings are coming so fast."[16]

Kapp's first task was to form a presidency.[17] For first counselor, she selected Patricia Terry Holland, who had served as a ward Young Women president and Relief Society president. Maurine Johnson Turley, Kapp's choice for second counselor, was the principal of the church seminary program at a junior high school in Bountiful, Utah, and was working toward a graduate degree in education.[18] The presidency worked closely with their administrative assistant, Carolyn J. Rasmus, an experienced teacher who earned a doctoral degree in physical education and special education before teaching in the College of Physical Education at BYU. She then served as administrative assistant to BYU presidents Dallin H. Oaks and Jeffrey R. Holland, Patricia Holland's husband, before coming to work for the Young Women presidency.[19] Because the counselors had heavy responsibilities beyond their Young Women assignments, Kapp and Rasmus often worked together to develop and implement ideas the full presidency had formulated. Over the course of Kapp's administration, her counselors changed three times, and a total of eighteen women served on the general board.[20]

Kapp, Holland, Turley, and Rasmus approached their new responsibilities methodically. Kapp had been told she would serve for about five years, and she was determined to establish a lasting foundation for the organization—something that would "fit all over the world" and still be relevant in ten years because, she knew, "it might take us that long to get the water to the end of the row."[21] Kapp understood that the review and approval processes established as part of the correlation movement might move slowly, but she also knew that the processes could result in broad support from church leadership, giving this new foundation staying power that had eluded other recent efforts at change.

Through this process of study and assessment, the presidency identified what they believed were clear deficiencies in the organization. On the ward level, the position of adult adviser for each Young Women class had been discontinued, leaving only the four members of the Young Women presidency to administer the entire program and build relationships with the young women. Responsibility for activities had been moved to the ward activities committee, which often did not coordinate with the youth organizations. There were therefore two entities—the Young Women organization and the activities committee—competing for the time of young women. Combined activities with young men—a hallmark of the program Kapp had helped design a decade earlier—had diminished in prominence. Kapp was also concerned that attendance rates for young women decreased as they grew older. Internal church studies showed that Latter-day Saint young women developed their identity in relation to the church through the Young Women organization, yet it seemed that fewer young women were becoming involved and that the organization had less to offer them.[22] As Kapp and her board considered these challenges, they gathered information from academic studies and from people in the community who worked with girls in organizations such as Girl Scouts and 4-H.[23]

Immediately upon her appointment, Kapp felt she needed to emphasize a few principles to guide young women: leadership experiences, responsibility and accountability in decision-making, prioritizing for eternal purposes, and developing a sense of values as a measuring stick. She also felt the Young Women organization needed a mission statement parallel to the scriptural mandate for the Aaronic Priesthood.[24] Based on their research, the presidency identified a list of twelve needs for the organization; emerging as the most important of those needs were a stronger sense of identity and increased recognition for young women, a developmental approach to personal progress that included more faith-building experiences and family involvement, and an increased feeling of worldwide sisterhood among young women.[25]

Kapp and her team set to work to put these principles into usable form. She knew it would be impossible to do everything they identified. Rather, they intended to focus on the unique spiritual needs of young women. In past generations, the organization had provided wide-ranging social and cultural experiences, but young women now found many of those types of activities through school and extracurricular channels. Changed times required a new vision. "What we were responsible for was to give them what no one else could give them," Kapp affirmed. The mission of the organization would be to help young women come to know God and realize their divine potential.[26]

IDENTIFYING VALUES FOR YOUNG WOMEN

On 6 and 7 August 1984, Kapp, Holland, Turley, and Rasmus held a retreat at a cabin in the mountains in Utah to begin solidifying a set of guiding values for the Young Women organization. They fasted in preparation and took time to share their feelings before engaging in quiet individual study in the scriptures. Then together they brainstormed concerns, desires, and needs of young women, which yielded a long list. Each woman then went individually into the woods to ponder and record what she felt the most important priorities were, and when they returned, they found that they had all identified the same principles. "The Spirit was unrestrained. We went home rejoicing," wrote Kapp.[27] A few weeks later, the entire board held an all-day working session in which board member Maren Mouritsen led the group in identifying the values the board thought were most critical for the organization, modifying and adding to those the presidency had previously identified. The resulting list served as the foundation for the rest of their work. They chose faith, divine nature, individual worth, knowledge, choice and accountability, and integrity; good works would be added to the list by the time the values were officially announced.[28]

The choice of mostly internal values was a contrast to prior approaches, which often focused on observable virtues. The areas of focus in the My Personal Progress program released in 1983 emphasized consistent devotional behaviors, cultural refinement, and domesticity.[29] While these emphases were consistent with the broader teaching in the church, Kapp wanted a different way to articulate what was important specifically for Latter-day Saint young women.[30] Though Kapp shared with other church leaders a concern about the moral challenges young women faced, the list of values did not include perennial moral categories such as chastity and modesty. Kapp and her board believed those virtues could be taught as examples of underlying spiritual characteristics. Sexuality, for example, could be discussed as an element of humans' inherent divine nature. Within the value of individual worth, young women could find motivation to respect their bodies and not seek validation through sexual attention. The value of integrity could encourage them to honor commitments to chaste living. The life pattern Kapp wanted to teach young women was fundamentally focused on a relationship with God—and morality would be a consequence of that focus. She believed a strong spiritual foundation would help young women address the moral dilemmas they faced. "They need a strong testimony to meet the challenges and to resist the temptations of these days," she said, echoing the words of generations of her predecessors.[31]

Unexpectedly, the term *values* became a sticking point as the proposed changes to the organization worked their way through the correlation approval process. By the 1980s, the term *values* was prominent in American culture, but it had several different associations. Politically, the term *family values* had been adopted by the Christian Right in the United States to express their opposition to abortion, feminism, and homosexuality, which they saw as threats to the traditional family. Latter-day Saints shared many of these same concerns.[32] *Values* had also become associated with the movement known as secular humanism, which argued that people were capable of being moral and ethical without religion and advocated a reliance on science, technology, and human cooperation and goodwill to solve the problems of humanity. Humanists believed that their values, such as "the preciousness and dignity of the individual person," were obstructed by religion.[33] In contrast to the use of *values* by the religious Right, secular humanists employed the term to separate morality from religion.

In a talk given in 1978, Neal A. Maxwell, one of the presidents of the Quorum of the Seventy, denounced secular humanism for engendering what he characterized as an intolerant, dangerously orthodox imperialism that would disallow a person's opinion when it was based upon a religious conviction. Maxwell also worried about secularized "value education" in schools.[34] In objecting to the term *values*, the correlation committee had identified a potential source of tension between Kapp's proposed framing and Maxwell's public messages. "It was at a time in the world when people were talking about humanistic values," Kapp recalled, "and so they [correlation staff members] felt that to use values in the context of the Church was totally inappropriate, and they also felt that we were establishing a new program that was placing more emphasis on values than it was on the gospel."[35] In the correlation process, however, such an objection did not end the conversation. Kapp had time to consider whether to choose an alternative label with less complex connotations or to make the case for keeping the term *values* in her proposal.

Kapp decided to make the case for retaining the term *values*. She had seen how some Latter-day Saints in business consulting were expanding conversations about values in yet another direction. She had been part of this trend while working with Charles Hobbs, whose major innovation in the time management field was to recommend that clients define their values and then organize their time around them.[36] Kapp's advocacy of values for young women built on her professional experience and her own ideas about the power of shaping one's life around one's most deeply held values.

Kapp felt that values provided a sound organizing principle for young women's religious and self-improvement efforts. Values were something one internalized (or already had), so they had more meaning in the short term and greater staying power later. Kapp also thought the shift she championed—from "areas of focus" to "values"—provided young women with a more specific Latter-day-Saint framing.[37] Kapp had been concerned since her service in Funk's presidency that Young Women materials were not teaching principles unique to the church.[38] The areas of focus in the existing My Personal Progress program (spiritual awareness; service and compassion; homemaking arts; recreation and the world of nature; cultural arts and education;

and personal and social refinement) would have been relevant for young people from a variety of religious backgrounds. In contrast, the Young Women values Kapp proposed were formulated to express Latter-day Saint doctrine, building on one another. Divine nature, for example, expressed the belief that all human beings are literal spirit children of God and have the potential to become like Him. Individual worth grew out of this truth—a young woman's identity as a daughter of God gave her inherent worth that was not dependent on worldly accomplishments or validation. Choice and accountability expressed the Latter-day Saint view that agency—the ability and responsibility to choose good over evil—was a central purpose of this life; young women who understood their divine nature and individual worth would be better prepared to make choices that would help them draw nearer to Christ. Each of the values was reinforced by scripture references. Divine nature, for example, was linked to 2 Peter 1:4–7, which speaks of Christians becoming "partakers of the divine nature." Individual worth reflected one of Joseph Smith's revelations that declared, "the worth of souls is great in the sight of God."[39] The secular humanist use of values distanced conversation about ethics and morals away from a religious center, but Kapp's move to derive values from church doctrine and make them central to the identities and decision-making of young women was a reclaiming of values in the other, explicitly religious, direction.

NAVIGATING APPROVALS AND LINES OF AUTHORITY

Kapp embraced the correlation principles she had learned during her tenure on the Youth Correlation Committee and in Funk's presidency a decade earlier. In the early months of her presidency, Kapp was part of a coordinating effort in which the presidents of the women-led organizations met with priesthood leaders to discuss the role of auxiliaries within the church structure. This group composed a document that set forth some basic principles for how auxiliaries were to work within the priesthood line. According to this document, the auxiliaries were to be the "eyes and ears" for the lead decision makers in the Quorum of the Twelve Apostles, reporting their observations and making recommendations. They were also to represent to those leaders the needs of those within their stewardship, and they were to help prepare resource materials for their organizations. The coordinating group also explored the need for more input from women when decisions were being made and considered forming a women's advisory council for that purpose.[40]

While the ideas presented in the document did not become binding, the process of creating it helped Kapp further internalize the principles it articulated, reinforcing her understanding that the Young Women general presidency was "a resource to the priesthood committees of the Church," rather than a decision-making

000089760421

Inspected By:Raquel_Aguilar

Sell your books at
World of Books!
Go to sell.worldofbooks.com
and get an instant price quote.
We even pay the shipping - see
what your old books are worth
today!

Sell your books at
World of Books!
Go to sell.worldofbooks.com
and get an instant price quote.
We even pay the shipping - see
what your old books are worth
today!

Inspected By: pedro_aguilar

0008670925421

body in its own right.[41] She told her board, "I believe our responsibility is to study the issues, to identify the concerns, and then, when we meet with the priesthood leaders, to be prepared to ask the most relevant questions," and, if asked, "be prepared to make a recommendation."[42]

Kapp believed this same relationship between priesthood and auxiliary leaders needed to exist at every level of church leadership—from general leadership down to wards and branches—if the organization was going to be effective. She insisted that Young Women "had to be just a piece of the priesthood organization, directed by the priesthood, with the responsibility for the success of this program resting upon the bishop and the stake president and the message being carried by the General Authorities." It was vital that priesthood leaders understand, as Kapp put it, "that the Young Women program is just the gospel of Jesus Christ for young women"; only then would they be as committed to its success as they were to that of the Aaronic Priesthood program for young men.[43] Kapp knew these ideals had been present in the 1970s when she helped reshape the organization through correlation principles; she also knew there was still some distance to go in realizing those ideals.

Kapp was also keenly aware of the limitations of her position within the larger structure of the church. The Young Women organization now reported through the Priesthood Department, which was led by a member of the Quorum of the Seventy as executive director and one or more additional seventies as managing directors, and then up to the Priesthood Executive Committee (PEC), which was made up of members of the Quorum of the Twelve Apostles.[44] Usually referring to the executive and managing directors of the Priesthood Department as the Young Women presidency's "priesthood leaders" or "advisers," Kapp viewed them not only as supervisors in the sense that they oversaw the presidency's work within the church's lines of reporting but also as counselors and advocates who facilitated, supported, encouraged, and made important contributions to the work of the Young Women.[45]

While this understanding brought clarity and a sense of direction, it also presented challenges. Kapp once wrote to the executive director of the Priesthood Department that the presidency wanted "to be as helpful and aggressive as is appropriate in doing our part to build the Kingdom."[46] But how aggressive was appropriate? Assuring male leaders that they were willing to take initiative in filling their responsibilities, the female leaders also felt it necessary to affirm that their assertiveness was not to be feared and would be expressed appropriately. Within those parameters, Kapp was determined to press forward and accomplish as much as possible. "I didn't want us to do *more* than we should, but I didn't want to do *less*," she explained, knowing she was not the final arbiter of where the line would fall.[47]

The Young Women organization's position within the lines of authority running through the Priesthood Department meant there were layers of hierarchy between Kapp and the ultimate decision makers who would render final approval on the organization's proposals. There was no provision for the Young Women presidency to meet regularly with the PEC. Instead, the executive director of the Priesthood Department represented them in regular meetings and arranged for the presidency to meet with the PEC only on some occasions. Likewise, the executive director often represented the work of the Young Women leaders to correlation committees. Members of the Young Women general presidency, therefore, were often not present in meetings that were vital to approval of their plans. When an item finally made it to the PEC or a correlation committee for approval, if anyone had a question that the executive representing the Young Women presidency could not answer, the Young Women presidency might have to wait another month or two before they or their representative would be on the agenda again and could answer it.[48] These dynamics were further complicated by the fact that during the eight years of Kapp's presidency, the executive director of the Priesthood Department changed five times. The person coming into the assignment needed to be oriented before issuing any approvals, and the time required for that orientation meant substantial delays and repeated work.[49] It was not until the month of Kapp's release that the women presidents of auxiliaries began meeting with the PEC.[50]

Kapp and her team approached these challenges with confidence and persistence. In September 1984, as they were preparing for the general women's meeting to be held in conjunction with October general conference, Kapp received a message that one of the speakers wanted to cede his time in the meeting to a video highlighting Sharlene Wells, who was recently crowned Miss America, the first Latter-day Saint to win that title since Colleen Kay Hutchins in 1951. For their first opportunity to speak to the young women of the church, however, the presidency wanted to send the message that young women did not have to be beautiful, popular, or academically successful to be valued. Their whole idea, Kapp said, "was to minimize the physical beauty that the world was putting such emphasis on." At the same time, only a few months into their administration, Kapp's presidency wanted to proceed carefully in questioning the decision because they were also trying to build trust and goodwill with priesthood leaders.[51]

As Kapp and her counselors discussed the matter, they wondered whether the decision to show the video had been a hasty one or something its originators felt was inspired. After reviewing an article by Spencer W. Kimball in which he decried swimsuit contests, they decided it had likely been hasty.[52] The four leaders—Kapp, Turley, Holland, and Rasmus—knelt together and prayed to know how to handle the issue, and while they were still kneeling, Kapp stated, "I feel a strong impression I should call Elder [Thomas S.] Monson." He was very warm on the phone and even called back to invite her to meet the following morning with several members of the Twelve who were in town at the time. He also asked her to bring the Relief Society and Primary general presidents. Kapp and her presidency decided to fast until after her meeting. She learned at the meeting that the decision had indeed been hasty and that it would be reversed. Additionally, Monson said it was important that priesthood leaders receive more input from the auxiliary leaders, and some of the leaders present thanked the women presidents for "keeping our feet to the fire."[53] Through her efforts, Kapp built trust and strong relationships with priesthood leaders, even if her interactions with them were sometimes intermittent and mediated.

THE KEY IS TURNED

The Young Women general board formally adopted the seven values and a preliminary five-year plan for the organization in November 1984.[54] The next step was a presentation to the PEC for their approval to move forward with the values and other aspects of their plan, including a satellite broadcast to reach young women throughout the church. The presentation would be a high-level, high-stakes opportunity.

On Sunday, 6 January 1985, Kapp awakened early and began to write as quickly as she could as ideas and inspiration flowed into her mind. All the pieces and parts, the data, problems, proposals—all these small, separate efforts came together in what seemed to her "like a magnificent mosaic." Eventually, she felt the elements fall into place for her proposal to the PEC, which she described as being presented "in behalf of the youth of the Church, particularly young women." After she finished her rough outline, she felt that this proposal had come after six months of careful labor but ultimately by revelation. She felt spiritually uplifted but physically and emotionally exhausted. She offered a prayer of gratitude, and then she called Carolyn Rasmus. "I've been to the mountain," she said, invoking scriptural stories that depicted revelation coming in mountain settings.[55]

Two days later, the presidency met with Dean L. Larsen, executive director of the Priesthood Department, and he scheduled the PEC presentation for 20 February 1985.[56] This gave Kapp and her team six weeks to prepare. Kapp's proposal document represented the culmination of almost a year's work as the new presidency had taken time to study, assess, and formulate ideas before presenting any proposals.[57] Because of Kapp's experience working with correlation processes as a member of Funk's presidency, she believed that priesthood leaders were looking to simplify and reduce church operations and did not want new programs. While in practice they retained little of what had come before, Kapp and her associates firmly maintained that they were refining the program already in place, enriching it so it had a distinctly Latter-day Saint focus and relating it to ordinances and covenants.[58]

The presidency had purchased a computerized system called VideoShow that displayed images and graphics.[59] Once the machine was loaded with materials about the state of the Young Women organization and the proposed values, Kapp began inviting members of the Twelve and the Seventy to stop by and see what the new system could do. Whenever Kapp met a decision maker in the lunchroom and he asked her how things were going, she told him the Young Women office had a new piece of equipment that she would love to show him if he ever had thirty minutes to stop by. One by one, about fifteen men came, and as each saw how the machine worked, he also learned about the presidency's plans. Most of them stayed an hour and offered advice so that by the date of the presentation, the materials were polished, and several priesthood leaders understood and acted as advocates for the Young Women presidency's plans.[60]

On the morning of 20 February, Kapp and her counselors met in a small room and knelt to pray one last time. They were preparing to meet with apostles Thomas S. Monson, David B. Haight, Neal A. Maxwell, and Ezra Taft Benson and with Carlos E. Asay of the Seventy, presiding bishop Victor L. Brown, and Dean L. Larsen.[61] "We sensed that this was really going to launch us in a direction, if it was approved," Kapp recalled. Kapp and her counselors, however, had no desire to see their plan adopted if it was a poor fit for the priorities of the church as a whole. They prayed that if it was right, the others at the meeting would hear them and understand and accept the proposals. If what they had prepared did not align with the will of God, they prayed that the priesthood leaders would not hesitate to stop them and that "their ears would be closed" to the proposal.[62]

The presentation unfolded in three sections: the current status of young women, perceived problems affecting them, and recommendations to address those problems. "We are anxious to share our findings so we might receive your counsel and direction and determine how you would wish us to serve as a resource and in what areas we have shared concerns," the introductory statement read.[63] The first section of the presentation identified a central question regarding the Young Women organization and the girls themselves: "What are they receiving as young women that will increase their conversion and commitment to the gospel?" Kapp listed five needs of young women: acceptable role models, positive learning experiences, recognition, appropriate validation and identity, and faith-promoting and spiritual experiences.[64]

Kapp then compared the experience of young women in the church with that of young men. While emphasizing that she was not suggesting young men and young women should have identical provisions, she laid out quantifiable disparities. Young men had at least six avenues of public recognition in the church, including priesthood ordination and duties, Scouting awards, and regular attention from the bishop. Young women had only two—one of which amounted to an attendance award. The Young Men organization was allocated up to eighteen adult leaders in the ward; the Young Women, only four. Priesthood leadership training for Young Men leaders was much more extensive than the minimal local training provided for Young Women leaders. By Kapp's count, the Young Women organization had 17 pages of published resource material, compared with 191 for Young Men (not including Scouting materials). And comparison of budget resources expended on each organization showed a "notable" difference.[65] Kapp cited academic studies showing that girls' self-esteem was significantly lower than boys' and posited that dynamics within the church were contributing to young women's problems. "Current Church practices appear to contribute to low self-esteem," she asserted. "The apparent ambiguity of the Young Women program may encourage many to seek approval and validation through popularity in the ways of the world."[66]

Having laid out this alarming picture, Kapp raised the issue of Young Women members and leaders having only limited access to people in positions of authority since the structural reorganization of the 1970s. She affirmed her support for having bishops, stake presidents, and general authorities more directly involved with Young Women while noting that the desired involvement was not always realized. She invited listeners to consider, "In what settings could Young Women leaders and priesthood leaders meet regularly (at every level) to address needs and hear the 'whole story' as well as serve as a resource to the priesthood leaders so that needs of young women might be considered in a responsible way?"[67]

She then offered the presidency's recommendations. Young women needed a structured program for validation and recognition, within an organization that allowed them to contribute to the mission of the church and that was based on fundamental gospel principles and guiding values. She listed and briefly explained those values: faith, divine nature, individual worth, knowledge, choice and accountability, good works, and integrity.[68] The values were the heart of the proposal, the culmination to which the rest of the presentation led. After presenting the values, Kapp ended the presentation with an offer and a call to arms. "Brethren, if you want to know about Young Men, you can hear about them at the annual priesthood restoration commemoration. If you want to know about Young Men, you can be aware of their annual Scouting conference. . . . But if you want to know about Young Women," she said, "the satellite screen is dark, the message vague, and the statistics alarming. . . . How can we help?"[69]

The leaders' responses were eager and heartfelt. Monson said, "We must address the challenge. . . . We must put our attention to this problem. . . . You have our strong endorsement of what has been said here." Maxwell emphasized that he believed they needed to delete nearly all other items from the PEC agenda, saying, "This is how strongly I feel about this." Benson asked the men to stand to signify the importance of what they had heard. Especially meaningful to Kapp was a comment by Benson, which she heard as a direct response to the presidency's prayer. He said that the men's "ears [were] opened."[70]

By the time Kapp returned to her office, someone from the meeting was already on the phone asking how soon the Young Women could have a satellite broadcast ready to present the new values to the worldwide church. In the chronology she wrote for her presidential tenure, Kapp wrote next to 20 February, "Today the key has been turned in behalf of young women"—an allusion to Joseph Smith's words at an early meeting of the Relief Society organization.[71] She saw the meeting as a crucial moment that would enable the Young Women organization to fulfill its potential in the lives of its young members, integrate more fully into the structure of the church, and help the young women of the church fulfill their own destinies.

The fireside itself would be a dramatic event. Kapp said it could not take place until November because she wanted everything to be thoroughly vetted and polished for the values launch. She wanted to present the values in a way that young women, their parents, and their leaders, male and female, would remember and understand. Knowing how long approvals could take, she wanted to be sure the presidency and board had enough time to produce a film for the fireside and a special issue of the *New Era* to distribute at the end of the event.[72]

Over the next several months, the Young Women presidency and board worked hard to prepare. Kapp and her team composed first-person statements for each value. The statement for choice and accountability, for example, read, "I will remain free by choosing good over evil and will accept responsibility for my choices." Kapp later explained that these statements were designed to be an affirmation, to identify a relationship, and to set an expectation.[73] The statements went through several drafts, and apostle Russell M. Nelson eventually sent a letter to the head of correlation staff to say they had been approved by the PEC, the Quorum of the Twelve Apostles, and the First Presidency.[74] But correlation committee members had two concerns about the approved statement for faith, which read, "I am a daughter of Heavenly Parents." The first was that this value statement would be the only one without some action involved for the young woman reciting the statement. The second concern was the reference to heavenly parents. While there was a long history of Latter-day Saint leaders teaching about a Heavenly Mother, those teachings did not appear in scripture.[75]

Each value statement was paired with a scripture in the proposal, so the board discussed the statement until they came to consensus on a revised draft—"I am a daughter of Heavenly Father, who loves me, and I have faith in His eternal plan"—and they proposed an accompanying scripture about God the Father. References to heavenly parents were retained in some other materials related to the values, but the final version of the values statement referenced faith in Heavenly Father rather than the more distinctively Latter-day Saint belief in heavenly parents.[76] The values worked their way through the approvals process, finally receiving full approval in August 1985.[77]

During this process, Young Women board members came to think a statement such as a pledge would be appropriate for young women and leaders to recite in conjunction with the values. With her background in curriculum design, Kapp understood that this statement should be built on a developmental sequence that addressed the questions *Who am I?*, *What am I to do?*, and *Why am I to do it?* The values were arranged in the statement to follow that sequence: understanding one's relationship to God engendered faith, faith brought a sense of divine identity and individual worth, and these principles built knowledge, which provided a basis for choices and good works. Integrity was a summation of all the values. The board members hoped that as young women repeated the pledge, they would internalize it and the values would become part of their core identity.[78]

Kapp's presidency formulated the pledge—which came to be called the Young Women theme—in collaboration with general authorities. J. Thomas Fyans, who had replaced Dean L. Larsen as the executive director of the Priesthood Department early in 1985, played a crucial role as facilitator. Fyans had told Kapp that her job was to seek and receive revelation for her assignment. Of his own role, he said, "You tell me where the big rocks in the road are, and my job is to try to remove the obstacles."[79] Fyans promised to facilitate general authority approval despite objections to the proposed theme and values from a forceful staff member of a correlation committee. As the theme struggled through the approvals process, Fyans took the unprecedented step of inviting the Young Women presidency to lunch at the temple with the seven presidents of the Quorum of the Seventy for a working meeting. In that setting, Fyans talked through the values with the male leaders. Then the women and men worked together to formulate the theme into almost-final form. This working session was exactly the kind of male-female engagement and collaboration Kapp hoped for, echoing the dynamics that had prevailed in the early years of correlation, as those in attendance collaborated to solve a problem and furthered Fyans's goal of removing obstacles.[80] The meeting was an important step for Kapp and her counselors in building support for their vision. Fyans served as managing director for only six months, but he played a crucial role in helping realize the Young Women presidency's plans.

When he was transferred to serve as an area president in South America, Kapp listed over two dozen changes he had facilitated, including the theme, several publications, and "enough exposure with the general authorities that they are aware and supportive of the concern for young women."[81]

An announcement made at the 9 October 1985 PEC meeting made clear that the First Presidency and the Quorum of the Twelve Apostles had approved the Young Women presidency's proposals. The presidency of the First Quorum of the Seventy also gave approval.[82] A year after the Young Women board first determined the values, the presidency had all the approvals they needed to launch those values, their accompanying value statements, and the Young Women theme at their satellite fireside, which had been scheduled for 10 November. The idea for two other events—an evening focused on values called "Young Women in Excellence" and a worldwide Young Women Day—were also approved.[83] The wording of the Young Women theme, as approved and presented at the satellite fireside, read as follows: "We are daughters of a Heavenly Father who loves us, and we love him. We will 'stand as witnesses of God at all times and in all things, and in all places . . .' as we strive to live the Young Women Values."[84]

FIRESIDE BY SATELLITE

On the evening of 10 November 1985, the lights in the Salt Lake Tabernacle dimmed, and a video began to play, with voice-over narration by Kapp. The scene was an ocean, with waves rolling dramatically against large rocks, sweeping onto the beach. "Stand with me at the sea shore," she invited. "Feel the breeze. Look out over the mighty ocean. . . . I can see the crest of a wave forming, a wave that will move across the earth, reaching every continent and every shore: Young women, we send out a call throughout all the world, a call that you hear with your heart and spirit. . . . Prepare to take your place in a great forward movement among the young women of the church."[85]

The fireside unfolded in an array of music, spoken word, and pageantry, broadcast by satellite to many of the organization's three hundred thousand members in meetinghouses around the world. The live audience in the Tabernacle also included many of the church's prominent leaders. Initially, some had been hesitant to accept Kapp's invitation. Apostle Boyd K. Packer explained that they worried a heavy presence of male leaders would contribute to the criticism that the church was run by men. But Kapp explained that she hoped general authorities would attend the fireside because she believed that collaboration between women and men created effective programs; Packer saw her reasoning.[86] Kapp also recognized that some of these men were the ultimate decision makers when it came to church programs and policies; she wanted them to understand the organization for young women and young women's needs when they made their decisions.

The support from priesthood leadership ultimately exceeded Kapp's expectations. Just five days before the fireside was to take place, ninety-year-old church president Spencer W. Kimball died.[87] Kapp initially thought that the fireside would be canceled altogether, but Russell M. Nelson called the next morning to assure her it would proceed. Furthermore, general authorities who had not planned to attend the fireside because of travel plans now canceled those plans to attend Kimball's funeral. Seven members of the Twelve, thirteen members of the Seventy, and Ezra Taft Benson, who succeeded Kimball as the church's president, attended the fireside.[88] Gordon B. Hinckley of the First Presidency and Nelson of the Twelve delivered earnest, optimistic remarks highlighting young women as daughters of God and daughters of Zion. Kapp delivered a stirring call for young women to stand up and lead out for righteousness. "To every young woman, throughout the entire Church, in every corner of the land: You are important, each one of you," she proclaimed.[89]

The video presentation in the Tabernacle then opened a sequence that formed the heart of the evening: an introduction of the Young Women values and theme. As viewers experienced the narration and orchestral music, a young woman named Astrid S. Tuminez appeared on the screen, walking along the shore. A twenty-year-old majoring in Russian and international relations at BYU, Astrid had trod a long path to the Tabernacle. The sixth of seven children, she spent her early childhood in the slums of Gomez Beach in Iloilo City on the Philippine island of Panay. Her makeshift home had no electricity or running water, and when the soles of her shoes wore out, she used candy wrappers to fill in the holes. Astrid joined the church as a child and attended the Iloilo Second Branch alongside fifty to sixty other Saints each week. Beginning when she was eleven, Astrid served as secretary of the Primary and Sunday School; at fifteen, she taught seminary. In 1982, she came to Utah, and her two older sisters—who were already in the United States—worked to fund her first year of college. Thereafter she obtained scholarships, working her way toward what would become a distinguished career in international relations and education.[90]

The choice to feature Astrid prominently in the video highlighted the presidency's desire to build a sense of worldwide sisterhood among young women and brought a vibrant global awareness to the production. This theme continued as the video introduced the values. Each value statement was recited by a young woman who then invited the audience to internalize it and live by it, as each value appeared on the screen in Spanish, French, and English. These young women represented a wide array of cultural backgrounds, including a young woman from the Catawba Nation in South Carolina, another from Mexico City, identical twins from Arizona, an African American young woman from Louisiana, and others from England, British Columbia, and Utah. Each young woman offered meaningful personal testimony of how each value pertained to the gospel of Jesus Christ as well as how it applied to everyday life.[91] While the speakers, choir, and other participants were mostly white, the clear message of the video was that Latter-day Saint young women lived all over the world, with varied heritages that were something to celebrate. Compared with racial representation in past churchwide events, the fireside was resoundingly diverse, though the board received some criticism that the event was not racially diverse enough.[92] For decades, as the church grew dramatically around the world, the primary model had been to export programs and an accompanying self-image that were fundamentally white, American, and Utah-centered. The Young Women presentation, consciously shaped by a more racially and geographically diverse sensibility, symbolized growing awareness of the need to balance the flow of influence between the church's cultural center and its global membership.

As the video faded, the lights in the Tabernacle came up to show Astrid standing at the front. "As young women of The Church of Jesus Christ of Latter-day Saints and daughters of a loving Heavenly Father," she said, "we believe as we come to accept and act upon these values, we will be prepared to make and keep sacred covenants, receive the ordinances of the temple, and enjoy the blessings of exaltation." As she named each value, groups of young women in the congregation stood to repeat the value and its statement, and a banner unfurled bearing the name of the value in English and one other language (a different one for each value). Maurine Turley then stood and led the congregation in repeating the Young Women theme. "Dear young women, we hope with all of our hearts that you will memorize this theme, write it in your journal, talk about it, ponder it, repeat it until it becomes a part of you," Turley urged.[93] A chorus of 130 young women then sang "I Walk by Faith," a song written especially for the event.[94]

In the fireside's grand finale, the choir (later joined by the congregation) sang an extended medley of well-known church hymns, featuring Ruth May Fox's anthem for youth, "Carry On," as the theme connecting them all. Dozens of young women filed in from the wings and marched up and down the aisles waving flags in all the colors representing the new values. The song and the waving flags, reminiscent of the 1930 centennial June Conference in which young women and young men first sang Fox's hymn, combined to offer a display that reflected both the heritage of the Young Women organization and its members and their new focus on identity and values.

Young Women fireside and worldwide satellite broadcast. 1985. In the fireside, Ardeth Greene Kapp and her presidency introduced the Young Women theme and values. Music at the fireside brought together new changes and past traditions as young women sang Ruth May Fox's 1930 MIA anthem, "Carry On," while holding aloft flags with colors representing each of the new values. (Courtesy *Church News*, copy at Church History Library, Salt Lake City.)

HARNESSING THE POWER OF MEDIA

The fireside itself was a multimedia spectacle, and its use of mass media and innovative technology was part of a broader churchwide movement. In 1974, newly ordained church president Spencer W. Kimball had urged the use of advances in media technology to further missionary work and other church efforts. He declared it imperative for leaders to make full use of these advances, particularly in broadcasting messages of faith to members and other interested people around the world.[95] By the 1980s, leaders were rolling out campaigns that included purchasing television spots for inspirational public service messages and invitations to receive church literature, which generated referrals for local missionaries. Satellite broadcasts also became increasingly prevalent. For example, the technology was used for seasonal broadcasts of church movies to local meetinghouses and for missionary open houses where apostles and other leaders could speak directly to individuals considering joining the church.[96]

Kapp's use of mass media and new technology became a hallmark of her tenure. Deeply aware of the impacts of popular media on young women, she harnessed newly available technology to combat the negative influence of media. Her emphasis on participatory experiences contrasted with traditional mass communication forms that worked in a one-way flow, such as a broadcast speaker sharing ideas to a passive listening audience. Participatory gestures such as having the fireside audience recite the new Young Women theme together or imagine themselves on the seashore helped Kapp cultivate a worldwide sense of sisterhood. She and her presidency mixed striking imagery and strong rhetorical approaches with these participatory elements to make the most of the available media. Kapp's presidency also prepared participatory training videos for Young Women leaders, including one interactive video that instructed participants to pause the video and discuss the principles being presented.[97]

Kapp also understood the importance of music in communicating the new message and pushing back against other negative messages. In the late 1970s and through the 1980s, an explosion of popular Latter-day Saint music began making musicians like Lex de Azevedo and Janice Kapp Perry into household names for Latter-day Saint families in the United States. Months before the fireside introducing the values, Kapp had approached Perry, to whom she was distantly related by marriage, to write a song incorporating all the new values for the satellite broadcast. The lyrics of Perry's song included each value in order, but having been written in early March before the wording of the value statements had been altered, it preserved the original language referencing both a Heavenly Father and a Heavenly Mother. "I Walk by Faith," it began, "a daughter of heavn'ly parents." It continued with the description of the remaining six values before concluding with a reminder of life's purpose: "Some day when God has proven me / I'll see Him face to face / But just for here and now I walk by faith."[98]

STRENGTHENING A SENSE OF WORLDWIDE SISTERHOOD

In the years after the November 1985 satellite broadcast introducing the Young Women values and theme, similar worldwide events further demonstrated the Kapp presidency's approach to mass communication.[99] The first was scheduled nearly a year after the fireside. Themed "The Rising Generation," the event was intended to help young women feel powerful, understand the potential of their influence, and increase their experience of young sisterhood as they participated together.[100] With these ideas in mind, the presidency invited young women around the world to write religious messages of testimony and hope, tie them to balloons, and gather locally on the same day to release them. They asked local groups to release their balloons in the morning to symbolize "the dawning of a new day for young women."[101] Some young women who were alone in a branch or who otherwise could not release balloons mailed their messages to Utah so they could still be included in the event.[102]

On the morning of 11 October 1986—according to their various time zones— tens of thousands of young women around the world released helium balloons, each with a personal message expressing their hope and faith. Many local leaders carefully chose the site of the balloon release to create for young women a connection between local landmarks and their faith. In Washington, DC, young women gathered at the Washington Monument to release balloons. In New York, they met at the Statue of Liberty. A group from the Cairo, Egypt, branch planned to snorkel in the Red Sea and release their messages sealed in bottles.[103]

In Los Altos, California, sisters Anne, Jane, and Rebecca Bennion were among the young women who participated. After gathering early at their stake center on 11 October, they boarded charter buses to San Francisco, where they joined hundreds of other young women from the region atop the Coit Tower hill. At the designated moment, they released balloons with their personal testimonies attached and watched them float into the distance. Fourteen-year-old Jane sent her balloon off with hopes that someone would find it. But for her, the experience was more about the sense of fellowship she felt. She was one of a small handful of members in her school, and the balloon release helped her feel connected with young women all over the world who were doing the same thing. That thought helped her feel less solitary in her faith. Her younger sister, Rebecca, who had turned twelve only a few months earlier, felt similarly. The Rising Generation event was one of her first experiences

The Rising Generation worldwide Young Women celebration, Buenos Aires, Argentina. 1986. On 11 October 1986, hundreds of thousands of young women around the globe released helium-filled balloons skyward with personal messages of love and testimony attached, expressing hope for unity and peace. (Church History Library, Salt Lake City.)

with the Young Women, and she loved it. Like Jane, she reveled in the feeling of worldwide sisterhood as she watched the balloons float across the bay.[104]

The messages of young women across the globe showed both their faith and their hope that the notes they wrote would reach someone who needed that message. Some wrote of their faith in God's love for everyone and of His perfect knowledge of His children's needs. Many emphasized the worth of each individual, the importance of family, and the common family of God's children, urging those who might read the note to promote love and peace. Many also wrote of their sincere belief in the gospel of Jesus Christ and the truth of the church to which they belonged.[105] Kerelayani Kalou Salaca from Lautoka, Fiji, shared her witness of Jesus as the Savior, of living prophets, and of the Book of Mormon before encouraging her reader to follow Paul's advice in Ephesians 4:32: "Be ye kind one to another, tenderhearted, forgiving one another, even as God for Christ's sake hath forgiven you." Valencia, from Italy, described how joining the church three years earlier had changed her life for good. "I want you to be able to have all this as well," she wrote. "For this reason I am writing this message, hoping that you will want to turn your own life around."[106]

After the event, Kapp's presidency received letters from some of the young women and their leaders, as well as from a few individuals who had found the messages and been touched by them. While visiting Henefer, Utah, a family who were not Latter-day Saints found three notes written by young women living in Jerusalem. These notes had been sent to Orem, Utah, and released from there.[107] A man from Hopkinsville, Kentucky, wrote to Mary Smith, who released her balloon from Fordyce, Arkansas. He explained that he almost ran over the message with his tractor but got off to see what it was. He told her, "That was the first time I ever found something like this, and it really gave me a good feeling inside knowing there was still some good people left in the world today." Mark Hilton from Salt Lake City wrote to Laura West to thank her for her note. He found it on the ground while working as a serviceman for a utility company and had a feeling he should pick it up. "I'm glad I did," he wrote. Already working to return to regular church participation after more than a decade away, Hilton said that Laura's letter inspired him to continue in his path. Several years later, another sister of Anne, Jane, and Rebecca Bennion learned personally of Mark's success in changing his life when she served a mission with his daughter, Antigone Hilton, in the Virginia Richmond Mission.[108]

Kapp's presidency held several other worldwide broadcasts and celebrations in the 1980s and early 1990s to make announcements and foster a sense of global sisterhood. In a 1987 broadcast, Kapp introduced a new Young Women logo, a colorful flaming torch that formed the profile of a young woman's face. She hoped the logo would spur young women to positive action: "Let this Young Women logo remind you," she said, "that every Christlike act, every kind word spoken, every vulgar word not spoken, every good thought, every honest act, every righteous choice, every scripture read, every prayer offered, every act of forgiveness, every effort to lift another will add to the light and through your righteous influence and your courageous example, even when it may not be popular, will help light the way for others."[109] In November 1989, members celebrated the 120th anniversary of the establishment of the Young Women organization. The presidency decided to announce the celebration a full year before the event—on 29 November 1988, church president Ezra Taft Benson went to the Lion House and rang the same bell that Brigham Young had rung over a century earlier to call his daughters in to establish what would become the Young Women organization.[110] The next year, as part of the commemoration, young women received little bells as a reminder of that heritage. They also listened to recorded messages from Benson and Kapp that were sent out on cassette tapes before the local celebration events.[111]

RESHAPING PERSONAL PROGRESS

One of Kapp's early goals had been to update the My Personal Progress program, and it was to this that she and her presidency turned after establishing the values and theme. At the end of the pivotal PEC presentation in February 1985, Thomas S. Monson had said, "We don't want a quick fix," and Kapp agreed.[112] For the next four years, even as the Young Women leaders planned and carried out fireside broadcasts and worldwide celebrations, a Personal Progress committee and then Kapp's presidency carefully revised and honed the program to directly address concerns about parental involvement, identity, and establishing developmental progress markers.[113]

The new Personal Progress committee held its first meeting on 13 March 1985.[114] Most of the members of the committee were married couples, both because Kapp had valued the cooperative insights of men and women during her time on the Youth Correlation Committee and because she wanted men involved to make sure the program facilitated a relationship between fathers and daughters. "We felt very strongly that a father and a mother have shared responsibility for a young woman," she said.[115] The committee's task was to carefully review the old program and recommend a new achievement structure and associated activities that were developmentally appropriate and globally minded.[116] For nearly two years, Jim and Louise Olsen Baird, the committee cochairs, met weekly with the dozen committee members, all of whom, like the Bairds, had significant professional experience in education and psychology.[117] Pulling from their professional backgrounds and considering their own family experiences, the committee decided they would refocus the program on the new values.

They wrote and rewrote their proposal before submitting it to the presidency for further polishing.[118]

Committee members structured the program around stages of adolescent development and sought to make it meaningful to youth around the globe. One of their important changes was increased focus on the temple. Despite added production cost, leaders chose to add to the new Personal Progress booklet a translucent onionskin page printed with an image of the Salt Lake Temple, which was designed to be overlaid on a depiction of Jesus Christ on the first page. "Through the temple you could see the Savior," Kapp said, describing the effect of the two opening pages. "And that is the message of the book: You prepare to make and keep sacred covenants, receive the ordinances of the temple, and go through the temple to develop that relationship with the Savior. Everything else that followed had that one goal in mind." Some leaders also instructed young women to paste their own image on the inside of the cover, so when the onionskin fell against it, they would see both Christ and themselves in the temple.[119]

The effort to orient young women toward the temple aligned with a new era of emphasis on the temple among Latter-day Saints. The church was beginning to mature in many places, as reflected in the creation of stakes and, especially, the construction of temples. In fact, the years 1983–1984 saw the dedication of twelve new temples in ten countries, including Australia, Guatemala, the Philippines, Samoa, and Taiwan.[120] By the end of the decade, forty-nine temples were in operation or under construction around the world.[121] This meant that an ever-increasing proportion of church members could participate in temple ordinances.

Kapp also believed that emphasizing the temple could address some of the concerns over complementarity of the programs for young women and young men. "If both young men and young women are preparing for the temple ordinances and exaltation, doctrinally and fundamentally there should be some principles in the programs for each group that are close," she explained.[122] She was not the only church leader in the era who saw the temple as the bridging link between young women and the broader doctrinal emphasis on priesthood. In a special issue of the *New Era* dedicated to Young Women, Russell M. Nelson referenced the temple endowment and sealing ordinances as central spiritual aspirations in a Latter-day Saint life.[123]

In addition to its temple emphasis, the new Personal Progress booklet presented three consequential changes. First, the Young Women values replaced the areas of focus as the basic structure for goal setting. As in the earlier program, the young women were to choose and work toward two goals related to each area of focus, or value, every year. Second, age-group awards and medallions replaced yearly progress certificates. Young women completed the Beehive, Mia Maid, and

Laurel requirements as they worked toward the culminating Young Womanhood Recognition award. Finally, although young women still retained a great deal of autonomy in choosing the goals related to each value, which were called value experiences, they chose from a list of options; the instructions allowed them to replace one value experience per year with a goal of their own design.

For Beehives, suggested value experiences included learning with friends or family members to sing a song about faith, committing to love and serve others for two weeks, and looking up the terms *moral* and *courage* in the dictionary and discussing them with parents or young women leaders. For Mia Maids, value experiences could include participating in a performance, reading a book on a gospel topic written by a general authority or general officer of the church, or spending a minimum of five hours in service outside their family (suggestions were provided).[124] Each year, young women also kept up regular practices such as scripture reading and journal writing. Laurels continued these practices, but instead of choosing and completing value experiences, they designed and carried out value projects.[125] The manual offered suggestions for the projects, and at least one per year had to involve service to others. Otherwise this part of the work remained largely up to the young women themselves, with the guidance and support of their parents and church leaders.

The new *Personal Progress* manual did maintain some elements of the old program, including its orientation toward service and family. The booklet continued to emphasize women's role as mothers, but now it referred to motherhood as a "sacred mission," adding a more powerful sense of divine calling, rather than focusing on natural gifts and cultural expectations.[126] In a section reflective of earlier booklets' focus on the process of setting and achieving goals and of Kapp's previous work in time management, the new booklet also provided a project plan sheet to guide young women through the steps of effectively establishing and carrying out goals.[127]

Young women throughout the church began working on the new Personal Progress program following its 1989 release. Some who had already been working on the previous program found they had to repeat some of the requirements and then fulfill new requirements to receive the Young Womanhood Recognition medallion.[128] Local papers occasionally reported on young women receiving this medallion and included descriptions of the service projects completed to attain it, so readers in places such as Utah, Texas, and New Jersey learned of Latter-day Saint young women achieving the highest award offered them by their church.[129] The projects included things like organizing a quilt drawing to raise money for a family whose children had a rare disease or studying sign language and teaching the other young women in the ward to use it in songs.

Ardeth Greene Kapp with Young Women logo and Personal Progress booklet. 1989. During her tenure from 1984 to 1992, Kapp reoriented the Young Women programs around a theme and values expressing Latter-day Saint beliefs. The torch logo and revised Personal Progress achievement program further solidified the organization's identity after rapid changes in the 1970s. (Church History Library, Salt Lake City.)

Katie Bennion, the younger sister of Anne, Jane, and Rebecca Bennion of Los Altos, California, was initially less enthusiastic. She entered Young Women in 1989, and for her, the Personal Progress program felt like little more than a massive checklist. But her mother prodded her to continue, and eventually the service she rendered as part of her culminating Laurel project became a life-changing experience. Katie's mother connected her with two elderly women who lived alone, neither of whom were Latter-day Saints. Katie's task was to visit them each once a month. One of these women was a Holocaust survivor named Sonja Loebner. Squeezing in the visits was difficult for Katie, who was involved in several extracurricular activities and had an after-school job. She found it challenging to carry on a conversation with the older woman, and sometimes she didn't want to go. But she felt good once she was there, and Loebner's willingness to share her life stories touched her. Katie already had an interest in World War II, but hearing Loebner's personal stories of surviving the Auschwitz concentration camp left her stunned. When Loebner passed away a few years later, she left Katie a painting she had done of St. Basil's Cathedral in Russia, because Katie had often admired it. Loebner's warmth and kindness gave Katie strength when she was just beginning to establish her religious identity.[130]

Elisabetta Calabrese, in the Florence district in Italy, was fourteen years old when the new program was introduced. Its focus on the temple was reinforced in her district by combined youth trips to the temple in Bern, Switzerland, nearly every year. Dozens of young men and young women, along with leaders and parents, boarded buses that drove them more than ten hours north to Bern. They stayed for a few days, lodging in nearby World War II–era underground bunkers that had been converted into youth hostels. The youth participated in baptisms for the dead at the temple, and they also enjoyed outdoor activities including swimming and biking. For Elisabetta the testimony meetings held in the local chapel were among the most meaningful aspects of these trips. As she listened to young people from her district share their testimonies, her own convictions were strengthened.[131]

The young women in Elisabetta's district did not meet regularly because of the small number of young women in her branch in Siena and the strain of traveling two hours to meet with other branches in Pisa, but they did work on Personal Progress and gather occasionally for activities. Their yearly camp provided an opportunity to complete value experiences. Church members in the district supported the young women in these efforts by holding a yearly bazaar where they purchased some of the goods the young women had made as part of their Personal Progress experiences. Pulling from their tight budgets, members purchased bookmarks, pillows, and other handmade goods, such as a painting depicting how the artist felt about a particular

Young Women value. The funds they raised helped the young women save money for their camp or temple trip that year.[132]

UPDATING *FOR THE STRENGTH OF YOUTH*

Another update to the Young Women organization that began early in Kapp's tenure but that likewise took several years to come to fruition was an updated version of the *For the Strength of Youth* booklet. Originally released in 1965, this guide to Latter-day Saint standards in areas such as dress, grooming, dating, and sexual purity had not been revised or given much attention in the youth organizations since 1972. In summer 1986, Kapp had a discussion with Thomas S. Monson about the need for a new edition.[133] The older version of the booklet talked about girls not wearing curlers in public, boys not wearing "grubbies," and other concerns that seemed trivial when compared with the temptations facing youth two decades later. "We thought about the challenges of today and felt like there really needed to be an updated version," Kapp recalled.[134]

The project became a collaborative undertaking with the Young Men general presidency, and it went through several stages and delays. One of the most difficult issues was striking the right balance in what to say and what not to say on matters of sexuality. One draft was rejected because reviewers felt it was too frank and could tempt young people to experiment by introducing sexual information they might not yet know. But the next draft received criticism for not dealing with "things of real consequence." The presidencies held focus groups with BYU freshmen, who told them the drafts used unclear and antiquated terminology. Eventually the Young Women and Young Men presidencies composed a draft they felt struck the right balance, but when they sent it for approval, it was rejected and lay dormant for several years. Meanwhile, the organizations continued to receive questions about standards for youth. Kapp felt mounting urgency about producing a definitive resource.[135]

She found an opportunity to express her concerns to Monson in a meeting on another subject in March 1990.[136] Kapp had previously resolved that if ever she had an opportunity to discuss *For the Strength of Youth* with top decision makers, she would be ready. When Monson asked whether she had anything else on her mind that day, she raised the issue, reminding him of their conversation years earlier. He asked how long it would take to prepare a new booklet. When Kapp answered that the new version was already prepared, Monson replied, "Leave it with me." A short time later, an assignment came from the PEC to prepare the publication. This time the Young Women and Young Men presidencies worked with a larger group that included representatives from the general leadership of the Sunday School, Church Education System, and even Welfare Services—every entity that had any responsibility for youth. It was the first time representatives of those organizations met together for a single purpose, as far as Kapp knew.[137] After years of waiting, the booklet was published in time for October 1990 general conference, where Monson spoke about it in two addresses.[138]

The cover of the new booklet conveyed a message of universality through its illustrations of many young women and young men of various races and ethnicities, and it was distributed in eighteen languages. The updated *For the Strength of Youth* booklet was divided into fourteen sections covering topics such as dating, dress and appearance, honesty, language, media, sexual purity, and spiritual help, among others. Each section contained a brief discussion of the topic, based in scripture. The language was direct and admonitory, though not harsh, combining definitions of standards with counsel about dos and don'ts. "Because sexual intimacy is so sacred, the Lord requires self-control and purity before marriage as well as full fidelity after marriage," the section on sexual purity stated. "Always stay in control of yourself and your physical feelings."[139] While the booklet addressed perennial concerns about modesty, chastity, and honesty, it also reflected worries that had arisen or intensified in the United States in the 1980s; the 1990 booklet admonished against profane language, sexual content in media, Satanism in music, and drug abuse.[140]

The rollout of *For the Strength of Youth* was designed to ensure it would be widely used and find a permanent place in the church's messaging to youth and parents.[141] Regional representatives and stake presidents received training from general authorities on how to use the booklet and teach its standards. Bishops, branch presidents, and parents were likewise encouraged to use *For the Strength of Youth* in teaching and counseling.[142] Bishops were instructed to personally ensure that the booklet had been distributed to every young person in their wards and to report back when the assignment was completed.[143] Within a few months of its release, one and a half million copies had been distributed. "This is not a one-time thing," affirmed Jack H. Goaslind of the Seventy, who served as Young Men general president at the time.[144] The *Church News*, the *Ensign*, and the *New Era* all supported the effort with regular articles discussing the booklet and the standards. A small wallet-size card that listed the standards and accompanied the booklet was intended to be easy for young people to carry with them, refer to often, and pull out in church settings for lessons and discussion.[145]

PARTICIPATING IN THE UPDATED PROGRAM

In the era after the introduction of the 1989 *Personal Progress* booklet, young women participated in weekly lessons and activities much as they had for the last decade. In contrast to the past eras of packed MIA calendars detailing weekly activities, more recent guides for leaders, like the *Young Women Handbook*, did not include explicit instructions concerning the activities themselves, leaving activities and planning up to local Young Women leaders.[146] The handbook advised them to make the new Young Women values a central focus of activity planning and included a new section titled "Planning with a Purpose," which included five steps for planning, carrying out, and evaluating activities that would help fulfill carefully chosen value experiences.[147]

The new handbook established "Help Strengthen Families" as one of the organization's basic principles and listed nine suggestions for accomplishing that goal. These included encouraging young women to take what they learned in lessons and apply it in their families—for instance, by planning activities that could include parents and other family members—and urging parents and families to become involved in the Personal Progress program with their young women.[148]

Three recurring annual events involving parents—New Beginnings, Young Women in Excellence, and a "standards event"—were part of the updated activity calendar. The New Beginnings meeting originated during Ruth Funk's tenure, and the overall format hadn't changed much: on an evening each January, the parents and bishop joined the ward or branch's young women to orient new members to the program and introduce the year's scriptural theme. Later in the year, at Young Women in Excellence, young women presented projects they had worked on to their parents and leaders. Projects might be anything—including arts and crafts, design, or engineering—so long as they reflected understanding of one or more of the Young Women values. Young women's parents also joined them for a yearly standards event that helped young women consider moral conduct, including sexual conduct, in light of eternal goals.[149]

Older elements of the organization carried over as well. Young women could participate in the Young Women sports program, under the direction of the ward sports director. The tradition of an annual Young Women camp remained, though in 1985 the board began to discuss how to integrate the Young Women values into camp and increase its focus on overtly religious experience.[150] The outdoor-skills emphasis of the 1960s also continued, with Campcrafter clinics and certifications remaining in place through the 1980s.[151] For Rebecca Bennion, the new values were meaningful, but it was the yearly camping, including the emphasis on outdoor skills, that became a formative part of her time as a young woman. She and her sisters attended Camp Liahona each year in the Sierra Nevada, where they could learn horseback riding and canoe on a lake. Like countless young women before her, Rebecca built campfires and sang songs ranging from the silly to the spiritual as she sat with her peers around the fire. Even more, Rebecca's stake had its own strong camp traditions that included increasingly difficult hikes each year, culminating in a three-day, two-night backpacking trip. Rebecca loved these. She loved recognizing that she could do hard things. She also loved being able to participate in activities, like backpacking trips, that she usually saw only the young men doing.[152]

General leaders continued looking for ways to emphasize the spiritual aspects of camping. While they continued to view connection with God as a by-product of time in nature, they began to treat spirituality as a skill that could be fostered through concrete goals and tasks. By 1992, when a new camp manual was released, it included directives such as "Each day while in camp, find a quiet spot and read from the scriptures for at least fifteen minutes. . . . Share your thoughts about God's creations with a leader or friend."[153] Traditional camping skills, supplemented by new references to caring for the environment, still formed the majority of requirements, but the spiritually focused activities established a new trajectory. Future Young Women general presidencies would build on this vision until they dropped certification altogether.

In the late 1980s, Elisabetta Calabrese experienced both the older outdoor-skills focus and the emerging religious emphasis at camp. Her local leaders felt strongly about the importance of camp, and the young women gathered as often as possible in the months leading up to it to prepare. This preparation included cultivating camping skills such as building fires and tying knots, as well as participating in activities focused on physical fitness.[154] In 1990, young women throughout Italy were invited to participate in a special countrywide camp called *Fiaccola Novanta*, or Torch 90, in reference to the Young Women logo and the year of the camp. Elisabetta's district spent the entire year planning for the massive event, dedicating every activity to some aspect of the preparation. This time, camp preparation included a challenge to read the entire Book of Mormon before the camp. When the young women arrived at the camp near a nature reserve in Abruzzo, Italy, they found open fields surrounded by wooded mountains with a nearby stream, but not a single building or camping accommodation. The young women were responsible for building basic structures such as bathrooms and tables. They cooked outside each day and undertook a difficult hike of several miles, for which they had prepared throughout the previous months. And although they were unable to bathe during the five days of the camp, the young women took turns washing in a small fountain of cold water. In these seemingly austere conditions, Elisabetta felt herself developing a sense of unity and sisterhood as she talked and shared faith with young women from different parts of Italy.[155]

Leaders also moved to restore a closer relationship between young women and young men in church activities. Coordination between the Young Men and Young Women organizations had fallen off in the 1970s, but in subsequent years leaders felt the previous tradition of social and spiritual interactions had served an important socializing function for youth, and they saw mixed-gender activities as preparation

Young women of Italy hiking as part of *Fiaccola Novanta*. 1990. Young women gathered to camp in a rugged area in Abruzzo, Italy, where half the region is dedicated to nature preserves. There they assembled basic structures for their camp, cooked their food outside, hiked several miles, and developed a common sense of identity as young women in The Church of Jesus Christ of Latter-day Saints. (Courtesy Elisabetta Calabrese.)

for compatible and lasting marriage.[156] From the earliest days of her tenure, Kapp looked for ways to refocus activities that included both young women and young men (now called "combined activities") on helping the youth develop relationships, including those that would lead them toward marriage. By 1988, the handbook guided leaders to plan joint activities where young people could "learn to support each other in righteousness and develop relationships as brothers and sisters in the ward family."[157] Combined activities were not intended to revive the vibrant conjoint programs and contests of the past, but leaders recognized that young women and young men would seek each other's company and looked for settings in which the church could "accommodate the need for the shared relationship between young men and young women."[158]

A FIRM FOUNDATION TO BUILD ON

Changes to the Young Women organization during the 1980s had helped the organization find its footing in the more centralized church structure. The Young Women values introduced a welcome stability after the rapidly changing names, achievement programs, and emphases in the 1970s. The use of a theme provided an anchor point through which young women could affirm their significance both in God's eyes and within the church. Creative strategies for using broadcast media gave general leadership new means to communicate with local leadership, recovering the lost communication lines between general and local leaders. Young Women general presidents' inclusion in settings like general conference provided another new avenue to communicate not only with young women and their leaders but also with the broader membership of the church.

Using both media promotion and memorable symbols, Kapp and her counselors had helped make Personal Progress recognizable to women of every age. For the next three decades, the values and theme would shape the experience of many young women and influence the broader sense of what it meant to be a woman in the church. Without any formal program encouraging them to do so, some women chose to work on Personal Progress after their teens—especially if they had a responsibility in the Young Women organization. Winnifred Cannon Jardine, born into the church many decades too early for Personal Progress, worked on the requirements from her home near Salt Lake City while she was in her nineties. In Rostov, Russia, where the church itself was young during the early 2000s, Relief Society members found satisfaction in pursuing the requirements and asserting their identities as daughters of God.[159]

In February 1993, a new Young Women general presidency gathered at the church's publishing facility to inspect the newly printed camp manuals and discuss the significance of the changes for an article in the *Church News*. Janette Callister Hales, who previously served as a counselor to Kapp, along with her counselors, Virginia Hinckley Pearce and Patricia Peterson Pinegar, posed for photos with the manuals, commenting on how the manual differed from past versions. Hales expressed a hope that the manual's basis in gospel principles and scripture would make it both adaptable and enduring.[160] It was, they noted, intended for an increasingly international cohort of young women. The work of helping young women all over the world develop strong individual identities as daughters of God would only grow in importance in the years to come.

ENGAGING THE WORLD

1992–2012

In 1994, nine-year-old Zandile Precious Qinisile and her young sister, Nqobile, moved to the Protea Glen suburb of Johannesburg, South Africa, to live with an aunt who took them in after their mother died. Zandile's aunt worked long hours as a nurse to support her three children and two nieces, so Zandile shouldered much of the family responsibility. As the oldest child in the home, she was in charge of cooking and cleaning in the morning and then dropping off her cousins at school and her sister at daycare before making the long walk to her own school. A few years later, tragedy struck again when Nqobile, by then living with her grandmother, died at age four.[1]

Many young people around the world faced similar situations. Those who grew up poor saw and experienced more health problems and death in their families and communities. Events like sudden moves and constraints like home responsibilities made it hard to develop networks of relationships for mentoring, helping in times of trouble, and identifying opportunities to meet short- and long-term needs. Girls and young women like Zandile also faced roadblocks in pursuing education.[2] Though she learned to be resourceful and hardworking in the face of her family's needs, Zandile didn't have the same tools for building toward future stability available to young women with better access to financial and social resources.

When Zandile was in her early teens, Latter-day Saint missionaries invited her neighbors to church, and Zandile went along. Zandile was moved by the community she found there. "I felt welcomed. I felt wanted. I felt special," she remembered of the isiZulu-speaking congregation she attended. She and one of her cousins soon joined the church. Later, so did her aunt and her other two cousins. From 1998 to 2002, Zandile participated in the Young Women organization. Although she felt welcomed by the congregation, she was still acutely aware of differences between her life and her peers'. Most had two parents. They had nicer clothes and could afford to have their hair done regularly. They attended better schools and spoke better English. At times, Zandile felt out of place around them at church and activities. She even heard some of them make fun of her. She continued to attend, however, because the church felt right. One year, while attending camp, she developed confidence that she was a daughter of a Heavenly Father. She felt a reassuring sense of belonging: "You are wanted," she remembered feeling, "you are needed, you are loved."[3]

In Zandile's Young Women experience, that sense of being wanted, needed, and loved was more important than any particular program. Recalling the influence of one leader, Zandile explained, "She was always there. She was just the person you can always go to about anything under the sun. And she would never judge you. She would advise you, help you. . . . She was just that person who was willing to go an extra mile, and I think that's why I'm so grateful for her. She molded me."[4] Though her leaders were working with limited resources and limited experience in the church, church structures provided them enough regular time with the girls to help them develop rich relationships. Zandile had lost two of her anchoring family relationships when her mother and sister died, but her relationships with God and her Young Women leader helped give her something to hold on to during a time of change in her own life and in the society around her. Latter-day Saint teaching promoted investment in traditional family structures, but in practice the church also nurtured the development of family-like relationships among members.

Zandile's positive experiences exemplified what Young Women general leaders wanted at the turn of the century. Her strong relationship with her local leader and her confidence as a daughter of God were fundamental elements that leaders hoped each girl would gain through her time in the organization. From 1992 to 2012, four general presidencies oversaw the Young Women organization. Leaders' concerns for the spiritual welfare of young women worldwide followed familiar patterns, even as they adjusted for new technological and cultural developments. Perennial worries over chastity and women's roles were compounded by the increasing influence of the internet. The leaders' work was informed by their perception that the family as the fundamental unit of society was deteriorating. And although presidencies since at least the 1930s had thought about cultural translation, leaders at the turn of the century were more focused than ever on developing programs that worked globally.

REACHING A MILESTONE OF INTERNATIONAL MEMBERSHIP

Experiences like Zandile's were increasingly typical. In the 1970s and 1980s, the church had expanded rapidly in Latin America and the Philippines. By the 1990s, waves of growth were also underway in Africa, some of Asia's industrializing economies, and the Global South more broadly.[5] Many members saw the growing presence of the church throughout the world as a fulfillment of both Jesus Christ's commission to teach and baptize "all nations" and Joseph Smith's prophecy that "the truth of God will go forth boldly, . . . till it has penetrated every continent, visited every clime, swept every country, and sounded in every ear."[6]

The church's growth in these areas came at a time of significant cultural crisis for many communities. Globalization, including shifts in the global centers of industrial production, proved deeply disorienting to many people and often served to erode traditional social structures. The church's message of strong religious faith combined with a structure for community and collective action resonated deeply in many societies in the Global South.[7] People like Zandile wanted opportunities to worship alongside others, to serve, and to experience mutual improvement through new relationships. Latter-day Saints' willingness to share their knowledge and experience within branches and wards helped people who were moving into cities and trying to find their place in the world. Church organizations strengthened individuals and communities, and new branches, wards, and stakes in turn strengthened the church. In 1996, shortly before Zandile's experience with Young Women began, church growth in the Global South had led to a major milestone: the number of church members outside the United States surpassed that of members inside the United States for the first time. Only a few years later, church leaders marked another milestone, noting that a majority of Latter-day Saints spoke something other than English as their primary language.[8]

Erika Aza was among the rapidly increasing number of young Latter-day Saint women growing up in the Global South. Baptized when she was eleven years old, after her family had been brought back into church activity by full-time missionaries in her area, she was one of a handful of young women in her tiny branch in Ipiales, Colombia, on the border with Ecuador. Because of the difficulty in traveling, Young Women leaders talked frequently with the girls over the phone to offer support and review goals. They also met all together in the branch one Saturday each month to work on Personal Progress and learn skills like cooking and sewing. Leaders helped Erika and other young women raise money to attend large youth conferences in Pasto, an hour to the north. One leader, Mary Rosero, helped the young women

Zandile Qinisile after Sunday church meetings, South Africa. Circa 1998. Zandile (left), her cousin Zamanguni Queeneth Dlamuka (right), and friend Yolanda Radebe (center) lived in Protea Glen, Johannesburg, and attended church together. The young women often returned from church to Yolanda's home to sit under a tree, where they chatted and discussed church activities. (Courtesy Zandile Qinisile.)

plant flower seeds to teach about faith and initiated a program for them to unite in daily prayer each morning: the girls knelt to pray each day at a designated time, then reported to Rosero over the phone about their experiences. These leaders guided Erika in becoming a faithful Latter-day Saint woman.[9]

As the church grew internationally, however, it maintained a strong association with the United States. The church was headquartered in the United States, and most church leaders were enmeshed in American culture; both facts had profoundly affected the culture of the church. Generations of North American church members had worked hard for acceptance, which had often involved emphasizing their American and European roots in a society that gave strong preference to white residents.[10] Norms and assumptions that were legacies of the Saints' efforts to be accepted as exemplary Americans sometimes complicated their embrace of a global identity.

General church leaders in Salt Lake City were increasingly aware of these challenges, even if they hadn't yet resolved them. Removing Americanisms in church policies and organizations and creating more globally relevant programs had, by now, become a decades-long goal. For leaders of the Young Women organization, part of working to meet the needs of an increasingly diverse membership included efforts at both continuity and simplification. In earlier eras, Young Women general presidencies and board members spent much of their time traveling to local stakes and wards or bringing local MIA leaders to Salt Lake City for instruction in running the complex and highly structured programs. Young Women general leaders in the 1990s, by contrast, followed the lead of Kapp by employing satellite technology to speak to youth directly.[11] Local leaders now worked to carry out a much simpler but less familiar program. General board members sometimes conducted training visits in stakes and wards within the United States, and the general presidency conducted them outside the United States, though these visits were less frequent than in previous decades.[12]

Continuity, simplicity, and emphasis on basic principles of belief became critical because, by the 1990s, Young Women general leaders served for a much shorter period. Kapp's eight-year presidency made her the last Young Women general president to serve longer than five years, a marked departure from the long tenures of women such as Martha Horne Tingey (twenty-four years) and Bertha Reeder (thirteen years). Standardized five-year terms allowed presidencies to anticipate and prepare for the completion of their service, but the brevity of the terms could mean releasing leaders just as they hit their stride in the positions.[13]

The first of these shorter presidencies, spanning from 1992 to 1997, was that of Janette Hales (who remarried during her time as president and thereafter went by Janette Hales Beckham). Hales was no stranger to high-profile leadership. She had served in the Utah state legislature, on the Primary general board, and as a counselor to Kapp in the Young Women general presidency. Hales saw her presidency's mission as continuing to implement the Kapp presidency's changes and further simplifying programs.[14] She chose as her counselors Virginia Pearce, who had served with her on the Primary general board, and Patricia Pinegar, to whom Hales had served as counselor in a ward Relief Society presidency. Pinegar had also served with her husband in leading the church's mission in south London and later the Missionary Training Center in Provo, Utah. These experiences gave her some understanding of the needs of Latter-day Saints outside the United States.[15]

As the presidency considered ways to simplify participation in the Young Women organization and make it accessible internationally, they took to heart the refrain repeated to them by general priesthood leaders: "We cannot export culture."[16] While some distinct Latter-day Saint practices were encouraged worldwide, by the 1990s church leaders worked to avoid Utah-centric practices like exporting elocution lessons to Australia or teaching young women around the world not to go out in public with curlers in their hair. To keep church programs relevant for Zandile and members like her, leaders in every church organization needed to find ways to recognize the life experiences and needs of church members around the world, especially in the Global South.

RISING TENSIONS IN THE GLOBAL NORTH

During the same period that the church was expanding in the Global South, there were growing tensions between the church's values and those of the Global North. Latter-day Saints and other observers watched with growing concern as an emphasis on sexual freedom and personal autonomy seemed to threaten the stability of family and community structures in new and more troubling ways.[17] Beginning in the late 1970s, internal church studies had been commissioned and committees formed to study issues affecting youth and their families, including teen intercourse and pregnancy, temple marriage rates, abortion, and homosexual relations. Metrics church leaders cared about often trended in directions that worried them; for example, rates of teen pregnancy in the 1980s were increasing even as rates of temple marriage were decreasing. Still, other indicators offered hope: Latter-day Saint teens in the United States tended to engage in premarital sex much less frequently than their peers, and marriages between Latter-day Saints were less likely to end in divorce.[18]

By the 1990s, two decades of rapidly shifting norms regarding family structure had led to major transformations in the lived experience of the church's young women. In the United States, overall divorce rates peaked in the 1980s, while divorce rates for individuals over age thirty-five continued to rise in the 1990s.[19] American teens and young adults, including members of the church, were increasingly likely to come from households with divorced parents. Even teens and young adults with married parents often worried about the possibility of their parents divorcing.

As marriage diminished in importance in Western society, Latter-day Saints continued to emphasize its centrality in their belief and practice. Members and leaders regularly affirmed that marriages sealed by the proper authority would remain intact through the eternities, which added weight to the project of building strong marriage partnerships in mortality.[20] Church leaders' investment in marriage was not only theological: they had long emphasized marriage, family, and parenting as vital to the health of a society. They believed stable two-parent families benefited people socially, emotionally, and economically. They also used the hope of a future family to motivate responsible choices and moral purity among the church's youth.[21] Both church members and leaders sought out forums for conversations with representatives of other religious and social organizations about how to promote the healthy function of families within supportive communities.[22]

During the same period, the gay rights movement in the United States was shifting its emphasis to advocate for legal recognition for same-sex relationships. Proponents of such changes were spurred to action in part by heartbreaking experiences during the AIDS epidemic, where life partners with no clear legal relationships were denied spousal rights during hospitalization or at death.[23] Hawaii was one of the first states to broach the question of whether marriage could be newly understood to encompass same-sex partnerships. In 1993, the Hawaii Supreme Court ruled that unless the state could provide a compelling rationale otherwise, a ban on gay or lesbian couples entering into durable legal agreements as intimate life partners was likely against the state's constitution.[24] Church leaders, however, had been speaking out against same-sex marriage since at least the 1980s, and in the coming years they would dedicate significant resources and energy to advocating against it.[25]

As the cultures of the Global North increasingly promoted individualism on matters of sexuality and reproduction, some scholars in the early 1990s began formulating a distinction between biological sex and gender. They argued sex was a biological assignment that was generally, though not always, made at birth, whereas gender was an identity constructed through social norms and behaviors, and it was something individuals could discover and create on their own.[26] Church leaders rejected these ideas, citing longstanding teachings that "the distinction between male and female . . . was an essential characteristic" of individuals' premortal and mortal existence that continued after death and resurrection.[27] Apostle Dallin H. Oaks taught in 1993 that gender differentiation—what he referred to as "maleness and femaleness"— was a fundamental reality of God's plan for His children.[28] Gender and family were deeply connected to Latter-day Saint beliefs about the purpose of life. Generations of

Latter-day Saint leaders had taught about a Mother as well as a Father in Heaven.[29] The Young Women value of divine nature reflected the Latter-day Saint understanding of humans' literal parent-child relationship with God and the belief that humans could grow ultimately to become gods like their heavenly parents.[30]

In the 1990s and early 2000s, church teachings reflected a growing concern over maintaining defined and separate gender roles, with a continuing emphasis on motherhood. These teachings had obvious implications for young women, who were learning what it meant to be faithful Latter-day Saint women. In general conference addresses throughout the first half of the 1990s, the term *gender* appeared more than four times as often as it had in any previous decade, and in the decade as a whole, use of the terms *mother* and *motherhood* increased by approximately 30 percent and 38 percent, respectively.[31]

YOUNG WOMEN AND THE FAMILY PROCLAMATION

On the evening of 23 September 1995, Relief Society general president Elaine Low Jack rose to address millions of women and young women gathered in groups around the world. As the first speaker in the general Relief Society meeting the week before general conference, she called on women to "make strengthening and nurturing your family your first priority." Jack and her counselors all spoke forcefully on the importance of families, and the meeting rose to its climax as recently ordained church president Gordon B. Hinckley read aloud a momentous new document: "The Family: A Proclamation to the World."[32]

This statement—a proclamation issued by the First Presidency and Quorum of the Twelve Apostles—did not introduce any new doctrine or policy but instead reviewed and summarized Latter-day Saint beliefs about the family.[33] "Marriage between a man and a woman is ordained of God," it declared, and "the family is central to the Creator's plan for the eternal destiny of His children." The proclamation then outlined that "plan of happiness": human beings are beloved spirit daughters and sons of heavenly parents, and God's plan is for His children to come to earth, obtain physical bodies, and progress toward increasing perfection and eternal life. Temple marriage was the key to this destiny: "Sacred ordinances and covenants available in holy temples make it possible for individuals to return to the presence of God and for families to be united eternally."[34]

The proclamation reiterated the church's longstanding opposition to sex outside of marriage and made explicit the assumption that heterosexual marriage was God's will. The proclamation made clear the church's stance that gender is an "essential characteristic" of individual identity and purpose and therefore discouraged conceptions of gender as fluid. Most of the proclamation's language, however, focused on the shared role of mothers and fathers as parents. Only two sentences of the proclamation described gendered roles: "By divine design, fathers are to preside over their families in love and righteousness and are responsible to provide the necessities of life and protection for their families. Mothers are primarily responsible for the nurture of their children." These descriptions were immediately followed by three sentences of qualifying language: "In these sacred responsibilities, fathers and mothers are obligated to help one another as equal partners. Disability, death, or other circumstances may necessitate individual adaptation. Extended families should lend support when needed." The text reflected the tension that had grown in the previous decade between the effort to promote a vision of equality and partnership in marriage and the desire to maintain defined gender roles and patriarchal leadership in families.[35]

The announcement of the family proclamation, as it came to be called, became a pivotal moment in clarifying and affirming the church's stance on issues surrounding gender, marriage, sexuality, and reproduction. The text itself was a concise 605 words, but in the years and decades after its publication, the proclamation was highly influential in defining church members' perspectives. Members were encouraged to display copies in prominent locations in their homes, and the statement readily lent itself to use in church classes, talks, and programs.[36]

Women from many parts of the world found the ideals of equal partnership and shared investment in family life transformative in their marital and familial relationships. In Japan, for example, Natsume Inagaki saw the focus on husbands and wives working together as equal partners as a refreshing change from a cultural expectation of wives serving husbands.[37] A woman from Botswana likewise appreciated the model of equal partnership and felt grateful for the larger role her husband took in caring for their children.[38] In South Africa, another woman delighted in the strength that mothers and fathers parenting as equal partners gave children and families, as well as the freedom it gave mothers and fathers to accomplish more in and outside the home.[39]

In Erika Aza's estimation, the descriptions of gendered expectations in the family proclamation simply supported what church leaders and her Colombian culture had already taught her. For her, as for many church members in the Global South in the 1990s, debates over issues such as gender stereotypes and legalizing marriage for same-sex couples held little resonance, if they made it into the news at all. More frequently, concerns over gender roles in Latin America had to do with cultural norms of male alcohol consumption and its effect on household economic stability. Men were seen as the head of the household and expected to provide for the family, even as their drinking habits frequently left their wives few financial resources to raise and care for the children.[40] Given this gendered reality, many female church members welcomed an official church document emphasizing male responsibility to home and family.[41]

For young women, the proclamation spoke mostly to future expectations. Marriage and childbearing were clearly delineated as the pinnacle of mortal and eternal achievement, elevating a rhetorical emphasis that had long permeated the Young Women organization. The ideal was a young woman who believed her eternal destiny was to participate in a family as a daughter, wife, and mother, with her roles based on the foundation of a mother and father who placed family at the center of their lives. In this ideal, a young woman anticipated a primary role of raising children, even though she was encouraged to prepare to provide economically for her family in case of need.

Still, many factors might interrupt a young woman's hope for the ideal. In the 1950s, when American young women watched friends marry at an average age of twenty and marriage rates were high, it had been easier to focus on marriage in the Young Women organization. By 2000, the average age of first marriage for American women was twenty-five—well past the age of participation in Young Women—and overall marriage rates were declining.[42] These and other demographic, social, and economic realities impacted individual expectations. In her ward or branch, a typical young woman saw many lives that did not follow the path presented as ideal—she encountered faithful women who had never married, had divorced, or had been unable to bear children. Economic circumstances could make the idea of one parent sufficing as a provider feel out of reach. And a young woman's sexual orientation or gender identity might affect her interest in being part of a male-female couple.

Young women's responses to the ideals laid out in the family proclamation were as varied as the young women themselves—some wrestled with them, while others felt assured of their truth. Bridey Jensen from Oklahoma, for example, had deep roots in the church and had served in Young Women class presidencies, but still she was told by a close friend that her feelings of same-sex attraction were the result of a "weak testimony." Grappling with such sentiments from some church members, Bridey felt different, lonely, and confused.[43] Other young women, such as Suzanne Fei, experienced loneliness in their desire to pursue a career. As Suzanne interacted with and observed the Latter-day Saint women she knew in the small towns she grew up in on the West Coast of the United States, she noted that none of the mothers she knew had careers—especially not in the science and technology field where her interests lay. Most of them had chosen motherhood over career, and she felt some pressure to abandon her ambition to pursue a career and follow the same path. This pressure was based in part on some members' belief that the proclamation's statement that "mothers are primarily responsible for the nurture of their children" meant a woman's highest calling—to raise children—precluded a career. Suzanne felt grateful, though, for the flexibility she found in the proclamation's clause on individual adaptation and for the support of teachers and parents, who helped her pursue her goals.[44] Finally, some, like Angela Fallentine in New Zealand, felt an assurance of the proclamation's truth and divine provenance. When she watched a video of Gordon B. Hinckley presenting the proclamation, she felt a powerful witness of its truth "literally from head to toe."[45]

TURNING HEARTS TO THE FAMILY

A month after the family proclamation was issued, Glenn L. Pace of the Quorum of the Seventy visited a meeting of Janette Beckham's Young Women general board with this directive: "See that it [the proclamation] is spread and does not fade." He shared many leaders' feeling that the family proclamation offered an effective solution to many of the world's problems.[46] The presidency and board members felt they had independent spiritual confirmation that a focus on family was the right direction for their organization, and they began planning ways to incorporate the proclamation into their work.[47]

As they considered family issues, board members discussed the disruptions of divorce and abuse, the need for role models, and the differences between ideals for how families could function and the realities young women lived. Although they may have been aware that teen pregnancy and teen abortion rates were in dramatic decline in the United States after a twenty-year high in 1990, the presidency still worried about early sexual activity and childbearing.[48] In February, board members held a special group retreat on Temple Square to discuss family life. They covered common challenges, demographic trends, and parenting best practices. After hours of discussion, the participants concluded that Young Women activities and camp could strengthen families, reinforce parents' teachings, and provide good role models.[49]

Despite sincere efforts to create a globally relevant program, cultural assumptions from the United States still informed many church programs and communications. The *Personal Progress* booklet's recommendation to bake a cake for a new neighbor, for example, made assumptions about cultural norms and available infrastructure. In India in the mid-1990s, Vilo and Gurcharan Singh Gill, who presided over the country's mission, had to remind American senior missionaries who wanted to teach cake baking that Indian church members didn't typically have conventional gas or electric ovens.[50] In France, a local Young Women leader named Deolinda Duriez helped young women adapt requirements from printed booklets because recommendations like making a cake for a neighbor were socially foreign.[51] The fire-building requirement in the camp manual similarly assumed a setting in which people didn't build fires at home but had reason to do so in outdoor settings. In rural parts of Africa, many young women built fires daily for cooking. In Japan, there were few outdoor settings where fire building was allowed or appropriate.

Amid the Young Women organization's efforts to adapt to a more global membership, a new Young Women general presidency was appointed in 1997, two years after the release of the family proclamation.[52] The new president, Margaret Dyreng Nadauld, had served in five ward Young Women presidencies and was serving on the Relief Society general board at the time she received her new assignment. Her first counselor, Carol Burdett Thomas, had been appointed only a few months earlier to serve as a counselor to Beckham. Second counselor Sharon Greene Larsen had served as president of her stake Young Women organization.[53] Like their predecessors, the new presidency made the family proclamation a priority. They regularly studied the document, and it informed their approach to teaching, training, and program design.[54]

In 1998, the Young Women general presidency announced a yearlong worldwide celebration under the theme of "turning hearts to the family." Over the course of the year, young women were invited to focus on family in several ways. They could, for example, study the family proclamation, interview a grandparent, research ancestors for whom temple ordinances could be performed, or perform acts of kindness and service for family members. Each ward or branch was to hold a culminating celebration activity at the end of the year designed to "help young women develop increased love for and understanding of the eternal nature of families." These activities could include plays, art exhibits, musical presentations, talent displays, and personal stories and testimonies.[55]

The presidency also emphasized the theme of families at the general Young Women meeting in March of that year. From 1978 to 1994, young women had been encouraged to participate in the general women's meeting, which took place before the October general conference and included all women ages twelve and up. Beginning in March 1994, the church started holding a separate meeting exclusively for young women a week before April general conference that was broadcast around the world through the church's satellite network system. The first general Young Women meeting featured the theme "Young Women of Faith." The meeting's format set the precedent for subsequent annual Young Women meetings: each member of the Young Women general presidency spoke, as did a member of the Quorum of the Twelve Apostles.[56]

At the 1998 general Young Women meeting, Nadauld taught that girls were part of three families—their current family, their future family, and their heavenly family—and that they should prepare in their youth for their future roles. Thomas reflected on numerous ways young women around the world supported their families, including by contributing to the spiritual tenor of their homes and doing family history and temple work.[57] Larsen invited the girls to become "titles of liberty" (a Book of Mormon term for a banner rallying people around a righteous cause) in their families by striving to protect against intruders such as selfishness, harshness, anger, and strife. "Your banner stands for peace and love and service to your families," she declared.[58]

The presidency believed young women's personal aspirations found ample accommodation within the principles of the family proclamation. In that same meeting, Nadauld connected education to the central focus on families, envisioning young women "who are getting an education and are preparing to bless others through it." For the sake of themselves and their future families, she exhorted, "Choose a fine education. Be qualified. Be well rounded. Work hard."[59] In a document the general presidency prepared to describe the Young Women organization and its goals, they presented education and marriage as complementary goals for young women that would bless a future family. "As opportunities for women increase," they wrote, "young couples seem to be developing a greater capacity for shared experiences." They noted that fathers were more involved in caring for young children than in previous generations, and they praised examples of high-achieving young women. The recently elected student body president at Stanford University, for example, attested that she had learned leadership skills in the Young Women organization. "This is the greatest time in the history of the world for young women," the presidency affirmed. They taught that with all the options available to them, young women needed to "be wise and set appropriate priorities for their lives."[60]

After what they felt was a successful yearlong effort to increase emphasis on the family, the Young Women leaders began considering lasting changes to achieve that end.[61] Since Kapp's presidency, the Young Women values and theme had been the expression of both young women's identity and the purpose of the organization. During an October 1998 board meeting, a committee on Personal Progress revisions proposed adding "nurture future generations" to the theme's list of priorities for which young women were preparing.[62] Upon further discussion, however, board members rejected the revision, concerned that *nurture* might be read as too exclusively connected with motherhood and might exclude those who never became parents.[63] A later proposal referenced "divine roles" in an "eternal plan" to evoke a wider range of meanings, but it was not until 2001 that they finally settled on a solution by adding "strengthen home and family." Unlike "nurture future generations," this phrase did not strike board members as too closely connected with future motherhood. "Young women," they believed, "can right now strengthen their families and prepare for the temple."[64] In announcing the change, Nadauld stressed its applicability to young women in any phase of life. "Strengthen the home of your youth and later your own family," she said.[65]

CONFRONTING INTERNET PORNOGRAPHY AND PROMOTING MODESTY

Over the course of the 1990s, public use of the internet skyrocketed and began to reshape the world. By the year 2000, just over half of American households had a computer, and 40 percent of homes had access to the internet.[66] By 2011, over 75 percent of Americans lived in a household with a computer, and 71 percent of households had internet access. With the increasing prevalence of smartphones in the 2010s, even households without computers could access the internet.[67] From the mid-2000s on, several key developments shaped users' online experience. High-speed internet connections made it easier to share large media files. Web platforms became more interactive and focused on user-generated content: blogs and social media channels rose to prominence and took on new life as people transitioned to mobile technology. By 2010 it was estimated that 30 percent of the worldwide population used the internet; by 2019 that number had grown to 57 percent, with half of internet users accessing it by mobile phone.[68]

Latter-day Saint leaders quickly embraced the internet's potential to connect Saints around the globe. In 1996, the church's first website for members, lds.org, went live, followed in 2001 by mormon.org, a site aimed at the general public.[69] By the end of the decade, the church had developed mobile apps like Gospel Library, which made scriptures, general conference reports, church magazines, lesson manuals, and many other resources available on users' devices.[70] In January 2010, a website dedicated to young Latter-day Saints (youth.lds.org) debuted in English, followed soon thereafter by versions in ten other languages. The site featured videos of young people sharing their experiences, messages from church leaders, and inspirational videos. It also contained resources for leaders and links to web content such as scriptures and the *New Era* magazine.[71]

During the same time period, people were quick to recognize the commercial potential of a system that allowed for the rapid flow of information around the world. Figures in the pornography industry were among the first to build personal fortunes in a digital attention economy.[72] Pornographic websites were certainly not the first ventures to tap into sexual desire for profit, but their scale of distribution was unprecedented.

Church leaders and secular experts were concerned about the objectification of women and girls in pornography and other media. In February 2005, the American

Psychological Association convened a task force with the charge to identify, study, and summarize the best research on the impact of cultural messages that sexualized girls. The study concluded that sexualization—that is, the tendency to view women and girls as sex objects and to evaluate them based on their physical characteristics— impeded the development of healthy sexuality and self-image. Psychologists linked sexualization with eating disorders, low self-esteem, and depression, which were the mental and emotional problems most common among women in the United States and other countries in the Global North at the time.[73]

Warnings against pornography became a regular theme of church leaders' addresses during the late 1990s and early 2000s.[74] Much of that focus was on the temptation that access to pornography posed for men, since men were its primary targets (though women were also part of the global audience for the industry).[75] Such concerns also opened rhetorical space for discussing the dangers posed by a culture that objectifies women through pornography and other tactics. The resulting discussions often emphasized modest dress as a defining standard for Latter-day Saint young women. Church leaders for decades had emphasized an equal standard of chastity for both young women and young men, but some members felt that discussions of modesty, which largely focused on young women, often created a double standard. These messages, both by implication and by direct statement, asserted that young women's clothing choices could lead men's minds toward unchaste thoughts. This could place the responsibility of men's purity of thought on young women who already struggled with image and identity issues.

Some leaders recognized this problem and worked to change the conversation about gender and chastity. In 1998, James E. Faust of the First Presidency spoke at the priesthood session of April general conference, building his remarks around the thirteenth article of faith. He pleaded with the men of the church to work toward greater consistency between their beliefs and their actions. This included standards of moral cleanliness. "There is no different or double standard for moral cleanliness for men and women in the Church. In fact, I believe holders of the priesthood have a greater responsibility to maintain standards of chastity before marriage and fidelity after marriage."[76]

In conjunction with discussions of sexual morality, dress had always been part of Young Women discourse. When the *For the Strength of Youth* booklet was first published in 1965, dress standards also addressed questions of formality and decorum, but by the end of the twentieth century, the cultural context for young women's clothing choices had shifted drastically. Young women were participating in sports, exercise, and physical activities at higher levels than ever before.[77] As a matter of course, they dressed in uniforms and athletic wear that might have been considered immodest by earlier standards but were increasingly regarded as practical and acceptable attire. At the same time, clothing standards in general had become more relaxed and oriented toward comfort.[78]

General-level church leaders around the beginning of the twenty-first century tried to focus the modesty conversation on identity. When Elaine Schwartz Dalton, second counselor in the Young Women general presidency, spoke to BYU students in 2004, she explained that modesty was more than dress, though the implication was that dress was still a central component. "When we truly know that we are daughters of God and have an understanding of our divine nature, it will be reflected in our countenance, our appearance, and our actions," she asserted. "It is an outward manifestation of an inner knowledge and commitment."[79] Speaking a year and a half later in October general conference, Young Women general president Susan Winder Tanner framed modesty in similar terms but invoked Paul's counsel to the Corinthians, which equated the sacredness of bodies with that of the temple. "We should dress and act in ways that reflect the sacred spirit inside us," she admonished. Then, echoing Dalton, she insisted, "Modesty is more than a matter of avoiding revealing attire. It describes not only the altitude of hemlines and necklines but the attitude of our hearts."[80] Tanner and Dalton taught that when young women had a clear understanding of their divine nature and the sacredness of their bodies and were committed to their covenants, they would naturally choose modest dress.

In a culture that increasingly valued individual expression, a person's sense of taste in music, film, or fashion was often seen as an important aspect of their personality.[81] Still, the standards promoted by church leaders resonated with many young women, and some shared leaders' concerns enough to adopt a more modest aesthetic as their own, even developing a niche market in the early 2000s for clothing that was intended to be both modest and stylish.[82] Divisions among young women over adherence to modesty guidelines could be painful. For a young woman who wore a tank top or sleeveless dress without intending to draw sexualized attention, it could feel like charges of immodesty were contributing more to objectification than the clothes were. What virtually all young women seemed to agree on, however, was that they did live in an atmosphere where their physical appearance was under regular, often discomfiting, scrutiny.

EXAMINING ASSUMPTIONS IN PERSONAL PROGRESS

As they weaved principles from the family proclamation into their organization, members of the Nadauld presidency also sought to understand and address unexamined American cultural assumptions in Young Women programs. They thought the programs were often unnecessarily complex and, despite past efforts, remained difficult for many young women globally. Nadauld's counselor Sharon Larsen was particularly concerned. Larsen had decades of experience with Young Women, having served on Ruth Funk's twenty-eight-member general board and later on Janette Beckham's eight-member board. She was also Ardeth Kapp's sister and had followed the Personal Progress program from its infancy. She was blunt about the need for continuing modification. While traveling internationally, Larsen saw how specific aspects of Personal Progress failed to translate. She made it a habit to run through global contexts in her mind and name specific places where a requirement or proposal simply would not work.[83]

For Zandile Qinisile in South Africa, for example, multiple obstacles complicated Personal Progress. Language was one. While a survey from church headquarters would have reported that most South African members spoke English, language fluency exists on a spectrum. Zandile was much more comfortable with the isiZulu spoken in church meetings than the written English of her Personal Progress materials. The *Personal Progress* booklet used vocabulary a young woman would never learn in a school class or through mass media. For Zandile, concepts like divine nature, individual worth, and charity were initially more mystifying than motivating. Her leaders, who were her source of mentoring and support, did not seem to understand the program well either, so informal spoken clarification was not a reliable alternative to print materials.

Other Personal Progress challenges were economic and logistical. Zandile and her oldest cousin, Zama, both had heavy cleaning responsibilities at home in addition to school assignments. Finding time to fulfill Personal Progress requirements was hard. The program's assumption of parental availability was also a barrier. Even when Zandile was able to understand and complete requirements for a Personal Progress goal, she felt unsure who should certify her completion, perhaps not realizing that the booklet allowed for an adult other than a parent or guardian to sign off. Her aunt was too busy to help, so Zandile felt stuck.[84] While many of her peers in the ward were economically better off, which gave them advantages in education and home life, they too struggled with the program. The result was that participation in Personal Progress never became a norm in the ward. Few girls completed the requirements.[85] Despite the steep learning curve, however, Zandile grew to appreciate the program as a reminder to look beyond the day-to-day concerns of her adolescence and prepare for a hopeful future.[86]

Tackling challenges like Zandile's proved difficult from church headquarters in Salt Lake City. One way Nadauld hoped to help members throughout the church was to maintain a critical mass of consistent participation in the program, so young women who finished would have the understanding and confidence to administer them as they grew up and were called to lead.[87] But she had to balance that ideal with the need for alteration and adaptation. To revise the Personal Progress program, Nadauld established a committee whose members included individuals with experience in the international church. Julie Bangerter Beck, who headed the committee, had lived in Brazil as a child when her parents oversaw a mission there.[88] Silvia Henriquez Allred, who also served on the committee, was born in El Salvador, had served as a public affairs missionary in Spain, and had led the church's mission in Asunción, Paraguay, with her husband.[89]

The presidency and committee worked on the project over several years. They were willing to sacrifice some of the physical, social, and intellectual breadth of the program for a simpler, more flexible version of Personal Progress that focused on devotional behaviors and a relationship with God. Like leaders before her, Nadauld felt progress depended on divine guidance accompanied by careful, attentive work. Reflecting on her administration, she emphasized that changes came by inspiration: "We have felt that these different things needed to happen," she explained. "Then we have put forth the effort, put pencil to paper, done the work and the homework, talked to people, researched, and done everything we needed to so that we would be able to receive the inspiration when it was time."[90]

Revisions to the Personal Progress program made requirements simpler and more specific, and the materials required to complete the requirements were pared down. The committee knew that not everyone could afford their own paper, so they decided to send a small journal with each Personal Progress booklet.[91] The required experiences for each value could all be accomplished with scriptures, the journal, and discussion with a parent or leader. For example, one faith value experience asked young women to read specific scriptural passages dealing with faith, pray each morning and night, discuss their experience with a parent or leader, and write about it in their journal.[92] Revisions also embraced flexibility. Following the required experiences for each value, young women were to complete three additional experiences, either from a list of proposed experiences or of their own creation. Young women could then design their own culminating value project or choose from a list. Example projects for the faith value included taking a church family history class and compiling stories of people who showed great faith, memorizing the apostles' recent proclamation titled "The Living Christ," or creating a story, poem, song, or artwork depicting faith. Next to these suggestions, the booklet provided space to describe a proposed project.[93] Providing this blank space gave young women clear permission to adapt the program to their circumstances rather than worry about doing the program incorrectly.

The new booklet also emphasized alternative options whenever it mentioned a parent.[94] It was clearer than ever before, for example, that young women could discuss how to prepare for motherhood with any mother they admired. A leader rather than a parent could sign off completed requirements.[95] The program also cut the age-specific aspects of previous versions, allowing young women to work through the program at their own pace. Once a young woman completed the requirements and received her Young Womanhood Recognition medallion, she became a mentor for others, so she could continue serving and growing while building unity within the group.[96] Nadauld explained that the young women who serve as mentors "don't move in and take the place of the parents, but there's another voice, another encouragement."[97] Subsequent revisions of the program introduced another award, the Honor Bee, for young women who mentored others, performed service, and fulfilled additional requirements.[98] The medallion itself was also redesigned. Instead of featuring a woman with European features and a long, flowing dress, the new medallion bore an image of the Salt Lake Temple.[99] While the temple was in Utah, it was perhaps the most well-known temple among Latter-day Saints worldwide, and its image symbolized temple covenants that were becoming increasingly available as the church expanded temple building throughout the world.

The members of the committee that worked on the Personal Progress revisions proved to have an extended influence on women's future experience in the church. Julie Beck and Elaine Dalton later served as counselors to Nadauld's successor, Susan Tanner. Beck also served as the Relief Society general president, with Silvia Allred as a counselor.[100] Nadauld felt the continual crossover of leadership among the women-led organizations—at both the general and local levels—provided consistency and helped young women transition more comfortably into Relief Society, which had been an area of concern since the separation of the programs for older and younger members of what had been the MIA in the 1970s.[101]

Although participating in the organization took less time by the beginning of the twenty-first century than it had in the decades when spiritualized recreation dominated the church's youth programs, young women still participated in Sunday classes and weeknight activities. Each year, local leaders used one of three Young Women manuals, each covering similar topics, to guide their Sunday instruction. An annual resource guide or supplement provided fresh ideas and support from the words of current church leaders, male and female. Nadauld's presidency began publishing the annual resource guides because they had not been authorized to prepare new curriculum but were concerned that the aging manuals, dating as far back as 1994, lacked up-to-date material on social and moral issues confronting young women.[102] By the early 2000s, the resource guide for the Young Women manuals was available online, with links to recent talks related to lesson topics like "Living the Gospel

Cultural celebration for Mexico City Mexico Temple rededication. 2008. Mexican youth celebrated the reopening of the Mexico City Mexico Temple through traditional music and dance before an audience of eighty-seven thousand in Estadio Azteca. International temple construction grew dramatically in the early twenty-first century. To commemorate temple dedications and rededications, youth participated in large cultural events—reminiscent of the large MIA festivals held in the mid-twentieth century—that featured their country's church history and traditional dance and music. (Courtesy *Church News*.)

Daily," "Creating a Spiritual Environment in the Home," "The Priesthood Can Bless Families," and "Learning to Share the Gospel."[103]

Important events such as New Beginnings and Young Women in Excellence continued as yearly traditions.[104] These evenings were especially memorable for Erika Aza in Colombia. Her leaders used them as an opportunity to talk about the values and their associated colors. At one such activity the young women dressed up for a fashion show, for which leaders helped them find stylish clothing and did their hair and makeup. As each girl walked in front of parents and leaders, the Young Women leaders announced her name and positive qualities, emphasizing her "true beauty." They wanted these young women, many of whom came from poor and rural circumstances, to see themselves as beautiful, feminine daughters of God.[105]

Youth conferences also continued, allowing young women and young men to gather for spiritual uplift and to meet and befriend other young church members, which remained especially important in areas where the church was less established.[106] Alongside such major events, weekly activities offered an opportunity to put Sunday lessons into practice or just bond as a group. For example, young women from several stakes in Southern California created a special fashion show of modest formal gowns that garnered headlines in the *Los Angeles Times*.[107] An article in the *New Era* featured activities from youth around the world as suggestions. Young women in Chile visited widows; youth in England hosted a "living history" evening with elderly ward members; youth in the state of Georgia in the United States held a cook-off starting with assigned ingredients; youth in Missouri made cakes and decorated them with scenes from the Book of Mormon. The article also recommended games, career nights connecting youth with ward members' work experience, and a scavenger hunt for service activities.[108]

GLOBAL CAMP EXPERIENCES

Just as Zandile Qinisile had struggled with Personal Progress, members around the world often struggled to make camp work, in part because they were unprepared for the complexity of planning and carrying out such an undertaking. In American culture, camping was considered a "back to the basics" wilderness experience, which made it easy to miss how much infrastructure was involved. Camping required accessible wilderness space where groups could get permission to stay, transportation to that space, and specialized supplies like tents, sleeping bags, and foods suited to camp preparation. Besides the physical infrastructure, Young Women camp required general camping experience. In countries where camping was common, the church could lean on skills people already had. Where group camping was not a common tradition, they had to work from scratch. Preparing for camp in such places could be exciting and baffling, frustrating and fulfilling.

In Mongolia, a decade of rapid church growth began when six senior missionary couples entered the country in 1992. Converts were disproportionately young and mostly lived in Ulaanbaatar, the nation's capital and home to half its population. In 1995, a mission was organized in the country, led by Richard and Mary Nielsen Cook.[109] That summer, Doka Tsedendorj and other Young Women leaders in Ulaanbaatar gathered at the Cooks' apartment to plan the church's first Young Women camp in their country. They were proud of the Mongolian steppes and often spent time during the summer riding horses and milking cows in the countryside, but the idea of a large, shared camp experience was new.[110] Most local leaders were barely older than the young women and the only church members in otherwise Buddhist families, and they didn't have any reference point for what a church camp might look like. Still, they enthusiastically participated in planning meetings as Mary Cook struggled to share her vision.[111]

The group needed shelter for the forty-three girls, seven leaders, and four senior missionaries who attended. Two young women were able to bring tents to share. Thanks to the church's developing Scouting program for young men in Mongolia, the Young Women had access to four more tents, making six tents for over fifty people. Transportation to the campsite over fifteen miles away was difficult. August monsoon rains had made the rough rural roads muddy. On the morning they planned to go, the bus they had hired did not arrive. It took two and a half hours for Tsedendorj and other leaders to persuade the driver of another bus to fulfill their unusual request.[112]

Food was simpler. Young women picked wild strawberries and cooked mutton dumpling soup over a fire. They drank warm sweet milk, a substitute for the traditional fermented mare's milk the young women had given up to adapt to their new religious commitment against alcohol. After sharing their sweetened milk, the group squeezed into a tiny cabin for a testimony meeting.[113] As night descended, so did the monsoon rains. Water quickly seeped through the tents and onto the young women crammed head to toe inside. Fortunately, their heavy wool blankets provided some protection.[114]

Return transportation was also difficult. With their chartered bus nowhere in sight after hours of waiting while the rain created muddy pools in the roads, the Young Women leaders worked to flag down another bus—no easy task so far outside the city. The next driver to pass by initially agreed to transport the group but balked when he saw the dozens of young women rushing up to the doors with huge bundles of equipment. Tsedendorj and another leader soon caught a ride to Ulaanbaatar in a vegetable

Young women camp in Mongolia. 1995. Young women in Mongolia squeezed into tents at the country's first camp. Despite torrential rains and transportation setbacks, the girls "loved every aspect" of their evening at camp and leaders did not hear a word of complaint (Mary N. Cook, "First Young Women Camp in Mongolia," *New Era*, June 2012, 27). Because the first missionaries were allowed into Mongolia only three years earlier, most campers and leaders were new members of the church. As membership continued to grow in new international areas, ongoing efforts to make the Young Women program culturally translatable became increasingly important. (Church History Library, Salt Lake City.)

truck, and at 5:30 that evening, the group was relieved to see the same bus from the day before bouncing down the road.[115] Though they had to pay the driver again, the weary group was able to return home.[115] As in other places, leaders would need time to decide whether the benefits of camp justified the challenges in the long term.

Local leaders in other countries often looked to missionaries for help in planning or adapting camp activities. In Albania in 1995, missionaries and local leaders scaled camp down to a day trip for their first attempt. Edlira Kocani, leader of the young women in a branch in Tirana, worked with two missionaries, Louise Holman and Patricia Cryer, to plan the event. After traveling by bus to a lake near Tirana, they found some shade and began with simple spiritual activities—a hymn, prayer, and recitation of the Young Women theme—before moving on to simple games with religious lessons.[116] That same summer, Elizabeth Adei-Manu, the stake Young Women president in Accra, Ghana, led ward and branch leaders in planning the country's first Young Women camp. Though there had been Latter-day Saints in Ghana for decades, girls' camp had not been a priority to that point. Adei-Manu acted with help from Lilian DeLong, an American expatriate living in Ghana. With about $400 from the stake, they rented a boarding school in Tema, to which they transported around one hundred young women and twenty leaders for a camp experience with various games and activities. Adei-Manu felt the camp was an overall success.[117]

Erika Aza was unable to participate in camp because her area in Colombia did not have the resources or the know-how to hold one, but she did join combined-gender youth conferences, during which she sometimes slept in a tent.[118] Likewise, Verónica Battista in Buenos Aires, Argentina, experienced combined-gender youth conferences rather than camp during her teenage years. When she became a Young Women leader herself in 2003, however, she and other local leaders tried holding a Young Women camp. They had no idea how to camp because no one in the stake had ever done it. But she and the other leaders pored over the manual, learning as much as they could, and jumped in. Her group ignored the camp certification requirements—they had no experience in them and no one to teach them. Still, Battista enjoyed the opportunity to find meaning in novel traditions. She loved the experience of cooking together with the girls, hearing their testimonies, and feeling the unity of the group.[119]

Members' experiments adapting an unfamiliar tradition often yielded powerful moments and greater unity for the young women who attended. In Ghana, Adei-Manu saw spiritual and social benefits to the camp she'd led with guidance from DeLong. The young women had learned Book of Mormon stories through fun skits. When she visited different wards after camp, young women knew her and were excited to see her, and she was pleased that she knew them as well. Members in Ghana continued camp after DeLong left. In Albania, Kocani valued the experience of the first camp in her country, but she did not plan a camp the next year because Louise Holman, who had helped organize the first camp, had returned home.[120] Though the experiment was fruitful, the degree of difficulty didn't justify continuing without outside energy and experience.

MAKING CAMP A PLACE OF RETREAT

These kinds of challenges were on the minds of new Young Women general president Susan Tanner and her counselors, Julie Beck and Elaine Dalton, when they were appointed in 2002. Tanner had extensive experience traveling internationally with her husband in his academic work and had served in several ward and stake women's leadership positions, including as stake Young Women president. In addition to her childhood years in Brazil, Beck had served on the Young Women general board before her appointment, as had Dalton, whose service also included time as a stake Young Women president.[121] The women considered both international issues and questions about the internet and media as they contemplated revising the camping program. During World War II, YWMIA leaders had viewed camp as a retreat from the stress of wartime realities. Now the Young Women presidency felt youth were facing a different kind of embattled reality: the constant bombardment of technology and media.[122] Tanner and her counselors understood that the internet's pressure was a constant, nearly inescapable presence that affected young women's mental health and commitment to religious virtue.[123] In almost every meeting with her board, Tanner discussed ways to combat internet pornography and sliding standards of dress and behavior portrayed in the media and to discourage Latter-day Saint young women from following such trends.[124] With these concerns in mind, the presidency sought ways to make camp less of a rugged outdoors experience, advocating instead for a peaceful retreat in nature.

Though practical questions remained about how to create an experience of refuge in different global settings, Tanner's presidency began to arrive at some clarity about camp's purpose. Young Women leaders felt an urgent need to create spaces where young women could escape the spiritual dangers that leaders saw encroaching ever more tenaciously.[125] Camp could be a space away from messages about female body image and objectification that pervaded online and broadcast media, a space where young women could find purpose and renewal.

In 2006, the church finished building a new Young Women camp in Heber Valley, Utah, as part of an ongoing investment in camping infrastructure. For decades, local church leaders in different areas had worked to secure and develop campsites.

Some sites, such as Mia Shalom in central Utah, served several individual stakes, whereas others, such as Brighton in Big Cottonwood Canyon near Salt Lake City, and Oakcrest in the mountains near Kamas, Utah, offered a supplement to ward and stake camps. In the early 2000s, over a dozen sites throughout the United States and Canada were being developed. In New England, for example, Gordon B. Hinckley enjoined leaders to purchase property and develop a camp for use by several stakes.[126] The Heber Valley camp, however, was the largest and reflected the latest thinking on the purpose of girls' camp.

Tanner and her counselors attended the new camp's dedication on 22 June. After driving past the seven Young Women value flags that welcomed visitors, they took their seats on the stage of the Lucy Mack Smith Amphitheater beside Dallin H. Oaks of the Quorum of the Twelve Apostles, Merrill J. Bateman of the presidency of the Seventy, and the two previous Young Women general presidents, Ardeth Kapp and Janette Beckham. Hundreds of campers and the facility's staff had left their activities to join the ceremony, taking their seats on split-log benches to listen to talks and a dedicatory prayer.[127]

The service demonstrated leaders' priorities, which were clearly no longer about certification. Tanner spoke on grounding young women in a sense of divine identity. She expressed her hope that camps would be a refuge where young women would learn about who they are as children of God and feel His love for them.[128] Bateman gave the dedicatory prayer, asking God that the camp be a haven from the evil in the world.[129]

STANDARDS OF CHASTITY

Positioning camp as a place apart from an increasingly evil world reflected a resurgent feeling of the need for defense and separation in the Young Women organization. Much discussion focused on what young women ought *not* do. Many young Latter-day Saints in the early 2000s did their best to uphold an identity that was often noteworthy in social situations for what it asked them not to drink, watch, or wear. One popular T-shirt at the time read simply, "I can't . . . I'm Mormon."[130]

For young women and young men, premarital sex and many physical expressions of passion were foremost on the list of don'ts. Not least because of the faith's continued strong emphasis for both genders on marriage and raising children, the ideal life path presented in church lessons involved abstinence until temple marriage. By the early 2000s, however, these ideals were competing with other prevalent cultural beliefs surrounding sexual experience. One analysis of how young Americans thought about virginity in film and in their own lives identified three main patterns: Some viewed their first sexual experience as a milestone in the maturation process. Others viewed virginity as having a stigma, suggesting immaturity or a lack of desirability. And still others viewed their first sexual experience as having heightened meaning as a gift and a marker of true love.[131] All three models left room for social pressure toward premarital sexual expression as a sign of maturation or a demonstration of the authenticity of deep romantic feelings. Researchers who studied religion and teenage sexuality found that Latter-day Saints had exceptionally high rates of commitment to chastity both in their intentions and in their behaviors.[132] Nevertheless, when the Young Women general presidency visited local congregations, local leaders regularly cited chastity as the top challenge facing their young women.[133]

Tanner and her presidency tried to focus the youth programs on positive formulations of sexual standards. They presented chastity not as simply the absence of sexual experience but as an active choice leading to increased spirituality. The 2007 theme of Especially for Youth—a BYU-sponsored program for high school students—was "Power in Purity." This theme was complemented by the 2007 churchwide theme for youth, "Let virtue garnish thy thoughts unceasingly; then shall thy confidence wax strong in the presence of God," which echoed the theme of a church antipornography booklet published the year before.[134] These messages emphasized the benefits of living a chaste life, like power and confidence.

Even with the church's strong emphasis on chastity, not all Latter-day Saint youth lived the ideal. About one in eight teenage Latter-day Saints who responded to the National Survey of Youth and Religion in 2002–2003 reported having had at least one sexual experience. More than half of that group reported returning to abstinence after a single experience.[135] In some cases, however, framing chastity as a matter of *purity* could lead to all-or-nothing thinking, discouragement, and complicated relationships between young women and local leaders.[136] Young women who were or had been sexually active were sometimes left feeling alienated. Because church messaging presented chastity as a defining feature of a good Latter-day Saint, their sense of self and their relationship with God could be disrupted by premarital sex.

Equating chastity and moral purity with virginity laid an even greater burden on young women who experienced sexual abuse or rape. Elizabeth Smart was a member of the Young Women organization in her ward when she was kidnapped from her Salt Lake City home in 2002 and repeatedly raped over the course of nine months. In later interviews, she praised the power of faith to bring hope and healing but also spoke frankly about how discussions at church that associated virginity with future desirability had been difficult for her. Smart's own internal dialogue after she was raped was influenced by past lessons on purity: "One of the first thoughts I had was, *No one is ever going to want to marry me now: I'm worthless, I'm filthy, I'm dirty.* I think every rape survivor feels those same feelings, but having that with the pressure of faith compounded on top—it was almost crippling."[137]

Long after her rapist was arrested and she was back with her family in safety, Smart found it difficult to listen to church lessons on chastity. In their attempts to discourage premarital sex, teachers sometimes used analogies implying that premarital sexual experiences changed a young woman in a permanent, negative way. "I just remember thinking, *This is terrible. Do they not realize I'm sitting in class? Do they not realize that I'm listening to what they're saying?* Those are terrible analogies," Smart said. While she recognized that teachers had no malice for victims of sexual assault, she found herself discouraged by the lack of consideration for the substantial percentage of young women who experienced rape or other abuse.[138]

In the early 2000s, church leaders made additional efforts to be mindful of diverse experiences among members, including young women. Leaders like Chieko Okazaki, former counselor in the Relief Society general presidency, and Richard G. Scott of the Quorum of the Twelve Apostles began to address the social and spiritual needs of sexual abuse victims in venues with higher visibility.[139] Church leaders also worked to be more mindful of young women who had chosen not to follow their religious standards of chastity for a time and then returned to living church standards. Increasingly, leaders worked to define attributes like purity as renewable, differentiating their calls for virtue from cultural conceptions of virginity as a quality that could be irretrievably lost. A 2006 general conference address on purity by Susan Tanner's counselor Elaine Dalton, for example, heavily emphasized repentance. Far from presenting a mistake as irreversible, she reminded listeners that "the Savior has promised forgiveness" and the path to the temple is made possible by "the redeeming and enabling power of the Atonement of Jesus Christ."[140] Over the next decade, general and local leaders continued to adjust how they presented chastity to better reflect this understanding.[141]

ADDING A NEW VALUE

Elaine Dalton was sustained as the new Young Women general president at the April 2008 general conference. She selected Mary Cook as her first counselor, with whom she had served in Tanner's presidency since 2007.[142] An educator by profession, Cook had also served with her husband as a mission leader.[143] Her second counselor, Ann Monson Dibb, held a degree in elementary education and served on the Young Women general board. As the daughter of church president Thomas S. Monson, Dibb had unique insight into general church leadership and the stories of Latter-day Saints worldwide.[144] A few days after being sustained, the three women donned hiking boots for their first meeting: a snowy, slippery morning hike up Ensign Peak.

The landmark, a hill overlooking the Salt Lake Valley, was given its name because Brigham Young had said, echoing language from Isaiah, that the peak was "a proper place to raise an ensign to the nations." Dalton and her counselors invoked Young's memory by surveying the valley from the same place he confirmed the future location of the Salt Lake Temple, which he later announced with the words, "Here we will build the temple of our God."[145]

While looking toward the temple, Dalton told her counselors, "We are going to help parents prepare the young women to be worthy to make and keep sacred covenants and receive the ordinances of the temple. That's our vision." Echoing Brigham Young's literal raising of an ensign in 1847, the Young Women presidency lifted and waved a gold shawl as "an ensign to the nations." They sang "High on the Mountain Top," a hymn that includes the words "a banner is unfurled. / Ye nations, now look up; / It waves to all the world."[146] For Dalton, the new banner they were waving stood for virtue.[147]

Years earlier, Dalton had arisen from a sleepless night with the conviction that the young women needed a return to virtue and a focus on the temple. When she explained her spiritual impressions to her husband while on a run the next morning, he stopped in the middle of the street and said, "Turn around and go home. You have to write this down."[148] The thoughts Dalton recorded that day guided her throughout the years of her presidency. As she later remarked, using virtue as a rallying cry was inherently linked with her impression to focus on the temple: "Virtue's the key that unlocks temple doors."[149]

At the October 2008 general conference, Dalton gave an address entitled "A Return to Virtue." Afterward, she and her presidency proposed adding virtue as one of the Young Women values—the first addition to the Kapp administration's inaugural 1985 list. To define the new value, Dalton used the broad definition of virtue found in *Preach My Gospel*, the missionary guide in circulation since 2004, as "a pattern of thought and behavior based on high moral standards," while noting "it encompasses chastity and moral purity."[150] That definition both reinforced the importance of chastity in Latter-day Saint belief and behavior and also allowed young women and leaders to think about broader patterns of moral behavior. Adding virtue as a value thus imbued it with a uniquely Latter-day Saint significance for the church's young women.[151] The Personal Progress revision incorporating the virtue value was the first version of the program released online.[152] "We are looking to a day," Dalton said of the new digital format, "when, at a click, anyone, anywhere in the world, will be able to access those things that are virtuous and lovely, that bless and strengthen homes and families, and that prepare young women everywhere to make and keep sacred temple covenants."[153]

For Dalton, the addition of virtue as a Young Women value was a kind of restoration, echoing the founding ideals of retrenchment at the origin of the Young
Women organization. "I looked up the word *retrench* as we were thinking about a
return to virtue," she remembered. "The dictionary says it is an additional interior
fortification. That is really what virtue is going to do for the young women. It's going
to give them a fortification, a strengthening, to stand as a witness of God in an ever
darkening world. It is going to help them have strength and courage."[154]

The structure of the new Personal Progress value experiences developed the virtue
theme more fully. Some of the required value experiences overtly addressed chastity.
Young women were to study the family proclamation, the section on "sexual purity"
in *For the Strength of Youth*, the thirteenth article of faith, and Proverbs 31:10–31 (on
the worth of a virtuous woman), and they were to write in their journals about the
blessings of committing to be chaste. Other experiences involved broader spiritual
strengthening. These focused on recognizing and maintaining the influence of the
Holy Ghost, preparing to participate in temple ordinances, and gaining greater appreciation for repentance. For the capstone value project, young women were to read
the entire Book of Mormon and record their thoughts, particularly regarding Jesus
Christ's example of virtue. Two pages were provided for young women to write their
testimonies of the Book of Mormon.[155]

Many Young Women groups celebrated the new value. In the Ipiranga Stake
in São Paulo, Brazil, Tatiana Christina dos Reis Dintof helped organize an activity
about virtue. She told the stories of Brigham Young identifying the Salt Lake Temple
site and the Young Women presidency raising a gold flag while looking toward the
temple and proclaiming a return to virtue. Channeling virtue's broad definition,
leaders asked the young women to develop three habits: praying every morning and
night, reading daily in the Book of Mormon, and smiling. They painted a logo representing these goals on a banner. "Each young woman stamped her hand on this banner. We are excited to prepare our young women to make covenants with the Lord in
the temple and help them come unto Christ," Dintof said.[156]

In practice, young women who chose to prioritize virtue often noticeably broke
with the social, dating, and sexual expectations of their peers. Zandile Qinisile in
South Africa was known as *umfundisi*, meaning "pastor's wife," in school because
of her knowledge of scripture and the standards she maintained. The feeling of not
fitting in with her peers was sometimes very difficult for her. She even turned down
a young man who wanted to date her, because he did not have the qualities she had
decided she wanted in a future husband. This made him angry, but Zandile was later
grateful for the Young Women lessons that taught her to expect something more.

Young women raising virtue banner, California. 2009. Following the example of President Elaine Schwartz Dalton, young women from the Concord Ward in California unfurled a gold banner atop a mountain as a "standard to the nations . . . calling for a return to virtue" (Elaine S. Dalton, "A Return to Virtue," *Ensign*, Nov. 2008, 79). Doing so symbolized their commitment to the new virtue value. Added to the Young Women program in 2008, the new value emphasized high moral standards, including chastity. Similar symbolic banner raisings occurred around the world. (Photograph by Laura Berrett.)

When she met the man who would become her husband, she recognized those qualities in him. "It was as simple as that," she realized.[157]

Almost four years after Dalton introduced virtue into the Young Women values, young people of the church experienced another major change. At the opening of the October 2012 general conference, it was announced that young women could serve missions at age nineteen, instead of age twenty-one, as had been the case since 1964.[158] Young men's age of eligibility was changed from nineteen to eighteen.[159] The announcement was greeted with excitement as well as an immediate outpouring of missionary applications from young women. Within a year of the age change, the female missionary force had risen over 140 percent, from about 8,100 to over 19,500.[160]

The 2012 age change for young missionaries marked the beginning of a new era in which Latter-day Saint youth engaged more with the core mission of the church, including through more outward-facing service and ministering efforts. But the concerns guiding leaders of young women continued much the same as before. As the church grew globally and faced rapid technological and social change, leaders sought ways not only to help young women grow and progress as they prepared for their future but also to protect and safeguard them in that journey.

As the first decade of the new millennium came to a close, the retrenchment efforts of recent presidencies gave way to an increased focus on expanding young women's horizons—and to consideration of what that might look like for young women in different parts of the world. Certainly, part of that expansion would be greater numbers of young women serving as missionaries, as well as a greater emphasis on preparing and encouraging young women to serve. Yet the next decade would see even greater changes to the organization for young Latter-day Saint women throughout the world, ushering in new opportunities for them to participate in the work of the church.

DISCIPLES OF CHRIST

2013–2024

On a chilly day in early May 2018, twenty-year-old Camila Ortega Aza stepped off an airplane in São Paulo, Brazil. Two days earlier, she had driven with her parents an hour and a half south from her home in Tuluá, Colombia, to Cali to be set apart as a missionary for The Church of Jesus Christ of Latter-day Saints. She worried about whether she would be able to master Portuguese and effectively share her testimony with the people in Manaus, Brazil. Shortly after she was set apart, several friends and family members wished her well as she boarded her flight at the airport. Despite her nervousness, she said goodbye with a smile that helped ease her mother's own worries. When Camila and four other arriving missionaries drove up to the Missionary Training Center in São Paulo, missionaries already in classes flung their arms out the windows to wave in welcome. She felt reassured as she settled in, but she felt most at home when she received her missionary name tag. Years of preparation had led her to this milestone. "Now," she thought, "I am a missionary."[1]

Camila was among tens of thousands of young Latter-day Saint women who excitedly submitted applications for missionary service in the years following the 2012 decrease in the minimum age requirement. By 2018, the number of young women serving missions had leveled off, but at over twenty thousand, it was still two and a half times greater than it had been in 2012.[2]

The lower age requirement had been a significant factor in Camila's decision to serve. From the time she was a little girl, she had wanted to be a missionary like her aunt Erika Aza, but she felt overwhelmed by the prospect of waiting until she was twenty-one years old. She was fourteen when she heard the announcement at general conference, and when she received her patriarchal blessing the following year, it included counsel for her to plan on serving a mission.[3] From that moment, Camila began sincerely preparing to do so, and the desire to serve shaped her experience in Young Women. Though she was not allowed to take the missionary preparation course offered in Sunday School until she was eighteen, she prepared in other ways by attending seminary, teaching alongside full-time missionaries in her area, and completing Personal Progress goals. After earning her Young Womanhood medallion, she helped a younger girl in the Beehive class complete her own work.[4]

In the seven years between when Camila learned she could serve at a younger age and when she finished her missionary service, young women became more integrated into the church's core work as they participated in family history and temple work, taught lessons, and served in their wards and communities. At the end of the decade, general leaders announced revisions to the church's youth organizations as sweeping as those that took place almost fifty years earlier. Young women and young men were asked more overtly than before to model their development after Jesus Christ and to think about their lifelong role as His disciples. Just as the missionary age changes early in the decade had brought the experiences of young women and young men closer together, changes in the 2020s to both Young Women and Young Men brought the organizations' programs and offerings closer to each other than they had been since the heyday of the MIA. While the initial rollout was complicated by the global COVID-19 pandemic, over the next few years, leaders refined Young Women programs to help young women participate in the work of the church and develop as mentors and future leaders. In the process, Young Women leaders worked to balance the recurring impulses toward retrenchment and engagement, in hopes of finally making the programs adaptable to the varied circumstances of the more than 540,000 Latter-day Saint young women throughout the world.[5]

CHANGING EXPECTATIONS FOR YOUNG WOMEN

Well before the restructuring of Young Women programs in the early 2020s, major changes were already taking place in the experience of the average Latter-day Saint young woman in the years after she turned eighteen. Higher rates of missionary service at younger ages for women after the missionary age change in 2012 were only part of that story. The larger social trend of lower marriage rates and older average age at marriage continued to affect Latter-day Saints. By the beginning of the century, a majority of adult members across the global church were single, widowed, or divorced rather than married. For some time, married members still made up a majority of Latter-day Saint adults in the United States and Canada, but even those regions would reach the same demographic tipping point by 2019.[6] Marriage and family relationships remained theologically and socially important for Latter-day Saints. But while generations of women had taken it for granted that they would primarily live their faith in the sphere of motherhood, in the 2010s, the need to prepare young women to act as disciples of Christ in diverse situations became more obvious.

In some ways, young women of the early twenty-first century were well prepared for this growing diversity of expectations about their futures. Researchers who studied generational differences divided young people during this period into two generational cohorts. Both cohorts—millennials (born between 1981 and 1996) and Generation Z (born between 1997 and 2012)—were generally understood to be more diverse demographically as well as more accepting of diversity than any previous generation. In the United States, these generations were also set apart by lower rates of religious affiliation than earlier generations.[7] In 2010, nearly one in four American adults under age thirty reported that they were no longer affiliated with the religious tradition they had been raised in. At the same time, however, most continued to believe in absolute standards of right and wrong.[8] Most members of both generations also expressed a strong desire to create a more equitable world.[9]

In some areas of advocacy, the hopes of these younger generations about the future could be in tension with Latter-day Saint teachings about gender, marriage, and family. In 2013, a majority of Americans recognized some degree of conflict between their religious beliefs and same-sex marriages, while 70 percent of American millennials supported legal recognition for same-sex marriage.[10] During that same period, Latter-day Saint leaders and members worked to balance teachings on chastity and marriage with the divine command to love all God's children. Church efforts included the 2012 launch and subsequent expansions of a website dedicated to promoting understanding of sexual orientation within a religious context, as well as the church's 2015 support for a model law in Utah designed to promote both religious freedom and nondiscrimination for LGBTQ individuals.[11] Still, there was a contrast between the attitudes of straightforward acceptance many young people preferred and the more complex range of attitudes in religious communities. In one 2014 survey, 31 percent of American millennials who had left their childhood religion cited concerns over the treatment of LGBTQ people as an important factor in their decision.[12]

In other arenas, Latter-day Saints were particularly well prepared to help young people take an active part in making a difference in the world. As they had in previous generations, church leaders and organizations worked to help empower young people to serve others. An increased focus on building missionary skills during the youth years was one striking example. Almost a decade before the missionary age change was announced, church leaders released a new missionary training manual titled *Preach My Gospel*. In contrast to previous missionary materials, *Preach My Gospel* was actively promoted for use by young women and young men before they were old enough for missionary service.[13]

After 2012, this emphasis on missionary preparation expanded even more explicitly to young women. Elaine Dalton, Young Women general president at the time of the announcement, felt that the organization's longstanding emphasis on temple worship dovetailed with mission preparation. "When a young woman is worthy to enter the temple, then she is also prepared to serve a mission," she explained. Dalton noted that Personal Progress requirements like reading the Book of Mormon or mentoring others prepared young women for missionary service and that values and goal-setting experiences would benefit those who served. "Heavenly Father loves and trusts His precious daughters, and now, as never before, is the time to flood the earth with their virtue, their strong spirits and their light," she stated.[14] With the growing number of young women serving missions shortly after their years in Young Women, outside observers took note. One article reported, "Waves of women . . . are taking part in the church's crucial coming-of-age ritual, returning home from their missions with unprecedented scriptural fluency, new confidence and new ideas about themselves."[15] While full-time missionary service played a role in strengthening this confidence and religious competence, for most Latter-day Saints who served, the missionary program built on a foundation laid during the teenage years.

Church leaders continued to work to strengthen that foundation for missionary service as well as lifelong service and leadership in the church. In 2013, the church introduced a new youth curriculum entitled *Come, Follow Me: Learning Resources for Youth* to promote topic-based gospel literacy.[16] In contrast to previous youth manuals, *Come, Follow Me* was designed for use both in mixed-gender youth Sunday School meetings and in Young Women and Young Men classes. It was the first time since the 1950s that young men and young women had shared the same curriculum. Like *Preach My Gospel*, the *Come, Follow Me* curriculum aimed to develop students' capacity for adaptive thinking about application of principles. Local leaders were encouraged to involve youth in teaching, allowing them to build a useful missionary skill and moving closer to the longstanding goal of youth leadership.[17]

EXPANDING THE VISION

The same year the *Come, Follow Me* curriculum was released, Bonnie Lee Green Oscarson was appointed Young Women general president. Oscarson had served three times as a ward Young Women president, twice in a stake Young Women presidency, and nine years as a seminary teacher but had no previous experience working at church headquarters.[18] "I think they deliberately wanted somebody that didn't have any experience, that hadn't come up through the ranks," she later reflected. "I was told by apostles, 'We need some fresh ideas and we want somebody to look at it with a fresh perspective.'"[19]

One way Oscarson and her counselors, Carol Foley McConkie and Neill Foote Marriott, sought fresh perspectives was through their board. In the months after being sustained, they began discussing the possibility of forming an international board to better represent the global church. In the past, women from international backgrounds had served on the board only while living within manageable travel distance of Salt Lake City. Digital communication technologies now allowed for simultaneous meetings from anywhere, and with encouragement from priesthood leaders at church headquarters and assistance from leaders in area offices around the world, the new presidency conducted a broader search.[20]

Their new board consisted of four women living in the Salt Lake City area, along with five others living in New York, Peru, Brazil, South Africa, and Japan. Dorah Mkhabela, who lived in South Africa, saw the calling as an opportunity to directly represent the circumstances and needs of young women in Africa. Carmela Melero de Hooker, who lived in Peru, likewise saw new possibility in the digital gatherings of the international board. "I think it is a great opportunity for Latin American women to share their experiences, challenges, strengths, hopes and testimonies more directly with the board," she said.[21] Oscarson assigned the new board members to visit Young Women meetings and activities and report back about what challenges they observed. Feedback from the international board members proved especially helpful in revising the camp program, which, despite earlier attempts at internationalization, was still "North American centric," as Oscarson put it.[22]

The new presidency also brought their own fresh perspectives. In addition to ward-level experience in Young Women, Oscarson and her counselors each had experience with missionary work. Oscarson had served alongside her husband in leading the Sweden Göteborg Mission.[23] Both her counselors had worked alongside their husbands in leading missions and remembered joining the church themselves. McConkie's family joined the church when she was a little girl, and being sealed to her family in the temple was a formative experience for her. Marriott converted as a young adult in Boston, Massachusetts.[24]

In 2015, Oscarson brought her past mission experience, as well as her connection to the church's young women, to a new assignment when she became the first woman to serve on the Missionary Executive Council, the leading council over missionary work. This change was part of a broader effort to integrate women as members of key councils at the top levels of church leadership: the Relief Society

Young women participating in worldwide indexing event, Salt Lake City. 2016. Youth from the Northpoint Second Ward indexed names on FamilySearch at their local stake family history center as part of a global push for youth participation in family history work. Youth in the 2010s engaged in temple and family history work on FamilySearch.org via computer or on FamilySearch mobile apps developed for smartphones in 2014. (Photograph by Brittany Chapman Nash.)

general president, Linda Kjar Burton, was appointed to the Priesthood Executive Council (renamed the Priesthood and Family Executive Council), and the Primary general president, Rosemary Mix Wixom, was placed on the Temple and Family History Executive Council. Each of these three committees, which had been established by Harold B. Lee in the correlation era, was led by a member of the Quorum of the Twelve Apostles.[25]

Ardeth Kapp, who had served on correlation committees under Lee's leadership, had predicted this kind of change in policy, envisioning a day when women would serve as members of these key committees.[26] Since the 1990s, church leaders had emphasized the importance of councils on the ward and stake level and had stressed the importance of women's full participation in them.[27] Until 2015, however, that emphasis had not been reflected in the church's highest councils. For Sheri L. Dew, former counselor in the Relief Society general presidency, the change represented a significant step in women's leadership in the church. "To now have the Relief Society, Young Women and Primary general presidents assigned as standing members of these three major committees signals how invaluable women are at all levels of church government on matters affecting all members," she explained.[28] While much of their work was still mediated by priesthood leaders, the presence of women leaders on these councils brought them into more direct participation in church decision-making than ever before.

TEMPLE COVENANTS AND FAMILY HISTORY WORK IN A DIGITAL ERA

These significant changes in women's participation in church leadership structures accompanied other developments in young women's church activities. Since Kapp's presidency in the mid-1980s, the temple had been continually emphasized by the Young Women organization. Most of that emphasis, however, was on preparing for the future, when women often receiving their temple endowment in preparation for, and shortly before, the marriage sealing ordinance. By the 2010s, however, a growing number of young women were receiving the endowment within a few years of turning eighteen, either in preparation for a mission or out of a personal desire for deeper spiritual commitment. Moreover, leaders envisioned young women in their teens carrying current temple recommends and attending the temple regularly to perform proxy baptisms, both of which would support them in maintaining high moral standards.[29] More young women than ever before could attend the temple regularly, as construction of temples had accelerated throughout the world. In 1997, the church dedicated its fiftieth temple; by the end of 2013, 141 temples were in operation, with temples on every inhabited continent.[30]

Youth at temple devotional, California. 2019. In the 2010s, an increased focus on the work of salvation and exaltation strengthened Latter-day Saint youth's commitment to temple attendance and ordinance work. These young men and women were among three thousand youth who attended a special devotional before the Oakland California Temple rededication. Youth devotionals began to replace youth cultural celebrations held before temple dedications and rededications. (The Church of Jesus Christ of Latter-day Saints.)

During the 2010s, church leaders also encouraged youth to become actively involved in the genealogical work that enabled proxy temple ordinances, drawing on the digital literacy that was now widespread among young people around the world. Apostle David A. Bednar suggested in 2011 that growing youth digital literacy might have a divine purpose. "Your fingers have been trained to text and tweet to accelerate and advance the work of the Lord—not just to communicate quickly with your friends," he said. "The skills and aptitude evident among many young people today are a preparation to contribute to the work of salvation."[31] In 2012, the First Presidency issued a letter encouraging youth and young adults to "use for temple work their own family names or the names of ancestors of their ward and stake members," which implied their participation in genealogical research and emphasized the temple as a site for current service rather than only as a symbol of future covenants.[32] Youth also became involved in efforts called "indexing," in which they downloaded images taken from sources such as handwritten parish rolls or probate records and then transcribed and uploaded the vital information in those sources in searchable form for use through the church's FamilySearch website.[33]

In Colombia, Camila Ortega Aza was among the many youth around the world who answered the call to become more involved in temple and family history work. A few years before her mission in 2018, she and other young women and men in her district in Tuluá accepted a challenge from their district president. They worked toward several goals related to indexing, preparing names for the temple, memorizing scriptures, and attending seminary. For weeks in the summer, youth in the three branches of the church in Tuluá met at the chapel on Sundays to peer at copies of old civic records on a computer screen. They also filled out their own family history records. On a few special occasions, youth joined in indexing marathons at the church. Throughout this time, their leaders encouraged them to pray for divine guidance so they could read and understand the old and unfamiliar handwriting and find the information they needed for their family history.

Then in October, the youth received a reward for their efforts: a special trip to Bogotá. There they spent an entire day at the temple doing baptisms for the people whose names they had indexed and then the next day enjoying themselves at an amusement park.[34] After the weeks of tedious indexing and the nine-hour bus trip to Bogotá, the time at the temple was a special experience for Camila. She felt her efforts in going through so many records had been worth it.[35]

Hundreds of thousands of young women around the world participated in similar family history and indexing efforts throughout the second decade of the 2000s. In the Hampton Ward in Mesa, Arizona, youth indexed over six thousand names in seven weeks. "It has made my temple experiences that much more meaningful," said

Aleece McLaws, a seventeen-year-old young woman who participated in the challenge and attended the temple weekly. Aleece said she received spiritual help after praying when she encountered difficult handwriting in the sources she was indexing.[36] In some places, church leaders appointed young women and men as family history consultants to help train others in the work, adding a new dimension to longstanding efforts at building youth leadership. In July 2016, Alycia Ames and Kalli Laing, young family history consultants in the North Salt Lake Legacy Stake in Utah, helped organize local participation in a churchwide indexing event that extended over a weekend. "This event is going to bless someone's life and your own," Alycia promised participants as she led out in training them.[37]

Throughout the decade, talks, articles, and activities invited youth to participate in temple and family history work.[38] Church publications highlighted positive experiences of young people involved in the work. The *Church News* featured a thirteen-year-old young woman from Utah, Ellie Tobiasson, who expressed her feelings in an artwork displayed at the Church History Museum at Temple Square. Ellie's piece depicted her great-grandmother holding her when she was a baby. As Ellie described it, her great-grandmother looked into the heavens and saw "the temple that binds her to me and to her posterity and us to our ancestors." Leaves in the painting represented a family tree. "I want to honor my ancestors' lives by shining my light and sharing what they have given me," Ellie said.[39] A few years later, the *New Era* spotlighted Rajane Samuels, a young woman in Jamaica. Rajane described how a family history goal helped her connect with her maternal grandmother and a paternal great-aunt. She further described feeling as though she had been led to some ancestors' headstones, gaining a sense of connection with the dead. When she performed temple ordinances on their behalf, Rajane said she could feel their excitement and joy. "All I wanted to do was thank them for giving me the opportunity to be a part of something so special," she said.[40]

Such efforts came at a time when young people and their adult leaders wrestled with the promise and peril of an increasingly digital world. Millennials were digitally savvy, and Gen Z were fully fluent, having had little to no life experience in the world as it existed before the advent of smartphones.[41] But technical proficiency did not necessarily imply social, emotional, or spiritual health. During this period, hundreds of articles and reports from scholars, news media, and religious leaders alike began asking questions about the benefits and damages of internet and social media use. Concerns included cyberbullying, internet addiction, and disconnection from family life.[42] Numerous Latter-day Saint leaders, including Young Women general president Bonnie L. Oscarson, addressed these issues in their messages.[43]

Youth temple trip, Guayaquil, Ecuador. 2018. These young women and men from Colombia brought to the temple several names they had extracted through family history indexing efforts. During the special temple trip, they were baptized vicariously for the individuals they had researched. (Courtesy Daniel Rosero.)

The Young Women organization and its members took advantage of new digital tools in many areas. Young women and local leaders were able to access more resources on specialized topics than were available in printed manuals. On its websites, the church published materials to help young people and their leaders more openly discuss issues such as mental health, sexual orientation, and questions about the church's history.[44] Genealogical work, however, presented a striking site of intersection between religion, generational differences, and technological change in the early twenty-first century.

SERVICE IN YOUNG WOMEN

Caring for those in need had been central to the work of the church since its founding, and for decades Young Women general leaders had emphasized service in their programs and directives to local leaders. In the 2010s and 2020s, a typical young woman in the church might participate in service projects organized during a midweek Young Women activity or as a special weekend event, in other church group projects, in personal service projects as an expression of her discipleship or to fulfill a Young Women requirement, in informal service as opportunities arose in her community, and in personal or family involvement with civic and interfaith relief efforts.

In 2012, researchers at the University of Pennsylvania reported that the average American Latter-day Saint dedicated roughly nine times as many hours to unpaid service than the average American.[45] But most of that service was centered in the local congregation; only about a fifth represented outreach beyond the church.[46] To assist members and others in finding volunteering opportunities outside their usual circles, the church turned toward a digital solution. In 2012, the church launched a website in North America called JustServe.org, which would later expand to other countries. The website helped connect people looking for service opportunities with groups seeking volunteer service.[47] JustServe was utilized unevenly, but leaders and young women in some places used it regularly to organize the service that was already deeply ingrained in the culture of Young Women.[48]

Large service efforts often arose in response to natural disasters around the world. In November 2013, one of the strongest tropical storms on record hit the Visayas region of the Philippines. The government's report on the typhoon's effects indicated that 800,000 people were preemptively evacuated, 16 million affected, and 6,300 or more killed by the storm.[49] Many young women in Tacloban, on Leyte island, were among those who left their homes before the storm hit to live temporarily in one of the two hundred Latter-day Saint meetinghouses used as evacuation centers. They joined ten thousand volunteers to assemble food and hygiene kits and distribute relief supplies, often under the auspices of the church's Helping Hands program, which

Youth community service project, Philippines. 2014. Donning iconic Helping Hands vests, Latter-day Saint youth from the San Mateo Ward in Rizal fixed and painted school chairs at the Casimiro A. Ynares Sr. Memorial National High School. Young women all over the world participated in similar events, ranging from community service to local and international disaster relief. (The Church of Jesus Christ of Latter-day Saints.)

was more oriented to disaster relief than was JustServe. Less-affected stakes on Cebu, west of Leyte, provided support to the hardest-hit stakes.[50] Youth were prepared to respond to dramatic needs through the culture of routine service. Young women regularly joined other Latter-day Saints in Helping Hands efforts to help with projects in education, health, and cleanup in public areas.[51]

Service activities were intended not only to address the immediate needs of those being served but also to foster a proactive service-oriented mindset in young people. Young women throughout the church were encouraged to watch for and take action to fill needs in their own homes, wards, and Young Women groups. In one general conference address, President Bonnie Oscarson commended young Latter-day Saints' desires to serve and make a difference in the world but added, "I also think that sometimes it's easy to miss some of the greatest opportunities to serve others because we are distracted or because we are looking for ambitious ways to change the world and we don't see that some of the most significant needs we can meet are within our own families, among our friends, in our wards, and in our communities."[52] She expressed hope that young women would act as disciples of Christ in the ways they directed their attention and efforts in their immediate circles.

A few young women in American Fork, Utah, incorporated this kind of local service into their regular ward experience. When Becca Sagers joined her Beehive class in 2012, her mother, Diana, was called as one of the Beehive leaders. Becca was born with a congenital cytomegalovirus (CMV) infection, which led to other conditions including cerebral palsy, hearing and sight loss, developmental delays, and epilepsy. Diana helped facilitate interactions between Becca and the other young women in her Beehive class.[53] Diana had heard from friends about young women who had completed the Personal Progress program by proxy for a classmate who had disabilities and proposed having Becca's classmates do the same for her. While the structure of the achievement program was not a good fit for Becca's abilities, improvising on that structure became a source of connection and joy. Some of the young women completed requirements with Becca, and others simply did them on her behalf. Rachel Weston painted a piece of art for Becca. From a photograph, she painted Becca at age two, with her glasses and hearing aids, and unable to sit up. On the other half of the canvas, she painted Becca as Rachel envisioned her after this life, when her disabilities would be healed. Diana had the painting professionally framed and hung it in Becca's room.[54] When they completed requirements for Becca, many of the young women shared their experiences in notes they gave her, and Diana and her family saw just how special the experience had been for those young women.[55] Members of the group felt bound together through their shared efforts at Christlike service.

Many young women in Utah learned to serve people with disabilities through a program called Special Needs Mutual. The program provided weeknight activities for people of all ages with disabilities and invited young women and men from nearby wards to help facilitate participation and socialization for the participants, giving people with disabilities a Young Women or Young Men experience of their own.[56] The program had begun in 1972 with a group of nine people participating in summer activities. That number swelled to twenty-seven two years later, with participants meeting every Thursday evening for drama and sports activities and spiritual discussions.[57] By the late 1990s, the program had expanded to include twelve groups in and around Salt Lake City and served around eight hundred people with all kinds of disabilities.[58] A decade later, the program had further expanded as far south as St. George, Utah, and was open to youth from any religious affiliation or practice. It was still going strong in the 2010s.[59]

SHIFTS IN EMPHASIS AND UNDERSTANDING

The April 2018 general conference began a period of major changes for the church. The church's president, Thomas S. Monson, had died in January, and Russell M. Nelson, the senior apostle, succeeded him. He had been ordained by the other members of the Quorum of the Twelve in January; he and a new First Presidency were sustained by church members during the April conference. Though Nelson was ninety-three years old at the time he took office, he was vigorous in mind and body and ready to lead the church through this period of change.

At the same conference, church members sustained a new Young Women general presidency whose significant leadership and missionary experience had prepared them to lead the Young Women organization in this dynamic period. Bonnie Hillam Cordon, who was sustained as the church's fifteenth Young Women general president, was a business executive and entrepreneur and had been serving as first counselor in the Primary general presidency at the time of her call. She had also served in various leadership positions in all three of the women's organizations of the church. She and her first counselor, Michelle Daines Craig, had both served full-time missions as young women, and Cordon had served as a mission leader with her husband in the Brazil Curitiba Mission. Rebecca Mitchell Craven, Cordon's second counselor, shared a similar experience, having recently served with her husband in presiding over the North Carolina Charlotte Mission.[60]

Later that year at the October general conference, leaders implemented sweeping changes meant to facilitate a greater emphasis on simplicity and adaptability. "It is time," Nelson stated in his opening remarks, "for a *home-centered Church,* supported by what takes place inside our branch, ward, and stake buildings," rather than thinking of "church" as something that happens primarily in the meetinghouse.[61] Changes announced during the previous April conference and in later conferences reflected this mindset. These changes included Nelson's announcement that the church's system of member visiting and service would be simplified and renamed *ministering*. Young women could now be assigned as "ministering sisters" at the age of fourteen, serving alongside an adult companion.[62] The most prominent change reduced the three-hour Sunday meeting block, in place since 1980, to a two-hour Sunday meeting schedule. Sacrament meetings would continue to take place every week, but Young Women Sunday class meetings (along with priesthood quorum and Relief Society meetings) would take place every other week, alternating with Sunday School. Church leaders encouraged members to replace the reduced communal worship time with individual or family gospel study. The church provided brief, image-rich manuals for families and individuals to use in their home gospel study and in Sunday School instruction. This curriculum adopted the title already in use for youth lessons: *Come, Follow Me.*[63]

The focus on simplicity and flexibility was tied to a broad, repeated emphasis throughout the church's messaging on the centrality of Jesus Christ and His Atonement. Also in October 2018, Nelson announced a "course correction," teaching that the church should be consistently referred to by its full name—The Church of Jesus Christ of Latter-day Saints—rather than nicknames like the "LDS Church" or the "Mormon Church." Nelson declared, "When we omit His name from His Church, we are inadvertently removing *Him* as the central focus of our lives."[64] Leaders sought to focus church members, including young women, on understanding their membership in the church not as an end in itself but as a means of making covenants with God, accessing spiritual power in their lives, and helping others along what Nelson and other leaders referred to as the covenant path.[65] This came to be expressed as "the work of salvation and exaltation."[66] The significant structural and programming changes to follow would seek to integrate young women more fully into this work.

Those changes would also be driven by shifts in understanding, language, and practice regarding women's relationship to priesthood authority. Those shifts had been ongoing throughout the church's history but took on new shape and urgency in the twenty-first century. The church had always ordained men exclusively. By the mid-1900s it was broadly understood that while women shared in the blessings made available by the priesthood, they did not hold or share its authority. This understanding animated the 1970s correlation movement.[67] It contributed to a divergence between the Young Men and Young Women organizations, as leaders sought to focus young men's programs on understanding and exercising their priesthood duties while retaining Boy Scouts as the activity channel. This shift had led to ongoing concerns about a lack of parity in the budgets and visibility of the Young Men and Young Women organizations.

Church leaders in the second decade of the twenty-first century worked to develop a new understanding about how women exercised the spiritual authority of the priesthood without ordination to priesthood offices. In a landmark 2014 general conference address, apostle Dallin H. Oaks explicated how the concept of priesthood authority included women. "We are not accustomed to speaking of women having the authority of the priesthood in their Church callings, but what other authority can it be?" he asked rhetorically. "Whoever functions in an office or calling received from one who holds priesthood keys exercises priesthood authority in performing her or his assigned duties." Oaks's formulation expanded the understanding of priesthood authority to include women.[68]

Adult women and young women were taught that they should understand their service within this framework. "As you perform the duties of your calling, you exercise priesthood authority," Bonnie Cordon affirmed while addressing Young Women class presidencies.[69] Many addresses and updates to curriculum focused on women's access to revelation and the centrality of councils in proper church administration.[70] These themes—acknowledging women's ability to exercise priesthood authority, expanding female stewardship, and focusing on personal revelation—marked a stark difference from the era of change fifty years before. Young women growing up in this new era would hear repeatedly and emphatically that the church valued receiving inspiration, speaking up in discussions, and accessing priesthood power in callings and covenants in their spiritual and religious lives.

INTRODUCING A NEW YOUTH PROGRAM

When Cordon, Craig, and Craven took office in March 2018, discussions were already well underway regarding how to create a more uniform, simplified, and gospel-centered youth program that would better meet the needs of a diverse global membership. The new Young Women presidency joined a working group to reconceptualize the church's Young Men and Young Women programs. The group knew the church would soon announce the end of its century-long affiliation with the Boy Scouts of America, and they were commissioned to make the broadest changes to the youth program since the correlation efforts of the 1970s.[71] In their discussions, Cordon felt spiritual direction that young women needed to understand three crucial things: their identity as daughters of God, their belonging within the church community, and their purpose in contributing to God's work of salvation and exaltation—what she termed "the cause of Christ."[72]

Service activity, Guatemala City, Guatemala. 2024. Young women in the Lo de Coy Ward learned to sow seeds and grow seedlings for families in need within their congregation. Recent shifts to simplify ministering efforts continued the focus on service that had remained strong in the Young Women organization since the reorientation of the youth programs in the 1970s. (Courtesy Oscar M. Abadillo.)

Among the first significant changes introduced was the age requirement for entry into the youth program, which for girls had stood at twelve since the 1930s. In December 2018, the church announced that incoming girls and boys would now advance as a group from Primary, the church's organization for children, into youth classes and quorums at the beginning of each year rather than at their birthday.[73] This meant that eleven-year-old girls joined Young Women each January.

More changes came in fall 2019. In a special broadcast in September, Cordon and other leaders introduced a new program, known simply as Children and Youth, to replace all other achievement programs for both girls and boys.[74] This meant that, for young women, Personal Progress was discontinued, along with the values and detailed requirements.

The Children and Youth program invited young people to center their personal development on Jesus Christ and set goals in the areas of intellectual, physical, spiritual, and social growth.[75] Its simple structure was oriented toward local initiative and individual inspiration, emphasizing the home-centered and church-supported framework.[76] A new Children and Youth website (the content of which was also accessible through the mobile Gospel Library app) provided extensive videos, articles, and ideas for goals and activities.[77]

By making individual and local adaptability the core of the program, rather than an added accessibility feature, leaders believed that the simplified program addressed the diverse needs of members. Cordon acknowledged that the "home-centered" ideal embedded in the program might be challenging for some young people who lived in homes where parents were not supportive of their religious efforts, but the hope was that everyone could find ways to bring gospel learning into the home, no matter their family situation. In that effort, the "church-supported" half of the equation remained fundamental. Local members—especially class presidencies and adult leaders—would play an essential role in ministering to young people and building a ward family where vulnerable youth would find the support they needed to live their religion.[78]

The new program maintained longstanding traditions, such as Young Women camps and jewelry and other tokens of recognition, though the new awards emphasized participation over achievement.[79] Church leaders hoped other activities, such as youth conferences and pioneer trek reenactments, would continue under local direction, with adaptation to local needs.[80] In addition, multiday youth gatherings known as For the Strength of Youth (FSY) conferences, which had formerly been held only in areas outside the United States and Canada, were made available to all youth worldwide on an alternating-year basis.[81] Though leaders in 2019 may not have recognized the precedent, these FSY gatherings could be seen as a fulfillment of hopes expressed as far back as 1975 that the large, vibrant gatherings that had characterized the MIA would be continued at local and regional levels.

In the October 2019 general conference, Cordon described further changes to the Young Women program. Eliciting an audible reaction from the audience, she announced that the Young Women organization's standard three-class division—along with the accompanying names of Beehive, Mia Maid, and Laurel—would be retired. While the decision to make this move had not been easy, it was based on internal research showing that most church units had a relatively small number of young women attending—an average of eleven worldwide but only nine in units outside the United States—making the three-class division difficult to implement.[82] Underscoring the importance of adaptation to varied circumstances, local units were to choose, based on their individual demographics, how many young women classes to organize in their branch or ward and what the age boundaries should be for each class.[83] Along with the new class structure came a reinvigoration of what had been called shadow leadership, first introduced fifty years earlier, now bolstered by an expanded understanding of women's authority to serve in the church.

Changes to the Young Men organization echoed iterations implemented (and ultimately reversed) in the 1970s. To align with scriptural guidance that bishops preside over the Aaronic Priesthood, ward-level Young Men presidencies were discontinued. Bishoprics would now directly oversee the Aaronic Priesthood quorums with adult men called as advisers. Young men serving as quorum presidencies would, like young women class leaders, take the lead, supported by the adults.[84] These sweeping changes meant the ward Young Women president would now work side by side and counsel directly with the bishop (bishops had previously had the option to delegate this role to one of their counselors), and bishops would hold increased responsibility for the oversight of youth programs generally. Significantly, ward budgets for youth activities would be divided equitably between the young men and the young women based on the number of each.[85]

Other changes announced at this conference also contributed to greater parity in the roles of men and women in the church. The first related to terminology. The term *auxiliary* would no longer be used, with each church entity (including Young Women) being called an *organization* and adult leaders referred to as *officers*.[86] The second, however, would have a direct and meaningful impact on the experience of young women. While records suggest that in the past women had served as formal witnesses to ordinances, including temple ordinances of baptism and marriage sealing, by the 1970s this function had come to be associated with priesthood office and therefore was performed only by men.[87] Church president

Russell M. Nelson announced that the witness role was open to both male and female members, including youth.[88] The opportunity to serve as witnesses during baptisms allowed young women to take part in creating a covenant community and to act in a recognized capacity in settings where women had formerly been observers. Shortly after this announcement, Grace Woodworth, a young woman from Victor, New York, served as a witness for the first time while participating in baptisms for the dead in the Palmyra New York Temple. "It was a special experience to be able to be a witness . . . for the first time. I remember making sure the person was fully submerged and nodding at the person marking the names," she reflected. "This change for young women to be witnesses for baptisms for the dead was meaningful because it allowed me to see that the Lord is eager for His daughters to participate in His work, and He trusts us to be instruments in His hands."[89]

NEW THEMES

The new changes extended to young people's week-to-week experiences, as leaders announced new themes for both young women and young men. Though young men previously had MIA slogans and the Boy Scout Oath, this was the first time the Young Men's organization had adopted a theme similar in nature to the Young Women theme. The Young Women organization, however, was updating a framework that had existed since the 1980s.

Initially, Cordon, Craig, and Craven expected that they would leave the theme largely untouched, though they had planned to remove the values and incorporate them into the new achievement program. Since Ardeth Kapp's introduction of the Young Women values and theme in the 1980s, the organization's general presidents had tried to preserve its basic structure as they introduced incremental changes. Cordon said, however, that they very quickly felt "an immense nudge" from the Spirit, spurring them to change the theme more extensively than they had planned. Now, through a collaborative process that included key input from the First Presidency, Cordon and her counselors arrived at a new theme they felt would express the principles that undergirded all the other changes happening in the church and in the organization at the time.[90] It read:

> I am a beloved daughter of heavenly parents, with a divine nature and eternal destiny.
> As a disciple of Jesus Christ, I strive to become like Him. I seek and act upon personal revelation and minister to others in His holy name.
> I will stand as a witness of God at all times and in all things and in all places.
> As I strive to qualify for exaltation, I cherish the gift of repentance and seek to improve each day. With faith, I will strengthen my home and family, make and keep sacred covenants, and receive the ordinances and blessings of the holy temple.[91]

The new theme resembled the one that had been at the heart of the organization for thirty-five years, but with substantial alterations, most notably an increased focus on Jesus Christ, the gift of the Holy Ghost, and covenant making. Recognizing that young women would stand and recite the theme in their Sunday meetings, Cordon and her presidency shifted the point of view from "we" to "I." It expressed Cordon's ideals of identity and belonging in three succinct phrases: "a beloved daughter of heavenly parents," "a disciple of Jesus Christ," and "a witness of God."[92] Though the theme closely resembled its predecessor in its concluding sentence, within the context of current church discourse, this statement reflected young women's engagement in the Lord's work of salvation and exaltation.[93]

Audrey Glende, a young woman from Salt Lake City who was in her final year in Young Women when the new theme was introduced, valued the new language on cherishing the gift of repentance: "It reminds us that we shouldn't be ashamed or fearful of the repentance process but rather appreciative of its availability." She also appreciated the implicit reference to a Heavenly Mother in the phrase "heavenly parents," which had been part of the initial proposed theme some thirty-four years earlier. Audrey was likewise moved by the more active, immediate, and personal language that moved beyond *preparation for* to *participation in* the work of salvation. And, though the church was continuing to globalize, Audrey said, the changes in the theme and programs helped her feel that a young woman's experience was becoming more individualized.[94]

The new Aaronic Priesthood quorum theme focused on similar principles. Announced in a special broadcast a month following general conference, the theme read:

I am a beloved son of God, and He has a work for me to do.

With all my heart, might, mind, and strength, I will love God, keep my covenants, and use His priesthood to serve others, beginning in my own home.

As I strive to serve, exercise faith, repent, and improve each day, I will qualify to receive temple blessings and the enduring joy of the gospel.

I will prepare to become a diligent missionary, loyal husband, and loving father by being a true disciple of Jesus Christ.

I will help prepare the world for the Savior's return by inviting all to come unto Christ and receive the blessings of His Atonement.[95]

MOVING FORWARD DURING A GLOBAL PANDEMIC

The church's new home-centered, church-supported paradigm became especially relevant when the worldwide SARS-CoV-2 (COVID-19) pandemic struck early in 2020, sending much of the world into lockdown and disrupting economies, education systems, and everyday lives. The church acted quickly to follow local public health directives by suspending meetings and gatherings, including regular Sunday worship services. Members were encouraged to worship in their families each week, and in many areas, priesthood holders, with authorization from their bishops, administered the sacrament in their homes.[96] It was a time of unprecedented adjustments and widespread uncertainty, particularly for young people, whose lives often revolved around friends and social activities. Unavoidably, implementation of the new Children and Youth program and other changes to the youth organizations was disrupted.

With both church meetings and school classes shifting to virtual formats, leaders looked for ways to help young women stay connected and build spiritual strength amid challenging circumstances. "Despite the challenges of our day, through technology, we can still counsel, we can still hold meetings, we can still care for one another, we can still minister," advised the Young Women general presidency.[97] In Copenhagen, Denmark, young women began holding virtual gatherings, during which they participated in a "positive minute," sharing spiritual thoughts and good experiences. In the Morada do Sol Ward in Brazil, class presidencies organized online meetings to discuss the gospel, set goals, and maintain commitment to living the gospel. Most of these girls were the only members of the church in their families, so the sustained connection and encouragement were critical.[98] In some stakes, virtual activities occurred on a much larger scale. One stake in Norway, for example, held a virtual youth conference in which over one hundred young people participated, and the St. George Utah Morningside Stake planned a virtual young women camp. These and similar activities were planned and led by the youth themselves. "The young women are our greatest resource to help us determine what young women need," the presidency observed.[99]

At headquarters, Cordon recognized almost immediately the potential for technology to enable many kinds of leadership training and communication that could no longer happen in person. The Young Women organization became the first of the five general church organizations to pilot stake leadership training through an online meeting platform called Zoom, holding the first such session on 29 April 2020, soon after pandemic restrictions were put in place in the United States. By the end of the year, the Young Women leadership had conducted over sixty online training sessions in North America. As they met virtually with local stake Young Women leaders, they paralleled the actions of their nineteenth- and early twentieth-century predecessors, who prioritized meeting with local leaders and traveled extensively to do so. Now, however, it was done from the convenience of home. Like many other adaptations that originated in the pandemic, these virtual meetings have continued.[100]

Work on other proposed initiatives continued during the pandemic. Of these, the most significant for the Young Women's organization was a thorough revision of the

For the Strength of Youth booklet. Established just before the pandemic and working throughout it, a committee comprising the Young Women and Young Men general presidencies, members of their boards, and staff members from various church departments reviewed the booklet and made recommendations for updating it.[101] Rather than including detailed lists of rules, the committee sought to emphasize Jesus Christ as the central figure of strength in the lives of youth and to highlight the value of understanding eternal truths and strengthening one's relationship with the Savior as the foundation for making inspired decisions.[102] As part of the process, the Young Women and Young Men presidencies each assigned a representative to pay close attention to the accessibility of the final language for a young, global audience. Language accessibility was an important consideration in another significant change, this one to church magazines. Fifty years after its inception, the *New Era* magazine was renamed *For the Strength of Youth*. The *New Era* had been available only in English, but the new magazine would be published in print and digitally each month in twenty-three languages and bimonthly in another twenty-four languages, with selected content posted online in an additional forty languages.[103]

Even as the Young Women organization continued to change, a sense of history and legacy remained important, and leaders had been planning for a meaningful sesquicentennial celebration in 2020.[104] Given pandemic conditions, there was no large-scale in-person event. Instead, the Young Women presidency issued a "My 150" challenge to young women, encouraging them to do something related to the number 150 to celebrate the anniversary.[105] Young women chose to complete activities such as reading 150 conference talks, running 150 miles, reading the Book of Mormon in 150 days, serving 150 meals to the homeless, raising $15,000 for diabetes research, and posting 150 inspiring messages on social media.[106] Many of the projects were related to the worldwide COVID-19 pandemic—young women offered service and support to the elderly, the sick, medical workers, and others who were affected.[107]

On 15 November 2020, Bonnie Cordon and her counselors shared these and other examples during a worldwide broadcast. Echoing the satellite broadcasts of the 1980s, it was a multicultural, multimedia production showcasing young women's talents, testimonies, and accomplishments. It opened with a montage of young women reciting the new Young Women theme in their own languages. A brief, animated video gave an overview of the organization's history and closed with an emphasis on young women's participation in God's work of salvation and exaltation in preparing the world for the second coming of Jesus Christ—emphasizing their integration into the work of the church rather than focusing on the organization itself.[108]

According to World Health Organization data, deaths related to the pandemic peaked in many regions in early 2021, with substantial spikes recurring through early 2022.[109] After observing a strong overall downward trend in cases over the next year, the World Health Organization declared an end to COVID-19's designation as a public health emergency in May 2023.[110] During the pandemic, relationships in the Young Women organization became a vital point of connection for many young women, and opportunities to provide service were meaningful. For many young women and local leaders, however, the goal-setting structure of the Children and Youth program fell by the wayside as simply maintaining connection became paramount. By 2023, ward and branch Young Women groups around the world were once again consistently meeting, but the degree to which they had implemented the new programs varied greatly.

THE ONGOING HISTORY

In November 2022, President Russell M. Nelson extended a call to Emily Belle Oswald Freeman to serve as the next general president of the Young Women organization. Freeman was well known in the Latter-day Saint community, especially in Utah, as an author and speaker, with a self-defined mission to help people connect to Jesus Christ. She taught in the Church Educational System for many years and developed expertise in the scriptures, which she shared in a popular podcast.[111]

Freeman's call was not publicly announced and confirmed by a sustaining vote until the April 2023 general conference, after which Freeman and her counselors had four additional months of transition time to learn from the previous presidency before formally taking office on 1 August. Freeman was grateful for the lengthy period of preparation. "Right when I got called, I started reading," she recalled.[112] Her primary focus during that period was the history of the Young Women organization. She took up volumes of the *Young Woman's Journal* and the 1911 *History*, underlined quotes from Susa Young Gates, examined photographs and reports of the 1925 MIA Jubilee, and thought back to her own memories as a young woman during the presidency of Ardeth Kapp and as a ward Young Women president during the presidency of Elaine Dalton. "From day one, it was my intent to go back to our roots," Freeman said. "What could we learn that would strengthen us now?"[113]

As counselors, Freeman called Tamara Wood Runia and Andrea Muñoz Spannaus. Runia had professional experience in journalism and nonprofit service experience with the Provo Food & Care Coalition. In 2018, she and her husband were called to lead the Australia Sydney Mission.[114] While there, Runia saw firsthand how the pandemic's isolation exacted a toll on young people—in 2020, Australia closed its borders while her youngest daughter, who was in her late teens, was in the United States.[115] Spannaus had served on the Relief Society Advisory Council just before her call to the Young Women general presidency. She and her husband had previously served as mission leaders in the Mexico Cuernavaca Mission.[116] Spannaus had joined the church at age nine and first served as a Young Women president in her home ward in Argentina at age eighteen. She later served as a local Young Women leader in several countries, including France, where she was called to serve even though she did not speak the language. Spannaus often found herself referring to a manual in English and then sharing her thoughts in Spanish for a bilingual counselor to translate into French. Experiences like these left her attuned to questions of how to best nourish faith and relationships across differences in setting, language, and culture.[117]

For one of their first meetings together, Freeman arranged to take Runia and Spannaus on a tour of the Lion House, which had recently been closed for stabilization and restoration, so they could experience the space where Brigham Young called his daughters together for the inaugural meetings of the Young Ladies' Department of the Ladies' Cooperative Retrenchment Association. Afterward, Freeman kept a replica of the Young family prayer bell on her desk as a reminder of how the whole Young Women organization had grown from something so small and personal as the ringing of a bell and a group of women gathering. She also prepared binders of readings to help her counselors join her study of the organization's history.

From April to August 2023, Freeman and her counselors were able to learn from the outgoing presidency and shadow them during meetings of the church's key councils. They also had dedicated space in the basement of the Relief Society Building to use for advance planning. The three hung butcher paper on the walls and filled it with notes about their insights and potential future directions for Young Women.[118] As they planned, Freeman and her counselors did not feel a need to re-create any given moment in the organization's history. "Over the years, some things have not worked," Freeman reflected, "but some things actually have."[119] The role of a modern leader, in her mind, was to sift through failed and successful past experiments to learn from both.

The study directly informed her actions. After reading about the young single women who served on the YLMIA board in the early twentieth century, Freeman felt inspired to call young single adult women to serve on her own advisory council, as the board was now called.[120] While planning for upcoming broadcasts, Freeman arranged to meet with and seek counsel from Ardeth Kapp. Reflecting on her own time as a young woman during Kapp's tenure, Freeman said, "She was a genius at helping you feel like you were a part of something bigger. . . . I remember how powerful it was."[121] Freeman, her counselors, and her council also revisited old questions about how the organization operated. What had been the purpose for and power in class names? What were the historical advantages and challenges of developing a strong conjoint relationship with the Young Men? How could their organization best foster strong relationships between young women and their local leaders?

Like every preceding presidency, Freeman and her counselors continued to wrestle with what it meant to be both an organization for youth and an organization for women. They felt strongly that their organization should prepare young women for lifelong discipleship and for local leadership roles across the global church. Every young woman, they concluded, needed to develop four foundational skills: how to run a presidency meeting, how to counsel, how to plan an activity, and how to minister. "If you can learn those things as part of your discipleship," Freeman said, "you can run the church everywhere."[122] As they considered plans for structured experiences and celebrations, developing those foundational skills was a constant underlying priority. Because both women and men serve in presidencies, plan events, and serve in the church's lay ministering system, strengthening those skills could provide impetus for shared efforts and programs with the young men.

At the same time, Freeman remained conscious of the distinctly female nature of the Young Women organization. During a visit with past president Elaine Dalton, Freeman sought counsel on the limits of what could be achieved by offering the same programs and written resources to young women and young men. "There are things that they will find strength in together," she remembered Dalton advising her, "and there's also strength to be found in their unique identities."[123] Ideas about women's roles had changed substantially over the course of the church's history, but Freeman remained attached to the idea of an underlying female strength.

Learning to identify that strength became a major goal for her. She looked for it in a passage of Latter-day Saint scripture addressed to Emma Hale Smith, the wife of Joseph Smith.[124] She looked for it in the members of the Young Women organization during an ambitious travel itinerary designed to give her deeper personal connection to the global church in her presidency's formative first year. And she felt it when she worked in the Relief Society Building, where she and many past presidents had their offices. "Imagine the creativity that has lived in these walls—and the wisdom, and the insight that came, and the revelation," she said. Working as a successor to past generations of female leaders reminded her of traditions from many cultures about women as figures who passed down wisdom. "You go down and stand in that Presidents Room and you feel the strength that only comes from women," she remarked. "There is a power there."[125]

In 1880, when Elmina Taylor was called as the first general president of the Young Ladies' Mutual Improvement Association, she presided over nearly two hundred largely autonomous local organizations. Taylor traveled thousands of miles by wagon and railroad to deliver messages of faith and encouragement to the church's young women and their leaders in the relatively compact geographical region where Latter-day Saints had gathered to build their Zion community. As the organization's sixteenth general president, Emily Belle Freeman presided over a complex organization with over half a million members in 182 countries.[126] She traveled around the globe by air and spoke to young women and their leaders around the world in person and via technology, harnessing social media and other online channels to reach the church's youth. For both presidents, as for all the women who served between them, a personal commitment to discipleship and a desire to help young women develop their own spiritual strength animated ongoing innovation and a quest for religious inspiration.

While these leaders believed in an eternal, unchanging God, they understood that organizational structures, communication tools, and the emphasis of their messages needed to be tailored to their moment. They understood that they would need to constantly engage with new questions about how to reach youth as culture changed and the church's belief in ongoing revelation brought about change to church policies and procedures. Leaders also revisited the same questions their predecessors had considered and often came to different conclusions about how to meet the demands of different times. The organization therefore changed cyclically, moving between poles of independence and collaboration with Young Men, between centrally issued prescriptions for running programs and space for local adaptation. Freeman recognized the shifting and pliable nature of the organization, even as it was built on a firm foundation. "We're going back to our roots," Freeman remarked, "but we're also living."[127]

The visions of individual discipleship that moved young women to organize their own retrenchment associations, the lofty aims of mutual improvement that inspired the individual and collective growth of members, and the religious values inspired by faith in the gospel of Jesus Christ have persisted through changes in policy, programs, and procedures. In 1890, Elmina Taylor rejoiced in the fruits she observed within those who participated in the fledgling Young Ladies' Mutual Improvement Association, stating, "The good seed which has been so abundantly sown has taken root in their hearts, and filled them with an increased desire for knowledge and an understanding of those truths which will tend to their most perfect development as daughters of God."[128] As they have nurtured divine identity and fostered commitment to the gospel of Jesus Christ, Taylor's successors have had—and will have—both the freedom and the obligation to revisit previous traditions and assumptions again and again. In each generation, after all, the core of the organization has never been its evolving programs or emphases, but the people it served during an important stage of life. As Michelle Craig observed in her 2020 sesquicentennial broadcast remarks, "The true beauty of our history is the young women who lived it."[129]

APPENDIX A: CHRONOLOGY

1870   27 May   Young Ladies' Department of the Ladies' Cooperative Retrenchment Association formed among Brigham Young's daughters.

1875   10 June   Junius F. Wells, commissioned by Brigham Young, organized first Young Men's Mutual Improvement Association (YMMIA).

1877   Young ladies' associations began adopting the name Young Ladies' Mutual Improvement Association (YLMIA).

1880   19 June   General presidencies established for each women's organization; Elmina Shepard Taylor appointed first general president of YLMIA.

1889   October   First issue of *Young Woman's Journal* published.

1893   First formal curriculum for YLMIA published: *Guide to the First Year's Course of Study*.

1896   30–31 May First conjoint annual conference (later known as June Conference) of YLMIA and YMMIA held.

1903   YLMIA subdivided into Senior and Junior classes.

1911   *History of the Young Ladies' Mutual Improvement Association* by Susa Young Gates published.

1912	First YLMIA summer camp held: Salt Lake City Liberty Stake young women camped near Murray, Utah.
1913	MIAs' growing recreation emphasis reflected in contests in storytelling, oratory, choral music, and athletics at annual June Conference.
1915	Bee-Hive Girls program established as a summer program for all YLMIA members, regardless of age.
1922	MIAs adopted gold and green as organizations' official colors.
	First Presidency defined purpose and function of auxiliaries; MIAs designated chief recreational agencies of the church.
1923	First YLMIA handbook published.
	First *Recreation Bulletin*, a joint bulletin with YMMIA, published.
1927	Bee-Hive Girls program established in Swiss-German Mission; Bee-Hive manual published in German.
	Gold and Green Balls and road shows added to official MIA calendar.
1929	*Young Woman's Journal* merged with *Improvement Era*.
1930	Various youth events held to honor the church's centennial.
	Treasures of Truth project established.
1934	Organization name changed to Young Women's Mutual Improvement Association (YWMIA). Age of entry set at twelve.
1937	Ruth May Fox became first Young Women general president to visit church members outside United States, touring Europe and England.
1940	First camp manual, *Camp-O-Rama*, published.

1942	June Conference and stake conventions canceled due to wartime conditions; June Conference next held in 1946.
1950	Enrollment in YWMIA made automatic for all young women in the church age twelve and above.
1956	*How Near to the Angels*, a YWMIA-commissioned film, released.
1960	Era of Youth section added to *Improvement Era*.
	Churchwide youth fireside featuring David O. McKay launched series of thirteen firesides transmitted to stakes around the world.
1961	Harold B. Lee announced All-Church Coordinating Council, commencing the modern correlation movement.
1962	Campcrafter program introduced with camp certification requirements.
1965	*For the Strength of Youth* booklet published, outlining standards for Latter-day Saint youth.
1969	Bishop's youth council established; bishops directed to appoint young women to class presidencies.
1971	*New Era* magazine for youth began publication along with two other correlated church magazines for adults and children.
	All-church sports and athletic tournaments and churchwide dance festivals discontinued.
1972	Youth organizations reorganized into Aaronic Priesthood Mutual Improvement Association (APMIA) for youth ages twelve to eighteen and Melchizedek Priesthood Mutual Interest Association (MPMIA) for those over age eighteen. Ruth Hardy Funk appointed president of APMIA Young Women.
1974	The name MIA discontinued; organizations renamed Young Women and Aaronic Priesthood.

		Behold Thy Handmaiden booklet introduced, offering suggested activities in six areas of focus and replacing earlier achievement programs for young women.
1975		Final June Conference held.
1977		My Personal Progress program introduced, building on six areas of focus introduced in Behold Thy Handmaiden.
1978	16 September	First general women's meeting broadcast from Salt Lake Tabernacle, for all women and young women ages twelve and older.
1980		Three-hour block schedule implemented for Sunday meetings, including regular Sunday instruction specifically for young women for the first time.
1985	10 November	In a Young Women satellite broadcast highlighting global sisterhood, President Ardeth Greene Kapp introduced Young Women theme and values.
1989		Young Women organization introduced new Personal Progress program structured around seven Young Women values.
1990		*For the Strength of Youth* revived, revised, and given vigorous churchwide rollout.
1993		New camp manual distributed, with focus on spirituality and global applicability.
1994	March	Annual general Young Women meeting became standard, held the week before April general conference.
1995	23 September	"The Family: A Proclamation to the World" issued by First Presidency.
1996		Church statisticians estimated that for the first time a majority of church members lived outside the United States.
		First church website launched.

2002 Personal Progress program revised, with new medallion featuring image of the Salt Lake Temple.

2008 President Elaine S. Dalton announced addition of virtue to Young Women values.

2010 Personal Progress program updated, with online progress tracking. Medallion updated to include a ruby and symbols for all three classes; Honor Bee charm introduced.

2012 Missionary age of service lowered to nineteen for young women.

2013 New youth curriculum titled *Come, Follow Me* released, intended to foster principle-based application.

2015 General presidents of Relief Society, Young Women, and Primary appointed to church's executive councils.

2019 New Children and Youth program announced, replacing Personal Progress.

   Multiday youth conferences, known as For the Strength of Youth, announced for worldwide implementation on alternate-year basis.

   President Bonnie H. Cordon announced new Young Women theme and changes to class names and structures.

2021 *New Era* magazine replaced by *For the Strength of Youth* print and digital publications, available in dozens of languages worldwide.

2022 Revised *For the Strength of Youth* booklet published, encouraging youth to make choices based on principles, spiritual guidance, and a relationship with Jesus Christ, rather than on specifically enumerated rules.

APPENDIX B: YOUNG WOMEN GENERAL PRESIDENCIES

Elmina Shepard Taylor, president, 1880–1904[1]
First counselor: Margaret (Maggie) Young Taylor, 1880–1887;[2] Maria Young Dougall, 1887–1904[3]
Second counselor: Martha (Mattie) Horne Tingey, 1880–1904[4]

Martha (Mattie) Horne Tingey, president, 1905–1929[5]
First counselor: Ruth May Fox, 1905–1929[6]
Second counselor: Mae Taylor Nystrom, 1905–1923;[7] Lucy Grant Cannon, 1923–1929[8]

Ruth May Fox, president, 1929–1937[9]
First counselor: Lucy Grant Cannon, 1929–1937[10]
Second counselor: Clarissa Alice Beesley, 1929–1937[11]

Lucy Grant Cannon, president, 1937–1948[12]
First counselor: Helen Spencer Williams, 1937–1944;[13]
Verna Wright Goddard, 1944–1948[14]
Second counselor: Verna Wright Goddard, 1937–
1944;[15] Lucy Taylor Andersen, 1944–1948[16]

Bertha Stone Reeder, president, 1948–1961[17]
First counselor: Emily Higgs Bennett, 1948–1961[18]
Second counselor: LaRue Carr Longden, 1948–1961[19]

Florence Smith Jacobsen, president, 1961–1972[20]
First counselor: Margaret Romney Jackson,
1961–1972[21]
Second counselor: Dorothy Porter Holt, 1961–1972[22]

Ruth Hardy Funk, president, 1972–1978[23]
First counselor: Hortense Hogan Child, 1972–1978[24]
Second counselor: Ardeth Greene Kapp, 1972–1978[25]

Elaine Anderson Cannon, president, 1978–1984[26]
First counselor: Arlene Barlow Darger, 1978–1984[27]
Second counselor: Norma Broadbent Smith,
1978–1984[28]

Ardeth Greene Kapp, president, 1984–1992[29]
First counselor: Patricia Terry Holland, 1984–1986;[30]
Maurine Johnson Turley, 1986–1987;[31] Jayne
Broadbent Malan, 1987–1992[32]
Second counselor: Maurine Johnson Turley, 1984–
1986; Jayne Broadbent Malan, 1986–1987; Elaine
Low Jack, 1987–1990;[33] Janette Callister Hales,
1990–1992[34]

**Janette Callister Hales Beckham, president,
1992–1997**[35]
First counselor: Virginia Hinckley Pearce,
1992–1997[36]
Second counselor: Patricia Peterson Pinegar, 1992–
1994;[37] Bonnie Dansie Parkin, 1994–1997;[38] Carol
Burdett Thomas, 1997[39]

Margaret Dyreng Nadauld, president, 1997–2002[40]
First counselor: Carol Burdett Thomas, 1997–2002[41]
Second counselor: Sharon Greene Larsen, 1997–2002[42]

Susan Winder Tanner, president, 2002–2008[43]
First counselor: Julie Bangerter Beck, 2002–2007;[44] Elaine Schwartz Dalton, 2007–2008[45]
Second counselor: Elaine Schwartz Dalton, 2002–2007;[46] Mary Nielsen Cook, 2007–2008[47]

Elaine Schwartz Dalton, president, 2008–2013[48]
First counselor: Mary Nielsen Cook, 2008–2013[49]
Second counselor: Ann Monson Dibb, 2008–2013[50]

Bonnie Lee Green Oscarson, president, 2013–2018[51]
First counselor: Carol Foley McConkie, 2013–2018[52]
Second counselor: Neill Foote Marriott, 2013–2018[53]

Bonnie Hillam Cordon, president, 2018–2023[54]
First counselor: Michelle Daines Craig, 2018–2023[55]
Second counselor: Rebecca (Becky) Mitchell Craven, 2018–2023[56]

Emily Belle Oswald Freeman, president, 2023–[57]
First counselor: Tamara Wood Runia, 2023–[58]
Second counselor: Andrea Muñoz Spannaus, 2023–[59]

Taylor, Lucy Grant Cannon, Tingey, Fox, Reeder, and Funk images courtesy Church History Library, Salt Lake City; Elaine Cannon and Beckham images courtesy Busath Photography, copies at CHL; Kapp, Dalton, Oscarson, Cordon, and Freeman images courtesy Busath Photography; Jacobsen and Nadauld images courtesy The Church of Jesus Christ of Latter-day Saints.

APPENDIX C:
CLASS CHART
AND LIST

This appendix presents a chart showing the classes in the Young Women organization from 1903 to 2019. An alphabetical listing of the classes is also included and gives a brief description of changes in the name and age grouping for each class. Determining factors for how young women were assigned to age groups varied over the years—for example, at times they were assigned by birth date, and at other times they were assigned based on their age at the beginning of the American school year.

The Young Ladies' Mutual Improvement Associations (YLMIAs) were first subdivided into Junior and Senior classes in 1903. Starting in the 1920s, further reconfiguration of age-grouped classes occurred frequently and sometimes paralleled similar groupings in the Young Men's Mutual Improvement Association (YMMIA). For many decades in the twentieth century, the organizations for young women and young men functioned largely on a joint basis and were collectively known as "the MIA." Until 1972, the MIA sponsored groups for adults; those groups are represented in this appendix. After 1972, the church's youth programs served only young people up to age eighteen, and activity and service groups for adults took a different trajectory, which is not traced here. In 2019, the Young Women general presidency announced that class names and age groupings were being retired. Instead, local church leaders would determine the number of classes for young women and, if needed, age groupings that would best meet the needs in their areas.

1903		Junior (ages 14–16)		Senior (ages 17 and over)		
1917		Junior/Bee-Hive Girls (ages 14–16)				
1919				Senior (ages 17–24)		Advanced Senior (ages 25 and up)
1921		Bee-Hive Girls (ages 14–15)	Intermediate (ages 16–17)	Senior (ages 18–24)		
1922			Junior (ages 16–17)			
1923				Senior/Gleaner (ages 18–23)		Advanced Senior (ages 23 and up)
1928				Gleaner (ages 18–23)		Adult (ages 24 and up)
1930	Bee-Hive Girls (ages 12–13 with parent permission; ages 14–15)		Junior (ages 15–16)	Gleaner (ages 17–23)		
1931	Nymph (ages 12–13 with parent permission)	Bee-Hive Girls (age 14)				
1932					Senior (ages 24–35)	Adult (ages 36 and up)
1934	Bee-Hive (ages 12–14)					
1936					Senior (ages 24–40)	Adult (ages 41 and up)
1939				Gleaner (ages 17–30) and Special Interest (optional for ages 25–30)		Adult (ages 31 and up)
1940				Gleaner (ages 17–24)	Special Interest (ages 25 and up)	
1950	Beehive (ages 12–13)	Mia Maid (ages 14–15)	Junior Gleaner (ages 16–18)	Gleaner (ages 19–25)	Special Interest (ages 26 and up)	
1959			Laurel (ages 16–18)		Young Marrieds and Mutual Study (ages 26 and up)	
1969					Mutual Interests (ages 26 and up)	
1970					Young Marrieds (married, any age) and Mutual Interests (unmarried, ages 26 and up)	
1972			Laurel (ages 16–17)			
2019	Age groups and class names retired; local units given flexibility to adjust to their needs.					

Adult (1928–1940)

This class provided educational and leisure opportunities for adult women and men, including those who were married. The Adult class replaced the Advanced Senior class in 1928 and ended in 1940, when it became part of the new Special Interest groups.

1928–1932: for ages 24 and up[1]
1932–1936: for ages 36 and up[2]
1936–1939: for ages 41 and up[3]
1939–1940: for ages 31 and up[4]

Advanced Senior (1917–1928)

This class provided educational and leisure opportunities for adult women and men. It was replaced by the Adult class in 1928.

1917–1923: for ages 25 and up[5]
1923–1928: for ages 23 and up[6]

Beehive (1915–2019)

Bee-Hive Girls was initially an optional summer program for all members of YLMIA. The lessons associated with this program later became the regular curriculum for the Junior class. When the Junior class was split into two age groups in 1921, the *Bee-Hive Girls* name was used for a separate class for 14- and 15-year-olds. The class eventually expanded to include 12- and 13-year-olds, and the class name was shortened to *Bee-Hive* and then finally to *Beehive*. In 1950, the class became a two-year program for ages 12 and 13 and remained as such until 2019, when the class name and age grouping were discontinued.

1915–1919: for ages 14 and up[7]
1919–1921: for ages 14–16; interchangeably called the Junior or Bee-Hive Girls class during these years[8]
1921–1930: for ages 14–15[9]
1930–1931: for ages 14–15; open to ages 12–13 with parental approval[10]
1931–1934: for age 14; open to ages 12–13 as part of the Nymph program with parental approval[11]
1934–1950: for ages 12–14[12]
1950–2019: for ages 12–13[13]

Gleaner (1922–1972)

Initially an optional program within the Senior class to provide young women with leadership opportunities, this group became known as the Gleaners in 1923. The Senior class name was changed to *Gleaner* in 1928. Gleaners often held lessons and activities with their YMMIA counterparts, the M Men, and these two classes became essentially a joint group over time. In 1972, this age group was placed in the Melchizedek Priesthood MIA program and the name *Gleaner* was discontinued.

1922–1923: for ages 18–24[14]
1923–1930: for ages 18–23[15]
1930–1939: for ages 17–23[16]
1939–1940: for ages 17–30[17]
1940–1950: for ages 17–24[18]
1950–1959: for ages 19–25, married or unmarried; women up to age 29 could remain in class[19]
1959–1960: for ages 18 and over, unmarried[20]
1960–1970: for those who were at least age 18, graduated from high school, and unmarried[21]
1970–1972: for ages 19–25, unmarried[22]

Intermediate (1921–1922)
This optional class was created when the original Junior class was dissolved and divided into two age groups in 1921. The Intermediate class was for those who had completed their Bee-Hive Girls coursework but were not old enough to be enrolled in the Senior class. This class was renamed *Junior Girls* in 1922 at the request of the young women themselves.

1921–1922: for ages 16–17[23]

Junior (1903–1921, 1922–1950)
One of the two original divisions in the organization, this class was created to meet the needs of younger girls and increase their participation. The Junior group was interchangeably called the Junior or Bee-Hive Girls class between 1919 and 1921, because the Bee-Hive Girls lessons became the regular curriculum for Juniors during that time. In 1921, the Junior class was dissolved and divided into two classes, Bee-Hive Girls and Intermediate. In 1922, the Intermediate class was renamed *Junior*. The Junior class was replaced by the Mia Maid and Junior Gleaner classes in 1950.

1903–1921: for ages 14–16[24]
1922–1930: for ages 16–17[25]
1930–1931: for ages 16–17; 17-year-olds could attend either the Junior or Gleaner group[26]
1931–1950: for ages 15–16[27]

Junior Gleaner (1950–1959)
Created in 1950 by combining the younger ages of the Gleaner group and the oldest year of the Junior class, the Junior Gleaner class was for young women ages 16–18.

This group held some classes and activities with their YMMIA counterparts, the Junior M Men. In 1959, the Junior Gleaner class was replaced by the Laurel class.

1950–1959: for ages 16–18[28]

Laurel (1959–2019)

A class for young women at least 16 years of age and still in high school, *Laurel* replaced *Junior Gleaner* as the class name in 1959. Laurels sometimes held classes and activities with their counterparts in church organizations for young men. The class name and age group were discontinued in 2019.

1959–1972: for ages 16–18[29]
1972–2019: for ages 16–17, or until young women graduated from high school[30]

Mia Maid (1950–2019)

This class for 14- and 15-year-olds was created by combining the youngest year of the Junior class and the oldest year of the Beehive class in 1950. The class name and age group were discontinued in 2019.

1950–2019: for ages 14–15[31]

Mutual Interests (1969–1972)

This class for adults was created to replace the Young Marrieds and Mutual Study classes. Mutual Interests was originally for those who had aged out of the M Men or Gleaner classes at age 26, regardless of marital status. In 1970 it changed to include only widows, widowers, divorced persons, and older singles. In 1972, this age group became part of the Melchizedek Priesthood MIA program and was no longer supervised by the Young Women and Young Men organizations.

1969–1970: for ages 26 and up, married or single[32]
1970–1972: for ages 26 and up, single[33]

Mutual Study (1959–1969)

This class, along with Young Marrieds, was for adult church members and was part of the Mutual Marrieds Department. The Mutual Marrieds Department replaced the Special Interest groups in 1959. Mutual Study was intended for older married couples but also for all adults of "middle age" and older. It was combined with Young Marrieds in 1969 to form the Mutual Interests class.

1959–1969: for all middle-aged adults and older[34]

Nymph (1931–1934)

The Nymph class was created for 12- and 13-year-olds as a segment of the Bee-Hive class. They could join with parental approval rather than stay in the Mi-Kan-Wee class for that age group in Primary. The Nymph class ended in 1934 when the age group was placed solely in the YWMIA as part of the Bee-Hive class.

1931–1934: for ages 12–13, connected to the Bee-Hive class[35]

Senior (1903–1928, 1932–1939)

One of the original class divisions in the organization, the Senior class was initially for young women ages 17 and over. In 1928, the Senior class was renamed *Gleaners*. The name *Senior* was briefly reintroduced for a joint class for adults in the 1930s.

1903–1917: for ages 17 and up[36]
1917–1921: for ages 17–24[37]
1921–1923: for ages 18–24[38]
1923–1928: for ages 18–23[39]
1932–1936: for ages 24–35[40]
1936–1939: for ages 24–40[41]

Special Interest (1939–1959)

This joint class presented elective study topics for older members of the Gleaner and M Men classes. It absorbed the Senior and Adult classes in 1940. The class was replaced by Mutual Study and Young Marrieds in 1959.

1939–1940: for ages 25–30, part of the Gleaner/M Men class[42]
1940–1950: for ages 25 and up[43]
1950–1959: for ages 26 and up; those aged 26–29 could remain in Gleaners or
     M Men if they wished[44]

Young Marrieds (1959–1969, 1970–1972)

This joint class, along with Mutual Study, was part of the Mutual Marrieds Department. The Mutual Marrieds Department replaced the Special Interest groups in 1959. The Young Marrieds class was intended for younger married couples raising families. It was combined with Mutual Study in 1969 to form the Mutual Interests class. In 1970 it was reintroduced as a class for married adults regardless of age. In 1972, this age group became part of the Melchizedek Priesthood MIA program.

1959–1969: for younger married couples[45]
1970–1972: for married adults regardless of age[46]

ACKNOWLEDGMENTS

This book has been many years in the making. In 2010, Brittany Chapman Nash, then a reference librarian in the Church History Library, and Jill Mulvay Derr, a senior research historian in the Church History Department, worked on a committee at the request of Young Women general president Elaine S. Dalton to begin exploring the possibility of preparing a history of the organization. That effort did not come to fruition at the time but resulted in much groundbreaking research. In 2016, historians Kate Holbrook and Lisa Olsen Tait proposed that the Church History Department's Publications Division produce a one-volume history of the Young Women. Department executives approved that proposal, and a team assembled to begin work. As it turned out, the need for extensive original research, coupled with changes in assignments and availability of various team members, meant that it took the better part of a decade to see the project through to publication. In the course of that process, many people have made significant contributions.

We give special thanks to administrators and officials of The Church of Jesus Christ of Latter-day Saints for sponsoring the project and to the management and staff of the Church History Library, where the majority of the documents cited in this volume are located. Leaders of the Young Women organization, including Bonnie H. Cordon and Emily Belle Freeman, their counselors, advisory councils, and administrative staff, gave feedback and enthusiastic support.

We acknowledge with appreciation the contributions of many individuals from the Church History Department. Jennifer Reeder provided formative research that shaped the opening chapter of the story. Mary Frances Rich, a service missionary, gave extensive research support and added valuable perspective from her broad experience in church service. Alison Kitchen Gainer, Kaytee R. Johnson, Jessica Anne Lawrence, Catherine Reese Newton, R. Eric Smith, Stephanie Steed, and Nathan N. Waite of the editorial staff also contributed. McKinsey Kemeny and Brenda Homer managed the huge task of securing intellectual property and privacy clearances. Ashley Woodworth Skinner skillfully typeset the volume.

Many research assistants, interns, and others helped with the enormous task of completing and managing research for the book. Katie Clark Blakesley, Jessica M. Nelson, and Charlotte Hansen Terry performed yeoman's work as research assistants. Charlotte Hansen Terry also took on the enormous task of preparing the appendixes for both the print book and the online version. Nicole Wechsler and Zachary Osborn worked as interns.

Jill Mulvay Derr, Colleen McDannell, and Laurel Thatcher Ulrich provided invaluable peer review of an early version of the manuscript.

We also wish to thank the management and staff at Deseret Book Company, Salt Lake City, for the professional help and advice they provided regarding the design, printing, and distribution of this volume. We especially appreciate the contributions of Sheri L. Dew, Laurel Christensen Day, Janiece L. Johnson, Garth Bruner, Heather Ward, Rachael Ward, Rebecca Datwyler, Derk Koldewyn, and Breanna Anderl.

Finally, we wish to remember with love and affection our beloved colleague Kate Holbrook, who passed away in 2022 as the book was nearing its last round of revision. Kate's leadership left countless indelible marks on the book and on our hearts, as she brought us together around good food and rigorous thinking.

NOTES

Most sources cited in this volume are referred to with a shortened citation. The "Works Cited" section provides full citation information for these shortened citations. Magazines and newspapers are cited in full in the notes and are not included in the list of works cited. The *Woman's Exponent*, the *Church News*, and the *Deseret News* and its variants, are all newspapers published in Salt Lake City. The *Latter-day Saints' Millennial Star* (later renamed the *Millennial Star*) is a newspaper published in England, initially in Manchester, later in Liverpool, and finally in London.

INTRODUCTION

1. M. A. Willie, Editorial, *Young Ladies' Companion* (East Bountiful, Utah Territory, manuscript newspaper), 15 July 1885, [4]–[5], copy at CHL.
2. "What the Bee-Hive Girls' Organization Has Done for Me," *Improvement Era*, May 1935, 298.
3. Adam C. Olson, "Making Progress Personal in Panama," *New Era*, Aug. 2006, 20–21.
4. See, for example, Jill Mulvay Derr, Janath Russell Cannon, and Maureen Ursenbach Beecher, *Women of Covenant: The Story of Relief Society* (Salt Lake City: Deseret Book, 1992); Maureen Ursenbach Beecher and Lavina Fielding Anderson, eds., *Sisters in Spirit: Mormon Women in Historical and Cultural Perspective* (Urbana: University of Illinois Press, 1987); Dave Hall, *A Faded Legacy: Amy Brown Lyman and Mormon Women's Activism, 1872–1959* (Salt Lake City: University of Utah Press, 2015); Carol Cornwall Madsen, *Emmeline B. Wells: An Intimate History* (Salt Lake City: University of Utah Press, 2017); and the Life Writings of Frontier Women series published by Utah State University Press.
5. See, for example, Laurel Thatcher Ulrich, *A House Full of Females: Plural Marriage and Women's Rights in Early Mormonism, 1835–1870* (New York: Alfred A. Knopf, 2017); Colleen McDannell, *Sister Saints: Mormon Women since the End of Polygamy* (New York: Oxford University Press, 2019); Jill Mulvay Derr, Carol Cornwall Madsen, Kate Holbrook, and Matthew J. Grow, eds., *The First Fifty Years of Relief Society: Key Documents in Latter-day Saint Women's History* (Salt Lake City: Church Historian's Press, 2016); The Discourses of Eliza R. Snow, Church Historian's Press, churchhistorianspress.org /eliza-r-snow; and The Diaries of Emmeline B. Wells, Church Historian's Press, churchhistorianspress .org/emmeline-b-wells.
6. Susa Young Gates, *History of the Young Ladies' Mutual Improvement Association of the Church of Jesus Christ of Latter-day Saints, from November 1869 to June 1910* (Salt Lake City: YLMIA General Board, 1911); Marba C. Josephson, *History of the YWMIA* (Salt Lake City: YWMIA, 1955).
7. Note that throughout the book, the term *organization* refers to the Young Women organization on the general and local levels, whereas *programs* refers to particular aspects of and initiatives within the organization, such as achievement and sports programs, which are intended to address specific needs that often change over time.

CHAPTER 1: RETRENCHMENT AND IMPROVEMENT, 1870–1890

1. Jones, "History," 2.
2. Elvira S. Barney, "My Visit South," *Woman's Exponent*, 15 Jan. 1876, 126; for more on "leading sisters," see Beecher, "Leading Sisters," 25–39.
3. See Arrington, Fox, and May, *Building the City of God*, 5–10, 135–154.
4. Jane Spiking Vance, Report, *Woman's Exponent*, 15 Dec. 1875, 106. Compare with Barney's comments in her own report: "I never saw before, nor do I think the world can boast of such noble intelligent, fine-looking marriageable young ladies as I saw in those settlements where I visited; they appeared neat and clean, comfortably dressed, but plain and as though their better judgment guided them." (Elvira S. Barney, "My Visit South," *Woman's Exponent*, 15 Jan. 1876, 126.)
5. Jones, "History," 2.
6. Jones, "History," 2.
7. See Helen Mar Whitney, "Life Incidents," *Woman's Exponent*, 15 Aug. 1880, 42; Holzapfel and Holzapfel, *Woman's View*, 35–36; and Winters, Reminiscences, 12, 13. As Anne M. Boylan has demonstrated, between 1790 and 1880 the number of voluntary Sunday school associations exploded in cities and towns throughout the newly formed United States. (Boylan, *Sunday School*, 1–3.)
8. "A Short Sketch of the Rise of the Young Gentlemen and Ladies Relief Society of Nauvoo," *Times and Seasons*, 1 Apr. 1843, 154.
9. Jed L. Woodworth, "Sunday Schools," in *Encyclopedia of Latter-day Saint History*, 1200–1202. Originally called the Parent Sunday School Union, it was renamed the Deseret Sunday School Union in 1872.
10. See, for example, Emerett Brown and Edith Smith, Report, *Woman's Exponent*, 1 Feb. 1875, 130.
11. *Deseret News 2013 Church Almanac*, 211.
12. "Remarks," *Deseret News*, 24 Nov. 1869, 496.
13. Crocheron, *Representative Women*, 20–21; "Pioneer Woman Goes to Her Rest," *Deseret Evening News*, 26 Aug. 1905, 3; Park, *Joseph Horne*, 51–53; Mary Elizabeth Horne Durrant, Biographical Sketches of Richard S., Joseph, and Mary Isabella Hales Horne, 4–9, Horne Family Collection, CHL.
14. Gamm and Putnam, "Growth of Voluntary Associations," 511–557; Boylan, *Sunday School*, 1–2. Particularly in the decade following the Civil War, virtually every new initiative was dubbed "cooperative," signifying, as one study defined it, "the willing pursuit of any enterprise, in whatever form that promised to benefit the whole body." (Arrington, Fox, and May, *Building the City of God*, 109.)
15. While the original name of the organization was the Ladies' Cooperative Retrenchment Society, it was known by several titles over the course of its existence. After the young women organized their own retrenchment associations, it was known for a time as the Senior and Junior Cooperative Retrenchment Association. Later it was called General Retrenchment (perhaps to distinguish it from the young ladies' groups) and then the Ladies' Semi-Monthly Meeting, reflecting its practice of meeting twice a month, which continued until 1904. (Derr et al., *First Fifty Years of Relief Society*, 343.)
16. Ladies' Cooperative Retrenchment Meeting, Minutes, 10 Feb. 1870, in Derr et al., *First Fifty Years of Relief Society*, 340, 341.
17. Report of Relief Society Jubilee, 17 Mar. 1892, in Derr et al., *First Fifty Years of Relief Society*, 616.
18. St. George Stake, General Minutes, 28 Oct. 1883.
19. Brooks, *Quicksand and Cactus*, 112. Andrew Karl Larson includes another version of this story, where the rebuttal is attributed to Mary Snow Gates, in his history of the Cotton Mission in southwestern Utah. (Larson, *Virgin River Basin*, 605–606.)
20. Ladies' Cooperative Retrenchment Meeting, Minutes, 10 Feb. 1870, in Derr et al., *First Fifty Years of Relief Society*, 341.
21. "Pen Sketch of an Illustrious Woman," *Woman's Exponent*, 1 Mar. 1881, 147.
22. Gates, *History of the YLMIA*, 6–7; Maria Young Dougall, "Reminiscences," *Young Woman's Journal*, Nov. 1919, 594.
23. Gates, *History of the YLMIA*, 6–9; "Historical Sketch of the Y. L. M. I. A.," *Young Woman's Journal*, Feb. 1892, 231–232; "A Biographical Sketch of the Life of Zina Young Williams Card," 6–7, Zina Card Brown Family Collection, CHL; Maria Young Dougall, "Reminiscences," *Young Woman's Journal*, Nov. 1919, 594–595.
24. Young Ladies' Department of the Ladies' Cooperative Retrenchment Association, Resolutions, 27 May 1870, in Derr et al., *First Fifty Years of Relief Society*, 353–354, 354n313; see also Lisa Olsen Tait, "Origins and Myths: Revisiting the Founding Story of the Latter-day Saint Young Women's Organization," *Journal of Mormon History* 51, no. 1 (Jan. 2025).

25. See, for example, 1 Timothy 2:9–10; 1 Peter 3:3–5; and Doctrine and Covenants 42:40.

26. Young Ladies' Department of the Ladies' Cooperative Retrenchment Association, Resolutions, 27 May 1870, in Derr et al., *First Fifty Years of Relief Society*, 355.

27. Young Ladies' Department of the Ladies' Cooperative Retrenchment Association, Resolutions, 27 May 1870, in Derr et al., *First Fifty Years of Relief Society*, 357. Ella (born 31 August 1847; daughter of Emeline Free; married 1865); Emily (born 1 March 1849; daughter of Emily Partridge; married January 1868); Zina (born 3 April 1850; daughter of Zina Diantha Huntington; married October 1868); Maria (born 10 December 1849; daughter of Clarissa Ross, raised by Zina Diantha Huntington; married June 1868); Caroline (born 1 February 1851; daughter of Emily Partridge; married October 1868); Dora (born 12 May 1852; daughter of Lucy Bigelow); Phebe (born 1 August 1854; daughter of Clarissa Ross, raised by Zina Diantha Huntington). At the time, Zina Young Williams was married to Thomas Williams. He died in 1874, and she later married Charles Ora Card, becoming known as Zina Young Card for most of her adult life.

28. As seen in the case of the Young Ladies' Retrenchment Association in Cedar City, the pattern of a president with six counselors was adopted in some early retrenchment associations, but the already-established pattern of a president with two counselors later prevailed.

29. Gates, *History of the YLMIA*, 59–60; "Resolutions," *Deseret Evening News*, 20 June 1870, [2]. The publication of this report alongside that of the original organization, dated within days of each other, further confirms the late May date as the founding date.

30. Gates, *History of the YLMIA*, 36–37, 61–67. A sampling of ward young ladies' association organization dates: Salt Lake Fourteenth Ward, 4 June 1870; Salt Lake Thirteenth Ward, 27 June 1870; Salt Lake Twentieth Ward, 8 July 1870; Salt Lake Eleventh Ward, 18 October 1872; Mill Creek Ward, 12 June 1874; Draper Ward, 30 November 1875; Sugar House Ward, 23 May 1877; West Jordan Ward, 7 February 1878. (Mill Creek Ward YLMIA Minutes, vol. 1, 12 June 1874, 1; Elnora Day, Report, *Woman's Exponent*, 15 Jan. 1876, 122; Sugar House Ward YLMIA Minutes, vol. 1, 23 May 1877, 2; Elizabeth Davis, Report, *Woman's Exponent*, 1 Mar. 1878, 146.)

31. See "A Representative Woman," *Woman's Exponent*, 15 Sept. 1882, 59.

32. May, "Demographic Portrait," 62.

33. See Strauss and Howe, *Generations*, 32–35, 441.

34. Lydia Alder, Report, *Woman's Exponent*, 15 Feb. 1878, 138.

35. No definitive contemporary listing of the Brigham Young household survives. These numbers are extrapolated from the lists of Young's wives and children in various sources. (See Orton and Slaughter, *40 Ways to Look at Brigham Young*, 119–123; Susa Young Gates, "Brigham Young and His Nineteen Wives," 3–12, Susa Young Gates Papers, Utah State Historical Society, Salt Lake City; and Susa Young Gates, "My Recollections," 1–4, Susa Young Gates Papers, Utah State Historical Society, Salt Lake City.)

36. Susa Young Gates, "Lucy Bigelow Young," 70, Susa Young Gates Papers, Utah State Historical Society, Salt Lake City.

37. See Gates, *History of the YLMIA*, 9–10; and Susa Young Gates, "Family Life among the Mormons," *North American Review*, Mar. 1890, 339–344.

38. Hunter, *How Young Ladies Became Girls*, 130, 140–145. According to Jane H. Hunter, the passage from childhood to womanhood in the Victorian-era United States unfolded on "a continuum which only later would be considered a distinct stage of life."

39. Salt Lake City was unquestionably the urban center of the Intermountain West, with a population of well over twelve thousand. Relative to the rest of the territory (and to many other places in the United States), it was a true city—with businesses, schools, social amenities, newspapers, and other urban cultural features. (Alexander and Allen, *Mormons and Gentiles*, 38–47.)

40. Hunter, *How Young Ladies Became Girls*, 394–395; Kett, *Rites of Passage*, 137–138.

41. Theriot, *Mothers and Daughters*, 62–65; see also Smith-Rosenberg, "Female World," 1–29.

42. Ellen Lunt, Report, *Woman's Exponent*, 15 Feb. 1876, 138.

43. Jones, "History," 3; "Died," *Latter-day Saints' Millennial Star*, 28 Apr. 1890, 272.

44. See, for example, Cedar City Ward YLMIA Minute Book, 29 July 1878, 23; 26 Aug. 1878, 24.

45. Lucinda Stratton and Eleanor Jepson, Report, *Woman's Exponent*, 15 June 1876, 10.

46. See, for example, "Resolutions," *Woman's Exponent*, 15 Mar. 1875, 154.

47. See Cunningham, *Reforming Women's Fashion*, 1–6.

48. Wayland-Smith, *Oneida*, 83.

49. Most of the extant sources that mention this clothing date to 1855, such as a letter written by George A. Smith, who told fellow apostle Franklin D. Richards, "The ladies are introducing a new fashion of dress, which they denominate the 'Deseret Costume.'" The Deseret Costume was developed under

the auspices of the Female Council of Health, suggesting that Latter-day Saint women's dress reforms were most closely aligned with the health reformers of the day (as opposed to those promoting political rights). (George A. Smith to Franklin D. Richards, 31 Aug. 1855, in Historian's Office, Letterpress Copybooks, vol. 1, p. 249; Derr, Cannon, and Beecher, *Women of Covenant*, 71; see also Sessions, Diary, 24 Apr. 1852.)

50. Entwistle, *Fashioned Body*, 11, 154–157.

51. Severa, *Dressed for the Photographer*, xv.

52. Bunker and Bitton, *Mormon Graphic Image*, 123–136.

53. Augusta Joyce Crocheron, "Origin of the Y. L. M. I. Association," *Woman's Exponent*, 15 June 1880, 10.

54. Maria Young Dougall, "Reminiscences," *Young Woman's Journal*, Nov. 1919, 595.

55. Maria Young Dougall, "Reminiscences," *Young Woman's Journal*, Nov. 1919, 595.

56. See, for example, "True Independence," *Woman's Exponent*, 15 Oct. 1873, 77; "Pride and Dress," *Woman's Exponent*, 1 Apr. 1884, 166; and "Report of First Ward Special Meeting—Association," *Woman's Exponent*, 1 Nov. 1877, 82.

57. The Beaver Relief Society had been organized in Pratt's home in 1870, and she served as both counselor and secretary for two years. (Ellsworth, *History of Louisa Barnes Pratt*, 345.)

58. Louisa Barnes Pratt, "A Lecture," *Woman's Exponent*, 1 May 1875, 183. This lecture was read before the Young Ladies' Retrenchment Association in Beaver on 13 March 1875.

59. Georgina Cuthbert, "Retrenchment," *Woman's Exponent*, 1 Apr. 1875, 163.

60. Nash, "Rethinking Republican Motherhood," 171–191; see also Mary Kelley, *Learning to Stand and Speak: Women, Education, and Public Life in America's Republic* (Chapel Hill: University of North Carolina Press, 2006).

61. See, for example, Mary Stuart, "An Essay Written for and Read before the Richmond Retrenchment Society," *Woman's Exponent*, 1 Jan. 1876, 114.

62. Eliza R. Snow, "Every Sister Should Come Forward," in Reeder and Holbrook, *At the Pulpit*, 74; "A Synopsis," *Woman's Exponent*, 1 May 1875, 178.

63. Mary Connelly, "Mary A. Freeze," *Young Woman's Journal*, Mar. 1912, 125; Gates, *History of the YLMIA*, 74.

64. Mary Ann Freeze, "The Blessings of Retrenchment Associations," *Woman's Exponent*, 15 Dec. 1876, 109.

65. Sarah M. Kimball, Report, *Woman's Exponent*, 1 Feb. 1874, 130; Mary Seegmiller, Report, *Woman's Exponent*, 1 May 1874, 178.

66. Jane Harrington, "Improvement," *Woman's Exponent*, 15 Apr. 1876, 171.

67. Howe, *What Hath God Wrought*, 244.

68. Crawford, "Mutual Improvement," 34–45. For a contemporary example, see William Allen, *Mutual Improvement; or, A Scheme for the Self-Adjustment of the Social Machine* (London: James Ridgway, 1846).

69. Henrotin, "Attitude of Women's Clubs," 527.

70. Bleak, Annals of the Southern Utah Mission, 1876 (Book B Continuation), 44.

71. In the 15 February 1876 issue of the *Woman's Exponent*, for example, Mary Ann Till of Goshen, Utah Territory, reported that a Young Ladies' Mutual Improvement Association had been organized in that small town, and Rebecca Allen of Hyrum, Utah Territory, reported that the name of the young ladies' association there had been changed to the Hyrum Young Ladies' Mutual Improvement Society. (Mary Ann Till, Report, and Rebecca Allen, Report, *Woman's Exponent*, 15 Feb. 1876, 138.)

72. Mary Ann Till, Report, *Woman's Exponent*, 15 Feb. 1876, 138.

73. Brigham City 3rd Ward YLMIA Minutes, vol. 1, 6 Apr. 1882, 76.

74. Mary Ann Freeze, "Retrenchment," *Woman's Exponent*, 15 Aug. 1874, 43.

75. See, for example, Jane Harrington, "Improvement," *Woman's Exponent*, 15 Apr. 1876, 171.

76. Reeder, "Making an (in)Delible Mark," 273–278.

77. Mary Ann Till, Report, *Woman's Exponent*, 15 Feb. 1876, 138.

78. Juie Ivins, "To the Little Girls," *Little Girls' Magazine* (St. George, Utah Territory, manuscript newspaper), 12 Nov. 1879, 10, copy at Utah State Historical Society, Salt Lake City; Reeder, "Making an (in) Delible Mark," 275–277; Tait, "Finding 'Cactus,'" 1–12.

79. See Kearl, Pope, and Wimmer, "Household Wealth," 477–496.

80. Jones, "History," 3.

81. This song-prayer-song pattern was typical of most nineteenth-century Latter-day Saint meetings.

82. Cedar City Ward YLMIA Minute Book, 20 Mar. 1876, 8–9.

83. The association's minute book contains detailed accounts of eight meetings in 1876 and a few meetings in 1877, and then it picks up again with extensive minutes in April 1878, by which time Henrietta had married Lehi Willard Jones. These breaks likely represent both the occasional hiatus in meetings and gaps in record keeping, likely more often the latter.

84. Jones, "History," 3. Association minutes for 23 September 1878 reference the bishop authorizing the association to conduct a store, though it is unclear whether the association actually did so. (Cedar City Ward YLMIA Minute Book, 23 Sept. 1878, 26.)

85. Cedar City Ward YLMIA Minute Book, 23 Sept. 1878, 25–26. The four women were Emily Newcombe Tucker (twenty-eight years old), Emeline Rosetta Haight Cosslett (nineteen years old), Caroline R. Adams (twenty years old), and Mary Anna Barnhurst (nineteen years old). (1920 U.S. Census, Cedar City, Iron Co., UT, 6A; 1880 U.S. Census, Cedar City, Iron Co., Utah Territory, 373D; 1870 U.S. Census, Cedar City, Iron Co., Utah Territory, 266[A]; Esshom, *Pioneers and Prominent Men*, 738.)

86. See Cedar City Ward YLMIA Minute Book, 21 Oct. 1878, 27; 4 Nov. 1878, 28; 10 Mar. 1879, 34.

87. Cedar City Ward YLMIA Minute Book, 10 Mar. 1879, 32; 27 Oct. 1879, 40.

88. Sarah Chatterly, "Cedar City," *Woman's Exponent*, 1 Feb. 1879, 189–190. This protest meeting was not their only venture into political activism in defense of their religion and way of life. The association also crafted a petition protesting the congressional bill that would later become the Edmunds Act. (Cedar City Ward YLMIA Minute Book, 23 Feb. 1882, 77–79.)

89. Mary Ann Lunt, Report, *Woman's Exponent*, 15 Apr. 1876, 171.

90. Junius F. Wells, "Historic Sketch of the Y. M. M. I. A.," *Improvement Era*, June 1925, 713–714; "History of the General Organization," *Contributor*, Oct. 1879, 22.

91. Walker, "Growing Up in Early Utah," 62–65.

92. Young Latter-day Saint men were not systematically ordained and advanced in Aaronic Priesthood offices until the twentieth century; thus, there was no institutional provision specifically for them at this time. There are scattered references to young men organizing before 1875 in a manner similar to the young women. In 1874, young men in Farmington, Utah Territory, were holding weekly meetings and forming resolutions. (Farmington Ward YMMIA Minutes, vol. 1, 8 Nov.–4 Dec. 1874, 40–44.)

93. In this period when Utah's and the United States' educational systems were still developing, the course of study at the university more closely paralleled what would now be considered a high school education. The institution was known as the University of Deseret until 1892, when its name was officially changed to the University of Utah. (Chamberlin, *University of Utah*, 130–133, 173.)

94. "Utah Native, Aged Church Worker, Dies," *Salt Lake Tribune*, 16 Apr. 1930, 30; Gates, *History of the YLMIA*, 80–82.

95. Junius F. Wells, "Historic Sketch of the Y. M. M. I. A.," *Improvement Era*, June 1925, 715.

96. "History of the General Organization," *Contributor*, Oct. 1879, 22.

97. Gates, *History of the YLMIA*, 82; see also Junius F. Wells, "Historic Sketch of the Y. M. M. I. A.," *Improvement Era*, June 1925, 715.

98. Junius F. Wells, "Historic Sketch of the Y. M. M. I. A.," *Improvement Era*, June 1925, 718, 720–721. The first four men assigned as YMMIA missionaries were Junius Wells, Milton Hardy, Morris Young, and John Henry Smith. Young was a son of Brigham Young, and Smith was a son of George A. Smith, a close friend of Brigham Young and a counselor in the First Presidency.

99. Junius F. Wells, "Historical Sketch of the Y. M. M. I. A.," *Improvement Era*, July 1925, 873, 875. Wells recalled that the missionaries were "chosen from the officers and active members of the Associations."

100. Junius F. Wells, "Historic Sketch of the Y. M. M. I. A.," *Improvement Era*, June 1925, 725; "The General Superintendency," *Contributor*, May 1880, 180–181.

101. Junius F. Wells, "Historic Sketch of the Y. M. M. I. A.," *Improvement Era*, June 1925, 721–722.

102. "Association Intelligence," *Contributor*, May 1880, 189; "Y. L. M. I. A.," *Woman's Exponent*, 1 Nov. 1881, 85.

103. "Home Affairs," *Woman's Exponent*, 1 Oct. 1877, 68.

104. Brigham Young to Don Carlos and Feramorz Little Young, 6 Aug. 1877, photocopy, George C. Young Collection, CHL.

105. See, for example, East Bountiful Ward YLMIA Minutes, vol. 1, 30 Oct. 1877.

106. See Hannah Cornaby, Report, *Woman's Exponent*, 1 Mar. 1878, 146; and Sarah Howard and Selina Sabine, Report, *Woman's Exponent*, 15 Apr. 1878, 170.

107. For example, when it was established in 1880, the first general YLMIA presidency included secretary Louie Wells, who was a daughter of Daniel H. Wells, a counselor in the First Presidency. Inaugural first counselor Margaret Young Taylor was married to John Taylor, who led the church after Young's death in 1877. (Jenson, *Latter-day Saint Biographical Encyclopedia*, 4:267, 270.)

108. Hartley, "Priesthood Reorganization of 1877," 3–36.

109. Gates, *History of the YLMIA*, 56–57.

110. For the establishment of stake Relief Society organizations, see Derr et al., *First Fifty Years of Relief Society*, 405–409, 425–427, 467–472.

111. "Home Affairs," *Woman's Exponent*, 15 July 1878, 29.

112. Gates, *History of the YLMIA*, 84–85; "Ladies Conference," *Deseret Evening News*, 23 Sept. 1878, [3]. For a sampling of reports of organizations of stake YLMIAs, see Elizabeth Davis, "Report of Trip North," *Woman's Exponent*, 1 Oct. 1878, 70; "Summit Stake Conference," *Deseret News*, 27 Nov. 1878, 679; Ida F. Hunt, Report, *Woman's Exponent*, 15 Nov. 1880, 94; and "Logan and Ogden Conferences," *Woman's Exponent*, 15 Sept. 1881, 60.

113. Gates, *History of the YLMIA*, 85–86; see also "Salt Lake Stake Relief Society Conference," *Woman's Exponent*, 1 July 1880, 22.

114. Susa Young Gates [Homespun, pseud.], "Biographical Sketch of Mrs. Elmina S. Taylor," *Young Woman's Journal*, Oct. 1890, 3.

115. Gates, *History of the YLMIA*, 93; Jenson, *Latter-day Saint Biographical Encyclopedia*, 1:634–635. In this era, leading sisters sometimes held multiple positions at the same time.

116. See, for example, Hannah Wickman, "Sanpete Stake," *Woman's Exponent*, 1 Apr. 1888, 166.

117. Gates, *History of the YLMIA*, 25–26, 87–88.

118. Gates, *History of the YLMIA*, 71; see also "Home Affairs," *Woman's Exponent*, 15 Mar. 1880, 156; "R. S. Reports," *Woman's Exponent*, 1 Apr. 1880, 166; and "R. S. Reports," *Woman's Exponent*, 1 May 1880, 183.

119. Gates, *History of the YLMIA*, 89. It is possible that Taylor and her counselors had been set apart when they were originally appointed in 1880 and the 1888 setting apart represented a reaffirmation or recognition of their position following the death of Eliza R. Snow, which may have been seen to terminate her (and her successors') oversight of the other women's organizations. When apostle Franklin D. Richards presented the names of women leaders for sustaining at the general conference the following April, he admitted that he did not know the names of all the YLMIA leaders, and only Taylor and her secretary were sustained. ("April Conference 1888," *Woman's Exponent*, 15 Apr. 1888, 172.)

120. "R. S. Reports," *Woman's Exponent*, 15 Feb. 1874, 138.

121. "The General Superintendency," *Contributor*, May 1880, 180.

122. Gates, *History of the YLMIA*, 179. Junius Wells noted that "mixed membership" had been permitted only "in a very few instances, where the population seemed so small that two associations could not be officered only at the expense of the membership." ("Membership and System," *Contributor*, Oct. 1880, 28.)

123. "The General Superintendency," *Contributor*, May 1880, 181.

124. "Membership and System," *Contributor*, Oct. 1880, 28.

125. Hannah Wickman, "Sanpete Stake," *Woman's Exponent*, 1 Apr. 1888, 166.

126. Junius F. Wells, "Historical Sketch of the Y. M. M. I. A.," *Improvement Era*, July 1925, 881–882.

127. Cedar City Ward YLMIA Minute Book, 22 Nov. 1884, 134.

128. "Membership and System," *Contributor*, Oct. 1880, 28–29.

129. See "Brigham City Notes," *Ogden (Utah Territory) Daily Herald*, 26 Jan. 1887, [4]; "Conjoint Meeting," *Home Sentinel* (Manti, Utah Territory), 21 May 1886, [4]; "First Joint Meeting," *Deseret Evening News*, 15 Dec. 1887, [3]; and "Local Briefs," *Salt Lake Herald*, 22 Nov. 1888, 8.

130. Junius F. Wells, "Salutation," *Contributor*, Oct. 1879, 12. Shortly after its establishment, the *Contributor* was sustained at a semiannual conference as the "organ of the Young Men's and Young Ladies' Mutual Improvement Associations." ("Association Intelligence," *Contributor*, Nov. 1880, 63.)

131. See Schneirov, *Dream of a New Social Order*, 27–28.

132. Susa Young Gates, "Novel Reading," *Young Woman's Journal*, July 1894, 498.

133. See Orson F. Whitney, "Home Literature," *Contributor*, June 1888, 297–302; and B. H. Roberts [Horatio, pseud.], "Legitimate Fiction," *Contributor*, Feb. 1889, 133–136. In the months following B. H. Roberts's call for "legitimate fiction," the magazine published his serialized novel, *Corianton*, which was based on a story in the Book of Mormon. (See [B. H. Roberts], "Corianton," *Contributor*, Mar. 1889, 171.)

134. "Association Intelligence," *Contributor*, Apr. 1880, 168; "Association Intelligence," *Contributor*, Apr. 1883, 279; Junius F. Wells, "Historical Sketch of the Y. M. M. I. A.," *Improvement Era*, July 1925, 880.

135. See "Association Intelligence," *Contributor*, May 1881, 256; and "Association Intelligence," *Contributor*, Nov. 1887, 38.

136. Junius F. Wells, "Historical Sketch of the Y. M. M. I. A.," *Improvement Era*, July 1925, 880. In 1888, probably to avoid conflict due to the already-full scheduling of meetings and buildings at general conference time, the YMMIA began holding its conferences around the first of June. This timing may have also been intended to honor Brigham Young as the organization's founder; his birthdate was 1 June. ("General Conference of the Y. M. M. I. A.," *Contributor*, Mar. 1888, 199; see also Strong, "History," 81.)

137. Gates, *History of the YLMIA*, 131.

CHAPTER 2: THE NEW YOUNG WOMAN, 1891–1910

1. The 1880 census found that Utah Territory had "more children under five years old, in proportion to its population, than any other division of the country," and over half the population was in their teens or younger. (Bitton, "Zion's Rowdies," 56, 66.)
2. Rowland, "Autobiographical Sketch," 1.
3. Rowland, "Autobiographical Sketch," 4.
4. "The Editor's Department," *Young Woman's Journal*, June 1891, 425.
5. See Bowman, *Mormon People*, 124–183. The standard studies of this critical period include Thomas G. Alexander, *Mormonism in Transition: A History of the Latter-day Saints, 1890–1930*, Illini Books ed. (Urbana: University of Illinois Press, 1996); Jan Shipps, *Mormonism: The Story of a New Religious Tradition* (Urbana: University of Illinois Press, 1985); Kathleen Flake, *The Politics of American Religious Identity: The Seating of Senator Reed Smoot, Mormon Apostle* (Chapel Hill: University of North Carolina Press, 2004); and Ethan R. Yorgason, *Transformation of the Mormon Culture Region* (Urbana: University of Illinois Press, 2003).
6. *Deseret News 2013 Church Almanac*, 212.
7. May, "Demographic Portrait," 56–57. May shows that this trend began in the 1880s.
8. In their study of generational dynamics in American history, researchers William Strauss and Neil Howe proposed a model of American generational cohorts based strictly on birth year. This model of pioneer, frontier, and railroad generations differs from Howe and Strauss's paradigm to emphasize the unique importance of Latter-day Saints' conversion experiences in defining generations at this particular historical moment. (See Strauss and Howe, *Generations*, 58–79; and Tait, "*Young Woman's Journal* and Its Stories," 112–120.)
9. Edward H. Anderson, "Effect of Wealth on Morals," *Contributor*, Oct. 1890, 465. For more on the generational crisis among Latter-day Saints in this period, see Tait, "*Young Woman's Journal*: Gender and Generations," 51–71; and Tait, "1890s Mormon Culture of Letters," 99–124.
10. See "Y. L. M. I. A. Conference," *Young Woman's Journal*, Feb. 1894, 258.
11. Gates, *History of the YLMIA*, 153.
12. Romania B. Pratt Penrose to Susa Young Gates, 26 June 1888, Susa Young Gates Papers, CHL.
13. Gates, *History of the YLMIA*, 33–35; see also "Thirteenth Meeting of the Ladies' Cooperative Retrenchment Association, Held July 23, 1870," Susa Young Gates Papers, CHL. It is unclear whether Gates was present at the inaugural meeting. She was living in the Lion House at the time and was seemingly old enough to have been included, but she never claimed to have been present, and it seems likely that she would have mentioned her attendance at that key meeting.
14. Joseph F. Smith to Susa Young Gates, 10 Aug. 1888, Susa Young Gates Papers, CHL; Wilford Woodruff to Susa Young Gates, 2 Oct. 1888, Susa Young Gates Papers, CHL.
15. Susa Young Gates to Elmina S. Taylor, Maria Young Dougall, and Martha Horne Tingey, 23 Aug. 1888, Susa Young Gates Papers, CHL. Tingey was known as Mattie J. Horne when she was first appointed to the presidency.
16. For a full account of the founding and business development of the *Young Woman's Journal*, see Tait, "Between Two Economies," 1–54.
17. "Letter of the Presidency," *Young Woman's Journal*, Oct. 1889, 19.
18. "The Editor's Department," *Young Woman's Journal*, Oct. 1889, 32.
19. See Okker, *Our Sister Editors*, 1–5; and Tait, "*Young Woman's Journal*: Gender and Generations," 51–71.
20. See Wiebe, *Search for Order*, xiii–xiv. The process Wiebe describes readily applies to the transformation of the loosely affiliated young ladies' associations into a unified, centrally directed YLMIA, as described in this chapter.
21. Alexander, *Mormonism in Transition*, 99–131.
22. "Y. L. M. I. A. Officers' Meeting," *Young Woman's Journal*, Nov. 1892, 94.
23. Gates, *History of the YLMIA*, 127.
24. "Y. L. M. I. A. General Conference," *Young Woman's Journal*, May 1890, 268–269. Invitations to serve may have been extended to some of the new aides in 1889, but they were all sustained in April 1890. (Gates, *History of the YLMIA*, 127–128, 131.)
25. Gates, *History of the YLMIA*, 132; Young Women General Board, Minutes, vol. 9, 30 Nov. 1921, 517.
26. Gates, *History of the YLMIA*, 128.
27. "Y. L. M. I. A. Officers' Meeting," *Young Woman's Journal*, Nov. 1892, 93; List of Officers, *Young Woman's Journal*, July 1899, 334; List of Officers, *Young Woman's Journal*, Jan. 1910, 54; Ann M. Cannon, "Our New Home," *Young Woman's Journal*, Apr. 1910, 181.

28. Rowland, "Autobiographical Sketch," 4; see also "Services Held Here for Fannie Rowland," *Springville (UT) Herald*, 20 June 1968, [4].

29. See, for example, Young Women General Board, Minutes, vol. 4, 7 Jan. 1903, 118. Until the early twentieth century, Latter-day Saint women often engaged in the practice of laying on hands and invoking the name of Jesus Christ to give blessings of healing, prophecy, or comfort. For more on female blessings in the nineteenth century, see Derr et al., *First Fifty Years of Relief Society*, 539–540; and Stapley and Wright, "Female Ritual Healing," 1–85.

30. "Ninth General Conjoint Conference," *Young Woman's Journal*, Aug. 1904, 370.

31. Gates, *History of the YLMIA*, 180.

32. *YMMIA Manual* [1891], 3, 12.

33. See Young Women General Board, Minutes, vol. 1, 7 Sept. 1892, 11–12.

34. Gates, *History of the YLMIA*, 181; "Y. L. M. I. A. Officers' Meeting," *Young Woman's Journal*, Nov. 1892, 93–94; *Guide to the First Year's Course of Study in the Young Ladies' Mutual Improvement Association* (Salt Lake City: George Q. Cannon and Sons, [1893]).

35. *Guide to the First Year's Course*, 12–13.

36. *Guide to the First Year's Course*, 12.

37. *Guide to the First Year's Course*, 5.

38. *Guide to the First Year's Course*, 13.

39. Young Women General Board, Minutes, vol. 1, 4 Dec. 1893, 19–20; 4 June 1894, 22. In 1894, Maria Young Dougall noted that some associations still did not use the *Guide*. ("Y. L. M. I. A. Conference," *Coalville [Utah Territory] Times*, 7 Sept. 1894, [2].)

40. *Guide to the Second Year's Course of Study in the Young Ladies' Mutual Improvement Association* (Salt Lake City: George Q. Cannon and Sons, 1896); "Ethics for Young Girls," *Young Woman's Journal*, Jan. 1900, 40.

41. Young Women General Board, Minutes, vol. 1, 6 June 1892, 10.

42. See, for example, *Guide to the First Year's Course*, 16; and "Ethics for Young Girls," *Young Woman's Journal*, Jan. 1900, 40–43.

43. *Guide to the First Year's Course*, 25.

44. *Guide to the First Year's Course*, 16.

45. Zina D. H. Young, "How I Gained My Testimony of the Truth," *Young Woman's Journal*, Apr. 1893, 317.

46. Tena Sorensen, "A Girl's Testimony," *Young Woman's Journal*, May 1898, 219–220.

47. See, for example, "Conjoint Conference," *Brigham City (UT) Bugler*, 27 Mar. 1897, [4].

48. "Faith and Repentance," *Young Woman's Journal*, Oct. 1892, 29.

49. "The Testimony of the Truth," *Young Woman's Journal*, Dec. 1892, 127.

50. "Culture versus Testimony," *Young Woman's Journal*, Jan. 1896, 189.

51. "The Testimony of the Truth," *Young Woman's Journal*, Dec. 1892, 127.

52. See "Testimony Meetings," *Young Woman's Journal*, Jan. 1902, 44; and "Guide Work," *Young Woman's Journal*, Aug. 1904, 372.

53. Pleasant View 1st Ward YLMIA Minutes, vol. 1, 7 Feb. 1898, 132–134.

54. Matthews, *Rise of the New Woman*, 3–35; see also Martha H. Patterson, ed., *The American New Woman Revisited: A Reader, 1894–1930* (New Brunswick, NJ: Rutgers University Press, 2008).

55. "Conventions of Women," *Young Woman's Journal*, July 1898, 334.

56. See Gates, *History of the YLMIA*, 89.

57. Mintz, *Huck's Raft*, 175, 197.

58. Hunter, *How Young Ladies Became Girls*, 170.

59. Buchanan, *Culture Clash*, 48, 50; *Twelfth Annual Report of the Public Schools*, 107–108, 110.

60. Monnett, "Mormon Church and Its Private School System," 98–120.

61. "The New B. Y. Academy," *Young Woman's Journal*, June 1892, 394. The Brigham Young Academy became Brigham Young University in 1903. (Wilkinson, *Brigham Young University*, 375–377.)

62. Hunter, *How Young Ladies Became Girls*, 260.

63. Rowland, "Autobiographical Sketch," 2.

64. Solomon, *In the Company of Educated Women*, 44, 63–64.

65. Simpson, *American Universities*, 2–3.

66. "Leaves from the Journal of a Medical Student," *Young Woman's Journal*, May 1891, 369–372; see also Tait, "Finding 'Cactus,'" 1–12.

67. Rowland, "Autobiographical Sketch," 2.

68. Matthews, *Rise of the New Woman*, 38–50.

69. Susa Young Gates [Mary Howe, pseud.], "Professional and Business Opportunities for Women," *Young Woman's Journal*, Oct. 1891, 24–25. The series' six installments ended with an article on dentistry. ("Dentists," *Young Woman's Journal*, Apr. 1892, 325–327.)

70. "Our Summer Work," *Young Woman's Journal*, Apr. 1904, 183.

71. Rowland, "Autobiographical Sketch," 2.

72. Gates, *History of the YLMIA*, 244–245.

73. Strauss and Howe, *Generations*, 239.

74. Mineau, Bean, and Skolnick, "Mormon Demographic History II," 439; "Median Age at First Marriage: 1890 to Present," Historical Marital Status Tables, U.S. Census Bureau, updated 21 Nov. 2023, census .gov; Skolnick et al., "Mormon Demographic History I," 14–15. This study found that in the 1890s, 36 percent of Latter-day Saint women married before age twenty; this was twelve percentage points lower than the previous decade, and in the 1900s the rate dropped even further to 32 percent. Surviving data do not capture the percentage of Latter-day Saint women who never married in this period.

75. James T. Duke, "Marriage: Eternal Marriage," in *Encyclopedia of Mormonism*, 2:857–859; see also Doctrine and Covenants 132:19–20.

76. See "Services Held Here for Fannie Rowland," *Springville (UT) Herald*, 20 June 1968, [4].

77. Rowland, "Autobiographical Sketch," 6.

78. Susa Young Gates, "Mrs. Elizabeth Claridge McCune," *Young Woman's Journal*, Aug. 1898, 339–343; "Our First Lady Missionaries," *Latter-day Saints' Millennial Star*, 28 July 1898, 472.

79. "Jennie Brimhall and Inez Knight," *Young Woman's Journal*, June 1898, 245–249.

80. Fanny Rowland to George Reynolds, 7 Apr. 1908, First Presidency, Missionary Calls and Recommendations, CHL.

81. Rowland, "Autobiographical Sketch," 4.

82. The six, with age at appointment, were Ann M. Cannon (twenty-two), Agnes Campbell (twenty-nine), Sarah Eddington (twenty-nine), May Booth Talmage (twenty-four), Rosetta Wallace Bennett (twenty-six), and Helen Winters Woodruff (twenty-four). Mae Taylor Nystrom, daughter of YLMIA president Elmina Taylor, had served on the board from 1892 (when she was twenty-one) to 1900 and rejoined the board in 1905, serving as a counselor to Martha Horne Tingey when Tingey became YLMIA president following Taylor's death. ("Ann Mousley Cannon, MIA Leader, 79, Dies in Denver," *Salt Lake Tribune*, 11 Nov. 1948, 18; "Church Worker Dies at Home Today," *Deseret News*, 19 Feb. 1942, 10; "Y. L. M. I. A. General Conference," *Young Woman's Journal*, May 1890, 269; "Y. L. M. I. A. Officers' Meeting," *Young Woman's Journal*, Nov. 1892, 93; "LDS Church Worker Dies at Ogden," *Salt Lake Tribune*, 7 Apr. 1944, 11; "Y. L. N. M. I. A. Officers' Meeting," *Young Woman's Journal*, Oct. 1896, 46; "Sen. Bennett's Mother, 88, Dies at Residence in S.L.," *Salt Lake Tribune*, 17 Mar. 1958, 20; "In Memoriam: Helen May Winters Woodruff," *Woman's Exponent*, July 1904, 12; May Booth Talmage, "Helen Winters Woodruff," *Young Woman's Journal*, July 1904, 292–294; "Mrs. Nystrom Succumbs in S.L. at 88," *Deseret News and Telegram*, 9 Dec. 1959, B17.)

83. Gates, *History of the YLMIA*, 174–175; Madelyn Stewart Silver, "A Story of Vision and Accomplishment," *Improvement Era*, Feb. 1950, 135.

84. Young Women General Board, Minutes, vol. 4, 7 Oct. 1899, 72–73; Gates, *History of the YLMIA*, 167.

85. See Barth, "Biography of Ann Mousley Cannon," 9.

86. Arrington, *Madelyn Cannon Stewart Silver*, 17–18, 25–39.

87. These women were Sarah Eddington, Joan Campbell, and Agnes Campbell. (Gates, *History of the YLMIA*, 145–149, 195–197.)

88. See, for example, "The Jenness-Miller System of Healthful and Artistic Dress," *Young Woman's Journal*, Feb. 1890, 157–159.

89. "Physical Culture," *Young Woman's Journal*, July 1893, 433–436; Maud May Babcock, "Physical Culture," *Young Woman's Journal*, Feb. 1894, 247–249; "Physical Culture," *Young Woman's Journal*, Mar. 1894, 296–298; "Delsarte," *Young Woman's Journal*, Apr. 1894, 358–360; "Physical Culture," *Young Woman's Journal*, May 1894, 405–408; "Biographical Sketch of Maud May Babcock, B. E.," *Young Woman's Journal*, June 1894, 410–413; "The Utah School of Physical Culture," *Young Woman's Journal*, July 1894, 457–461.

90. *Transactions of the National Council of Women*, 9.

91. *Transactions of the National Council of Women*, 23; "A Glimpse of Washington," *Woman's Exponent*, 1 Mar. 1891, 132. The organization first referred to itself in its own proceedings as the Young Ladies' National Mutual Improvement Association in the 6 October 1893 general conference, according to its minutes. This change in name was never made official or used exclusively, and in May 1904 the board voted to discontinue its use. (Young Women General Board, Minutes, vol. 2, 6 Oct. 1893, 19; vol. 4, 25 May 1904, 292; "With the Editor," *Young Woman's Journal*, Feb. 1899, 92.)

92. See, for example, "Editor's Department," *Young Woman's Journal*, Feb. 1895, 234.

93. "Editor's Department," *Young Woman's Journal*, Apr. 1893, 326–327.

94. Tenth Ward YLMIA History, 2.

95. See "Editor's Department," *Young Woman's Journal*, Apr. 1893, 326.

96. Susa Young Gates, "Utah Women at the National Council of Women," *Young Woman's Journal*, June 1895, 393.

97. Susa Young Gates provides the most detailed account, though her coverage of earlier years is incomplete. (Gates, *History of the YLMIA*, 153–156.)

98. See, for example, "Grand Necktie and Apron Ball," *Wasatch Wave* (Heber City, Utah Territory), 11 Nov. 1890, [3]; "Delightful Entertainment," *Brigham City (Utah Territory) Bugler*, 25 Apr. 1891, 1; "Snowville Briefs," *Standard* (Ogden, Utah Territory), 17 Nov. 1892, 8; "Y L M I A Kirmess," *Republic* (Nephi, UT), 3 July 1897, [4]; "A Party at Vermillion," *Southern Censor* (Richfield, UT), 27 Aug. 1897, [3]; and "Local Points," *Journal* (Logan, UT), 28 Sept. 1897, [8].

99. Gates, *History of the YLMIA*, 156; "Y. L. M. I. A. Officers' Meeting," *Young Woman's Journal*, Nov. 1892, 94. Two dollars in 1892 is equal to about fifty-seven dollars in modern currency.

100. Gates, *History of the YLMIA*, 156–157, 159; Young Women General Board, Minutes, vol. 1, 4 Sept. 1893, 17–18; "Officers' Conference," *Young Woman's Journal*, May 1894, 394–395. In modern currency, $763 would equal approximately $22,000.

101. Gates, *History of the YLMIA*, 157–158. For more about Sunday School nickel day, see *Jubilee History*, 31.

102. Gates, *History of the YLMIA*, 158–159; Young Women General Board, Minutes, vol. 1, 4 Sept. 1894, 25.

103. "Our Annual Day," *Young Woman's Journal*, Aug. 1895, 529. At first the board permitted stakes to retain one-fourth of the dime funds collected each year, but in 1897 they requested that all money collected be sent to them. (Gates, *History of the YLMIA*, 159.)

104. For a complete account of the magazine in its first decade, see Tait, "Between Two Economies," 1–54.

105. Editorial, *Young Woman's Journal*, June 1897, 426; "Annual Report of the Y. L. N. M. I. Associations," *Young Woman's Journal*, Sept. 1897, 582; Tait, "Between Two Economies," 17, 42–43, 45.

106. Elmina S. Taylor to Susa Young Gates, 17 Oct. 1896, Susa Young Gates Papers, CHL; see also Tait, "Between Two Economies," 44–45.

107. Gates, *History of the YLMIA*, 108–110. Gates's wealthy friend Elizabeth Claridge McCune also made a substantial donation of five hundred dollars. The *Journal* suspended publication for the last three months of 1897; when it resumed in 1898, the issues were numbered to coincide with the calendar year instead of beginning in October as done previously. ("Salutation," *Young Woman's Journal*, Jan. 1898, 43.)

108. "New Year's Greetings," *Young Woman's Journal*, Jan. 1901, 38–39.

109. Preston Nibley, "Y. M. M. I. A. Publications," *Improvement Era*, June 1925, 756–757. On the front cover of the November 1897 issue, the new magazine listed top church leaders and YMMIA officials Joseph F. Smith, B. H. Roberts, Heber J. Grant, and Thomas Hull as editors and business managers.

110. When Joseph F. Smith became part of the church's First Presidency in 1901, he retained at least figure-head editorship of the *Improvement Era*. While most of the editorial work was done by others, Smith published a monthly column reflecting his vigorous leadership and doctrinal teachings. By 1910, the *Improvement Era* had become the official magazine of the church's priesthood quorums as well as the YMMIA. By 1915, the *Era* had also become the organ of the church schools. (See the front covers of the November 1910 and November 1915 issues of the *Improvement Era*.)

111. Young Women General Board, Minutes, vol. 1, 8 Apr. 1896, 68–70; Elmina S. Taylor to Susa Young Gates, 1 May 1896, Susa Young Gates Papers, CHL.

112. "Y. L. M. I. A. General Conference," *Young Woman's Journal*, May 1890, 268; "First Territorial Annual Conference of the Y. L. M. I. Association," *Young Woman's Journal*, Nov. 1891, 88–94; Ann M. Cannon, "Y. L. M. I. A. Officers' Meeting," *Young Woman's Journal*, Nov. 1892, 93–95.

113. "In Woman's Sphere," *Deseret Evening News*, 22 Oct. 1892, 5.

114. "Should the Mutual Improvement Associations Unite?," *Young Woman's Journal*, Aug. 1896, 503–504. The writer of this piece signed himself "Union"; in the *Contributor*, Thomas Hull identified himself as the writer. (Thomas Hull, Letter to the Editor, *Contributor*, Oct. 1896, 741.)

115. Young Women General Board, Minutes, vol. 1, 8 Apr. 1896, 70.

116. "M. I. A. Conference," *Deseret Evening News*, 29 May 1896, 10; "M. I. Associations," *Salt Lake Herald*, 31 May 1896, 6; "Mutual Improvement," *Salt Lake Herald*, 1 June 1896, 6; see also Young Women General Board, Minutes, vol. 1, 4 May 1896, 71.

117. See Reeder and Holbrook, *At the Pulpit*, xix.

118. "Mutual Improvement," *Salt Lake Herald*, 1 June 1896, 6. The Young Men's *Contributor* ceased publication before printing a report of the conference, and the *Young Woman's Journal* did not publish anything about the conference for several months. (See "Y. L. N. M. I. A. Officers Meeting," *Young Woman's Journal*, Oct. 1896, 45.)

119. Young Women General Board, Minutes, vol. 1, 6 July 1896, 74.

120. The Utah Stake was headquartered in Provo and included most of Utah County until it was divided in 1901. (Jenson, *Encyclopedic History*, 907–908.)

121. "Y. L. N. M. I. A. Conference," *Young Woman's Journal*, May 1897, 387–389.

122. For examples of conjoint conferences or sessions prior to 1896, see "Improvement in the Far North," *Deseret Evening News*, 9 Mar. 1885, [3]; "Conjoint Conference," *Journal* (Logan, Utah Territory), 17 May 1893, [5]; and "M. I. A. Work in Emery Stake," *Daily Enquirer* (Provo, Utah Territory), 30 Apr. 1894, 4.

123. Young Women General Board, Minutes, vol. 1, 4 Jan. 1897, 88.

124. Young Women General Board, Minutes, vol. 2, 1 Mar. 1897, 68–70.

125. "Shall the Mutual Improvement Associations Unite?," *Young Woman's Journal*, Aug. 1896, 505. It is not clear whether Hull was expressing his own ideas or whether his proposal had broader support within the YMMIA.

126. "Shall the Mutual Improvement Associations Unite?," *Young Woman's Journal*, Aug. 1896, 504.

127. "Shall the Mutual Improvement Associations Unite?," *Young Woman's Journal*, Aug. 1896, 505.

128. See Young Women General Board, Minutes, vol. 1, 7 Sept. 1896, 80.

129. "Y. L. N. M. I. A. Officers Meeting," *Young Woman's Journal*, Oct. 1896, 45.

130. While *presidency* was by far the more common term used for the women leaders, *superintendency* was sometimes used to parallel the term always used in the young men's organization. YLMIA leaders seem to have used the terms interchangeably. On 5 November 1894, Elmina Taylor asked the board to vote on the term by which she would be called. The minutes record the following: "The term Superintendent was used when she was set apart to her office. But she had joined the National Council as President and Vice-Presidents in conformity to custom. Felt that if there was any serious objection the point should be settled. After discussion all were in favor of the appellation of President." (Young Women General Board, Minutes, vol. 1, 5 Nov. 1894, 37.)

131. Hartley, "From Men to Boys," 80–136.

132. Milton H. Hardy, "Government of the Associations," *Contributor*, May 1888, 257–258; *YMMIA Manual* [1891], 12. Sources do not provide a clear rationale for why "superintendent" or "president" was favored in any given situation or if there was any distinction between the two terms.

133. Young Women General Board, Minutes, vol. 2, 1 Mar. 1897, 69; "Mutual Improvement Conference," *Young Woman's Journal*, Aug. 1897, 528–529.

134. See, for example, "Eighth General Conference M. I. A.," *Young Woman's Journal*, July 1903, 332.

135. *Instructions to the Y. L. M. I. A. Officers*, 8; *Y. L. M. I. A. Hand Book* [1926], 78. There is no publication date on this pamphlet, but internal evidence and general board minutes suggest that it dates to 1904. (Young Women General Board, Minutes, vol. 4, 31 Dec. 1902, 111; 23 Mar. 1904, 268.)

136. "M. I. Associations," *Salt Lake Herald*, 31 May 1896, 6.

137. "Union," *Young Woman's Journal*, Mar. 1897, 288.

138. "The M. I. A. Conference," *Young Woman's Journal*, July 1899, 336.

139. "The M. I. A. Conference," *Young Woman's Journal*, July 1899, 336.

140. The first Sunday School convention was held in 1898. (*Jubilee History*, 35.)

141. "Our Work," *Improvement Era*, Sept. 1900, 870; Young Women General Board, Minutes, vol. 4, 1 Oct. 1902, 87–88; 2 Dec. 1902, 102–103; "Eighth General Conference M. I. A.," *Young Woman's Journal*, July 1903, 333. Some YLMIAs held conventions on their own initiative before the general plan was established. (See "Officers' Notes," *Young Woman's Journal*, Oct. 1903, 469.)

142. Gates, *History of the YLMIA*, 224–226.

143. "Officers' Notes," *Young Woman's Journal*, Nov. 1903, 519–520.

144. "Officers' Notes," *Young Woman's Journal*, Oct. 1903, 469.

145. Utah Stake YLMIA Minutes, vol. 1, 23 Sept. 1906, 226–228.

146. Young Women General Board, Minutes, vol. 4, 3 Dec. 1902, 103; see also "Officers' Page," *Young Woman's Journal*, Feb. 1903, 88; and "Eighth General Conference M. I. A.," *Young Woman's Journal*, July 1903, 333.

147. Utah Stake YLMIA Officers Minutes, 16 Dec. 1906; 20 Jan. 1907.

148. Utah Stake YLMIA Officers Minutes, 16 Dec. 1906.

149. "Conjoint Meetings," *Improvement Era*, Dec. 1903, 149. Leaders encouraged associations to hold joint sessions on "Sunday evening, the evening of the Fast Day being selected for that purpose whenever possible." ("Our Work," *Improvement Era*, Aug. 1898, 778.)

150. *YMMIA Manual* [1901], 4–7. YMMIA leaders worried that "our meetings are not sufficiently attractive and therefore literary societies and other organizations are detracting from our work." (YMMIA Minutes, vol. 3, 31 May 1900, 39.)

151. "Officers' Notes," *Young Woman's Journal*, Oct. 1903, 469–470.

152. Shipps, May, and May, "Sugar House Ward," 323–326, 329.

153. Mintz, *Huck's Raft*, 196; Hall, *Adolescence*, 1:ix–xv.

154. Mintz, *Huck's Raft*, 196–197.

155. "The Responsibility of Officers," *Young Woman's Journal*, July 1904, 330.

156. Hickman did not cite a specific work by Coe. He had almost certainly encountered Coe's work in the course of his career as an educator at various church academies. By 1904, Coe had published several important books: *The Spiritual Life: Studies in the Science of Religion* (1900), *The Religion of a Mature Mind* (1902), and *Education in Religion and Morals* (1904). He had also published over twenty articles, many of which dealt specifically with the intersection of adolescence and religion. (See Coe, "Adolescence," 14–22; and Helen Allan Archibald, "George Albert Coe," Database: Christian Educators of the 20th Century, Biola University, biola.edu.)

157. "The Responsibility of Officers," *Young Woman's Journal*, July 1904, 330.

158. Hall, *Adolescence*, 1:xix.

159. See, for example, "Y. L. M. I. A. Officers' Meeting," *Young Woman's Journal*, Nov. 1890, 79; and "The Conference of the Y. L. M. I. A of the Cache Stake," *Young Woman's Journal*, Aug. 1895, 518.

160. *Guide for the Junior Department* [1903], 2. The Sunday Schools and the YMMIA had graded their classes a few years earlier. (*Latter-day Saints' Sunday School Treatise*, 10–11, 19–20; YMMIA Minutes, vol. 3, 31 May 1900, 38–39.)

161. *Guide for the Junior Department* [1903], 2.

162. "Officers' Notes," *Young Woman's Journal*, Apr. 1904, 183; "A Biographical Sketch of President Elmina S. Taylor," *Young Woman's Journal*, Jan. 1905, 6.

163. "Y. L. N. M. I. A. Conference," *Young Woman's Journal*, May 1897, 388.

164. "A Biographical Sketch of President Elmina S. Taylor," *Young Woman's Journal*, Jan. 1905, 3–5.

165. Young Women General Board, Minutes, vol. 4, 5 Apr. 1905, 390.

166. "Martha Horne Tingey," *Young Woman's Journal*, June 1905, 260–261; Emmeline B. Wells, "Martha Jane Horne Tingey," *Young Woman's Journal*, Jan. 1891, 146, 150.

167. Gates, *History of the YLMIA*, 290–295; Jenson, *Latter-day Saint Biographical Encyclopedia*, 4:264. LDS College was a forerunner of LDS Business College, known after 2020 as Ensign College.

168. See Springville 4th Ward YLMIA Minutes, vol. 2, 30 Oct. 1906, 236.

169. The women who went to college were Lillian Condie, Ora Roylance, Hannah Condie, Lena Condie, Ivy Hall, Henrietta Palfreyman, Jessie Robertson, and Lola White. ("Springville," *Salt Lake Herald-Republican*, 3 Dec. 1911, sec. 2, p. 18; Maycock, "Esther Palfreyman Condie," 2; "B. Y. U. Students Make Their Protest Public," *Salt Lake Tribune*, 16 Mar. 1911, 1; Carr and Russell, "History of Henrietta Palfreyman Clyde," 3; Walker and Walker, *Glimpses of Pleasant Grove Schools*, 74; "Lola B. White Succumbs of Heart Attack," *Springville [UT] Herald*, 1 May 1975, 8.)

170. "Services Held Here for Fannie Rowland," *Springville (UT) Herald*, 20 June 1968, [4]; "Louisa Rowland, Ex-Librarian, Services Held," *Springville Herald*, 30 Sept. 1971, 15; Death Certificate for Ada Isabell Henline, 25 Apr. 1923, Charleston, Wasatch Co., UT, Utah Death Certificates, 1904–1965, FamilySearch.org; "Lola B. White Succumbs of Heart Attack," *Springville Herald*, 1 May 1975, 8; "Funeral Services Held for Lena Maycock," *Springville Herald*, 10 Sept. 1964, 1; "Louise Wiscombe Will Be Honored on 80th Birthday," *Pleasant Grove (UT) Review*, 5 Mar. 1970, [4]; "Cora G. Scott," *Salt Lake Tribune*, 27 Nov. 1964, B10.

171. Springville 4th Ward YLMIA Minutes, vol. 2, 15 Jan. 1907, 242–243. On 15 January 1907, the Fourth Ward YLMIA leadership was reorganized with Rowland as president. Two seventeen-year-old young women were also assigned as "missionaries," but the minutes do not clearly reflect what that meant, and it was not an officially prescribed position in the YLMIA.

172. Springville 4th Ward YLMIA Minutes, vol. 2, 28 Aug. 1906, 231.

173. Young Women General Board, Minutes, vol. 5, 9 and 16 Aug. 1906, 57–58, 59.

174. Springville 4th Ward YLMIA Minutes, vol. 2, 28 Aug. 1906, 231.

175. See Springville 4th Ward YLMIA Minutes, vol. 2, 18 Sept. 1906, 232; 2, 16, 23, and 30 Oct. 1906, 233–236.

176. Springville 4th Ward YLMIA Minutes, vol. 2, 22 Jan. 1907, 244.

177. Springville 4th Ward YLMIA Minutes, vol. 2, 22 Jan. 1907, 244; "How the Savior Taught by Parables [pt. 2]," *Young Woman's Journal*, Dec. 1906, 574.

178. "Summer Meetings," *Young Woman's Journal*, May 1906, 224; "Summer Meetings," *Young Woman's Journal*, May 1907, 227.

179. Springville 4th Ward YLMIA Minutes, vol. 2, 17 and 31 July 1906, 228–229; vol. 3, 16 July 1907, 7.

180. Springville 4th Ward YLMIA Minutes, vol. 3, 7 May 1907, 1.

181. See Ellen Jakeman, "The Western Boom," *Young Woman's Journal*, May 1890, 241–246.

182. Springville 4th Ward YLMIA Minutes, vol. 3, 20 Aug. 1907, 9; "Society News," *Springville (UT) Herald*, 15 Aug. 1935, 1.

183. Springville 4th Ward YLMIA Minutes, vol. 3, 16 July 1907, 7.

184. Springville 4th Ward YLMIA Minutes, vol. 3, 10, 17, and 24 Sept. 1907, 10–12; 15 Oct. 1907, 14.

185. See Young Women General Board, Minutes, vol. 3, 4 Dec. 1899, 81; 7 Oct. 1901, 280. Gates suffered from severe health problems from 1902 to 1904 and juggled many responsibilities, but she never lost sight of the project and seems to have resumed work on it in earnest in 1905. Several entries in the YLMIA general board minutes trace the publication of the book. It was publicly announced in November 1911. (Young Women General Board, Minutes, vol. 4, 15 Nov. 1905, 462; vol. 7, 17 June 1911, 41–42; 10 and 17 Aug. 1911, 47, 49; 9 and 19 Oct. 1911, 57, 59; "History of the Y. L. M. I. A.," *Young Woman's Journal*, Nov. 1911, 642, 644.)

186. Susa Young Gates, "Historical Sketch of the Y. L. M. I. A.," *Young Woman's Journal*, Feb. 1892, 231–232; see also Lisa Olsen Tait, "Origins and Myths: Revisiting the Founding Story of the Latter-day Saint Young Women's Organization," *Journal of Mormon History* 51, no. 1 (Jan. 2025). In the *History*, Gates wrote that this account was based on memories of Bathsheba Smith, who was present for the occasion. (Gates, *History of the YLMIA*, 6.)

187. See discussion in chapter 1, p. 7 herein.

188. Gates, *History of the YLMIA*, 9.

189. Gates, *History of the YLMIA*, 82. Wells's account originated in a talk he gave at the June Conference in 1905; Gates's text of the speech, included in chapter 4 of her book, seems to be the only extant source. (See also "Our Work," *Improvement Era*, July 1905, 711; and Junius F. Wells, "Historic Sketch of the Y. M. M. I. A.," *Improvement Era*, June 1925, 714–715.)

190. See Mary Connelly, "The Place of the Y. L. M. I. A. in the Church," *Young Woman's Journal*, July 1912, 386–388.

191. May Booth Talmage, "Our Jubilee Year," *Young Woman's Journal*, Nov. 1919, 578; Ruth May Fox, "Fifty Years Ago," *Young Woman's Journal*, Nov. 1919, 592.

192. *Y. L. M. I. A. Hand Book* [1923], 7–8; *Hand Book of the Young Men's and Young Ladies' Mutual Improvement Associations* [1928], 16.

193. George Q. Morris, "The Necessity of Co-operation in M. I. Work," *Young Woman's Journal*, Aug. 1909, 394.

CHAPTER 3: MAKING THE MIA, 1911–1930

1. "Officers' Notes," *Young Woman's Journal*, June 1911, 339; Jenson, *Latter-day Saint Biographical Encyclopedia*, 4:263; "Salt Lake's Population Is 92,777," *Salt Lake Herald-Republican*, 15 Nov. 1910, 1.

2. Walter J. Sloan, "Evolution of a Traction System," *Evening Telegram* (Salt Lake City), 28 Aug. 1909, 14.

3. Nichols, *Prostitution, Polygamy, and Power*, 178–181.

4. Peiss, *Cheap Amusements*, 67–77.

5. Peiss, *Cheap Amusements*, 41–45, 163–164; see also Moore and Hedges, "Trends in Labor," 4–5.

6. Peiss, *Cheap Amusements*, 5, 51–54, 104–114, 132–138, 158–162.

7. Hine, *Rise and Fall of the American Teenager*, 177–202; Savage, *Teenage*, 197–216.

8. For a contemporary account of how American life had changed by the end of the 1920s, see Frederick Lewis Allen, *Only Yesterday: An Informal History of the 1920s* (New York: Harper and Brothers, 1931).

9. *Deseret News 2013 Church Almanac*, 212; Plewe, *Mapping Mormonism*, 174.

10. "Samoa Mapusaga M.I.A. Record," 1; Young Women General Board, Minutes, vol. 8, 13 Jan. 1915, 113; Puketapu Branch YLMIA Minutes, 8 May 1921.

11. Kimball, *Autobiography*, 6–8.

12. Flanagan, *America Reformed*, 42–48, 81–84, 171–173; McGerr, *Fierce Discontent*, xii–xvi, 28–32, 79–81, 99–104, 133–134, 235–238.

13. Peiss, *Cheap Amusements*, 164–165.

14. Bowman, *Mormon People*, 152–183; McDannell, *Sister Saints*, 35–38; Alexander, *Mormonism in Transition*, 39–62, 134–135.

15. Edith R. Lovesy, "Social Affairs," *Young Woman's Journal*, Sept. 1911, 509, 511.

16. Edward H. Anderson, "Social Affairs," *Young Woman's Journal*, Sept. 1911, 512, 514–515.

17. "By Mrs. Zina B. Cannon," *Young Woman's Journal*, Sept. 1911, 519.

18. "By Mrs. Rachel Grant Taylor," *Young Woman's Journal*, Sept. 1911, 520; see also "New Member of Board," *Young Woman's Journal*, Aug. 1911, 457.

19. "By Mrs. Zina B. Cannon," *Young Woman's Journal*, Sept. 1911, 518.

20. Kimball, *Autobiography*, 7, 10–21.
21. "M. I. Work in San Francisco," *Improvement Era*, Feb. 1900, 315. While the YLMIA records for the San Francisco Branch are not available, the YMMIA records include details from conjoint meetings with YLMIA members starting on 22 November 1910. (San Francisco Branch YMMIA Minutes, vol. 1, 22 Nov. 1910.)
22. Edith R. Lovesy, "Social Affairs," *Young Woman's Journal*, Sept. 1911, 511.
23. Edward H. Anderson, "Social Affairs," *Young Woman's Journal*, Sept. 1911, 512.
24. Curtis, *Play Movement*, 3–8.
25. See, for example, Addie Cannon Howells, "The Playground Movement," *Young Woman's Journal*, Aug. 1913, 463–469; and Nicholas Byhower, "Public Parks," *Young Woman's Journal*, Mar. 1914, 160–162. Byhower was the superintendent of parks in Salt Lake City.
26. "Reception at Deseret 'Gym,'" *Deseret Evening News*, 5 Sept. 1910, 6; "Deseret Gymnasium Is a Beauty," *Evening Telegram* (Salt Lake City), 20 Sept. 1910, 10; see also Kimball, *Sports in Zion*, 66–83.
27. Fischer-Tiné, Huebner, and Tyrrell, *Spreading Protestant Modernity*, 2–3, 7; Sims, *YWCA*, 18, 74.
28. Embry, *Spiritualized Recreation*, 8, 22; Kimball, "Muscular Mormonism," 550–551; see also Moore, "Learning to Play," 89–106.
29. See Doctrine and Covenants 29:34; 88:15.
30. B. H. Roberts, "Physical Development," *Young Woman's Journal*, Aug. 1912, 454–456.
31. MIA Day, a conjoint event, gradually supplanted the Annual Day that had been observed by the YLMIA since the 1890s. (See pp. 42–43 herein.)
32. Edward H. Anderson, "Social Affairs," *Young Woman's Journal*, Sept. 1911, 515.
33. "M. I. A. Meets in Barratt Hall," *Salt Lake Herald*, 9 June 1906, 12; Kimball, *Sports in Zion*, 101.
34. "General M. I. A. Annual Field Day," *Improvement Era*, July 1911, 846–847.
35. "M. I. A. Athletic Tourney Starts," *Evening Telegram* (Salt Lake City), 3 June 1911, 14.
36. Mattie Read Evans, "Musical Contests," *Young Woman's Journal*, Oct. 1912, 588–589.
37. "Music and Musicians," *Inter-mountain Republican* (Salt Lake City), 7 Mar. 1909, Society section, 4.
38. Mattie Read Evans, "Musical Contests," *Young Woman's Journal*, Oct. 1912, 588.
39. "M. I. A. Oratorical Prizes Go to Heber and Midway," *Daily Herald* (Provo, UT), 9 June 1913, 1.
40. "M. I. A. Oratorical Prizes Go to Heber and Midway," *Daily Herald* (Provo, UT), 9 June 1913, 1.
41. "B.Y.C. to Have New Program," *Salt Lake Tribune*, 18 May 1925, 2.
42. "How Near to the Angels," *Improvement Era*, Oct. 1956, 709. Coleman's married name was Tatge.
43. "'The Mailbox' Star Dies in Midway," *Daily Herald* (Provo, UT), 3 Feb. 1986, 4.
44. Iosepa Branch YMMIA and YLMIA Record Book, 4 and 25 May 1913, 3, 5; 8 and 22 June 1913, 7, 9.
45. Oscar A. Kirkham, "M. I. A. Day: Definition and Purpose," *Young Woman's Journal*, Aug. 1913, 494–495.
46. May Green, "Execution," *Young Woman's Journal*, Aug. 1913, 498.
47. Emily Caldwell Adams, "The Spirit of Contest," *Young Woman's Journal*, Aug. 1914, 506–507.
48. Oscar A. Kirkham, "M. I. A. Day: Definition and Purpose," *Young Woman's Journal*, Aug. 1913, 494.
49. "Contest Work and M. I. A. Day Activities," *Young Woman's Journal*, Feb. 1915, 118–120.
50. "Special Activities," *Young Woman's Journal*, Aug. 1915, 518; "Special Activities," *Young Woman's Journal*, Mar. 1916, 187.
51. "Contest in Food Preservation," *Young Woman's Journal*, July 1917, 408.
52. Nancy Ferguson and Jennifer Burch, "Religious Camps: Common Roots and New Sprouts," *Camping Magazine*, Nov./Dec. 2011, 49–53.
53. "Emily Rachel Hillam Higgs," 2–5.
54. Emily H. Higgs et al., "Liberty Glen Camp," *Young Woman's Journal*, Jan. 1913, 31.
55. Josephson, *History of the YWMIA*, 136.
56. Josephson, *History of the YWMIA*, 135; Emily H. Higgs et al., "Liberty Glen Camp," *Young Woman's Journal*, Jan. 1913, 31; see also Jenson, *Latter-day Saint Biographical Encyclopedia*, 2:468–470.
57. Emily H. Higgs et al., "Liberty Glen Camp," *Young Woman's Journal*, Jan. 1913, 32.
58. Josephson, *History of the YWMIA*, 136; Higgs, "First MIA Summer Camp," 2.
59. Emily H. Higgs et al., "Liberty Glen Camp," *Young Woman's Journal*, Jan. 1913, 32.
60. Josephson, *History of the YWMIA*, 136; "Girl Campers Enjoy Outing," *Deseret Evening News*, 18 July 1912, 8.
61. Josephson, *History of the YWMIA*, 136; Emily H. Higgs et al., "Liberty Glen Camp," *Young Woman's Journal*, Jan. 1913, 32–33.
62. Emily H. Higgs et al., "Liberty Glen Camp," *Young Woman's Journal*, Jan. 1913, 33.
63. Josephson, *History of the YWMIA*, 136; Jenson, *Latter-day Saint Biographical Encyclopedia*, 1:619.

64. Josephson, *History of the YWMIA*, 137; "Emily Rachel Hillam Higgs," 7; Executive Board Minutes, 10 Oct. 1916, in Young Women General Board, Minutes, vol. 8.

65. Josephson, *History of the YWMIA*, 137.

66. Higgs, "First MIA Summer Camp," 1–3.

67. *Handbook for Scout Masters*, 1, 4, 24, 308.

68. "The Boy Scout Movement in Utah," *Improvement Era*, Apr. 1911, 541–542; see also YMMIA Minutes, vol. 11, 8 and 22 Mar. 1911, 28–29, 37.

69. Eugene L. Roberts, "The Boy Pioneers of Utah," *Improvement Era*, Oct. 1911, 1088–1091.

70. YMMIA Minutes, vol. 11, 29 Nov. 1911, 115.

71. Lyman R. Martineau, "M. I. A. Scouts," *Improvement Era*, Mar. 1912, 354–361.

72. YMMIA Minutes, vol. 13, 8 Jan. 1913, 2, 4, 5.

73. YMMIA Minutes, vol. 13, 26 Feb. 1913, 40–41.

74. YMMIA Minutes, vol. 13, 5 Mar. 1913, 41–42; 23 Apr. 1913, 84. Taylor was married to YLMIA board member Rachel Grant Taylor. For more on the process and discussions of affiliation, see George Q. Morris, "Thirty-Five Years of Scouting in the Church," *Improvement Era*, May 1948, 274.

75. For example, the first Boy Scout motto, "Be prepared," appeared in the first (1908) edition of the Scouting handbook. (Baden-Powell, *Scouting for Boys*, pt. 1, p. 20.)

76. "Flourishing Norwegian M. I. A.," *Improvement Era*, July 1904, 728–729.

77. Nameplate, *Young Woman's Journal*, Sept. 1904, 387; "The Twenty-Fourth," *Salt Lake Daily Herald*, 24 July 1880, [3]. Elmina Taylor had used this phrase in 1882. (Emily G. Cluff and Annie L. Jones, Report, *Woman's Exponent*, 1 Dec. 1882, 102.)

78. In fact, two slogans were introduced at June Conference in 1914: "We stand for a sacred Sabbath and a weekly half holiday," and "We stand for an eleven o'clock closing of amusements." ("Officers' Notes," *Young Woman's Journal*, June 1914, 387.)

79. For the slogans for 1914–1929, see *Hand Book of the Young Men's and Young Ladies' Mutual Improvement Associations* (1928), 85–86.

80. *Y. L. M. I. A. Hand Book* (1923), 62–63; "Suggestions for Putting the Slogan into Action," *Young Woman's Journal*, Feb. 1925, 116–117.

81. *Hand Book of the Young Men's and Young Ladies' Mutual Improvement Associations* (1928), 85.

82. Miller, *Growing Girls*, 23–28; Edward Marshall, "Campfire Girls of America Is the Name of a New Organization," *New York Times*, 17 Mar. 1912, pt. 5, p. 3.

83. Madelyn Stewart Silver, "A Story of Vision and Accomplishment," *Improvement Era*, Feb. 1950, 107; Young Women General Board, Minutes, vol. 7, 8 and 22 May 1913, 30, 32.

84. Charlotte Stewart, "Bee-Hive Girls and Camp Fire Girls," *Young Woman's Journal*, Apr. 1918, 202.

85. Miller, *Growing Girls*, 5, 13; Gulick, *Written Thoughts*, 3.

86. Miller, *Growing Girls*, 16.

87. Miller, *Growing Girls*, 5–6.

88. Deloria, *Playing Indian*, 111–114; Ann M. Cannon, "Wohelo," *Young Woman's Journal*, June 1913, 363–365.

89. "Suggestions for Camp Fire Work," *Young Woman's Journal*, May 1914, 315–316.

90. Arrington, *Madelyn Cannon Stewart Silver*, 32–33.

91. Charlotte Stewart, "Bee-Hive Girls and Camp Fire Girls," *Young Woman's Journal*, Apr. 1918, 202; Madelyn Stewart Silver, "A Story of Vision and Accomplishment," *Improvement Era*, Feb. 1950, 107, 134.

92. Charlotte Stewart, "Bee-Hive Girls and Camp Fire Girls," *Young Woman's Journal*, Apr. 1918, 202; Ann M. Cannon, "Origin of the Bee-Hive Girls' Organization," *Improvement Era*, May 1935, 283; Madelyn Stewart Silver, "A Story of Vision and Accomplishment," *Improvement Era*, Feb. 1950, 107, 134. One notice reported that nearly seven hundred Granite Stake young women had earned a total of 23,000 beads that summer. In an example of local adaptation of the program, the same notice reported that 123 special beads had been awarded to young women who read the Book of Mormon. ("Granite Stake Camp Fire," *Young Woman's Journal*, Dec. 1914, 765.)

93. "Summer Work," *Young Woman's Journal*, Mar. 1915, 192.

94. Horn, *Bees in America*, 19.

95. Horn, *Bees in America*, 55–58, 76–81, 93. Charles Penrose described the hive and honeybees as a "communal coat of arms" for Latter-day Saints, representing their "industry, harmony, order and frugality," as well as the "sweet results of their toil, union and intelligent cooperation." (Charles W. Penrose, "Deseret," *Deseret Evening News*, 11 Oct. 1881, [2].)

96. Young Women General Board, Minutes, vol. 8, 8 Oct. 1914, 84.

97. "Summer Work," *Young Woman's Journal*, Mar. 1916, 188; see also Ann M. Cannon, "Origin of the Bee-Hive Girls' Organization," *Improvement Era*, May 1935, 283.

98. Elen Wallace, "The Bee-Hive Symbolism," *Young Woman's Journal*, July 1916, 390.

99. *Hand Book for the Bee-Hive Girls* (1915), 8.

100. Elen Wallace, "The Bee-Hive Symbolism," *Young Woman's Journal*, July 1916, 391–393.

101. *Hand Book for the Bee-Hive Girls* (1915), 3–5.

102. *Hand Book for the Bee-Hive Girls* (1915), 10–11.

103. Elen Wallace, "The Bee-Hive Symbolism," *Young Woman's Journal*, July 1916, 394; *Hand Book for the Bee-Hive Girls* (1915), 5–7.

104. *Hand Book for the Bee-Hive Girls* (1915), 5.

105. "The Day of the Swarm," *Young Woman's Journal*, Nov. 1915, 695. These events received frequent mention in newspapers and the *Journal*. (See, for example, "Bee Hive Notes," *Millard County Chronicle* [Delta, UT], 12 Sept. 1918, [8].)

106. Arrington, *Madelyn Cannon Stewart Silver*, 35.

107. *Hand Book for the Bee-Hive Girls* (1915), 3.

108. Alexander, *Mormonism in Transition*, 133–166; Hall, *Faded Legacy*, 70–82.

109. Plewe, *Mapping Mormonism*, 132–133.

110. Alexander, *Mormonism in Transition*, 118.

111. Hartley, "Priesthood Reform Movement," 137–144; Joseph F. Smith, Address, 6 Apr. 1906, in *76th Annual Conference*, 3.

112. Milton H. Hardy, "Government of the Associations," *Contributor*, May 1888, 259–260; Milton H. Hardy and George H. Brimhall, "M. I. Manual, Part II," *Contributor*, Jan. 1895, 187–188. The Relief Society was not generally classified as an auxiliary until the twentieth century, since it occupied a special position parallel to the priesthood, having been organized by Joseph Smith in 1842. Not long after Joseph F. Smith took office, he began referring to the Relief Society as an auxiliary, albeit the "oldest" one and one that occupied a special position in the church. The Relief Society's transition to auxiliary status was particularly difficult, given its past autonomy. (Derr, Cannon, and Beecher, *Women of Covenant*, 154, 172, 212–214, 240–242; Joseph F. Smith, Address, 6 Apr. 1906, in *76th Annual Conference*, 3–4.)

113. Joseph F. Smith, Address, 4 Apr. 1913, in *Eighty-Third Annual Conference*, 7.

114. Joseph F. Smith, Address, 6 Apr. 1906, in *76th Annual Conference*, 3.

115. Joseph F. Smith, "Dress and Social Practices," *Improvement Era*, Dec. 1916, 172–173.

116. "Communication on Dress," and "Instructions on Social Work," *Young Woman's Journal*, Apr. 1917, 225–228; Alexander, "Between Revivalism," 25–26.

117. Alexander, "Between Revivalism," 25–30; John A. Widtsoe, "Preliminary Recommendation of the Recreation Committee of the Correlation Board," John A. Widtsoe Papers, CHL. Religion Classes were established in 1890 to provide after-school religious instruction for children and were listed among the church's auxiliaries until 1929, when Religion Class functions were absorbed by the Primary Association. ("Religion Class," in *Encyclopedia of Latter-day Saint History*, 998.)

118. Young Women General Board, Minutes, vol. 8, 15 and 22 Nov. 1917, 193, 196.

119. "Timely Hints to Girls Given at Bee-Hive Meeting," *Deseret Evening News*, 8 June 1918, sec. 2, p. 8; see also Charlotte Stewart, "The Bee Hive Girl of 1918," *Young Woman's Journal*, July 1918, 365–369.

120. "Utah Stake Y. L. M. I. A. Workers Make Great Record in War Service," *Provo (UT) Post*, 24 Jan. 1919, 1.

121. *Mission* here refers to the districts and branches within a particular geographic area that are administered by a mission presidency until local membership grows to a large enough number that the units may be converted into stakes and wards.

122. "Y. L. M. I. A. Report of War Emergency Work for the Year, 1918," *Young Woman's Journal*, June 1919, 338–339. Likewise, in 1917 local YLMIA organizations responded to a contest sponsored by the general board and preserved almost 350,000 pounds of food. ("Food Drying Contest," *Young Woman's Journal*, Mar. 1918, 166.)

123. "A Timely Word," *Young Woman's Journal*, Dec. 1918, 697–698.

124. "M. I. A. Notes," *Young Woman's Journal*, Jan. 1919, 45, 61; "M. I. A. Conditions," *Young Woman's Journal*, Feb. 1919, 113.

125. "Editorial Department," *Young Woman's Journal*, Mar. 1919, 172–173.

126. Fass, *The Damned and the Beautiful*, 13–25; George A. Coe, *What Ails Our Youth?* (New York: Charles Scribner's Sons, 1924).

127. Mintz, *Huck's Raft*, 213–232; Fass, *The Damned and the Beautiful*, 21–25; Gordon, *Moral Property*, 125–168.

128. Fass, *The Damned and the Beautiful*, 15–16.

129. "The Ward Social Center," *Young Woman's Journal*, Aug. 1920, 481.

130. See, for example, Social Advisory Committee, Minutes, vol. 2, 30 Mar. 1920.

131. Clarissa A. Beesley, "The National Conference of Social Work," *Young Woman's Journal*, June 1920, 322–323; "Delegates Returning Home," *Salt Lake Telegram*, 21 Apr. 1920, sec. 2, p. 1.

132. Mary C. Kimball, "Clarissa A. Beesley," *Young Woman's Journal*, May 1929, 321–322.

133. Clarissa A. Beesley, "The National Conference of Social Work," *Young Woman's Journal*, June 1920, 322–323.

134. Arthur L. Beeley, "Problems in Leadership," *Improvement Era*, Sept. 1920, 1024.

135. Arthur L. Beeley, "Problems in Leadership," *Improvement Era*, Sept. 1920, 1027.

136. See, for example, Social Advisory Committee, Minutes, vol. 2, 7 and 14 Sept. 1920; and Correlation–Social Advisory Committee, Minutes, vol. 1, 30 Nov. 1920.

137. Social Advisory Committee, Minutes, vol. 2, 5 Apr. 1920.

138. Arthur L. Beeley, "A Statistical Study of Social Dancing," *Young Woman's Journal*, Mar. 1920, 162–165. Beeley did not say what girls' second-place choices were, nor did he offer further information about how the other recreational choices on the survey were ranked.

139. Social Advisory Committee, Minutes, vol. 2, ca. July 1920.

140. See McGerr, *Fierce Discontent*, 52–54, 65–66.

141. Social Advisory Committee, Minutes, vol. 2, 5 Apr. 1920.

142. "Practical Nursing to be Featured by Church," *Deseret Evening News*, 3 Apr. 1920, sec. 2, p. 12.

143. Kimball, *Sports in Zion*, 60–65; Jackson, *Places of Worship*, 135–208.

144. Goodman, "Correlation: The Early Years," 321–329; Alexander, "Between Revivalism," 31–35.

145. Correlation–Social Advisory Committee, Report to the First Presidency, 12 Apr. 1921, in Correlation–Social Advisory Committee, Minutes, vol. 2; Correlation–Social Advisory Committee, Minutes, vol. 1, 16 Nov. 1920.

146. First Presidency, Letter to Chairman of the Committee on Priesthood Outlines and Courses of Study and to the General Superintendents and Presidencies of Auxiliary Associations, 5 Oct. 1922, in Correlation–Social Advisory Committee, Minutes, vol. 3.

147. "Suggestions," in Correlation–Social Advisory Committee, Minutes, vol. 3. This document, which immediately follows the 5 October 1922 letter from the First Presidency in the committee minutes, lists action items, presumably in response to the letter.

148. *Recreation Bulletin No. 1* ([Salt Lake City]: MIA General Boards, 1923).

149. Social Advisory Committee, Minutes, vol. 2, 5 Apr. 1920.

150. Fass, *The Damned and the Beautiful*, 20–25; Savage, *Teenage*, 197, 201–202, 206–207, 209.

151. *Hand Book for the Bee-Hive Girls* (1915), 5; see also "Bee-Hive Girls," *Young Woman's Journal*, June 1920, 347; "Bee-Hive Girls," *Young Woman's Journal*, Mar. 1921, 168; "Bee-Hive Girls' Department," *Young Woman's Journal*, May 1921, 296; Felix J. Koch, "Sheepskins and Cherries," *Young Woman's Journal*, July 1921, 407; Agnes Lovendahl Stewart, "What Shall I Do?," *Young Woman's Journal*, Nov. 1927, 718; and Harrison R. Merrill, "This Hair Question," *Young Woman's Journal*, June 1926, 385.

152. Fern Chipman Eyring, "Nature-Loving under Leadership," *Young Woman's Journal*, Oct. 1924, 545.

153. Agnes Lovendahl Stewart, "You Are Pretty," *Young Woman's Journal*, Aug. 1925, 499.

154. Harrison R. Merrill, "This Hair Question," *Young Woman's Journal*, June 1926, 385–386.

155. "Bee-Hive Girls," *Young Woman's Journal*, July 1925, 443.

156. Alma P. Burton, "Endowment," in *Encyclopedia of Mormonism*, 2:454–456.

157. Martha Horne Tingey et al., Editorial, *Young Woman's Journal*, Jan. 1916, 44.

158. Joseph F. Smith, *Temple Instructions to the Bishops* (1918), in Clark, *Messages of the First Presidency*, 5:110.

159. "Dress," *Young Woman's Journal*, Mar. 1917, 175–176.

160. Martha Horne Tingey, "To Our Officers," *Young Woman's Journal*, July 1917, 364.

161. "Temple Garments Greatly Modified," *Salt Lake Tribune*, 4 June 1923, 12; Alexander, *Mormonism in Transition*, 316–317.

162. See George F. Richards, "Modesty," *Young Woman's Journal*, June 1916, 323.

163. See "Fa-ho-cha Swarm" (photograph), *Young Woman's Journal*, Oct. 1929, 700.

164. Peiss, *Hope in a Jar*, 97–133.

165. "Why, Oh Why?," *Young Woman's Journal*, July 1921, 444.

166. *Y. L. M. I. A. Hand Book* (1923), 38; "Mothers and Daughters of St. George Stake Join in Grand Outing," *Young Woman's Journal*, Aug. 1925, 505.

167. "Mothers' and Daughters' Day," *Young Woman's Journal*, Jan. 1928, 41.

168. "Mothers' and Daughters' Party," *Young Woman's Journal*, June 1927, 398.

169. Elen Wallace, "Green and Gold—MIA Colors," *Young Woman's Journal*, July 1922, 400.

170. "The M. I. A. Plan for 1927–28," *Young Woman's Journal*, July 1927, 464. For examples of early Gold and Green Balls, see "Layton," *Weekly Reflex* (Kaysville, UT), 31 Jan. 1925, 8; "Washington,"

Washington County News (St. George, UT), 20 Jan. 1926, [5]; and "Big Contest On," *Iron County Record* (Cedar City, UT), 10 Dec. 1926, [1].

171. *Hand Book of the Young Men's and Young Ladies' Mutual Improvement Associations* (1928), 119.

172. "The Gold and Green Ball," *Young Woman's Journal*, Mar. 1927, 188.

173. "The Gold and Green Ball," *Young Woman's Journal*, Mar. 1929, 189–190; "Candidates for Queen of Ball Announced," *Deseret News*, 23 Jan. 1929, sec. 2, p. 1.

174. On the Latter-day Saints and drama, see Givens, *People of Paradox*, 143–151.

175. *Y. L. M. I. A. Hand Book* (1923), 77–78; see also Maud May Babcock, "Technique of Play Production," *Young Woman's Journal*, Oct. 1921, 559.

176. "Influence," *Young Woman's Journal*, Mar. 1929, 196.

177. "Preaching the Gospel of Better Recreation," *Young Woman's Journal*, May 1924, 258–259; "Granite Stake Road Show Big Success," *Salt Lake Telegram*, 8 Mar. 1924, sec. 2, p. 1.

178. Iletta Dowdell, "Panguitch Stake," *Young Woman's Journal*, May 1927, 330–331.

179. Marguerite Gordon and Velma Wing, "A Bee-Hive Girl's Fantasy," *Young Woman's Journal*, Aug. 1925, 510–511.

180. "The Latter-day Saint Girl," *Young Woman's Journal*, Aug. 1925, 521–528.

181. Elizabeth Eames King to Catherine Folsom, 10 Oct. 1925, in *Young Woman's Journal*, Dec. 1925, 756.

182. "The Glory of God Is Intelligence," *Young Woman's Journal*, June 1925, 372–373. The YLMIA also agreed to adopt the YMMIA motto taken from Doctrine and Covenants 93:36 as a unified MIA theme: "The Glory of God Is Intelligence." Before 1925, the motto of the YLMIA had been "Improvement our motto, Perfection our aim."

183. "Y. M. M. I. A. Jubilee," *Young Woman's Journal*, Feb. 1925, 116. The MIAs had attempted to reach the goal of one hundred thousand members in the YLMIA jubilee year of 1919 but had fallen short. During this era, membership in the MIAs was highly encouraged and even expected for young Latter-day Saints, but it was still voluntary and required participants to enroll themselves in the organizations. ("Campaign for 100,000," *Young Woman's Journal*, Sept. 1919, 496; "Working for 50,000 Membership," *Improvement Era*, Aug. 1919, 923–924.)

184. "The Jubilee Year—a Year of Testimony," *Young Woman's Journal*, May 1925, 305.

185. "Special Joint Program for Sunday Evening, June 7," *Young Woman's Journal*, June 1925, 377.

186. "Fourth Day of M. I. A. Session Draws Crowds," *Salt Lake Telegram*, 9 June 1925, sec. 2, pp. 1, 6.

187. "Record Crowds Attend M. I. A. Jubilee Meet," *Davis County Clipper* (Bountiful, UT), 12 June 1925, [2]; "No One Lost," *Young Woman's Journal*, Aug. 1925, 500–501.

188. "M. I. A. Pageant Unequalled in City's History," *Salt Lake Tribune*, 11 June 1925, 1; "M. I. A. Jubilee Pageant Forms Immense Line," *Salt Lake Telegram*, 10 June 1925, 2.

189. "M. I. A. Pageant Unequalled in City's History," *Salt Lake Tribune*, 11 June 1925, 11.

190. "Our Jubilee," *Young Woman's Journal*, July 1925, 437.

191. See, for example, "Summer Vacations Made Easy by New Camp," *Salt Lake Telegram*, 8 July 1921, 12; and "Y. L. M. I. A. Summer Homes," *Young Woman's Journal*, June 1924, 311.

192. *Hand Book of the Young Men's and Young Ladies' Mutual Improvement Associations* (1928), 140; "Summer Camps are Calling!," *Young Woman's Journal*, May 1928, 287.

193. "Extract from Camp Log Brighton M. I. A. Home," *Young Woman's Journal*, July 1929, 474.

194. Charlotte Stewart, "Camp Activities," *Young Woman's Journal*, Aug. 1922, 453–455.

195. *Hand Book of the Young Men's and Young Ladies' Mutual Improvement Associations* (1928), 141. The program was written by Ruth May Fox. For other examples of pioneer memory being ritualized, see Bitton, "Ritualization of Mormon History," 67–85.

196. "New Member of the General Board," *Young Woman's Journal*, Nov. 1927, 721. Elsie Hogan Van Noy said that Moss took training in "camping and leadership activities" at Columbia University in New York. (Van Noy, "Summer Camps," 2.)

197. Claire N. Hulme, "Is Summer Camping Worth While for Y. L. M. I. A.?," *Young Woman's Journal*, June 1924, 313–314.

198. "Preliminary Study of Temple and Non-temple Marriages," 1, 3, 11–14.

199. "Preliminary Study of Temple and Non-temple Marriages," 19.

200. "'The Mailbox' Star Dies in Midway," *Daily Herald* (Provo, UT), 3 Feb. 1986, 4.

201. Knowles, *Howard W. Hunter*, 14–17, 57. John William Hunter later joined the church in 1927.

202. Kimball, *Autobiography*, 21–24.

203. See, for example, "The Latter-day Saint Woman," *Young Woman's Journal*, Aug. 1914, 513–521, running monthly through Nov. 1914, 706–714; and "Latter-day Saint Ideals of Home and Home Life," *Young Woman's Journal*, Aug. 1928, 514–523, running monthly through Apr. 1929, 212–227.

204. "Courtship," *Young Woman's Journal*, Nov. 1921, 655.

205. Allen, Embry, and Mehr, *Hearts Turned to the Fathers*, 33–90.

206. Heber J. Grant, "A Marvelous Work and a Wonder," *Improvement Era*, May 1928, 612.

207. H. David Burton, "Baptism for the Dead: LDS Practice," in *Encyclopedia of Mormonism*, 1:95–96; see also Allen Claire Rozsa, "Temple Ordinances," in *Encyclopedia of Mormonism*, 4:1444–1445; and Elma W. Fugal, "Salvation of the Dead," in *Encyclopedia of Mormonism*, 3:1257–1259. Baptism for the dead is mentioned in the New Testament. (See 1 Corinthians 15:29.)

208. Zola Bunker, "Bee-Hive Work a Great Success," *Young Woman's Journal*, June 1929, 423.

209. "Is Religion Still Being Taught in the M. I. A.?," *Young Woman's Journal*, Oct. 1928, 665.

210. See Florence Barclay, "The Meaning of Marriage, of Wifehood, and Motherhood," *Young Woman's Journal*, June 1917, 330; and "The Latter-day Saint Woman," *Young Woman's Journal*, Aug. 1914, 513. The lesson is entitled "Woman's Mission—A Home Maker."

211. For example, the lead article in the March 1921 edition of the *Young Woman's Journal* describes in glowing terms the visit of Dr. Caroline Hedger to give lectures on "the development of soul and body in young children and adolescents." The article also includes a detailed report of her research and findings. (Frank R. Arnold, "A Distinguished Visitor to Utah," *Young Woman's Journal*, Mar. 1921, 127–130.)

212. An example of the board responding to feedback from local officers can be found in the introduction of the Senior and Junior departments in the first YLMIA handbook. Related to the Senior class, the writers note "growing demand" for opportunities for leadership and self-expression, whereas the Junior department was introduced to "meet a need which was felt to exist in many stakes." The handbook also notes that "the departments in the Y. L. M. I. A. are the outgrowth of systematic study." (*Y. L. M. I. A. Hand Book* [1923], 28–31.)

213. "The Bee-Hive Girls," *Young Woman's Journal*, Sept. 1919, 496–497; "Junior Course of Study," *Young Woman's Journal*, Sept. 1920, 535.

214. *Y. L. M. I. A. Hand Book* (1923), 31–32.

215. "Age for Entrance into the Bee-Hive Girls' Organization," *Young Woman's Journal*, Jan. 1923, 38. By the 1920s, it had become standard to ordain boys as deacons at age twelve. (Hartley, "From Men to Boys," 115–116.)

216. "Age for Membership in the Y. L. M. I. A.," *Young Woman's Journal*, Oct. 1920, 567–568.

217. *Supplement to the Bee Hive Girls Handbook* (1931), 3–4; *Handbook for the Bee-Hive Girls* (1934), 9.

218. See, for example, "The Savior of the World," *Young Woman's Journal*, Mar. 1926, 214–215.

219. *Y. L. M. I. A. Hand Book* (1923), 32.

220. *Y. L. M. I. A. Hand Book* (1926), 53–54.

221. "Junior Girls," *Young Woman's Journal*, July 1924, 381.

222. *Y. L. M. I. A. Hand Book* (1923), 28–29.

223. "Senior Class Organization," *Young Woman's Journal*, Sept. 1922, 496–497; *Y. L. M. I. A. Hand Book* (1923), 29–30.

224. Ruth May Fox, who was serving as a counselor in the YLMIA general presidency at the time, suggested *Gleaners* as the name for the senior organizations at a general board meeting, and the name was approved the next day. (Young Women General Board, Minutes, vol. 10, 9 May 1923, 209.)

225. "The Gleaners," *Young Woman's Journal*, Aug. 1923, 453–454.

226. "The Beginnings of the Gleaner Organization," *Young Woman's Journal*, Sept. 1925, 585.

227. "Sheaf for 1927–28," *Young Woman's Journal*, Aug. 1927, 530–532.

228. Young Women General Board, Minutes, vol. 13, 27 Oct. 1937, 389. This is the earliest reference in YWMIA archives to a sheaf-binding ceremony. However, the earliest reference to sheaf binding, though not indicating an actual ceremony, is a "Sheaf Binding song of the Gleaner Girls" in 1927. ("Y. L. M. I. A.," *Deseret News*, 11 June 1927, sec. 2, p. 8.)

229. *Gleaner Manual* (1937), iv, 227; *Gleaner Manual* (1938), ii; *Program for Junior M Men and Junior Gleaners* (1950), sec. 3, pp. 2, 4; Josephson, *History of the YWMIA*, 79.

230. As an example of such a sheaf-binding ceremony, see "Sixth Ward Gleaner Girls Hold Sheaf Binding Rites," *Daily Herald* (Provo, UT), 4 Dec. 1940, sec. 2, p. 1.

231. The age range for this class also fluctuated for some years.

232. Lucy W. Smith, "Guide Work 1917–18," *Young Woman's Journal*, Aug. 1917, 463.

233. "To Advanced Senior Class Work Committees," *Young Woman's Journal*, Oct. 1922, 552–553.

234. "M. I. A. Calendar," *Young Woman's Journal*, Aug. 1923, 453.

235. "Advanced Senior Class, Attention!," *Young Woman's Journal*, Dec. 1923, 673.

236. "Advanced Senior Class, Attention!," *Young Woman's Journal*, Oct. 1923, 576; "Attention Advanced Senior Workers," *Young Woman's Journal*, Nov. 1923, 616.

237. "Is Religion Still Being Taught in the M. I. A.?," *Young Woman's Journal*, Oct. 1928, 664.

238. *Hand Book of the Young Men's and Young Ladies' Mutual Improvement Associations* (1928), 5–11. This

handbook incorporated and added to material from earlier manuals. Much of the recreational theory was also found in *Recreation Organization and Leadership: Official Recreation Guide* (Salt Lake City: MIA General Boards, 1926). Richard Ian Kimball calls the recreational program laid out in the 1920s the "ideological apex of Mormon religious recreation." (Kimball, *Sports in Zion*, 48.)

239. *Hand Book of the Young Men's and Young Ladies' Mutual Improvement Associations* (1928), 30.

240. The full committee was Ephraim E. Ericksen, Nicholas G. Morgan, Heber C. Iverson, James Gunn McKay, W. O. Robinson, Martha G. Smith, Emily C. Adams, Charlotte Stewart, Elen Wallace, Elsie T. Brandley, Vida F. Clawson, and Elva Moss. (*Hand Book of the Young Men's and Young Ladies' Mutual Improvement Associations* [1928], 52.)

241. "Change in the Personnel of the General Board," *Young Woman's Journal*, Aug. 1914, 512; Lally, "Life and Educational Contributions," 19–25.

242. Young Women General Board, Minutes, vol. 9, 17 Apr. 1921, 417.

243. Charlotte Stewart, "Putting Over the Recreational Program," *Improvement Era*, Aug. 1923, 924.

244. Ericksen, *Memories and Reflections*, 83–88; Kenney, "E. E. Ericksen," 16–27; see also "Dr. Ephraim Ericksen, Former Dean at U., Dies," *Salt Lake Tribune*, 24 Dec. 1967, C5; Simpson, *American Universities*, 86–90; and Walker, Whittaker, and Allen, *Mormon History*, 39–40.

245. *Hand Book of the Young Men's and Young Ladies' Mutual Improvement Associations* (1928), 16.

246. *Hand Book of the Young Men's and Young Ladies' Mutual Improvement Associations* (1928), 16–17.

247. *Hand Book of the Young Men's and Young Ladies' Mutual Improvement Associations* (1928), 19.

248. *Hand Book of the Young Men's and Young Ladies' Mutual Improvement Associations* (1928), 46.

249. *Hand Book of the Young Men's and Young Ladies' Mutual Improvement Associations* (1928), 10–11.

250. *Hand Book of the Young Men's and Young Ladies' Mutual Improvement Associations* (1928), 18.

251. *Hand Book of the Young Men's and Young Ladies' Mutual Improvement Associations* (1928), 9–10.

252. *Hand Book of the Young Men's and Young Ladies' Mutual Improvement Associations* (1928), 58–67.

253. *Hand Book of the Young Men's and Young Ladies' Mutual Improvement Associations* (1928), 94–95.

254. YMMIA Minutes, vol. 26, 12 Sept. 1928, 184.

255. *Hand Book of the Young Men's and Young Ladies' Mutual Improvement Associations* (1928), 71. The Bee-Hive manual had reflected this term a decade earlier, and it seems to have arisen at least by the 1890s. (*Hand Book for the Bee-Hive Girls* [1915], 4; "Mutual Improvement," *Young Woman's Journal*, Sept. 1892, 565.)

256. Ruth May Fox, "The Birthday of the Women's General Boards," *Young Woman's Journal*, June 1928, 393–395.

257. "The June Conference," *Young Woman's Journal*, July 1929, 477.

258. Elsie Talmage Brandley, Autobiographical Sketch, in Brandley, Journal, 1933–1935.

259. Elmina Taylor had mentioned the possibility of publishing a joint paper with the YMMIA in 1896. (Young Women General Board, Minutes, vol. 2, 5 Oct. 1896, 66.)

260. *Improvement Era Semi-centennial Year Book*, 1; "Financial," 6 May 1929, *Improvement Era*, Proposed Campaign, 1929, CHL.

261. "New Size and Style," 6 May 1929, *Improvement Era*, Proposed Campaign, 1929, CHL.

262. Young Women General Board, Minutes, vol. 11, 8 May 1929, 484.

263. Young Women General Board, Minutes, vol. 11, 14 May 1929, 487.

264. Young Women General Board, Minutes, vol. 11, 15 May 1929, 488.

265. Agnes S. Campbell, "Young Woman's Journal," *Young Woman's Journal*, Oct. 1929, 683.

266. See "The Era in Every Home," *Improvement Era*, Sept. 1929, 948.

267. Elsie Talmage Brandley, Autobiographical Sketch, in Brandley, Journal, 1933–1935.

268. Tingey had been appointed as a counselor to Elmina Taylor in the first general presidency in 1880. (Clarissa A. Beesley, "President Martha H. Tingey," *Young Woman's Journal*, May 1929, 309–311.)

269. Elsie Talmage Brandley, "Ruth May Fox," *Young Woman's Journal*, May 1929, 313, 314.

270. Marba C. Josephson, "Careers of Service to Young Womanhood," *Improvement Era*, Dec. 1937, 790–791. Cannon's father was Heber J. Grant.

271. May Booth Talmage, "Lucy Grant Cannon," *Young Woman's Journal*, May 1929, 317–319; Young Women General Board, Minutes, vol. 9, 7 Feb. 1918, 14; 8 June 1918, 60; 2 Jan. 1919, 96; 3 June 1920, 292; Mary C. Kimball, "Clarissa A. Beesley," *Young Woman's Journal*, May 1929, 321–322; Alexander, "Between Revivalism," 30, 32.

272. "Annual Statistical and Financial Report of the Y. L. M. I. A.," *Young Woman's Journal*, Nov. 1928, 746–747; Young Women General Board, Minutes, vol. 11, 17 Oct. 1928, 402.

273. Lucy W. Smith, "Youth's Heritage," *Young Woman's Journal*, Feb. 1929, 105.

274. "Greetings," *Young Woman's Journal*, June 1925, 336.

CHAPTER 4: MODERN MUTUALS, 1930–1948

1. "Priesthood Celebrate Centenary; Hear Message," *Deseret News*, 7 Apr. 1930, 1.
2. Ruth May Fox, "The Heavenly Gift," *Improvement Era*, Apr. 1930, 381.
3. Davidson, *Our Latter-day Hymns*, 284–285.
4. Warwick C. Lamoreaux, "The Challenge," *Improvement Era*, Aug. 1930, 687.
5. "The June Conference," *Improvement Era*, June 1930, 573; "M Men–Gleaner Session of the June Conference, 1930," *Improvement Era*, Aug. 1930, 707.
6. "M Men–Gleaner Session of the June Conference, 1930," *Improvement Era*, Aug. 1930, 707.
7. "A Centennial Gathering of Youth," *Improvement Era*, Aug. 1930, 684.
8. Bennion, *Gleaning*, 123; see also "The Project," *Improvement Era*, Oct. 1930, 823. B. H. Roberts's *Comprehensive History of the Church of Jesus Christ of Latter-day Saints: Century I* was a monumental project published on the church's centennial, 6 April 1930. (Walker, Whittaker, and Allen, *Mormon History*, 35–37; Douglas D. Alder, "Comprehensive History of the Church," in *Encyclopedia of Mormonism*, 1:303–304.)
9. Bennion, *Gleaning*, 123.
10. Bennion, *Gleaning*, 124.
11. Cadet notebook fillers were sold two for five cents, for example, as were writing tablets. ("ZCMI Downstairs Dept. Store," *Deseret News*, 1 Nov. 1934, 20.)
12. Bennion, *Gleaning*, 124.
13. Eleanor Larsen, Treasures of Truth, [1], [2], [7], [8], Mette and Soren Larsen Family Collection, CHL.
14. South Davis Stake, Gleaners' Treasure Book, CHL; "Funeral of Miss Pack," *Deseret Evening News*, 16 Aug. 1905, 2; see also "Young Girl's Sudden Death," *Deseret Evening News*, 14 Aug. 1905, 1.
15. Jefferson Ward, Treasures of Truth, CHL; see also Stapley and Wright, "Female Ritual Healing," 1–85.
16. *Building a Life*, 88–89.
17. *Hand Book for the Bee-Hive Girls* (1931), 10, 20.
18. "Contest Events for Bee-Hive Girls," *Improvement Era*, Jan. 1931, 169.
19. *1940–1941 Junior Manual*, 45.
20. *Junior Manual, 1947–48*, 32.
21. See *Mia Maid Manual, 1950–51*, sec. 3, p. 15.
22. Plewe, *Mapping Mormonism*, 104–105, 132, 144–145; see also Arrington and Bitton, *Mormon Experience*, 139–140.
23. The first chapel in Germany was dedicated in 1929; the first in Denmark in 1931. The Washington Chapel, Washington, DC—dedicated in 1933—was the first in the eastern United States since the 1840s. ("The New German-Austrian Chapel," *Latter-day Saints' Millennial Star*, 5 Sept. 1929, 573; Minert, *In Harm's Way*, 310; "Widtsoes Leave Saturday for N. Y.," *Salt Lake Tribune*, 23 May 1931, 26; Historic American Buildings Survey, *Washington Chapel*, 1, 2.)
24. Ardis Parshall, email to James Goldberg, 1 Nov. 2021.
25. Louise Puenzieux, "Une Guerison Miraculeuse," French Mission President's Files, CHL.
26. Louise Puenzieux, "Une Guerison Miraculeuse," French Mission President's Files, CHL. The quotes are translated from the original French.
27. Louise Puenzieux, "Une Guerison Miraculeuse," French Mission President's Files, CHL.
28. *Handbuch für die Bienenkorbmädchen* [Handbook for the Bee-Hive Girls], Helga Meyer Collection, CHL.
29. Meyer and Galli, *Under a Leafless Tree*, 54. Helga's experiences as a Bee-Hive Girl are also found in *Saints*, 3:346–349.
30. *Handbuch für die Bienenkorbmädchen*, Helga Meyer Collection, CHL.
31. "First Group of Bee-Hive Girls on European Continent," *Young Woman's Journal*, Sept. 1927, 594; *Handbuch für die Bienenkorbmädchen*, 18.
32. *Handbuch für die Bienenkorbmädchen*, 18–19.
33. *Hand Book for the Bee-Hive Girls* (1927), 52; *Handbuch für die Bienenkorbmädchen*, 136–139.
34. *Handbuch für die Bienenkorbmädchen*, 140.
35. "Basel Branch, Switzerland," *Young Woman's Journal*, Sept. 1927, 594.
36. "Conference of the Presidents of Relief Societies," 28–29.
37. See *Bijenkorfmeisjes Handboek: Kerk van Jezus Christus van de Heiligen der Laatste Dagen* (Rotterdam: Nederlandsche Zending, 1934); and *Håndbok for Bi-kube Piker i Unge Kvinners Gjensidige Utdannelses Forening* (Oslo: Norske Misjon, 1934).
38. Amy Brown Lyman, "General Conference of the Relief Society," *Relief Society Magazine*, Dec. 1916, 663; "Mrs. Lalene H. Hart," *Relief Society Magazine*, June 1931, 335–338.
39. "Conference of the Presidents of Relief Societies," 16–17.

40. "Conference on Womans Activity," 6.
41. "Conference on Womans Activity," 7–9.
42. Conkling, "Members without a Church," 191–214.
43. Tullis, "Shepherd to Mexico's Saints," 127–138.
44. Mexican Mission Manuscript History and Historical Reports, vol. 4, pt. 2, 9 May 1926; vol. 5, pt. 1, 24 Sept. 1934; Shepherd and Shepherd, *Mormon Passage*, 100; Tullis, "Shepherd to Mexico's Saints," 137.
45. "1,200 Mexican Members Return to Church during Pres. Smith's Visit," *Church News*, 15 June 1946, 1, 4.
46. Bureau of Economic and Business Research, "Measures of Economic Changes in Utah," 23; Alexander, *Utah*, 311, 312, 315, 317. Twenty-five banks in Utah failed between 1929 and 1933.
47. Mintz, *Huck's Raft*, 234.
48. Peterson and Cannon, *Awkward State of Utah*, 271–272.
49. Savage, *Teenage*, 277–280.
50. YMMIA Minutes, vol. 28, 8 Nov. 1933, 60.
51. See Ericksen, *Memories and Reflections*, 83–105.
52. "Salt Lake Writer Taken by Death," *Salt Lake Tribune*, 3 Aug. 1935, 26.
53. Quinn, *Elder Statesman*, 49–65.
54. Brandley, Journal, 26 Oct. 1933.
55. Young Women General Board, Minutes, vol. 12, 13 Nov. 1933, 520, 522.
56. See *Hand Book of the Young Men's and Young Ladies' Mutual Improvement Associations* (1928), 85–86.
57. Members of the Survey Committee from the YLMIA were Ruth May Fox, Lucy Grant Cannon, and Clarissa A. Beesley (the YLMIA presidency), Rose Wallace Bennett, Rachel G. Taylor, Grace C. Neslen, Elsie Talmage Brandley, and Elsie Hogan. (Young Women General Board, Minutes, vol. 12, 22 Nov. 1933, 523; see also Young Women General Board, Minutes, vol. 12, 15 Nov. 1933, 519; 20 Dec. 1933, 529.)
58. YMMIA Minutes, vol. 28, Jan.–Feb. 1934, 81–154.
59. Brandley, Journal, 3 Jan. 1934.
60. Brandley, Journal, 6 Feb. 1934.
61. Brandley, Journal, 20 Feb. 1934.
62. YMMIA Minutes, vol. 28, 7 Feb. 1934, 94–95.
63. YMMIA Minutes, vol. 28, 24 Jan. 1934, 85.
64. YMMIA Minutes, vol. 28, 7 Feb. 1934, 89–90.
65. YMMIA Minutes, vol. 28, 28 Feb. 1934, 132.
66. YMMIA Minutes, vol. 28, 28 Feb. 1934, 112, 113, 117, 140–141.
67. YMMIA Minutes, vol. 28, 28 Feb. 1934, 123.
68. YMMIA Minutes, vol. 28, 28 Feb. 1934, 112.
69. YMMIA Minutes, vol. 28, 28 Feb. 1934, 141.
70. YMMIA Minutes, vol. 28, 7 Feb. 1934, 100.
71. YMMIA Minutes, vol. 28, 28 Feb. 1934, 147.
72. YMMIA Minutes, vol. 28, 7 Feb. 1934, 98.
73. YMMIA Minutes, vol. 28, 7 and 28 Feb. 1934, 85, 118–119, 123. Arthur L. Beeley, John F. Bowman, and Rose W. Bennett made this assertion.
74. YMMIA Minutes, vol. 28, 7 and 28 Feb. 1934, 88–90, 151.
75. For more on fundamentalist views and the fundamentalist-modernist controversy, see Reid et al., *Dictionary of Christianity in America*, 461–468, 646–648.
76. McDannell, "Christianity in the United States," 236–251; Handy, "American Religious Depression," 3–16; Carpenter, "Fundamentalist Institutions," 62–75.
77. Marty, *Modern American Religion*, 304.
78. Brandley, Journal, 24 Feb. 1934.
79. YMMIA Minutes, vol. 28, 7 Feb. 1934, 102.
80. YMMIA Minutes, vol. 28, 28 Feb. 1934, 119–122.
81. YMMIA Minutes, vol. 28, 14 Mar. 1934, 169.
82. "Report of the Committee on M. I. A. Survey," 2. Versions of the report in the YLMIA and YMMIA minutes were rendered verbatim but were paginated differently due to the respective secretaries' formatting when the report was typed into the record.
83. "Report of the Committee on M. I. A. Survey," 4.
84. "Report of the Committee on M. I. A. Survey," 5.
85. "Report of the Committee on M. I. A. Survey," 11.
86. YMMIA Minutes, vol. 28, 14 Mar. 1934, 169.
87. YMMIA Minutes, vol. 28, 21 Mar. 1934, 173.

88. Elsie Talmage Brandley, "The Religious Crisis of Today," *Improvement Era*, Aug. 1934, 467–468, 496; see also Reeder and Holbrook, *At the Pulpit*, 135–143.

89. See Young Women General Board, Minutes, vol. 13, 2 May 1934, 39.

90. Melvin J. Ballard, "Morality and the New Day," *Improvement Era*, Sept. 1934, 515–516, 527.

91. Oscar A. Kirkham, "Latter-day Saint Youth and the New Day," *Improvement Era*, Aug. 1934, 463–464, 497; Joseph Fielding Smith, "The Glorious Possibilities for Us of the Religious Crisis," *Improvement Era*, Aug. 1934, 466.

92. "M. I. A. Slogan—1934–35," *Deseret News*, 2 June 1934, Church section, 3.

93. Clarissa A. Beesley, "New Phases of Our Program for 1934–35," *Improvement Era*, Sept. 1934, 558.

94. Clarissa A. Beesley, "New Phases of Our Program for 1934–35," *Improvement Era*, Sept. 1934, 557–558.

95. See Young Women General Board, Minutes, vol. 12, 14 Sept. 1932, 399; vol. 13, 21 Mar. 1934, 21.

96. Young Women General Board, Minutes, vol. 13, 28 Mar. 1934, 25.

97. YLMIA General Presidency to Heber J. Grant and Anthony W. Ivins, 24 May 1934, in Young Women General Board, Minutes, vol. 13, inserted between pp. 24 and 25.

98. Heber J. Grant and Anthony W. Ivins to Ruth May Fox, Lucy Grant Cannon, and Clarissa A. Beesley, 29 May 1934, in Young Women General Board, Minutes, vol. 13, inserted between pp. 24 and 25.

99. "Comments on Church News of the Week," *Deseret News*, 2 June 1934, Church section, 8.

100. "Report of the Committee on M. I. A. Survey," 20.

101. "Objectives," *M. I. A. Leader*, Aug. 1934, 1.

102. Brandley, Journal, 14 Sept.–6 Oct. 1934.

103. Brandley, Journal, 15–17 Sept. 1934.

104. Brandley, Journal, 20 Sept. 1934.

105. "Flashes from the Missions," *M. I. A. Leader*, Jan. 1938, 3.

106. "Music Festivals," *M. I. A. Leader*, Apr. 1938, 2.

107. R. DeRell Litster, "M. I. A. for the Blind," *Improvement Era*, June 1940, 369.

108. Adelaide Thompson Poananga, "How It's Done in New Zealand," *Improvement Era*, Mar. 1938, 156, 176.

109. Mexican Mission Manuscript History and Historical Reports, vol. 5, pt. 1, 14–15 Dec. 1935.

110. Guillermo Balderas, Life History, 1985, 13–19, Guillermo Balderas Papers, CHL; Balderas Family History, 14–15, Balderas Family Scrapbooks, CHL; see also correspondence between Guillermo Balderas and Porfiria Monroy, 1935–1937, Balderas Family Scrapbooks, CHL.

111. Parker and Jensen, "*Hui Tau*," 123, 127.

112. Adelaide Thompson Poananga, "How It's Done in New Zealand," *Improvement Era*, Mar. 1938, 156, 176.

113. "What One Mission District Has Done," *M. I. A. Leader*, Mar. 1938, 3–4.

114. "Mutual Messages," *Improvement Era*, Aug. 1938, 496.

115. "Germany Holds M. I. A. 'Echo of Joy' Festival," *Deseret News*, 18 July 1936, Church section, 2; see also "Mutual Messages," *Improvement Era*, Sept. 1937, 582; and Young Women General Board, Minutes, vol. 14, 16 Mar. 1938, 21.

116. "Holland Holds Small Replica of Salt Lake's Annual June Conference," *Deseret News*, 27 June 1936, Church section, 8.

117. "The Dawn of a New Day," *Latter-day Saints' Millennial Star*, 20 June 1935, 388.

118. See, for example, "An Anniversary," *Latter-day Saints' Millennial Star*, 11 Apr. 1935, 238; and "In Reminiscence," *Latter-day Saints' Millennial Star*, 2 May 1935, 287.

119. David O. McKay, "Teaching the Word of Wisdom," *Latter-day Saints' Millennial Star*, 9 Oct. 1924, 649; Hilda Payne, "Every Little Helps," *Latter-day Saints' Millennial Star*, 24 Oct. 1914, 684–685.

120. For more on flannel dances, see Horwood, *Keeping Up Appearances*, 95–96.

121. "The Dawn of a New Day," *Latter-day Saints' Millennial Star*, 20 June 1935, 388–391, 396–397; Joseph J. Cannon, "A Glorious Occasion," *Latter-day Saints' Millennial Star*, 20 June 1935, 392–393.

122. "The Dawn of a New Day," *Latter-day Saints' Millennial Star*, 20 June 1935, 388–391; Wendell J. Ashton, "Memories of Kidderminster," *Latter-day Saints' Millennial Star*, 11 June 1936, 371–374.

123. "President Grant's European Itinerary," *Improvement Era*, Aug. 1937, 467; Richard R. Lyman, "The Visit of President Grant," *Latter-day Saints' Millennial Star*, 24 June 1937, 392–393; Parry D. Sorensen, "President Grant Arrives," *Latter-day Saints' Millennial Star*, 1 July 1937, 405.

124. Lucy Grant Cannon, "The Log of a European Tour," *Improvement Era*, Aug. 1937, 482.

125. Lucy Grant Cannon, "The Log of a European Tour," *Improvement Era*, Sept. 1937, 578, 590; Parry D. Sorensen, "After One Hundred Years in Britain," *Improvement Era*, Sept. 1937, 576.

126. Parry D. Sorensen, "Centennial Memories," and "Achievement Awards," *Latter-day Saints' Millennial Star*, 19 Aug. 1937, 533–535, 538–541, 543–544.

127. Young Women General Board, Minutes, vol. 13, 25 Aug. 1937, 374.

128. Lucy Grant Cannon, "The Log of a European Tour," *Improvement Era*, Nov. 1937, 708.

129. Marba C. Josephson, "Service to the Young Women of the Church," *Improvement Era*, July 1948, 430; Young Women General Board, Minutes, vol. 13, 3 and 20 Nov. 1937, 391, 400.

130. "Mrs. Goddard, Mrs. Williams Win Positions," *Deseret News*, 6 Nov. 1937, 1, 8.

131. Josephson, *History of the YWMIA*, 333–334.

132. Marba C. Josephson, "Service to the Young Women of the Church," *Improvement Era*, July 1948, 430.

133. Hugh B. Brown, "A Farewell to Our Missionaries," and "A Message to the Saints and Friends of the Church in Great Britain," *Latter-day Saints' Millennial Star*, 14 Sept. 1939, 578–579, 584–585.

134. "All European Missionaries to Return to United States," *Deseret News*, 26 Sept. 1939, 1.

135. "War Forces Church Change," *Deseret News*, 29 Jan. 1940, 9.

136. "Brev fra den Norske Ungdomsforening," *Skandinaviens Stjerne*, Feb. 1943, 33.

137. Norman Dunn, "Birmingham District Whitsuntide M.I.A. Convention," *Latter-day Saints' Millennial Star*, 6 June 1940, 432.

138. "The New M.I.A. Boards," *Latter-day Saints' Millennial Star*, 11 Feb. 1943, 95.

139. "District Activities," *Millennial Star*, Aug. 1945, 242; "District Activities," *Millennial Star*, June 1945, 185.

140. Schrum, *Some Wore Bobby Sox*, 12–13.

141. Schrum, *Some Wore Bobby Sox*, 4, 18–19.

142. Schrum, *Some Wore Bobby Sox*, 12, 15.

143. *M. I. A. Manual for Executives* (1939), 18–19, 28.

144. *M. I. A. Manual for Executives* (1939), 28, 34–37, 115. Honor Night was sometimes also called Honor Day.

145. Young Women General Board, Minutes, vol. 14, 30 Mar. 1938, 25; "Creative Work in Stakes and Wards," *M. I. A. Leader*, Nov. 1938, 5; "Theme Festival Week," *M. I. A. Leader*, Nov. 1938, 5; "May 2nd—Ward Theme Festival and Honor Night," *M. I. A. Leader*, Nov. 1938, 6; *M. I. A. Manual for Executives* (1939), 21–22.

146. "Tenth Ward Sets Theme Festival," *Herald-Journal* (Logan, UT), 30 Apr. 1940, 8.

147. Lucy Grant Cannon, Helen S. Williams, and Verna W. Goddard to Stake Executives of YWMIA, 20 Feb. 1942, in Young Women General Board, Minutes, vol. 15, p. 29.

148. "Y. W. M. I. A. Executives and Gleaner Leaders," *M. I. A. Leader*, Nov. 1940, 3.

149. All requirements were laid out in the *M. I. A. Leader* in 1940, with some minor clarifications provided in 1941. ("Y. W. M. I. A. Executives and Gleaner Leaders," *M. I. A. Leader*, Nov. 1940, 3–4; "Changes in Golden Gleaner Plan," *M. I. A. Leader*, May 1941, 2.)

150. "Golden Gleaner Event Sunday," *Times-News* (Nephi, UT), 3 May 1945, 1; see also "South Ward Girls Bind Sheaf First," *Manti (UT) Messenger*, 21 Mar. 1941, 1; "Golden Gleaner Awards Presented to Nine," *Voice of Sharon* (Provo, UT), 17 Apr. 1941, 1.

151. "Sixth Ward Gleaner Girls Hold Sheaf Binding Rites," *Daily Herald* (Provo, UT), 4 Dec. 1940, sec. 2, p. 1; see also Widtsoe, *Your Questions Answered*, 130; and *Program for Junior M Men and Junior Gleaners* (1950), sec. 3, p. 36.

152. Christensen, "Impact of World War II," 509; Powell, *Utah Remembers World War II*, xi–xii.

153. She is better known by her later married name, Emma Lou Thayne. ("Emma Lou Warner Thayne," *Deseret News*, 10 Dec. 2014, B6.)

154. See, for example, "Three Utahns Reported as Casualties," *Salt Lake Tribune*, 7 June 1944, pt. 2, p. 15; "2 Utahns Die in War Zones," *Salt Lake Tribune*, 8 June 1944, pt. 2, p. 13; and "Killed, Missing in Battle Zones," *Salt Lake Tribune*, 9 June 1944, pt. 2, p. 17.

155. Bruce Weber, "Homer Warner, 90, Pioneering Physiologist," *New York Times*, 14 Dec. 2012, B10.

156. Meyer, "Emma Lou Thayne," 185; see also Thayne, *Place of Knowing*, 173.

157. Mintz, *Huck's Raft*, 256–260; Kennedy, *Freedom from Fear*, 747–748; Adams, *Best War Ever*, 127.

158. Roger D. Launius, "World War II in Utah," in Powell, *Utah History Encyclopedia*, 646–647.

159. Allen, "Crisis on the Home Front," 409; Geddes, *Migration*, 7.

160. Roger D. Launius, "World War II in Utah," in Powell, *Utah History Encyclopedia*, 646–647.

161. Geddes, *Migration*, 7–8.

162. Mary Lue Knell McCune, Personal History, private possession.

163. Mary Lue Knell McCune, Personal History, private possession.

164. "An Urgent Message," *M. I. A. Leader*, Jan. 1942, 2–3.

165. Heber J. Grant, J. Reuben Clark, and David O. McKay, "Notice to Church Officers," *Improvement Era*, Feb. 1942, 74; "Ward Conventions," *M. I. A. Leader*, Aug. 1942, 2.

166. *M. I. A. Manual for Executives* (1943), 45–48; Heber J. Grant, J. Reuben Clark, and David O. McKay, "Conference Notice," *Improvement Era*, Oct. 1942, 640.

167. Allen, "Crisis on the Home Front," 407, 410–411.

168. On 1 April 1920, the First Presidency and Council of the Twelve approved "the Bee-Hive House to be used as a girls' home." (Young Women General Board, Minutes, vol. 9, 8 Apr. 1920, 265; see also Young Women General Board, Minutes, vol. 9, 17 June 1920, 305–306.)

169. Young Women General Board, Minutes, vol. 15, 28 Apr. 1943, 120–121.

170. "They All Belong to Us!," *M. I. A. Leader*, Oct. 1942, 1–2.

171. "Membership Plans in the Y. W. M. I. A.," *M. I. A. Leader*, Oct. 1942, 2–3.

172. Young Women General Board, Minutes, vol. 15, 9 Feb. 1944, 178.

173. YWMIA General Presidency to "M.I.A. Girls," Feb. 1944, in Young Women General Board, Minutes, vol. 15, 9 Feb. 1944, 179.

174. *M. I. A. Manual for Executives* (1939), 47–48.

175. See Young Women General Board, Minutes, vol. 11, 17 Nov. 1926, 123; 19 Jan. 1927, 146; vol. 13, 8 Aug. 1934, 63.

176. "Where Are Our Hundred and Fifty Thousand?," *M. I. A. Leader*, Mar. 1944, 3.

177. See YLMIA General Presidency to YLMIA Stake Presidents, 19 Mar. 1932, in Young Women General Board, Minutes, vol. 12, pp. 333, 335; Young Women General Board, Minutes, vol. 12, 9 Apr. 1932, 341; "Pamphlets on Tobacco and Liquor," *M. I. A. Leader*, Jan. 1937, 3; "Mormon Youth Program Reinforces Spirituality," *Deseret News*, 7 June 1941, Church section, 1; and "Clean Life Scrolls Given to President," *Deseret News*, 30 May 1942, Church section, 1. Herbert Maw of the YMMIA general board introduced the Word of Wisdom theme at the 1931 June Conference. (Young Women General Board, Minutes, vol. 12, 12 June 1931, 218.)

178. "Special Folder for Y. W. M. I. A. Girls," *M. I. A. Leader*, May 1941, 3; Alvin G. Pack, "New Pioneers— On the March," *Improvement Era*, July 1941, 427.

179. Adams, *Best War Ever*, 124–125; Pfau, "Allotment Annies," 100, 105–106.

180. Melvin J. Ballard, "Morality and the New Day," *Improvement Era*, Sept. 1934, 515.

181. "An Urgent Message," *M. I. A. Leader*, Jan. 1942, 2.

182. Richard L. Evans, "For Tomorrow We Die," *Improvement Era*, Aug. 1942, 512.

183. Marba C. Josephson, "Challenge to Youth," *Improvement Era*, Aug. 1942, 512.

184. D'Emilio and Freedman, *Intimate Matters*, 178–180, 261–262.

185. Hugh B. Brown, "To the Girls behind the Men behind the Guns," *Improvement Era*, Feb. 1943, 80–82.

186. Young Women General Board, Minutes, vol. 15, 9 Dec. 1942, 89.

187. See Hiltner, *Taking Leave*, 1–9.

188. "Women's Leader Urges Child Welfare Program," *Salt Lake Telegram*, 16 June 1943, sec. 2, p. 13; see also Young Women General Board, Minutes, vol. 15, 28 Apr. 1943, 120–121.

189. In Utah, carnal knowledge of a female between thirteen and eighteen years old, now called *statutory rape*, has been a felony since at least 1898. (*Revised Statutes of the State of Utah*, 902; see also "Authorities Explain Laws Governing Cases of Assault," *Salt Lake Telegram*, 15 Jan. 1943, sec. 2, p. 17; Smith, "Rape Law," 228; Cocca, *Jailbait*, 9–28; and State v. Tellay, 100 Utah 25, 110 P.2d 342 [1941].)

190. Smith, "Rape Law," 228. Reports of immoral conduct (defined as sexual behavior that could spread venereal disease) were also on the rise. ("Is Your Daughter a 'Victory Girl?,'" *Deseret News*, 14 Feb. 1944, 4.)

191. Marba C. Josephson, "Challenge to Youth," *Improvement Era*, Aug. 1942, 512.

192. Young Women General Board, Minutes, vol. 15, 28 Apr. 1943, 120–121.

193. Lucy Grant Cannon and George Q. Morris to Harold B. Lee, 5 Nov. 1942, in Young Women General Board, Minutes, vol. 15, pp. 81–82; Young Women General Board, Minutes, vol. 15, 4 Nov. 1942, 78.

194. Meyer, "Emma Lou Thayne," 185.

195. [Heber C. Kimball] to William Kimball, 21 Dec. 1854, in Historian's Office, Letterpress Copybooks, vol. 1, p. 50; Heber C. Kimball to Franklin D. Richards, 31 Aug. 1855, in *Latter-day Saints' Millennial Star*, 17 Nov. 1855, 730–731; Robison, "Historic Structures Report," pt. 2, pp. 13–14.

196. Robison, "Historic Structures Report," pt. 2, pp. 15–16; "In Lion House and Social Hall," *Deseret Evening News*, 15 Sept. 1900, 20; "Lion House Has Been Remodeled and Now Contains a Modern Cooking School," *Salt Lake Herald*, 24 Mar. 1907, 3; Harrison R. Merrill, "Welcome, Come In," *Improvement Era*, May 1933, 394–397.

197. Young Women General Board, Minutes, vol. 12, 7 Dec. 1932, 424.

198. "Lion House Opens as Center Jan. 3," *Deseret News*, 24 Dec. 1932, Church section, 2.

199. *Y. L. M. I. A. Lion House Social Center*, [2]–[4].

200. "Defense Work at Lion House Attracts Many," *Deseret News*, 24 Jan. 1942, Society section, 3; "Lion House Asks Women Join Clubs," *Deseret News*, 21 Mar. 1942, Society section, 2; "Lion House Social Center Schedules Week's Events," *Salt Lake Tribune*, 11 Jan. 1942, 6D.

201. "Some Ingenious Projects," *Improvement Era*, Jan. 1943, 50.

202. "Gleaners," *Improvement Era*, Apr. 1943, 243.

203. "M.I.A. Day, May 11," *Improvement Era*, May 1943, 302.

204. Clarissa A. Beesley, "M.I.A. Offering to Youth," *Improvement Era*, Nov. 1943, 702.

205. "The Wartime Summer Way for M.I.A.," *Improvement Era*, May 1943, 302.

206. See "The Next Steps in M. I. A. for Ward Officers," *M. I. A. Leader*, Apr. 1942, 1.

207. "Summer Recreation Leadership Institute," *M. I. A. Leader*, May 1936, [2]; Young Women General Board, Minutes, vol. 13, 17 June 1936, 285; "Mutual Messages," *Improvement Era*, May 1936, 313; see also Young Women General Board, Minutes, vol. 13, 3 Mar. 1937, 335.

208. Young Women General Board, Minutes, vol. 14, 3 Apr. 1940, 165.

209. "Summer Camping for Girls," *M. I. A. Leader*, Apr. 1940, 4; "Value of Summer Camps for Girls Discussed at Y.W.M.I.A. Session," *Deseret News*, 7 Apr. 1941, 6.

210. "Mutual Dell Outing Open Monday," *Lehi (UT) Sun*, 18 June 1942, [8]; "Outing Dates Announced for Mutual Dell," *Lehi Sun*, 25 June 1942, [5]; "A. F. Wards at Mutual Dell," *American Fork (UT) Citizen*, 3 July 1942, [4].

211. *Y. W. M. I. A. Camp-O-Rama* (Salt Lake City: YWMIA General Board, 1940).

212. *Cooking Out-of-Doors: A Supplement to Camp-O-Rama* (Salt Lake City: YWMIA General Board, 1947); see also "Camp Supplement," *M. I. A. Leader*, Apr. 1942, 4.

213. *Y. W. M. I. A. Camp-O-Rama* (1940), 5.

214. *Y. W. M. I. A. Camp-O-Rama* (1946), 29–32.

215. *Cooking Out-of-Doors*, 15, 17, 20, 24–25; *Y. W. M. I. A. Camp-O-Rama* (1946), 38–41. One suggestion was to build a tin-can stove—but *Cooking Out-of-Doors* provided no accompanying instructions for how to build such an apparatus.

216. *Y. W. M. I. A. Camp-O-Rama* (1946) 80, 83, 101–102. Examples of these "Indian handcrafts" include headdresses, gourd rattles, beadwork, bows and arrows, totem poles, and other crafts perceived as being part of Native American culture. Pioneer handcraft projects might have included making molasses candy and pioneer dolls.

217. *Camptivities*, 1.

218. Young Women General Board, Minutes, vol. 15, 24 Mar. 1943, 110; 19 Apr. 1944, 193–195. YWMIA general board discussions included a yearly report on certain members' attendance at a Pacific Camp Convention held in California each year. Those reporting noted that camp was a way to prevent juvenile delinquency, help youth adversely affected by the war, and instill leadership and other desirable qualities in young people.

219. Young Women General Board, Minutes, vol. 15, 16 Aug. 1944, 217.

220. *Camptivities*, 1, 5–7, 12–14, 18, 37.

221. Derr, Cannon, and Beecher, *Women of Covenant*, 310–312; see also Benson, *Labor of Love*, 12–35; and Bergera, "Ezra Taft Benson's 1946 Mission to Europe," 73–112.

222. Kuehne, *Mormons as Citizens of a Communist State*, 367–383.

223. For more on Latter-day Saint assimilation throughout the first half of the twentieth century, see Mauss, *Angel and the Beehive*, 60–101.

224. Stephen L Richards, Address, 6 Oct. 1945, in *One Hundred Sixteenth Semi-annual Conference*, 52.

225. Young Women General Board, Minutes, vol. 16, 9 Jan. 1946, 1, 3. Membership in 1941–42 was 76,867. (Young Women General Board, Minutes, vol. 15, 14 Oct. 1942, 74a.)

226. Young Women General Board, Minutes, vol. 16, 9 Jan. 1946, 3.

227. Young Women General Board, Minutes, vol. 15, 13 June 1945, 285; 19 Sept. 1945, 298.

228. Young Women General Board, Minutes, vol. 16, 20 Jan. 1946, 7.

229. J. Reuben Clark, "Plain Talk to Girls," *Improvement Era*, Aug. 1946, 492–493.

230. Young Women General Board, Minutes, vol. 16, 20 Jan. 1946, 9.

231. "Resume of M.I.A. June Conference," *Improvement Era*, July 1946, 424, 456.

232. George Q. Morris, "Introducing the M.I.A. Theme for 1946–1947," *Improvement Era*, July 1946, 428.

233. See Young Women General Board, Minutes, vol. 16, 20 Jan. 1946, 9.

234. "Bee-hive Girls Plan Church-Wide Camps as Centennial Activity," *Church News*, 8 Mar. 1947, 4.

235. Henry A. Smith, "Mission Activities Will Make Utah Centennial World-Wide," *Church News*, 8 Mar. 1947, 1, 5.

CHAPTER 5: SHOWCASING YOUTH, 1948–1961

1. These and many other activities are evident in Myrna's Treasures of Truth book and in newspaper reports of Wellington and Carbon stake MIA activities. (See, for example, "Wellington Second Ward

Stages Gold and Green Ball," *Sun-Advocate* [Price, UT], 28 Jan. 1954, [9]; "Wellington Second Ward to Hear Seminary Students," *Sun-Advocate*, 18 Mar. 1954, 10; "Stake MIA Speech Festival Ends in Three-Way Tie," *Sun-Advocate*, 13 May 1954, 8; "Wellington MIA Drama Festival Rates Praise," *Sun-Advocate*, 15 Dec. 1955, 7; and "Food and Fun Party Staged by MIA of Wellington 2nd Ward," *Sun-Advocate*, 1 July 1954, 8.)

2. "Wellington MIA Workers Attend Confab," *Sun-Advocate* (Price, UT), 28 June 1956, 3.

3. "The Standards of the Church," *Latter-day Saints' Millennial Star*, 12 Mar. 1942, 171; "The Standards of the Church," *Improvement Era*, Aug. 1957, 594.

4. Patterson, *Grand Expectations*, 61–67.

5. Mintz and Kellogg, *Domestic Revolutions*, 178–180.

6. Mintz, *Huck's Raft*, 285.

7. Mintz, *Huck's Raft*, 267; see also Hine, *Rise and Fall of the American Teenager*, 139–140.

8. Mintz, *Huck's Raft*, 286–295.

9. See "YW Sports-Camp-Games," and "Athletics," *MIA Stake Leader*, Sept. 1959, special insert, [3]; and LaRue C. Longden, "It's Smart to Be a Latter-day Saint," *Improvement Era*, June 1955, 392.

10. Spencer W. Kimball, "A Style of Our Own," *Church News*, 28 Feb. 1951, 5.

11. "The Church Moves On," *Improvement Era*, Mar. 1952, 136.

12. Bertha S. Reeder, Reminiscences, [10], [11], [17], [21].

13. "The Newly Appointed Presidency," *Improvement Era*, July 1948, 477–478; Bertha S. Reeder, interview by Jill C. Mulvay, 29 Apr. 1974, 25; LaRue C. Longden, interview by Jill C. Mulvay, 2 Jan. 1974, 15–16; Florence S. Jacobsen, interview by Gordon Irving, 7 Nov. 1991, 244–246; Ruth Hardy Funk, interview by Gordon Irving, 5 Feb. 1979, 95–97.

14. Young Women General Board, Minutes, vol. 16, 11 Dec. 1946, 77.

15. The issue had been raised in 1934. (See "Report of the Committee on M. I. A. Survey," 25.)

16. "Bee Hive," *MIA Stake Leader*, Apr. 1950, 4; *Handbook for the Bee Hive Girls* (1950), 8. Before 1950, the Bee Hive class included fourteen-year-olds.

17. "Department Suggestions for April Leadership Meeting," *MIA Stake Leader*, Apr. 1950, 2–5.

18. "M.I.A. June Conference 1950," 8, June Conference Files, CHL.

19. *Mia Maid Manual, 1950–51*, sec. 1, p. 8; Young Women General Board, Minutes, vol. 16, 13 Sept. 1950, 369.

20. "Junior Girls to Be Named MIA Maids by General Board," *Church News*, 12 Mar. 1950, 5.

21. See *Mia Maid Manual, 1950–51*, sec. 1, p. 8.

22. "'New MIA Maid Rose' Flower Beautifies Chapel Grounds," *Church News*, 15 May 1954, 6; Hortense Child Smith, interview by Gordon Irving, 30 Nov. 1978, 56–57.

23. *Mia Maid Manual, 1951–52*, sec. 2, pp. 3–4.

24. *Mia Maid Manual, 1950–51*, sec. 1, pp. 15–16.

25. "Wellington MIA Girls Stage Rose Ceremony," *Sun-Advocate* (Price, UT), 10 June 1954, 6.

26. Albert L. Zobell Jr., "A Light to All the World," *Improvement Era*, Aug. 1958, 621.

27. "2 New Departments to Serve Youth Enrolled in MIA Emphasize Activity," *Church News*, 19 Mar. 1950, 5; *Program for Junior M Men and Junior Gleaners* (1950), sec. 3, pp. 33–35.

28. *Mia Maid Manual, 1950–51*, sec. 1, p. 8.

29. *Program for Junior M Men and Junior Gleaners* (1950), sec. 3, p. 33.

30. Young Women General Board, Minutes, vol. 16, 28 June 1950, 359.

31. "Announcing the Program for Latter-day Saint Girls," 10–13. The program also laid out plans for a parallel organization at the stake level.

32. Young Women General Board, Minutes, vol. 16, 18 Jan. 1950, 321.

33. *Mia Maid Manual, 1950–51*, sec. 1, pp. 14–15; Young Women General Board, Minutes, vol. 16, 18 Jan. 1950, 322; *Girls' Program* (1950), 4.

34. *Girls' Program* (1950), 12–13.

35. *Girls' Program* (1950), 5; "Stake Report for Girls (Ages 12 to 19) for October 1950," [1], YWMIA Stake and Mission Reports, CHL.

36. *Girls' Program* (1950), 5.

37. "Stake Report for Girls (Ages 12 to 19) for October 1950," [1]–[2], YWMIA Stake and Mission Reports, CHL; "Stake Report for Girls (Age 12–19) for October 1960," [1]–[4], YWMIA Stake and Mission Reports, CHL.

38. Young Women General Board, Minutes, vol. 16, 14 Sept. 1949, 293–294.

39. *Executive Manual for Officers* (1950), sec. A.

40. Ardeth G. Kapp, interview by Gordon Irving, 14 Dec. 1978, 23. Kapp, who would later serve as Young Women general president, served as a ward YWMIA president in the 1950s.

41. See, for example, *M Man–Gleaner Manual, 1955–1956*, 10–12.

42. *M Man–Gleaner Manual, 1955–1956*, 8–9.

43. *M Man–Gleaner Manual, 1955–1956*, 57–58.

44. *Mia Maid Manual, 1951–52*, sec. 1, pp. 2–3; sec. 2, pp. 3–8.

45. See, for example, *Executive Manual for Officers* (1950), sec. A, pp. 5–26.

46. See *M Man–Gleaner Manual, 1955–1956*, 10–12.

47. *M. I. A. in the Missions*, 3–5.

48. Adam S. Bennion, "MIA Youth Conference West German Mission," *Improvement Era*, Mar. 1957, 148–149.

49. Young Women General Board, Minutes, vol. 17, 6 June 1956, 223; "New Zealand MIA Holds Four-Day Meet," *Church News*, 9 June 1956, 12.

50. Pittsburgh Branch Bulletin, 11 Dec. 1955; 29 Jan 1956; 25 Mar. 1956; 16 Sept. 1956; 1 Nov. [1 Dec.], 1956, Pittsburgh Stake Files, CHL.

51. Pittsburgh Branch, General Minutes, vol. 15, 29 May 1955, 18–19.

52. "Recreation," *MIA Stake Leader*, May 1950, 7; *1951–52 Y.W.M.I.A. Sports Supplement*, 3–7.

53. "Y. W. Sports," *MIA Stake Leader*, Dec. 1953, 5; "Mrs. Reeder Pleased with YWMIA Record," *Church News*, 16 June 1956, 10.

54. Florence S. Jacobsen, interview by Lavina Fielding Anderson, 5 Apr. 1984, 23–24; Bertha S. Reeder, "The Young Women's Mutual Improvement Association," *Improvement Era*, Nov. 1956, 844.

55. Bertha S. Reeder, interview by Jill C. Mulvay, 29 Apr. 1974, 37–38.

56. Ruth Hardy Funk, interview by Gordon Irving, 5 Feb. 1979, 82–83.

57. Bertha S. Reeder, interview by Jill C. Mulvay, 29 Apr. 1974, 38.

58. *Camp Standards*, 9.

59. "Bee Hive," *MIA Stake Leader*, Aug. 1956, 6.

60. Edna K. Pay, "Enjoy Good Food in the Out-of-Doors," *Improvement Era*, July 1953, 546–547.

61. Jack M. Reed, "MIA Opens Camp Institute Today," *Salt Lake Tribune*, 14 June 1950, 12.

62. Lia Davis, interview by Kate Holbrook, 17 Aug. 2021, 6.

63. Ruth Hardy Funk, interviews by Gordon Irving, 5 Feb. 1979, 85–86, 93; 6 Feb. 1979, 116, 118–120.

64. Marba C. Josephson, "Youth in Action," *Improvement Era*, Aug. 1949, 512.

65. "Dance-Drama Festival Thrills Huge Crowd," *Deseret News and Salt Lake Telegram*, 18 June 1956, A5.

66. Young Women General Board, Minutes, vol. 16, 5 Mar. 1952, 454; "Telecasts Feature Stellar Foursomes," *Church News*, 6 Mar. 1954, 12; "M. I. A. June Conference Report, June 11, 12, 13, 14, 1959," June Conference Files, CHL. The first evidence of a telecast of the full June Conference was in 1966. ("1966 June Conference," in Young Women General Board, Minutes, June 1966. For more on the rise of television in American culture, see Livingstone, "Half a Century of Television," 155.)

67. Ruth Hardy Funk, interview by Gordon Irving, 5 Feb. 1979, 85.

68. "Chief Scout Executive Speaks at 7 Departmental Sessions," *Church News*, 21 June 1958, 7.

69. Rebecca Franklin, "A Mighty People in the Rockies," *New York Times*, 3 Apr. 1955, 17, 26, 28, 30, 32, 34; Andrew Hamilton, "Those Amazing Mormons," *Coronet*, Apr. 1952, 26–30.

70. Ruth Hardy Funk, interview by Gordon Irving, 6 Feb. 1979, 121.

71. Hunt, "American Sport Policy," 274; "Induction Statistics," Selective Service System, sss.gov/history -and-records/induction-statistics.

72. Young Women General Board, Minutes, vol. 17, 12 Nov. 1958, 378; "President's Council on Youth Fitness," *Journal of Health, Physical Education, Recreation*, Sept. 1960, 35. Romney had previously addressed the board about how the MIA could further the national cause. (Young Women General Board, Minutes, vol. 17, 22 Oct. 1958, 374.)

73. "Meet the Editors of the Era of Youth," *Improvement Era*, July 1960, 513.

74. Ruth Hardy Funk, interview by Gordon Irving, 5 Feb. 1979, 93–95.

75. Walter King, "Queen of Beauty," *Allied Youth*, Sept. 1952, 3; "Colleen Kay Hutchins, Miss America of 1952," *Listen: A Journal of Better Living*, Apr.–June 1952, 5.

76. Doyle L. Green, "Colleen Hutchins, Miss America, 1952," *Improvement Era*, June 1952, 396.

77. John G. Kinnear, "MIA in the Missions," *Improvement Era*, Sept. 1961, 641; "YM Athletics," *MIA Leader*, Sept. 1963, 6; see also Marba C. Josephson, "Meet Me at Mutual," *Improvement Era*, Jan. 1952, 10.

78. Doyle L. Green, "A Decade of Service 1948–1958," *Improvement Era*, July 1958, 525–526; see also "Thirty Young Converts Spark Activity in Ft. Wayne Branch," *Church News*, 6 July 1957, 8.

79. Josephson, *History of the YWMIA*, 210.

80. "Virtue Is Its Own Reward," 1956, copy at CHL. These posters were part of a campaign entitled "Be Honest with Yourself," which ran from 1956 through 1961. The earliest poster was "Beauty Is More than Skin Deep."

81. Astle and Burton, "History of Mormon Cinema," 78, 80.
82. "How Near to the Angels," *Improvement Era*, Oct. 1956, 765.
83. "How Near to the Angels," *Improvement Era*, Oct. 1956, 764–765.
84. *How Near to the Angels*, 3:12–3:24.
85. *How Near to the Angels*, 19:58–21:30.
86. Mintz and Kellogg, *Domestic Revolutions*, 178–181; "Median Age at First Marriage: 1890 to Present," Historical Marital Status Tables, U.S. Census Bureau, updated 21 Nov. 2023, census.gov.
87. Carol Hinckley Cannon, "If I Were in My Teens," *Improvement Era*, Oct. 1954, 761.
88. Meyerowitz, "Liberal 1950s," 297–319.
89. Patterson, *Grand Expectations*, 353–361.
90. Spencer W. Kimball, "A Style of Our Own," *Church News*, 28 Feb. 1951, 5.
91. Mark E. Petersen, *The Sacredness of Sex: Chastity in Its Holy Mission* (Provo, UT: Brigham Young University, 1953), copy at CHL.
92. Helena M. Williams Allen, interview by Lavina Fielding Anderson, 13 Mar. 1984, 4.
93. Petersen, *Sacredness of Sex*, 8–9; Spencer W. Kimball, "A Style of Our Own," *Church News*, 28 Feb. 1951, 5. Official translations of addresses using these terms, along with other contemporary sources, help reveal their meaning. (Ardis Parshall, "Necking and Petting," *Keepapitchinin* [blog], 12 Feb. 2018, keepapitchinin.org.)
94. *Junior M Men–Junior Gleaner Manual* (1951), sec. 4, p. 44.
95. *Mia Maid Manual, 1952–1953*, 185.
96. *1956–57 Junior M Men Junior Gleaner Manual*, 237; *Mia Maid Manual* (1955), 95. Under Lucy Grant Cannon's leadership, the YWMIA began holding standards nights in the 1940s, spurred by alarming reports that soldiers passing through Salt Lake City had found many young Latter-day Saint women willing to grant sexual favors. In 1961, the standards event for Laurels and their mothers became known as How Laurels Grow, and the event for Mia Maids took on the name Sacred to Me. (Helena M. Williams Allen, interview by Lavina Fielding Anderson, 13 Mar. 1984, 4; "Is Your Daughter a 'Victory Girl?,'" *Deseret News*, 14 Feb. 1944, 4; "Ensign-Laurel," *MIA Stake Leader*, Jan. 1961, 5; "Mia Maid," *MIA Stake Leader*, June 1961, 5.)
97. *1956–57 Junior M Men Junior Gleaner Manual*, 237. These pamphlets bear various names, including *Strength through Clean Living*, *Whene'er My Heart Is Pure*, and *How Near to the Angels*.
98. Teaiwa, "bikinis," 87, 91–92; Tiffany Webber-Hanchett, "Bikini," in *Encyclopedia of Clothing and Fashion*, 155–157.
99. Moapa Stake YWMIA Presidency to Bertha S. Reeder, 6 Dec. 1950, YWMIA Correspondence, CHL.
100. YWMIA General Presidency to David O. McKay, 15 Dec. 1950, YWMIA Correspondence, CHL.
101. Spencer W. Kimball, "A Style of Our Own," *Church News*, 28 Feb. 1951, 5.
102. Petersen, *Sacredness of Sex*, 8.
103. Blakesley, "A Style of Our Own," 22.
104. LaRue C. Longden, "It's Smart to Be a Latter-day Saint," *Improvement Era*, June 1955, 392.
105. *Spirit of the Hive* (1956), 9.
106. *Spirit of the Hive* (1956), 88–89.
107. May, *Homeward Bound*, 150–151, 176–178. These ideas made their way into Relief Society lessons. (See, for example, Annie M. Ellsworth, "Homemaking, the Ideal Career for Women," *Relief Society Magazine*, Jan. 1957, 4–7; and Vesta Barnett, "Work Meeting—Managing a Home," *Relief Society Magazine*, July 1958, 471–472.)
108. A youth program of the United States Department of Agriculture, 4-H originated in the early twentieth century to offer vocational training in farming and housekeeping in rural areas. Myrna and her sister LaRene headed a 4-H group called the Cookerettes. (Buck, "Amusements and Recreations," 69–84; "Fifty-Four Women from Southeast Utah Attend Judging School," *Sun-Advocate* [Price, UT], 12 Aug. 1954, 12; "Achievement Awards to 600 Carbon 4-Hers," *Sun-Advocate*, 11 Nov. 1954, 7.)
109. *Spirit of the Hive* (1954), 229–230, 232.
110. Marba C. Josephson, "If I Were in My Teens," *Improvement Era*, Oct. 1953, 800.
111. Mintz and Kellogg, *Domestic Revolutions*, 181.
112. *Mia Maid Manual, 1958–1959*, 279–287.
113. Iris Parker, "If I Were in My Teens," *Improvement Era*, Aug. 1953, 608–609; see also "On Being a Lady," *Improvement Era*, Sept. 1959, 710–711; and "On Being a Lady, a Shining You," *Improvement Era*, Oct. 1959, 777–778.
114. See, for example, *Mia Maid, 1954–5*, 116–120; *Mia Maid Manual, 1958–1959*, 263–287; and *Mia Maid Manual, 1952–1953*, 194–245.
115. *Mia Maid Manual, 1952–1953*, 212–213.

116. *Mia Maid Manual, 1958–1959*, 273–274.

117. May, "Demographic Portrait," 128.

118. Plewe, *Mapping Mormonism*, 156–157, 174–175.

119. Ruth Hardy Funk, interview by Gordon Irving, 5 Feb. 1979, 87–88.

120. Plewe, *Mapping Mormonism*, 174, 207.

121. Ruth Hardy Funk, interview by Gordon Irving, 5 Feb. 1979, 87–88; "Recreational-Social Event Readied for 7000 Young People," *Church News*, 17 Apr. 1954, 5, 12; "Southern California M I A Conference," *Improvement Era*, Oct. 1954, 714–715, 735.

122. "Southern California M I A Conference," *Improvement Era*, Oct. 1954, 714–715, 735; "16,000 Attend Closing Session of Mormons," *Los Angeles Times*, 9 Aug. 1954, 2.

123. Young Women General Board, Minutes, vol. 17, 30 June 1956, 224i.

124. Young Women General Board, Minutes, vol. 17, 28 Apr. 1954, 69.

125. Young Women General Board, Minutes, vol. 17, 5 Sept. 1956, 226.

126. El Paso 3rd Ward Members, interview by James Goldberg, 20 Sept. 2014, 1, 7–9.

127. El Paso 3rd Ward Members, interview by James Goldberg, 20 Sept. 2014, 15, 22–23.

128. El Paso 3rd Ward Members, interview by James Goldberg, 20 Sept. 2014, 23.

129. Plewe, *Mapping Mormonism*, 174.

130. Margot J. Butler, interview by Mary Frances Rich, 29 Dec. 2020, 3, 6.

131. "Stake Report for Girls (Age 12–19) for October 1960," YWMIA Stake and Mission Reports, CHL.

132. Margot J. Butler, interview by Mary Frances Rich, 29 Dec. 2020, 7.

133. Margot J. Butler, interview by Mary Frances Rich, 29 Dec. 2020, 5.

134. David O. McKay, Diary, 17 May 1957, in Heath, *Confidence amid Change*, 174.

135. Reeve and Parshall, *Mormonism: A Historical Encyclopedia*, 130; Larry R. Skidmore, "Firesides," in *Encyclopedia of Latter-day Saint History*, 377.

136. See "Weber Stake Notes," *Ogden (UT) Standard*, 20 Jan. 1906, 5; and "Lecturer to Speak at Midvale First Ward Sunday Nite," *Sentinel* (Murray, UT), 2 Nov. 1939, [1].

137. Henry A. Smith, "Nearly 200,000 Listen to President's Special Message," and "Interest in Firesides Assured By 'Kick-Off,'" *Church News*, 9 Jan. 1960, 3, 12.

138. Henry A. Smith, "Firesides to Have Wide Radio Coverage," *Church News*, 19 Dec. 1959, 5.

139. Henry A. Smith, "Church Plans Massive Effort to Reach Youth," *Church News*, 5 Dec. 1959, 9; "'Dating, Ultimate Marriage' Title of Final Fireside Talk," *Church News*, 26 Mar. 1960, 4. Prerecorded talks were provided to those in areas not reached by radio.

140. "Elder Marion D. Hanks Dies at 89," *Church News*, 13 Aug. 2011, 7; "Elder Marion D. Hanks," *Ensign*, Nov. 1984, 100–101.

141. See, for example, "Elder Kimball Will Make Tour of European Nations," *Church News*, 12 Mar. 1955, 2; "Elder Lee Observes Steady Advancement," *Church News*, 30 June 1956, 7; Thomas S. Monson, "Mark E. Petersen," *Ensign*, Mar. 1984, 6–13; England, "Small and Piercing Voice," 77–90; Advertisement, *Deseret News and Salt Lake Telegram*, 11 Dec. 1957, 8D; Advertisement, *Salt Lake Tribune*, 16 Nov. 1957, 18; and "Elder Brown's Sermons in New Book," *Church News*, 1 Dec. 1956, 3.

142. Margot J. Butler, interview by Mary Frances Rich, 29 Dec. 2020, 8.

143. "MIA Leaders Counseled in Right Living," *Church News*, 15 June 1957, 5; Addresses, *Church News*, 22 June 1957, 3–7, 13; David O. McKay, "If Any Will Do His Will," and Stephen L Richards, "MIA Prepares the Missionary," *Improvement Era*, Sept. 1957, 624–627; LeGrand Richards, "The Worth of MIA," *Improvement Era*, Oct. 1957, 708–710, 764–766.

144. In the 1950s, for example, the *Improvement Era* published only ten items authored by members of the YWMIA presidency, an average of one per year.

145. Henry A. Smith, "Pres. McKay Leads Church in Period of Phenominal Growth," *Church News*, 2 Apr. 1960, 3.

146. "YWMIA Enrollment Exceeds 100,000 First Time in History," *Deseret News*, 4 Jan. 1950, Church section, 6.

147. "LDS Add 600,000 during 1950s," *Salt Lake Tribune*, 7 Apr. 1960, 8.

CHAPTER 6: A PROGRAM OF DEFENSE, 1961–1972

1. Florence S. Jacobsen, interview by Lavina Fielding Anderson, 5 Apr. 1984, 24–26.

2. Florence S. Jacobsen, interview by Lavina Fielding Anderson, 5 Apr. 1984, 26–29.

3. Florence S. Jacobsen, interview by Lavina Fielding Anderson, 5 Apr. 1984, 16–20.

4. Patterson, *Grand Expectations*, 450–451; Pope, "Traditional Values," 234–235.

5. Florence S. Jacobsen, interview by Gordon Irving, 18 Nov. 1991, 266.

6. Harold B. Lee, Address, 30 Sept. 1961, in *One Hundred Thirty-First Semi-annual Conference*, 79–80.

7. Harold B. Lee, Address, 30 Sept. 1961, in *One Hundred Thirty-First Semi-annual Conference*, 81.

8. Florence S. Jacobsen, interview by Gordon Irving, 18 Nov. 1991, 266–267; Young Women General Board, Minutes, 6 Nov. 1961.

9. Florence S. Jacobsen, interview by Gordon Irving, 18 Nov. 1991, 264.

10. Florence S. Jacobsen, interview by Gordon Irving, 18 Nov. 1991, 263–268.

11. Chieko N. Okazaki, interviews by Brian D. Reeves, 21 Feb. 1991, 1, 4, 8; 7 Mar. 1991, 18–19.

12. Chieko N. Okazaki, interview by Brian D. Reeves, 14 Mar. 1991, 31; see also Florence S. Jacobsen, interview by Gordon Irving, 18 Nov. 1991, 264.

13. Though Armenians were counted as white under early twentieth-century United States law, Badwagan Piranian (who joined the church in Switzerland and was appointed president of the Palestine-Syrian Mission in 1933) stands out as an early church leader not from a northwestern European background. The global proliferation of stakes in the 1960s expanded opportunities for nonwhite leadership: Percy J. Rivers (whose ancestry was Samoan with some Chinese and German) appears to have been the first nonwhite stake president. Adney Komatsu, another Japanese American, served as a mission president and later a general authority Seventy. (Turkish Mission Manuscript History and Historical Reports, vol. 2, pt. 2, 21 May 1933, 29; "Eligibility of Armenians," *Boston Daily Globe*, 24 Nov. 1909, 7; "Citizenship for Armenians," *New York Times*, 25 Dec. 1909, 3; Percy J. Rivers, interview by R. Lanier Britsch, 10 Jan. 1974, 2, 20–21; "Elder Komatsu," *Church News*, 5 Mar. 2011, 13.)

14. For a list of committees at the outset of Jacobsen's presidency, see "YWMIA Committee, November 1961," in Young Women General Board, Minutes, 6 Nov. 1961.

15. "YWMIA Committee, November 1961," in Young Women General Board, Minutes, 6 Nov. 1961.

16. The Articles of Faith are statements of basic Latter-day Saint beliefs, formulated by Joseph Smith in 1842 and now canonized as scripture in the Pearl of Great Price.

17. Young Women General Board, Minutes, vol. 17, 3 Dec. 1958, 382.

18. *Ensign-Laurel Manual* (1959), 267–269.

19. Florence S. Jacobsen, interview by Lavina Fielding Anderson, 5 Apr. 1984, 23–24.

20. Bette Lou Sims, interview by Nicholas B. Shrum, 25 Sept. 2018, 8.

21. Florence S. Jacobsen, interview by Lavina Fielding Anderson, 5 Apr. 1984, 23–24, 34.

22. *YWMIA Campcrafter Certification Program*, A.

23. *YWMIA Campcrafter Certification Program*, B, F.

24. "2,117,451 Listed by Church," *Deseret News*, 6 Apr. 1964, 8A. Enrollment of young men in this year was 220,449.

25. "Church Presents Statistical Report," *Deseret News*, 6 Apr. 1970, A9. Enrollment of young women was 366,749.

26. Vicki Noyce Barrett, interview by Mary Frances Rich and Lisa Olsen Tait, 16 Apr. 2021, 7, 8.

27. Ruth Hardy Funk, interview by Gordon Irving, 6 Feb. 1979, 126–127.

28. Funk, "Ruth, Come Walk with Me," 119.

29. First Presidency to General Priesthood Committee, 24 Mar. 1960, in Romney, "History of the Correlation of L.D.S. Church Auxiliaries," sec. I. Lee quoted from this letter extensively in his October 1961 address. (Harold B. Lee, Address, 30 Sept. 1961, in *One Hundred Thirty-First Semi-annual Conference*, 79–80.)

30. Bowman, *Mormon People*, 193–195; see also Elaine A. Cannon, interview by Gordon Irving, 5 Sept. 1984, 81.

31. See Goodman, "Correlation: The Turning Point," 259–284.

32. Funk, "Ruth, Come Walk with Me," 119–121.

33. Wendell J. Ashton, interview by Gordon Irving, 17 May 1984, 150.

34. Hortense Child Smith, interview by Gordon Irving, 25 Jan. 1979, 123–124.

35. Elaine A. Cannon, interview by Gordon Irving, 28 Dec. 1984, 101; Ardeth G. Kapp, interviews by Gordon Irving, 29 Dec. 1978, 49–50; 12 June 1979, 84.

36. Pulsipher, *Ruth Hardy Funk*, 113–114.

37. Wendell J. Ashton, interview by Gordon Irving, 17 May 1984, 152.

38. Hortense Child Smith, interview by Gordon Irving, 25 Jan. 1979, 124; Funk, "Ruth, Come Walk with Me," 122.

39. Harold B. Lee, Address, 30 Sept. 1961, in *One Hundred Thirty-First Semi-annual Conference*, 78–79; Goodman, "Correlation: The Early Years," 321–338.

40. Harold B. Lee, Address, 30 Sept. 1961, in *One Hundred Thirty-First Semi-annual Conference*, 81.

41. Mauss, *Angel and the Beehive*, 3–16, 85–99; Bowman, *Mormon People*, 205.

42. Wilson, *Adorned in Dreams*, 162, 164–166, 191–193; Magidson and Albrecht, *Mod New York*, 28–29, 57.

43. Kermit Mehlinger, "The Sexual Revolution," *Ebony*, Aug. 1966, 60.

44. Stone, "Sexual Expression," 22–25; Allyn, *Make Love, Not War*, 60–65; Strub, *Obscenity Rules*, 1–4.

45. See, for example, Kermit Mehlinger, "The Sexual Revolution," *Ebony*, Aug. 1966, 57–62; and [Jane Howard], "Betty Friedan's Pet Pique: The Feminine Mystique," *Life,* 1 Nov. 1963, 88.

46. Although sociological studies suggest that premarital sex was not generally accepted in the United States until the late 1960s, MIA leaders were attuned to the many changes brewing before then. (Putnam and Campbell, *American Grace*, 91–94; Chafe, *Unfinished Journey*, 123–128, 328–336; Irvine, *Disorders of Desire*, 32; Mauss, *Angel and the Beehive*, 93–95.)

47. Marvin J. Ashton, "Accentuate the Positive," *MIA Leader*, May 1962, 1.

48. The age of sixteen may have been taken from its widespread use in the United States as a legal driving age. (See "Elder Kimball Speaks on 'Youth and the Car,'" *Church News*, 20 Feb. 1960, 3; for early reactions to the policy of waiting to date until age sixteen, see Gina Grow, Letter to the Editor, *Y'ldcat* [Provo, UT], 2 Feb. 1962, 2.)

49. Florence S. Jacobsen, interview by Gordon Irving, 25 Nov. 1991, 291–292. For an example of general authority queries and responses, see Joseph Fielding Smith to Florence S. Jacobsen, 30 Sept. 1963, Florence S. Jacobsen Papers, CHL; and General YWMIA Presidency and General YMMIA Superintendency to Joseph Fielding Smith, 15 Oct. 1963, Florence S. Jacobsen Papers, CHL.

50. "June Conference Chaperoning, Governing, Dating," *MIA Leader*, May 1964, 2.

51. Delbert L. Stapley, "Leaders of Youth, Anything Short of Your Full Potential Isn't Good Enough," *Improvement Era*, Aug. 1964, 643, 662.

52. Spencer W. Kimball, "Save the Youth of Zion," *Improvement Era*, Sept. 1965, 800; see also "Character Is Reflected in Dress, Speech," *Church News*, 3 July 1965, 16.

53. See *For the Strength of Youth* (1965), 3.

54. "For the Strength of Youth," *MIA Leader*, Sept. 1965, 2.

55. For an example of an earlier piece directed at leaders, see "Communication on Dress," *Young Woman's Journal*, Apr. 1917, 225–226.

56. Jepson, "Study of the *For the Strength of Youth* Pamphlet," 51–53.

57. *For the Strength of Youth* (1965), 12–13.

58. *For the Strength of Youth* (1970), 12.

59. Young Women General Board, Minutes, 16 Sept. 1964.

60. *For the Strength of Youth* (1970), 3–5. "Figure-hugging" probably referred to the style of "hip hugger" jeans first introduced in the late 1950s, which would later come to be identified with the hippie aesthetic.

61. *For the Strength of Youth* (1965), 8; Blakesley, "A Style of Our Own," 28–29.

62. "On Standards and Parties," *MIA Leader*, Nov. 1965, 2.

63. *For the Strength of Youth* (1965), 9.

64. *For the Strength of Youth* (1965), 16.

65. Plewe, *Mapping Mormonism*, 174.

66. Nenita Reyes Gapiz, interview by Godofredo Hilario Esguerra and Wayne Crosby, 27 Feb. 2011, 6:33–6:38.

67. Ruben and Nenita Reyes Gapiz, interview by Chad M. Orton, Nov. 1994, 1–14.

68. Jorgensen was referring to the *Small MIA* handbook, which was published in 1966 and contained a simplified outline of MIA objectives along with some lessons and suggestions for activities that could be adapted for any age group. (*Lessons and Activities: The Small MIA* [Salt Lake City: MIA General Boards, 1966].)

69. Elaine L. Jorgensen to Florence S. Jacobsen, 10 Apr. 1969, CHL; "Italy: Church Chronology," Global Histories, history.ChurchofJesusChrist.org.

70. Netherlands Amsterdam Mission Manuscript History and Historical Reports, vol. 13, pt. 2, 12 Aug. 1965; "Sister van Mondfrans and Sister Willy Beekhuizen," in George Tuffin, Notes on 1960s Dutch Girls Camps, copy in authors' possession; George Tuffin, email to Brittany Chapman Nash, 4 Mar. 2017; George Tuffin, email to Kate Holbrook, 13 May 2022.

71. George Tuffin, Notes on 1960s Dutch Girls Camps, copy in authors' possession.

72. Linda McCall and Hayden Bogle, interview by James Goldberg, 30 Apr. 2021, 29.

73. Linda McCall, interview by Mary Francis Rich, 27 Jan. 2021, 4–5.

74. Linda McCall and Hayden Bogle, interview by James Goldberg, 30 Apr. 2021, 15–17, 22–25, 29, 33, 34.

75. Oral History no. 30, interview by Caroline Kline, 24 Oct. 2009, 4, Claremont Mormon Women Oral History Collection, Claremont Colleges Library, Claremont, CA.

76. Mary Frances Rich, Maurine Jensen Proctor, and Carol Clark, interview by James Goldberg, 26 Aug. 2021, 1:24:54–1:24:58.

77. *Utonian 1968*, 34, 42.

78. Mary Frances Rich, Maurine Jensen Proctor, and Carol Clark, interview by James Goldberg, 26 Aug. 2021, 1:07:08–1:07:14, 1:25:28–1:25:38.

79. Mary Frances Rich, Maurine Jensen Proctor, and Carol Clark, interview by James Goldberg, 26 Aug. 2021, 1:00:38–1:00:45, 1:12:07–1:12:22.

80. Mary Frances Rich, Maurine Jensen Proctor, and Carol Clark, interview by James Goldberg, 26 Aug. 2021, 59:10–1:00:00, 1:18:00–1:19:00.

81. Mary Frances Rich, Maurine Jensen Proctor, and Carol Clark, interview by James Goldberg, 26 Aug. 2021, 54:00–54:56.

82. Jan Christiansen Smith, interview by James Goldberg, 27 Aug. 2021, 1:18:00–1:20:20.

83. See Elaine A. Cannon, "LDS Student Association," in *Encyclopedia of Mormonism*, 2:817.

84. Mary Frances Rich, Maurine Jensen Proctor, and Carol Clark, interview by James Goldberg, 26 Aug. 2021, 1:51:30–1:53:06.

85. Mary Frances Rich, Maurine Jensen Proctor, and Carol Clark, interview by James Goldberg, 26 Aug. 2021, 1:28:00–1:30:00.

86. Jan Christiansen Smith, interview by James Goldberg, 27 Aug. 2021, 31:00–32:10.

87. Mary Frances Rich, Maurine Jensen Proctor, and Carol Clark, interview by James Goldberg, 26 Aug. 2021, 1:23:30–1:24:45, 1:56:55–1:59:45.

88. "Getting to Know You," *Improvement Era*, Jan. 1970, 74.

89. "In the Beginning," *Improvement Era*, May 1970, 70.

90. G. Homer Durham, "The Racial Revolution in America," *Improvement Era*, Oct. 1968, 93–95.

91. Kimball, "Spencer W. Kimball," 4–78; Reeve, *Religion of a Different Color*, 253–260.

92. Linda McCall and Hayden Bogle, interview by James Goldberg, 30 Apr. 2021, 18–19.

93. Linda McCall, Treasures of Truth, transcription, in Linda McCall, email to James Goldberg, 4 May 2021.

94. Linda McCall and Hayden Bogle, interview by James Goldberg, 30 Apr. 2021, 18–19.

95. The 28 November 1869 founding date given by Susa Young Gates in her history was the prevailing understanding. (See p. 57 herein.)

96. "1969 June Conference," in Young Women General Board, Minutes, June 1969; Mabel Jones Gabbott, "The Centennial Festivities—Churchwide and Yearlong," *Improvement Era*, May 1969, 68.

97. "MIA Salutes 'Ideal American Girl,'" *Salt Lake Tribune*, 28 June 1969, 4; "1969 June Conference," in Young Women General Board, Minutes, June 1969; "Color, Precision Highlight Dance Festival," *Church News*, 5 July 1969, 4.

98. See "President McKay Praises YWMIA," *Church News*, 5 July 1969, 4.

99. "1969 June Conference," in Young Women General Board, Minutes, June 1969; "A Huge 5-Layer Centennial Cake," *Church News*, 5 July 1969, 5.

100. Mabel Jones Gabbott, "The Centennial Festivities—Churchwide and Yearlong," *Improvement Era*, May 1969, 68–69.

101. Florence S. Jacobsen, "MIA Confrontation," *Improvement Era*, May 1969, 16–20.

102. See Patterson, *Grand Expectations*, 710–711.

103. Kenneth W. Godfrey, "A Growing Generation," *Improvement Era*, Nov. 1969, 8–9.

104. De Schweinitz, "Holding On to the 'Chosen Generation,'" 286, 289.

105. Kenneth W. Godfrey, "A Growing Generation," *Improvement Era*, Nov. 1969, 9.

106. See *Laurel Manual 1965–66*, 41–42; *Gateway to a Wonderful You*, 40–41; and *M Man–Gleaner Manual 1965–66*, 29–30.

107. *MIA Executive Manual Supplement*, 17–18. The M Men–Gleaner program continued to function on the stake level with conjoint leadership councils.

108. Stephen W. Gibson, "New Bishop's Youth Council," *Church News*, 3 May 1969, 4.

109. "Laurel Conference to Draw 2,500 Girls to Y. Campus," *Church News*, 14 Mar. 1970, 4; Margrit F. Lohner, interview by Sylvia Bruening, Aug. 1972, 48.

110. "LDS Laurels Launch Meet at BYU," *Salt Lake Tribune*, 24 Aug. 1970, 30.

111. "For Laurels," *MIA Leader*, Sept. 1970, 5.

112. In 1960, Cannon and Marion G. Hanks had been appointed coeditors of the "Era of Youth" insert of the *Improvement Era*. (Advertisement, *Church News*, 25 June 1960, 17; "Meet the Editors of the Era of Youth," *Improvement Era*, July 1960, 513.)

113. *New Era*, Jan. 1971.

114. Young Women General Board, Minutes, 7 Apr. 1971, [1].

115. YWMIA General Presidency to Spencer W. Kimball, 5 Apr. 1967, Florence S. Jacobsen Papers, CHL; Priesthood Correlation Executive Committee, Meeting Minutes, vol. 2, 1 July 1970, 369; Belle S. Spafford, "Report and Official Instructions," *Relief Society Magazine*, Nov. 1970, 815.

116. "Athletic Program Changed for Greater Participation," *Church News*, 26 June 1971, 10; "Big Changes

in MIA Programs," *New Era*, Sept. 1971, 44–45; "Programs and Policies Newsletter," *Ensign*, Sept. 1971, 76.

117. Florence S. Jacobsen, interview by Lavina Fielding Anderson, 5 Apr. 1984, 36–39. Jacobsen did not specify which member of the First Presidency said this; the members of the First Presidency at this time were Harold B. Lee, N. Eldon Tanner, and Marion G. Romney.

118. "2 Priesthood-Oriented MIAs," *Church News*, 11 Nov. 1972, 3, 8.

119. "2 Priesthood-Oriented MIAs," *Church News*, 11 Nov. 1972, 3, 8–9, 11.

120. See Doctrine and Covenants 107:13, 15.

121. "2 Priesthood-Oriented MIAs," *Church News*, 11 Nov. 1972, 8, 11.

CHAPTER 7: YWMIA TO YOUNG WOMEN, 1972–1984

1. Ardeth G. Kapp, interview by Gordon Irving, 12 June 1979, 89; Hortense Child Smith, interview by Gordon Irving, 11 June 1979, 183. This chapter relies heavily on oral histories conducted with Kapp and Child shortly after their service ended in 1978. Child married Eldred G. Smith soon after her release from Young Women; we have referred to her as Child in the text since this is the name she was known by at the time. Interviews with Ruth Funk were conducted in 1979 but covered only her life and church service up to 1962 (cataloged as OH 1020). Unfortunately, for unknown reasons, interviews covering the remaining years of her service, including her presidency, were never completed. She later gave a short interview to Andrew Kimball, which we have cited when applicable.

2. Ardeth G. Kapp, interview by Gordon Irving, 12 June 1979, 89–90; Brown, *Bishop Victor L. Brown*, 67; Hortense Child Smith, interview by Gordon Irving, 11 June 1979, 183. Child and Brown both stated in later reminiscences that Lee presented the proposal, but Kapp wrote in her journal that Brown presented it. It is possible Brown presented the proposal and Lee added his own thoughts.

3. Hortense Child Smith, interview by Gordon Irving, 11 June 1979, 183; Jack H. Goaslind, interview by Gordon Irving, 3 Feb. 1982, 135–136; Ardeth G. Kapp, interview by Gordon Irving, 12 June 1979, 89–90.

4. Basic organizational changes announced in November 1972 had been worked out by members of the Correlation Executive Committee with Lee "looking over their shoulders," according to Hortense Child. (Hortense Child Smith, interview by Gordon Irving, 11 June 1979, 169–170; see also Priesthood Correlation Executive Committee, Meeting Minutes, vol. 2, 3 Feb. 1971, 397.)

5. Hortense Child Smith, interview by Gordon Irving, 11 June 1979, 170–171.

6. APMIA Executive Committee, Meeting Minutes, 11 Jan.–20 Mar. 1973.

7. Hortense Child Smith, interview by Gordon Irving, 11 June 1979, 167; Brown, *Bishop Victor L. Brown*, 66–67.

8. APMIA Executive Committee, Meeting Minutes, 6 Feb. and 20 Mar. 1973.

9. APMIA Executive Committee, Meeting Minutes, 20 Mar. 1973; Hortense Child Smith, interview by Gordon Irving, 11 June 1979, 174.

10. "Aaronic Priesthood MIA," *Church News*, 14 Apr. 1973, 8–9, 11; Hortense Child Smith, interview by Gordon Irving, 11 June 1979, 171.

11. "Leaders Explain Aaronic Priesthood MIA," *Church News*, 30 June 1973, 6–7, 10.

12. Brown, *Bishop Victor L. Brown*, 68.

13. Vaughn J. Featherstone, interview by Gordon Irving, 23 Feb. 1982, 137; Ardeth G. Kapp, interview by Gordon Irving, 12 June 1979, 94–95.

14. J M. Heslop, "Priesthood to Direct Youth of the Church," *Church News*, 29 June 1974, 3, 14–15; "To Strengthen Youth of Church," *Church News*, 29 June 1974, 8–9.

15. Vaughn J. Featherstone, interview by Gordon Irving, 23 Feb. 1982, 137.

16. Hortense Child Smith, interview by Gordon Irving, 3 Nov. 1980, 286.

17. Hortense Child Smith, interview by Gordon Irving, 11 June 1979, 185.

18. See "Church Defines Ecclesiastical, Temporal Lines," *Church News*, 5 Feb. 1977, 8–9.

19. Victor L. Brown, Journal Entry, 31 Oct. 1976, Victor L. Brown Files, CHL.

20. "Youth Programs Are Restructured," *Church News*, 14 May 1977, 3.

21. Hortense Child Smith, interview by Gordon Irving, 3 Nov. 1980, 285.

22. Neil D. Schaerrer, interview by Gordon Irving, 14 Dec. 1979, 4.

23. Hortense Child Smith, interview by Gordon Irving, 3 Nov. 1980, 281.

24. Ardeth G. Kapp, interview by Gordon Irving, 13 June 1979, 129.

25. Hortense Child Smith, interview by Gordon Irving, 11 June 1979, 175; Ardeth G. Kapp, interview by Gordon Irving, 13 June 1979, 127–129.

26. "To Strengthen Youth of Church," *Church News*, 29 June 1974, 8–9, 15.

27. Ardeth G. Kapp, interview by Gordon Irving, 12 June 1979, 98–99.

28. Hortense Child Smith, interviews by Gordon Irving, 11 June 1979, 186; 31 Oct. 1980, 228.

29. Brown, *Bishop Victor L. Brown*, 67–68; see also Robert L. Backman, interview by Ronald G. Watt, 27 May 1993, 171.

30. Hortense Child Smith, interview by Gordon Irving, 22 Oct. 1980, 192.

31. "June Conferences to End, Pres. Kimball Tells Session," *Church News*, 28 June 1975, 3, 5; see also "Historic Conferences End," *Church News*, 5 July 1975, 3; and *Lengthening Our Stride: June Conference 1975*, 4–7, Young Women Programs, CHL.

32. Hortense Child Smith, interviews by Gordon Irving, 18 Jan 1979, 89; 11 June 1979, 178–187.

33. Hortense Child Smith, interview by Gordon Irving, 11 June 1979, 186–187.

34. Ruth Hardy Funk, interview by Andrew Kimball, 27 Nov. 1979, Spencer W. Kimball Biography Research Files, CHL.

35. Hortense Child Smith, interview by Gordon Irving, 4 Nov. 1980, 313.

36. "To Strengthen Youth of Church," *Church News*, 29 June 1974, 8–9.

37. Ardeth G. Kapp, interview by Gordon Irving, 12 June 1979, 102.

38. Victor L. Brown, Journal Entry, 31 Oct. 1976, Victor L. Brown Files, CHL.

39. Ardeth G. Kapp, interview by Gordon Irving, 29 Dec. 1978, 79.

40. See Hortense Child Smith, interviews by Gordon Irving, 22 Oct. 1980, 203; 31 Oct. 1980, 219, 221; 3 Nov. 1980, 281–282.

41. Ardeth G. Kapp, interviews by Gordon Irving, 29 Dec. 1978, 78; 12 June 1979, 101.

42. Young Women General Board, Minutes, 17 Mar. 1968; "Changes Readied for 1969–70 YWMIA Program," *Church News*, 6 Sept. 1969, 5; Eleanor Knowles, "New Directions in MIA," *Improvement Era*, Aug. 1970, 30–31.

43. Eleanor Knowles, "New Directions in MIA," *Improvement Era*, Aug. 1970, 30–31; "Girls' Achievement Program to Be Started in January," *Church News*, 26 Dec. 1970, 3.

44. Young Women General Board, Minutes, 6 May 1970. This may have originally been intended to be a combined meeting with parents, their daughter, and the bishop, as noted in a 1970 *Church News* article, but it does not appear to have functioned this way. ("3 New YW Programs Introduced," *Church News*, 27 June 1970, 4; *Aaronic Priesthood and Young Women's Personal Achievement Program Leadership Guide*, 5.)

45. Ardeth G. Kapp and Carolyn J. Rasmus, interview by Gordon Irving, 4 May 1992, 57, 59.

46. APMIA Executive Committee, Meeting Minutes, 14 Nov. 1972; 6 Feb. 1973; Florence S. Jacobsen, interview by Gordon Irving, 25 Nov. 1991, 292.

47. Ardeth G. Kapp, interview by Gordon Irving, 13 June 1979, 145.

48. APMIA Executive Committee, Meeting Minutes, 11 Oct. 1973.

49. Ardeth G. Kapp, interview by Gordon Irving, 13 June 1979, 145.

50. APMIA Executive Committee, Meeting Minutes, 11 Oct. 1973.

51. APMIA Executive Committee, Meeting Minutes, 17 Jan. 1974.

52. Ardeth G. Kapp, interview by Gordon Irving, 13 June 1979, 144.

53. "Behold Thy Handmaiden," *Church News*, 22 June 1974, 8–9; Ardeth G. Kapp, interview by Gordon Irving, 12 June 1979, 99–100; Pulsipher, *Ruth Hardy Funk*, 168–169. Luke 1:38 reports that Mary said, "Behold the handmaid of the Lord; be it unto me according to thy word."

54. Hortense Child Smith, interview by Gordon Irving, 22 Oct. 1980, 200; *Behold Thy Handmaiden* [Guidelines for adult leaders], 3–5.

55. Ardeth G. Kapp, interview by Gordon Irving, 13 June 1979, 144–146; Young Women General Board, Minutes, 9 Nov. 1973.

56. "Behold Thy Handmaiden," *Church News*, 22 June 1974, 8–9.

57. *Behold Thy Handmaiden* [Guidelines for adult leaders], 1, 6, 11.

58. *Behold Thy Handmaiden* [Girls' booklet], [2]–[3]; see also 3 Nephi 13:33.

59. The following survey of the women's movement relies on Orleck, *Rethinking American Women's Activism*, 77–132; Schulman, *The Seventies*, 159–189; and Dicker, *History of U.S. Feminisms*, 57–101.

60. Orleck, *Rethinking American Women's Activism*, 86–87.

61. Bushman, "Women in Dialogue," 5–6.

62. Peterson, "Somewhere Inbetween," 74–76.

63. Thomas S. Monson, "The Women's Movement: Liberation or Deception?," *Ensign*, Jan. 1971, 17–19.

64. "Excerpts from Talks Given at the 1973 Priesthood MIA June Conference," *New Era*, Nov. 1973, 146–147.

65. "Behold Thy Handmaiden," *Church News*, 22 June 1974, 8–9.

66. "'Lengthening Our Stride' in the Arts of Making an Eternal Home," Young Women Resource Library Files, CHL.

67. Ardeth G. Kapp, interview by Gordon Irving, 13 June 1979, 145; Hortense Child Smith, interview by Gordon Irving, 22 Oct. 1980, 200.

68. Ardeth G. Kapp, interview by Gordon Irving, 12 June 1979, 99–100; Pulsipher, *Ruth Hardy Funk*, 168–169; Hortense Child Smith, interview by Gordon Irving, 22 Oct. 1980, 200–201.

69. Hortense Child Smith, interview by Gordon Irving, 22 Oct. 1980, 200.

70. Ardeth G. Kapp, interview by Gordon Irving, 12 June 1979, 99–100. A biography of Ruth Funk said that the direction had come from the First Presidency, while Young Women general board minutes indicate that Marion D. Hanks, managing director of youth programs, recommended the change after consulting with several other church leaders. (Pulsipher, *Ruth Hardy Funk*, 168–169; Young Women General Board, Minutes, 5 Jan. 1977, 2.)

71. Gerry Avant, "Progress Is Its Own Reward for Young Women in Gaining Goals," *Church News*, 17 Sept. 1977, 7.

72. Hortense Child explained the choice of painting in comments in a *Church News* article that announced the new program: "We encourage the girls to emulate Mary's spirit of devotion," she said. (Gerry Avant, "Progress Is Its Own Reward for Young Women in Gaining Goals," *Church News*, 17 Sept. 1977, 7.)

73. *My Personal Progress* (1977), 8–9, 12–16, 63–64; Gerry Avant, "Progress Is Its Own Reward for Young Women in Gaining Goals," *Church News*, 17 Sept. 1977, 7; *General Handbook of Instructions* (1983), 11.

74. Hortense Child Smith, interviews by Gordon Irving, 11 June 1979, 186–187; 22 Oct. 1980, 203.

75. Sharon Taylor Shimp, Karen Taylor Asay, and Rama Taylor Cowley, interview by Amber Taylor, 26 Aug. 2021, 47:10–58:00, 1:14:00–1:16:00, 1:17:20–1:18:00, 1:26:00–1:26:50, 1:28:00–1:29:00.

76. Dorothy Kay (Dottie) Boone Jones, interview by Lisa Olsen Tait, 21 Apr. 2021, 1, 5, 6–7, 19–22, 31.

77. Merydith Garfield Sandell, interview by Jessica M. Nelson, 10 May 2018, 4–8.

78. Hortense Child Smith, interview by Gordon Irving, 11 June 1979, 167, 174.

79. "Leaders Explain Aaronic Priesthood MIA," *Church News*, 30 June 1973, 6.

80. Hortense Child Smith, interview by Gordon Irving, 3 Nov. 1980, 269–270.

81. David Croft, "Aaronic Priesthood Leaders Called to Serve with Action," *Church News*, 29 June 1974, 7; Ardeth G. Kapp, interview by Gordon Irving, 12 June 1979, 99.

82. Hortense Child Smith, interviews by Gordon Irving, 11 June 1979, 179; 3 Nov. 1980, 269. In another setting, Ardeth Kapp emphasized that youth leadership was the fundamental element of the new plans that had been approved in the March 1973 temple meeting. (Ardeth G. Kapp, interview by Gordon Irving, 12 June 1979, 91.)

83. Hortense Child Smith, interview by Gordon Irving, 11 June 1979, 180.

84. "'Death to Tumbleweeds!' Say Torrance Youth," *New Era*, Sept. 1976, 39.

85. "Fighting Fire with Service Projects," *New Era*, Jan./Feb. 1979, 49.

86. "A Night of Sharing," *New Era*, May 1980, 41.

87. Mary Frances Rich and Lisa Olsen Tait, Notes on Interviews with Charlene Holmstrom, 1–11.

88. "Welfare Services in Perspective," *Ensign*, Feb. 1979, 12–18.

89. Sharon Taylor Shimp, email to Amber Taylor, 31 Aug. 2021; Karen Taylor Asay, email to Amber Taylor, 31 Aug. 2021.

90. This idea was discussed in 1973 and codified in the 1975 *Young Women Handbook*, which was the first such publication released after the reworking of the organization that began in 1972. ("New AP MIA Program Discussed by Leaders," *Church News*, 30 June 1973, 10; *Young Women Handbook* [1975], 7, 14–15.)

91. Ardeth G. Kapp, interview by Gordon Irving, 7 Sept. 1979, 167; Hortense Child Smith, interview by Gordon Irving, 18 Jan. 1979, 88–89.

92. Hortense Child Smith, interview by Gordon Irving, 3 Nov. 1980, 284–285.

93. *Activity Book*, xi, xxv.

94. Ardeth G. Kapp, interview by Gordon Irving, 7 Sept. 1979, 172.

95. Ruth Hardy Funk, interview by Andrew Kimball, 27 Nov. 1979, Spencer W. Kimball Biography Research Files, CHL. For more on the church's response to the women's movement and the Equal Rights Amendment, see Bradley, *Pedestals and Podiums*, vii–xxiv.

96. Ruth Hardy Funk, interview by Andrew Kimball, 27 Nov. 1979, Spencer W. Kimball Biography Research Files, CHL; Ardeth G. Kapp, interview by Gordon Irving, 12 June 1979, 108–109.

97. Ardeth G. Kapp, interview by Gordon Irving, 12 June 1979, 109–113. Women leaders' tenure in office decreased substantially at this point. Bertha S. Reeder was YWMIA general president for thirteen years, and her successor, Florence S. Jacobsen, was president for eleven. Both Funk and her successor, Elaine A. Cannon, served for six years. In the first two decades of the twenty-first century, each Young Women general president served for five years.

98. Elaine A. Cannon, interview by Gordon Irving, 17 July 1990, 158–159.
99. "New Young Women Leaders," *Church News*, 15 July 1978, 3; Lynne Hollstein, "New YW Counselor Is Eager to Serve," *Church News*, 29 July 1978, 13; Gerry Avant, "Her Love's Evolved," *Church News*, 5 Aug. 1978, 6.
100. Elaine A. Cannon, interview by Gordon Irving, 17 July 1990, 161.
101. "Young Men–Young Women: 1973–1977 Trend Comparison," YWMIA History Records, CHL.
102. Elaine A. Cannon, interview by Gordon Irving, 17 July 1990, 161.
103. Elaine A. Cannon, "Program for All Women Over 18 in the Church of Jesus Christ of Latter-day Saints," 4–5, Elaine A. Cannon Papers, BYU.
104. Elaine A. Cannon, interview by Gordon Irving, 17 July 1990, 162.
105. "New Leaders Named for Young Women," *New Era*, Nov. 1978, 38.
106. Pulsipher, *Ruth Hardy Funk*, 172.
107. Spencer W. Kimball, "Privileges and Responsibilities of Sisters," *Ensign*, Nov. 1978, 103.
108. Barbara B. Smith, "Women's Greatest Challenge," *Ensign*, Nov. 1978, 109.
109. Ruth Hardy Funk, "Come, Listen to a Prophet's Voice," *Ensign*, Nov. 1978, 106; "The First Presidency of Church Issues Statement on Abortion," *Church News*, 27 Jan. 1973, 7; see also *General Handbook Supplement* (1976), 6.
110. Ruth Hardy Funk, "Come, Listen to a Prophet's Voice," *Ensign*, Nov. 1978, 107.
111. Elaine A. Cannon, "If We Want to Go Up, We Have to Get On," *Ensign*, Nov. 1978, 108.
112. *Young Women Handbook* (1975), 10; Elaine A. Cannon, interview by Gordon Irving, 17 July 1990, 180.
113. Elaine A. Cannon, interview by Gordon Irving, 28 Dec. 1984, 111–112; Young Women General Board, Minutes, 17 Mar. 1968.
114. Debra Hovik Stewart, email to Kate Holbrook, 12 Oct. 2020.
115. Ardeth G. Kapp and Carolyn J. Rasmus, interview by Gordon Irving, 4 May 1992, 41; Elaine A. Cannon, interview by Gordon Irving, 17 July 1990, 174.
116. Elaine A. Cannon, interview by Gordon Irving, 17 July 1990, 180–182.
117. Elaine A. Cannon, interview by Gordon Irving, 17 July 1990, 178.
118. Patricia Brown Jake, interview by Amber Taylor, 11 Sept. 2021, 1:58–5:12, 15:55–22:03, 25:50–31:01, 57:14–1:00:05, 1:00:29–1:05:25.
119. Elaine A. Cannon, interview by Gordon Irving, 21 Aug. 1990, 192–196.
120. Elaine A. Cannon, interview by Gordon Irving, 21 Aug. 1990, 195.
121. Rhonda Shelby, interview by Alan Cherry, 22 Feb. 1985, 4, 12, African American Oral History Project Transcripts, BYU.
122. Rhonda Shelby, interview by Alan Cherry, 22 Feb. 1985, 31–32, African American Oral History Project Transcripts, BYU.
123. Rhonda Shelby, interview by Alan Cherry, 22 Feb. 1985, 14, African American Oral History Project Transcripts, BYU.
124. Rhonda Shelby, interview by Alan Cherry, 22 Feb. 1985, 16, African American Oral History Project Transcripts, BYU.
125. Kendra Bybee, "I'm a Pioneer: The Perseverance of the First Black Sister Missionary Called to Serve," LDS Living, 18 July 2022, ldsliving.com; Bruce R. McConkie, "All Are Alike unto God," CES Religious Educators' Symposium, Provo, UT, 18 Aug. 1978, speeches.byu.edu.
126. *My Personal Progress* (1983), 1, 2.
127. Elaine A. Cannon, interview by Gordon Irving, 27 Aug. 1985, 156–157.
128. Elaine A. Cannon, interview by Gordon Irving, 17 July 1990, 182.
129. Elaine A. Cannon, interview by Gordon Irving, 21 Aug. 1990, 194.
130. Elaine A. Cannon, interview by Gordon Irving, 17 July 1990, 187–188.
131. Elaine A. Cannon, interviews by Gordon Irving, 17 July 1990, 176; 21 Aug. 1990, 191.
132. Elaine A. Cannon, interview by Gordon Irving, 17 July 1990, 175.
133. Elaine A. Cannon, interview by Gordon Irving, 27 Aug. 1985, 156; see also 2 Kings 5:1–4.

CHAPTER 8: STANDING AS WITNESSES OF GOD, 1984–1992

1. Ardeth G. Kapp and Carolyn J. Rasmus, interview by Gordon Irving, 29 Apr. 1992, 26–31.
2. Ardeth G. Kapp and Carolyn J. Rasmus, interview by Gordon Irving, 29 Apr. 1992, 4, 10–21.
3. Rasmus, Ardeth G. Kapp Biography, 232–233; Kapp, Journal, 27 Jan. 1983, 19–21.

4. Ardeth G. Kapp and Carolyn J. Rasmus, interview by Gordon Irving, 29 Apr. 1992, 23–27.

5. Ardeth G. Kapp and Carolyn J. Rasmus, interview by Gordon Irving, 29 Apr. 1992, 31.

6. Haws, *Mormon Image*, 79–91; Bradley, *Pedestals and Podiums*, vii–xxiv.

7. Wheatley-Pesci, "Expanded Definition of Priesthood," 35–36; see also Ulrich, "Mormon Women," 45–63.

8. Reeder and Holbrook, *At the Pulpit*, 346–347.

9. Ardeth G. Kapp and Carolyn J. Rasmus, interview by Gordon Irving, 4 May 1992, 55.

10. Ardeth G. Kapp and Carolyn J. Rasmus, interview by Gordon Irving, 4 May 1992, 57; "Young Women Presentation to PEC," 20 Feb. 1985, 2, in Young Women General Board, Minutes, 27 Feb. 1985; Johnson, *Sleepwalking through History*, 150–151; Brumberg, *Body Project*, 119–124, 182–189, 201–206; see also Patterson, *Restless Giant*, 184; and Hine, *Rise and Fall of the American Teenager*, 288–289.

11. In 1984, church membership reached over 5.6 million, an increase of 2.2 million in a decade. (*Deseret News 1991–1992 Church Almanac*, 335.)

12. Chawla, *Situation of Youth*, 14–28, 36–37.

13. John Sagers (data analyst, Church Membership and Statistical Records Department), email to Nicholas B. Shrum, 13 Sept. 2021; Elaine A. Cannon, interview by Gordon Irving, 17 July 1990, 161, 168. It is not clear how much the decreased activity rates in the late 1970s and 1980s were related to engagement with the Young Women program and how much they were related to activity rates in the larger church.

14. Ardeth G. Kapp and Carolyn J. Rasmus, interview by Gordon Irving, 4 May 1992, 42–43; see also Elaine A. Cannon, interview by Gordon Irving, 17 July 1990, 161.

15. Ardeth G. Kapp and Carolyn J. Rasmus, interview by Gordon Irving, 4 May 1992, 40; Kapp, Journal, 11 Apr. 1984.

16. Kapp, Journal, 11 and 22 Apr. 1984; Ardeth G. Kapp and Carolyn J. Rasmus, interview by Gordon Irving, 4 May 1992, 40.

17. Ardeth G. Kapp and Carolyn J. Rasmus, interview by Gordon Irving, 29 Apr. 1992, 30–32.

18. "First Presidency Calls Young Women Counselors," *Church News*, 20 May 1984, 7.

19. Ardeth G. Kapp and Carolyn J. Rasmus, interviews by Gordon Irving, 29 Apr. 1992, 10–11, 30; 4 May 1992, 43–45; Carolyn J. Rasmus, email to Kate Holbrook, 15 Sept. 2020.

20. See Appendix B: Young Women General Presidencies, p. 335 herein.

21. Ardeth G. Kapp and Carolyn J. Rasmus, interview by Gordon Irving, 4 May 1992, 62.

22. Ardeth G. Kapp and Carolyn J. Rasmus, interview by Gordon Irving, 4 May 1992, 42–43; "Young Women Presentation to PEC," 20 Feb. 1985, 1, in Young Women General Board, Minutes, 27 Feb. 1985. Much of the content of this assessment came from a 1982 study of activity and inactivity performed by the Research and Correlation Division of the church, cited in the presidency's presentation to the PEC. Though Kapp expressed concern about young women's attendance rates in some areas being lower than young men's, which would have been a break with prior norms, church data indicate that the overall attendance percentage for young women in 1985 remained slightly higher than for young men. (John Sagers, email to Nicholas B. Shrum, 13 Sept. 2021.)

23. Ardeth G. Kapp and Carolyn J. Rasmus, interview by Gordon Irving, 4 May 1992, 40–43, 51, 58, 73.

24. Ardeth G. Kapp and Carolyn J. Rasmus, interview by Gordon Irving, 4 May 1992, 40; see also Doctrine and Covenants 20:46–60; 84:111.

25. Ardeth G. Kapp and Carolyn J. Rasmus, interview by Gordon Irving, 4 May 1992, 55–58.

26. Ardeth G. Kapp and Carolyn J. Rasmus, interview by Gordon Irving, 4 May 1992, 52, 54.

27. Kapp, Journal, 7 Aug. 1984; Ardeth G. Kapp and Carolyn J. Rasmus, interview by Gordon Irving, 4 May 1992, 54–55.

28. Turley, Journal, 28 Sept. 1984, 58–59; Ardeth G. Kapp and Carolyn J. Rasmus, interview by Gordon Irving, 4 May 1992, 60; Young Women General Board, Minutes, 28 Sept. 1984, 2.

29. *My Personal Progress* (1977), 10–11.

30. See Spencer W. Kimball, "The Blessings and Responsibilities of Womanhood," *Ensign*, Mar. 1976, 70–73; and Spencer W. Kimball, "The Role of Righteous Women," *Ensign*, Nov. 1979, 102–104.

31. "Ardeth Greene Kapp: Young Women General President," *Ensign*, May 1984, 98.

32. Dowland, "Family Values," 607–609, 630.

33. Paul Kurtz and Edwin H. Wilson, "Humanist Manifesto II," *Humanist*, Sept./Oct. 1973, 4–9; Tibor Machan and Lansing Pollock, "Interview with Paul Kurtz," *Reason*, Mar. 1982, reason.com.

34. Neal A. Maxwell, "Meeting the Challenges of Today," BYU Devotional, Provo, UT, 10 Oct. 1978, 1–3, speeches.byu.edu.

35. Ardeth G. Kapp and Carolyn J. Rasmus, interview by Gordon Irving, 4 May 1992, 75; [Ardeth G. Kapp], "A Big Rock: History of the Young Women Values," 2, Young Women Files, CHL.

36. Hobbs, *Time Power*, 42. Latter-day Saint Stephen Covey would soon be famous for making similar recommendations in books such as *First Things First*, *Principle-Centered Leadership*, and the

phenomenally successful *The Seven Habits of Highly Effective People*. He wrote on the same ideas for a specifically Latter-day Saint audience as well.

37. Ardeth G. Kapp and Carolyn J. Rasmus, interview by Gordon Irving, 4 May 1992, 54.

38. Ardeth G. Kapp, interview by Gordon Irving, 29 Dec. 1978, 54–55; Ardeth G. Kapp and Carolyn J. Rasmus, interview by Gordon Irving, 4 May 1992, 54.

39. "Young Women Values," *New Era*, Nov. 1985 (Young Women special issue), 30, 32; Doctrine and Covenants 18:10.

40. Ardeth G. Kapp and Carolyn J. Rasmus, interview by Gordon Irving, 4 May 1992, 67.

41. Ardeth G. Kapp, interview by Gordon Irving, 7 Sept. 1979, 185.

42. Ardeth G. Kapp and Carolyn J. Rasmus, interview by Gordon Irving, 4 May 1992, 60.

43. Ardeth G. Kapp and Carolyn J. Rasmus, interview by Gordon Irving, 4 May 1992, 57.

44. The Priesthood Department oversaw the work of all the church auxiliary organizations—the Primary, Relief Society, Young Women, Young Men, and Sunday School—as well as military relations, church music, and Aaronic and Melchizedek Priesthood functions. This organizational structure has remained essentially unchanged since it was established in 1977. (*Deseret News 1987 Church Almanac*, 27; *Deseret News 1978 Church Almanac*, 246–247, 252–254.)

45. Ardeth G. Kapp and Carolyn J. Rasmus, interview by Gordon Irving, 29 May 1992, 146–164.

46. Ardeth G. Kapp to J. Thomas Fyans, 4 Mar. 1985, Ardeth G. Kapp Files, CHL.

47. Ardeth G. Kapp and Carolyn J. Rasmus, interview by Gordon Irving, 4 May 1992, 66.

48. Ardeth G. Kapp and Carolyn J. Rasmus, interview by Gordon Irving, 29 May 1992, 154.

49. Ardeth G. Kapp, interview by Jared Jepson, 21 Jan. 2005, 9–10.

50. Ardeth G. Kapp and Carolyn J. Rasmus, interview by Gordon Irving, 4 June 1992, 211–212.

51. Ardeth G. Kapp and Carolyn J. Rasmus, interview by Gordon Irving, 4 May 1992, 100–102.

52. See Kimball, "A Style of Our Own," 163–164.

53. Turley, Journal, 20 Sept. 1984, 55–57; Ardeth G. Kapp and Carolyn J. Rasmus, interview by Gordon Irving, 4 May 1992, 103.

54. Young Women General Board, Minutes, Nov. 1984, 3–4.

55. Ardeth G. Kapp and Carolyn J. Rasmus, interview by Gordon Irving, 4 May 1992, 73–74, 78.

56. Kapp and Rasmus, "Chronology," 248–249.

57. Ardeth G. Kapp and Carolyn J. Rasmus, interview by Gordon Irving, 4 May 1992, 50.

58. Ardeth G. Kapp and Carolyn J. Rasmus, interview by Gordon Irving, 4 May 1992, 54.

59. VideoShow, created by General Parametrics, was a briefcase-size computer dedicated solely to displaying slideshows from floppy disks. In 1984, the unit cost $2,400. ("VideoShow Adds Polish to Slide Shows," *InfoWorld*, 18 June 1984, 55.)

60. Ardeth G. Kapp and Carolyn J. Rasmus, interview by Gordon Irving, 4 May 1992, 64–65.

61. Priesthood Executive Council, Minutes, 20 Feb. 1985, 1, 3.

62. Ardeth G. Kapp and Carolyn J. Rasmus, interview by Gordon Irving, 4 May 1992, 63.

63. "Young Women Presentation," 1, 8, Young Women Files, CHL.

64. "Young Women Presentation," 2, Young Women Files, CHL.

65. "Young Women Presentation," 4–7, Young Women Files, CHL.

66. "Young Women Presentation to PEC," 20 Feb. 1985, 5–6, in Young Women General Board, Minutes, 27 Feb. 1985.

67. "Young Women Presentation," 8, Young Women Files, CHL.

68. "Young Women Presentation," 10, Young Women Files, CHL.

69. Ardeth G. Kapp and Carolyn J. Rasmus, interview by Gordon Irving, 4 May 1992, 65, 79.

70. Turley, Journal, 20 Feb. 1985, 75, 77; see also Priesthood Executive Council, Minutes, 20 Feb. 1985, 3–4.

71. Kapp and Rasmus, "Chronology," 249. A month and a half after the founding of the Relief Society, Joseph Smith told the membership, "I now turn the <u>key</u> to you in the name of God and this Society shall rejoice and knowledge and intelligence shall flow down from this time." (Nauvoo Relief Society Minute Book, 28 Apr. 1842, in Derr et al., *First Fifty Years of Relief Society*, 59.)

72. Young Women General Board, Minutes, 27 Feb. 1985, 2; Ardeth G. Kapp and Carolyn J. Rasmus, interview by Gordon Irving, 4 May 1992, 64–65. The *New Era* produced a special Young Women issue for November 1985 that was in many respects a print version of the fireside, including printed versions of Kapp's and Nelson's talks and profiles of the young women who represented the values. (Russell M. Nelson, "Daughters of Zion," and Ardeth G. Kapp, "Stand Up, Lead Out," *New Era*, Nov. 1985 [Young Women special issue], 4–9, 22–26.)

73. Young Women General Board, Minutes, 26 June 1985, 4–5; 21 Aug. 1985, 3; "Young Women Values," *New Era*, Nov. 1985 (Young Women special issue), 27; Ardeth G. Kapp and Carolyn J. Rasmus, interview by Gordon Irving, 4 May 1992, 63.

74. Russell M. Nelson to Daniel H. Ludlow, 25 June 1985, photocopy, Young Women Files, CHL.

75. For a survey of historical teachings on Mother in Heaven, see Paulsen and Pulido, "A Mother There," 71–97.

76. Young Women General Board, Minutes, 21 Aug. 1985, 4.

77. Kapp and Rasmus, "Chronology," 251.

78. Ardeth G. Kapp and Carolyn J. Rasmus, interviews by Gordon Irving, 20 May 1992, 140; 4 June 1992, 194.

79. Ardeth G. Kapp and Carolyn J. Rasmus, interview by Gordon Irving, 29 May 1992, 150.

80. Kapp, Journal, 20 Sept. 1985.

81. Ardeth G. Kapp, "Thanks to Elder J. Thomas Fyans, A Tender Tutor, A Magnificent Mentor," Oct. 1985, in Fyans, Journals, CHL; "Elder Jack H. Goaslind, Elder Robert L. Backman of the Presidency of the First Quorum of the Seventy," *Ensign*, Nov. 1985, 100.

82. Priesthood Executive Council, Minutes, 9 Oct. 1985; First Quorum of the Seventy, Minutes, 10 Oct. 1985, in Fyans, Journal, 10 Oct. 1985.

83. Priesthood Executive Council, Minutes, 26 Sept. 1985, 1; Turley, Journal, 25 Sept. 1985, 113; Ardeth G. Kapp and Carolyn J. Rasmus, interview by Gordon Irving, 29 May 1992, 176.

84. Gerry Avant, "Young Women Are Challenged: 'Stand for Truth and Righteousness,'" *Church News*, 17 Nov. 1985, 10. The second sentence quotes a Book of Mormon verse, Mosiah 18:9.

85. "Stand for Truth and Righteousness" (10 Nov. 1985 broadcast), 4, General Young Women Meeting Satellite Broadcast Records, CHL; "The 1st Young Women's Fireside: Stand for Truth and Righteousness," 36:26–37:11.

86. Carolyn J. Rasmus, Journal Entry, 16 Nov. 1985, [1]–[2], Carolyn J. Rasmus Office Papers, CHL. For membership estimate, see "300,000 Young Women Send Balloon Messages of Hope Worldwide," *Ensign*, Nov. 1986, 102. According to church statistics, about 144,000 of the 300,000 girls on the Young Women rolls were regularly involved in the program in 1985. (John Sagers, email to Nicholas B. Shrum, 13 Sept. 2021.)

87. Kimball, *Lengthen Your Stride*, 413–416.

88. Carolyn J. Rasmus, Journal Entry, 16 Nov. 1985, [2], [7], Carolyn J. Rasmus Office Papers, CHL.

89. "Stand for Truth and Righteousness" (10 Nov. 1985 broadcast), 2, General Young Women Meeting Satellite Broadcast Records, CHL; "The 1st Young Women's Fireside: Stand for Truth and Righteousness," 19:47–19:58.

90. Tuminez, "Coming Home," 88, 96–97, 102–103; Astrid S. Tuminez, "Education Carves Path from Manila to Microsoft," *News Deeply*, 23 May 2016, deeply.thenewhumanitarian.org; "Asia Vision Series: Dr. Astrid S. Tuminez," Stories Asia, Microsoft Asia News Center, 18 Sept. 2017, news.microsoft .com/apac/features; Astrid S. Tuminez, email to Kate Holbrook, 24 June 2018; Young Women General Board, Minutes, 13 Nov. 1985, 4; Iloilo 2nd Branch, General Minutes, 5 Oct. and 2 Nov. 1975; 11 Jan. 1976; see also Marjorie Cortez, "UVU Gains New President," *Deseret News*, 21 Apr. 2018, A1, A6.

91. "The 1st Young Women's Fireside: Stand for Truth and Righteousness," 38:00–43:25; "Young Women Values," *New Era*, Nov. 1985 (Young Women special issue), 28–40.

92. Young Women General Board, Minutes, 13 Nov. 1985, 4.

93. "The 1st Young Women's Fireside: Stand for Truth and Righteousness," 46:50–52:24.

94. "The 1st Young Women's Fireside: Stand for Truth and Righteousness," 52:56–53:21.

95. Spencer W. Kimball, "When the World Will Be Converted," *Ensign*, Oct. 1974, 10–14.

96. Watkins, "History of Media," pt. 1, pp. 9–10, 21–25, 80–84.

97. Ardeth G. Kapp and Carolyn J. Rasmus, interview by Gordon Irving, 29 May 1992, 179–180.

98. Young Women General Board, Minutes, 7 Mar. 1985, 1; Perry, *Songs from My Heart*, 81.

99. See, for example, Kellene Ricks, "Worldwide Anniversary Celebrates 'Tie to Past, Commitment to Future,'" *Church News*, 25 Nov. 1989, 8–9; and Sheridan R. Sheffield, "Walk in the Light," *Church News*, 28 Nov. 1992, 8–9.

100. "The Rising Generation: Young Women Worldwide," 11 Apr. 1986, 1, Carolyn J. Rasmus Office Papers, CHL; see also Alma 5:49.

101. "The Rising Generation: Young Women Worldwide," 11 Apr. 1986, 2, Carolyn J. Rasmus Office Papers, CHL.

102. "The Rising Generation: Young Women Worldwide," 11 Apr. 1986, 8, Carolyn J. Rasmus Office Papers, CHL; Young Women General Board, Minutes, 26 Feb. 1986, 5; 3 Sept. 1986, 5.

103. Young Women General Board, Minutes, 8 Oct. 1986, 2; LeeAnn Fackrell to Kathleen Lubeck, 31 Aug. 1986, Carolyn J. Rasmus Office Papers, CHL; "300,000 Young Women Send Balloon Messages of Hope Worldwide," *Ensign*, Nov. 1986, 102.

104. Anne Hinckley Bennion et al., interview by Amber Taylor, 14 Mar. 2021, 35–41.

105. Rising Generation Compilation, CHL.

106. Valencia signed only her first name. These letters are representative of those collected in a binder of young women's messages in the authors' possession entitled "The Rising Generation: Young Women Worldwide."

107. "Jerusalem Balloon Sendoff," 1986, Carolyn J. Rasmus Office Papers, CHL.

108. Rising Generation Compilation, CHL; Anne Hinckley Bennion et al., interview by Amber Taylor, 14 Mar. 2021, 37–39; along with follow-up emails.

109. "Logo Symbolic That Girls Will Hold Up the Light of Christ," *Church News*, 24 Oct. 1987, 7; "Follow 'Stars' to Destination," *Church News*, 24 Oct. 1987, 3.

110. Ardeth G. Kapp and Carolyn J. Rasmus, interview by Gordon Irving, 29 May 1992, 166, 178; Kellene Ricks, "Prophet Rings Bell 119 Years Later to Commemorate Founding of Y.W.," *Church News*, 10 Dec. 1988, 3–4. The prevailing understanding at the time was still based on Susa Young Gates's date of 28 November 1869 for the founding of the Young Ladies' Retrenchment Association.

111. "Bells to Ring During YW Commemoration," *Church News*, 14 Jan. 1989, 5; Kellene Ricks, "Worldwide Anniversary Celebrates 'Tie to Past, Commitment to Future,'" *Church News*, 25 Nov. 1989, 8–9.

112. Ardeth G. Kapp and Carolyn J. Rasmus, interview by Gordon Irving, 4 June 1992, 201–202.

113. Ardeth G. Kapp and Carolyn J. Rasmus, interview by Gordon Irving, 4 June 1992, 235.

114. Young Women Personal Progress Program Revision Committee, Minutes, 13 Mar. 1985, [1], Young Women Minutes, 1984–1992, CHL.

115. Ardeth G. Kapp and Carolyn J. Rasmus, interview by Gordon Irving, 4 June 1992, 203; Young Women Personal Progress Program Revision Committee, Minutes, 10 Apr. 1985, [2], Young Women Minutes, 1984–1992, CHL.

116. Ardeth G. Kapp and Carolyn J. Rasmus, interview by Gordon Irving, 4 June 1992, 201; Young Women Personal Progress Program Revision Committee, Minutes, 13 Mar. 1985, [1], Young Women Minutes, 1984–1992, CHL.

117. Louise Baird, interview by Kate Holbrook, 9 Feb. 2018, 1–3; Alvin H. Price, Journal, 1985–1986, private possession; Ardeth G. Kapp and Carolyn J. Rasmus, interview by Gordon Irving, 4 June 1992, 201–202.

118. Louise Baird, interview by Kate Holbrook, 9 Feb. 2018, 3–4, 8–9; Ardeth G. Kapp and Carolyn J. Rasmus, interview by Gordon Irving, 4 June 1992, 202–205; Young Women Personal Progress Program Revision Committee, Minutes, 30 July 1985, [1], Young Women Minutes, 1984–1992, CHL; Alvin H. and Barbara W. Price, interview by Kate Holbrook, 14 Feb. 2018, 11.

119. Ardeth G. Kapp and Carolyn J. Rasmus, interview by Gordon Irving, 4 June 1992, 204–205.

120. *Deseret News 1985 Church Almanac*, 9.

121. *Deseret News 1991–1992 Church Almanac*, 6.

122. Ardeth G. Kapp and Carolyn J. Rasmus, interview by Gordon Irving, 4 May 1992, 57.

123. Russell M. Nelson, "Daughters of Zion," *New Era*, Nov. 1985 (Young Women special issue), 9.

124. *Personal Progress* (1989), 19, 21, 39, 62, 64.

125. *Personal Progress* (1989), 75.

126. *Personal Progress* (1989), 4.

127. *Personal Progress* (1989), 76–80.

128. Darlene Kearl, "Award for Kristen Bindrup," *Morgan County News* (Morgan, UT), 22 Feb. 1991, 4A.

129. See, for example, "Young Womenhood Recognition Award," *Manti (UT) Messenger*, 7 Feb. 1991, 3; "Ward Cites Miss Clark," *Item of Millburn (NJ) and Short Hills*, 26 Sept. 1991, 7; and "Odessan Receives Award," *Odessa (TX) American*, 3 Aug. 1991, 14.

130. Anne Hinckley Bennion et al., interview by Amber Taylor, 14 Mar. 2021, 27–28; Katie Bennion Jepsen, email to Amber Taylor, 19 Sept. 2021.

131. Elisabetta J. Calabrese, interview by Phillip and Doreen Lear, 13 Nov. 2017, 24:30–27:50.

132. Elisabetta J. Calabrese, interview by Phillip and Doreen Lear, 13 Nov. 2017, 27:50–29:15.

133. Kapp and Rasmus, "Chronology," 254.

134. Ardeth G. Kapp and Carolyn J. Rasmus, interview by Gordon Irving, 4 June 1992, 216.

135. Ardeth G. Kapp and Carolyn J. Rasmus, interview by Gordon Irving, 4 June 1992, 216–218.

136. Kapp and Rasmus, "Chronology," 265.

137. Ardeth G. Kapp and Carolyn J. Rasmus, interview by Gordon Irving, 4 June 1992, 218–219.

138. Thomas S. Monson, "That We May Touch Heaven," and "The Lighthouse of the Lord," *Ensign*, Nov. 1990, 45–47, 95–99.

139. *For the Strength of Youth* (1990), 15.

140. *For the Strength of Youth* (1990), 10–14.

141. Ardeth G. Kapp and Carolyn J. Rasmus, interview by Gordon Irving, 4 June 1992, 220.

142. "The Lord's Standards Haven't Changed," *Ensign*, Sept. 1991, 7–10.

143. Ardeth G. Kapp and Carolyn J. Rasmus, interview by Gordon Irving, 4 June 1992, 220.

144. "The Lord's Standards Haven't Changed," *Ensign*, Sept. 1991, 9.

145. See, for example, "For the Strength of Youth," *Church News*, 12 Jan. 1991, 4; and "Tough Questions, Solid Answers," *New Era*, Feb. 1991, 38–39.

146. See *Young Women Handbook* (1989), 6–10.

147. *Young Women Handbook* (1989), 7.

148. *Young Women Handbook* (1989), 2.

149. *Young Women Handbook* (1989), 8–9.

150. Young Women General Board, Minutes, 26 June 1985, 5; 21 Aug. 1985, 7; 12 Mar. 1986, 7; "Young Women's Personal Achievement Program Structure," 5, in Young Women General Board, Minutes, Aug. 1985.

151. *Young Women Handbook* (1989), 9–10.

152. Anne Hinckley Bennion et al., interview by Amber Taylor, 14 Mar. 2021, 7–8, 18–19.

153. *Young Women Camp Manual* (1992), 8.

154. Elisabetta J. Calabrese, interview by Phillip and Doreen Lear, 13 Nov. 2017, 10:25–14:00.

155. Elisabetta J. Calabrese, interview by Phillip and Doreen Lear, 13 Nov. 2017, 17:50–24:25.

156. See Hortense Child Smith, interview by Gordon Irving, 3 Nov. 1980, 285.

157. *Young Women Handbook* (1988), 10; see also *Young Women Handbook* (1989), 10.

158. Ardeth G. Kapp and Carolyn J. Rasmus, interview by Gordon Irving, 4 May 1992, 71.

159. Marissa Bodily, "Aging in Place: 50 Years in Winnifred Jardine's Home," *Voices of Utah* (blog), 3 Apr. 2014, voices-of-utah.com; Alvin H. and Barbara W. Price, interview by Kate Holbrook, 14 Feb. 2018, 1–2.

160. Sheridan R. Sheffield, "New Young Women Camp Manual Written 'for Today,'" *Church News*, 20 Feb. 1993, 3.

CHAPTER 9: ENGAGING THE WORLD, 1992–2012

1. Zandile Precious Qinisile, interview by Khumbulani D. Mdletshe, 9 Feb. 2019, 1–3.

2. See Gupta, de Wit, and McKeown, "Impact of Poverty," 667–672.

3. Zandile Precious Qinisile, interview by Khumbulani D. Mdletshe, 9 Feb. 2019, 5–7, 12–14.

4. Zandile Precious Qinisile, interview by Khumbulani D. Mdletshe, 9 Feb. 2019, 12.

5. Plewe, *Mapping Mormonism*, 166–173. For more on the rise of the term *Global South*, see Dados and Connell, "Global South," 12–13.

6. David B. Haight, "Filling the Whole Earth," *Ensign*, May 1990, 23; Matthew 28:19–20; Joseph Smith, "Church History," 1 Mar. 1842, in *JSP*, H1:500.

7. For more on the expanding influence of Christianity in the Global South, see Jenkins, *Next Christendom*, xi–xiii.

8. Jay M. Todd, "More Members Now Outside U.S. Than in U.S.," *Ensign*, Mar. 1996, 76–77; Jay M. Todd, "Historic Milestone Achieved: More Non-English-Speaking Members Now Than English-Speaking," *Ensign*, Sept. 2000, 76–77; see also Sarah Petersen, "The Majority of Mormons Live Outside the US," *Deseret News*, 30 Aug. 2013, deseret.com.

9. Erika Aza Rosero, interview by Amber Taylor, 11 Mar. 2021, 22:00–33:00, 34:55–37:00, 42:53–43:30.

10. Bowman, *Mormon People*, xix–xxi; Reeve, *Religion of a Different Color*, 1–13.

11. Janette Hales Beckham, interview by Kate Holbrook, 23 Aug. 2016, 9, 14–16, 25.

12. Margaret D. Nadauld, interview by Christine R. Marin, 17 Sept. 2002, 16.

13. See, for example, Elaine S. Dalton, interview by Justin Bray, 25 June 2014, 19–20.

14. Janette Hales Beckham, interview by Kate Holbrook, 23 Aug. 2016, 2–5, 9.

15. "New Young Women General Presidency Called," *Ensign*, May 1992, 106; Janette Hales Beckham, interview by Kate Holbrook, 23 Aug. 2016, 6–7.

16. Janette Hales Beckham, interview by Kate Holbrook, 23 Aug. 2016, 9.

17. Bellah et al., *Habits of the Heart*, 55, 142; see also MacIntyre, *After Virtue*, 1–5.

18. "Premarital Pregnancy among Mormons," 8 June 1983, draft, 1–2, Relief Society Research and Evaluation Services Reports, CHL; Priesthood Executive Council, Minutes, 19 Sept. 1990, 1, 2; see also Heaton, Bahr, and Jacobson, *Statistical Profile of Mormons*, 89, 105.

19. Norton and Miller, *Marriage, Divorce, and Remarriage*, 1–21; Kennedy and Ruggles, "Breaking Up Is Hard to Count," 587–598.

20. See James E. Talmage, "The Eternity of Sex," *Young Woman's Journal*, Oct. 1914, 600–604.

21. See, for example, David O. McKay, "To Parents in the Church," in *Family Home Evening Manual* (1968), iv; Spencer W. Kimball, "Strengthening the Family—the Basic Unit of the Church," *Ensign*, May 1978, 45–48; Barbara B. Smith, "A Safe Place for Marriages and Families," *Ensign*, Nov. 1981, 83–85; and James E. Faust, "The Greatest Challenge in the World—Good Parenting," *Ensign*, Nov. 1990, 32–35.

22. For example, BYU law professor Richard Wilkins began forging relationships with other representatives concerned about family at the United Nations Habitat II conference in Istanbul in 1996. Wilkins went on to establish the World Family Policy Center, which operated from 1999 to 2008 at BYU, to influence discourse on family-related issues at the UN. During this period, Wilkins facilitated church leaders' involvement in the World Congress of Families. In 1999, Wilkins's World Family Policy Center was a sponsor of the World Congress of Families' annual conference at a UN facility in Geneva, Switzerland. Young Women general president Margaret D. Nadauld spoke at the conference. Civil and human rights groups later raised concerns about the World Congress of Families because of its connections with ethnic nationalism in some countries and its influence on authoritarian measures to limit free speech around gay rights. (Richard G. Wilkins, "Defending the Family," BYU Devotional, Provo, UT, 6 July 1999, speeches.byu.edu; "Brigham Young University. World Family Policy Center," University Organizational History Project, Harold B. Lee Library, BYU, byuorg.lib.byu.edu; "Church Participates in World Congress of Families," *Ensign*, Feb. 2000, 76–77; "World Congress of Families," Extremist Files, Southern Poverty Law Center, splcenter.org.)

23. Philip S. Gutis, "Small Steps Toward Acceptance Renew Debate on Gay Marriage," *New York Times*, 5 Nov. 1989, sec. 4, p. 24.

24. Jeffrey Schmalz, "In Hawaii, Step Toward Legalized Gay Marriage," *New York Times*, 7 May 1993, sec. A, p. 14.

25. See *The Church and the Proposed Equal Rights Amendment*, 2, 9; Dallin H. Oaks, "Principles to Govern Possible Public Statement on Legislation Affecting Rights of Homosexuals," 7 Aug. 1984; and Gordon B. Hinckley, "Reverence and Morality," *Ensign*, May 1987, 46–47.

26. Butler, "From *Gender Trouble*," 503.

27. James E. Talmage, "The Eternity of Sex," *Young Woman's Journal*, Oct. 1914, 600–604.

28. Dallin H. Oaks, "The Great Plan of Happiness," *Ensign*, Nov. 1993, 72.

29. Paulsen and Pulido, "A Mother There," 71–97.

30. "Becoming Like God," Gospel Topics Essays, ChurchofJesusChrist.org.

31. According to a corpus of general conference talks from Latter-day Saint leaders, *gender* was used seventeen times from 1990 to 1994, while it was used only four times in the 1980s. *Mother* was used 707 times in the 1980s and 919 times in the 1990s. *Motherhood* was used 26 times in the 1980s and 36 times in the 1990s. (LDS General Conference Corpus, lds-general-conference.org.)

32. Elaine L. Jack, "Relief Society: A Balm in Gilead," and Gordon B. Hinckley, "Stand Strong against the Wiles of the World," *Ensign*, Nov. 1995, 92, 100–101; see also Chieko N. Okazaki, "A Living Network," and Aileen H. Clyde, "What Is Relief Society For?," *Ensign*, Nov. 1995, 93–98.

33. An 1841 revelation had instructed Joseph Smith and early church leaders to write "a solemn proclamation of my gospel" to "all the kings of the world." Since then, church leaders have issued only a few such proclamations. (Doctrine and Covenants 124:2–4; Scott Taylor, "Proclamations Are Rare Events in Church History," *Church News*, 12 Apr. 2020, 4–5.)

34. First Presidency and Council of the Twelve Apostles, *The Family: A Proclamation to the World* (Salt Lake City: The Church of Jesus Christ of Latter-day Saints, 1995).

35. First Presidency and Council of the Twelve Apostles, *The Family: A Proclamation to the World* (Salt Lake City: The Church of Jesus Christ of Latter-day Saints, 1995); Bushman, *Contemporary Mormonism*, 38–42.

36. Bushman, *Contemporary Mormonism*, 38–42.

37. Natsume Inagaki, email to Melissa Inouye, 27 Sept. 2020.

38. Anonymous, interview by Deidre Green, 9 June 2015, interview 1, p. 9, Gender, Narrative, and Religious Practice in Southern Africa Oral History Collection, Special Collections, Claremont Colleges Library, Claremont, CA.

39. Oral History no. 155, interview by Caroline Kline, 30 Nov. 2016, 14–16, Claremont Mormon Women Oral History Collection, Claremont Colleges Library, Claremont, CA.

40. See Drogus, "Private Power or Public Power," 62–63; and Bergunder, "Pentecostal Movement," 168.

41. Erika Aza Rosero, interview by Amber Taylor, 11 Mar. 2021, 1:17:40–1:19:40.

42. "Median Age at First Marriage: 1890 to Present," Historical Marital Status Tables, U.S. Census Bureau, updated 21 Nov. 2023, census.gov.

43. Bridey Jensen, "Understanding Who She Is," interview by Krisanne Hastings, 20 June 2012, LDS Women Project, ldswomenproject.com.

44. Suzi Fei, "Coded in the DNA," interview by Kathryn Peterson, 4 Oct. 2013, LDS Women Project, ldswomenproject.com.

45. Angela Fallentine, "Recorded in Heaven," interview by Lydia Defranchi, 6 Sept. 2013, LDS Women Project, ldswomenproject.com.

46. Young Women General Board, Minutes, 26 Oct. 1995, [2].

47. Young Women General Board, Minutes, 11 Jan. 1996, [2]–[3].

48. Young Women General Board, Minutes, 11 Jan. 1996, [3]; Gretchen Livingston and Deja Thomas, "Why Is the Teen Birth Rate Falling?," Pew Research Center, 2 Aug. 2019, pewresearch.org; Kost, Maddow-Zimet, and Arpaia, *Pregnancies, Births, and Abortions*, 9–10. The 1990 high never reached the peak teen pregnancy numbers from the 1950s.

49. "Notes from Family Retreat," in Young Women General Board, Minutes, 8 Feb. 1996, [1]–[4].

50. Gurcharan Singh Gill, email to James Goldberg, 17 Sept. 2020.

51. Olivier Duriez and Deolinda Duriez, interview by Jay G. Burrup, 1 June 2002, 18–19, 21. Steven L. Olsen assisted the authors by clarifying some French passages from this interview. His notes and translations are in the authors' possession.

52. "New Presidency for Young Women," *Church News*, 11 Oct. 1997, 5.

53. "Margaret D. Nadauld," and "Sharon G. Larsen," *Ensign*, Nov. 1997, 103; "Carol B. Thomas," *Ensign*, May 1997, 109.

54. Young Women General Board, Minutes, 8 Jan. 1998, [3]–[4].

55. Julie A. Dockstader, "Young Women Turning 'Hearts to the Family,'" *Church News*, 24 Jan. 1998, 5.

56. "Young Women Will Be Instructed by Leaders in General Meeting," *Church News*, 12 Mar. 1994, 10; Julie A. Dockstader, "Trusting Lord Brings True Security," *Church News*, 2 Apr. 1994, 3.

57. Carol B. Thomas, "Understanding Our True Identity," *Ensign*, May 1998, 91–92.

58. Sharon G. Larsen, "Young Women—Titles of Liberty," *Ensign*, May 1998, 93.

59. Margaret D. Nadauld, "Turning Hearts to the Family," *Ensign*, May 1998, 90.

60. "Young Women," 4–5, in Young Women General Board, Minutes, 29 Jan. 1998.

61. Julie A. Dockstader, "Young Women Worldwide Celebration Is 'Turning Hearts to the Family,'" *Church News*, 28 Nov. 1998, 8–9, 11.

62. Young Women General Board, Minutes, 15 Oct. 1998, 4.

63. Young Women General Board, Minutes, 29 Oct. 1998, 8.

64. Young Women General Board, Minutes, 10 Feb. 2000, [3]; 9 Aug. 2001, [1].

65. Julie Dockstader Heaps, "Personal Progress: Temple Preparation," *Church News*, 27 Oct. 2001, 4.

66. Newburger, *Home Computers and Internet Use*, 1.

67. File, *Computer and Internet Use*, 2, 10–12.

68. "2010 Statistics Update" (newsletter no. 61), Internet World Stats News, 30 Mar. 2011, internetworld stats.com; Luke Pensworth, "2019 Internet Statistics, Trends, and Data," DailyWireless, 7 Mar. 2020, dailywireless.org.

69. "Technology Used by Church from Early Years," Newsroom, 1 Jan. 2007, newsroom.Church ofJesusChrist.org.

70. "New Mobile Apps Available," Tech Forum, 3 June 2010, tech.ChurchofJesusChrist.org/forum.

71. R. Scott Lloyd, "New Web Site for Youth," *Church News*, 9 Jan. 2010, 3–4.

72. See Kushner, *Players Ball*, 1–8, 87–104.

73. American Psychological Association, Task Force on the Sexualization of Girls, *Report*, v, 2, 4.

74. See, for example, Thomas S. Monson, "Pornography, the Deadly Carrier," *Ensign*, July 2001, 2–5.

75. See, for example, M. Russell Ballard, "Keeping Covenants," *Ensign*, May 1993, 6–9; Gordon B. Hinckley, "Loyalty," *Ensign*, May 2003, 58; and Gordon B. Hinckley, "A Tragic Evil among Us," *Ensign*, Nov. 2004, 59–62.

76. James E. Faust, "We Seek After These Things," *Ensign*, May 1998, 44–45.

77. From 1972 to 2012, women's participation in school-sponsored sports grew from fewer than 300,000 to over 3.2 million. In basketball, for example, high school girls' participation grew from 132,000 in 1972 to 454,000 by 1998. (Cahn, *Coming on Strong*, 285; "High School Athletics Participation History (1969–2008)," National Federation of State High School Associations, updated 8 Sept. 2023, nfhs.org.)

78. Tortora, *Dress, Fashion, and Technology*, 178, 181; Fashion History Timeline: 1990–1999, Fashion Institute of Technology, updated 24 Sept. 2020, fashionhistory.fitnyc.edu.

79. Elaine S. Dalton, "Arise and Shine Forth," BYU Women's Conference Address, Provo, UT, 30 Apr. 2004, speeches.byu.edu.

80. Susan W. Tanner, "The Sanctity of the Body," *Ensign*, Nov. 2005, 14.

81. See Rocamora, "Personal Fashion Blogs," 407–424.

82. See, for example, Rodger L. Hardy, "Desire for Modesty Turns into Business," "More Modest Fashion in Utah County," and Rodger L. Hardy, "Sales Take Off for Business That Sells Modest Swimwear," *Deseret Morning News*, 9 Mar. 2006, Utah Valley Life section, 3, 6, 7. These businesses were based in the Latter-day Saint cultural region centered in Utah, but because of the rise of internet commerce, they could also serve church members throughout the United States and beyond.

83. Sharon G. Larsen, interview by Christine R. Marin, 17 Sept. 2002, 3, 5, 13, 31.

84. Zandile Precious Qinisile, interview by Khumbulani D. Mdletshe, 9 Feb. 2019, 8, 10–11.

85. Zandile Precious Qinisile, interview by Khumbulani D. Mdletshe, 9 Feb. 2019, 11.

86. Zandile Precious Qinisile, interview by Khumbulani D. Mdletshe, 9 Feb. 2019, 14.

87. Sharon G. Larsen, interview by Christine R. Marin, 17 Sept. 2002, 27.

88. "Julie Bangerter Beck," *Ensign*, Nov. 2002, 124.

89. "Silvia H. Allred," *Ensign*, May 2007, 127.

90. Margaret D. Nadauld, interview by Christine R. Marin, 17 Sept. 2002, 17, 20.

91. Carol B. Thomas, interview by Christine R. Marin, 17 Feb. 2002, 12–13; "Teaming Up for Youth," *Ensign*, Jan. 2002, 10.

92. *Young Women Personal Progress* (2001), 13.

93. *Young Women Personal Progress* (2001), 16–17; "The Living Christ," *Church News*, 1 Jan. 2000, 3.

94. *Young Women Personal Progress* (2001), 9, 13.

95. *Young Women Personal Progress* (2001), 20.

96. *Young Women Personal Progress* (2001), 8, 64.

97. Julie Dockstader Heaps, "Personal Progress: Temple Preparation," *Church News*, 27 Oct. 2001, 4.

98. *Young Women Personal Progress* (2009), 83–84.

99. See *Young Women Personal Progress* (2001), cover.

100. Beck served as first counselor in the Young Women general presidency from 2002 to 2007 and as president of the Relief Society from 2007 to 2012. Dalton served as second counselor in the Young Women general presidency from 2002 to 2007, first counselor from 2007 to 2008, and president from 2008 to 2013. Allred served as first counselor in the Relief Society general presidency from 2007 to 2012.

101. Margaret D. Nadauld, interview by Christine R. Marin, 17 Sept. 2002, 17–18.

102. Margaret D. Nadauld, interview by Christine R. Marin, 17 Sept. 2002, 13–14.

103. See, for example, "Resource Guide for *Young Women Manual 3*," *Ensign*, Nov. 2001, 107; and the online version at ChurchofJesusChrist.org; see also Erickson, "Doctrinal and Historical Analysis of Young Women's Education," 186–192.

104. "'New Beginnings' in a New Year," *Church News*, 13 Jan. 2013, 14.

105. Erika Aza Rosero, interview by Amber Taylor, 11 Mar. 2021, 1:11:30–1:17:30.

106. Margaret D. Nadauld, interview by Christine R. Marin, 17 Sept. 2002, 19–20.

107. Naomi Frandsen, "Young Women Are Models of Modesty," *Ensign*, Jan. 2003, 75–77; William Lobdell, "Modest, Style-Conscious, and Frustrated No More," *Los Angeles Times*, 11 Oct. 2002, 1.

108. David Dickson, "15 Awesome Mutual Activity Ideas," *New Era*, Oct. 2015, 24–27.

109. Mary N. Cook, "A Mighty Change in Mongolia," *Liahona*, Feb. 1997, 10–13; Mary N. Cook, interview by Brittany Chapman Nash, 2 Mar. 2017, 2.

110. Mary N. Cook and Ulaanbaatar Branch Young Women to Cook Family, 30 Aug. 1994, Mary N. Cook Papers, CHL; Mary N. Cook, interview by Brittany Chapman Nash, 2 Mar. 2017, 3.

111. Mary N. Cook, interview by Brittany Chapman Nash, 2 Mar. 2017, 2, 3–5.

112. Mary N. Cook to Cook Family, 15 Aug. 1995, Mary N. Cook Papers, CHL.

113. Mary N. Cook, interview by Brittany Chapman Nash, 2 Mar. 2017, 5–6.

114. Mary N. Cook, interview by Brittany Chapman Nash, 2 Mar. 2017, 5, 6.

115. Mary N. Cook, interview by Brittany Chapman Nash, 2 Mar. 2017, 7–8.

116. Myzejen Kocani and Edlira Kocani, interview by Matthew K. Heiss, 11 May 1996, 18–19.

117. Elizabeth A. Adei-Manu, interview by Brent G. Thompson, 12 Sept. 1998, 8–9.

118. Erika Aza Rosero, Interview by Amber Taylor, 11 Mar. 2021, 50:00–1:04:00.

119. Verónica Battista, email to Amber Taylor, 13 Dec. 2022.

120. Elizabeth A. Adei-Manu, interview by Brent G. Thompson, 12 Sept. 1998, 9–10; Myzejen Kocani and Edlira Kocani, interview by Matthew K. Heiss, 11 May 1996, 18, 20; see also the full bibliographic entry for Laurel L. Holman Papers, 1994–1998, in the CHL catalog.

121. "New General Presidency Is Called for Young Women Organization," *Church News*, 12 Oct. 2002, 4; "Susan Winder Tanner," *Ensign*, Nov. 2002, 123.

122. "Young Women Program: Study of Needs," 25 Apr. 2007, 5, Elaine S. Dalton Miscellaneous Files, CHL; see also Young Women General Board, Minutes, 5 June 2003, [2].

123. Mary N. Cook, interview by Amber Taylor, 12 May 2019, file 5, 9:00–11:00.

124. Mary N. Cook, interview by Amber Taylor, 12 May 2019, file 5, 15:00–20:00.

125. Susan W. Tanner, interview by Amber Taylor, 3 June 2019, 11:00–29:00.

126. Deb Pouliot, email to Amber Taylor, 28 Oct. 2020.

127. Greg Hill, "Retreat to Mountain Sanctuary," *Church News*, 1 July 2006, 8–10.

128. Greg Hill, "Retreat to Mountain Sanctuary," *Church News*, 1 July 2006, 10.

129. Merrill J. Bateman, "Heber Valley Camp Dedicatory Prayer," 22 June 2006, CHL.

130. Tad Walch, "BYU Newspaper Yanks T-Shirt Ad," *Deseret Morning News*, 25 Sept. 2004, B1–B2.

131. Carpenter, "Virginity Loss in Reel/Real Life," 804–827.

132. See Regnerus, *Forbidden Fruit*, 123, 133.

133. See, for example, Young Women General Board, Minutes, 29 May 2003, [2]; 5 June 2003, [4]; 21 Aug. 2003, [2]; 5 Feb. 2004, [2]; 26 Jan. 2006, [2]; 8 June 2006, [2].

134. Brittanie Morris, "EFY Change Supports Church's Focus," *Daily Universe* (Provo, UT), 23 Jan. 2007, universe.byu.edu; "New Mutual Theme Announced for 2007," *Ensign*, Nov. 2006, 127–128; *Let Virtue Garnish Thy Thoughts* (Salt Lake City: The Church of Jesus Christ of Latter-day Saints, 2006); see also Young Women General Board, Minutes, 19 Oct. 2006, [2].

135. Regnerus, *Forbidden Fruit*, 133.

136. See, for example, Stone, "Young Women in Mormon Homelands," 127–129, 164–165.

137. Molly Oswaks, "Elizabeth Smart Is Standing Up for Rape Victims—And Tearing Down Purity Culture," *Vice*, 1 Sept. 2016, vice.com.

138. Molly Oswaks, "Elizabeth Smart Is Standing Up for Rape Victims—And Tearing Down Purity Culture," *Vice*, 1 Sept. 2016, vice.com.

139. Okazaki, "Healing from Sexual Abuse," 1–12; Richard G. Scott, "To Heal the Shattering Consequences of Abuse," *Ensign*, May 2008, 40–43; Camille West, "Bringing Hope and Healing to Victims of Abuse," *Church News*, 4 Nov. 2018, 22–23.

140. Elaine S. Dalton, "Look toward Eternity!," *Ensign*, Nov. 2006, 31–32.

141. In 2016, for example, leaders removed the Book of Mormon verse Moroni 9:9 from Personal Progress materials. (Kerr, "'Virtue' in Moroni 9:9," 260–265.)

142. "The Sustaining of Church Officers," *Ensign*, May 2008, 7. Julie B. Beck was called as the fifteenth general president of the Relief Society in April 2007. ("The Sustaining of Church Officers," *Ensign*, May 2007, 6.)

143. Sarah Jane Weaver, "Choose Happiness, Young Women Leader Counsels," *Church News*, 9 June 2007, 11.

144. Sarah Jane Weaver, "Childhood Event Becomes Cornerstone of Testimony," *Church News*, 9 Aug. 2008, 6.

145. Elaine S. Dalton, interview by Justin Bray, 25 June 2014, 7–8; Wright and Westrup, "Ensign Peak," 29, 41–42; Jacob Olmstead, email to Kate Holbrook, 11 Apr. 2022.

146. "High on the Mountain Top," Hymn 5, in *Hymns* (1985).

147. Elaine S. Dalton, interview by Justin Bray, 25 June 2014, 8.

148. Elaine S. Dalton, interview by Justin Bray, 25 June 2014, 11.

149. Elaine S. Dalton, interview by Justin Bray, 25 June 2014, 15.

150. Elaine S. Dalton, "A Return to Virtue," *Ensign*, Nov. 2008, 79; *Preach My Gospel*, 118.

151. Dictionary definitions of the word *virtue* indicate high moral character, goodness, valor, and capability, before listing *chastity* (in sixth and last place in the list of definitions) as a comparable idea. ("Virtue," in Merriam-Webster Dictionary, merriam-webster.com/dictionary/virtue.)

152. The First Presidency approved the general presidency's proposal and announced the addition of virtue to the Young Women values in a letter dated 28 November 2008. ("New Value: Virtue," *Church News*, 20 Dec. 2008, 3.)

153. Sarah Jane Weaver, "Personal Progress Online," *Church News*, 30 Oct. 2010, 14.

154. "Standing for Virtue," *New Era*, Nov. 2009, 18.

155. *Young Women Personal Progress* (2009), 69–74.

156. "Standing for Virtue," *New Era*, Nov. 2009, 19.

157. Zandile Precious Qinisile, interview by Khumbulani D. Mdletshe, 9 Feb. 2019, 15.

158. Embry, "Oral History and Mormon Women Missionaries," 174.

159. "Feel the Spirit of the Lord," *Church News*, 14 Oct. 2012, 3.

160. "Thousands More Mormons Choose Missionary Service," Newsroom, 3 Oct. 2013, newsroom.ChurchofJesusChrist.org.

CHAPTER 10: DISCIPLES OF CHRIST, 2013–2024

1. Camila Ortega Aza, interview by Amber Taylor, 1 Apr. 2021, 21:00–24:00.

2. Trent Toone, "A 'Spectacular Success': How Sister Missionaries Have Dispelled Myths for 120 Years," *Deseret News*, 8 June 2018, deseret.com.

3. A patriarchal blessing is a special blessing, given by a man ordained as a patriarch, that "provides inspired direction from the Lord" and includes "a declaration of a person's lineage in the house of Israel." ("Patriarchal Blessings," Topics and Questions, ChurchofJesusChrist.org.)

4. Camila Ortega Aza, interview by Amber Taylor, 1 Apr. 2021, 8:35–10:30, 12:16–12:50, 28:00–31:15.

5. John Sagers (data analyst, Church Membership and Statistical Records Department), email to Nicholas B. Shrum, 13 Sept. 2021.

6. Gerrit W. Gong, "Room in the Inn," *Liahona*, May 2021, 26.

7. "What Are the Core Characteristics of Generation Z?," Annie E. Casey Foundation, 12 Jan. 2021, aecf .org; Michael Dimock, "Defining Generations: Where Millennials End and Generation Z Begins," Pew Research Center, 17 Jan. 2019, pewresearch.org.

8. "Religion among the Millennials," Pew Research Center, 17 Feb. 2010, pewresearch.org.

9. "What Are the Core Characteristics of Generation Z?," Annie E. Casey Foundation, 12 Jan. 2021, aecf.org.

10. "Growing Support for Gay Marriage: Changed Minds and Changing Demographics," Pew Research Center, 20 Mar. 2013, pewresearch.org.

11. "Church Updates Official 'Mormon and Gay' Website," Newsroom, 25 Oct. 2016, newroom .ChurchofJesusChrist.org; "Transcript of News Conference on Religious Freedom and Non-discrimination," Newsroom, 27 Jan. 2015, newsroom.ChurchofJesusChrist.org; Laurie Goodstein, "Utah Passes Antidiscrimination Bill Backed by Mormon Leaders," *New York Times*, 12 Mar. 2015, nytimes.com.

12. Emily Fetsch, "Are Millennials Leaving Religion over LGBT Issues?," Public Religion Research Institute, 13 Mar. 2014, prri.org; Daniel Cox, Juhem Navarro-Rivera, and Robert P. Jones, "A Shifting Landscape: A Decade of Change in American Attitudes about Same-Sex Marriage and LGBT Issues," Public Religion Research Institute, 26 Feb. 2014, prri.org.

13. M. Russell Ballard, "The Greatest Generation of Missionaries," *Ensign*, Nov. 2002, 46–49; Shaun D. Stahle, "Preach My Gospel," *Church News*, 6 Nov. 2004, 8, 13.

14. Sarah Jane Weaver, "Young Women Prepare for Option of Missionary Service," *Church News*, 2 Dec. 2012, 6–7.

15. Jodi Kantor and Laurie Goodstein, "Missions Signal a Growing Role for Mormon Women," *New York Times*, 1 Mar. 2014, nytimes.com.

16. This program provided topics and outlines for lessons for youth Sunday School and for Young Women and Young Men Sunday instruction. It was a precursor to the churchwide *Come, Follow Me* curriculum implemented in 2019, which standardized the curriculum for all church members from Primary age to adults. (Camille West, "New Resources for Home, Primary, Sunday School," *Church News*, 15 July 2018, 2.)

17. Richardson, "Come, Follow Me," 23–47.

18. "Sister Bonnie L. Oscarson" (Leader Biography), Newsroom, newsroom.ChurchofJesusChrist.org.

19. Bonnie L. Oscarson, interview by Lisa T. Clayton, 28 June 2018, 83.

20. Sarah Jane Weaver, "International Representation on New Young Women General Board," *Church News*, 16 Feb. 2014, 5.

21. "New Members Announced for Young Women General Board," Newsroom, 14 Feb. 2014, newsroom .ChurchofJesusChrist.org; Bonnie L. Oscarson, interview by Lisa T. Clayton, 28 June 2018, 85–86; Sarah Jane Weaver, "International Representation on New Young Women General Board," *Church News*, 16 Feb. 2014, 5.

22. Bonnie L. Oscarson, interview by Lisa T. Clayton, 28 June 2018, 89–90.

23. "Bonnie L. Oscarson," *Ensign*, May 2013, 143.

24. "Carol F. McConkie," and "Neill F. Marriott," *Ensign*, May 2013, 144.

25. Tad Walch, "In a Significant Move, Women to Join Key, Leading LDS Church Councils," *Deseret News*, 19 Aug. 2015, deseret.com. By 2021, two women served on each of the executive councils. (Sydney Walker, "Inside Church Headquarters: A Look at 3 of the Church's Executive Councils and What They Do," *Church News*, 24 July 2021, 5–7.)

26. Turley, Journal, 20 Sept. 1984, 57; Kapp, Journal, 22 Sept. 1984.

27. See, for example, M. Russell Ballard, "Strength in Counsel," *Ensign*, Nov. 1993, 76–78; "Counseling with Our Councils," *Ensign*, May 1994, 24–26; and M. Russell Ballard, *Counseling with Our Councils: Learning to Minister Together in the Church and in the Family* [Salt Lake City: Deseret Book, 1997].

28. Tad Walch, "In a Significant Move, Women to Join Key, Leading LDS Church Councils," *Deseret News*, 19 Aug. 2015, deseret.com.

29. Elaine S. Dalton, interview by Justin Bray, 25 June 2014, 16.

30. *Deseret News 2003 Church Almanac,* 472–475; Elaine S. Dalton, interview by Justin Bray, 25 June 2014, 16; Brook P. Hales, "Statistical Report, 2013," *Ensign*, May 2014, 28.

31. David A. Bednar, "The Hearts of the Children Shall Turn," *Ensign*, Nov. 2011, 26.

32. First Presidency to "Members of the Church," 8 Oct. 2012, ChurchofJesusChrist.org.

33. "Why Indexing Matters," *New Era*, Oct. 2014, 16–17.

34. Series of email exchanges between Camila Ortega Aza and Amber Taylor, 9–13 Apr. and 17 June 2021.

35. Series of email exchanges between Camila Ortega Aza and Amber Taylor, 9–13 Apr. 2021.

36. Jill B. Adair, "Indexing Project: Youth Log 6,159 Names," *Church News*, 19 Apr. 2008, 5.

37. Cheri Peacock Hendricks, "Worldwide Indexing Event: How One Area's Youth Led the Way," *FamilySearch Blog*, 26 July 2016, familysearch.org/en/blog.

38. See, for example, Quentin L. Cook, "Roots and Branches," *Ensign*, May 2014, 44–48; "Special Section: Their Story, Your Story," *New Era*, Oct. 2014, 2–25; and Megan Armknecht, "How You Can Help with Temple Work," *New Era*, Aug. 2017, 10–11.

39. R. Scott Lloyd, "Helping Redeem the Dead," *Church News*, 30 Dec. 2012, 7, 12.

40. Sally Johnson Odekirk, "Three Ways to Be Involved in Family History," *New Era*, Feb. 2017, 34.

41. In 2001, education writer Marc Prensky coined the term *digital native* to describe students who had grown up with the exploratory and adaptive logics of digital interaction, in contrast to the *digital immigrants* of older generations, whose training emphasized step-by-step paradigms of task completion. (Prensky, "Digital Natives, Digital Immigrants," 1, 3–6.)

42. See, for example, O'Keefe, Clarke-Pearson, and Council on Communications and Media, "Impact of Social Media," 800–804; Carroll and Kirkpatrick, *Impact of Social Media*, 1–6; and Bob Smithouser, "Using Social Media to Engage with Your Teen," Focus on the Family, 2014, focusonthefamily.com.

43. See, for example, "Things as They Really Are," Strive to Be, 6 Oct. 2011, youtube.com; Bonnie L. Oscarson, "The Needs before Us," *Ensign*, Nov. 2017, 25; Russell M. Nelson and Wendy W. Nelson, "Hope of Israel," Worldwide Youth Devotional, Salt Lake City, UT, 3 June 2018, ChurchofJesusChrist.org; and Jeffrey R. Holland, "Angels and Astonishment," Seminaries and Institutes Annual Training Broadcast, Salt Lake City, UT, 12 June 2019, ChurchofJesusChrist.org.

44. See Mental Health, mentalhealth.ChurchofJesusChrist.org; "Same-Sex Attraction" (Topic), Newsroom, newsroom.ChurchofJesusChrist.org; "Church Provides Context for Recent Media Coverage on Gospel Topics Pages," Newsroom, 11 Nov. 2014, newsroom.ChurchofJesusChrist.org; and M. Russell Ballard, "The Opportunities and Responsibilities of CES Teachers in the 21st Century," Address to CES Religious Educators, 26 Feb. 2016, ChurchofJesusChrist.org.

45. Cnaan, Evans, and Curtis, "Called to Serve," [16].

46. Cnaan, Evans, and Curtis, "Called to Serve," [8].

47. *JustServe: Community Service Guidebook,* 2.

48. See, for example, Kurt Francom, "Implementing JustServe.org in Your Area: An Interview with Autumn Stringham," 9 June 2019, *Leading Saints Podcast*, 21:29–21:35, leadingsaints.org.

49. Republic of the Philippines, National Disaster Risk Reduction and Management Council, "NDRRMC Update: Final Report re Effects of Typhoon 'Yolanda' (Haiyan)," 6–9 Nov. 2013, pp. 1–3, ndrrmc.gov.ph.

50. "Helping Hands for Typhoon Survivors," Newsroom (Philippines), 25 Nov. 2013, news-ph.Churchof JesusChrist.org; "Remembering Yolanda," Newsroom (Philippines), 8 Nov. 2015, news-ph.Churchof JesusChrist.org.

51. See "Election Cleanup by Mormon Helping Hands," Newsroom (Philippines), 26 May 2016, news-ph .ChurchofJesusChrist.org.

52. Bonnie L. Oscarson, "The Needs before Us," *Ensign*, Nov. 2017, 25–26.

53. Diana Sagers, interview by James Goldberg, 4 Jan. 2021, 2–4.

54. Diana Sagers, interview by James Goldberg, 4 Jan. 2021, 5–7.

55. Diana Sagers, interview by James Goldberg, 4 Jan. 2021, 5, 7, 26–27.

56. Lisa Larson, "Part of the Group," *Daily Spectrum* (St. George, UT), 16 May 2009, D1; Jason Swensen, "Special Needs Mutual Experiences a Prom to Remember," Church News, 1 May 2015, ChurchofJesusChrist.org.

57. "MIA for Handicapped," *Davis County Clipper* (Bountiful, UT), 25 Feb. 1972; "Special Youth Find Pleasure in Aaronic Priesthood MIA," *Church News*, 9 Mar. 1974, 10.

58. Julie A. Dockstader, "Sweet Is the Work," *Church News*, 4 Dec. 1999, 8–9, 13.

59. Lisa Larson, "Part of the Group," *Daily Spectrum* (St. George, UT), 16 May 2009, D1; Jason

Swensen, "Special Needs Mutual Experiences a Prom to Remember," *Church News*, 1 May 2015, ChurchofJesusChrist.org.

60. "New Young Women General Presidency Announced," *Church News*, 8 Apr. 2018, 7.

61. Russell M. Nelson, "Opening Remarks," *Ensign*, Nov. 2018, 7.

62. Sarah Jane Weaver and Marianne Holman Prescott, "A New Chapter in the History of the Church," *Church News*, 8 Apr. 2018, 20.

63. "Church Consolidates Meeting Schedules," *Ensign*, Mar. 1980, 73–78; Quentin L. Cook, "Deep and Lasting Conversion to Heavenly Father and the Lord Jesus Christ," *Ensign*, Nov. 2018, 8–10.

64. Russell M. Nelson, "The Correct Name of the Church," *Ensign*, Nov. 2018, 87, 88.

65. See Russell M. Nelson, "Come, Follow Me," *Ensign*, May 2019, 91; Michelle D. Craig, "Spiritual Capacity," *Ensign*, Nov. 2019, 19–21; Gerrit W. Gong, "Covenant Belonging," *Ensign*, Nov. 2019, 80–83; Quentin L. Cook, "Great Love for Our Father's Children," *Ensign*, May 2019, 76–80; and Bonnie H. Cordon, "Becoming a Shepherd," *Ensign*, Nov. 2018, 74–76.

66. *General Handbook* (2020), sec. 1.2, pp. 4–5; see also Gary E. Stevenson, "Divinely Appointed Responsibilities, Heavenly Blessings," BYU Devotional Address, 2 Mar. 2021, speeches.byu.edu.

67. Tait, "What Is Women's Relationship to Priesthood?," 252–262.

68. Dallin H. Oaks, "The Keys and Authority of the Priesthood," *Ensign*, May 2014, 51; see also Tait, "What Is Women's Relationship to Priesthood?," 268–269.

69. Bonnie H. Cordon, "Beloved Daughters," *Ensign*, Nov. 2019, 69; see also, for example, Dale G. Renlund and Ruth Lybbert Renlund, *The Melchizedek Priesthood: Understanding the Doctrine, Living the Principles* (Salt Lake City: Deseret Book, 2018); Jean B. Bingham, "United in Accomplishing God's Work," *Ensign*, May 2020, 60–63; and Aubrey Eyre, "Women Are Endowed with Priesthood Power," *Church News*, 12 May 2019, 10–11.

70. See, for example, Quentin L. Cook, "The Blessing of Continuing Revelation to Prophets and Personal Revelation to Guide Our Lives," *Ensign*, May 2020, 96–100; Laudy Ruth Kaouk, "How the Priesthood Blesses Youth," *Ensign*, May 2020, 56–57; and Russell M. Nelson, "Hear Him," *Ensign*, May 2020, 88–92.

71. Jason Swensen, "Historic Changes for Children and Youth," *Church News*, 13 May 2018, 3, 16. The disaffiliation took effect 1 January 2020.

72. Bonnie H. Cordon, interview by Anne Berryhill and Lisa Olsen Tait, 21 Apr. 2023, 1–2, 14.

73. "Age Changes for Youth Progression and Ordination Announced," Newsroom, 14 Dec. 2018, newsroom.ChurchofJesusChrist.org; Tad Walch, "What Church Changes for 11-Year-Olds Mean for 2019 and Beyond," *Deseret News*, 14 Dec. 2018, deseret.com.

74. "Special Children and Youth Broadcast," 38:12–38:20.

75. These areas corresponded to a description of Jesus Christ's youth in the New Testament: "Jesus increased in wisdom and stature, and in favour with God and man." (Luke 2:52.)

76. *Children and Youth of The Church of Jesus Christ of Latter-day Saints: An Introductory Guide for Parents and Leaders* (Salt Lake City: Church of Jesus Christ of Latter-day Saints, 2019). On nearly every page, the booklet describes how the home-centered, church-supported framework should look. The four areas of focus are on page 3.

77. Children and Youth, ChurchofJesusChrist.org/youth/childrenandyouth.

78. Bonnie H. Cordon, interview by Anne Berryhill and Kate Holbrook, 20 Nov. 2019, 5–6, 28–31.

79. See "Children and Youth Emblems," Inspiration, 16 Aug. 2021, ChurchofJesusChrist.org/inspiration/children-and-youth-emblems.

80. "Leaders Outline Church's New Children and Youth Program," Newsroom, 17 Nov. 2019, newsroom.ChurchofJesusChrist.org.

81. "Church Expands Global Youth Conference Program," Newsroom, 19 July 2019, newsroom.ChurchofJesusChrist.org. International FSY conferences were modeled on the Especially For Youth (EFY) program that originated at Brigham Young University as a weeklong summer experience for Latter-day Saint youth. ("What is EFY?," Especially For Youth, efy.byu.edu/about; Bytheway, "History of 'Especially For Youth,'" 46–84.)

82. See Bonnie H. Cordon, Michelle D. Craig, and Becky Craven, "Strengthening Young Women" (slide-show presentation to First Presidency, 2019), copy in authors' possession.

83. Bonnie H. Cordon, "Beloved Daughters," *Ensign*, Nov. 2019, 68.

84. At the stake and general level, adult Young Men presidencies would continue, with a stake high councilor serving as Young Men president, alongside high councilors assigned to oversee Young Women and Primary as part of a stake Aaronic Priesthood–Young Women committee including the stake Young Women president and chaired by a counselor in the stake presidency.

85. Quentin L. Cook, "Adjustments to Strengthen Youth," *Ensign*, Nov. 2019, 41–42.

86. See *General Handbook* (2020), sec. 7.6, pp. 36–38; and Quentin L. Cook, "Adjustments to Strengthen Youth," *Ensign*, Nov. 2019, 42–43.

87. Jonathan A. Stapley, "The Witness of Women: Historical Context," *By Common Consent* (blog), 2 Oct. 2019, bycommonconsent.com; see also Stapley, *Power of Godliness*, 94.

88. Russell M. Nelson, "Witnesses, Aaronic Priesthood Quorums, and Young Women Classes," *Ensign*, Nov. 2019, 38–39; Sarah Jane Weaver, "Women, Youth, Children Can Serve as Witnesses," *Church News*, 6 Oct. 2019, 3. Any baptized member could serve as a witness to baptisms of living persons outside the temple or proxy baptisms in the temple, and any endowed member could serve as a witness for marriage sealings in the temple.

89. Grace Woodworth, personal message to Ashley Woodworth Skinner, 26 Apr. 2024.

90. Bonnie H. Cordon, interview by Anne Berryhill and Lisa Olsen Tait, 21 Apr. 2023, 9–11.

91. Bonnie H. Cordon, "Beloved Daughters," *Ensign*, Nov. 2019, 67.

92. Bonnie H. Cordon, interview by Anne Berryhill and Lisa Olsen Tait, 21 Apr. 2023, 2, 5.

93. Young Women Theme (2019), ChurchofJesusChrist.org; Bonnie H. Cordon, interview by Anne Berryhill and Lisa Olsen Tait, 21 Apr. 2023, 3.

94. Audrey Glende, talk, 15 Jan. 2020, copy in authors' possession.

95. Sydney Walker, "Children and Youth: 'Strive to Be' Like Christ," *Church News*, 24 Nov. 2019, 24; "Linking Arms with a Worldwide Brotherhood," *Church News*, 1 Dec. 2019, 17. The new Young Men theme was announced in a special "Face to Face" meeting broadcast to youth, as well as their parents and leaders.

96. "Update: Gatherings of Church Members Temporarily Suspended Worldwide," Newsroom, 12 Mar. 2020, newsroom.ChurchofJesusChrist.org; "COVID-19 Prompts Temporary Adjustments," *Church News*, 22 Mar. 2020, 4–5; "First Presidency Provides Guidance on How to Administer the Church in Challenging Times," Newsroom, 17 Apr. 2020, newsroom.ChurchofJesusChrist.org.

97. "Staying Connected: Loving, Leading from a Distance," *Church News*, 19 Apr. 2020, 26.

98. "Why Class Presidencies Are Needed More Than Ever," *Church News*, 18 Oct. 2020, 18.

99. "Staying Connected: Loving, Leading from a Distance," *Church News*, 19 Apr. 2020, 26–27.

100. Young Women Presidency, "2020 Articles and Talks Status Sheet," copy in authors' possession.

101. Jenifer Greenwood (director of policies and training support), email to Anne Berryhill, 16 Nov. 2022.

102. The new booklet was published in fall 2022, titled *For the Strength of Youth: A Guide for Making Choices*.

103. Sydney Walker, "Church Announces Magazine Changes," *Church News*, 16 Aug. 2020, 5–6.

104. This event was timed to mark the 1870 likely founding date rather than the 1869 traditionally remembered founding date that had been used as a basis for the centennial. Its occurrence in November rather than May was happenstance and not meant to commemorate the traditional date.

105. "Young Women Organization Celebrates 150 Years in 2020," Newsroom, 27 May 2020, newsroom .ChurchofJesusChrist.org.

106. "Face to Face with the YW General Presidency," 26:59–27:55, 33:36–35:10, 53:20–55:55.

107. "Face to Face with the YW General Presidency," 31:50–36:50.

108. "Face to Face with the YW General Presidency," 8:43–12:30.

109. "Number of Weekly COVID-19 Deaths Reported to WHO," WHO COVID-19 Dashboard, updated 7 Apr. 2024, data.who.int/dashboards/covid19/deaths.

110. "WHO Chief Declares End to COVID-19 as a Global Health Emergency," UN News, 5 May 2023, news.un.org.

111. Mary Richards, "Deep and Abiding Belief in Jesus Christ," *Church News*, 3 June 2023, 16–17; Emily Belle Freeman homepage, emilybellefreeman.com. Freeman's podcast, which she cohosted with David Butler, was called *Don't Miss This*.

112. Emily Belle Freeman, interview by Lisa Olsen Tait, Brittany Chapman Nash, Amber Taylor, and James Goldberg, 20 Mar. 2024, 15:32–15:40.

113. Emily Belle Freeman, interview by Lisa Olsen Tait, Brittany Chapman Nash, Amber Taylor, and James Goldberg, 20 Mar. 2024, 16:20–16:31.

114. "Tamara W. Runia," General Church Leadership, updated 20 Feb. 2024, ChurchofJesusChrist.org.

115. Tamara W. Runia and Andrea Muñoz Spannaus, interview by Amber Taylor, James Goldberg, and Brittany Chapman Nash, 26 Mar. 2024, 11:47–12:35.

116. "Andrea Muñoz Spannaus," General Church Leadership, updated 20 Feb. 2024, ChurchofJesusChrist .org.

117. Tamara W. Runia and Andrea Muñoz Spannaus, interview by Amber Taylor, James Goldberg, and Brittany Chapman Nash, 26 Mar. 2024, 1:40–3:32, 35:41–38:40.

118. Tamara W. Runia and Andrea Muñoz Spannaus, interview by Amber Taylor, James Goldberg, and Brittany Chapman Nash, 26 Mar. 2024, 7:48–8:20, 12:56–14:40, 22:00–23:53.

119. Emily Belle Freeman, interview by Lisa Olsen Tait, Brittany Chapman Nash, Amber Taylor, and James Goldberg, 20 Mar. 2024, 17:20–17:26.

120. "14 Women Newly Called to Serve on Young Women General Advisory Council," *Church News*, 9 Sept. 2023, 20–21. The change from *general board* to *advisory council* had been formalized in the church's 2021 General Handbook. (Sydney Walker, "Words and Phrases No Longer Used in Handbook," *Church News*, 2 Oct. 2021, 8.)

121. Emily Belle Freeman, interview by Lisa Olsen Tait, Brittany Chapman Nash, Amber Taylor, and James Goldberg, 20 Mar. 2024, 21:15–21:20, 22:59–23:05.

122. Emily Belle Freeman, interview by Lisa Olsen Tait, Brittany Chapman Nash, Amber Taylor, and James Goldberg, 20 Mar. 2024, 11:10–11:40.

123. Emily Belle Freeman, interview by Lisa Olsen Tait, Brittany Chapman Nash, Amber Taylor, and James Goldberg, 20 Mar. 2024, 32:49–33:00.

124. See Doctrine and Covenants 25.

125. Emily Belle Freeman, interview by Lisa Olsen Tait, Brittany Chapman Nash, Amber Taylor, and James Goldberg, 20 Mar. 2024, 23:57–24:22.

126. John Sagers (data analyst, Church Membership and Statistical Records Department), email to Nicholas B. Shrum, 13 Sept. 2021.

127. Emily Belle Freeman, interview by Lisa Olsen Tait, Brittany Chapman Nash, Amber Taylor, and James Goldberg, 20 Mar. 2024, 5:50–5:56.

128. Elmina S. Taylor, Maria Y. Dougall, and Martha H. Tingey, "To the Officers and Members of the Y. L. M. I. Associations," *Young Woman's Journal*, Oct. 1890, 28.

129. "Face to Face with the YW General Presidency," 13:56–14:00.

APPENDIX B: YOUNG WOMEN GENERAL PRESIDENCIES

1. Salt Lake Stake Relief Society, Report, 18 and 19 June 1880, in Derr et al., *First Fifty Years of Relief Society*, 472; Gates, *History of the YLMIA*, 93, 266.

2. Salt Lake Stake Relief Society, Report, 18 and 19 June 1880, in Derr et al., *First Fifty Years of Relief Society*, 472; Gates, *History of the YLMIA*, 94–95.

3. Gates, *History of the YLMIA*, 98–99.

4. Salt Lake Stake Relief Society, Report, 18 and 19 June 1880, in Derr et al., *First Fifty Years of Relief Society*, 472; Gates, *History of the YLMIA*, 287.

5. Gates, *History of the YLMIA*, 281–283, 288–289; "Our Reorganization," *Young Woman's Journal*, May 1905, 245; "A Tribute," *Young Woman's Journal*, May 1929, 307.

6. Gates, *History of the YLMIA*, 285; "The Executive Officers of the General Board of the Y. L. M. I. A.," *Young Woman's Journal*, June 1905, 259.

7. Gates, *History of the YLMIA*, 285; "The Executive Officers of the General Board of the Y. L. M. I. A.," *Young Woman's Journal*, June 1905, 259; "Change in the Presidency," *Young Woman's Journal*, Aug. 1923, 457.

8. "Change in the Presidency," *Young Woman's Journal*, Aug. 1923, 457.

9. Elsie T. Brandley, "Ruth May Fox," *Young Woman's Journal*, May 1929, 313–314; John A. Widtsoe, "The New Y.W.M.I.A. Presidency," *Improvement Era*, Dec. 1937, 760.

10. May Booth Talmage, "Lucy Grant Cannon," *Young Woman's Journal*, May 1929, 317.

11. Mary C. Kimball, "Clarissa A. Beesley," *Young Woman's Journal*, May 1929, 322.

12. "Greetings from the New Presidency of the Young Women's Mutual Improvement Association," *Improvement Era*, Dec. 1937, 741; John A. Widtsoe, "The New Y. W. M. I. A. Presidency," *Improvement Era*, Dec. 1937, 760; Marba C. Josephson, "Service to the Young Women of the Church," *Improvement Era*, July 1948, 430, 476.

13. "Greetings from the New Presidency of the Young Women's Mutual Improvement Association," *Improvement Era*, Dec. 1937, 741; John A. Widtsoe, "The New Y. W. M. I. A. Presidency," *Improvement Era*, Dec. 1937, 760; "Y.W.M.I.A. Counselor," *Improvement Era*, Aug. 1944, 494.

14. "Y.W.M.I.A. Counselor," *Improvement Era*, Aug. 1944, 494.

15. "Greetings from the New Presidency of the Young Women's Mutual Improvement Association," *Improvement Era*, Dec. 1937, 741; John A. Widtsoe, "The New Y. W. M. I. A. Presidency," *Improvement Era*, Dec. 1937, 760.

16. Helena W. Larson, "Lucy Taylor Andersen," *Improvement Era*, Aug. 1944, 493; "Y.W.M.I.A. Counselor," *Improvement Era*, Aug. 1944, 494.

17. Marba C. Josephson, "Bertha S. Reeder," *Improvement Era*, May 1948, 265; Marba C. Josephson, "Service to the Young Women of the Church," *Improvement Era*, July 1948, 431, 477–478; "Changes Made at Fall Conference," *Improvement Era*, Nov. 1961, 796; Marba C. Josephson, "Recently Released YWMIA General Presidency," *Improvement Era*, Jan. 1962, 28–29, 68.

18. Marba C. Josephson, "Service to the Young Women of the Church," *Improvement Era*, July 1948, 431, 477–478.

19. Marba C. Josephson, "Service to the Young Women of the Church," *Improvement Era*, July 1948, 431, 478.

20. "Changes Made at Fall Conference," *Improvement Era*, Nov. 1961, 796; Marba C. Josephson, "Recently Appointed YWMIA General Presidency," *Improvement Era*, Jan. 1962, 26–27, 69–71; "2 Priesthood-Oriented MIAs," *Church News*, 11 Nov. 1972, 3.

21. Marba C. Josephson, "Recently Appointed YWMIA General Presidency," *Improvement Era*, Jan. 1962, 27, 69.

22. Marba C. Josephson, "Recently Appointed YWMIA General Presidency," *Improvement Era*, Jan. 1962, 69–71.

23. "2 Priesthood-Oriented MIAs," *Church News*, 11 Nov. 1972, 3, 8, 11; "New Young Women Presidency Announced," *Ensign*, Sept. 1978, 76.

24. "2 Priesthood-Oriented MIAs," *Church News*, 11 Nov. 1972, 3, 8, 11. Hortense Hogan Child was a widow when she was called in 1972; she married Eldred G. Smith in 1977.

25. "2 Priesthood-Oriented MIAs," *Church News*, 11 Nov. 1972, 3, 8, 11.

26. "New Young Women Leaders," *Church News*, 15 July 1978, 3; "New Young Women Presidency Announced," *Ensign*, Sept. 1978, 76; "Ardeth Greene Kapp, Young Women General President," *Ensign*, May 1984, 98.

27. "New Young Women Presidency Announced," *Ensign*, Sept. 1978, 76.

28. "New Young Women Presidency Announced," *Ensign*, Sept. 1978, 76.

29. "Ardeth Greene Kapp, Young Women General President," *Ensign*, May 1984, 98; "New Young Women General Presidency Called," *Ensign*, May 1992, 106–107.

30. "Two Called to Young Women General Presidency," *Ensign*, July 1984, 75; Gordon B. Hinckley, "Solemn Assembly and Sustaining of Church Officers," *Ensign*, May 1986, 75.

31. Gordon B. Hinckley, "Solemn Assembly and Sustaining of Church Officers," *Ensign*, May 1986, 75; Thomas S. Monson, "The Sustaining of Church Officers," *Ensign*, May 1987, 19.

32. Thomas S. Monson, "The Sustaining of Church Officers," *Ensign*, May 1987, 19.

33. Thomas S. Monson, "The Sustaining of Church Officers," *Ensign*, May 1987, 19; "New Young Women Counselor," *Ensign*, May 1990, 111.

34. "New Young Women Counselor," *Ensign*, May 1990, 111.

35. "New Young Women General Presidency Called," *Ensign*, May 1992, 106–107; "Changes in Members of Seventies Quorums; New Young Women Presidency," *Ensign*, Nov. 1997, 102. Janette C. Hales was a widow when she was called to be the Young Women general president in 1992. She married Raymond E. Beckham in 1995.

36. "New Young Women General Presidency Called," *Ensign*, May 1992, 106–107.

37. "New Young Women General Presidency Called," *Ensign*, May 1992, 106–107; "New Seventies, Primary Presidency, and Young Women Counselor Called," *Ensign*, Nov. 1994, 104.

38. "New Seventies, Primary Presidency, and Young Women Counselor Called," *Ensign*, Nov. 1994, 104; "New Leaders Called, Three New Quorums of Seventy Formed," *Ensign*, May 1997, 101.

39. "New Leaders Called, Three New Quorums of Seventy Formed," *Ensign*, May 1997, 101.

40. "Changes in Members of Seventies Quorums; New Young Women Presidency," *Ensign*, Nov. 1997, 102; "New Leaders Called, Policies Announced," *Ensign*, Nov. 2002, 120.

41. "Changes in Members of Seventies Quorums; New Young Women Presidency," *Ensign*, Nov. 1997, 102.

42. "Changes in Members of Seventies Quorums; New Young Women Presidency," *Ensign*, Nov. 1997, 102.

43. "New Leaders Called, Policies Announced," *Ensign*, Nov. 2002, 120; Dieter F. Uchtdorf, "The Sustaining of Church Officers," *Ensign*, May 2008, 6–7.

44. "New Leaders Called, Policies Announced," *Ensign*, Nov. 2002, 120; Thomas S. Monson, "The Sustaining of Church Officers," *Ensign*, May 2007, 5–6.

45. Thomas S. Monson, "The Sustaining of Church Officers," *Ensign*, May 2007, 5–6.

46. "New Leaders Called, Policies Announced," *Ensign*, Nov. 2002, 120; Thomas S. Monson, "The Sustaining of Church Officers," *Ensign*, May 2007, 5–6.

47. Thomas S. Monson, "The Sustaining of Church Officers," *Ensign*, May 2007, 5–6.

48. Dieter F. Uchtdorf, "The Sustaining of Church Officers," *Ensign*, May 2008, 6–7; "183rd Annual General Conference Includes Sustaining of New Young Women General Presidency," *Ensign*, May 2013, 134.

49. Dieter F. Uchtdorf, "The Sustaining of Church Officers," *Ensign*, May 2008, 6–7.

50. Dieter F. Uchtdorf, "The Sustaining of Church Officers," *Ensign*, May 2008, 6–7.

51. "183rd Annual General Conference Includes Sustaining of New Young Women General Presidency," *Ensign*, May 2013, 134; Dallin H. Oaks, "The Sustaining of Church Officers," *Ensign*, May 2018, 28–29.

52. "183rd Annual General Conference Includes Sustaining of New Young Women General Presidency," *Ensign*, May 2013, 134.

53. "183rd Annual General Conference Includes Sustaining of New Young Women General Presidency," *Ensign*, May 2013, 134.

54. Dallin H. Oaks, "The Sustaining of Church Officers," *Ensign*, May 2018, 28–29; Dallin H. Oaks, "Sustaining of General Authorities, Area Seventies, and General Officers," *Liahona*, May 2023, 32–33.

55. Dallin H. Oaks, "The Sustaining of Church Officers," *Ensign*, May 2018, 28–29.

56. Dallin H. Oaks, "The Sustaining of Church Officers," *Ensign*, May 2018, 28–29.

57. Dallin H. Oaks, "Sustaining of General Authorities, Area Seventies, and General Officers," *Liahona*, May 2023, 32–33.

58. Dallin H. Oaks, "Sustaining of General Authorities, Area Seventies, and General Officers," *Liahona*, May 2023, 32–33.

59. Dallin H. Oaks, "Sustaining of General Authorities, Area Seventies, and General Officers," *Liahona*, May 2023, 32–33.

APPENDIX C: CLASS CHART AND LIST

1. "Special Instruction for M. I. A. Officers," *Young Woman's Journal*, May 1928, 312; "The Adult Department," *Young Woman's Journal*, July 1928, 434; "The Adult Department," *Young Woman's Journal*, Aug. 1928, 498–499; *Hand Book of the Young Men's and Young Ladies' Mutual Improvement Associations* (1928), 221–222; Josephson, *History of the YWMIA*, 230; *Hand Book of the Young Men's and Young Ladies' Mutual Improvement Associations* (1931), 63, 103.

2. "Adult," *Improvement Era*, Sept. 1932, 686.

3. *M. I. A. Guide for Executives* (1936), 32; "Important Announcement," *M. I. A. Leader*, Apr. 1940, 1.

4. Young Women General Board, Minutes, vol. 14, 8 Feb. 1939, 71; "Announcement of Enlarged M Men and Gleaner Departments," *Improvement Era*, May 1939, 301; Bennion, *Youth and Its Religion*, 9, 252.

5. Lucy W. Smith, "Guide Work 1917–18," *Young Woman's Journal*, Aug. 1917, 463; "Advanced Senior Classes," *Young Woman's Journal*, Oct. 1917, 562.

6. "Ages for Enrollment in M. I. A. Classes," *Young Woman's Journal*, Jan. 1923, 38; *Y. L. M. I. A. Hand Book* (1923), 57; "Special Instruction for M. I. A. Officers," *Young Woman's Journal*, May 1928, 312; "The Adult Department," *Young Woman's Journal*, Aug. 1928, 498–499; Josephson, *History of the YWMIA*, 230.

7. *Hand Book for the Bee-Hive Girls* (1915), 4; "Summer Work," *Young Woman's Journal*, Mar. 1915, 192; Ann M. Cannon, "Junior Work," *Young Woman's Journal*, July 1919, 397.

8. Ann M. Cannon, "Junior Work," *Young Woman's Journal*, July 1919, 397–399; "Courses of Study," and "The Bee-Hive Girls," *Young Woman's Journal*, Sept. 1919, 496–497; "Juniors—Bee-Hive Girls," *Young Woman's Journal*, Dec. 1919, 673; "Junior Course of Study," *Young Woman's Journal*, Sept. 1920, 535.

9. "Class Work," *Young Woman's Journal*, Aug. 1921, 494; *Y. L. M. I. A. Hand Book* (1923), 32.

10. Young Women General Board, Minutes, vol. 12, 5 Oct. 1930, 129.

11. *Hand Book of the Young Men's and Young Ladies' Mutual Improvement Associations* (1931), 148; *Hand Book for the Bee-Hive Girls* (1931), 10; "Placing Bee Hive Girls Entering M. I. A.," and "Nymphs," *Improvement Era*, Nov. 1931, 49, 50; *Supplement to the Bee Hive Girls Handbook* (1931), 3.

12. "Bee Hive Girls," *Improvement Era*, Sept. 1934, 562; Heber J. Grant and Anthony W. Ivins to Stake Presidents, 3 Aug. 1934, in "Officers' Notes," *Children's Friend*, Sept. 1934, 311; *Hand Book of the Young Men's and Young Women's Mutual Improvement Associations* (1934), 64.

13. "Bee Hive," *MIA Stake Leader*, Apr. 1950, 4; Bonnie H. Cordon, "Beloved Daughters," *Ensign*, Nov. 2019, 68.

14. "Senior Class Organization," *Young Woman's Journal*, Sept. 1922, 496; "Senior Girls Organization," *Young Woman's Journal*, Dec. 1922, 672.

15. "The Gleaners," *Young Woman's Journal*, Aug. 1923, 453–454; *Y. L. M. I. A. Hand Book* (1923), 29–30; "The Gleaner Department," *Young Woman's Journal*, July 1928, 434–435; *Hand Book of the Young Men's and Young Ladies' Mutual Improvement Associations* (1928), 269.

16. Bennion, *Gleaning*, 122; Beesley, *Believing and Doing*, 103; *Hand Book of the Young Men's and Young Ladies' Mutual Improvement Associations* (1931), 103.

17. Bennion, *Youth and Its Religion*, 9, 252.

18. "Important Announcement," *M. I. A. Leader*, Apr. 1940, 1; Lloyd, *Learning to Live*, 203.

19. "M Men–Gleaner," *MIA Stake Leader*, Apr. 1950, 3; *Executive Manual for Officers* (1951), 33.

20. *Executive MIA, 1959–1960*, 105–106; "M Man–Gleaner Department," *MIA Stake Leader*, Sept. 1959, insert, [2].

21. *Executive MIA, 1960–1961*, 109; *MIA Executive Manual* (1963), 269.

22. "Adult MIA Program Expands," *Church News*, 27 June 1970, 4; *MIA Executive Manual* (1972), sec. 16, pp. 1–2; "2 Priesthood-Oriented MIAs," *Church News*, 11 Nov. 1972, 3, 8–9.

23. "New Plans for Intermediate Girls," *Young Woman's Journal*, Aug. 1921, 494; "Intermediate Girls," *Young Woman's Journal*, Sept. 1921, 529; "Intermediate Girls," *Young Woman's Journal*, Feb. 1922, 103; "Junior Girls," *Young Woman's Journal*, Aug. 1922, 463–464; *Outline of Courses of Study for Junior Classes* (1922), 3.

24. *Guide for the Junior Department* (1903), 2; "Officers' Page," *Young Woman's Journal*, Feb. 1903, 88; "Guide Department," *Young Woman's Journal*, Aug. 1903, 381; "Junior Classes," *Young Woman's Journal*, Oct. 1903, 469; Gates, *History of the YLMIA*, 183–185; Ann M. Cannon, "Junior Work," *Young Woman's Journal*, July 1919, 397–399; "Bee-Hive Girls," *Young Woman's Journal*, Aug. 1921, 494; *Y. L. M. I. A. Hand Book* (1923), 32.

25. "Junior Girls," *Young Woman's Journal*, Aug. 1922, 463–464; *Y. L. M. I. A. Hand Book* (1923), 31.

26. Beesley, *Believing and Doing*, 103.

27. *Building a Life*, 87; *Hand Book of the Young Men's and Young Ladies' Mutual Improvement Associations* (1931), 121; "Junior," *MIA Stake Leader*, Apr. 1950, 4.

28. "Junior M Men–Junior Gleaner," *MIA Stake Leader*, May 1950, 5; *Program for Junior M Men and Junior Gleaners* (1950), sec. 3, p. 6; "Ensign-Laurel," *MIA Stake Leader*, Sept. 1959, insert, [2].

29. *Executive MIA, 1959–1960*, 106–107; "Ensign-Laurel," *MIA Stake Leader*, Sept. 1959, insert, [2]; *Ensign-Laurel Manual* (1959), 268; *MIA Executive Manual* (1963), 272; *MIA Executive Manual* (1970), 286.

30. *MIA Executive Manual* (1972), sec. 18, p. 5; *Young Women Handbook* (1975), 1; Bonnie H. Cordon, "Beloved Daughters," *Ensign*, Nov. 2019, 68.

31. "Junior," *MIA Stake Leader*, Apr. 1950, 4; Bonnie H. Cordon, "Beloved Daughters," *Ensign*, Nov. 2019, 68.

32. *MIA Executive Manual Supplement, 1969–70*, 16; "Mutual Interests," *MIA Leader*, Aug. 1969, 3.

33. "Adult MIA Program Expands," *Church News*, 27 June 1970, 4; *MIA Executive Manual* (1972), sec. 16, p. 3; "2 Priesthood-Oriented MIAs," *Church News*, 11 Nov. 1972, 3, 8–9.

34. "Mutual Marrieds," *MIA Stake Leader*, Sept. 1959, insert, [2]; *Executive MIA, 1959–1960*, 101–102; "Mutual Interests," *MIA Leader*, Aug. 1969, 3; *MIA Executive Manual Supplement, 1969–70*, 16. The manuals and handbooks containing this information did not delineate what ages were included in "middle age."

35. *Supplement to the Bee Hive Girls Handbook* (1931), 3; "Placing Bee Hive Girls Entering M. I. A.," and "Nymphs," *Improvement Era*, Nov. 1931, 49–50; *Hand Book for the Bee-Hive Girls* (1931), 10; *Hand Book of the Young Men's and Young Ladies' Mutual Improvement Associations* (1931), 148; *Handbook for the Officers* (1930), 87, 165; "Bee Hive Girls," *Improvement Era*, Sept. 1934, 562.

36. *Guide for the Junior Department* (1903), 2; "Officers' Page," *Young Woman's Journal*, Feb. 1903, 88; "Guide Department," *Young Woman's Journal*, Aug. 1903, 381; "Junior Classes," *Young Woman's Journal*, Oct. 1903, 469.

37. Lucy W. Smith, "Guide Work 1917–18," *Young Woman's Journal*, Aug. 1917, 463; "Advanced Seniors and Seniors," *Young Woman's Journal*, Dec. 1919, 673.

38. "New Plans for Intermediate Girls," *Young Woman's Journal*, Aug. 1921, 494; *Outline of Courses of Study for Junior Classes* (1922), 3.

39. "Ages for Enrollment in M. I. A. Classes," *Young Woman's Journal*, Jan. 1923, 38; *Y. L. M. I. A. Hand Book* (1923), 29.

40. "Seniors," *Improvement Era*, Sept. 1932, 686.

41. *M. I. A. Guide for Executives* (1936), 32; Bennion, *Youth and Its Religion*, 9, 252.

42. "Special Interest Groups," *M. I. A. Leader*, Nov. 1939, 4; *M. I. A. Manual for Executives* (1939), 52; "Important Announcement," *M. I. A. Leader*, Apr. 1940, 1.

43. "Important Announcement," *M. I. A. Leader*, Apr. 1940, 1; *Brochure for Special Interest Groups* (1940), 5.

44. "M Men-Gleaner," *MIA Stake Leader*, Apr. 1950, 3; *Executive Manual for Officers* (1951), 32–33; "Mutual Marrieds," *MIA Stake Leader*, June 1959, 3; "Mutual Marrieds," *MIA Stake Leader*, Sept. 1959, insert, [2].

45. "Mutual Marrieds," *MIA Stake Leader*, Sept. 1959, insert, [2]; *Executive MIA, 1959–1960*, 101–102; "Mutual Interests," *MIA Leader*, Aug. 1969, 3; *MIA Executive Manual Supplement, 1969–70*, 16.

46. "Adult MIA Program Expands," *Church News*, 27 June 1970, 4; *MIA Executive Manual* (1972), sec. 16, p. 2; "2 Priesthood-Oriented MIAs," *Church News*, 11 Nov. 1972, 3, 8–9.

WORKS CITED

This list serves as a guide to sources cited in *Carry On: The Latter-day Saint Young Women Organization, 1870–2024*. Sources cited in this volume are referred to on first and subsequent occurrences by a conventional shortened citation. For convenience, some documents are referred to by editorial titles rather than by their original titles or by the titles given in the catalogs of their current repositories, in which case the list of works cited provides the editorial title followed by full bibliographic information. In entries for manuscript sources, dates typically identify when the manuscript was created, which is not necessarily the time period the manuscript covers. Many manuscript sources and church publications cited in this volume are available at the Church History Library of The Church of Jesus Christ of Latter-day Saints, Salt Lake City, and are freely available online at catalog.ChurchofJesusChrist.org. Some of the books and pamphlets cited in this volume that are now in the public domain can be fully accessed through websites created by various commercial and nonprofit organizations or institutional partnerships of university and public libraries. These include Google Books, HathiTrust Digital Library, and Internet Archive.

The following abbreviations are used in this list of sources cited:

BYU   L. Tom Perry Special Collections, Harold B. Lee Library, Brigham Young University, Provo, Utah

CHL   Church History Library, The Church of Jesus Christ of Latter-day Saints, Salt Lake City

Aaronic Priesthood and Young Women's Personal Achievement Program Leadership Guide. Salt Lake City: Presiding Bishopric, 1970.

The Activity Book. Salt Lake City: The Church of Jesus Christ of Latter-day Saints, 1977.

Adams, Michael C. C. *The Best War Ever: America and World War II*. Baltimore: Johns Hopkins University Press, 1994.

Adei-Manu, Elizabeth A. Interview by Brent G. Thompson, 12 Sept. 1998. Transcript. CHL.

WORKS CITED

African American Oral History Project Transcripts, BYU / African American Oral History Project Transcripts, Case Files, and Other Material, 1980–1995. Charles Redd Center for Western Studies Oral History Project Records. BYU.

Alexander, Thomas G. "Between Revivalism and the Social Gospel: The Latter-day Saint Social Advisory Committee, 1916–1922." *BYU Studies* 23, no. 1 (Winter 1983): 19–39.

———. *Mormonism in Transition: A History of the Latter-day Saints, 1890–1930*. 3rd ed. Salt Lake City: Greg Kofford Books, 2012.

———. *Utah: The Right Place*. 2nd rev. ed. Salt Lake City: Gibbs Smith, 2003.

Alexander, Thomas G., and James B. Allen. *Mormons and Gentiles: A History of Salt Lake City*. Western Urban History Series 5. Boulder, CO: Pruett, 1984.

Allen, Helena M. Williams. Interview by Lavina Fielding Anderson, 13 Mar. 1984. Transcript. CHL.

Allen, James B. "Crisis on the Home Front: The Federal Government and Utah's Defense Housing in World War II." *Pacific Historical Review* 38, no. 4 (Nov. 1969): 407–428.

Allen, James B., Jessie L. Embry, and Kahlile B. Mehr. *Hearts Turned to the Fathers: A History of the Genealogical Society of Utah, 1894–1994*. Provo, UT: BYU Studies, 1995.

Allyn, David. *Make Love, Not War: The Sexual Revolution: An Unfettered History*. New York: Routledge, 2016.

American Psychological Association, Task Force on the Sexualization of Girls. *Report of the APA Task Force on the Sexualization of Girls*. Washington, DC: American Psychological Association, 2007.

"Announcing the Program for Latter-day Saint Girls," 1945. CHL.

APMIA Executive Committee, Meeting Minutes / Aaronic Priesthood MIA Executive Committee. Meeting Minutes, 1972–1975. CHL.

Arrington, Leonard J. *Madelyn Cannon Stewart Silver: Poet, Teacher, Homemaker*. Salt Lake City: Publishers Press, 1998.

Arrington, Leonard J., and Davis Bitton. *The Mormon Experience: A History of the Latter-day Saints*. 2nd ed. Urbana: University of Illinois Press, 1992.

Arrington, Leonard J., Feramorz Y. Fox, and Dean L. May. *Building the City of God: Community and Cooperation among the Mormons*. 2nd ed. Urbana: University of Illinois Press, 1992.

Ashton, Wendell J. Interviews by Gordon Irving, Jan. 1984–May 1985. Transcript. CHL.

Astle, Randy, and Gideon O. Burton. "A History of Mormon Cinema." *BYU Studies* 46, no. 2 (2007): 12–163.

Aza, Camila Ortega. Interview by Amber Taylor, 1 Apr. 2021. Audio file. Copy in authors' possession.

Backman, Robert L. Interviews by Ronald G. Watt, Mar.–Oct. 1993. Transcript. CHL.

Baden-Powell, Robert. *Scouting for Boys. A Handbook for Instruction in Good Citizenship*. London: Horace Cox, 1908.

Baird, Louise. Interview by Kate Holbrook, 9 Feb. 2018. Transcript. CHL.

Balderas, Guillermo. Papers, 1951–1985. Digital files. CHL.

Balderas Family Scrapbooks, 1910–1991. CHL.

Barrett, Vicki Noyce. Interview by Mary Frances Rich and Lisa Olsen Tait, 16 Apr. 2021. Transcript. CHL.

Barth, Ruth Stewart. "Needs: The Biography of Ann Mousley Cannon," no date. Special Collections, J. Willard Marriott Library, University of Utah, Salt Lake City. Digital copy available at familysearch.org.

Bateman, Merrill Joseph. "Heber Valley Camp Dedicatory Prayer," 22 June 2006. CHL.

Beckham, Janette Hales. Interview by Kate Holbrook, 23 Aug. 2016. Transcript. CHL.

Beecher, Maureen Ursenbach. "The 'Leading Sisters': A Female Hierarchy in Nineteenth-Century Mormon Society." *Journal of Mormon History* 9 (1982): 25–39.

Beesley, Clarissa A. *Believing and Doing: A Course of Study for the Junior Department of the Y. L. M. I. A., 1930–31*. [Salt Lake City]: YLMIA General Board, 1930.

Behold Thy Handmaiden [Girls' booklet]. Salt Lake City: The Church of Jesus Christ of Latter-day Saints, 1974.

Behold Thy Handmaiden [Guidelines for adult leaders]. Salt Lake City: The Church of Jesus Christ of Latter-day Saints, 1974.

Bellah, Robert N., Richard Madsen, William M. Sullivan, Ann Swidler, and Steven M. Tipton. *Habits of the Heart: Individualism and Commitment in American Life*. Berkeley: University of California Press, 1985.

Bennion, Adam S. *Gleaning: A Course of Study for the Gleaner Department of the Y. L. M. I. A., 1930–31*. Salt Lake City: YLMIA General Board, 1930.

Bennion, Anne Hinckley, Jane Noble Bennion, Rebecca Jacobsen Bennion Zimmer, Katherine Elizabeth Bennion Jepsen, Ruth Bennion Gollnick, and Rachel Carolyn Bennion. Interview by Amber Taylor, 14 Mar. 2021. Transcript. CHL.

Bennion, Lowell L. *Youth and Its Religion: Joint M Men and Gleaner Activities, Special Interest Groups, M Men Program, Gleaner Program, 1939–1940*. [Salt Lake City]: MIA General Boards, 1939.

Benson, Ezra Taft. *A Labor of Love: The 1946 European Mission of Ezra Taft Benson*. Salt Lake City: Deseret Book, 1989.

Bergera, Gary James. "Ezra Taft Benson's 1946 Mission to Europe." *Journal of Mormon History* 34, no. 2 (Spring 2008): 73–112.

Bergunder, Michael. "The Pentecostal Movement and Basic Ecclesial Communities in Latin America: Sociological Theories and Theological Debates." *International Review of Mission* 91, no. 361 (Apr. 2002): 163–186.

Bible. See *Holy Bible*.

Bitton, Davis. "The Ritualization of Mormon History." *Utah Historical Quarterly* 43, no. 1 (Winter 1975): 67–85.

———. "Zion's Rowdies: Growing Up on the Mormon Frontier." In *The Ritualization of Mormon History and Other Essays*, 54–68. Urbana: University of Illinois Press, 1994.

Blakesley, Katie Clark. "'A Style of Our Own': Modesty and Mormon Women, 1951–2008." *Dialogue: A Journal of Mormon Thought* 42, no. 2 (Summer 2009): 20–53.

Bleak, James Godson. Annals of the Southern Utah Mission, ca. 1903–1906. CHL.

The Book of Mormon: Another Testament of Jesus Christ. Salt Lake City: The Church of Jesus Christ of Latter-day Saints, 2013.

Bowman, Matthew. *The Mormon People: The Making of an American Faith*. New York: Random House, 2012.

Boylan, Anne M. *Sunday School: The Formation of an American Institution, 1790–1880*. New Haven, CT: Yale University Press, 1988.

Bradley, Martha Sonntag. *Pedestals and Podiums: Utah Women, Religious Authority, and Equal Rights*. Salt Lake City: Signature Books, 2005.

Brandley, Elsie Talmage. Journal, 1933–1935. Electronic file. Posted 11 Aug. 2014, in "Elsie Talmage," FamilySearch (Person ID: KWCF-N9P), familysearch.org.

Brigham City 3rd Ward YLMIA Minutes / Brigham City 3rd Ward, Brigham City Stake, Young Women's Mutual Improvement Association. Minutes and Records, 1878–1972. CHL.

Brochure for Special Interest Groups of the Mutual Improvement Associations, 1940–1941. Salt Lake City: MIA General Boards, 1940.

Brooks, Juanita. *Quicksand and Cactus: A Memoir of the Southern Mormon Frontier*. Salt Lake City: Howe Brothers, 1982.

Brown, Victor L. *Bishop Victor L. Brown: Personal History, Compiled 1984*. [Salt Lake City]: By the author, 1984.

———. Files, 1961–1989. CHL.

Brumberg, Joan Jacobs. *The Body Project: An Intimate History of American Girls*. New York: Vintage Books, 1998.

Buchanan, Frederick S. *Culture Clash and Accommodation: Public Schooling in Salt Lake City, 1890–1994*. San Francisco: Smith Research Associates in association with Signature Books, 1996.

Buck, Holly. "'Amusements and Recreations . . . Makes Our Working Hours Profitable': Utah 4-H, 1940–1960." *Utah Historical Quarterly* 72, no. 1 (Winter 2004): 69–84.

Building a Life: A Course of Study, for the Junior Department of the Y. L. M. I. A., 1931–32. Salt Lake City: YLMIA General Board, 1931.

Bunker, Gary L., and Davis Bitton. *The Mormon Graphic Image, 1834–1914: Cartoons, Caricatures, and Illustrations*. Salt Lake City: University of Utah Press, 1983.

Bureau of Economic and Business Research, School of Business, University of Utah. "Measures of Economic Changes in Utah, 1847–1947." *Utah Economic and Business Review* 7, no. 1 (Dec. 1947): 1–105.

Bushman, Claudia L. *Contemporary Mormonism: Latter-day Saints in Modern America*. Lanham, MD: Rowman and Littlefield, 2008.

———. "Women in Dialogue: An Introduction." *Dialogue: A Journal of Mormon Thought* 6, no. 2 (Summer 1971): 5–8.

Butler, Judith. "From *Gender Trouble: Feminism and the Subversion of Identity*." In *Feminist Theory: A Reader*, edited by Wendy K. Kolmar and Frances Bartkowski, 496–504. 2nd ed. Boston: McGraw-Hill Higher Education, 2005.

Butler, Margot J. Interview by Mary Frances Rich, 29 Dec. 2020. Transcript. CHL.

Bytheway, John G. "A History of 'Especially for Youth'—1976–1986." Master's thesis, Brigham Young University, 2003.

Cahn, Susan K. *Coming on Strong: Gender and Sexuality in Women's Sport*. 2nd ed. Urbana: University of Illinois Press, 2015.

Calabrese, Elisabetta J. Interview by Phillip Lear and Doreen Lear, 13 Nov. 2017. CHL.

Camp Standards. Salt Lake City: YWMIA, [1948].

Camptivities for Summer Camps of Y. W. M. I. A. [Salt Lake City]: YWMIA General Board, 1944.

Cannon, Elaine A. Interviews by Gordon Irving, Apr. 1979–Aug. 1990. Transcript. CHL.

———. Papers, 1832–2003. BYU.

WORKS CITED

Carpenter, Joel A. "Fundamentalist Institutions and the Rise of Evangelical Protestantism, 1929–1942." *Church History* 49, no. 1 (Mar. 1980): 62–75.

Carpenter, Laura M. "Virginity Loss in Reel/Real Life: Using Popular Movies to Navigate Sexual Initiation." *Sociological Forum* 24, no. 4 (Dec. 2009): 804–827.

Carr, Dianne Clyde, and Carma Clyde Russell. "History of Henrietta Palfreyman Clyde." Posted 25 Jan. 2018, in "Henrietta Palfreyman," FamilySearch (Person ID: KWCW-SWN), familysearch.org.

Carroll, J. A., and R. L. Kirkpatrick. *Impact of Social Media on Adolescent Behavioral Health in California*. Oakland: California Adolescent Health Collaborative, 2011.

Cedar City Ward YLMIA Minute Book / "Cedar City Ward Y. L. M. I. A Minute Book 'A,' 1876 to 1894." Cedar Ward Young Women's Mutual Improvement Association, Minutes and Records, 1876–1907. CHL.

Chafe, William H. *The Unfinished Journey: America since World War II*. New York: Oxford University Press, 1986.

Chamberlin, Ralph V. *The University of Utah: A History of Its First Hundred Years, 1850 to 1950*. Edited by Harold W. Bentley. Salt Lake City: University of Utah Press, 1960.

Chawla, Sandeep. *The Situation of Youth in the 1980s and Prospects and Challenges for the Year 2000*. New York: United Nations, 1986.

Christensen, John E. "The Impact of World War II." In *Utah's History*, edited by Richard D. Poll et al., 497–514. Logan: Utah State University Press, 1989.

The Church and the Proposed Equal Rights Amendment: A Moral Issue. Insert in March 1980 *Ensign*. Salt Lake City: Ensign Magazine, 1980.

Claremont Mormon Women Oral History Collection. Claremont Colleges Library, Claremont, CA.

Clark, James R. *Messages of the First Presidency of The Church of Jesus Christ of Latter-day Saints*. Vol. 5, *1916–1934*. Salt Lake City: Bookcraft, 1971.

Cnaan, Ram, Van Evans, and Daniel W. Curtis. "Called to Serve: The Prosocial Behavior of Active Latter-day Saints." Research report, University of Pennsylvania School of Social Policy and Practice, 2012.

Cocca, Carolyn E. *Jailbait: The Politics of Statutory Rape Laws in the United States*. Albany: State University of New York Press, 2004.

Coe, George A. "Adolescence—the Religious Point of View." *Journal of Childhood and Adolescence* 2, no. 1 (Jan. 1902): 14–22.

"A Conference of the Presidents of Relief Societies of the European Missions, Held at Durham House, 295 Edge Lane, Liverpool, August 16–21, 1929." European Mission, Relief Society Presidents' Conference Minutes, 1929. CHL.

"Conference on Womans Activity in European Missions, Basel, June 18–28, 1930." In "Widtsoe, Leah D., 1930 June 18–28," Alphabetical Subject Files, General Correspondence, Susa Young Gates Papers, ca. 1870–1933. CHL.

Conkling, J. Christopher. "Members without a Church: Japanese Mormons in Japan from 1924 to 1948." *BYU Studies* 15, no. 2 (Winter 1975): 191–214.

Cook, Mary N. Interview by Amber Taylor, 12 May 2019. Audio files. Copy in authors' possession.

———. Interview by Brittany Chapman Nash, 2 Mar. 2017. Transcript. CHL.

———. Papers, 1994–2001. CHL.

Cooking Out-of-Doors: A Supplement to "Camp-O-Rama." Salt Lake City: YWMIA General Board, 1947.

Cordon, Bonnie H. Interview by Anne Berryhill and Kate Holbrook, 20 Nov. 2019. Transcript. CHL.

———. Interview by Anne Berryhill and Lisa Olsen Tait, 21 Apr. 2023. Transcript. Copy in authors' possession.

Correlation–Social Advisory Committee. Minutes, 1920–1922. CHL.

Crawford, John C. "Mutual Improvement and Library Activity: Overviewing the Evidence." *Library and Information History* 32, nos. 1–2 (Feb./May 2016): 34–45.

Crocheron, Augusta Joyce. *Representative Women of Deseret, a Book of Biographical Sketches, to Accompany the Picture Bearing the Same Title*. Salt Lake City: J. C. Graham, 1884.

Cunningham, Patricia A. *Reforming Women's Fashion, 1850–1920: Politics, Health, and Art*. Kent, OH: Kent State University Press, 2003.

Curtis, Henry S. *The Play Movement and Its Significance*. New York: MacMillan, 1917.

Dados, Nour, and Raewyn Connell. "The Global South." *Contexts* (American Sociological Association) 11, no. 1 (Winter 2012): 12–13.

Dalton, Elaine S. Interview by Justin Bray, 25 June 2014. Transcript. CHL.

———. Miscellaneous Files, 2000–2011. CHL.

Davidson, Karen Lynn. *Our Latter-day Hymns: The Stories and the Messages*. Rev. ed. Salt Lake City: Deseret Book, 2009.

Davis, Lia. Interview by Kate Holbrook, 17 Aug. 2021. Transcript. Copy in authors' possession.

Deloria, Philip. *Playing Indian*. New Haven, CT: Yale University Press, 1998.

WORKS CITED

D'Emilio, John, and Estelle B. Freedman. *Intimate Matters: A History of Sexuality in America.* 3rd ed. Chicago: University of Chicago Press, 2012.

Derr, Jill Mulvay, Carol Cornwall Madsen, Kate Holbrook, and Matthew J. Grow, eds. *The First Fifty Years of Relief Society: Key Documents in Latter-day Saint Women's History.* Salt Lake City: Church Historian's Press, 2016.

Derr, Jill Mulvay, Janath Russell Cannon, and Maureen Ursenbach Beecher. *Women of Covenant: The Story of Relief Society.* Salt Lake City: Deseret Book, 1992.

De Schweinitz, Rebecca. "Holding On to the 'Chosen Generation': The Mormon Battle for Youth in the Late 1960s and Early 1970s." In *Out of Obscurity: Mormonism since 1945*, edited by Patrick Q. Mason and John G. Turner, 278–301. New York: Oxford University Press, 2016.

Deseret News 1978 Church Almanac. Salt Lake City: Deseret News, 1978.

Deseret News 1985 Church Almanac. Salt Lake City: Deseret News, 1984.

Deseret News 1987 Church Almanac. Salt Lake City: Deseret News, 1987.

Deseret News 1991–1992 Church Almanac. Salt Lake City: Deseret News, 1990.

Deseret News 2003 Church Almanac. Salt Lake City: Deseret News, 2002.

Deseret News 2013 Church Almanac. Salt Lake City: Deseret News, 2013.

Dicker, Rory. *A History of U.S. Feminisms.* Berkeley, CA: Seal Press, 2008.

The Doctrine and Covenants of The Church of Jesus Christ of Latter-day Saints: Containing Revelations Given to Joseph Smith, the Prophet, with Some Additions by His Successors in the Presidency of the Church. Salt Lake City: The Church of Jesus Christ of Latter-day Saints, 2013.

Dowland, Seth. "'Family Values' and the Formation of a Christian Right Agenda." *Church History* 78, no. 3 (Sept. 2009): 606–631.

Drogus, Carol Ann. "Private Power or Public Power: Pentecostalism, Base Communities, and Gender." In *Power, Politics, and Pentecostals in Latin America*, edited by Edward L. Cleary and Hannah W. Stewart-Gambino, 55–76. New York: Routledge, 2018.

Duriez, Olivier, and Deolinda Duriez. Interview by Jay G. Burrup, 1 June 2002. Transcript. CHL.

East Bountiful Ward YLMIA Minutes / East Bountiful Ward, Davis Stake, Young Women's Mutual Improvement Association. Minutes and Records, 1870–1908. CHL.

Eighty-Third Annual Conference of the Church of Jesus Christ of Latter-day Saints. Salt Lake City: Deseret News, 1913.

Ellsworth, S. George, ed. *The History of Louisa Barnes Pratt: Being the Autobiography of a Mormon Missionary Widow and Pioneer.* Life Writings of Frontier Women 3. Logan: Utah State University Press, 1998.

El Paso 3rd Ward Members. Interview by James Goldberg, 20 Sept. 2014. Transcript. CHL.

Embry, Jessie L. "Oral History and Mormon Women Missionaries: The Stories Sound the Same." *Frontiers: A Journal of Women Studies* 19, no. 3 (1998): 171–188.

———. *Spiritualized Recreation: Mormon All-Church Athletic Tournaments and Dance Festivals.* Provo, UT: Charles Redd Center for Western Studies, Brigham Young University, 2008.

"Emily Rachel Hillam Higgs—Her Story." Posted 29 June 2022, in "Emily Rachel Hillam," FamilySearch (Person ID: KWCQ-M6R), familysearch.org.

Encyclopedia of Clothing and Fashion. Vol. 1, *Academic Dress to Eyeglasses.* Edited by Valerie Steele. Detroit: Charles Scribner's Sons, 2005.

Encyclopedia of Latter-day Saint History. Edited by Arnold K. Garr, Donald Q. Cannon, and Richard O. Cowan. Salt Lake City: Deseret Book, 2000.

Encyclopedia of Mormonism. Edited by Daniel H. Ludlow. 5 vols. New York: Macmillan, 1992.

England, Eugene. "A Small and Piercing Voice: The Sermons of Spencer W. Kimball." *BYU Studies* 25, no. 4 (Fall 1985): 77–90.

Ensign-Laurel Manual. Salt Lake City: MIA, 1959.

Entwistle, Joanne. *The Fashioned Body: Fashion, Dress, and Modern Social Theory.* 2nd ed. Malden, MA: Polity, 2015.

Ericksen, Ephraim E. *Memories and Reflections: The Autobiography of E. E. Ericksen.* Edited by Scott G. Kenney. Salt Lake City: Signature Books, 1987.

Erickson, Andrea. "Doctrinal and Historical Analysis of Young Women's Education in The Church of Jesus Christ of Latter-day Saints." Master's thesis, Brigham Young University, 2009.

Esshom, Frank. *Pioneers and Prominent Men of Utah: Comprising Photographs, Genealogies, Biographies.* Salt Lake City: Utah Pioneers Book, 1913.

Executive Manual for Officers of the Young Men's and Young Women's Mutual Improvement Associations, 1950–1951. [Salt Lake City]: MIA General Boards, 1950.

Executive Manual for Officers of the Young Men's and Young Women's Mutual Improvement Associations, 1951–1952. [Salt Lake City]: MIA General Boards, 1951.

Executive MIA, 1959–1960. [Salt Lake City]: The Church of Jesus Christ of Latter-day Saints, 1959.

Executive MIA, 1960–1961. [Salt Lake City]: The Church of Jesus Christ of Latter-day Saints, 1960.

"Face to Face with the YW General Presidency: Celebrating 150 Years." Video, 1:12:45, 15 Nov. 2020. Media Library, The Church of Jesus Christ of Latter-day Saints, ChurchofJesusChrist.org.

Family Home Evening Manual. Salt Lake City: Council of the Twelve Apostles, 1968.

Farmington Ward YMMIA Minutes / Farmington Ward, Davis Stake, Young Men's Mutual Improvement Association. Minutes and Records, 1874–1943. CHL.

Fass, Paula S. *The Damned and the Beautiful: American Youth in the 1920's*. New York: Oxford University Press, 1977.

Featherstone, Vaughn J. Interviews by Gordon Irving, 1981–1982. CHL.

File, Thom. *Computer and Internet Use in the United States: Population Characteristics*. Current Population Survey Reports P20-569. Washington, DC: U.S. Census Bureau, 2013.

First Presidency. Missionary Calls and Recommendations, 1877–1918. CHL.

"The 1st Young Women's Fireside: Stand for Truth and Righteousness (1985)." Video, 1:33:33, 12 Sept. 2016. Hard-to-Find Mormon Videos, youtube.com/watch?v=B451SzXC7fo.

Fischer-Tiné, Harald, Stefan Huebner, and Ian Tyrrell, eds. *Spreading Protestant Modernity: Global Perspectives on the Social Work of the YMCA and YWCA, 1889–1970*. Perspectives on the Global Past Series. Honolulu: University of Hawai'i Press, 2021.

Flanagan, Maureen A. *America Reformed: Progressives and Progressivisms, 1890s–1920s*. New York: Oxford University Press, 2006.

Freeman, Emily Belle. Interview by Lisa Olsen Tait, Brittany Chapman Nash, Amber Taylor, and James Goldberg, 20 Mar. 2024. Audio file. Copy in authors' possession.

French Mission President's Files, 1935–1964. CHL.

For the Strength of Youth: LDS Standards. Salt Lake City: The Church of Jesus Christ of Latter-day Saints, 1965.

For the Strength of Youth: LDS Standards. Salt Lake City: The Church of Jesus Christ of Latter-day Saints, 1970.

For the Strength of Youth. Salt Lake City: The Church of Jesus Christ of Latter-day Saints, 1990.

Funk, Ruth Hardy. Interviews by Gordon Irving, Jan.–Feb. 1979. Transcript. CHL.

———. "Ruth, Come Walk with Me." In *He Changed My Life: Personal Experiences with Harold B. Lee*, edited by L. Brent Goates, 118–126. Salt Lake City: Bookcraft, 1988.

Fyans, John Thomas. Journals, ca. 1940–1989. Microfilm. CHL.

Gamm, Gerald, and Robert D. Putnam. "The Growth of Voluntary Associations in America, 1840–1940." *Journal of Interdisciplinary History* 29, no. 4 (Spring 1999): 511–557.

Gapiz, Nenita Reyes. Interview by Godofredo Hilario Esguerra and Wayne Crosby, 27 Feb. 2011. Audio file. CHL.

Gapiz, Ruben and Nenita Reyes Gapiz. Interview by Chad M. Orton, Nov. 1994. Transcript. CHL.

Gates, *History of the YLMIA* / Gates, Susa Young. *History of the Young Ladies' Mutual Improvement Association of the Church of Jesus Christ of Latter-day Saints, from November 1869 to June 1910*. Salt Lake City: YLMIA General Board, 1911.

Gates, Susa Young. Papers, ca. 1870–1933. CHL.

———. Papers, 1852–1932. Utah State Historical Society, Salt Lake City.

Gateway to a Wonderful You [Mia Maid manual]. Salt Lake City: YWMIA General Board, 1965.

Geddes, Joseph A. *Migration: A Problem of Youth in Utah*. Utah Agricultural Experiment Station Bulletin 323. Logan: Utah State Agricultural College, 1946.

Gender, Narrative, and Religious Practice in Southern Africa Oral History Collection. Special Collections, Claremont Colleges Library, Claremont, CA.

General Handbook of Instructions. Salt Lake City: The Church of Jesus Christ of Latter-day Saints, 1983.

General Handbook: Serving in The Church of Jesus Christ of Latter-day Saints, March 2020. Salt Lake City: The Church of Jesus Christ of Latter-day Saints, 2020.

General Handbook Supplement, Number 1: July 1, 1976. Salt Lake City: The Church of Jesus Christ of Latter-day Saints, 1976.

General Young Women Meeting Satellite Broadcast Records, 1985–1987. CHL.

The Girls' Program. Salt Lake City: YWMIA, 1950.

Givens, Terryl L. *People of Paradox: A History of Mormon Culture*. New York: Oxford, 2007.

Gleaner Manual: Youth and Its Culture by Carlton and Edna Ball Culmsee. Joint Gleaner and M Men Activities, Gleaner Activities. Manual for the Gleaner Department of the Y. W. M. I. A., 1938–39. Salt Lake City: MIA General Boards, 1938.

Gleaner Manual: Youth's Opportunities. Salt Lake City: MIA General Boards, 1937.

Goaslind, Jack H. Interviews by Gordon Irving, 1981–1982. Transcript. CHL.

Goodman, Michael A. "Correlation: The Early Years." In *A Firm Foundation: Church Organization and*

WORKS CITED

Administration, edited by David J. Whittaker and Arnold K. Garr, 319–338. Provo, UT: Religious Studies Center, Brigham Young University, 2011.

———. "Correlation: The Turning Point (1960s)." In *Salt Lake City: The Place Which God Prepared*, edited by Scott C. Esplin and Kenneth L. Alford, 259–284. Provo, UT: Religious Studies Center, Brigham Young University, 2011.

Gordon, Linda. *The Moral Property of Women: A History of Birth Control Politics in America*. Urbana: University of Illinois Press, 2002.

Guide for the Junior Department of the Young Ladies' National Mutual Improvement Associations, 1903–1904. Salt Lake City: General Board, 1903.

Guide to the First Year's Course of Study in the Young Ladies' Mutual Improvement Association. Salt Lake City: George Q. Cannon and Sons, [1893].

Gulick, Luther H. *Written Thoughts, WAPA I: Camp Fire Girls and the New Relation of Women to the World*. No place: Camp Fire Girls, 1912.

Gupta, Rita Paul-Sen, Margaret L. de Wit, and David McKeown. "The Impact of Poverty on the Current and Future Health Status of Children." *Journal of Paediatrics and Child Health* 12, no. 8 (Oct. 2007): 667–672.

Hall, Dave. *A Faded Legacy: Amy Brown Lyman and Mormon Women's Activism, 1872–1959*. Salt Lake City: University of Utah Press, 2015.

Hall, G. Stanley. *Adolescence: Its Psychology and Its Relations to Physiology, Anthropology, Sociology, Sex, Crime, Religion, and Education*. 2 vols. New York: D. Appleton, 1905.

Handbook for Scout Masters, Boy Scouts of America. New York: Boy Scouts of America, 1914.

Hand Book for the Bee-Hive Girls of the Y. L. M. I. A. Salt Lake City: YLMIA General Board, 1915.

Hand Book for the Bee-Hive Girls of the Y. L. M. I. A. 9th ed. Salt Lake City: YLMIA General Board, 1927.

Hand Book for the Bee-Hive Girls of the Y. L. M. I. A. 11th ed. Salt Lake City: YLMIA General Board, 1931.

Handbook for the Bee-Hive Girls of the Y. W. M. I. A. 12th ed. Salt Lake City: YWMIA General Board, 1934.

Hand Book for the Bee Hive Girls of the Y. W. M. I. A. Salt Lake City: YWMIA General Board, 1950.

A Handbook for the Officers and Teachers in the Primary Association (Religion Class) of the Church of Jesus Christ of Latter-day Saints. [Salt Lake City]: General Board of Primary Associations, 1930.

Hand Book of the Young Men's and Young Ladies' Mutual Improvement Associations. Official Guide for the Leisure-Time and Recreation Program of the Church of Jesus Christ of Latter-day Saints. [Salt Lake City]: MIA General Boards, 1928.

Hand Book of the Young Men's and Young Ladies' Mutual Improvement Associations. Official Guide for the Leisure-Time and Recreation Program of the Church of Jesus Christ of Latter-day Saints. [Salt Lake City]: MIA General Boards, 1931.

Hand Book of the Young Men's and Young Women's Mutual Improvement Associations of the Church of Jesus Christ of Latter-day Saints. [Salt Lake City]: MIA General Boards, 1934.

Handbuch für die Bienenkorbmädchen des Fortbildungsvereins für junge Damen. 2nd ed. Basel, Switzerland: Swiss-German and German-Austrian Mission, 1928.

Handy, Robert T. "The American Religious Depression, 1925–1935." *Church History* 29, no. 1 (Mar. 1960): 3–16.

Hartley, William G. "From Men to Boys: LDS Aaronic Priesthood Offices, 1829–1996." *Journal of Mormon History* 22, no. 1 (Spring 1996): 80–136. Also in William G. Hartley, *My Fellow Servants: Essays on the History of the Priesthood*, 37–86. Provo, UT: BYU Studies, 2010.

———. "The Priesthood Reform Movement, 1908–1922." *BYU Studies* 13, no. 2 (1973): 137–156.

———. "The Priesthood Reorganization of 1877: Brigham Young's Last Achievement." *BYU Studies* 20, no. 1 (Fall 1979): 3–36.

Haws, J. B. *The Mormon Image in the American Mind: Fifty Years of Perception*. New York: Oxford University Press, 2013.

Heath, Harvard S., ed. *Confidence amid Change: The Presidential Diaries of David O. McKay, 1951–1970*. Salt Lake City: Signature Books, 2019.

Heaton, Tim B., Stephen J. Bahr, and Cardell K. Jacobson. *A Statistical Profile of Mormons: Health, Wealth, and Social Life*. Mellen Studies in Sociology 43. Lewiston, NY: Edwin Mellen Press, 2004.

Henrotin, Ellen M. "The Attitude of Women's Clubs and Associations toward Social Economics." *Bulletin of the Department of Labor* 23 (July 1899): 501–545.

Higgs, Emily Hillam. "The First MIA Summer Camp for Girls—1912: Notes from the Journal of Emily H. Higgs, YWMIA Liberty Stake President," no date. Typescript. CHL.

Hiltner, Aaron. *Taking Leave, Taking Liberties: American Troops on the World War II Home Front*. Chicago: University of Chicago, 2020.

Hine, Thomas. *The Rise and Fall of the American Teenager*. New York: Perennial, 2000.

Historian's Office. Letterpress Copybooks, 1854–1879, 1885–1886. CHL.

WORKS CITED

Historic American Buildings Survey. *Washington Chapel, Church of Jesus Christ of the Latter-day Saints (Unification Church), 2810 Sixteenth Street Northwest, Washington, District of Columbia.* HABS DC-539. Washington, DC: National Park Service, U.S. Department of the Interior, 2015.

Hobbs, Charles R. *Time Power.* 1st Perennial Library ed. New York: Harper and Row, 1988.

The Holy Bible, Containing the Old and New Testaments Translated out of the Original Tongues: And with the Former Translations Diligently Compared and Revised, by His Majesty's Special Command. Authorized King James Version with Explanatory Notes and Cross References to the Standard Works of The Church of Jesus Christ of Latter-day Saints. Salt Lake City: The Church of Jesus Christ of Latter-day Saints, 2013.

Holzapfel, Jeni Broberg, and Richard Neitzel Holzapfel, eds. *A Woman's View: Helen Mar Whitney's Reminiscences of Early Church History.* Provo, UT: Religious Studies Center, Brigham Young University, 1997.

Horn, Tammy. *Bees in America: How the Honey Bee Shaped a Nation.* Lexington: University Press of Kentucky, 2005.

Horne Family Collection, 1872–1978. CHL.

Horwood, Catherine. *Keeping Up Appearances: Fashion and Class between the Wars.* Gloucestershire, England: History Press, 2011.

Howe, Daniel Walker. *What Hath God Wrought: The Transformation of America, 1815–1848.* New York: Oxford University Press, 2007.

How Near to the Angels. Directed by Wetzel Whitaker, BYU Motion Picture Studios, 1956. 42 min.

Hunt, Thomas M. "American Sport Policy and the Cultural Cold War: The Lyndon B. Johnson Presidential Years." *Journal of Sport History* 33, no. 3 (Fall 2006): 273–297.

Hunter, Jane H. *How Young Ladies Became Girls: The Victorian Origins of American Girlhood.* New Haven, CT: Yale University Press, 2002.

Hymns of The Church of Jesus Christ of Latter-day Saints. Salt Lake City: The Church of Jesus Christ of Latter-day Saints, 1985.

Iloilo 2nd Branch, Philippines Cebu City Mission. General Minutes, 1975–1977. CHL.

Improvement Era (Corporation). Proposed Campaign, 1929. CHL.

The Improvement Era Semi-centennial Year Book, 1897–1947. [Salt Lake City]: Improvement Era, [1946].

Instructions to the Y. L. M. I. A. Officers. [Salt Lake City]: YLMIA General Board, [1904].

Iosepa Branch YMMIA and YLMIA Record Book, 1913. Translated by Bella Lin Kee. Edited by Kenneth W. Baldridge. Typescript. CHL.

Irvine, Janice M. *Disorders of Desire: Sexuality and Gender in Modern American Sexuality.* Rev. ed. Philadelphia: Temple University Press, 2005.

Jackson, Richard W. *Places of Worship: 150 Years of Latter-day Saint Architecture.* Provo, UT: Religious Studies Center, Brigham Young University, 2003.

Jacobsen, Florence S. Interview by Lavina Fielding Anderson, 5 Apr. 1984. Transcript. CHL.

———. Interviews by Gordon Irving, 1981, 1991, 1997. Transcript. CHL.

———. Papers, ca. 1950–1985. CHL.

Jake, Patricia Brown. Interview by Amber Taylor, 11 Sept. 2021. Audio file. Copy in authors' possession.

Jefferson Ward, Grant Stake (Salt Lake City). Treasures of Truth, 1931–1932. CHL.

Jenkins, Philip. *The Next Christendom: The Coming of Global Christianity.* 3rd ed. New York: Oxford University Press, 2011.

Jenson, Andrew. *Encyclopedic History of the Church of Jesus Christ of Latter-day Saints.* Salt Lake City: Deseret News, 1941.

———. *Latter-day Saint Biographical Encyclopedia: A Compilation of Biographical Sketches of Prominent Men and Women in the Church of Jesus Christ of Latter-day Saints.* 4 vols. Salt Lake City: Andrew Jenson History Co., 1901–1936.

Jepson, Jared A. "A Study of the *For the Strength of Youth* Pamphlet, 1965–2004." Master's thesis, Brigham Young University, 2005.

Johnson, Haynes. *Sleepwalking through History: America in the Reagan Years.* New York: Anchor Books, 1992.

Jones, Dorothy Kay (Dottie) Boone. Interview by Lisa Olsen Tait, 21 Apr. 2021. Transcript. CHL.

Jones, Henrietta Lunt. "History of the First Retrenchment Organization in Cedar City, 1869–1885," no date. Typescript, Sept. 1938. Copy at CHL.

Jorgensen, Elaine L. Letter to Florence S. Jacobsen, 10 Apr. 1969. CHL.

Josephson, Marba C. *History of the YWMIA.* Salt Lake City: YWMIA, 1955.

JSP, H1 / Davidson, Karen Lynn, David J. Whittaker, Mark Ashurst-McGee, and Richard L. Jensen, eds. *Histories, Volume 1: Joseph Smith Histories, 1832–1844.* Vol. 1 of the Histories series of *The Joseph Smith Papers,* edited by Dean C. Jessee, Ronald K. Esplin, and Richard Lyman Bushman. Salt Lake City: Church Historian's Press, 2012.

Jubilee History of Latter-day Saints Sunday Schools, 1849–1899. Salt Lake City: Deseret Sunday School Union, 1900.

June Conference Files, 1890–1972. CHL.

Junior Manual, 1947–48: Life to Enjoy. Salt Lake City: YWMIA General Board, 1947.

Junior M Men–Junior Gleaner Manual, 1951–52. Salt Lake City: MIA General Boards, 1951.

JustServe: Community Service Guidebook. Salt Lake City: The Church of Jesus Christ of Latter-day Saints, 2018.

Kapp, Ardeth G. Files, 1984–1992. CHL.

———. Interview by Jared Jepson, 21 Jan. 2005. Transcript. CHL.

———. Interviews by Gordon Irving, Dec. 1978–Sept. 1979. Transcript. CHL.

———. Journals, 1948–2020. Ardeth G. Kapp Papers, 1948–2020. CHL.

Kapp, Ardeth G., and Carolyn J. Rasmus. "Chronology of Important Dates for Young Women during the Administration of Ardeth G. Kapp." In Ardeth G. Kapp and Carolyn J. Rasmus, Interviews by Gordon Irving, Apr.–June 1992, 244–267. Transcript. CHL.

———. Interviews by Gordon Irving, Apr.–June 1992. Electronic transcript. CHL.

Kearl, James R., Clayne L. Pope, and Larry T. Wimmer. "Household Wealth in a Settlement Economy: Utah, 1850–1870." *Journal of Economic History* 40, no. 3 (Sept. 1980): 477–496.

Kennedy, David M. *Freedom from Fear: The American People in Depression and War, 1929–1945.* New York: Oxford University Press, 1999.

Kennedy, Sheela, and Steven Ruggles. "Breaking Up Is Hard to Count: The Rise of Divorce in the United States, 1980–2010." *Demography* 51, no. 2 (Apr. 2014): 587–598.

Kenney, Scott G. "E. E. Ericksen: Loyal Heretic." *Sunstone* 3, no. 5 (July–Aug. 1978): 16–27.

Kerr, Jason A. "'Virtue' in Moroni 9:9." *Journal of Book of Mormon Studies* 26, no. 1 (2017): 260–265.

Kett, Joseph F. *Rites of Passage: Adolescence in America, 1790 to the Present.* New York: Basic Books, 1977.

Kimball, Camilla Eyring. *Autobiography of Camilla Eyring Kimball.* No place: By the author, 1975.

Kimball, Edward L. *Lengthen Your Stride: The Presidency of Spencer W. Kimball.* Salt Lake City: Deseret Book, 2005.

———. "Spencer W. Kimball and the Revelation on Priesthood." *BYU Studies* 47, no. 2 (2008): 4–78.

Kimball, Richard Ian. "Muscular Mormonism." *International Journal of the History of Sport* 25, no. 5 (Apr. 2008): 549–578.

———. *Sports in Zion: Mormon Recreation, 1890–1940.* Urbana: University of Illinois Press, 2003.

Kimball, Spencer W. "A Style of Our Own." In *Faith Precedes the Miracle: Based on Discourses of Spencer W. Kimball,* 161–168. Salt Lake City: Deseret Book, 1977.

Knowles, Eleanor. *Howard W. Hunter.* Salt Lake City: Deseret Book, 1994.

Kocani, Myzejen, and Edlira Kocani. Interview by Matthew K. Heiss, 11 May 1996. Transcript. CHL.

Kost, Kathryn, Isaac Maddow-Zimet, and Alex Arpaia. *Pregnancies, Births, and Abortions among Adolescents and Young Women in the United States, 2013: National and State Trends by Age, Race, and Ethnicity.* New York: Guttmacher Institute, 2017.

Kuehne, Raymond. *Mormons as Citizens of a Communist State: A Documentary of the Church of Jesus Christ of Latter-day Saints in East Germany, 1945–1990.* Salt Lake City: University of Utah Press, 2010.

Kushner, David. *The Players Ball: A Genius, a Con Man, and the Secret History of the Internet's Rise.* New York: Simon and Schuster, 2019.

Lally, Robert C. "The Life and Educational Contributions of Charlotte Stewart." Master's thesis, University of Utah, 1950.

Larsen, Sharon G. Interview by Christine R. Marin, 17 Sept. 2002. Transcript. CHL.

Larson, Andrew Karl. *"I Was Called to Dixie": The Virgin River Basin: Unique Experiences in Mormon Pioneering.* [Salt Lake City]: Deseret News, 1961.

Latter-day Saints' Sunday School Treatise. 2nd ed. Salt Lake City: Deseret Sunday School Union, 1898.

Laurel Manual 1965–66. Salt Lake City: YWMIA, 1965.

Little Girls' Magazine. St. George, Utah Territory. Manuscript Newspaper. 1879. Copy at Utah State Historical Society Archives, Salt Lake City.

Livingstone, Sonia. "Half a Century of Television in the Lives of Our Children." *Annals of the American Academy of Political and Social Science* 625 (Sept. 2009): 151–163.

Lloyd, Wesley P. *Learning to Live: Joint M Men and Gleaner Activities, M Men Lessons, Gleaner Program, 1940–1941.* [Salt Lake City]: MIA General Boards, 1940.

Lohner, Margrit F. Interview by Sylvia Bruening, Aug. 1972. CHL.

Longden, LaRue C. Interviews by Jill C. Mulvay, 2, 7, 24, and 31 Jan. 1974. Transcript. CHL.

MacIntyre, Alasdair. *After Virtue: A Study in Moral Theory.* 3rd ed. Notre Dame, IN: University of Notre Dame Press, 2007.

Magidson, Phyllis, and Donald Albrecht, eds. *Mod New York: Fashion Takes a Trip*. New York: Monacelli Press, 2017.

Marty, Martin E. *Modern American Religion*. Vol. 2, *The Noise of Conflict, 1919–1941*. Chicago: University of Chicago Press, 1991.

Matthews, Jean V. *The Rise of the New Woman: The Women's Movement in America, 1875–1930*. Chicago: Ivan R. Dee, 2003.

Mauss, Armand L. *The Angel and the Beehive: The Mormon Struggle with Assimilation*. Urbana: University of Illinois Press, 1994.

May, Dean L. "A Demographic Portrait of the Mormons, 1830–1980." In *After 150 Years: The Latter-day Saints in Sesquicentennial Perspective*, edited by Thomas G. Alexander and Jessie L. Embry, 38–69. Provo, UT: Charles L. Redd Center for Western Studies, 1983. Revised edition published in *The New Mormon History: Revisionist Essays on the Past*, edited by D. Michael Quinn, 121–135. Salt Lake City: Signature Books, 1992.

May, Elaine Tyler. *Homeward Bound: American Families in the Cold War Era*. Rev. ed. New York: Basic Books, 2017.

Maycock, Annie Selena Condie. "Esther Palfreyman Condie, Wife of Gibson Sharp Condie." Posted 5 Aug. 2018, in "Esther May Palfreyman," FamilySearch (Person ID: KWJ4-WCY), familysearch.org.

McCall, Linda. Interview by Mary Frances Rich, 27 Jan. 2021. Linda McCall, Interviews, 27 Jan. and 30 Apr. 2021. Transcript. CHL.

McCall, Linda, and Hayden Bogle. Interview by James Goldberg, 30 Apr. 2021. Linda McCall, Interviews, 27 Jan. and 30 Apr. 2021. Transcript. CHL.

McCune, Mary Lue Knell. Personal History, no date. Private possession. Copy in authors' possession.

McDannell, Colleen. "Christianity in the United States During the Inter-war Years." In *The Cambridge History of Christianity*, vol. 9, *World Christianities, c. 1914–c. 2000*, edited by Hugh McLeod, 236–251. Cambridge: Cambridge University Press, 2006.

———. *Sister Saints: Mormon Women since the End of Polygamy*. New York: Oxford, 2019.

McGerr, Michael. *A Fierce Discontent: The Rise and Fall of the Progressive Movement in America, 1870–1920*. New York: Free Press, 2003.

Mette and Soren Larsen Family Collection, 1843–2015. CHL.

Mexican Mission Manuscript History and Historical Reports, 1874–1977. CHL.

Meyer, Casualene. "Emma Lou Thayne and the Art of Peace." *BYU Studies Quarterly* 53, no. 3 (Fall 2014): 181–191, 193–194.

Meyer, Helga. Collection, 1944–1958, 2016–2018. CHL.

Meyer, Helga, and Lark Evans Galli. *Under a Leafless Tree: The Story of a Mormon Girl from East Prussia*. Bloomington, IN: iUniverse, 2013.

Meyerowitz, Joanne. "The Liberal 1950s? Reinterpreting Postwar American Sexual Culture." In *Gender and the Long Postwar: The United States and the Two Germanys, 1945–1989*, edited by Karen Hagemann and Sonya Michel, 297–319. Washington, DC: Woodrow Wilson Center Press, 2014.

MIA Executive Manual. Salt Lake City: MIA General Boards, 1963.

MIA Executive Manual. Salt Lake City: MIA General Boards, 1970.

MIA Executive Manual. Salt Lake City: MIA General Boards, 1972.

MIA Executive Manual Supplement, 1969–70. Salt Lake City: MIA General Boards, 1969.

M. I. A. Guide for Executives and Community Activity Committees, 1936–37. [Salt Lake City]: MIA General Boards, 1936.

M. I. A. in the Missions. [Salt Lake City]: [MIA General Boards], ca. 1955. Copy at CHL.

The Mia Maid, 1954–5. Salt Lake City: YWMIA, 1954.

Mia Maid Manual, 1950–51: Life to Enjoy. Salt Lake City: YWMIA General Board, 1950.

Mia Maid Manual, 1951–52. Salt Lake City: YWMIA General Board, 1951.

Mia Maid Manual, 1952–1953. Salt Lake City: YWMIA General Board, 1952.

Mia Maid Manual. Salt Lake City: YWMIA, 1955.

Mia Maid Manual, 1958–1959. Salt Lake City: YWMIA, 1958.

M. I. A. Manual for Executives and Community Activity Committees, 1939–1940. Salt Lake City: MIA General Boards, 1939.

M. I. A. Manual for Executives and Community Activity Committees, 1943–1944. Salt Lake City: MIA General Boards, 1943.

Mill Creek Ward YLMIA Minutes / Mill Creek Ward, Cottonwood Stake, Young Women's Mutual Improvement Association. Minutes and Records, 1874–1949. CHL.

Miller, Susan A. *Growing Girls: The Natural Origins of Girls' Organizations in America*. New Brunswick, NJ: Rutgers University Press, 2007.

Mineau, Geraldine P., Lee L. Bean, and Mark Skolnick. "Mormon Demographic History II: The Family Life Cycle and Natural Fertility." *Population Studies* 33, no. 3 (Nov. 1979): 429–446.

Minert, Roger P. *In Harm's Way: East German Latter-day Saints in World War II*. Provo, UT: Religious Studies Center, Brigham Young University, 2009.

Mintz, Steven. *Huck's Raft: A History of American Childhood*. Cambridge, MA: Belknap Press of Harvard University Press, 2004.

Mintz, Steven, and Susan Kellogg. *Domestic Revolutions: A Social History of American Family Life*. New York: Free Press, 1988.

M Man–Gleaner Manual, 1955–1956. Salt Lake City: MIA General Boards, 1955.

M Man–Gleaner Manual 1965–66. Salt Lake City: MIA General Boards, 1965.

Monnett, John D., Jr. "The Mormon Church and Its Private School System in Utah: The Emergence of the Academies, 1880–1892." PhD diss., University of Utah, 1984.

Moore, Geoffrey H., and Janice Neipert Hedges. "Trends in Labor and Leisure." *Monthly Labor Review* 94, no. 2 (Feb. 1971): 3–11.

Moore, R. Laurence. "Learning to Play: The Mormon Way and the Way of Other Americans." *Journal of Mormon History* 16 (1990): 89–106.

My Personal Progress. Salt Lake City: The Church of Jesus Christ of Latter-day Saints, 1977.

My Personal Progress. Salt Lake City: The Church of Jesus Christ of Latter-day Saints, 1983.

Nadauld, Margaret D. Interview by Christine R. Marin, 17 Sept. 2002. Transcript. CHL.

Nash, Margaret A. "Rethinking Republican Motherhood: Benjamin Rush and the Young Ladies' Academy of Philadelphia." *Journal of the Early Republic* 17, no. 2 (Summer 1997): 171–191.

Netherlands Amsterdam Mission Manuscript History and Historical Reports, 1841–1977. CHL.

Newburger, Eric C. *Home Computers and Internet Use in the United States: August 2000*. Current Population Report P23-207. Washington, DC: U.S. Census Bureau, 2001.

Nichols, Jeffrey. *Prostitution, Polygamy, and Power: Salt Lake City, 1847–1918*. Urbana: University of Illinois Press, 2002.

1951–52 Y.W.M.I.A. Sports Supplement. Salt Lake City: YWMIA General Board, [1951].

1956–57 Junior M Men Junior Gleaner Manual. Salt Lake City: MIA General Boards, 1956.

1940–1941 Junior Manual. Salt Lake City: YWMIA General Board, 1940.

Norton, Arthur J., and Louisa F. Miller. *Marriage, Divorce, and Remarriage in the 1990's*. Current Population Report P23-180. Washington, DC: U.S. Bureau of the Census, 1992.

Okazaki, Chieko N. "Healing from Sexual Abuse." Embracing Hope Discourse, Provo, UT, 23 Oct. 2002. Available at ChurchofJesusChrist.org/bc/content/ldsorg/topics/welfare/pdf/Healing-from-Sexual-Abuse -Okazaki.pdf.

———. Interviews by Brian D. Reeves, Feb.–Apr. 1991. Transcript. CHL.

O'Keefe, Gwenn Schurgin, Kathleen Clarke-Pearson, and Council on Communications and Media. "The Impact of Social Media on Children, Adolescents, and Families." *Pediatrics* 127, no. 4 (Apr. 2011): 800–804.

Okker, Patricia. *Our Sister Editors: Sarah J. Hale and the Tradition of Nineteenth-Century American Women Editors*. Athens: University of Georgia Press, 1995.

One Hundred Sixteenth Semi-annual Conference of the Church of Jesus Christ of Latter-day Saints, Held in the Tabernacle, Salt Lake City, Utah, October 5, 6, and 7, 1945, with Report of Discourses. Salt Lake City: The Church of Jesus Christ of Latter-day Saints, 1945.

One Hundred Thirty-First Semi-annual Conference of the Church of Jesus Christ of Latter-day Saints, Held in the Tabernacle, Salt Lake City, Utah, September 29, 30, and October 1, 1961, with Report of Discourses. Salt Lake City: The Church of Jesus Christ of Latter-day Saints, 1961.

Orleck, Annelise. *Rethinking American Women's Activism*. New York: Routledge, 2015.

Orton, Chad M., and William W. Slaughter. *40 Ways to Look at Brigham Young: A New Approach to a Remarkable Man*. Salt Lake City: Deseret Book, 2008.

Oscarson, Bonnie L. Interviews by Lisa T. Clayton, 27 and 28 June 2018. Transcript. CHL.

An Outline of Courses of Study for Junior Classes of the Young Ladies' Mutual Improvement Association. Number Two. [Salt Lake City]: YLMIA General Board, 1922.

Park, Clara Horne. *Joseph Horne, Pioneer of 1847*. [Salt Lake City]: Family Organization of Joseph Horne, [1961].

Parker, Rangi, and Emily W. Jensen. "The *Hui Tau*: Cultural Heart of the New Zealand Mission." In *Pioneers in the Pacific: Memory, History, and Cultural Identity among the Latter-day Saints*, edited by Grant Underwood, 121–131. Provo, UT: Religious Studies Center, Brigham Young University, 2005.

Patterson, James T. *Grand Expectations: The United States, 1945–1974*. New York: Oxford University Press, 1996.

WORKS CITED

———. *Restless Giant: The United States from Watergate to* Bush v. Gore. New York: Oxford University Press, 2005.

Paulsen, David L., and Martin Pulido. "'A Mother There': A Survey of Historical Teachings about Mother in Heaven." *BYU Studies* 50, no. 1 (2011): 71–97.

Peiss, Kathy. *Cheap Amusements: Working Women and Leisure in Turn-of-the-Century New York.* Philadelphia: Temple University Press, 1986.

———. *Hope in a Jar: The Making of America's Beauty Culture.* Philadelphia: University of Pennsylvania Press, 2011.

Perry, Janice Kapp. *Songs from My Heart: The Stories behind the Songs.* Sandy, UT: Sounds of Zion, 2000.

Personal Progress. Salt Lake City: The Church of Jesus Christ of Latter-day Saints, 1989.

Petersen, Mark E. *The Sacredness of Sex: Chastity in Its Holy Mission.* Provo, UT: Brigham Young University, 1953. Copy at CHL.

Peterson, Charles S., and Brian Q. Cannon. *The Awkward State of Utah: Coming of Age in the Nation, 1896–1945.* Salt Lake City: University of Utah Press, 2015.

Peterson, Grethe Ballif. "Somewhere Inbetween." *Dialogue: A Journal of Mormon Thought* 6, no. 2 (Summer 1971): 74–76.

Pfau, Ann. "Allotment Annies and Other Wayward Wives: Wartime Concerns about Female Disloyalty and the Problem of the Returned Veteran." In *The United States and the Second World War: New Perspectives on Diplomacy, War, and the Home Front,* edited by G. Kurt Piehler and Sidney Pash, 99–128. New York: Fordham University Press, 2010.

Pittsburgh Branch, Eastern States Mission. General Minutes, 1925–1974. CHL.

Pittsburgh Pennsylvania Stake. Files, 1831–1986. CHL.

Pleasant View 1st Ward YLMIA Minutes / Pleasant View 1st Ward, Provo Utah Sharon East Stake, Young Women's Mutual Improvement Association. Minutes and Records, 1891–1972. CHL.

Plewe, Brandon S., ed. *Mapping Mormonism: An Atlas of Latter-day Saint History.* 2nd ed. Provo, UT: Brigham Young University Press, 2014.

Pope, Liston. "Traditional Values in Transition." In *Values and Ideals of American Youth,* edited by Eli Ginzberg, 229–235. New York: Columbia University Press, 1961.

Powell, Allan Kent, ed. *Utah History Encyclopedia.* Salt Lake City: University of Utah Press, 1994.

———. *Utah Remembers World War II.* Logan: Utah State University Press, 1991.

Preach My Gospel: A Guide to Missionary Service. Salt Lake City: The Church of Jesus Christ of Latter-day Saints, 2004.

"Preliminary Study of Temple and Non-temple Marriages" (Studies in Church Work, no. 2), June 1921. In Correlation–Social Advisory Committee, Minutes, vol. 2, CHL.

Prensky, Marc. "Digital Natives, Digital Immigrants Part 1." *On the Horizon* 9, no. 5 (Oct. 2001): 1–6.

Price, Alvin H. Journal, 1985–1986. Private possession.

Price, Alvin H., and Barbara W. Price. Interview by Kate Holbrook, 14 Feb. 2018. Transcript. CHL.

Priesthood Correlation Executive Committee. Meeting Minutes, 1961–1972. CHL.

Priesthood Executive Council. Minutes, 1982–1985. Priesthood and Family Executive Council, Minutes and Records, 1982–1985, 2012–2018. CHL.

Program for Junior M Men and Junior Gleaners: Course of Study—"We Believe," by T. Edgar Lyon, 1950–1951. Salt Lake City: MIA General Boards, 1950.

Puketapu Branch YLMIA Minutes / Puketapu Branch, New Zealand Mission, Young Women's Mutual Improvement Association. Minutes and Records, 1921–1924. CHL.

Pulsipher, Nancy Ruth Funk. *Ruth Hardy Funk: A Journey of Joy and Gratitude.* Salt Lake City: Marcus C. Funk Family History Association, 2000.

Putnam, Robert D., and David E. Campbell. *American Grace: How Religion Divides and Unites Us.* New York: Simon and Schuster, 2010.

Qinisile, Zandile Precious. Interview by Khumbulani D. Mdletshe, 9 Feb. 2019. Transcript. CHL.

Quinn, D. Michael. *Elder Statesman: A Biography of J. Reuben Clark.* Salt Lake City: Signature Books, 2002.

Rasmus, Carolyn J. Ardeth G. Kapp Biography, Sept. 1985. Ardeth G. Kapp Papers, 1948–2020. CHL.

———. Office Papers, 1984–1993. CHL.

Reeder, Bertha S. (Bertha J. Stone Richards). Interviews by Jill C. Mulvay, 29 Apr. and 1 May 1974. Transcript. CHL.

———. Reminiscences, ca. 1974. Bertha J. Stone Richards Collection, ca. 1893–1980. CHL.

Reeder, Jennifer. "Making an (in)Delible Mark: Nineteenth-Century Mormon Girls and Their Manuscript Newspapers." *Utah Historical Quarterly* 85, no. 3 (Summer 2017): 273–278.

Reeder, Jennifer, and Kate Holbrook, eds. *At the Pulpit: 185 Years of Discourses by Latter-day Saint Women.* Salt Lake City: Church Historian's Press, 2017.

Reeve, W. Paul. *Religion of a Different Color: Race and the Mormon Struggle for Whiteness*. New York: Oxford University Press, 2015.

Reeve, W. Paul, and Ardis E. Parshall, eds. *Mormonism: A Historical Encyclopedia*. Santa Barbara, CA: ABC-CLIO, 2010.

Regnerus, Mark D. *Forbidden Fruit: Sex and Religion in the Lives of American Teenagers*. New York: Oxford University Press, 2007.

Reid, Daniel G., Robert D. Linder, Bruce L. Shelley, and Harry S. Stout, eds. *Dictionary of Christianity in America: A Comprehensive Resource on the Religious Impulse that Shaped a Continent*. Downers Grove, IL: InterVarsity Press, 1990.

Relief Society Research and Evaluation Services Reports, 1981–1983. CHL.

"Report of the Committee on M. I. A. Survey," Mar. 1934. In Young Women General Board, Minutes, vol. 13. CHL.

Revised Statutes of the State of Utah, in Force Jan. 1, 1898. Lincoln, NE: State Journal, 1897.

Rich, Mary Frances, and Lisa Olsen Tait. Notes on Interviews with Charlene Holmstrom. Copy in authors' possession.

Rich, Mary Frances, Maurine Jensen Proctor, and Carol Clark. Interview by James Goldberg, 26 Aug. 2021. Audio file. Copy in authors' possession.

Richardson, Matthew O. "Come, Follow Me: Learning Resources for Youth." *Religious Educator* 14, no. 3 (2013): 23–47.

The Rising Generation Compilation, 1986–1987. CHL.

Rivers, Percy J. Interview by R. Lanier Britsch, 10 Jan. 1974. Transcript. CHL.

Robison, Elwin C. "Historic Structures Report of the Brigham Young Estate: Beehive House, Offices, and Lion House," 15 Jan. 2011 (amended 6 Feb. 2011). Report for Historic Sites Division, Church History Department, Salt Lake City. Copy in authors' possession.

Rocamora, Agnès. "Personal Fashion Blogs: Screens and Mirrors in Digital Self-Portraits." *Fashion Theory* 15, no. 4 (2011): 407–424.

Romney, Antone K. "History of the Correlation of L.D.S. Church Auxiliaries," Aug. 1961. CHL.

Rosero, Erika Aza. Interview by Amber Taylor, 11 Mar. 2021. Audio file. Copy in authors' possession.

Rowland, Fanny. "Autobiographical Sketch of Fanny Rowland." Posted 14 Feb. 2017, in "Fanny Rowland," FamilySearch (Person ID: KWJ8-8ZH), familysearch.org.

Runia, Tamara W., and Andrea Muñoz Spannaus. Interview by Amber Taylor, James Goldberg, and Brittany Chapman Nash, 26 Mar. 2024. Audio file. Copy in authors' possession.

Sagers, Diana L. Interview by James Goldberg, 4 Jan. 2021. Transcript. CHL.

Saints: The Story of the Church of Jesus Christ in the Latter Days. Vol. 3, *Boldly, Nobly, and Independent, 1893–1955*. Salt Lake City: The Church of Jesus Christ of Latter-day Saints, 2022.

"Samoa Mapusaga M.I.A. Record," 1909–1916. Mapusaga Ward, Pago Pago Samoa West Stake, Young Men's Mutual Improvement Association Minutes and Records, 1909–1973. CHL.

Sandell, Merydith Garfield. Interview by Jessica M. Nelson, 10 May 2018. Transcript. CHL.

San Francisco Branch YMMIA Minutes / San Francisco Branch, California Mission, Young Men's Mutual Improvement Association. Minutes and Records, 1910–1965. CHL.

Savage, Jon. *Teenage: The Prehistory of Youth Culture, 1875–1945*. New York: Penguin, 2007.

Schaerrer, Neil D. Interview by Gordon Irving, 14 Dec. 1979. Transcript. CHL.

Schneirov, Matthew. *The Dream of a New Social Order: Popular Magazines in America, 1893–1914*. New York: Columbia University Press, 1994.

Schrum, Kelly. *Some Wore Bobby Sox: The Emergence of Teenage Girls' Culture 1920–1945*. New York: Palgrave Macmillan, 2004.

Schulman, Bruce J. *The Seventies: The Great Shift in American Culture, Society, and Politics*. New York: Da Capo Press, 2001.

Sessions, Patty Bartlett. Diary, 1851–1853. Patty Bartlett Sessions, Diaries and Account Book, 1846–1866, 1880. CHL.

76th Annual Conference of the Church of Jesus Christ of Latter-day Saints: Held in the Tabernacle, Salt Lake City, Utah, April Sixth, Seventh, Eighth, Nineteen Hundred and Six, with a Full Report of the Discourses. Salt Lake City: Deseret News, 1906.

Severa, Joan L. *Dressed for the Photographer: Ordinary Americans and Fashion, 1840–1900*. Kent, OH: Kent State University Press, 1995.

Shepherd, Gary, and Gordon Shepherd. *Mormon Passage: A Missionary Chronicle*. Urbana: University of Illinois Press, 1998.

Shimp, Sharon Taylor, Karen Taylor Asay, and Rama Taylor Cowley. Interview by Amber Taylor, 26 Aug. 2021. Audio file. Copy in authors' possession.

Shipps, Jan, Cheryll L. May, and Dean L. May. "Sugar House Ward: A Latter-day Saint Congregation." In *American Congregations*, vol. 1, *Portraits of Twelve Religious Communities*, edited by James P. Wind and James W. Lewis, 293–348. Chicago: University of Chicago Press, 1994.

Simpson, Thomas W. *American Universities and the Birth of Modern Mormonism, 1867–1940*. Chapel Hill: University of North Carolina Press, 2016.

Sims, Bette Lou. Interview by Nicholas B. Shrum, 25 Sept. 2018. Transcript. CHL.

Sims, Mary S. *The YWCA—an Unfolding Purpose*. New York: Woman's Press, 1950.

Skolnick, Mark, Lee L. Bean, Dean L. May, V. Arbon, K. de Nevers, and P. Cartwright. "Mormon Demographic History I: Nuptiality and Fertility of Once-Married Couples." *Population Studies* 32, no. 1 (1978): 5–19.

Smith, Hortense Child. Interviews by Gordon Irving, Nov. 1978–Nov. 1980. Transcript. CHL.

Smith, Jan Christiansen. Interview by James Goldberg, 27 Aug. 2021. Audio file. Copy in authors' possession.

Smith, Michaele. "Rape Law in the Mid-twentieth Century: Sexual Violence in Salt Lake City." *Utah Historical Quarterly* 85, no. 3 (Summer 2017): 225–237.

Smith-Rosenberg, Carroll. "The Female World of Love and Ritual: Relations between Women in Nineteenth-Century America." *Signs: Journal of Women in Culture and Society* 1, no. 1 (Fall 1975): 1–29.

Social Advisory Committee. Minutes, 1916–1920. CHL.

Solomon, Barbara Miller. *In the Company of Educated Women: A History of Women and Higher Education in America*. New Haven, CT: Yale University Press, 1985.

South Davis Stake. Gleaners' Treasure Book, ca. 1934–1937. CHL.

"Special Children and Youth Broadcast Featuring President M. Russell Ballard." Video, 48:29, 29 Sept. 2019. Children and Youth, The Church of Jesus Christ of Latter-day Saints, ChurchofJesusChrist.org.

Spencer W. Kimball Biography Research Files, 1924–1980. CHL.

Spirit of the Hive for Bee Hive Girls, YWMIA. Salt Lake City: YWMIA General Board, 1954.

Spirit of the Hive for Bee Hive Girls, YWMIA. Salt Lake City: YWMIA General Board, 1956.

Springville 4th Ward YLMIA Minutes / Springville 4th Ward, Springville Stake, Young Women's Mutual Improvement Association. Minutes and Records, 1892–1973. CHL.

Stapley, Jonathan A. *The Power of Godliness: Mormon Liturgy and Cosmology*. New York: Oxford University Press, 2018.

Stapley, Jonathan A., and Kristine Wright. "Female Ritual Healing in Mormonism." *Journal of Mormon History* 37, no. 1 (Winter 2011): 1–85.

St. George Stake. General Minutes, 1864–1935, 1960–1977. CHL.

Stone, Geoffrey R. "Sexual Expression and Free Speech: How Our Values Have (D)evolved." *Human Rights* (American Bar Association) 43, no. 4 (Oct. 2018): 22–25.

Stone, Heather Joy. "Young Women in Mormon Homelands, 1975–2000: An Oral History Project." PhD diss, University of Utah, 2018.

Strauss, William, and Neil Howe. *Generations: The History of America's Future, 1584 to 2069*. New York: William Morrow, 1991.

Strong, Leon M. "A History of the Young Men's Mutual Improvement Association, 1875–1938." Master's thesis, Brigham Young University, 1939.

Strub, Whitney. *Obscenity Rules: Roth v. United States and the Long Struggle over Sexual Expression*. Lawrence: University Press of Kansas, 2013.

Sugar House Ward YLMIA Minutes / Sugar House Ward, Sugar House Stake, Young Women's Mutual Improvement Association. Minutes and Records, 1877–1971. CHL.

Supplement to the Bee Hive Girls Handbook: Program for the Nymphs, the Youngest Group of Bee-Hive Girls. Salt Lake City: YLMIA General Board, 1931.

Tait, Lisa Olsen. "Between Two Economies: The Business Development of the *Young Woman's Journal*, 1889–1900." *Journal of Mormon History* 38, no. 4 (Fall 2012): 1–54.

———. "The 1890s Mormon Culture of Letters and the Post-Manifesto Marriage Crisis: A New Approach to Home Literature." *BYU Studies Quarterly* 52, no. 1 (2013): 99–124.

———. "Finding 'Cactus': My Search for One Mormon Writer." Unpublished paper, 23 May 2009. Delivered at Mormon Historical Association Conference, Springfield, IL, 2009. Copy in authors' possession.

———. "What Is Women's Relationship to Priesthood?" *BYU Studies Quarterly* 60, no. 3 (2021): 241–272.

———. "*The Young Woman's Journal* and Its Stories: Gender and Generations in 1890s Mormondom." PhD diss., University of Houston, 2010.

———. "*The Young Woman's Journal*: Gender and Generations in a Mormon Women's Magazine." *American Periodicals* 22, no. 1 (2012): 51–71.

Tanner, Susan W. Interview by Amber Taylor, 3 June 2019. Audio file. CHL.

Teaiwa, Teresia K. "bikinis and other s/pacific n/oceans." *Contemporary Pacific* 6, no. 1 (Spring 1994): 87–109.

WORKS CITED

Tenth Ward YLMIA History / "History of the Young Ladies Mutual Improvement Association of the Tenth Ward, 1886–1903." In Tenth Ward, Park Stake, Young Women's Mutual Improvement Association, Minutes and Records, 1870–1973, vol. 5, 1886–1904. CHL.

Thayne, Emma Lou. *The Place of Knowing: A Spiritual Biography*. Bloomington, IN: iUniverse, 2011.

Theriot, Nancy M. *Mothers and Daughters in Nineteenth-Century America: The Biosocial Construction of Femininity*. Lexington: University Press of Kentucky, 1996.

"Things as They Really Are." Video, 3:27, 6 Oct. 2011. Media Library, The Church of Jesus Christ of Latter-day Saints, ChurchofJesusChrist.org.

Thomas, Carol B. Interview by Christine R. Marin, 17 Feb. 2002. Transcript. CHL.

Tortora, Phyllis G. *Dress, Fashion, and Technology: From Prehistory to Present*. London: Bloomsbury, 2015.

Transactions of the National Council of Women of the United States, Assembled in Washington, D.C., February 22 to 25, 1891. Edited by Rachel Foster Avery. Philadelphia: National Council of Women, 1891.

Tuffin, George. Notes on 1960s Dutch Girls Camps, no date. Copy in authors' possession.

Tullis, F. LaMond. "A Shepherd to Mexico's Saints: Arwell L. Pierce and the Third Convention." *BYU Studies* 37, no. 1 (1997–1998): 127–157.

Tuminez, Astrid S. "Coming Home." In *Silent Notes Taken*, 87–107. New York: Mormon Artists Group Press, 2002.

Turkish Mission Manuscript History and Historical Reports, 1884–1951. CHL.

Turley, Maurine J. Journals, ca. 1984–1992. Maurine J. Turley Papers, ca. 1984–1992. CHL.

Twelfth Annual Report of the Public Schools of Salt Lake City for the Year Ending June 30th, 1902. Salt Lake City: Salt Lake City Board of Education, 1902.

Ulrich, Laurel Thatcher. "Mormon Women in the History of Second-Wave Feminism." *Dialogue: A Journal of Mormon Thought* 43, no. 2 (Summer 2010): 45–63.

Utah Stake YLMIA Minutes / Provo Utah Central Stake Young Women's Mutual Improvement Association. Minutes and Records, 1881–1971. CHL.

Utah Stake YLMIA Officers Minutes / Utah Stake Young Ladies' Mutual Improvement Association. Officers Minutes, 1901–1908, 1910. CHL.

Utonian 1968. Vol. 62. Salt Lake City: Associated Students of the University of Utah, 1968.

Van Noy, Elsie Ellen Hogan. "Summer Camps." In "Young Ladies (Later Young Womens) Mutual Improvement Association—from April, 1927 to Dec. 1937," ca. 1957. Typescript. CHL.

"Virtue Is Its Own Reward," 1956. Copy at CHL.

Walker, Lucile H., and Harold S. Walker. *Glimpses of Pleasant Grove Schools, 1850–1950*. Provo, UT: BYU Press, 1962.

Walker, Ronald W. "Growing Up in Early Utah: The Wasatch Literary Association, 1874–1878." *BYU Studies* 43, no. 1 (2004), 61–79.

Walker, Ronald W., David J. Whittaker, and James B. Allen. *Mormon History*. Urbana: University of Illinois Press, 2001.

Watkins, Jordan, comp. "History of Media in The Church of Jesus Christ of Latter-day Saints," 2009. CHL.

Wayland-Smith, Ellen. *Oneida: From Free Love Utopia to the Well-Set Table*. New York: Picador, 2016.

Wheatley-Pesci, Meg. "An Expanded Definition of Priesthood? Some Present and Future Consequences." *Dialogue: A Journal of Mormon Thought* 18, no. 3 (Fall 1985): 33–42.

Widtsoe, John A. Papers. CHL.

———. *Your Questions Answered: Joint M Men and Gleaner Program, the M Men Lessons, the Gleaner Program, 1943–1944*. MIA General Boards, 1943.

Wiebe, Robert H. *The Search for Order, 1877–1920*. New York: Hill and Wang, 1967.

Wilkinson, Ernest L., ed. *Brigham Young University: The First One Hundred Years*. Vol. 1. Provo, UT: Brigham Young University Press, 1975.

Wilson, Elizabeth. *Adorned in Dreams: Fashion and Modernity*. London: I. B. Tauris, 2003.

Winters, Mary Ann Stearns. Reminiscences, no date. Typescript. CHL.

Wright, Dennis A., and Rebekah E. Westrup. "Ensign Peak: A Historical Review." In *Salt Lake City: The Place Which God Prepared*, edited by Scott C. Esplin and Kenneth L. Alford, 27–46. Provo, UT: Religious Studies Center, Brigham Young University, 2011.

Y. L. M. I. A. Hand Book: A Guide for Stake and Ward Officers of the Young Ladies' Mutual Improvement Associations of the Church of Jesus Christ of Latter-day Saints. [Salt Lake City]: General Board, 1923.

Y. L. M. I. A. Hand Book: A Guide for Stake and Ward Officers of the Young Ladies' Mutual Improvement Associations of the Church of Jesus Christ of Latter-day Saints. 3rd ed. [Salt Lake City]: General Board, 1926.

Y. L. M. I. A. Lion House Social Center for Girls and Women. [Salt Lake City]: YLMIA, [1933].

YMMIA Manual [1891] / L. D. S. Young Men's Mutual Improvement Associations. Manual. Part One, 1891–92. Salt Lake City: [YMMIA General Board], 1891.

WORKS CITED

YMMIA Manual [1901] / *Young Men's Mutual Improvement Associations Manual, 1901–1902. Subject: Principles of the Gospel, Part I.* Salt Lake City: YMMIA General Board, 1901.

YMMIA Minutes / Young Men Mutual Improvement Association, Minutes, 1898–1972. Young Men, Minutes, 1898–1989, 1991–1997, 2001–2003. CHL.

Young, George C. Collection, 1857–1963. Photocopy. CHL.

Young Ladies' Companion. East Bountiful, Utah Territory. Manuscript newspaper, 1877–1891. Copy at CHL.

Young Women Camp Manual. Salt Lake City: The Church of Jesus Christ of Latter-day Saints, 1992.

Young Women Files, 1984–1990. CHL.

Young Women General Board. Minutes, 1891–1992, 1997–2008. CHL.

Young Women Handbook. Salt Lake City: The Church of Jesus Christ of Latter-day Saints, 1975.

Young Women Handbook. Salt Lake City: The Church of Jesus Christ of Latter-day Saints, 1988.

Young Women Handbook. Salt Lake City: The Church of Jesus Christ of Latter-day Saints, 1989.

Young Women Minutes, 1984–1992. CHL.

Young Women Personal Progress: Standing as a Witness of God. Salt Lake City: The Church of Jesus Christ of Latter-day Saints, 2001.

Young Women Personal Progress: Standing as a Witness of God. Salt Lake City: The Church of Jesus Christ of Latter-day Saints, 2009.

Young Women Programs, 1961–1976. CHL.

Young Women Resource Library Files, 1915, 1938–1978. CHL.

YWMIA Campcrafter Certification Program. [Salt Lake City]: [YWMIA], [1962].

Y. W. M. I. A. Camp-O-Rama. Salt Lake City: YWMIA General Board, 1940.

Y. W. M. I. A. Camp-O-Rama. Salt Lake City: YWMIA General Board, 1946.

YWMIA Correspondence / Young Women's Mutual Improvement Association Correspondence, 1946–1972, 1997–2002. CHL.

YWMIA History Records / Young Women's Mutual Improvement Association History Records, 1957–1983. CHL.

YWMIA Stake and Mission Reports / Young Women's Mutual Improvement Association Stake and Mission Reports, 1950–1972. CHL.

Zina Card Brown Family Collection, 1806–1972. CHL.

INDEX

A

Aaronic Priesthood: age for, 201; and bishop's youth council, 197; religious instruction in, 224; teachers in, 18; theme, 320; and young men's program, 48, 206, 318, 351n92

Aaronic Priesthood Mutual Improvement Association (APMIA), 200 (illus.), 201, 203–206, 207 (illus.)

abortion, 213, 223

abstinence and chastity, 117, 121, 164–165, 185, 256, 281, 292–294, 296, 375n96

achievement programs: for Bee-Hive Girls, 149, 198 (illus.), 256; Behold Thy Handmaiden program, 212–213, 215; Children and Youth program, 317–318; for Gleaner Girls, 130, 149; for Junior Gleaners, 148, 149; for Laurel class, 256; for Mia Maids, 146–148, 149, 256; My Personal Progress program, 215–216, 227, 236, 237; and performance demonstrations, 129–130; Personal Achievement program, 211–212. See also Personal Progress program

Activity Book, The, 216, 220

Adams, Caroline R., 351n85

Addams, Jane, 78

Adei-Manu, Elizabeth, 290

Adler, Felix, 78

adolescence, defining, 10–12, 51–52, 129

Adult class, 340

Advanced Senior class, 96–97, 340

Africa: family culture in, 275; youth programs in, 267, 278, 283, 290–291, 296–298

age: of adolescence, 10–12, 51–52, 129; of adulthood, 201; for dating, 184, 185; for entry into mission service, 298, 299–300; for entry into youth programs, 94–95, 145–146, 317; generational dynamics, 9–12, 28, 77, 83, 301, 353n8, 394n41; and leadership, 54; and marriage, 10, 38, 54, 93, 163, 276, 355n74

Albania, youth programs in, 290, 291

alcohol consumption, 70–71, 134, 149, 275

All-Church Coordinating Council: establishment of, 178; goals of, 182–184; Youth Correlation Committee initiatives, 185–187

Alldridge, Ann Blunt, 12

Allen, Rebecca, 350n71

Allred, Silvia Henriquez, 284, 285, 391n100

American Red Cross, 76, 136

Ames, Alycia, 308

Anderson, Edward, 61, 64

anniversary celebrations: pioneer centennial (1947), 141; Young Women centennial (1969), 194–196, 195 (illus.); Young Women Jubilee (1925), 87–89; Young Women sesquicentennial (2020), 322

Annual Day (Dime Day), 42–43, 356n103. See also MIA Day

APMIA (Aaronic Priesthood Mutual Improvement Association), 200 (illus.), 201, 203–206, 207 (illus.)

apostles. See Quorum of the Twelve Apostles

Argentina, youth programs in, 252 (illus.), 290

Articles of Faith, 180, 377n16

Asay, Carlos E., 242

Ashton, Marvin J., 184

Ashton, Wendell, 183

athletic programs, 64, 152–155, 390n77

attendance records, 146, 149–150, 172

Australia: pandemic in, 323; youth programs in, 172

authority. See leadership

auxiliary status of church organizations, 74–76, 238–239, 318, 362n112

awards. See achievement programs

Aza, Camila Ortega, 299–300, 307

Aza, Erika, 269–271, 287, 290, 299

Azevedo, Lex de, 250

B

Babcock, Maud May, 40, 41 (illus.), 84

Backman, Robert L., 204, 207 (illus.)

Baird, Jim, 254

Baird, Louise Olsen, 254
Balderas, Guillermo, 124–125
Ballard, Melvin J., 100, 101, 121
balloon release event (1986), 251–253, 252 (illus.)
balls (Gold and Green Balls), 83–84, 124, 152, 162 (illus.)
baptism, 193
baptisms for the dead, 93–94, 193, 305–308, 319
Barney, Elvira Stevens, 3–4, 348n4
Barnhurst, Mary Anna, 351n85
Barnhurst, Priscilla, 24
Bateman, Merrill J., 292
Battista, Verónica, 290
beauty, 7, 83, 240, 287
Beck, Julie Bangerter, 284, 285, 291, 391n100
Beckham, Janette Callister Hales, 265, 271, 292, 335
Bednar, David A., 307
Bee-Hive Girls: achievement awards, 149, 198 (illus.), 256; age range for, 94–95, 145–146, 340; beehive symbolism, 72–73, 361n95; camps, 138–139, 141, 155; discontinuation of, 318; establishment of, 71–72; femininity ideals, 81, 167; health diaries, 81–82; in missions, 110–113, xi; plays about, 86; purpose and curriculum, 73–74, 167–168, 340; scrapbook projects, 108; temple trips, 93; value experiences, 256; war service pin, 76
Bee-Hive Girl's Fantasy, A (Marguerite Gordon and Velma Wing), 86
Beehive House (Salt Lake City), 132–133
Beekhuizen, Willy, 189
Beeley, Arthur, 79, 119
Beesley, Clarissa A., 78–79, 100, 102, 122, 127, 368n57
Behold Thy Handmaiden program, 212–213, 215. See also My Personal Progress program
Bennett, Emily Higgs, 145, 149
Bennett, Rosetta Wallace, 96, 101, 118, 355n82, 368n57
Bennion, Anne, 251
Bennion, Jane, 251
Bennion, Katie, 258
Bennion, Rebecca, 251, 261–262
Benson, Ezra Taft, 140, 158, 166, 174, 179, 242, 244, 247, 254
bishops. See Presiding Bishopric; priesthood
bishop's youth committee, 205
bishop's youth council, 196
Black communities and church members, 189, 192–193, 226–227
Blechert, Bertha, 108
blessings: baptisms for the dead, 93–94, 193, 305–308, 319; of healing, 108; patriarchal, 193, 393n3; women giving, 31, 354n29
boarding houses, 132–133
boards. See general boards
Bogle, Yvonne, 190
Bond, Julian, 191
Book of Mormon, 34, 171, 213, 227, 262, 296
Boone, Dottie, 217
Boy Scouts of America (BSA), 69–70, 74, 315
Bradfield, Shirley, 225

Brandley, Elsie Talmage, 100, 101, 115, 116–117, 119, 121, 123–124, 368n57
Brazil, youth programs in, 296, 321
Brigham Young Academy, 34, 36
Brigham Young University (BYU), 161, 165, 166, 231–232
Brighton Girls Camp, 90, 91 (illus.), 294
Brimhall, George, 50
Brimhall, Lucy Jane "Jennie," 38–39
Britain: church centennial celebration in, 141; mission leadership during World War II, 128–129; youth programs in, 113, 125–128, 189–190
Brown, Hugh B., 128, 135
Brown, Patty, 225
Brown, Victor L., 201, 203, 206, 207 (illus.), 208, 209, 210, 242
BSA (Boy Scouts of America), 69–70, 74, 315
budgets. See funding
Bunker, Zola Woodbury, 93
Burton, Linda Kjar, 305
Butler, Margot, 172, 174
BYU (Brigham Young University), 161, 165, 166, 231–232

C

Calabrese, Elisabetta, 258, 262
Caley, Lucy, 193
California, youth programs in, 169–171, 306 (illus.)
Campbell, Agnes, 31, 355n82
Campcrafter program, 180, 261
Camp Fire Ceremonial, 90
Camp Fire Girls, 71–72, 155
Camp Liahona, 261
Camp-O-Rama (camping manual), 139, 155
Camp Pinnacle, 67
camps: activities, 69, 90, 139, 155, 261–262; international, 262, 263 (illus.), 277–278, 287–291, 289 (illus.); manuals and training for, 139–140, 155, 180, 262, 264–265; program and site development, 67–69, 89–90, 91 (illus.), 138–139, 155, 291–292; spiritual purpose of, 69, 90–92, 155, 262, 291, 292
Canada, youth programs in, 124, 125
Cannon, Abraham, 43, 45
Cannon, Ann Mousley, 39, 45, 71, 72, 355n82
Cannon, Carol Hinckley, 163
Cannon, Elaine Anderson, 335; correlation committee service, 183; leadership as president, 221, 222–225, 227–228, 232; life experience, 221, 225; New Era editorship, 197–199; in White House Conference on Youth, 159
Cannon, George Q., 46; Life of Joseph Smith, 33, 34
Cannon, Hugh, 68, 101
Cannon, Lucy Grant, 334; at British youth conference, 127, 128; leadership as president, 141, 210; life experience, 92, 128; member of MIA Service Committee, 368n57
Cannon, Zina Bennion, 61–62
Card, Zina Young Williams, 7, 13

careers. *See* employment

Catholicism, 118

centennial celebrations: pioneer arrival (1947), 141; YWMIA (1969), 194–196, 195 (illus.)

certification programs, 180

chastity, 117, 121, 164–165, 185, 256, 281, 292–294, 296, 375n96. *See also* modesty

Chicagoland Music Festival, 159

Child, Hortense Hogan, 207 (illus.); correlation committee service 183; leadership as counselor, 201, 203, 204, 206, 208, 209, 217, 382n72

Children and Youth program, 317–318

Children's Friend (magazine), 197

Christ. *See* Jesus Christ

Christiansen, Jan, 191–192

Church Education System, 259–260

Church News (newspaper), 175, 260, 265, 308

Church of Jesus Christ of Latter-day Saints: celebration of pioneer centennial (1947), 141; growth of, 28, 60, 105, 109, 169, 180, 188, 233, 255, 269; Jesus Christ as focus of, 314; membership record, 133–134; public image, 158–160, 187; temple participation, 92–94, 193, 255, 285, 305, 306 (illus.), 309 (illus.), 318–319

civil rights movement, 192

Clark, Bertha, 166

Clark, Carol, 191–192

Clark, J. Reuben, Jr., 115–116, 119, 141, 163–164

Clawson, Emily Young, 9, 349n27

Clean Life campaign, 134

clothing: and cosmetics, 83; dress reform movements and modesty standards, 7–9, 13–14, 75–76, 83, 165–167, 185–187, 281–282, 349n49; fashion shows, 83; for physical activity, 39, 81; style changes, 78, 81, 83, 165, 184, 189, 378n60; temple garments, 82–83

Cluff, Ann, 35

Coe, George A., 52, 358n156

Cohen, Sidney, 191

Coleman, Lethe, 65, 92

Colombia: family culture in, 275–276; youth programs in, 269–271, 287, 290, 307, 309 (illus.)

combined activities, 262–264

Come, Follow Me (curriculum), 302, 314, 393n16

Community Activities Committee, 97

community outreach and service work, 76, 136–138, 217–220, 219 (illus.), 310–313, 311 (illus.), 314, 316 (illus.). *See also* social work

Condie, Hannah, 358n169

Condie, Lena, 358n169

Condie, Lillian, 358n169

conferences: board member attendance of, 50; general Young Women meetings, 278–279; in missions, 123–128, 152, 189, 190, 269, 321; on social work, 78–79; For the Strength of Youth (FSY), 317–318; virtual, 321; YLMIA–YMMIA collaborations, 25, 45–49 (*see also* June Conference); on youth leadership, 197. *See also* conventions

Conjoint Conference (1896), 45–46. *See also* June Conference

conjoint movement, 23–25, 45–49, 50–51, 58

Connelly, Mary, 64

contests, 64–67, 85 (illus.), 122, 123

Contributor (magazine), 25, 45. *See also* Improvement Era

conventions: board member attendance of, 50; function of, 49–50; YLMIA–YMMIA collaborations, 49, 50–51

Cook, Mary Nielsen, 288, 294–295

Cook, Richard, 288

Copier, Jantje, xi

Cordon, Bonnie Hillam, 313, 315, 318, 319, 322, 337

correlation ideology and initiatives, 178, 182–184, 197–199

Correlation–Social Advisory Committee, 80–81

Corry, Rachel, 18

cosmetics, 83

Cosslett, Emeline Rosetta Haight, 351n85

counterculture movement (1960s), 190–191, 199

courtship and dating, 77, 124–125, 148, 184

Covey, Stephen, 385n36

COVID-19 pandemic, 320–321, 322–323

Craig, Michelle Daines, 313, 319, 326

Craven, Rebecca Mitchell, 313, 319

Cressey, George, 132

Croxall, Caroline Young, 9, 349n27

Cryer, Patricia, 290

cultural identity, and spirituality, 124, 125–127, 189. *See also* race and ethnicity

Curtis, LeGrand R., Sr., 207 (illus.)

Cuthbert, Maureen, 190

D

Dalton, Elaine Schwartz, 282, 285, 291, 294–296, 302, 325, 336, 391n100

dancing and dances: Gold and Green Balls, 83–84, 124, 152, 162 (illus.); modesty standards, 75, 185; social studies on, 79; style changes, 184

Darger, Arlene Barlow, 222

dating and courtship, 77, 124–125, 148, 184

daughters of God, identity as, 227, 238, 247, 264, 268, 282, 292, 319

Davis, Lia, 156

Day of the Swarm ceremony, 74

Dear to My Heart program, 165

defense industries (wartime), 131–132

DeLong, Lilian, 290–291

DeMille, Cecil B., 158

Denmark, youth programs in, 113, 153 (illus.), 321

depression (economic), 114–115, 117, 233

depression (mental), 280

Deseret Book, 174

Deseret Costume, 13, 349n49

Deseret Gymnasium, 64, 68

deseret symbolism, 72

devotionals, 306 (illus.)

Dew, Sheri L., 305

Dibb, Ann Monson, 294–295

Dime Day (Annual Day), 42–43, 356n103. *See also* MIA Day

Dintof, Tatiana Christina dos Reis, 296

disabilities, and service work, 312–313

divine nature, as value, 238, 245, 274

divorce rates, 272–273

Dlamuka, Zamanguni Queeneth, 270 (illus.)

Dobbs, Sareta, 227

domestic skills, 73–74, 167–168. *See also* family life; marriage

Dougall, Maria Young, 7, 9, 11 (illus.), 13, 29, 32 (illus.), 349n27

Doxey, Roy, 208

draft (military), 130

drama productions, 84–87. *See also* film productions

dress. *See* clothing; modesty

Durham, G. Homer, 193

Duriez, Deolinda, 277

E

Eardley, Adella Woolley, 31

Eastin, Catherine, 148

eating disorders, 280

economic depression and recession, 114–115, 117, 233

economic growth, 144

Eddington, Sarah, 31, 42, 355n82

education: expansion of opportunities for women, 36–37; increased high school enrollment, 36, 129; and societal focus on domesticity, 168; Sunday class meetings, 224–225, 285–287, 314; youth program curriculum, 33–35, 94–97, 302, 314, 393n16

Eisenhower, Dwight D., 158, 159

Empey, Ella Young, 9, 10, 11 (illus.), 13–14, 349n27

employment: career-family life balance, 225–226, 276; in defense industries, 131–132; expansion of opportunities for women, 37–38; and housing demand, 132–133; and societal focus on domesticity, 168; unemployment rates, 115

endowment ordinance, 82, 193, 255, 305

England. *See* Britain

Ensign (magazine), 197, 260

Ensign Peak, 294–295

Equal Rights Amendment, 213, 220, 232

Ericksen, Ephraim, 97, 119

eternal progression theology, 61

ethnicity. *See* race and ethnicity

Evans, Mattie Read, 65

evolutionary theory, 60

Eyring, Fern Chipman, 81

Eyring (later Kimball), Camilla, 60, 62, 92, 115, 123

F

faith. *See* spirituality and faith

Fallentine, Angela, 277

family life: balancing career with, 225–226, 276; church proclamation on, 274–277; and domestic skills, 73–74, 167–168; emphasized in youth programs, 278–280; and fatherhood, 276; and heavenly parents, 274; and motherhood, 214–215, 256, 274, 276, 279; and parental involvement in youth programs, 83, 165, 254, 261, 283, 284–285, 317; shifting societal norms in, 272–273; women's sacred roles in, 214–215, 222–223. *See also* marriage

family values, as term, 236

fashion shows, 83. *See also* clothing

father-daughter activities, 254

fatherhood, 276

Faust, James E., 281

Featherstone, Vaughn J., 207 (illus.)

Fei, Suzanne, 276

Feminine Mystique, The (Betty Friedan), 213

femininity: archetypal, 71–72; and beauty, 7, 83, 240, 287; and clothing, 187; emphasized in youth programs, 81, 167–169

feminism and women's movement, 213–215, 220–221, 222, 232

Fiaccola Novanta (Torch 90), 262, 263 (illus.)

film productions, 161–163. *See also* theater productions

firesides, 173–175, 221, 222, 244, 246–248, 249 (illus.)

First Presidency: and All-Church Coordinating Council, 178; appointment of youth organization presidents, 102, 177, 199–201, 221, 231, 323; approval of youth organization initiatives, 122–123, 149, 244, 246; correlation initiative, 178, 182; and establishment of APMIA, 203; family proclamation, 274–275; firesides, 173–175, 221, 222; messages in *Improvement Era*, 123; oversight of youth organizations, 115–116, 179, 210. *See also specific presidents*

Florida, youth programs in, 124

Foote, Louisa, 35

For the Strength of Youth (booklet), 185–187, 186 (illus.), 259–260, 321–322

For the Strength of Youth (FSY) conferences, 317–318

For the Strength of Youth (magazine), 322

4-H, 212, 234

Fox, Ruth May, 334; at British youth conference, 127; "Carry On," 105–106, 248; "The Heavenly Gift," 105; leadership as counselor, 54, 72, 365n224; leadership as president, 102, 122, 128; life experience, 127; mentioned, 57, 137, 368n57; on women's leadership, 99–100

France, youth programs in, 113, 277

Freeman, Emily Belle Oswald, 323–326, 337

Freeze, Lelia "Lillie" Tuckett, 31, 47

Freeze, Mary Ann Burnham, 14–15, 16, 21

Friedan, Betty, *The Feminine Mystique*, 213

Friend (magazine), 197

frontier generation, 28, 53

FSY (For the Strength of Youth) conferences, 317–318

funding: centralization of auxiliary budgets, 199; equitable youth program budgets, 318; fundraising initiatives, 42–45, 68, 356n103, 356n107

Funk, Ruth Hardy, 207 (illus.), 335 (illus.); correlation committee service, 181, 182, 183; on June Conference performances, 156, 158, 181; leadership as president, 201, 203–204, 210, 220–221; on women's issues, 214–215, 222, 223

Future Homemakers of America, 212

Fyans, J. Thomas, 245–246

G

Gapiz, Ruben, 188

Garfield, Merydith, 217

Gates, Susa Young: *History of the Young Ladies' Mutual Improvement Association*, 56–57, 359n185; life experience, 29, 353n13; mentioned, 7, 46; on New Woman ideal, 36; oversight of *Young Woman's Journal*, 29–30, 33–34, 40, 43, 47; on political involvement, 40; on YLMIA–YMMIA collaboration, 47–48, 49

gay rights movement, 213, 273. *See also* homosexuality

gender dynamics: and attraction, 168–169; and co-educational public schools, 36; and combined activities, 262–264; and conjoint movement, 23–25, 46, 47; courtship and dating, 77, 124–125, 148, 184; disparities between Young Women and Young Men, 168–169; equality and parity, 99–100, 183, 213–214, 245, 303–305, 318–319; fatherhood, 276; motherhood, 214–215, 256, 274, 276, 279; and priesthood authority, 48–49, 203, 210, 239, 243, 246–247, 303–305, 314–315; women's movement, 213–215, 220–221, 222, 232. *See also* femininity; marriage; sex and sexuality

gender vs. biological sex, 273, 274

genealogical work, 93, 106–108, 304 (illus.), 307–308

general boards, 32 (illus.); discussion of family life, 277; discussion of joint magazine proposal, 101; discussion of modern spirituality crisis, 116–119; duties of, 31, 50, 150, 180–181; expansion of, 30–33, 179; First Presidency guidance for, 115–116, 179; international members, 303; Survey Committee's report to, 116, 119–120, 122–123, 368n57; and youth leadership conference, 197. *See also* presidencies, general

general presidencies. *See* presidencies, general

generational dynamics, 9–12, 28, 77, 83, 301, 353n8, 394n41

Generation Z, 301, 308

Germany: World War II aftermath, 140; youth programs in, 110–113, 152

Ghana, youth programs in, 291

Gill, Gurcharan Singh, 277

Gill, Vilo, 277

Ginsberg, Allen, 191

Girl Guides, 71

Girl Scouts, 71, 234

Girls' Friendly Society, 61

Girls' Program (Program for Latter-day Saint Girls), 149

Gleamenight, 151

Gleaner Girls: achievement awards, 130, 149; age range for, 341; curriculum, 95–96, 340–341, 365n224; low interest in, 191; in missions, 125; mixed-gender social activities, 99, 106, 151; name, 95, 365n224; Treasures of Truth program, 106–108. *See also* Junior Gleaners

Glende, Audrey, 320

global expansion. *See* missions

Goaslind, Jack H., 207 (illus.), 260

Goddard, George, 42

Goddard, Verna Wright, 128

Godfrey, Fannie Jones, 68

Godfrey, James, 68

Godfrey, Kenneth, 196

Gold and Green Balls, 83–84, 124, 152, 162 (illus.)

Golden Gleaner awards, 130, 149

Gonzalez, Sandra, 171–172

Gordon, Marguerite, *A Bee-Hive Girl's Fantasy* (with Velma Wing), 86

Gospel Library (mobile app), 280

Grant, Heber J., 93, 102, 134, 174, 356n109

Great Britain. *See* Britain

Green, May, 67

Guatemala, youth programs in, 316 (illus.)

Guide to the First Year's Course of Study, 33–34

Gulick, Charlotte, 71–72

Gulick, Luther, 71–72

H

Haight, David B., 242

Hale, Ruth, 161

Hales (later Beckham), Janette Callister, 265, 271, 292, 335

Hall, G. Stanley, *Adolescence*, 51–52

Hall, Ivy, 358n169

handbooks, 94, 97–99, 112–113, 216, 260–261, 353n238, 378n68, 382n90

Hanks, Marion D., 159, 174, 208, 382n70

Hardy, Milton, 351n98

Hawaii: same-sex marriage in, 273; youth programs in, 124, 141

healing, miraculous, 108, 110

health and hygiene, emphasized in youth programs, 73, 81–82. *See also* physical activity

heavenly parents, 244–245, 250, 274, 319, 320

Heber Valley Camp, 291–292

Hedger, Caroline, 365n211

Heim, Jacques, 165

Helping Hands, 311 (illus.), 312

Heston, Charlton, 158

Hickman, Josiah, 52, 358n156

Higgs, Brentnall, 68

Higgs, Emily Hillam, 68, 69

Hilton, Antigone, 253

Hilton, Mark, 253

Hinckley, Bryant, 50

Hinckley, Gordon B., 231, 232, 247, 274, 292

History of the Young Ladies' Mutual Improvement Association (Susa Gates), 56–57, 359n185

Hobbs, Charles, 232, 237

Hogan, Elsie, 368n57

Holland, Jeffrey R., 234

Holland, Patricia Terry, 234, 240

Holman, Louise, 290, 291

Holmstrom, Charlene, 218

Holt, Dorothy Porter, 178

homosexuality, 213, 273, 276, 301

honeybee symbolism, 72–73

Honor Bee award, 149, 285

Hooker, Carmela Melero de, 303

Horne, Martha "Mattie." *See* Tingey, Martha Horne

Horne, Mary Isabella Hales, 5–6, 53

Houchen, William, 24

housing, wartime, 132–133

Houtz, Vida, 54

Hovik, Debra, 224

Hoving, Luisina "Lucy," 46

Howe, Neil, 353n8

How Laurels Grow program, 375n96

How Near to the Angels (film), 65, 161–163, 171, 173, 187

Huber, Gladys, 84

Hui Tau (New Zealand cultural event), 125

Hull, Thomas, 45, 47, 356n109

Hull House, 159

Hulme, Claire N., 90

Hunter, Howard W., 92, 174

Hunter, Jane H., 349n38

Hunter, John William, 92

Hunter, Mary Ann, 24

Hunter, Nellie Marie Rasmussen, 92

Hutchins, Colleen Kay, 159–160

I

Improvement Era (magazine): coverage of Gold and Green Balls, 84; coverage of Miss America, 159–160; discontinuation of, 197 (*see also New Era*); editorship of, 356n110; establishment of, 45, 356n109; First Presidency messages in, 123; "If I Were a Teen" series, 163; merger with *Young Woman's Journal*, 100–101, 366n259; motto of, 70; series on Black community outreach, 192; series on camping, 155; series on fatalism, 134–135; series on modesty, 166–167

Inagaki, Natsume, 275

indexing, 304 (illus.), 307–308

India, youth programs in, 277

individual worth, as value, 236, 238, 245

influenza pandemic (1918–1919), 76–77

Instructor (magazine), 197

integrity, as value, 236, 245

Intermediate class, 341

International Council of Women, 40

international expansion. *See* missions

internet: church use of, 280, 285–287, 307, 321; negative influences of, 280–281, 291, 310; rise of, 268

Italy, youth programs in, 188–189, 258–259, 262, 263 (illus.)

J

Jack, Elaine Low, 274

Jackson, Margaret Romney, 178

Jacobsen, Florence Smith, 334; leadership as president, 179, 180, 185, 199–201; life experience, 177–178; at YWMIA centennial celebration, 194

Japan: family culture in, 275; youth programs in, 114, 278

Jardine, Winnifred Cannon, 264

Jensen, Bridey, 276

Jensen, Katie C., 133

Jensen, Maurine, 191–192

Jesus Christ: centrality of, 314, 322; as model, 296, 319; relationship with, 255

Jones, Hyrum, 24

Jorgensen, Elaine Lewis, 188

Josephson, Marba Cannon, 136, 141, 160, 168

June Conference: 1909, 58; 1911, 59, 61; 1912, 64; 1913, 65; 1930, 105–106; 1934, 121–122; 1941, 134; 1946, 141; 1956, 158; and APMIA announcement, 203, 205–206; centennial celebration (1969), 194; contests and performance showcases at, 64, 65, 66 (illus.), 67, 86–87, 122, 156, 157 (illus.), 158, 181; discontinuation of, 209–210; Jubilee celebration (1925), 87–89; and leadership development, 155, 156–158; praise for women's leadership of, 159; priesthood speakers at, 174; slogans, 71, 122, 361n78; Southern California conference modeled on, 169–171

Junior class: age range for, 94, 341; curriculum, 94–95, 341, 365n212; mentioned, 99; Treasures of Truth program, 108–109

Junior Gleaners: achievement awards, 148, 149; chastity ideal, 165; establishment of, 146; mixed-gender social activities, 151; purpose of, 149, 341–342. *See also* Laurel class

Junior M Men, 148, 151

JustServe.org, 310

K

Kapp, Ardeth Greene, 207 (illus.), 257 (illus.), 335 (illus.); appointed as Young Women general president, 231; correlation committee service, 183; and Emily Belle Freeman, 324; leadership as counselor, 201, 203, 204, 208, 210, 211, 382n82; leadership as ward Young Women president, 373n40; life experience, 231–232; mentioned, 292, 305; leadership as general president: assessment of challenges and needs, 232–235; authority dynamics, 238–241; Personal Progress update, 254–256; *For the Strength of Youth* update, 259–260; tenure length, 271; use of mass media and new technology, 242, 250, 253–254; values initiative, 235–238, 241–246

Kennedy, John F., 213

Kerr, Marion, 135

Kimball, Camilla Eyring, 60, 62, 92, 115, 123

Kimball, Heber C., 4

Kimball, Richard Ian, 365n238

Kimball, Spencer W.: appointment of youth organization presidents, 221; on chastity, 164, 166, 185; death of, 247; and establishment of APMIA, 206; on June Conference discontinuation, 209–210; marriage, 92; mentioned, 171, 240; public profile; racial inclusion initiatives, 226; and women's issues, 221, 222; on youth organization quality, 145

King, Elizabeth Eames, 87

King, Lueen Jensen, 165

King, Martin Luther, Jr., 192

Kirkham, Oscar A., 65, 121

Knell, Mary Lue, 131–132

Knight, Inez, 38–39

Kocani, Edlira, 290, 291

Komatsu, Adney, 377n13

L

Ladies' Cooperative Retrenchment Association, 5–6, 348n15. *See also* Young Ladies' Department of the Ladies' Cooperative Retrenchment Association

Laing, Kalli, 308

language: barriers, 131–132, 283; translations, 112–113, 125, 260, 322

Larsen, Dean L., 241, 242

Larsen, Eleanor, 107

Larsen, Sharon Greene, 278, 279, 283

Latter-day Saint Student Association (LDSSA), 192

Laurel class: achievement awards, 256; age range for, 342; chastity ideal, 375n96; discontinuation of, 318; establishment of, 180; leadership conference, 197; value projects, 256; Young Womanhood Recognition, 216

lds.org, 280

LDSSA (Latter-day Saint Student Association), 192

leadership: and certification programs, 180; establishment of centralized, 21–23; fostering culture of, in youth, 196–197, 217–220, 325; manuals, 150–151; mentorship, 285; in missions, 113–114, 128–129; shadow, 217–218, 318; and spiritual qualifications, 120; virtual training meetings, 321; women seated on Tabernacle stand, 231, 232; women's membership in church councils, 303–305. *See also* First Presidency; general boards; presidencies, general; priesthood

Leary, Timothy, 191

Lee, Harold B.: correlation initiative, 178, 305; death of, 206; and establishment of APMIA, 203, 205, 208, 210; at June Conference, 141; and LDSSA, 192; mentioned, 178, 222; public profile

LGBTQ community, 213, 273, 276, 301

Liberty Glen Camp, 68–69

Lindsay, Lisle, 65

Lion House (Salt Lake City), 7, 8 (illus.), 10, 57, 136–138, 194, 324

Little Girls' Magazine, 16

Lloyd, LaVern McClellan, 108

Loebner, Sonja, 258

logos, 253–254, 257 (illus.)

Longden, LaRue Carr, 145, 149, 159, 166–167

Lord's Supper, 150

Lovesy, Edith Rossiter, 59, 61

Lund, Anthon H., 50

Lunt, Florence, 24

Lunt, Henrietta, 3, 4, 9, 12, 16–18

Lunt, Mary Ann, 12, 18

Lyman, Francis M., 50

Lyman, Richard R., 99, 102

M

MacCarthy, Shane, 159

Macdonald, Julia Ivins, 16, 37

Macfarlane, May, 24

Maeterlinck, Maurice, *Life of the Bee*, 72–73

Mailbox, The (church video), 65

manuals: camping, 139–140, 155, 180, 262, 264–265; codes of conduct, 185–187, 186 (illus.), 259–260, 321–322; leadership, 150–151, 260; mission, 188, 295, 301–302; program handbooks, 94, 97–99, 112–113, 216, 260–261, 353n238, 378n68, 382n90; Sunday class meetings, 285

Māori culture, 125

marriage: and age, 10, 38, 54, 93, 163, 276, 355n74; and courtship, 124–125, 148, 163; divorce rates, 272–273; plural, 7, 18, 27, 28; promotion of ideal, 160–163, 173, 273, 274–275; and race, 93, 171, 193, 226; as sacred, 38, 273, 274; same-sex, 273, 301; shifting societal norms, 272–273, 300–301; temple, 92, 173, 274; YLMIA–YMMIA collaboration compared to, 49

Marriott, Neill Foote

Mary imagery, 212, 215, 227, 382n72

Maw, Herbert, 118

Maxwell, Neal A., 237, 242, 244

McCahon, Linda, 189–190, 193, 226

McConkie, Carol Foley, 303

McCune, Elizabeth Claridge, 356n107

McKay, David O., 158, 166, 171, 173, 174, 177, 183

McKay, Quinn, 208

McLaws, Aleece, 308

Mead, Wilma, 163

media: church use of, 161–163, 250–251, 280, 307, 321; negative influences of, 164, 184, 233, 280, 291, 308; rise of the internet, 280

Meiszus, Helga, 110–112

Melchizedek Priesthood, 48

Melchizedek Priesthood Mutual Interest Association (MPMIA), 201

mental health, 280

mentorship, 285

Mexico, youth programs in, 114, 123–125, 286 (illus.)

MIA. *See* Young Ladies'/Women's Mutual Improvement Association; Young Men's Mutual Improvement Association

MIA Day, 64. *See also* Theme Festival and Honor Night

Mia Joy awards, 146, 149

MIA Leader (newsletter), 123, 155

Mia Maids: achievement awards, 146–148, 149, 256; age range for, 342; chastity ideal, 165, 375n96; discontinuation of, 318; establishment of, 146; femininity ideals, 167; mixed-gender social activities, 151; name, 146; purpose of, 148; rose symbolism, 146; value experiences, 256

Mia Shalom Recreation Camp, 292

migration, voluntary, 132–134

military service, World War II, 130–131

millennials, 301, 308

ministering system, 314

miracles: of healing, 108, 110; testimonies of, 34

Miss America pageant, 159–160, 214, 240

Missionary Executive Council, 303

missions: and conversion rates, 160, 169; expansion and growth, 109, 188, 233, 255, 269; leadership of, 113–114, 128–129; manuals, 188, 295, 301–302; preparing youth for service, 301–302; race, and serving in, 193, 226–227; reduction in age of eligibility for service, 298, 299–300; training for service, 19; women's acceptance into full-time service, 38–39; youth program activities and events at, 110–113, 123–128, 129, 151–152, 172, 188–190, 269–271, 287–74, 288–291, 321; and youth program global relevancy efforts, 271, 272, 283–285; youth program guiding assumptions vs. local circumstances in, 172–173, 188, 271, 277–278, 282–283, 287–288

mixed-gender activities, 262–264

Mkhabela, Dorah, 303

M Men, 99, 106, 125, 148, 151

modesty, 75–76, 83, 165–167, 185–187, 282. *See also* chastity

Moffat, S. A., 70

Mongolia, youth programs in, 288–290, 289 (illus.)

Monroy, Porfiria, 124–125

Monson, Thomas S., 214, 241, 242, 244, 254, 259, 313

morality: sexual, chastity ideal, 117, 121, 164–165, 185, 256, 281, 292–294, 296, 375n96; sexual, loosening norms of, 60, 121, 134–135, 163–164, 184, 272, 273, 280–281; sexual, modesty ideal, 75–76, 83, 165–167, 185–187, 282; and thirteenth article of faith, 180, 281; and values, 236, 295; visual campaigns to promote, 160–163; and Word of Wisdom, 134, 144, 149. *See also* values

Moreno, Mayka, xi–xii

mormon.org, 280

Morris, George Q., 58, 99, 117, 141

Moss, Elva, 90

mother-daughter activities, 83, 165

motherhood, 214–215, 256, 274, 276, 279

mottos and slogans, 70–71, 122, 361n78. *See also* themes

Mouritsen, Maren, 236

MPMIA (Melchizedek Priesthood Mutual Interest Association), 201

music: as communication tool, 105–106, 250; contests, 65, 66 (illus.)

Mutual Dell Camp, 139

Mutual Interests class, 342

Mutual Study class, 342

My Personal Progress program, 215–216, 227, 236, 237. *See also* Personal Progress program

My Story—Lest I Forget project, 108–109

N

Nadauld, Margaret Dyreng, 279, 280, 283–284, 285, 336, 389n22

National Council of Women (NCW), 40, 159

National Defense Committees, 76

National Organization for Women (NOW), 213

National Woman Suffrage Association, 40

National Women's Conference (1977), 222

Native American imagery, 72, 139, 372n216

natural disasters, and service work, 310–312

Navas, Andrea, xi

NCW (National Council of Women), 40, 159

Neff, Estelle, 38

Nelson, Russell M., 244, 247, 255, 314, 319, 323

Neslen, Grace C., 368n57

Netherlands, youth programs in, 113, 189, xi

New Beginnings event, 261, 287

New Era (magazine): coverage of genealogical work, 308; coverage of global youth activities, 287; coverage of service work, 218; coverage of values program, 244, 385n72; establishment of, 197–199; internet access to, 280; renamed, 322 (*see also For the Strength of Youth* [magazine]); series on *For the Strength of Youth*, 260; series on temple ordinances, 255

New Woman ideal: emergence of, 35–36; impact on women's opportunities, 36–39; impact on YLMIA, 39–40, 54

New Zealand, youth programs in, 60, 124, 125, 152, 162 (illus.)

Noall, Elizabeth "Libbie," 46

Norway, youth programs in, 128, 321

NOW (National Organization for Women), 213

Noyce, Vicki, 181

nursing courses, 77

Nymph class, 342–343

Nystrom, Mae Taylor, 54, 355n82

O

Oakcrest Girls Camp, 292

Oaks, Dallin H., 234, 273, 292, 315

Okazaki, Chieko N., 179, 180, 294

Oscarson, Bonnie Lee Green, 302–303, 308, 312, 336

Our Little Gem (newspaper), 17 (illus.)

outdoor programs. *See* camps; Scouting programs

P

Pace, Glenn L., 277

Pack, Belle, 108

Pack, Jessie Stirling, 108

Packer, Boyd K., 246

Palfreyman, Henrietta, 358n169

pandemic: 1918–1919, 76–77; 2020–2023, 320–321, 322–323

Papa and the Playhouse (play), 181

parental involvement, 83, 165, 254, 261, 283, 284–285, 317

Parker, Iris, 168

patriarchal blessings, 193, 393n3

Paul, Joshua Hughes, 69

Pearce, Virginia Hinckley, 265, 272

PEC. *See* Priesthood Executive Committee

Pennsylvania, youth programs in, 152

Penrose, Charles, 361n95

performance activities: contests and showcases, 65, 66 (illus.), 85 (illus.), 156, 158, 181; drama productions, 84–87; film productions, 161–163

Perry, Janice Kapp, 250

Personal Achievement program, 211–212

Personal Progress program: cultural assumptions in, 277–278, 282–283; discontinuation of, 317; global relevancy efforts, 283–285; impact of, 256–259, xi–xii; as update to My Personal Progress, 254–256; values in, 255–256, 296

Petersen, LaRene, 146, 375n108

Petersen, Mark E., 164, 166

Petersen, Myrna, 143–144, 145, 160, 165, 375n108

Peterson, H. Burke, 207 (illus.)

Peterson, Mary, 35

Philippines, youth programs in, 188, 311 (illus.)

physical activity: athletic programs, 64, 152–155, 390n77; clothing for, 39, 81; and health and hygiene, 73, 81–82; and New Woman ideal, 39–40, 41 (illus.); physical fitness programs, 159; and progressive reformers, 64

Pinegar, Patricia Peterson, 265, 272

pioneer generation, 9, 28, 53, 106–107

Piranian, Badwagan, 377n13

plural marriage, 7, 18, 27, 28

Poananga, Adelaide Thompson, 124, 125

pornography, 280–281

poster campaigns, 160

Pratt, Lona, 9

Pratt, Louisa Barnes, 14, 350n57

Preach My Gospel (missionary manual), 295, 301–302

preliminary programs, 51, 55

premarital sex and chastity, 117, 121, 164–165, 185, 256, 281, 292–294, 296, 375n96.

Prensky, Marc, 394n41

presidencies, class, 196–197

presidencies, general: auxiliary relationship with priesthood, 238–239; chronology, 333–337; communication challenges, 209–211, 239–241; establishment and structure of, 21–23; in organizational restructuring, 206–208, 318, 395n84; tenure length, decline in, 271, 382n97; terminology, 357n130; transitions, 53–54, 102, 128, 145, 178, 199–201, 221, 231, 234, 271, 278, 285, 291, 294, 302, 313, 323. *See also specific presidents*

Presidency, First. *See* First Presidency

Presiding Bishopric, 196, 201, 203, 204, 206–208, 210

priesthood: church organizations as auxiliaries to, 74–76, 238–239, 362n112; firesides, 173–175; gender-hierarchy dynamics, 48–49, 203, 210, 239, 243, 246–247, 303–305, 314–315; modern spirituality crisis as threat to, 117–118; and moral cleanliness, 281; oversight of youth organizations, 48, 196, 200 (illus.), 201, 203, 206–208, 211, 239–244, 246, 318; and race, 193, 226; reform movements, 21, 75; and temple participation of women, 255; women's priesthood authority, 315. *See also* Aaronic Priesthood; First Presidency; Quorum of the Seventy; Quorum of the Twelve Apostles

Priesthood Executive Committee (PEC), 239–240, 241–244, 246, 259, 305, 385n44

Primary Association, 21, 22, 113, 305

Program for Latter-day Saint Girls (Girls' Program), 149

Progressive Era, 61

Protestantism, mainstream, 118–119

psychology: of religion, 52; of sexualization, 280

public speaking: contests, 65; emphasized in youth programs, 16, 19; expansion of opportunities for women, 46

Puenzieux, Louise, 109–110

purity discourse, 293–294. *See also* chastity

Q

Qinisile, Nqobile, 267

Qinisile, Zandile Precious, 267–268, 270 (illus.), 283, 296

Quorum of the Seventy, 174, 208, 239, 245, 246

Quorum of the Twelve Apostles: correlation initiative, 182; and establishment of APMIA, 203; family proclamation, 274–275; firesides, 174–175; oversight of youth organizations, 20, 185, 208, 238, 239, 244, 246

R

race and ethnicity: and church leadership, 179, 377n13; diversity and inclusion efforts, 210, 226–227, 247–248, 260; and marriage, 93, 171, 193, 226; and migration patterns, 192–193; and racism, 171–172, 192, 193, 226

Radebe, Yolanda, 270 (illus.)

railroad generation, 28

rape and sexual abuse, 293–294

Rasmus, Carolyn J., 234, 240, 241

Rasmussen, Nellie Marie, 92

Réard, Louis, 165

recession, economic, 233

recreation: achievement programs, 129–130, 146, 147 (illus.), 149, 198 (illus.); *The Activity Book,* 216, 220; contests, 64–67, 66 (illus.), 85 (illus.), 122, 123; decline in emphasis on, 218–220, 235; general board committees for, 180–181; Gold and Green

Balls, 83–84, 124, 152, 162 (illus.); at the Lion House, 136–138; during meetings, 151; in missions, 110–113, 123–128, 129, 151–152, 172, 188–190, 269–271, 287–74, 288–291, 321; preliminary programs, 51, 55; and shift in approach under APMIA, 205; significance of, in Young Women experience, 216–217; spiritual emphasis, 62–64, 69, 80–81, 90–92, 97, 119–120, 262, 291, 292; ward buildings for, 80; wartime, 135–136. *See also* camps; physical activity; Scouting programs; social work

Recreation Bulletin, 80

Red Cross, 76, 136

Reeder, Bertha Stone, 334; leadership as president, 145–146, 149, 152–155, 165–166, 180, 210, 271; life experience, 145; mentioned, 175, 177

Rees, Edith, 129

Relief Society: auxiliary status, 362n112; leadership structure, 21, 22–23, 113–114; leadership transitions, 285, 391n100; mission branches, 113–114; nursing courses, 77; Personal Progress participation, 264; political involvement, 40; relationship with Young Women organization, 224, 228; representation in church councils, 303–305; and retrenchment, 5–6, 12; scholarship on, xii; Joseph Smith on, 244, 385n71; and Social Advisory Committee, 75–76; teachers in, 18; YLMIA hosting events for, 56

Relief Society Magazine, 197

repentance, gift of, 294, 319, 320

retrenchment: and dress reform, 7–9, 13–14, 349n49; vs. improvement, 14–16; movement origins, 5–6

Reyes, Nenita, 188

Reynolds, George, 42

Richards, Franklin D., 352n119

Richards, Jane Snyder, 21

Richards, Stephen L, 76, 78, 81, 140

Rivers, Percy J., 377n13

road shows, 86

Roberts, B. H., 46, 64, 69, 70, 356n109

Robertson, Jessie, 358n169

Romney, Marion G., 181

Romney, Ott, 159

Rosero, Mary, 269–271

rose symbolism, 146

Rose Tying Ceremony (Mia Maids), 146–148

Ross, Mark, 169

Rowland, Fanny: education and career, 36–37, 38; on experience as single woman, 38; leadership experience, 27, 31, 54, 55, 56, 358n171; life experience, 27; missionary service, 39

Rowland, Louisa, 56

Roylance, Ora, 358n169

Rückert, Friedrich, 113

Runia, Tamara Wood, 323

S

sacrament meetings, 150

Sacredness of Sex, The (pamphlet), 164

Sacred to Me program, 165, 375n96

Sagers, Becca, 312

Sagers, Diana, 312

Salaca, Kerelayani Kalou, 253

Saltair Resort, 68

Salt Lake City: housing demand in, 132–133; Lion House, 7, 8 (illus.), 10, 57, 136–138, 194, 324; population growth, 59

Salvation Army, 67

same-sex marriage, 273, 301

Samoa, youth programs in, 60

Samuels, Rajane, 308

Schaerrer, Neil, 208

science, reconciling faith with, 118–119

Scott, Richard G., 294

Scouting programs: secular organizations, 69–70, 71–72, 74, 234, 315; for young men, 69–70, 99, 158, 288, 315; for young women (*see* Bee-Hive Girls; camps)

sealing ordinance, 255

secular humanism, 237

secular influences and societal changes: camp as refuge from, 291, 292; commercialized recreation, 98; counterculture movement, 178, 190–191, 199; and crisis of modern spirituality, 114–119, 121–122; and economic depression, 114–115; family structure, shifting norms of, 272–273; negative influences of popular media, 164, 184, 233, 280, 291, 308; in Progressive Era, 59–61, 77–78; and public education, 36–37, 129; secular humanism, 237; sexuality, loosening norms of, 60, 121, 134–135, 163–164, 184, 272, 273, 280–281; women's movement, 213–215, 232. *See also* New Woman ideal

self-esteem, 243, 281

Senior class, 95–96, 343, 365n212. *See also* Advanced Senior class; Gleaner Girls

service work, 76, 136–138, 217–220, 219 (illus.), 310–313, 311 (illus.), 314, 316 (illus.). *See also* social work

sesquicentennial celebration (Young Women, 2020), 322

sex and sexuality: double standards, 135, 164–165, 281; and individual worth, 236; loosening norms of, 60, 121, 134–135, 163–164, 184, 272, 273, 280–281; as sacred, 164

sexual abuse and rape, 293–294

sexualization, 280

shadow leadership, 217–218, 318

sheaf-binding ceremonies, 96, 148

Shelby, Rhonda, 226

Sherratt, Rosy May, 24

Silver Gleaner awards, 148, 149

Sims, Bette Lou, 180

sisterhood, 247, 250, 251–253, 262

slogans and mottos, 70–71, 122, 361n78. *See also* themes

Small MIA handbook, 378n68

Smart, Elizabeth, 293–294

Smith, Barbara Bradshaw, 222

Smith, Bathsheba, 359n186

Smith, Emma Hale, 325

Smith, George A., 349n49, 351n98

Smith, John Henry, 47, 351n98

Smith, Joseph: allusions to, 244, 385n71; as prophet, 119; visions and revelations of, 117, 118, 238, 269, 389n33

Smith, Joseph F., 24, 29, 46, 48, 74–75, 356n109, 356n110, 362n112

Smith, Joseph Fielding, 118, 121

Smith, Mary, 253

Smith, Mary A., 18

Smith, Nicholas G., 118

Smith, Norma Broadbent, 221, 222

Snow, Eliza Roxcy: on generational conflict, 9; leadership roles, 5, 7, 19, 20, 21, 22, 23; on spiritual development, 14

Snow, Erastus, 6

Social Advisory Committee, 75–76, 78, 79–80. *See also* Correlation–Social Advisory Committee

social work: conferences on, 78–79; defined, 78; Social Advisory Committee initiatives, 78, 79–80; and volunteer service work, 76, 136–138, 217–220, 219 (illus.), 310–313, 311 (illus.), 314, 316 (illus.)

South Africa: family culture in, 275; youth programs in, 267, 283, 296–298

South Carolina, youth programs in, 60

Southern California conference, 169–171

Spannaus, Andrea Muñoz, 323–324

Special Interest class, 343

Special Needs Mutual, 313

spirituality and faith: in achievement programs, 210; and baptisms for the dead, 93–94; and concern for temple participation, 92–94; crisis of modern, 114–119, 121–122; and cultural identity, 124, 125–127, 189; daughters of God, identity as, 227, 238, 247, 264, 268, 282, 292, 319; as fundamental to YLMIA, 57; and genealogical work, 93, 106–108, 304 (illus.), 307–308; and psychology of religion, 52; and recreation, 62–64, 69, 80–81, 90–92, 97, 119–120, 262, 291, 292; Sunday religious instruction, 224–225, 285–287, 314; and temple ordinances, 82, 193, 255, 305; and temple participation, 92–94, 193, 255, 285, 305, 306 (illus.), 309 (illus.), 318–319; testimonies of, 34–35, 57, 251–253; and Treasures of Truth program, 106–110. *See also* Jesus Christ; morality; values

Spofford, Grace, 159

sports programs, 64, 152–155, 390n77

stake conventions. *See* conventions

standards events, 261

Stapley, Delbert L., 185

Stark, Hilda, 16

Stewart, Charlotte, 97

Stewart, Madelyn, 72, 74

Strauss, William, 353n8

summer activities. *See* camps; Scouting programs

Sunday class meetings, for young women, 224–225, 285–287, 314

Sunday School: attendance records, 150, 172; in early church history, 4; funding, 42; and Social Advisory Committee, 76; *For the Strength of Youth* update, 259–260

superintendency, as term, 357n130

Sweden, youth programs in, 125

Switzerland, youth programs in, 109–110, 113

T

Tabernacle Choir, 158

Tait, John, 24

Talmage, James E., 115

Talmage, May Booth, 54, 57, 355n82

Tanner, Susan Winder, 282, 285, 291, 292, 293, 336

Taylor, Elmina Shepard, 32 (illus.), 333; death, 53; leadership as president, 22, 24, 29, 31, 33, 40, 42, 43, 45, 46, 53, 325, 352n119, 357n130; life experience, 22, 53; mentioned, 52; on YLMIA–YMMIA collaboration, 24, 47, 49, 366n259

Taylor, George, 22

Taylor, John, 21

Taylor, John H., 70, 361n74

Taylor, Karen, 216

Taylor, Margaret Young, 22, 351n107

Taylor, Rachel Grant, 62, 361n74, 368n57

Taylor, Rama, 216

Taylor, Sharon, 216

teenager, as term, 129

temple garments, 82–83

temple marriage, 92, 173, 274

temple participation, 92–94, 193, 255, 285, 305, 306 (illus.), 309 (illus.), 318–319

testimonies of faith, 34–35, 57, 251–253

Tew, Melvina, 54, 55

Texas, youth programs in, 171

Thatcher, Fanny Young, 22

theater productions, 84–87. *See also* film productions

Theme Festival and Honor Night, 129–130

themes, 245, 246, 319–320. *See also* mottos and slogans

Third Convention (Mexico), 114

Thomas, Carol Burdett, 279

Till, Mary Ann, 350n71

Tingey, Martha Horne, 32 (illus.), 333; leadership as counselor, 22, 29, 366n268; leadership as president, 53–54, 82, 102, 271

tobacco use, 134, 149

Tobiasson, Ellie, 308

transfer card system, 133–134, 149

Treasures of Truth program, 106–110, 211, 212

Tsedendorj, Doka, 288

Tucker, Emily Newcombe, 351n85

Tuminez, Astrid S., 247, 248

Turley, Maurine Johnson, 234, 240, 248

U

University of Utah, 19, 191, 192, 351n93

urbanization, 59–60

INDEX

V

values: fireside on, 244, 246–248, 249 (illus.); identification of, for Young Women, 235–238; initiative proposal and approval, 241–245, 246; integrated in camp programs, 261; integrated in Personal Progress program, 255–256, 296; as term, 236–237; theme, 245, 246; virtue added to list of, 295–298

Vanguards, 99

Van Mondfrans, Cornelia, 189

Vietnam War (1955–1975), 191

virginity and chastity, 117, 121, 164–165, 185, 256, 281, 292–294, 296, 375n96. *See also* modesty; morality

virtue, as value, 295–298, 297 (illus.). *See also* morality

visions, 34, 108, 117, 118

vocation. *See* employment

volunteer service, 76, 136–138, 217–220, 219 (illus.), 310–313, 311 (illus.), 314, 316 (illus.). *See also* social work

W

Wallace, Bernadine, 169

Wallace, Elen, 50, 72–73

Warhol, Andy, 191

Warner, Emma Lou, 130–131

Washington (state), youth programs in, 125

Watson, Mary Frances, 191–192

Welfare Services, 259–260

Wells, Daniel H., 19

Wells, Junius, 19, 23–24, 25, 57, 351n98, 352n122, 359n189

Wells, Leah, 148

Wells, Louisa "Louie," 22, 351n107

Wells, Sharlene, 240

West, Laura, 253

Western Boom, The (serialized novel), 56

Wheat, Jacklyn, 225

Wheeler, Gloria, 192

White, Lola, 54, 358n169

Whitney, Orson F., *History of Utah*, 33

Widtsoe, John A., 119, 120

Wilkins, Richard, 389n22

Williams, Helen Spencer, 117, 128

Williams, Zina, 9, 349n27

Willie, M. A., xi

Wing, Velma, *A Bee-Hive Girl's Fantasy* (with Marguerite Gordon), 86

witnesses, women serving as, 318–319, 396n88

Wixom, Rosemary Mix, 305

Woman's Exponent (newspaper), 16, 18, 20, 30

women's movement, 213–215, 220–221, 222, 232

Wood, Ada, 24

Woodruff, Helen Winters, 355n82

Woodruff, Wilford, 29

Woodstock (1969), 194–196

Woodworth, Grace, 319

Word of Wisdom, 134, 144, 149

World Congress of Recreation and Leisure, 159

World War I (1914–1918), 76

World War II (1939–1945): beginning of, 128; defense industries, 131–132; end and aftermath, 140–141; military service, 130–131; mission leadership during, 128–129; moral standards during, 134–135; youth programs during, 132

writing pursuits: emphasized in youth programs, 16, 25; Treasures of Truth program, 106–110, 211, 212. *See also Improvement Era*; *Young Woman's Journal*

Y

Yates, Sara, 180

YLMIA/YWMIA. *See* Young Ladies'/Women's Mutual Improvement Association

YMMIA. *See* Young Men's Mutual Improvement Association

Young, Brigham: family of, 7–9, 10, 11 (illus.), 12; identification of Salt Lake Temple site, 295, 296; improvement association initiative, 19, 20, 23, 56–57, 98; priesthood quorum initiative, 21; retrenchment initiative, 5, 7

Young, Dora, 9, 349n27

Young, Morris, 351n98

Young, Phebe, 9, 349n27

Young, Zina D. H., 34

Young Ladies' Department of the Ladies' Cooperative Retrenchment Association: dress reform, 13–14, 349n49; establishment of, 7–9; generational dynamics, 9–12; improvement emphasis, 14–16. *See also* Young Ladies'/Women's Mutual Improvement Association (YLMIA/YWMIA)

Young Ladies' Gem (newspaper), 16

Young Ladies'/Women's Mutual Improvement Association (YLMIA/YWMIA): age requirements, 94–95, 145–146; autonomy of, efforts to preserve, 47–48, 72, 199; centennial celebration (1969), 194–196, 195 (illus.); and centralization of auxiliary budgets, 199; classes and programs, 339–343 (*see also* achievement programs; Bee-Hive Girls; Gleaner Girls; June Conference; Junior class; Junior Gleaners; Laurel class; Mia Maids; recreation; Senior class); codes of conduct, 185–187, 186 (illus.); education initiatives and curriculum, 33–35, 94–97; enrollment and attendance campaigns, 149–150; enrollment and attendance statistics, 133, 140, 150, 172, 175, 181, 364n183; film productions, 161–163; fostering culture of youth leadership, 196–197; fundraising initiatives, 42–45, 68, 356n103, 356n107; Susa Gates' *History*, 56–57, 359n185; goals of, 14–16; handbooks, 94, 97–99, 112–113, 172, 188, 365n238, 378n68; leadership manuals, 150–151; leadership structure (*see* general boards; presidencies, class; presidencies, general); magazines and newsletters (*see Improvement Era*; *MIA Leader*; *New Era*; *Young Woman's Journal*); meeting protocols and calendar, 16–18, 54–56, 122, 129, 151;

mission branches, challenges of, 172–173, 188; mission branches, leadership of, 114; mottos and slogans, 70–71, 122, 361n78; name changes, 15, 20, 122–123, 206, 350n71; and New Woman ideal, 39–40, 54; organizational restructuring, 199–201, 200 (illus.), 203–206 (*see also* Young Women organization); response to World War I and influenza pandemic, 76–77; response to World War II, 132, 135–136; service work, 76, 136–138; transfer card system, 133–134, 149; YMMIA partnership and collaboration dynamics, 23–26, 45–49, 50–51, 55, 58, 97, 99–100

Young Marrieds class, 343

Young Men organization: codes of conduct, 259–260, 321–322; disparities with Young Women organization, 242–243; name changed to, 208; organizational restructuring, 318; relationship with Young Women organization, 208, 220, 235, 262–264, 325; theme, 319

Young Men's Christian Association (YMCA), 64

Young Men's Mutual Improvement Association (YMMIA): classes and programs, 69–70, 99, 106, 125, 148, 151, 158, 288, 315; codes of conduct, 185–187, 186 (illus.); efforts to revive, 45, 47; establishment of, 19–20, 57; handbooks, 97–99, 365n238; magazines and newsletters (*see Contributor*; *Improvement Era*; *MIA Leader*); mottos and slogans, 70–71, 122, 361n78; organizational restructuring, 199–201, 200 (illus.), 203–208 (*see also* Young Men organization); and Social Advisory Committee, 76; YLMIA partnership and collaboration dynamics, 23–26, 45–49, 50–51, 55, 58, 97, 99–100 (*see also* June Conference)

Young Womanhood Recognition medallion, 216, 285

Young Woman's Journal (magazine), 44 (illus.); coverage of Gold and Green Balls, 84; coverage of influenza pandemic and war, 76–77; coverage of Jubilee, 89; coverage of National Council of Women activity, 40; establishment of, 29–30; female office staff, 38; funding, 43, 356n107; lessons in, 34; merger with *Improvement Era*, 100–101, 366n259; motto of, 70; read at YLMIA meetings, 56; series on drama productions, 86, 87; series on mainstream higher education, 37; series on physical activity, 39–40, 41 (illus.), 64, 81, 365n211; series on social work, 78; series on spirituality, 93–94; series on vocational opportunities, 37–38

Young Women Handbook, 260–261, 382n90

Young Women in Excellence event, 261, 287

Young Women organization: achievement programs, 211–213, 215–216, 217 (*see also* Personal Progress program); activity planning and events, 260–261, 285–287; age requirements, 317; anniversary celebration (1988), 254; budget for, 318; chronology, 327–331; classes, 339–343 (*see also* Bee-Hive Girls; Laurel class; Mia Maids); codes of conduct, 259–260, 321–322; enrollment and attendance statistics, 222, 384n22, 386n86, 390n77; fostering culture of youth leadership, 217–220, 325;

genealogical work, 307–308; global relevancy efforts, 271, 272, 283–285; handbooks, 216, 260–261, 382n90; logo, 253–254, 257 (illus.); missionary preparation, 301–302; mission branches, challenges of, 271; organizational restructuring, 206–208, 315–318; relationship with Young Men organization, 208, 220, 235, 262–264, 325; scholarship on, xii–xiv; service work, 217–220, 219 (illus.), 310–313, 311 (illus.), 314, 316 (illus.); sesquicentennial celebration (2020), 322; Sunday class meetings, 224–225, 285–287, 314; themes, 245, 246, 319–320. *See also* values; Young Ladies'/Women's Mutual Improvement Association (YLMIA/YWMIA)

Young Women's Bible Training Movement, 67

Young Women's Christian Association (YWCA), 61, 64

youth, defining, 10–12, 51–52, 129

youth.lds.org, 280

Z

Zabriskie, Alva, 55